Enterprise Networking, Security, and Automation Companion Guide (CCNAv7)

Cisco Press

Enterprise Networking, Security, and Automation Companion Guide (CCNAv7)

Cisco Networking Academy

Copyright© 2020 Cisco Systems, Inc.

Published by:
Cisco Press

1 2020

Library of Congress Control Number: 2020935515

ISBN-13: 978-0-13-663432-4

ISBN-10: 0-13-663432-X

Warning and Disclaimer

This book is designed to provide information about the Cisco Networking Academy Enterprise Networking, Security, and Automation (CCNAv7) course. Every effort has been made to make this book as complete and as accurate as possible, but no warranty or fitness is implied.

The information is provided on an "as is" basis. The authors, Cisco Press, and Cisco Systems, Inc. shall have neither liability nor responsibility to any person or entity with respect to any loss or damages arising from the information contained in this book or from the use of the discs or programs that may accompany it.

The opinions expressed in this book belong to the author and are not necessarily those of Cisco Systems, Inc.

Editor-in-Chief
Mark Taub

Alliances Manager, Cisco Press
Arezou Gol

Director, ITP Product Management
Brett Bartow

Senior Editor
James Manly

Managing Editor
Sandra Schroeder

Development Editor
Ellie Bru

Senior Project Editor
Tonya Simpson

Copy Editor
Kitty Wilson

Technical Editor
Bob Vachon

Editorial Assistant
Cindy Teeters

Cover Designer
Chuti Prasertsith

Composition
codeMantra

Indexer
Ken Johnson

Proofreader
Betty Pessagno

Trademark Acknowledgments

All terms mentioned in this book that are known to be trademarks or service marks have been appropriately capitalized. Cisco Press or Cisco Systems, Inc., cannot attest to the accuracy of this information. Use of a term in this book should not be regarded as affecting the validity of any trademark or service mark.

Special Sales

For information about buying this title in bulk quantities, or for special sales opportunities (which may include electronic versions; custom cover designs; and content particular to your business, training goals, marketing focus, or branding interests), please contact our corporate sales department at corpsales@pearsoned.com or (800) 382-3419.

For government sales inquiries, please contact governmentsales@pearsoned.com.

For questions about sales outside the U.S., please contact intlcs@pearson.com.

Feedback Information

At Cisco Press, our goal is to create in-depth technical books of the highest quality and value. Each book is crafted with care and precision, undergoing rigorous development that involves the unique expertise of members from the professional technical community.

Readers' feedback is a natural continuation of this process. If you have any comments regarding how we could improve the quality of this book, or otherwise alter it to better suit your needs, you can contact us through email at feedback@ciscopress.com. Please make sure to include the book title and ISBN in your message.

We greatly appreciate your assistance.

Americas Headquarters	Asia Pacific Headquarters	Europe Headquarters
Cisco Systems, Inc.	Cisco Systems (USA) Pte. Ltd.	Cisco Systems International BV Amsterdam,
San Jose, CA	Singapore	The Netherlands

Cisco has more than 200 offices worldwide. Addresses, phone numbers, and fax numbers are listed on the Cisco Website at www.cisco.com/go/offices.

Cisco and the Cisco logo are trademarks or registered trademarks of Cisco and/or its affiliates in the U.S. and other countries. To view a list of Cisco trademarks, go to this URL: www.cisco.com/go/trademarks. Third party trademarks mentioned are the property of their respective owners. The use of the word partner does not imply a partnership relationship between Cisco and any other company. (1110R)

About the Contributing Authors

Bob Vachon is a professor at Cambrian College (Sudbury, Ontario) and Algonquin College (Ottawa, Ontario). He has more than 30 years of computer, networking, and information technology teaching experience and has collaborated on many Cisco Networking Academy courses, including CCNA, CCNA Security, CCNP, Cybersecurity, and more as team lead, lead author, and subject matter expert. Bob enjoys playing guitar by a campfire with friends and family.

Allan Johnson entered the academic world in 1999, after 10 years as a business owner/operator, to dedicate his efforts to his passion for teaching. He holds both an M.B.A. and an M.Ed. in training and development. He taught CCNA courses at the high school level for 7 years and has taught both CCNA and CCNP courses at Del Mar College in Corpus Christi, Texas. In 2003, Allan began to commit much of his time and energy to the CCNA Instructional Support Team, providing services to Networking Academy instructors worldwide and creating training materials. He now works full time for Cisco Networking Academy as Curriculum Lead.

Contents at a Glance

Reader Services

Register your copy for convenient access to downloads, updates, and corrections as they become available. To start the registration process, go to www.ciscopress.com/register and log in or create an account*. Enter the product ISBN 9780136634324 and click Submit. When the process is complete, you will find any available bonus content under Registered Products.

*Be sure to check the box that you would like to hear from us to receive exclusive discounts on future editions of this product.

Contents

Command Syntax Conventions

The conventions used to present command syntax in this book are the same conventions used in the IOS Command Reference. The Command Reference describes these conventions as follows:

- **Boldface** indicates commands and keywords that are entered literally as shown. In actual configuration examples and output (not general command syntax), boldface indicates commands that are manually input by the user (such as a **show** command).

- *Italic* indicates arguments for which you supply actual values.

- Vertical bars (|) separate alternative, mutually exclusive elements.

- Square brackets ([ ]) indicate an optional element.

- Braces ({ }) indicate a required choice.

- Braces within brackets ([{ }]) indicate a required choice within an optional element.

Introduction

Enterprise Networking, Security, and Automation Companion Guide (CCNAv7) is the official supplemental textbook for the Cisco Network Academy CCNA Enterprise Networking, Security, and Automation version 7 course. Cisco Networking Academy is a comprehensive program that delivers information technology skills to students around the world. The curriculum emphasizes real-world practical application and provides opportunities to gain the skills and hands-on experience needed to design, install, operate, and maintain networks in small to medium-sized businesses as well as enterprise and service provider environments.

This book provides a ready reference that explains the same networking concepts, technologies, protocols, and devices as the online curriculum. This book emphasizes key topics, terms, and activities and provides some alternative explanations and examples to supplement the course. You can use the online curriculum as directed by your instructor and then use this *Companion Guide*'s study tools to help solidify your understanding of all the topics.

Who Should Read This Book

The book, like the course it accompanies, is designed as an introduction to data network technology for those pursuing careers as network professionals as well as those who need an introduction to network technology for professional growth. Topics are presented concisely, starting with the most fundamental concepts and progressing to a comprehensive understanding of network communication. The content of this text provides the foundation for additional Cisco Networking Academy courses and preparation for the CCNA certification.

Book Features

The educational features of this book focus on supporting topic coverage, readability, and practice of the course material to facilitate your full understanding of the course material.

Topic Coverage

The following list gives you a thorough overview of the features provided in each chapter so that you can make constructive use of your study time:

- **Objectives:** Listed at the beginning of each chapter, the objectives reference the core concepts covered in the chapter. The objectives match the objectives listed in the corresponding chapters of the online curriculum; however, the question format in the *Companion Guide* encourages you to think about finding the answers as you read the chapter.

- **Notes:** These are short sidebars that point out interesting facts, timesaving methods, and important safety issues.

- **Summary:** At the end of each chapter is a summary of the chapter's key concepts. It provides a synopsis of the chapter and serves as a study aid.

- **Practice:** At the end of each chapter is a full list of all the labs, class activities, and Packet Tracer activities to refer to at study time.

Readability

The following features are provided to help you understand networking vocabulary:

- **Key terms:** Each chapter begins with a list of key terms, along with a page-number reference to find the term used inside the chapter. The terms are listed in the order in which they are explained in the chapter. This handy reference allows you to find a term, flip to the page where the term appears, and see the term used in context. The Glossary defines all the key terms.

- **Glossary:** This book contains an all-new Glossary that defines more than 1000 terms.

Practice

Practice makes perfect. This *Companion Guide* offers you ample opportunities to put what you learn into practice. You will find the following features valuable and effective in reinforcing the instruction that you receive:

Interactive Graphic

Video

- **Check Your Understanding questions and answer key:** Review questions are presented at the end of each chapter as a self-assessment tool. These questions match the style of questions in the online course. Appendix A, "Answers to the Check Your Understanding Questions," provides an answer key to all the questions and includes an explanation of each answer.

- **Labs and activities:** Throughout each chapter, you are directed back to the online course to take advantage of the activities provided to reinforce concepts. In addition, at the end of each chapter is a "Practice" section that lists all the labs and activities to provide practice with the topics introduced in this chapter.

- **Page references to online course:** After most headings is a number in parentheses—for example, (1.1.2). This number refers to the page number in the online course so that you can easily jump to that spot online to view a video, practice an activity, perform a lab, or review a topic.

About Packet Tracer Software and Activities

Interspersed throughout the chapters, you'll find a few Cisco Packet Tracer activities. Packet Tracer allows you to create networks, visualize how packets flow in a network, and use basic testing tools to determine whether a network would work. When you see this icon, you can use Packet Tracer with the listed file to perform a task suggested in this book. The activity files are available in the online course. Packet Tracer software is available only through the Cisco Networking Academy website. Ask your instructor for access to Packet Tracer.

How This Book Is Organized

This book corresponds closely to the Cisco Networking Academy Enterprise Networking, Security, and Automation v7 course and is divided into 14 chapters, one appendix, and a glossary of key terms:

- **Chapter 1, "Single-Area OSPFv2 Concepts":** This chapter explains single-area OSPF. It describes basic OSPF features and characteristics, packet types, and single-area operation.

- **Chapter 2, "Single-Area OSPFv2 Configuration":** This chapter explains how to implement single-area OSPFv2 networks. It includes router ID configuration, point-to-point configuration, DR/BDR election, single-area modification, default route propagation, and verification of a single-area OSPFv2 configuration.

- **Chapter 3, "Network Security Concepts":** This chapter explains how vulnerabilities, threats, and exploits can be mitigated to enhance network security. It includes descriptions of the current state of cybersecurity, tools used by threat actors, malware types, common network attacks, IP vulnerabilities, TCP and UDP vulnerabilities, network best practices, and cryptography.

- **Chapter 4, "ACL Concepts":** This chapter explains how ACLs are used to filter traffic, how wildcard masks are used, how to create ACLs, and the difference between standard and extended IPv4 ACLs.

- **Chapter 5, "ACLs for IPv4 Configuration":** The chapter explains how to implement ACLs. It includes standard IPv4 ACL configuration, ACL modifications using sequence numbers, applying an ACL to vty lines, and extended IPv4 ACL configuration.

- **Chapter 6, "NAT for IPv4":** This chapter explains how to enable NAT services on a router to provide IPv4 address scalability. It includes descriptions of the purpose and function of NAT, the different types of NAT, and the advantages and disadvantages of NAT. Configuration topics include static NAT, dynamic NAT, and PAT. NAT64 is also briefly discussed.

- **Chapter 7, "WAN Concepts":** This chapter explains how WAN access technologies can be used to satisfy business requirements. It includes descriptions of the purpose of a WAN, how WANs operate, traditional WAN connectivity options, modern WAN connectivity options, and internet-based connectivity options.

- **Chapter 8, "VPN and IPsec Concepts":** This chapter explains how VPNs and IPsec are used to secure communications. It includes descriptions of different types of VPNs and an explanation of how the IPsec framework is used to secure network traffic.

- **Chapter 9, "QoS Concepts":** This chapter explains how network devices use QoS to prioritize network traffic. It includes descriptions of network transmission characteristics, queuing algorithms, different queueing models, and QoS implementation techniques.

- **Chapter 10, "Network Management":** This chapter explains how to use a variety of protocols and techniques to manage a network, including CDP, LLDP, NTP, SNMP, and Syslog. In addition, this chapter discusses the management of configuration files and IOS images.

- **Chapter 11, "Network Design":** This chapter explains the characteristics of scalable networks. It includes descriptions of network convergence, considerations for designing scalable networks, and switch and router hardware.

- **Chapter 12, "Network Troubleshooting":** This chapter describes how to troubleshoot networks. It includes explanations of network documentation, troubleshooting methods, and troubleshooting tools. The chapter also demonstrates how to troubleshoot symptoms and causes of network problems using a layered approach.

- **Chapter 13, "Network Virtualization":** This chapter describes the purpose and characteristics of network virtualization. It includes descriptions of cloud computing, the importance of virtualization, network device virtualization, software-defined network, and controllers used in network programming.

- **Chapter 14, "Network Automation":** This chapter explains network automation. It includes descriptions of automation, data formats, APIs, REST, configuration management tools, and Cisco DNA Center.

- **Appendix A, "Answers to the 'Check Your Understanding' Questions":** This appendix lists the answers to the questions in the "Check Your Understanding Questions" section at the end of each chapter.

- **Glossary:** The Glossary provides definitions for all the key terms identified in each chapter.

Figure Credits

Figure 5-4, screenshot of Remote Access from PC1 © Tera Term Project

Figure 5-5, screenshot of Remote Access Attempt from PC2 © Tera Term Project

Figure 8-9, screenshot of Wireshark of Encapsulated Protocols © Wireshark

Figure 10-24, screenshot of Example of Using Tera Term to Backup a Configuration © Tera Term Project

Figure 10-25, screenshot of Example of Using Tera Term to Send a Configuration © Tera Term Project

Figure 12-16, screenshot of Wireshark Capture © Wireshark

Figure 13-1, screenshot of AWS Management Console © 2020, Amazon Web Services, Inc

Figure 14-1, screenshot of HTML Example and Resulting Web Page © WHATWG

CHAPTER 1

Single-Area OSPFv2 Concepts

Objectives

Upon completion of this chapter, you will be able to answer the following questions:

- What are the basic features and characteristics of OSPF?

- What OSPF packet types are used in single-area OSPF?

- How does single-area OSPF operate?

Key Terms

This chapter uses the following key terms. You can find the definitions in the Glossary.

Introduction (1.0)

Imagine that it is time for your family to visit your grandparents. You pack your bags and load them into the car. But the process takes a bit longer than you planned, and now you are running late. You pull out your map. There are three different routes. One route is no good because there is a lot of construction on the main road, and it is temporarily closed. Another route is very scenic, but it takes an additional hour to get to your destination. The third route is not as pretty but it includes a highway, which is much faster. In fact, it is so much faster that you might actually be on time if you take it.

In networking, packets do not need to take the scenic route. The *fastest available* route is always the best. *Open Shortest Path First (OSPF)* is designed to find the fastest available path for a packet from source to destination. This chapter covers the basic concepts of single-area *OSPFv2*. Let's get started!

OSPF Features and Characteristics (1.1)

OSPF is a popular multivendor, open-standard, *classless* link-state routing protocol. In this section you will learn how OSPF operates.

Introduction to OSPF (1.1.1)

This section provides a brief overview of Open Shortest Path First (OSPF), including *single-area OSPF* and *multiarea OSPF*. OSPFv2 is used for IPv4 networks, while *OSPFv3* is used for IPv6 networks. In addition, OSPFv3 with address families supports both IPv4 and IPv6. The primary focus of this chapter is on single-area OSPFv2.

OSPF is a link-state routing protocol that was developed as an alternative for the distance vector protocol Routing Information Protocol (RIP). RIP was an acceptable routing protocol in the early days of networking and the internet. However, RIP's reliance on hop count as the only metric for determining best route quickly became problematic. Using hop count does not scale well in larger networks with multiple paths of varying speeds. OSPF has significant advantages over RIP in that it offers faster convergence and scales to much larger network implementations.

OSPF is a link-state routing protocol that uses the concept of *areas*. A network administrator can divide the routing domain into distinct areas that help control routing update traffic. A link is an interface on a router. A link is also a network segment that connects two routers, or a stub network such as an Ethernet LAN that is connected to a single router. Information about the state of a link is known as link-state information; this information includes the network prefix, prefix length, and cost.

This chapter covers basic, single-area OSPF implementations and configurations.

Components of OSPF (1.1.2)

All routing protocols share similar components. They all use routing protocol messages to exchange route information. The messages help build data structures, which are then processed using a routing algorithm.

The components of OSPF are as follows:

- Routing protocol messages
- Data structures
- Algorithm

Routing Protocol Messages

Routers running OSPF exchange messages to convey routing information using five types of packets. These packets, as shown in Figure 1-1, are as follows:

- *Hello packet*
- *Database description (DBD) packet*
- *Link-state request (LSR) packet*
- *Link-state update (LSU) packet*
- *Link-state acknowledgment (LSAck) packet*

Hello packets
Database description packets
Link-state Request packets
Link-state Update packets
Link-state Acknowledgement packets

Figure 1-1   OSPF Packets

These packets are used to discover neighboring routers and also to exchange routing information to maintain accurate information about the network.

Data Structures

OSPF messages are used to create and maintain three OSPF databases:

- *Adjacency database*: This creates the *neighbor table*.
- *Link-state database (LSDB)*: This creates the *topology table*.
- *Forwarding database*: This creates the routing table.

Each of these tables contains a list of neighboring routers to exchange routing information. The tables are kept and maintained in RAM. In Table 1-1, take a particular note of the command used to display each table.

Table 1-1   OSPF Databases

Database	Table	Description
Adjacency database	Neighbor table	■ Lists all neighbor routers to which a router has established bidirectional communication. ■ This table is unique for each router. ■ Can be viewed using the **show ip ospf neighbor** command.
Link-state database	Topology table	■ Lists information about all other routers in the network. ■ This database represents the network topology. ■ All routers within an area have identical LSDBs. ■ Can be viewed using the **show ip ospf database** command.
Forwarding database	Routing table	■ Lists routes generated when an algorithm is run on the link-state database. ■ The routing table of each router is unique and contains information on how and where to send packets to other routers. ■ Can be viewed using the **show ip route** command.

Algorithm

A router builds a topology table by using results of calculations based on *Dijkstra's algorithm*. The *shortest-path first (SPF) algorithm* is based on the cumulative cost to reach a destination.

The SPF algorithm creates an SPF tree by placing each router at the root of the tree and calculating the shortest path to each node, as shown in Figure 1-2. The SPF tree is then used to calculate the best routes. OSPF places the best routes into the forwarding database, which is used to make the routing table.

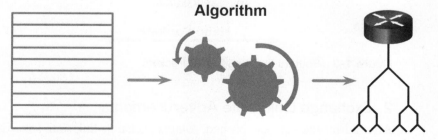

Figure 1-2   Algorithm Creates SPF Tree

Link-State Operation (1.1.3)

To maintain routing information, OSPF routers complete a generic link-state routing process to reach a state of *convergence*. In the following figures, the topology consists of five routers. The links between the routers have been labeled with cost values. In OSPF, cost is used to determine the best path to the destination. A router completes the following link-state routing steps:

Step 1.   Establish neighbor adjacencies.

Step 2.   Exchange link-state advertisements.

Step 3.   Build the link-state database.

Step 4.   Execute the SPF algorithm.

Step 5.   Choose the best route.

1. Establish Neighbor Adjacencies

OSPF-enabled routers must recognize each other on the network before they can share information. An OSPF-enabled router sends Hello packets out all OSPF-enabled interfaces to determine if neighbors are present on those links, as shown in Figure 1-3. If a neighbor is present, the OSPF-enabled router attempts to establish a neighbor adjacency with that neighbor.

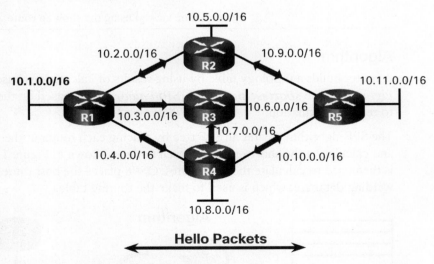

Figure 1-3   Routers Exchange Hello Packets

2. Exchange Link-State Advertisements

After adjacencies are established, routers exchange link-state advertisements (LSAs), as shown in Figure 1-4. An LSA contains the state and cost of each directly connected link. Routers flood their LSAs to adjacent neighbors. Adjacent neighbors receiving the LSA immediately flood the LSA to other directly connected neighbors, until all routers in the area have all LSAs.

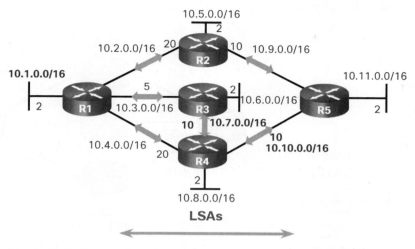

Figure 1-4   Routers Exchange LSAs

3. Build the Link-State Database

After LSAs are received, OSPF-enabled routers build the topology table (LSDB) based on the received LSAs, as shown in Figure 1-5. This database eventually holds all the information about the topology of the area.

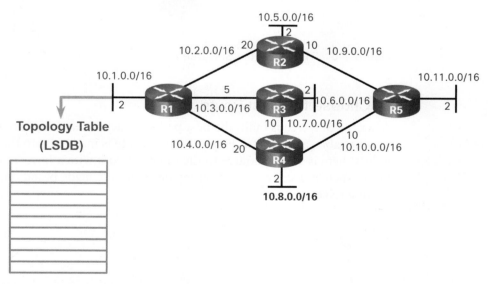

Figure 1-5   R1 Creates Its Topology Table

4. Execute the SPF Algorithm

When the LSDB is built, routers then execute the SPF algorithm. The gears in Figure 1-6 for this step are used to indicate the execution of the SPF algorithm. The SPF algorithm creates the SPF tree.

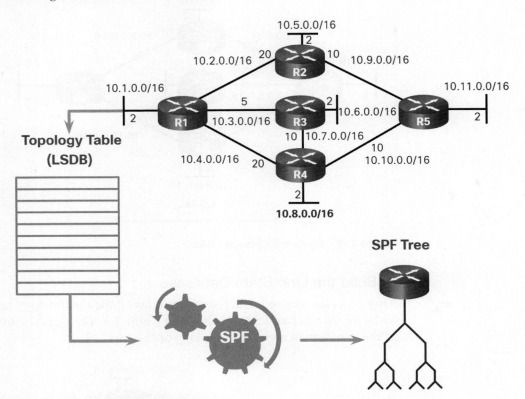

Figure 1-6   R1 Creates the SPF Tree

5. Choose the Best Route

After the SPF tree is built, the best paths to each network are offered to the IP routing table, as shown in Figure 1-7. The route is inserted into the routing table unless there is a route source to the same network with a lower administrative distance, such as a static route. Routing decisions are made based on the entries in the routing table.

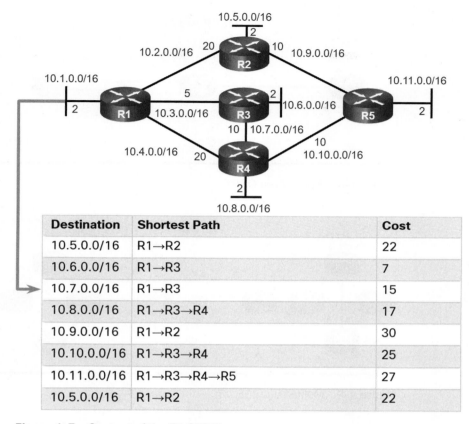

Destination	Shortest Path	Cost
10.5.0.0/16	R1→R2	22
10.6.0.0/16	R1→R3	7
10.7.0.0/16	R1→R3	15
10.8.0.0/16	R1→R3→R4	17
10.9.0.0/16	R1→R2	30
10.10.0.0/16	R1→R3→R4	25
10.11.0.0/16	R1→R3→R4→R5	27
10.5.0.0/16	R1→R2	22

Figure 1-7 Content of the R1 SPF Tree

Single-Area and Multiarea OSPF (1.1.4)

To make OSPF more efficient and scalable, OSPF supports hierarchical routing using areas. An *OSPF area* is a group of routers that share the same link-state information in their LSDBs. OSPF can be implemented in one of two ways:

- **Single-area OSPF:** All routers are in one area, as shown in Figure 1-8. Best practice is to use area 0.

- **Multiarea OSPF:** OSPF is implemented using multiple areas, in a hierarchical fashion, as shown in Figure 1-9. All areas must connect to the *backbone area* (area 0). Routers interconnecting the areas are referred to as *area border routers (ABRs).*

The focus of this chapter is on single-area OSPFv2.

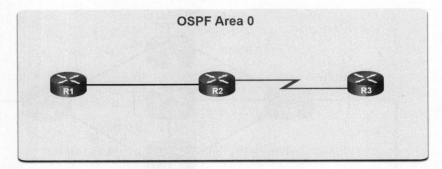

Figure 1-8   Single-Area OSPF

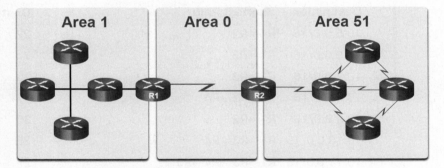

Figure 1-9   Multiarea OSPF

Multiarea OSPF (1.1.5)

With multiarea OSPF, one large routing domain can be divided into smaller areas to support hierarchical routing. Routing still occurs between the areas (*interarea routing*), and many of the processor-intensive routing operations, such as recalculating the database, are kept within an area.

For instance, any change regarding the link-state information (including the addition, deletion, or modification of a link) causes the router connected to that link to send out a new LSA. Any time a router receives new information about a topology change within the area, the router must rerun the SPF algorithm, create a new SPF tree, and update the routing table. The SPF algorithm is CPU intensive, and the time it takes for calculation depends on the size of the area.

Note

Routers in other areas receive updates regarding topology changes, but these routers only update the routing table; they do not rerun the SPF algorithm.

Too many routers in one area would make the LSDBs very large and increase the load on the CPU. Therefore, arranging routers into areas effectively partitions a potentially large database into smaller and more manageable databases.

The hierarchical topology design options with multiarea OSPF can offer the following advantages:

- **Smaller routing tables:** Tables are smaller because there are fewer routing table entries. This is because network addresses can be summarized between areas. *Route summarization* is not enabled by default.

- **Reduced link-state update overhead:** Designing multiarea OSPF with smaller areas minimizes processing and memory requirements.

- **Reduced frequency of SPF calculations:** Multiarea OSPF localize the impact of a topology change within an area. For instance, it minimizes routing update impact because LSA flooding stops at the area boundary.

For example, in Figure 1-10, R2 is an ABR for area 51. A topology change in area 51 would cause all area 51 routers to rerun the SPF algorithm, create a new SPF tree, and update their IP routing tables. The ABR, R2, would send an LSA to routers in area 0, which would eventually be flooded to all routers in the OSPF routing domain. This type of LSA does not cause routers in other areas to rerun the SPF algorithm. They only have to update their LSDB and routing table.

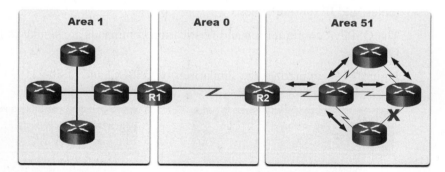

Figure 1-10   Link Change Impacts Local Area Only

Note the following in Figure 1-10:

- Link failure affects the local area only (area 51).

- The ABR (R2) isolates the flooding of a specific LSA to area 51.

- Routers in areas 0 and 1 do not need to run the SPF algorithm.

OSPFv3 (1.1.6)

OSPFv3 is the version of OSPF used for exchanging IPv6 prefixes. Recall that in IPv6, the network address is referred to as the *prefix*, and the subnet mask is called the *prefix length*.

Similar to its IPv4 counterpart, OSPFv3 exchanges routing information to populate the IPv6 routing table with remote prefixes.

> **Note**
>
> With the OSPFv3 address families feature, OSPFv3 includes support for both IPv4 and IPv6. The OSPF address families feature is beyond the scope of this book.

OSPFv2 runs over the IPv4 network layer, communicating with other OSPF IPv4 peers and advertising only IPv4 routes.

OSPFv3 has the same functionality as OSPFv2 but uses IPv6 as the network layer transport, communicating with OSPFv3 peers and advertising IPv6 routes. OSPFv3 also uses the SPF algorithm as the computation engine to determine the best paths throughout the routing domain.

OSPFv3 has separate processes from its IPv4 counterpart. The processes and operations are basically the same as in the IPv4 routing protocol, but they run independently. OSPFv2 and OSPFv3 each have separate adjacency tables, OSPF topology tables, and IP routing tables.

The OSPFv3 configuration and verification commands are similar to those used in OSPFv2.

Figure 1-11 summarizes the similarities of OSPFv2 and OSPFv3.

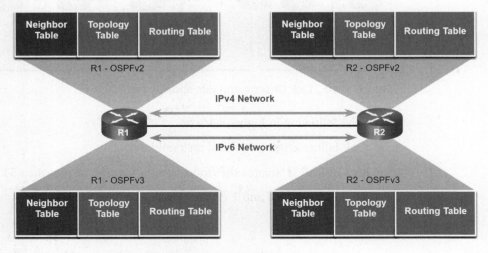

Figure 1-11   OSPFv2 and OSPFv3 Data Structures

Check Your Understanding—OSPF Features and Characteristics (1.1.7)

Refer to the online course to complete this activity.

OSPF Packets (1.2)

In this section you will learn about the types of packets used to establish and maintain an OSPF neighbor relationship.

Video—OSPF Packets (1.2.1)

Refer to the online course to view this video.

Types of OSPF Packets (1.2.2)

OSPF uses link-state packets to determine the fastest available route for a packet. OSPF uses the following *link-state packets (LSPs)* to establish and maintain neighbor adjacencies and exchange routing updates. Each packet serves a specific purpose in the OSPF routing process:

- **Type 1: Hello packet:** This packet is used to establish and maintain adjacency with other OSPF routers.

- **Type 2: Database Description (DBD) packet:** This packet contains an abbreviated list of the LSDB of the sending router and is used by receiving routers to check against the local LSDB. The LSDB must be identical on all *link-state routers* within an area to construct an accurate SPF tree.

- **Type 3: Link-State Request (LSR) packet:** Receiving routers can request more information about any entry in the DBD by sending an LSR.

- **Type 4: Link-State Update (LSU) packet:** This packet is used to reply to LSRs and to announce new information. LSUs contain several different types of LSAs.

- **Type 5: Link-State Acknowledgment (LSAck) packet:** When an LSU is received, the router sends an LSAck to confirm receipt of the LSU. The LSAck data field is empty.

Table 1-2 summarizes the five different types of LSPs used by OSPFv2. OSPFv3 has similar packet types.

Table 1-2   OSPF Packet Types

Type	Packet Name	Description
1	Hello	Discovers neighbors and builds adjacencies between them.
2	Database Description (DBD)	Checks for database synchronization between routers.
3	Link-State Request (LSR)	Requests specific link-state records from router to router.
4	Link-State Update (LSU)	Sends specifically requested link-state records.
5	Link-State Acknowledgment (LSAck)	Acknowledges the other packet types.

Link-State Updates (1.2.3)

Routers initially exchange Type 2 DBD packets. A DBD packet is an abbreviated list of the LSDB of the sending router. It is used by receiving routers to check against the local LSDB.

The receiving routers use a Type 3 LSR packet to request more information about an entry in the DBD.

The Type 4 LSU packet is used to reply to an LSR packet.

A Type 5 packet is used to acknowledge the receipt of a Type 4 LSU.

LSUs are also used to forward OSPF routing updates, such as link changes. Specifically, an LSU packet can contain 11 different types of OSPFv2 LSAs; some of the most common OSPFv2 LSAs are shown in Figure 1-12. OSPFv3 renamed several of these LSAs and also contains two additional LSAs.

Note

The difference between the LSU and LSA terms can sometimes be confusing because these terms are often used interchangeably. However, an LSU contains one or more LSAs.

Note the following in Figure 1-12:

- An LSU contains one or more LSAs.

- LSAs contain route information for destination networks.

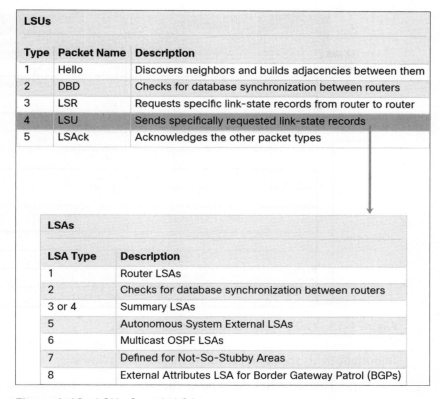

LSUs

Type	Packet Name	Description
1	Hello	Discovers neighbors and builds adjacencies between them
2	DBD	Checks for database synchronization between routers
3	LSR	Requests specific link-state records from router to router
4	LSU	Sends specifically requested link-state records
5	LSAck	Acknowledges the other packet types

LSAs

LSA Type	Description
1	Router LSAs
2	Checks for database synchronization between routers
3 or 4	Summary LSAs
5	Autonomous System External LSAs
6	Multicast OSPF LSAs
7	Defined for Not-So-Stubby Areas
8	External Attributes LSA for Border Gateway Patrol (BGPs)

Figure 1-12   LSUs Contain LSAs

Hello Packet (1.2.4)

The OSPF Type 1 packet is the Hello packet. Hello packets are used to do the following:

- Discover OSPF neighbors and establish neighbor adjacencies.
- Advertise parameters on which two routers must agree to become neighbors.
- Elect the *designated router (DR)* and *backup designated router (BDR)* on multiaccess networks such as Ethernet networks. Point-to-point links do not require DR or BDR.

Figure 1-13 displays the fields contained in the OSPFv2 Type 1 Hello packet.

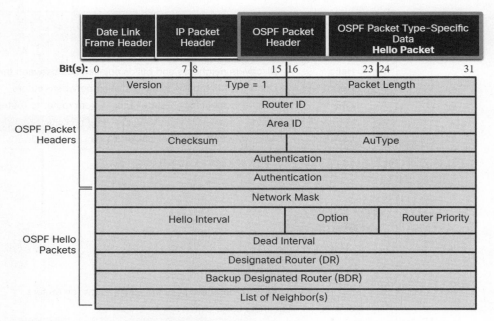

Figure 1-13   OSPF Hello Packet Content

Important fields shown in the figure include the following:

- **Type:** This identifies the type of packet. The value 1 indicates a Hello packet. The value 2 identifies a DBD packet, 3 an LSR packet, 4 an LSU packet, and 5 an LSAck packet.

- *Router ID*: A 32-bit value expressed in dotted decimal notation (like an IPv4 address) is used to uniquely identify the originating router.

- **Area ID:** This is the number of the area from which the packet originated.

- **Network Mask:** This is the subnet mask associated with the sending interface.

- *Hello Interval*: This specifies the frequency, in seconds, at which a router sends Hello packets. The default Hello interval on multiaccess networks is 10 seconds. This timer must be the same on neighboring routers; otherwise, an adjacency is not established.

- *Router Priority*: This is used in a DR/BDR election. The default priority for all OSPF routers is 1, but it can be manually altered to a value from 0 to 255. The higher the value, the more likely the router is to become the DR on the link.

- *Dead Interval*: This is the time, in seconds, that a router waits to hear from a neighbor before declaring the neighboring router out of service. By default, the router Dead Interval is four times the Hello Interval. This timer must be the same on neighboring routers; otherwise, an adjacency is not established.

- **Designated Router (DR):** This is the router ID of the DR.

- **Backup Designated Router (BDR):** This is the router ID of the BDR.

- **List of Neighbors:** This list identifies the router IDs of all adjacent routers.

Check Your Understanding—OSPF Packets (1.2.5)

Refer to the online course to complete this activity.

OSPF Operation (1.3)

In this section you will learn how OSPF achieves convergence.

Video—OSPF Operation (1.3.1)

Refer to the online course to view this video.

OSPF Operational States (1.3.2)

Now that you know about the OSPF link-state packets, this section explains how they work with OSPF-enabled routers. When an OSPF router is initially connected to a network, it attempts to:

- Create adjacencies with neighbors

- Exchange routing information

- Calculate the best routes

- Reach convergence

Table 1-3 details the states OSPF progresses through while attempting to reach convergence:

Table 1-3   Description of OSPF Operational States

State	Description
Down state	■ No Hello packets received = Down. ■ Router sends Hello packets. ■ Transition to *Init state*.
Init state	■ Hello packets are received from the neighbor. ■ Hello packets contain the Router ID of the sending router. ■ Transition to *Two-Way state* when the router sees its router ID being advertised in a neighbor's Hello packet.

State	Description
Two-Way state	■ In this state, communication between the two routers is bidirectional. ■ On multiaccess links, the routers elect a DR and a BDR. ■ Transition to *ExStart state*.
ExStart state	■ On point-to-point networks, the two routers decide which router will initiate the DBD packet exchange. ■ Next, they decide on the initial DBD packet sequence number.
Exchange state	■ Routers exchange DBD packets. ■ If additional router information is required, transition to Loading; otherwise, transition to the *Full state*.
Loading state	■ LSRs and LSUs are used to gain additional route information. ■ Routes are processed using the SPF algorithm. ■ Transition to the Full state.
Full state	■ The link-state database of the router is fully synchronized. OSPF has converged.

Establish Neighbor Adjacencies (1.3.3)

When OSPF is enabled on an interface, the router must determine if there is another OSPF neighbor on the link. To accomplish this, the router sends a Hello packet that contains its router ID out all OSPF-enabled interfaces. The Hello packet is sent to the reserved All OSPF Routers IPv4 multicast address 224.0.0.5. Only OSPFv2 routers process these packets. The OSPF router ID is used by the OSPF process to uniquely identify each router in the OSPF area. A router ID is a 32-bit number formatted like an IPv4 address and assigned to uniquely identify a router among OSPF peers.

When a neighboring OSPF-enabled router receives a Hello packet with a router ID that is not within its neighbor list, the receiving router attempts to establish an adjacency with the initiating router.

1. Down State to Init State

When OSPFv2 is enabled, the enabled Gigabit Ethernet 0/0 interface transitions from the Down state to the Init state, as shown in Figure 1-14. R1 starts sending Hello packets out all OSPF-enabled interfaces to discover OSPF neighbors to develop adjacencies with.

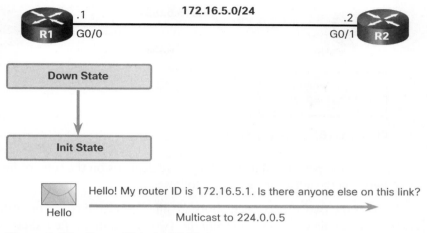

Figure 1-14   Down State to Init State

2. The Init State

R2 receives the Hello packet from R1 and adds the R1 router ID to its neighbor list. R2 then sends a Hello packet to R1, as shown in Figure 1-15. The packet contains the R2 router ID and the R1 router ID in its list of neighbors on the same interface.

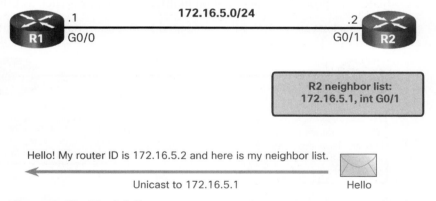

Figure 1-15   The Init State

3. Two-Way State

R1 receives the Hello packet and adds the R2 router ID to its list of OSPF neighbors, as shown in Figure 1-16. It also notices its own router ID in the list of neighbors of the Hello packet. When a router receives a Hello packet with its router ID listed in the list of neighbors, the router transitions from the Init state to the Two-Way state.

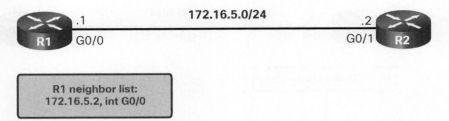

Figure 1-16   Two-Way State

The action performed in Two-Way state depends on the type of interconnection between the adjacent routers, as follows:

- If the two adjacent neighbors are interconnected over a point-to-point link, they immediately transition from the Two-Way state to the ExStart state.

- If the routers are interconnected over a common Ethernet network, then a designated router DR and a BDR must be elected.

4. Elect the DR and BDR

Because R1 and R2 are interconnected over an Ethernet network, a DR and BDR election takes place. As shown in Figure 1-17, R2 becomes the DR, and R1 is the BDR. This process occurs only on multiaccess networks such as Ethernet LANs.

Hello packets are continually exchanged to maintain router information.

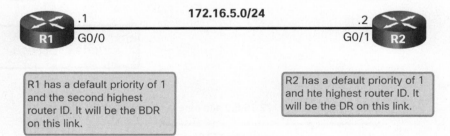

Figure 1-17   Elect the DR and BDR

Synchronizing OSPF Databases (1.3.4)

After the Two-Way state, routers transition to database synchronization states. The Hello packet was used to establish neighbor adjacencies, and the other four types of

OSPF packets are used during the process of exchanging and synchronizing LSDBs. This is a three-step process:

Step 1.   Decide which is the first router.

Step 2.   Exchange DBDs.

Step 3.   Send an LSR.

1. Decide First Router

In the ExStart state, the two routers decide which router will send the DBD packets first. The router with the higher router ID will be the first router to send DBD packets during the Exchange state. In Figure 1-18, R2 has the higher router ID and sends its DBD packets first.

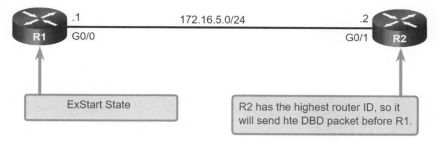

Figure 1-18   Decide Which Router Sends the First DBD

2. Exchange DBDs

In the Exchange state, the two routers exchange one or more DBD packets. A DBD packet includes information about the LSA entry header that appears in the LSDB of the router. The entries can be about a link or about a network. Each LSA entry header includes information about the link-state type, the address of the advertising router, the cost of the link, and the sequence number. The router uses the sequence number to determine the newness of the received *link-state information*.

In Figure 1-19, R2 sends a DBD packet to R1. When R1 receives the DBD, it performs the following actions:

Step 1.   It acknowledges the receipt of the DBD using the LSAck packet.

Step 2.   R1 then sends DBD packets to R2.

Step 3.   R2 acknowledges R1.

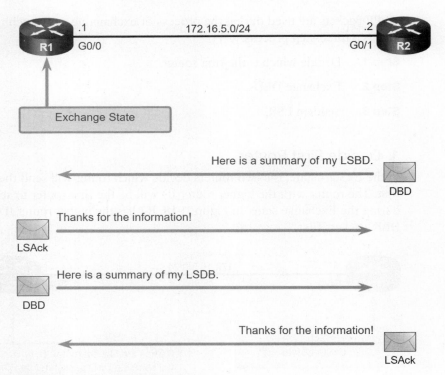

Figure 1-19 Exchange DBD Packets

3. Send an LSR

R1 compares the information received with the information it has in its own LSDB. If the DBD packet has a more current link-state entry, the router transitions to the Loading state.

For example, in Figure 1-20, R1 sends an LSR regarding network 172.16.6.0 to R2. R2 responds with the complete information about 172.16.6.0 in an LSU packet. Again, when R1 receives an LSU, it sends an LSAck. R1 then adds the new link-state entries into its LSDB.

After all LSRs have been satisfied for a given router, the adjacent routers are considered synchronized and in a Full state. Updates (LSUs) are sent only to neighbors in the following conditions:

- When a change is perceived (incremental updates)
- Every 30 minutes

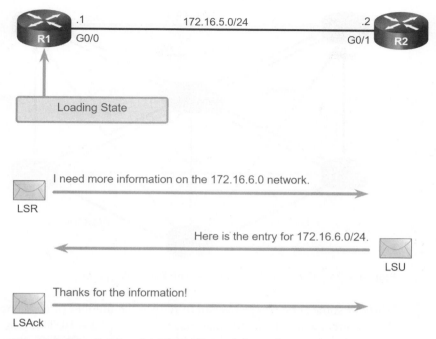

Figure 1-20   Getting Additional Route Information

The Need for a DR (1.3.5)

Why is a DR and BDR election necessary?

Multiaccess networks can create two challenges for OSPF regarding the flooding of LSAs:

- **Creation of multiple adjacencies:** Ethernet networks could potentially interconnect many OSPF routers over a common link. Creating adjacencies with every
  router is unnecessary and undesirable. It would lead to an excessive number of
  LSAs exchanged between routers on the same network.

- **Extensive flooding of LSAs:** Link-state routers flood their LSAs any time OSPF
  is initialized or when there is a change in the topology. This flooding can become
  excessive.

To understand the problem with multiple adjacencies, we must study a formula:
For any number of routers (designated as n) on a multiaccess network, there are
$n (n - 1) / 2$ adjacencies. For example, Figure 1-21 shows a simple topology of five
routers, all of which are attached to the same multiaccess Ethernet network.

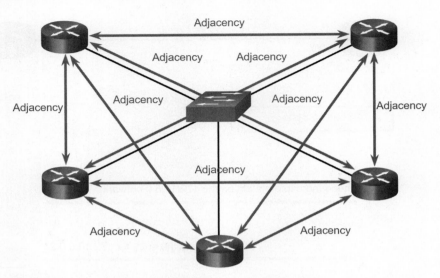

Figure 1-21   Creating Adjacencies with Every Neighbor

Without some type of mechanism to reduce the number of adjacencies, collectively these routers would form 10 adjacencies: 5 (5 − 1) / 2 = 10. This may not seem like much, but as routers are added to the network, the number of adjacencies increases dramatically. For example, a multiaccess network with 20 routers would create 190 adjacencies.

LSA Flooding with a DR (1.3.6)

A dramatic increase in the number of routers also dramatically increases the number of LSAs exchanged between the routers. This flooding of LSAs significantly impacts the operation of OSPF.

Flooding LSAs

To understand the problem of extensive flooding of LSAs , refer to Figure 1-22.

In the figure, R2 sends out an LSA, which triggers every other router to also send out an LSA. Not shown in the figure are the required acknowledgments sent for every LSA received. If every router in a multiaccess network had to flood and acknowledge all received LSAs to all other routers on that same multiaccess network, the network traffic would become quite chaotic.

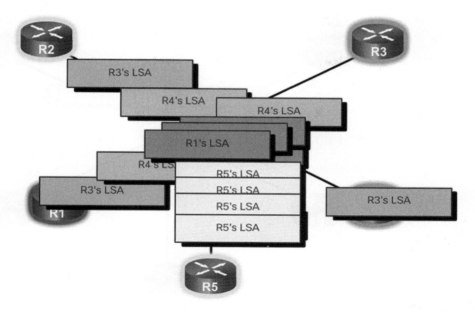

Figure 1-22   Flooding LSAs

LSAs and DR

The solution to managing the number of adjacencies and the flooding of LSAs on a multiaccess network is the designated router (DR). On multiaccess networks, OSPF elects a DR to be the collection and distribution point for LSAs sent and received. A backup designated router (BDR) is also elected in case the DR fails. All other routers become *DROTHERs*. A DROTHER is a router that is neither the DR nor the BDR.

> **Note**
>
> The DR is only used for the dissemination of LSAs. The router will still use the best next-hop router indicated in the routing table for the forwarding of all other packets.

Figure 1-23 shows the role of the DR to be the collector and distributer of LSAs in a multiaccess network.

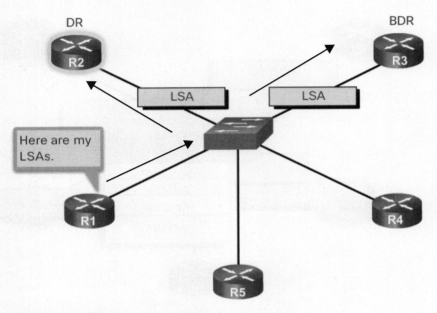

Figure 1-23   R1 Sends LSAs to the DR and BDR

Check Your Understanding—OSPF Operation (1.3.7)

Refer to the online course to complete this activity.

Interactive
Graphic

Summary (1.4)

The following is a summary of the sections in this chapter.

OSPF Features and Characteristics

Open Shortest Path First (OSPF) is a link-state routing protocol that was developed as an alternative for the distance vector protocol Routing Information Protocol (RIP). OSPF has significant advantages over RIP in that it offers faster convergence and scales to much larger network implementations. OSPF is a link-state routing protocol that uses the concept of areas for scalability. A link is an interface on a router. A link is also a network segment that connects two routers, or a stub network such as an Ethernet LAN that is connected to a single router. Link-state information includes the network prefix, prefix length, and cost. All routing protocols use routing protocol messages to exchange route information. The messages help build data structures, which are then processed using a routing algorithm. Routers running OSPF exchange messages to convey routing information using five types of packets: the Hello packet, the Database Description packet, the Link-State Request packet, the Link-State Update packet, and the Link-State Acknowledgment packet. OSPF messages are used to create and maintain three OSPF databases: the adjacency database creates the neighbor table, the link-state database (LSDB) creates the topology table, and the forwarding database creates the routing table. The router builds the topology table using results of calculations based on Dijkstra's SPF (shortest-path first) algorithm. The SPF algorithm is based on the cumulative cost to reach a destination. In OSPF, cost is used to determine the best path to the destination. To maintain routing information, OSPF routers complete a generic link-state routing process to reach a state of convergence:

Step 1.   Establish neighbor adjacencies.

Step 2.   Exchange link-state advertisements.

Step 3.   Build the link-state database.

Step 4.   Execute the SPF algorithm.

Step 5.   Choose the best route.

With single-area OSPF, any number can be used for the area, but best practice is to use area 0. Single-area OSPF is useful in small networks with few routers. With multi-area OSPF, one large routing domain can be divided into smaller areas to support hierarchical routing. Routing still occurs between the areas (interarea routing), and many of the processor-intensive routing operations, such as recalculating the database, are kept within an area. OSPFv3 is the OSPFv2 equivalent for exchanging IPv6 prefixes. Recall that in IPv6, the network address is referred to as the prefix, and the subnet mask is called the prefix length.

OSPF Packets

OSPF uses the following link-state packets (LSPs) to establish and maintain neighbor adjacencies and exchange routing updates: Hello (Type 1), DBD (Type 2), LSR (Type 3), LSU (Type 4), and LSAck (Type 5). LSUs are also used to forward OSPF routing updates, such as link changes. Hello packets are used to:

- Discover OSPF neighbors and establish neighbor adjacencies.

- Advertise parameters on which two routers must agree to become neighbors.

- Elect the designated router (DR) and backup designated router (BDR) on multi-access networks like Ethernet networks. Point-to-point links do not require a DR or BDR.

Some important fields in the Hello packet are Type, Router ID, Area ID, Network Mask, Hello Interval, Router Priority, Dead Interval, DR, BDR, and List of Neighbors.

OSPF Operation

When an OSPF router is initially connected to a network, it attempts to:

- Create adjacencies with neighbors
- Exchange routing information
- Calculate the best routes
- Reach convergence

The states that OSPF progresses through to do this are Down state, Init state, Two-Way state, ExStart state, Exchange state, Loading state, and Full state. When OSPF is enabled on an interface, the router must determine if there is another OSPF neighbor on the link by sending a Hello packet that contains its router ID out all OSPF-enabled interfaces. The Hello packet is sent to the reserved All OSPF Routers IPv4 multicast address 224.0.0.5. Only OSPFv2 routers process these packets. When a neighboring OSPF-enabled router receives a Hello packet with a router ID that is not within its neighbor list, the receiving router attempts to establish an adjacency with the initiating router. After the Two-Way state, routers transition to database synchronization states, which is a three-step process:

Step 1. Decide which is the first router.

Step 2. Exchange DBDs.

Step 3. Send an LSR.

Multiaccess networks can create two challenges for OSPF regarding the flooding of LSAs: the creation of multiple adjacencies and extensive flooding of LSAs. A dramatic increase in the number of routers also dramatically increases the number of LSAs exchanged between the routers. This flooding of LSAs significantly impacts the operation of OSPF. If every router in a multiaccess network had to flood and acknowledge all received LSAs to all other routers on that same multiaccess network, the network traffic would become quite chaotic. This is why DR and BDR election is necessary. On multiaccess networks, OSPF elects a DR to be the collection and distribution point for LSAs sent and received. A BDR is also elected in case the DR fails.

Practice

There are no labs or Packet Tracer activities for this chapter.

Check Your Understanding

Complete all the review questions listed here to test your understanding of the topics and concepts in this chapter. The appendix "Answers to the 'Check Your Understanding' Questions" lists the answers.

1. Which OSPF data structure is identical in all routers in an OSPF area after convergence?

   A. Adjacency database

   B. Link-state database

   C. Routing table

   D. SPF tree

2. Which statements describe features of the OSPF topology table? (Choose three.)

   A. After convergence, the table contains only the lowest-cost route entries for all known networks.

   B. All routers in an area have identical topology tables.

   C. It is a link-state database that represents the network topology.

   D. Its contents are the result of running the SPF algorithm.

   E. The table can be viewed via the **show ip ospf database** command.

   F. The topology table contains information on how and where to send packets to other routers.

3. What is used to create the OSPF neighbor table?

    A. Adjacency database

    B. Link-state database

    C. Forwarding database

    D. Routing table

4. What is a function of OSPF Hello packets?

    A. To discover neighbors and build adjacencies between them

    B. To ensure database synchronization between routers

    C. To request specific link-state records from neighbor routers

    D. To send specifically requested link-state records

5. Which OPSF packet contains one or more link-state advertisements?

    A. Hello

    B. DBD

    C. LSAck

    D. LSR

    E. LSU

6. What are the purposes of an OSPF router ID? (Choose two.)

    A. To enable the SPF algorithm to determine the lowest-cost path to remote networks

    B. To facilitate router participation in the election of the designated router

    C. To facilitate the establishment of network convergence

    D. To facilitate the transition of the OSPF neighbor state to Full

    E. To uniquely identify the router within the OSPF domain

7. Which statement describes a multiarea OSPF network?

    A. It consists of multiple network areas that are daisy-chained together.

    B. It has a core backbone area with other areas connected to the backbone area.

    C. It has multiple routers that run multiple routing protocols simultaneously, and each protocol consists of an area.

    D. It requires a three-layer hierarchical network design approach.

8. What are the advantages of using multiarea OSPF? (Choose two.)

   A. A backbone area is not required.

   B. It allows OSPFv2 and OSPFv3 to run together.

   C. It enables multiple routing protocols to run in a large network.

   D. It improves routing efficiency by reducing the routing table and link-state update overhead.

   E. It improves routing performance by dividing the neighbor table into separate smaller ones.

   F. Topology changes in one area do not cause SPF recalculations in other areas.

9. Which command can be used to verify the contents of the LSDB in an OSPF area?

   A. **show ip ospf database**

   B. **show ip ospf interface**

   C. **show ip ospf neighbor**

   D. **show ip route ospf**

10. Which of the following facilitates hierarchical routing in OSPF?

    A. Auto-summarization

    B. Frequent SPF calculations

    C. The election of designated routers

    D. The use of multiple areas

11. Which step does an OSPF-enabled router take immediately after the OSPF router builds the topology table?

    A. Chooses the best path

    B. Establishes an adjacency with another router

    C. Exchanges link-state advertisements

    D. Executes the SPF algorithm

12. Which type of OSPFv2 packet contains an abbreviated list of the LSDB of a sending router and is used by receiving routers to check against the local LSDB?

    A. Database Description

    B. Link-State Acknowledgment

    C. Link-State Request

    D. Link-State Update

13. Which OSPF states are performed prior to two routers forming a neighbor adjacency? (Choose three.)

    A. Down

    B. Exchange

    C. ExStart

    D. Init

    E. Loading

    F. Two-Way

14. In an OSPF network, when are DR and BDR elections required?

    A. When all the routers in an OSPF area cannot form adjacencies

    B. When the routers are interconnected over a common Ethernet network

    C. When the two adjacent neighbors are in two different networks

    D. When the two adjacent neighbors are interconnected over a point-to-point link

15. When an OSPF network is converged and no network topology change has been detected by a router, how often are LSU packets sent to neighboring routers?

    A. Every 10 seconds

    B. Every 40 seconds

    C. Every 15 minutes

    D. Every 30 minutes

CHAPTER 2

Single-Area OSPFv2 Configuration

Objectives

Upon completion of this chapter, you will be able to answer the following questions:

- How do you configure an OSPFv2 router ID?

- How do you configure single-area OSPFv2 in a point-to-point network?

- How do you configure the OSPF interface priority to influence the DR/BDR election in a multiaccess network?

- How do you implement modifications to change the operation of single-area OSPFv2?

- How do you configure OSPF to propagate a default route?

- How do you verify a single-area OSPFv2 implementation?

Key Terms

This chapter uses the following key terms. You can find the definitions in the Glossary.

broadcast multiaccess   *page 49*

reference bandwidth   *page 63*

OSPF Hello and Dead intervals   *page 70*

propagate a default route   *page 74*

edge router   *page 74*

autonomous system boundary router (ASBR)   *page 74*

Introduction (2.0)

Now that you know about single-area OSPFv2, you can probably think of many ways it could benefit your own network. As a link-state protocol, OSPF is designed to not only find the fastest available route, it is designed to *create* fast, available routes. You may prefer a bit more control over some areas of your network, and OSPF gives you several ways to manually override the DR election process and create your own preferred routes. With OSPF, your network can combine the automated processes with your own choices to make a network that you could troubleshoot in your sleep! You know you want to learn how to do this!

OSPF Router ID (2.1)

In this section you will configure the OSPF router ID.

OSPF Reference Topology (2.1.1)

This section discusses the foundation on which OSPF bases its entire process: the OSPF router ID. Figure 2-1 shows the topology used for configuring OSPFv2 in this chapter.

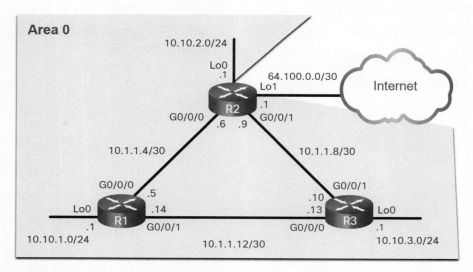

Figure 2-1   OSPF Reference Topology

The routers in this topology have a starting configuration, including interface addresses. There is currently no static routing or dynamic routing configured on any of the routers. All interfaces on R1, R2, and R3 (except the Loopback 1 interface on R2) are within the OSPF backbone area. The ISP router is used as the gateway to the internet of the routing domain.

> **Note**
>
> In this topology the loopback interface is used to simulate the WAN link to the internet and a LAN connected to each router. This is done to allow this topology to be duplicated for demonstration purposes on routers that only have two Gigabit Ethernet interfaces.

Router Configuration Mode for OSPF (2.1.2)

OSPFv2 is enabled using the **router ospf** *process-id* global configuration mode command, as shown in Example 2-1 for R1. The *process-id* value is a number between 1 and 65,535 and is selected by the network administrator. The *process-id* value is locally significant, which means that it does not have to be the same value on the other OSPF routers to establish adjacencies with those neighbors. It is considered best practice to use the same *process-id* on all OSPF routers.

Example 2-1   OSPF Router Configuration Commands

```
R1(config)# router ospf 10
R1(config-router)# ?
  area                 OSPF area parameters
  auto-cost            Calculate OSPF interface cost according to bandwidth
  default-information  Control distribution of default information
  distance             Define an administrative distance
  exit                 Exit from routing protocol configuration mode
  log-adjacency-changes Log changes in adjacency state
  neighbor             Specify a neighbor router
  network              Enable routing on an IP network
  no                   Negate a command or set its defaults
  passive-interface    Suppress routing updates on an interface
  redistribute         Redistribute information from another routing protocol
  router-id            router-id for this OSPF process
R1(config-router)#
```

After you enter the **router ospf** *process-id* command, the router enters router configuration mode, as indicated by the **R1(config-router)#** prompt. Enter a question mark (**?**) to view all the commands available in this mode. The list of commands shown in Example 2-1 has been altered to display only the commands that are relevant to this chapter.

Router IDs (2.1.3)

An OSPF router ID is a 32-bit value, represented as an IPv4 address. The router ID is used to uniquely identify an OSPF router. Every OSPF packet includes the router ID of the originating router. Every router requires a router ID to participate in an OSPF domain. The router ID can be defined by an administrator or automatically assigned by the router. The router ID is used by an OSPF-enabled router to do the following:

- **Participate in the synchronization of OSPF databases:** During the Exchange state, the router with the highest router ID sends its Database Descriptor (DBD) packets first.

- **Participate in the election of the designated router (DR):** In a multiaccess LAN environment, the router with the highest router ID is elected the DR. The routing device with the second-highest router ID is elected the backup designated router (BDR).

Note

The DR and BDR election process is discussed in more detail later in this chapter.

Router ID Order of Precedence (2.1.4)

How does a router determine the router ID? As illustrated in Figure 2-2, Cisco routers derive the router ID based on one of three criteria.

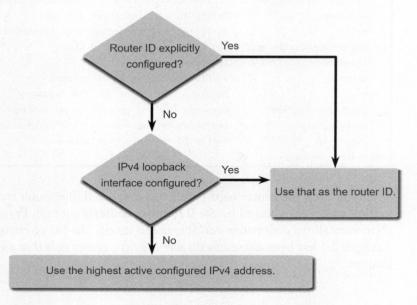

Figure 2-2 Three Criteria for Choosing the Router ID

The router ID is explicitly configured using the OSPF **router-id** *rid* router configuration mode command. The *rid* value is any 32-bit value expressed as an IPv4 address. This is the recommended method to assign a router ID.

If the router ID is not explicitly configured, the router chooses the highest IPv4 address of any of the configured loopback interfaces. This is the next best alternative to assigning a router ID.

If no loopback interfaces are configured, the router chooses the highest active IPv4 address of any of its physical interfaces. This is the least recommended method because it makes it more difficult for administrators to distinguish between specific routers.

Configure a Loopback Interface as the Router ID (2.1.5)

In the reference topology shown in Figure 2-1, only the physical interfaces are configured and active. The loopback interfaces have not been configured. When OSPF routing is enabled on the router, the routers pick the following highest active configured IPv4 addresses as the router IDs:

- **R1:** 10.1.1.14 (G0/0/1)
- **R2:** 10.1.1.9 (G0/0/1)
- **R3:** 10.1.1.13 (G0/0/0)

Note

OSPF does not need to be enabled on an interface for that interface to be chosen as the router ID.

Instead of relying on the physical interface, the router ID can be assigned to a loopback interface. Typically, the IPv4 address for this type of loopback interface should be configured using a 32-bit subnet mask (255.255.255.255). This effectively creates a host route. A 32-bit host route would not get advertised as a route to other OSPF routers.

Example 2-2 shows how to configure a loopback interface on R1. Assuming that the router ID was not explicitly configured or previously learned, R1 uses IPv4 address 1.1.1.1 as its router ID. Assume in this case that R1 has not yet learned a router ID.

Example 2-2   Using the Loopback Address as the Router ID

```
R1(config-if)# interface Loopback 1
R1(config-if)# ip address 1.1.1.1 255.255.255.255
R1(config-if)# end
R1#
R1# show ip protocols | include Router ID
  Router ID 1.1.1.1
R1#
```

Explicitly Configure a Router ID (2.1.6)

In Figure 2-3, the topology has been updated to show the router ID for each router:

- **R1:** 1.1.1.1

- **R2:** 2.2.2.2

- **R3:** 3.3.3.3

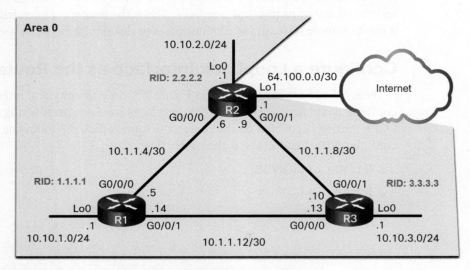

Figure 2-3 OSPF Reference Topology with Router IDs

Use the **router-id** *rid* router configuration mode command to manually assign a router ID. In Example 2-3, the router ID 1.1.1.1 is assigned to R1. Use the **show ip protocols** command, as shown in this example, to verify the router ID.

Example 2-3 Configuring and Verifying the Router ID

```
R1(config)# router ospf 10
R1(config-router)# router-id 1.1.1.1
R1(config-router)# end
*May 23 19:33:42.689: %SYS-5-CONFIG_I: Configured from console by console
R1#
R1# show ip protocols | include Router ID
  Router ID 1.1.1.1
R1#
```

Modify a Router ID (2.1.7)

After a router selects a router ID, an active OSPF router does not allow the router ID to be changed until the router is reloaded or the OSPF process is reset.

In Example 2-4 R1, the configured router ID has been removed and the router reloaded.

Example 2-4   Modifying the Router ID

```
R1# show ip protocols | include Router ID
   Router ID 10.10.1.1
R1#
R1# conf t
Enter configuration commands, one per line.  End with CNTL/Z.
R1(config)# router ospf 10
R1(config-router)# router-id 1.1.1.1
% OSPF: Reload or use "clear ip ospf process" command, for this to take effect
R1(config-router)# end
R1#
R1# clear ip ospf process
Reset ALL OSPF processes? [no]: y
*Jun  6 01:09:46.975: %OSPF-5-ADJCHG: Process 10, Nbr 3.3.3.3 on GigabitEthernet0/0/1
   from FULL to DOWN, Neighbor Down: Interface down or detached
*Jun  6 01:09:46.975: %OSPF-5-ADJCHG: Process 10, Nbr 2.2.2.2 on GigabitEthernet0/0/0
   from FULL to DOWN, Neighbor Down: Interface down or detached
*Jun  6 01:09:46.981: %OSPF-5-ADJCHG: Process 10, Nbr 3.3.3.3 on GigabitEthernet0/0/1
   from LOADING to FULL, Loading Done
*Jun  6 01:09:46.981: %OSPF-5-ADJCHG: Process 10, Nbr 2.2.2.2 on GigabitEthernet0/0/0
   from LOADING to FULL, Loading Done
R1#
R1# show ip protocols | include Router ID
   Router ID 1.1.1.1
R1#
```

Notice that the current router ID is 10.10.1.1, which is the Loopback 0 IPv4 address. The router ID should be 1.1.1.1. Therefore, R1 is configured with the command **router-id 1.1.1.1**.

Notice that an informational message appears, stating that the OSPF process must be cleared or the router must be reloaded. R1 already has adjacencies with other neighbors using the router ID 10.10.1.1, and those adjacencies must be renegotiated using the new router ID 1.1.1.1. Use the **clear ip ospf process** command to reset the adjacencies. You can then verify that R1 is using the new router ID with the **show ip protocols** command piped to display only the router ID section.

Clearing the OSPF process is the preferred method to reset the router ID.

> **Note**
>
> Using the **router-id** command is the preferred method for assigning an OSPF router ID. Otherwise, the router chooses the highest IPv4 loopback interface address or the highest active IPv4 address of any of its physical interfaces.

Interactive Graphic

Syntax Checker—Configure R2 and R3 Router IDs (2.1.8)

Refer to the online course to complete this activity.

Interactive Graphic

Check Your Understanding—OSPF Router ID (2.1.9)

Refer to the online course to complete this activity.

Point-to-Point OSPF Networks (2.2)

In this section, you will configure a point-to-point single-area OSPF network.

The network Command Syntax (2.2.1)

One type of network classified by OSPF is a point-to-point network. You can specify the interfaces that belong to a point-to-point network by configuring the **network** router configuration command. You can also configure OSPF directly on the interface with the **ip ospf** interface configuration command, as you will see later in this chapter. Both commands are used to determine which interfaces participate in the routing process for an OSPFv2 area.

The basic syntax for the **network** command is as follows:

```
Router(config-router)# network network-address wildcard-mask area area-id
```

In this syntax:

- *network-address wildcard-mask* syntax is used to enable OSPF on interfaces. Any interfaces on a router that match the network address in the **network** command are enabled to send and receive OSPF packets.

- **area** *area-id* refers to the OSPF area. When configuring single-area OSPFv2, the **network** command must be configured with the same *area-id* value on all routers. Although any area ID can be used, it is good practice to use an area ID of 0 with single-area OSPFv2. Following this convention makes it easier if the network is later altered to support multiarea OSPFv2.

The Wildcard Mask (2.2.2)

The wildcard mask is typically the inverse of the subnet mask configured on the interface. In a subnet mask, binary 1 indicates a match, and binary 0 is not a match. In a wildcard mask, the reverse is true, as shown here:

- **Wildcard mask bit 0:** Matches the corresponding bit value in the address.
- **Wildcard mask bit 1:** Ignores the corresponding bit value in the address.

The easiest method for calculating a wildcard mask is to subtract the network subnet mask from 255.255.255.255, as shown for the /24 and /26 subnet masks in Figure 2-4.

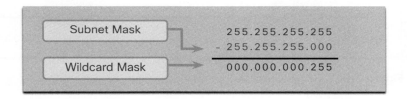

Calculating a Wildcard Mask for /26

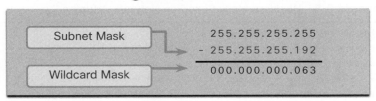

Figure 2-4   Wildcard Mask Calculation

Check Your Understanding—The Wildcard Masks (2.2.3)

Refer to the online course to complete this activity.

Configure OSPF Using the network Command (2.2.4)

Within routing configuration mode, there are two ways to identify the interfaces that will participate in the OSPFv2 routing process. Figure 2-5 shows the reference topology for this section.

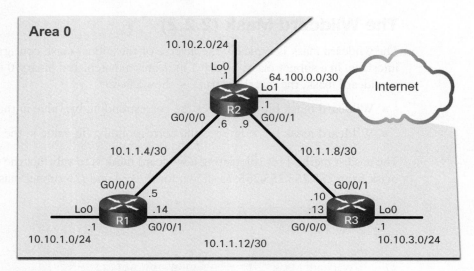

Figure 2-5   OSPF Reference Topology

In Example 2-5, the wildcard mask identifies the interface based on the network addresses. Any active interface that is configured with an IPv4 address belonging to that network will participate in the OSPFv2 routing process.

Example 2-5   Wildcard Mask Based on Network Address

```
R1(config)# router ospf 10
R1(config-router)# network 10.10.1.0 0.0.0.255 area 0
R1(config-router)# network 10.1.1.4 0.0.0.3 area 0
R1(config-router)# network 10.1.1.12 0.0.0.3 area 0
R1(config-router)#
```

Note

Some IOS versions allow the subnet mask to be entered instead of the wildcard mask. IOS then converts the subnet mask to the wildcard mask format.

As an alternative, Example 2-6 shows how OSPFv2 can be enabled by specifying the exact interface IPv4 address using a quad-zero wildcard mask. Entering **network 10.1.1.5 0.0.0.0 area 0** on R1 tells the router to enable interface Gigabit Ethernet 0/0/0 for the routing process. As a result, the OSPFv2 process will advertise the network that is on this interface (10.1.1.4/30).

Example 2-6   Wildcard Based on the Interface IPv4 Address

```
R1(config)# router ospf 10
R1(config-router)# network 10.10.1.1 0.0.0.0 area 0
R1(config-router)# network 10.1.1.5 0.0.0.0 area 0
R1(config-router)# network 10.1.1.14 0.0.0.0 area 0
R1(config-router)#
```

The advantage of specifying the interface is that the wildcard mask calculation is not necessary. Notice that in all cases, the **area** argument specifies area 0.

Interactive
Graphic

Syntax Checker—Configure R2 and R3 Using the network Command (2.2.5)

Refer to the online course to complete this activity.

Configure OSPF Using the ip ospf Command (2.2.6)

You can configure OSPF directly on the interface instead of by using the **network** command. To configure OSPF directly on the interface, use the **ip ospf** interface configuration mode command. The syntax is as follows:

```
Router(config-if)# ip ospf process-id area area-id
```

For R1, remove the **network** commands by using the **no** form of the **network** commands. Then go to each interface and configure the **ip ospf** command, as shown in Example 2-7.

Example 2-7   Configuring OSPF on the Interfaces

```
R1(config)# router ospf 10
R1(config-router)# no network 10.10.1.1 0.0.0.0 area 0
R1(config-router)# no network 10.1.1.5 0.0.0.0 area 0
R1(config-router)# no network 10.1.1.14 0.0.0.0 area 0
R1(config-router)# exit
R1(config)#
R1(config)# interface GigabitEthernet 0/0/0
R1(config-if)# ip ospf 10 area 0
R1(config-if)# exit
R1(config)#
R1(config)# interface GigabitEthernet 0/0/1
R1(config-if)# ip ospf 10 area 0
R1(config-if)# exit
R1(config)#
R1(config)# interface Loopback 0
R1(config-if)# ip ospf 10 area 0
R1(config-if)#
```

Interactive
Graphic
Syntax Checker—Configure R2 and R3 Using the ip ospf Command (2.2.7)

Refer to the online course to complete this activity.

Passive Interface (2.2.8)

By default, OSPF messages are forwarded out all OSPF-enabled interfaces. However, these messages really only need to be sent out interfaces that are connecting to other OSPF-enabled routers.

Refer to the topology in Figure 2-6.

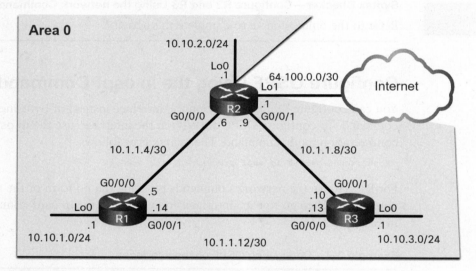

Figure 2-6   OSPF Passive Interface Reference Topology

OSPFv2 messages are forwarded out the three loopback interfaces even though no OSPFv2 neighbor exists on these simulated LANs. In a production network, these loopbacks would be physical interfaces to networks with users and traffic. Sending out unneeded messages on a LAN affects the network in three ways:

- **Inefficient use of bandwidth:** Available bandwidth is consumed by transporting unnecessary messages.

- **Inefficient use of resources:** All devices on the LAN must process and eventually discard the message.

- **Increased security risk:** Without additional OSPF security configurations, OSPF messages can be intercepted with packet sniffing software. Routing updates can be modified and sent back to the router, corrupting the routing table with false metrics that misdirect traffic.

Configure Passive Interfaces (2.2.9)

Use the **passive-interface** router configuration mode command to prevent the transmission of routing messages through a router interface, but still allow that network to be advertised to other routers. The configuration in Example 2-8 identifies the R1 Loopback 0/0/0 interface as passive.

Example 2-8   Configuring and Verifying Passive Interfaces

```
R1(config)# router ospf 10
R1(config-router)# passive-interface loopback 0
R1(config-router)# end
R1#
*May 23 20:24:39.309: %SYS-5-CONFIG_I: Configured from console by console
R1#
R1# show ip protocols
*** IP Routing is NSF aware ***
(output omitted)
Routing Protocol is "ospf 10"
  Outgoing update filter list for all interfaces is not set
  Incoming update filter list for all interfaces is not set
  Router ID 1.1.1.1
  Number of areas in this router is 1. 1 normal 0 stub 0 nssa
  Maximum path: 4
  Routing for Networks:
  Routing on Interfaces Configured Explicitly (Area 0):
    Loopback0
    GigabitEthernet0/0/1
    GigabitEthernet0/0/0
  Passive Interface(s):
    Loopback0
  Routing Information Sources:
    Gateway         Distance      Last Update
    3.3.3.3              110      01:01:48
    2.2.2.2              110      01:01:38
  Distance: (default is 110)
R1#
```

Note

The loopback interface in this example is representing an Ethernet network. In production networks, loopback interfaces are not required to be passive.

The **show ip protocols** command is used to verify that the Loopback 0 interface is listed as passive. The interface is still listed under the heading "Routing on Interfaces

Configured Explicitly (Area 0)," which means that this network is still included as a route entry in OSPFv2 updates that are sent to R2 and R3.

Interactive Graphic

Syntax Checker—Configure R2 and R3 Passive Interfaces (2.2.10)

Use Syntax Checker to configure the loopback interfaces on R2 as passive. As an alternative, all interfaces can be made passive using the **passive-interface default** command. Interfaces that should not be passive can be re-enabled using the **no passive-interface** command. Configure R3 with the **passive-interface default** command and then re-enable the Gigabit Ethernet interfaces.

Refer to the online course to complete this activity.

OSPF Point-to-Point Networks (2.2.11)

By default, Cisco routers elect a DR and BDR on Ethernet interfaces, even if there is only one other device on the link. You can verify which routers have been chosen as DR or BDR using the **show ip ospf interface** command, as shown in Example 2-9 for G0/0/0 of R1.

Example 2-9   Verifying the OSPF Network Type

```
R1# show ip ospf interface GigabitEthernet 0/0/0
GigabitEthernet0/0/0 is up, line protocol is up
  Internet Address 10.1.1.5/30, Area 0, Attached via Interface Enable
  Process ID 10, Router ID 1.1.1.1, Network Type BROADCAST, Cost: 1
  Topology-MTID    Cost     Disabled     Shutdown      Topology Name
        0           1          no           no             Base
  Enabled by interface config, including secondary ip addresses
  Transmit Delay is 1 sec, State BDR, Priority 1
  Designated Router (ID) 2.2.2.2, Interface address 10.1.1.6
  Backup Designated router (ID) 1.1.1.1, Interface address 10.1.1.5
  Timer intervals configured, Hello 10, Dead 40, Wait 40, Retransmit 5
    oob-resync timeout 40
    Hello due in 00:00:08
  Supports Link-local Signaling (LLS)
  Cisco NSF helper support enabled
  IETF NSF helper support enabled
  Index 1/2/2, flood queue length 0
  Next 0x0(0)/0x0(0)/0x0(0)
  Last flood scan length is 1, maximum is 1
  Last flood scan time is 0 msec, maximum is 0 msec
  Neighbor Count is 1, Adjacent neighbor count is 1
    Adjacent with neighbor 2.2.2.2  (Designated Router)
  Suppress hello for 0 neighbor(s)
R1#
```

As shown in Example 2-9, in this case, R1 is the BDR and R2 is the DR. The DR/BDR election process is unnecessary as there can only be two routers on the point-to-point network between R1 and R2. Notice in this output that the router has designated the network type as BROADCAST.

To change this to a point-to-point network, use the **ip ospf network point-to-point** interface configuration command on all interfaces where you want to disable the DR/BDR election process. Example 2-10 shows this configuration for R1. The OSPF neighbor adjacency status will go down for a few milliseconds.

Example 2-10   Changing and Verifying the OSPF Network Type

```
R1(config)# interface GigabitEthernet 0/0/0
R1(config-if)# ip ospf network point-to-point
*Jun  6 00:44:05.208: %OSPF-5-ADJCHG: Process 10, Nbr 2.2.2.2 on GigabitEthernet0/0/0
  from FULL to DOWN, Neighbor Down: Interface down or detached
*Jun  6 00:44:05.211: %OSPF-5-ADJCHG: Process 10, Nbr 2.2.2.2 on GigabitEthernet0/0/0
  from LOADING to FULL, Loading Done
R1(config-if)# exit
R1(config)#
R1(config)# interface GigabitEthernet 0/0/1
R1(config-if)# ip ospf network point-to-point
*Jun  6 00:44:45.532: %OSPF-5-ADJCHG: Process 10, Nbr 3.3.3.3 on GigabitEthernet0/0/1
  from FULL to DOWN, Neighbor Down: Interface down or detached
*Jun  6 00:44:45.535: %OSPF-5-ADJCHG: Process 10, Nbr 3.3.3.3 on GigabitEthernet0/0/1
  from LOADING to FULL, Loading Done
R1(config-if)# end
R1#
R1# show ip ospf interface GigabitEthernet 0/0/0
GigabitEthernet0/0/0 is up, line protocol is up
  Internet Address 10.1.1.5/30, Area 0, Attached via Interface Enable
  Process ID 10, Router ID 1.1.1.1, Network Type POINT_TO_POINT, Cost: 1
  Topology-MTID    Cost    Disabled    Shutdown    Topology Name
        0           1         no          no           Base
  Enabled by interface config, including secondary ip addresses
  Transmit Delay is 1 sec, State POINT_TO_POINT
  Timer intervals configured, Hello 10, Dead 40, Wait 40, Retransmit 5
    oob-resync timeout 40
    Hello due in 00:00:04
  Supports Link-local Signaling (LLS)
  Cisco NSF helper support enabled
  IETF NSF helper support enabled
  Index 1/2/2, flood queue length 0
  Next 0x0(0)/0x0(0)/0x0(0)
  Last flood scan length is 1, maximum is 2
  Last flood scan time is 0 msec, maximum is 1 msec
  Neighbor Count is 1, Adjacent neighbor count is 1
    Adjacent with neighbor 2.2.2.2
  Suppress hello for 0 neighbor(s)
R1#
```

Notice that the Gigabit Ethernet 0/0/0 interface now lists the network type as POINT_TO_POINT and that there is no DR or BDR on the link.

Loopbacks and Point-to-Point Networks (2.2.12)

We use loopbacks to provide additional interfaces for a variety of purposes. In this case, we are using loopbacks to simulate more networks than the equipment can support. By default, loopback interfaces are advertised as /32 host routes. For example, R1 would advertise the 10.10.1.0/24 network as 10.10.1.1/32 to R2 and R3, as shown in Example 2-11.

Example 2-11   Verifying That R2 Has a Route to the R1 Loopback Interface

```
R2# show ip route | include 10.10.1
O        10.10.1.1/32 [110/2] via 10.1.1.5, 00:03:05, GigabitEthernet0/0/0
R2#
```

To simulate a real LAN, the Loopback 0 interface is configured as a point-to-point network so that R1 will advertise the full 10.10.1.0/24 network to R2 and R3, as shown in Example 2-12.

Example 2-12   Configuring the Loopback to Simulate a Point-to-Point Network

```
R1(config-if)# interface Loopback 0
R1(config-if)# ip ospf network point-to-point
R1(config-if)#
```

Now R2 receives the more accurate, simulated LAN network address of 10.10.1.0/24, as shown in Example 2-13.

Example 2-13   Verifying That R2 Now Has a /24 Route to the Loopback Network

```
R2# show ip route | include 10.10.1
O        10.10.1.0/24 [110/2] via 10.1.1.5, 00:00:30, GigabitEthernet0/0/0
R2#
```

Note

At the time of this writing, Packet Tracer does not support the **ip ospf network point-to-point** interface configuration command on Gigabit Ethernet interfaces. However, it does support this command on loopback interfaces.

Packet Tracer—Point-to-Point Single-Area OSPFv2 Configuration (2.2.13)

In this Packet Tracer activity, you will configure single-area OSPFv2 as follows:

- Explicitly configure router IDs.

- Configure the **network** command on R1 using a wildcard mask based on the subnet mask.

- Configure the **network** command on R2 using a quad-zero wildcard mask.

- Configure the **ip ospf** interface command on R3.

- Configure passive interfaces.

- Verify OSPF operation using the **show ip protocols** and **show ip route** commands.

Multiaccess OSPF Networks (2.3)

In this section, you will configure the OSPF interface priority to influence the DR/BDR election.

OSPF Network Types (2.3.1)

Another type of network that uses OSPF is the multiaccess OSPF network. Multiaccess OSPF networks are unique in that one router controls the distribution of LSAs. The router that is elected for this role should be determined by the network administrator through proper configuration.

OSPF may include additional processes, depending on the type of network. The topology in the previous section (refer to Figure 2-6) uses point-to-point Ethernet links between the routers. However, routers can be connected to the same switch to form a multiaccess Ethernet network, as shown in Figure 2-7.

Ethernet LANs are the most common example of *broadcast multiaccess* networks. In broadcast networks, all devices on the network see all broadcast and multicast frames.

OSPF Designated Router (2.3.2)

Recall that in multiaccess networks, OSPF elects a DR and BDR as a solution to manage the number of adjacencies and the flooding of link-state advertisements (LSAs). The DR is responsible for collecting and distributing LSAs sent and received. The DR uses the multicast IPv4 address 224.0.0.5, which is meant for all OSPF routers.

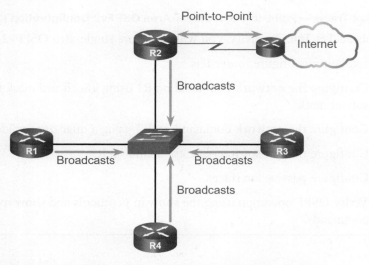

Figure 2-7   R2 Connected to Different Network Types

A BDR is also elected in case the DR fails. The BDR listens passively and maintains a relationship with all the routers. If the DR stops producing Hello packets, the BDR promotes itself and assumes the role of DR.

Every other router becomes a DROTHER (a router that is neither the DR nor the BDR). DROTHERs use the multiaccess address 224.0.0.6 (all designated routers) to send OSPF packets to the DR and BDR. Only the DR and BDR listen for 224.0.0.6.

In Figure 2-8, R1 sends LSAs to the DR. Notice that only the DR and the BDR process the LSA sent by R1 using the multicast IPv4 address 224.0.0.6.

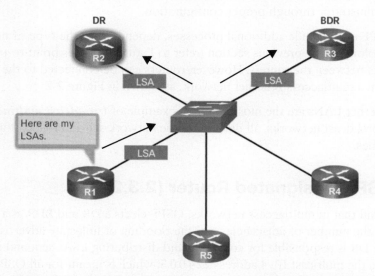

Figure 2-8   Role of the DR: Forming Adjacencies with the DR and the BDR Only

In Figure 2-9, R1, R5, and R4 are DROTHERs. The DR sends out the LSA to all OSPF routers using the multicast IPv4 address 224.0.0.5.

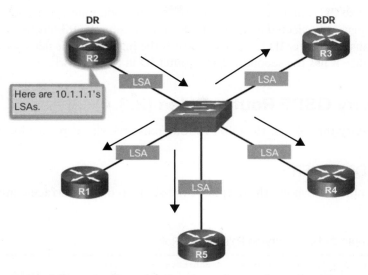

Figure 2-9   Role of the DR: Sending LSAs to Other Routers

OSPF Multiaccess Reference Topology (2.3.3)

In the multiaccess topology shown in Figure 2-10, there are three routers interconnected over a common Ethernet multiaccess network, 192.168.1.0/24.

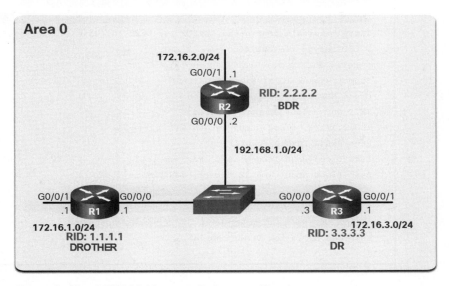

Figure 2-10   OSPF Multiaccess Reference Topology

Each router is configured with the indicated IPv4 address on the Gigabit Ethernet 0/0/0 interface.

Because the routers are connected over a common multiaccess network, OSPF has automatically elected a DR and BDR. In this example, R3 has been elected as the DR because its router ID is 3.3.3.3, which is the highest in this network. R2 is the BDR because it has the second-highest router ID in the network.

Verify OSPF Router Roles (2.3.4)

To verify the roles of the OSPFv2 router, use the **show ip ospf interface** command.

R1 DROTHER

Example 2-14 shows the output of the **show ip ospf interface** command generated on R1.

Example 2-14   Verifying R1's Router Role

```
R1# show ip ospf interface GigabitEthernet 0/0/0
GigabitEthernet0/0/0 is up, line protocol is up
   Internet Address 192.168.1.1/24, Area 0, Attached via Interface Enable
   Process ID 10, Router ID 1.1.1.1, Network Type BROADCAST, Cost: 1
   Topology-MTID    Cost    Disabled    Shutdown      Topology Name
          0           1        no          no             Base
   Enabled by interface config, including secondary ip addresses
   Transmit Delay is 1 sec, State DROTHER, Priority 1
   Designated Router (ID) 3.3.3.3, Interface address 192.168.1.3
   Backup Designated router (ID) 2.2.2.2, Interface address 192.168.1.2
   Timer intervals configured, Hello 10, Dead 40, Wait 40, Retransmit 5
     oob-resync timeout 40
     Hello due in 00:00:07
   Supports Link-local Signaling (LLS)
   Cisco NSF helper support enabled
   IETF NSF helper support enabled
   Index 1/1/1, flood queue length 0
   Next 0x0(0)/0x0(0)/0x0(0)
   Last flood scan length is 0, maximum is 1
   Last flood scan time is 0 msec, maximum is 1 msec
   Neighbor Count is 2, Adjacent neighbor count is 2
     Adjacent with neighbor 2.2.2.2  (Backup Designated Router)
     Adjacent with neighbor 3.3.3.3  (Designated Router)
   Suppress hello for 0 neighbor(s)
R1#
```

As shown in Example 2-14, R1 is not the DR or BDR; rather, it is a DROTHER with a default priority of 1. The DR is R3, with router ID 3.3.3.3 at IPv4 address 192.168.1.3, and the BDR is R2, with router ID 2.2.2.2 at IPv4 address 192.168.1.2. This output also shows that R1 has two adjacencies: one with the BDR and one with the DR.

R2 BDR

Example 2-15 shows the output of the **show ip ospf interface** command generated on R2.

Example 2-15   Verifying R2's Router Role

```
R2# show ip ospf interface GigabitEthernet 0/0/0
GigabitEthernet0/0/0 is up, line protocol is up
  Internet Address 192.168.1.2/24, Area 0, Attached via Interface Enable
  Process ID 10, Router ID 2.2.2.2, Network Type BROADCAST, Cost: 1
  Topology-MTID    Cost    Disabled    Shutdown    Topology Name
       0            1         no          no            Base
  Enabled by interface config, including secondary ip addresses
  Transmit Delay is 1 sec, State BDR, Priority 1
  Designated Router (ID) 3.3.3.3, Interface address 192.168.1.3
  Backup Designated router (ID) 2.2.2.2, Interface address 192.168.1.2
  Timer intervals configured, Hello 10, Dead 40, Wait 40, Retransmit 5
    oob-resync timeout 40
    Hello due in 00:00:01
  Supports Link-local Signaling (LLS)
  Cisco NSF helper support enabled
  IETF NSF helper support enabled
  Index 1/1, flood queue length 0
  Next 0x0(0)/0x0(0)
  Last flood scan length is 0, maximum is 1
  Last flood scan time is 0 msec, maximum is 0 msec
  Neighbor Count is 2, Adjacent neighbor count is 2
    Adjacent with neighbor 1.1.1.1
    Adjacent with neighbor 3.3.3.3   (Designated Router)
  Suppress hello for 0 neighbor(s)
R2#
```

As shown in this example, R2 is the BDR, with a default priority of 1. The DR is R3, with router ID 3.3.3.3 at IPv4 address 192.168.1.3, and the BDR is R2, with router ID 2.2.2.2 at IPv4 address 192.168.1.2. R2 has two adjacencies: one with a neighbor with router ID 1.1.1.1 (R1) and the other with the DR.

R3 DR

Example 2-16 shows the output of the **show ip ospf interface** command generated by R3.

Example 2-16   Verifying R3's Router Role

```
R3# show ip ospf interface GigabitEthernet 0/0/0
GigabitEthernet0/0/0 is up, line protocol is up
  Internet Address 192.168.1.3/24, Area 0, Attached via Interface Enable
  Process ID 10, Router ID 3.3.3.3, Network Type BROADCAST, Cost: 1
  Topology-MTID    Cost    Disabled    Shutdown     Topology Name
        0            1        no          no            Base
  Enabled by interface config, including secondary ip addresses
  Transmit Delay is 1 sec, State DR, Priority 1
  Designated Router (ID) 3.3.3.3, Interface address 192.168.1.3
  Backup Designated router (ID) 2.2.2.2, Interface address 192.168.1.2
  Timer intervals configured, Hello 10, Dead 40, Wait 40, Retransmit 5
    oob-resync timeout 40
    Hello due in 00:00:06
  Supports Link-local Signaling (LLS)
  Cisco NSF helper support enabled
  IETF NSF helper support enabled
  Index 1/1/1, flood queue length 0
  Next 0x0(0)/0x0(0)/0x0(0)
  Last flood scan length is 2, maximum is 2
  Last flood scan time is 0 msec, maximum is 0 msec
  Neighbor Count is 2, Adjacent neighbor count is 2
    Adjacent with neighbor 1.1.1.1
    Adjacent with neighbor 2.2.2.2   (Backup Designated Router)
  Suppress hello for 0 neighbor(s)
R3#
```

As shown in this example, R3 is the DR, with a default priority of 1 and router ID 3.3.3.3 at IPv4 address 192.168.1.3, and the BDR is R2, with router ID 2.2.2.2 at IPv4 address 192.168.1.2. R3 has two adjacencies: one with a neighbor with router ID 1.1.1.1 (R1) and the other with the BDR.

Verify DR/BDR Adjacencies (2.3.5)

To verify the OSPFv2 adjacencies, use the **show ip ospf neighbor** command. The state of neighbors in multiaccess networks can be as follows:

- **FULL/DROTHER:** This is a DR or BDR router that is fully adjacent with a non-DR or BDR router. These two neighbors can exchange Hello packets, updates, queries, replies, and acknowledgments.

- **FULL/DR:** The router is fully adjacent with the indicated DR neighbor. These two neighbors can exchange Hello packets, updates, queries, replies, and acknowledgments.

- **FULL/BDR:** The router is fully adjacent with the indicated BDR neighbor. These two neighbors can exchange Hello packets, updates, queries, replies, and acknowledgments.

- **2-WAY/DROTHER:** The non-DR or BDR router has a neighbor relationship with another non-DR or BDR router. These two neighbors exchange Hello packets.

The normal state for an OSPF router is usually FULL. If a router is stuck in another state, it is an indication that there are problems in forming adjacencies. The only exception to this is the 2-WAY state, which is normal in a multiaccess broadcast network. For example, DROTHERs form a 2-WAY neighbor adjacency with any DROTHERs that join the network. When this happens, the neighbor state displays as 2-WAY/DROTHER.

The following sections show the output for the **show ip ospf neighbor** command on each router.

R1 Adjacencies

In Example 2-17, the output generated by R1 confirms that R1 has adjacencies with the following routers:

- R2 with router ID 2.2.2.2 is in a FULL state, and the role of R2 is BDR.

- R3 with router ID 3.3.3.3 is in a FULL state, and the role of R3 is DR.

Example 2-17   R1's Neighbor Table

```
R1# show ip ospf neighbor
Neighbor ID     Pri    State       Dead Time    Address        Interface
2.2.2.2          1     FULL/BDR    00:00:31     192.168.1.2    GigabitEthernet0/0/0
3.3.3.3          1     FULL/DR     00:00:39     192.168.1.3    GigabitEthernet0/0/0
R1#
```

R2 Adjacencies

In Example 2-18, the output generated by R2 confirms that R2 has adjacencies with the following routers:

- R1 with router ID 1.1.1.1 is in a FULL state, and R1 is neither the DR nor the BDR.

- R3 with router ID 3.3.3.3 is in a FULL state, and the role of R3 is DR.

Example 2-18   R2's Neighbor Table

```
R2# show ip ospf neighbor
Neighbor ID     Pri    State           Dead Time   Address       Interface
1.1.1.1          1     FULL/DROTHER    00:00:31    192.168.1.1   GigabitEthernet0/0/0
3.3.3.3          1     FULL/DR         00:00:34    192.168.1.3   GigabitEthernet0/0/0
R2#
```

R3 Adjacencies

In Example 2-19, the output generated by R3 confirms that R3 has adjacencies with the following routers:

- R1 with router ID 1.1.1.1 is in a FULL state, and R1 is neither the DR nor the BDR.

- R2 with router ID 2.2.2.2 is in a FULL state, and the role of R2 is BDR.

Example 2-19   R3's Neighbor Table

```
R3# show ip ospf neighbor
Neighbor ID     Pri    State           Dead Time   Address       Interface
1.1.1.1          1     FULL/DROTHER    00:00:37    192.168.1.1   GigabitEthernet0/0/0
2.2.2.2          1     FULL/BDR        00:00:33    192.168.1.2   GigabitEthernet0/0/0
R3#
```

Default DR/BDR Election Process (2.3.6)

How do the DR and BDR get elected? The OSPF DR and BDR election decision is based on the several criteria.

The routers in the network elect the router with the highest interface priority as the DR. The router with the second-highest interface priority is elected as the BDR. The priority can be configured to be any number between 0 and 255. If the interface priority value is set to 0, that interface cannot be elected as DR or as BDR. The default priority of multiaccess broadcast interfaces is 1. Therefore, unless otherwise configured, all routers have an equal priority value and must rely on another tie-breaking method during the DR/BDR election.

If the interface priorities are equal, then the router with the highest router ID is elected the DR. The router with the second-highest router ID is the BDR.

Recall that the router ID is determined in one of the following three ways:

- The router ID can be manually configured.

- If no router IDs are configured, the router ID is determined by the highest loopback IPv4 address.

- If no loopback interfaces are configured, the router ID is determined by the highest active IPv4 address.

In Figure 2-11, all Ethernet router interfaces have a default priority of 1.

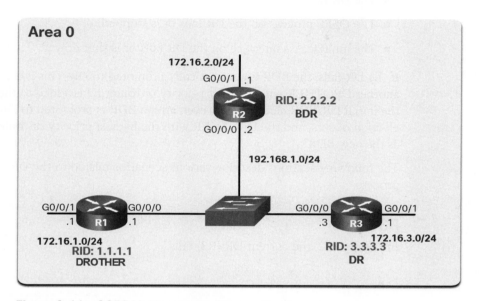

Figure 2-11   OSPF Multiaccess Reference Topology

As a result, based on the selection criteria listed above, the OSPF router ID is used to elect the DR and BDR. R3, with the highest router ID, becomes the DR; and R2, with the second-highest router ID, becomes the BDR.

The DR and BDR election process takes place as soon as the first router with an OSPF-enabled interface is active on the multiaccess network. This can happen when the preconfigured OSPF routers are powered on or when OSPF is activated on the interface. The election process takes only a few seconds. If all of the routers on the multiaccess network have not finished booting, it is possible for a router with a lower router ID to become the DR.

OSPF DR and BDR elections are not preemptive. That is, if a new router with a higher priority or higher router ID is added to the network after the DR and BDR election, the newly added router does not take over the DR or the BDR role. This is because those roles have already been assigned. The addition of a new router does not initiate a new election process.

DR Failure and Recovery (2.3.7)

After the DR is elected, it remains the DR until one of the following events occurs:

- The DR fails.

- The OSPF process on the DR fails or is stopped.

- The multiaccess interface on the DR fails or is shut down.

If the DR fails, the BDR is automatically promoted to DR. This is the case even if another DROTHER with a higher priority or router ID is added to the network after the initial DR/BDR election. However, after a BDR is promoted to DR, a new BDR election occurs, and the DROTHER with the highest priority or router ID is elected as the new BDR.

The following sections describe various scenarios related to the DR and BDR election process.

R3 Fails

In Figure 2-12, the current DR (R3) fails.

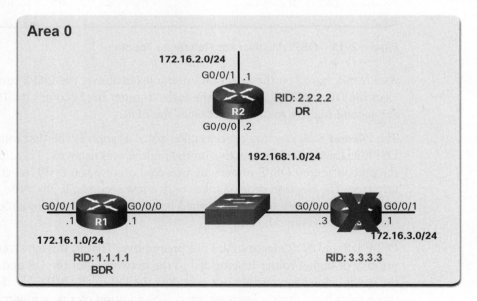

Figure 2-12 R3 Fails

Therefore, the pre-elected BDR (R2) assumes the role of DR. Subsequently, an election is held to choose a new BDR. Because R1 is the only DROTHER, it is elected as the BDR.

R3 Rejoins Network

In Figure 2-13, R3 has rejoined the network after several minutes of being unavailable.

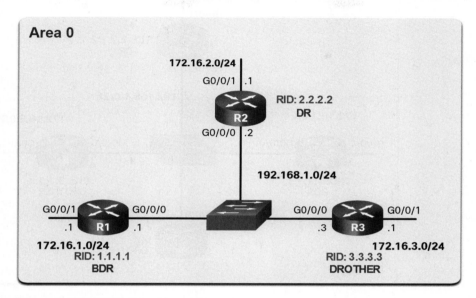

Figure 2-13   R3 Rejoins Network

Because the DR and BDR already exist, R3 does not take over either role. Instead, it becomes a DROTHER.

R4 Joins Network

In Figure 2-14, a new router (R4) with a higher router ID is added to the network.

The DR (R2) and the BDR (R1) retain the DR and BDR roles. R4 automatically becomes a DROTHER.

R2 Fails

In Figure 2-15, R2 has failed.

The BDR (R1) automatically becomes the DR, and an election process selects R4 as the BDR because it has the higher router ID.

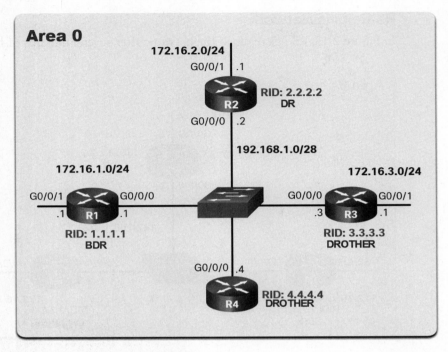

Figure 2-14 R4 Joins Network

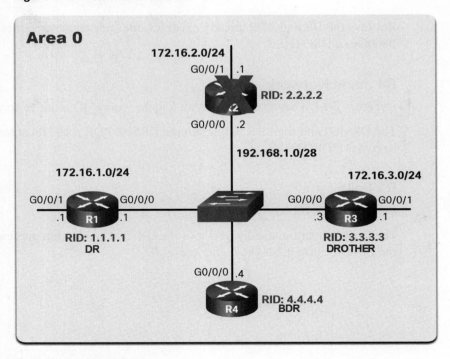

Figure 2-15 R2 Fails

The ip ospf priority Command (2.3.8)

If the interface priorities are equal on all routers, the router with the highest router ID is elected the DR. It is possible to configure the router ID to manipulate the DR/BDR election. However, this process works only if there is a stringent plan for setting the router ID on all routers. Configuring the router ID can help control this. However, in large networks, this can be cumbersome.

Instead of relying on the router ID, it is better to control the election by setting interface priorities. This also allows a router to be the DR in one network and a DROTHER in another. To set the priority of an interface, use the **ip ospf priority** *value* interface configuration command, where *value* is 0 to 255. A *value* of 0 does not become a DR or a BDR. A *value* of 1 to 255 on the interface makes it more likely that the router becomes the DR or the BDR.

Configure OSPF Priority (2.3.9)

In the reference topology in Figure 2-11, the **ip ospf priority** interface configuration command will be used to change the DR and BDR as follows:

- R1 should be the DR and will be configured with a priority of 255.
- R2 should be the BDR and will be left with the default priority of 1.
- R3 should never be a DR or BDR and will be configured with a priority of 0.

Example 2-20 shows a change of the R1 G0/0/0 interface priority from 1 to 255.

Example 2-20 Configuring R1's OSPF Priority

```
R1(config)# interface GigabitEthernet 0/0/0
R1(config-if)# ip ospf priority 255
R1(config-if)# end
R1#
```

Example 2-21 shows a change of the R3 G0/0/0 interface priority from 1 to 0.

Example 2-21 Configuring R3's OSPF Priority

```
R3(config)# interface GigabitEthernet 0/0/0
R3(config-if)# ip ospf priority 0
R3(config-if)# end
R3#
```

Example 2-22 shows how to clear the OSPF process on R1. The **clear ip ospf process** privileged EXEC command also must be entered on R2 and R3 (not shown). Notice the OSPF state information that is generated.

Example 2-22   Clearing OSPF on R1

```
R1# clear ip ospf process
Reset ALL OSPF processes? [no]: y
R1#
*Jun  5 03:47:41.563: %OSPF-5-ADJCHG: Process 10, Nbr 2.2.2.2 on GigabitEthernet0/0/0
  from FULL to DOWN, Neighbor Down: Interface down or detached
*Jun  5 03:47:41.563: %OSPF-5-ADJCHG: Process 10, Nbr 3.3.3.3 on GigabitEthernet0/0/0
  from FULL to DOWN, Neighbor Down: Interface down or detached
*Jun  5 03:47:41.569: %OSPF-5-ADJCHG: Process 10, Nbr 2.2.2.2 on GigabitEthernet0/0/0
  from LOADING to FULL, Loading Done
*Jun  5 03:47:41.569: %OSPF-5-ADJCHG: Process 10, Nbr 3.3.3.3 on GigabitEthernet0/0/0
  from LOADING to FULL, Loading Done
```

In Example 2-23, the output from the **show ip ospf interface g0/0/0** command on R1 confirms that R1 is now the DR, with a priority of 255, and identifies the new neighbor adjacencies of R1.

Example 2-23   Verifying That R1 Is Now the DR

```
R1# show ip ospf interface GigabitEthernet 0/0/0
GigabitEthernet0/0/0 is up, line protocol is up
   Internet Address 192.168.1.1/24, Area 0, Attached via Interface Enable
   Process ID 10, Router ID 1.1.1.1, Network Type BROADCAST, Cost: 1
   Topology-MTID    Cost    Disabled    Shutdown       Topology Name
         0            1        no          no              Base
   Enabled by interface config, including secondary ip addresses
   Transmit Delay is 1 sec, State DR, Priority 255
   Designated Router (ID) 1.1.1.1, Interface address 192.168.1.1
   Backup Designated router (ID) 2.2.2.2, Interface address 192.168.1.2
   Timer intervals configured, Hello 10, Dead 40, Wait 40, Retransmit 5
     oob-resync timeout 40
     Hello due in 00:00:00
   Supports Link-local Signaling (LLS)
   Cisco NSF helper support enabled
   IETF NSF helper support enabled
   Index 1/1/1, flood queue length 0
   Next 0x0(0)/0x0(0)/0x0(0)
   Last flood scan length is 1, maximum is 2
   Last flood scan time is 0 msec, maximum is 1 msec
   Neighbor Count is 2, Adjacent neighbor count is 2
     Adjacent with neighbor 2.2.2.2  (Backup Designated Router)
     Adjacent with neighbor 3.3.3.3
   Suppress hello for 0 neighbor(s)
R1#
```

Syntax Checker—Configure OSPF Priority (2.3.10)

Refer to the online course to complete this activity.

Packet Tracer—Determine the DR and BDR (2.3.11)

In this activity, you will complete the following:

- Examine the DR and BDR roles and watch the roles change when there is a change in the network.

- Modify the priority to control the roles and force a new election.

- Verify that routers are filling the desired roles.

Modify Single-Area OSPFv2 (2.4)

In this section, you will learn how OSPF uses cost to determine the best path and see how to configure OSPF interface settings to improve network performance.

Cisco OSPF Cost Metric (2.4.1)

Recall that a routing protocol uses a metric to determine the best path of a packet across a network. A metric gives an indication of the overhead that is required to send packets across a certain interface. OSPF uses cost as a metric. A lower cost indicates a better path than a higher cost.

Note

The OSPF RFC does not specify what "cost" is. Cisco uses the cumulative bandwidth for route calculations.

The Cisco cost of an interface is inversely proportional to the bandwidth of the interface. Therefore, a higher bandwidth indicates a lower cost. The formula used to calculate the OSPF cost is

Cost = reference bandwidth / interface bandwidth

The default *reference bandwidth* is 10^8 (100,000,000); therefore, the formula is

Cost = 100,000,000 bps / interface bandwidth in bps

The table in Figure 2-16 breaks down the cost calculation.

Interface Type	Reference Bandwidth in bps		Default Bandwidth in bps	Cost
10 Gigabit Ethernet 10 Gbps	100,000,000	÷	10,000,000,000	0.01 = 1
Gigabit Ethernet 1 Gbps	100,000,000	÷	1,000,000,000	0.1 = 1
Fast Ethernet 100 Mbps	100,000,000	÷	100,000,000	1
Ethernet 10 Mbps	100,000,000	÷	10,000,000	1

Same Costs due to reference bandwidth

Figure 2-16   Default Cisco OSPF Costs

Because the OSPF cost value must be an integer, FastEthernet, Gigabit Ethernet, and 10 Gigabit Ethernet (10GigE) interfaces share the same cost. To correct this situation, you can:

- Adjust the reference bandwidth with the **auto-cost reference-bandwidth** router configuration command on each OSPF router.

- Manually set the OSPF cost value with the **ip ospf cost** interface configuration command on necessary interfaces.

Adjust the Reference Bandwidth (2.4.2)

The cost value must be an integer. If something less than an integer is calculated, OSPF rounds up to the nearest integer. Therefore, the OSPF cost assigned to a Gigabit Ethernet interface with the default reference bandwidth of 100,000,000 bps would equal 1 because the nearest integer for 0.1 is 0 instead of 1:

Cost = 100,000,000 bps / 1,000,000,000 = 1

For this reason, all interfaces faster than Fast Ethernet have the same cost value (1) as a Fast Ethernet interface. To assist OSPF in making the correct path determination, the reference bandwidth must be changed to a higher value to accommodate networks with links faster than 100 Mbps. Changing the reference bandwidth does not actually affect the bandwidth capacity on the link; rather, it simply affects the calculation used to determine the metric. To adjust the reference bandwidth, use the **auto-cost reference-bandwidth** *Mbps* router configuration command:

```
Router(config-router)# auto-cost reference-bandwidth Mbps
```

This command must be configured on every router in the OSPF domain. Notice that the value is expressed in Mbps; therefore, to adjust the costs for Gigabit Ethernet, use the **auto-cost reference-bandwidth 1000** router configuration command. For 10 Gigabit Ethernet, use the **auto-cost reference-bandwidth 10000** router configuration command. To return to the default reference bandwidth, use the **auto-cost reference-bandwidth 100** command.

Whichever method is used, it is important to apply the configuration to all routers in the OSPF routing domain. Table 2-1 shows the OSPF cost if the reference bandwidth is adjusted to accommodate 10 Gigabit Ethernet links. The reference bandwidth should be adjusted any time there are links faster than FastEthernet (100 Mbps).

Table 2-1   OSPF Reference Bandwidths and Costs

Interface Type	Reference Bandwidth in bps		Default Bandwidth in bps	Cost
10 Gigabit Ethernet 10 Gbps	10,000,000,000	÷	10,000,000,000	1
Gigabit Ethernet 1 Gbps	10,000,000,000	÷	1,000,000,000	10
Fast Ethernet 100 Mbps	10,000,000,000	÷	100,000,000	100
Ethernet 10 Mbps	10,000,000,000	÷	10,000,000	1000

Use the **show ip ospf interface g0/0/0** command to verify the current OSPFv2 cost assigned to the R1 Gigabit Ethernet 0/0/0 interface. In Example 2-24, notice that the output displays a cost of 1. Then, after adjusting the reference bandwidth, the cost is 10. This allows for scaling to 10 Gigabit Ethernet interfaces in the future without having to adjust the reference bandwidth again.

Note

The **auto-cost reference-bandwidth** command must be configured consistently on all routers in the OSPF domain to ensure accurate route calculations.

Example 2-24   Configuring and Verifying R1's Reference Bandwidth

```
R1# show ip ospf interface gigabitethernet0/0/0
GigabitEthernet0/0/0 is up, line protocol is up
  Internet Address 10.1.1.5/30, Area 0, Attached via Interface Enable
  Process ID 10, Router ID 1.1.1.1, Network Type POINT_TO_POINT, Cost: 1
(output omitted)
R1# config t
Enter configuration commands, one per line.  End with CNTL/Z.
R1(config)# router ospf 10
R1(config-router)# auto-cost reference-bandwidth 10000
% OSPF: Reference bandwidth is changed.
        Please ensure reference bandwidth is consistent across all routers.
```

```
R1(config-router)#
R1(config-router)# do show ip ospf interface gigabitethernet0/0/0
GigabitEthernet0/0 is up, line protocol is up
  Internet address is 172.16.1.1/24, Area 0
  Process ID 10, Router ID 1.1.1.1, Network Type BROADCAST, Cost: 10
  Transmit Delay is 1 sec, State DR, Priority 1
(output omitted)
```

OSPF Accumulates Costs (2.4.3)

The cost of an OSPF route is the accumulated value from one router to the destination network. Assuming that the **auto-cost reference-bandwidth 10000** command has been configured on all three routers, the cost of the links between each pair of routers is now 10. The loopback interfaces have a default cost of 1, as shown in Figure 2-17.

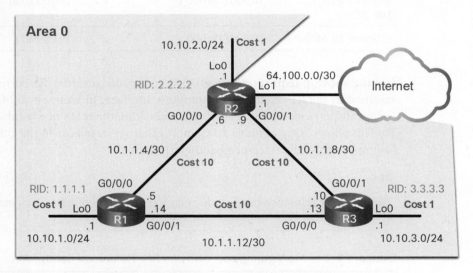

Figure 2-17   OSPF Reference Topology with Cost Values

Therefore, we can calculate the cost for each router to reach each network. For example, the total cost for R1 to reach the 10.10.2.0/24 network is 11. This is because the link to R2 cost is 10, and the loopback default cost is 1, and 10 + 1 = 11.

The routing table of R1 in Example 2-25 confirms that the metric to reach the R2 LAN is a cost of 11.

Example 2-25   Verifying R1's Metric

```
R1# show ip route | include 10.10.2.0
O          10.10.2.0/24 [110/11] via 10.1.1.6, 01:05:02, GigabitEthernet0/0/0
R1#
R1# show ip route 10.10.2.0
Routing entry for 10.10.2.0/24
  Known via "ospf 10", distance 110, metric 11, type intra area
  Last update from 10.1.1.6 on GigabitEthernet0/0/0, 01:05:13 ago
  Routing Descriptor Blocks:
  * 10.1.1.6, from 2.2.2.2, 01:05:13 ago, via GigabitEthernet0/0/0
        Route metric is 11, traffic share count is 1
R1#
```

Manually Set OSPF Cost Value (2.4.4)

OSPF cost values can be manipulated to influence the route chosen by OSPF.
For example, in the current configuration, R1 is load balancing to the 10.1.1.8/30
network. It will send some traffic to R2 and some traffic to R3. You can see this in
the routing table in Example 2-26.

Example 2-26   R1: Load Balancing Traffic to 10.1.1.8/30

```
R1# show ip route ospf | begin 10
      10.0.0.0/8 is variably subnetted, 9 subnets, 3 masks
O          10.1.1.8/30 [110/20] via 10.1.1.13, 00:54:50, GigabitEthernet0/0/1
                       [110/20] via 10.1.1.6, 00:55:14, GigabitEthernet0/0/0
(output omitted)
R1#
```

Note

Changing the cost of links may have undesired consequences. Therefore, interface cost values
should be adjusted only when the outcome is fully understood.

An administrator may want traffic to go through R2 and use R3 as a backup route in
case the link between R1 and R2 goes down.

Another reason to change the cost value is that other vendors may calculate OSPF in
a different manner. By manipulating the cost value, the administrator can make sure
the route costs shared between OSPF multivendor routers are accurately reflected in
routing tables.

To change the cost value reported by the local OSPF router to other OSPF routers,
use the **ip ospf cost** *value* interface configuration command. In Figure 2-18, we need

to change the cost of the loopback interfaces to 10 to simulate Gigabit Ethernet speeds. In addition, we will change the cost of the link between R2 and R3 to 30 so that this link is used as a backup link.

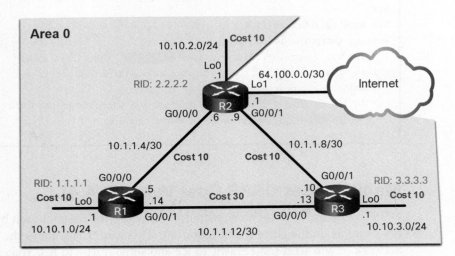

Figure 2-18 OSPF Reference Topology with Manually Adjusted Cost Values

Example 2-27 shows the configuration for R1.

Example 2-27 Cost Configuration on R1

```
R1(config)# interface g0/0/1
R1(config-if)# ip ospf cost 30
R1(config-if)# interface lo0
R1(config-if)# ip ospf cost 10
R1(config-if)# end
R1#
```

Assuming that OSPF costs for R2 and R3 have been configured to match the topology in Figure 2-18, the OSPF routes for R1 would have the cost values shown in Example 2-28. Notice that R1 is no longer load balancing to the 10.1.1.8/30 network. In fact, all routes go through R2 via 10.1.1.6, as desired by the network administrator.

Example 2-28 R1's OSPF Cost Values

```
R1# show ip route ospf | begin 10
      10.0.0.0/8 is variably subnetted, 9 subnets, 3 masks
O        10.1.1.8/30 [110/20] via 10.1.1.6, 01:18:25, GigabitEthernet0/0/0
O        10.10.2.0/24 [110/20] via 10.1.1.6, 00:04:31, GigabitEthernet0/0/0
O        10.10.3.0/24 [110/30] via 10.1.1.6, 00:03:21, GigabitEthernet0/0/0
R1#
```

Note

Although using the **ip ospf cost** interface configuration command is the recommended method to manipulate the OSPF cost values, an administrator could also manipulate the values by using the **bandwidth** *kbps* interface configuration command. However, that would work only if all the routers are Cisco routers.

Test Failover to Backup Route (2.4.5)

What happens if the link between R1 and R2 goes down? We can simulate that by shutting down the Gigabit Ethernet 0/0/0 interface and verifying that the routing table is updated to use R3 as the next-hop router. In Example 2-29, notice that R1 can now reach the 10.1.1.4/30 network via 10.1.1.13 through R3, with a cost value of 50.

Example 2-29   Simulating Failover to the Backup Route

```
R1(config)# interface g0/0/0
R1(config-if)# shutdown
*Jun  7 03:41:34.866: %OSPF-5-ADJCHG: Process 10, Nbr 2.2.2.2 on GigabitEthernet0/0/0
  from FULL to DOWN, Neighbor Down: Interface down or detached
*Jun  7 03:41:36.865: %LINK-5-CHANGED: Interface GigabitEthernet0/0/0, changed state
  to administratively down
*Jun  7 03:41:37.865: %LINEPROTO-5-UPDOWN: Line protocol on Interface GigabitEther-
  net0/0/0, changed state to down
R1(config-if)# end
R1#
R1# show ip route ospf | begin 10
      10.0.0.0/8 is variably subnetted, 8 subnets, 3 masks
O        10.1.1.4/30 [110/50] via 10.1.1.13, 00:00:14, GigabitEthernet0/0/1
O        10.1.1.8/30 [110/40] via 10.1.1.13, 00:00:14, GigabitEthernet0/0/1
O        10.10.2.0/24 [110/50] via 10.1.1.13, 00:00:14, GigabitEthernet0/0/1
O        10.10.3.0/24 [110/40] via 10.1.1.13, 00:00:14, GigabitEthernet0/0/1
R1#
```

Interactive Graphic

Syntax Checker—Modify the Cost Values for R2 and R3 (2.4.6)

Refer to the online course to complete this activity.

Hello Packet Intervals (2.4.7)

As shown in Figure 2-19, OSPFv2 Hello packets are transmitted to multicast address 224.0.0.5 (all OSPF routers) every 10 seconds. This is the default timer value on multiaccess and point-to-point networks.

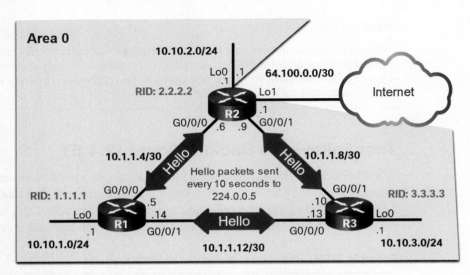

Figure 2-19   OSPF Reference Topology with Hello Packets

Note

Hello packets are not sent on the simulated LAN interfaces because those interfaces were set to passive by using the **passive-interface** router configuration command.

The Dead interval is the period that the router waits to receive a Hello packet before declaring the neighbor down. If the Dead interval expires before the routers receive a Hello packet, OSPF removes that neighbor from its link-state database (LSDB). The router floods the LSDB with information about the down neighbor out all OSPF-enabled interfaces. Cisco uses a default of 4 times the Hello interval. This is 40 seconds on multiaccess and point-to-point networks.

Note

On nonbroadcast multiaccess (NBMA) networks, the default Hello interval is 30 seconds, and the default Dead interval is 120 seconds. NBMA networks are beyond the scope of this chapter.

Verify Hello and Dead Intervals (2.4.8)

The *OSPF Hello and Dead intervals* are configurable on a per-interface basis. The OSPF intervals must match, or a neighbor adjacency does not occur. To verify the currently configured OSPFv2 interface intervals, use the **show ip ospf interface** command, as shown in Example 2-30. The Gigabit Ethernet 0/0/0 Hello and Dead intervals are set to the default 10 seconds and 40 seconds, respectively.

Example 2-30   Hello and Dead Intervals on R1 G0/0/0

```
R1# show ip ospf interface g0/0/0
GigabitEthernet0/0/0 is up, line protocol is up
  Internet Address 10.1.1.5/30, Area 0, Attached via Interface Enable
  Process ID 10, Router ID 1.1.1.1, Network Type POINT_TO_POINT, Cost: 10
  Topology-MTID    Cost     Disabled     Shutdown       Topology Name
        0           10         no           no              Base
  Enabled by interface config, including secondary ip addresses
  Transmit Delay is 1 sec, State POINT_TO_POINT
  Timer intervals configured, Hello 10, Dead 40, Wait 40, Retransmit 5
    oob-resync timeout 40
    Hello due in 00:00:06
  Supports Link-local Signaling (LLS)
  Cisco NSF helper support enabled
  IETF NSF helper support enabled
  Index 1/2/2, flood queue length 0
  Next 0x0(0)/0x0(0)/0x0(0)
  Last flood scan length is 1, maximum is 1
  Last flood scan time is 0 msec, maximum is 0 msec
  Neighbor Count is 1, Adjacent neighbor count is 1
    Adjacent with neighbor 2.2.2.2
  Suppress hello for 0 neighbor(s)
R1#
```

Use the **show ip ospf neighbor** command to see the Dead Time counting down from 40 seconds, as shown in Example 2-31. By default, this value is refreshed every 10 seconds when R1 receives a Hello from the neighbor.

Example 2-31   Dead Intervals Counting Down on R1

```
R1# show ip ospf neighbor
Neighbor ID      Pri   State     Dead Time    Address       Interface
3.3.3.3            0   FULL/  -   00:00:35     10.1.1.13     GigabitEthernet0/0/1
2.2.2.2            0   FULL/  -   00:00:31     10.1.1.6      GigabitEthernet0/0/0
R1#
```

Modify OSPFv2 Intervals (2.4.9)

It may be desirable to change the OSPF timers so that routers detect network failures in less time. Doing this increases traffic, but sometimes quick convergence is more important than the extra traffic it creates.

> **Note**
>
> The default Hello and Dead intervals are based on best practices and should be altered only in rare situations.

OSPFv2 Hello and Dead intervals can be modified manually using the following interface configuration mode commands:

```
Router(config-if)# ip ospf hello-interval seconds
Router(config-if)# ip ospf dead-interval seconds
```

Use the **no ip ospf hello-interval** and **no ip ospf dead-interval** commands to reset the intervals to their defaults.

In Example 2-32, the Hello interval for the link between R1 and R2 is changed to 5 seconds. Immediately after changing the Hello interval, Cisco IOS automatically modifies the Dead interval to four times the Hello interval. However, you can document the new Dead interval in the configuration by manually setting it to 20 seconds, as shown.

As displayed by the highlighted OSPFv2 adjacency message, when the Dead timer on R1 expires, R1 and R2 lose adjacency. This occurs because the R1 and R2 must be configured with the same Hello interval. Use the **show ip ospf neighbor** command on R1 to verify the neighbor adjacencies. Notice that the only neighbor listed is the 3.3.3.3 (R3) router and that R1 is no longer adjacent with the 2.2.2.2 (R2) neighbor.

Example 2-32   Modified Hello and Dead Intervals on R1 Causing a Loss in Adjacency with R2

```
R1(config)# interface g0/0/0
R1(config-if)# ip ospf hello-interval 5
R1(config-if)# ip ospf dead-interval 20
R1(config-if)#
*Jun  7 04:56:07.571: %OSPF-5-ADJCHG: Process 10, Nbr 2.2.2.2 on GigabitEthernet0/0/0
  from FULL to DOWN, Neighbor Down: Dead timer expired
R1(config-if)# end
R1#
R1# show ip ospf neighbor
Neighbor ID     Pri   State       Dead Time   Address        Interface
3.3.3.3           0   FULL/  -    00:00:37    10.1.1.13      GigabitEthernet0/0/1
R1#
```

To restore adjacency between R1 and R2, the R2 Gigabit Ethernet 0/0/0 interface Hello interval is set to 5 seconds, as shown in Example 2-33. Almost immediately, the IOS displays a message that adjacency has been established with a state of FULL. Verify the interface intervals by using the **show ip ospf interface** command. Notice that the Hello time is 5 seconds and that the Dead Time was automatically set to 20 seconds instead of the default 40 seconds.

Example 2-33   Adjusting the Hello Interval to Restore Adjacency with R2

```
R2(config)# interface g0/0/0
R2(config-if)# ip ospf hello-interval 5
*Jun  7 15:08:30.211: %OSPF-5-ADJCHG: Process 10, Nbr 1.1.1.1 on GigabitEthernet0/0/0
  from LOADING to FULL, Loading Done
R2(config-if)# end
R2#
R2# show ip ospf interface g0/0/0 | include Timer
  Timer intervals configured, Hello 5, Dead 20, Wait 20, Retransmit 5
R2#
R2# show ip ospf neighbor
Neighbor ID     Pri   State        Dead Time    Address      Interface
3.3.3.3           0   FULL/   -    00:00:38     10.1.1.10    GigabitEthernet0/0/1
1.1.1.1           0   FULL/   -    00:00:17     10.1.1.5     GigabitEthernet0/0/0
R2#
```

Syntax Checker—Modifying Hello and Dead Intervals on R3 (2.4.10)

The Hello and Dead intervals are set to 5 and 20, respectively, on R1 and R2. Use Syntax Checker to modify the Hello and Dead intervals on R3 and verify that adjacencies are reestablished with R1 and R2.

Refer to the online course to complete this activity.

Packet Tracer—Modify Single-Area OSPFv2 (2.4.11)

In this Packet Tracer activity, you will complete the following:

- Adjust the reference bandwidth to account for Gigabit Ethernet and faster speeds.
- Modify the OSPF cost value.
- Modify the OSPF Hello timers.
- Verify that the modifications are accurately reflected in the routers.

Default Route Propagation (2.5)

In this section, you will configure OSPF to propagate a default route.

Propagate a Default Static Route in OSPFv2 (2.5.1)

Your network users will need to send packets out of your network to non-OSPF networks, such as the internet. You will therefore need to have a default static route that they can use. In the topology in Figure 2-20, R2 is connected to the internet and should *propagate a default route* to R1 and R3.

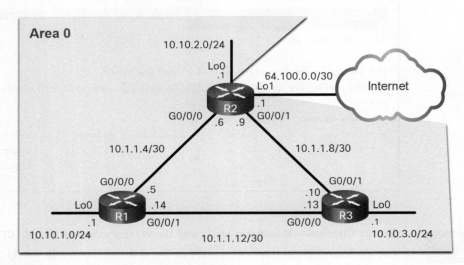

Figure 2-20   OSPF Reference Topology

The router connected to the internet is sometimes called the *edge router*, or the gateway router. However, in OSPF terminology, the router located between an OSPF routing domain and a non-OSPF network is called the *autonomous system boundary router (ASBR)*.

All that is required for R2 to reach the internet is a default static route to the service provider.

Note

In this example, a loopback interface with IPv4 address 64.100.0.1 is used to simulate the connection to the service provider.

To propagate a default route, the edge router (R2) must be configured with the following:

■ A default static route using the **ip route 0.0.0.0 0.0.0.0** [*next-hop-address* | *exit-intf*] global configuration command.

■ The **default-information originate** router configuration command. This instructs R2 to be the source of the default route information and propagate the default static route in OSPF updates.

In Example 2-34, R2 is configured with a loopback to simulate a connection to the internet. Then a default route is configured and propagated to all other OSPF routers in the routing domain.

Note

When configuring static routes, best practice is to use the next-hop IP address. However, when simulating a connection to the internet, there is no next-hop IP address. Therefore, we use the *exit-intf* argument

Example 2-34   Simulating and Propagating a Default Route

```
R2(config)# interface lo1
R2(config-if)# ip address 64.100.0.1 255.255.255.252
R2(config-if)# exit
R2(config)#
R2(config)# ip route 0.0.0.0 0.0.0.0 loopback 1
%Default route without gateway, ifnot a point-to-point interface, may impact
  performance
R2(config)#
R2(config)# router ospf 10
R2(config-router)# default-information originate
R2(config-router)# end
R2#
```

Verify the Propagated Default Route (2.5.2)

You can verify the default route settings on R2 by using the **show ip route** command, as shown in Example 2-35.

Example 2-35   R2's Routing Table

```
R2# show ip route | begin Gateway
Gateway of last resort is 0.0.0.0 to network 0.0.0.0
S*       0.0.0.0/0 is directly connected, Loopback1
         10.0.0.0/8 is variably subnetted, 9 subnets, 3 masks
C           10.1.1.4/30 is directly connected, GigabitEthernet0/0/0
L           10.1.1.6/32 is directly connected, GigabitEthernet0/0/0
C           10.1.1.8/30 is directly connected, GigabitEthernet0/0/1
L           10.1.1.9/32 is directly connected, GigabitEthernet0/0/1
O           10.1.1.12/30 [110/40] via 10.1.1.10, 00:48:42, GigabitEthernet0/0/1
                         [110/40] via 10.1.1.5, 00:59:30, GigabitEthernet0/0/0
O           10.10.1.0/24 [110/20] via 10.1.1.5, 00:59:30, GigabitEthernet0/0/0
C           10.10.2.0/24 is directly connected, Loopback0
```

```
L          10.10.2.1/32 is directly connected, Loopback0
O          10.10.3.0/24 [110/20] via 10.1.1.10, 00:48:42, GigabitEthernet0/0/1
        64.0.0.0/8 is variably subnetted, 2 subnets, 2 masks
C          64.100.0.0/30 is directly connected, Loopback1
L          64.100.0.1/32 is directly connected, Loopback1
R2#
```

You can also use this command to verify that R1 and R3 each received a default route, as shown in Examples 2-36 and 2-37.

Example 2-36 R1's Routing Table

```
R1# show ip route | begin Gateway
Gateway of last resort is 10.1.1.6 to network 0.0.0.0
O*E2  0.0.0.0/0 [110/1] via 10.1.1.6, 00:11:08, GigabitEthernet0/0/0
        10.0.0.0/8 is variably subnetted, 9 subnets, 3 masks
C          10.1.1.4/30 is directly connected, GigabitEthernet0/0/0
L          10.1.1.5/32 is directly connected, GigabitEthernet0/0/0
O          10.1.1.8/30 [110/20] via 10.1.1.6, 00:58:59, GigabitEthernet0/0/0
C          10.1.1.12/30 is directly connected, GigabitEthernet0/0/1
L          10.1.1.14/32 is directly connected, GigabitEthernet0/0/1
C          10.10.1.0/24 is directly connected, Loopback0
L          10.10.1.1/32 is directly connected, Loopback0
O          10.10.2.0/24 [110/20] via 10.1.1.6, 00:58:59, GigabitEthernet0/0/0
O          10.10.3.0/24 [110/30] via 10.1.1.6, 00:48:11, GigabitEthernet0/0/0
R1#
```

Example 2-37 R3's Routing Table

```
R3# show ip route | begin Gateway
Gateway of last resort is 10.1.1.9 to network 0.0.0.0
O*E2  0.0.0.0/0 [110/1] via 10.1.1.9, 00:12:04, GigabitEthernet0/0/1
        10.0.0.0/8 is variably subnetted, 9 subnets, 3 masks
O          10.1.1.4/30 [110/20] via 10.1.1.9, 00:49:08, GigabitEthernet0/0/1
C          10.1.1.8/30 is directly connected, GigabitEthernet0/0/1
L          10.1.1.10/32 is directly connected, GigabitEthernet0/0/1
C          10.1.1.12/30 is directly connected, GigabitEthernet0/0/0
L          10.1.1.13/32 is directly connected, GigabitEthernet0/0/0
O          10.10.1.0/24 [110/30] via 10.1.1.9, 00:49:08, GigabitEthernet0/0/1
O          10.10.2.0/24 [110/20] via 10.1.1.9, 00:49:08, GigabitEthernet0/0/1
C          10.10.3.0/24 is directly connected, Loopback0
L          10.10.3.1/32 is directly connected, Loopback0
R3#
```

Notice that the route source on R1 and R3 is O*E2, signifying that it was learned using OSPFv2. The asterisk identifies this as a good candidate for the default route. The E2 designation identifies that it is an external route. (The meaning of E1 and E2 is beyond the scope of this chapter.)

Packet Tracer—Propagate a Default Route in OSPFv2 (2.5.3)

In this activity, you will configure an IPv4 default route to the internet and propagate that default route to other OSPF routers. You will then verify that the default route is in downstream routing tables and that hosts can now access a web server on the internet.

Verify Single-Area OSPFv2 (2.6)

In this section, you will verify single-area OSPFv2.

Verify OSPF Neighbors (2.6.1)

If you have configured single-area OSPFv2, you will need to verify your configurations. This section details the many commands that you can use to verify OSPF.

As you know, the following two commands are particularly useful for verifying routing:

- **show ip interface brief:** This verifies that the desired interfaces are active with correct IP addressing.
- **show ip route:** This verifies that the routing table contains all the expected routes.

Additional commands for determining that OSPF is operating as expected include the following:

- **show ip ospf neighbor**
- **show ip protocols**
- **show ip ospf**
- **show ip ospf interface [brief]**

Figure 2-21 shows the OSPF reference topology used to demonstrate these commands.

You can use the **show ip ospf neighbor** command to verify that a router has formed an adjacency with its neighboring routers. If the router ID of the neighboring router is not displayed, or if it does not show as being in a state of FULL, the two routers have not formed an OSPFv2 adjacency.

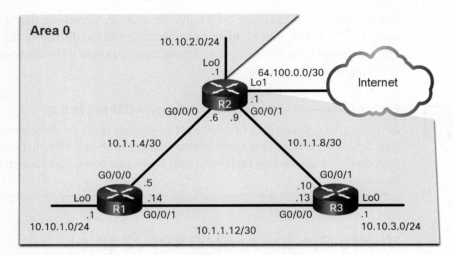

Figure 2-21   OSPF Reference Topology

If two routers do not establish adjacency, link-state information is not exchanged. Incomplete LSDBs can cause inaccurate SPF trees and routing tables. Routes to destination networks may not exist or may not be the most optimum paths.

Note

A non-DR or non-BDR router (that is, a DROTHER) that has a neighbor relationship with another non-DR or non-BDR router will display a 2-WAY adjacency instead of FULL.

Example 2-38 displays the neighbor table of R1.

Example 2-38   R1's OSPF Neighbor Table

```
R1# show ip ospf neighbor
Neighbor ID     Pri    State         Dead Time    Address      Interface
3.3.3.3           0    FULL/  -      00:00:19     10.1.1.13    GigabitEthernet0/0/1
2.2.2.2           0    FULL/  -      00:00:18     10.1.1.6     GigabitEthernet0/0/0
R1#
```

For each neighbor, the **show ip ospf neighbor** command displays the following:

- **Neighbor ID:** This is the router ID of the neighboring router.

- **Pri:** This is the OSPFv2 priority of the interface. This value is used in the DR/BDR election.

- **State:** This is the OSPFv2 state of the interface. FULL state means that the router and its neighbor have identical OSPFv2 LSDBs. On multiaccess networks, such as Ethernet, two routers that are adjacent may have their states displayed as 2WAY. The dash indicates that no DR or BDR is required because of the network type.

- **Dead Time:** This is the amount of time remaining that the router waits to receive an OSPFv2 Hello packet from the neighbor before declaring the neighbor down. This value is reset when the interface receives a Hello packet.

- **Address:** This is the IPv4 address of the interface of the neighbor to which this router is directly connected.

- **Interface:** This is the interface on which this router has formed adjacency with the neighbor.

Two routers may not form an OSPFv2 adjacency if the following occurs:

- The subnet masks do not match, causing the routers to be on separate networks.

- The OSPFv2 Hello or Dead timers do not match.

- The OSPFv2 network types do not match.

- There is a missing or incorrect OSPFv2 **network** command.

Verify OSPF Protocol Settings (2.6.2)

Using the **show ip protocols** command is a quick way to verify vital OSPF configuration information, as shown in Example 2-39.

Example 2-39   Verifying OSPF Protocol Settings

```
R1# show ip protocols
*** IP Routing is NSF aware ***
(output omitted)
Routing Protocol is "ospf 10"
  Outgoing update filter list for all interfaces is not set
  Incoming update filter list for all interfaces is not set
  Router ID 1.1.1.1
  Number of areas in this router is 1. 1 normal 0 stub 0 nssa
  Maximum path: 4
  Routing for Networks:
  Routing on Interfaces Configured Explicitly (Area 0):
    Loopback0
    GigabitEthernet0/0/1
    GigabitEthernet0/0/0
  Routing Information Sources:
    Gateway         Distance      Last Update
    3.3.3.3              110       00:09:30
    2.2.2.2              110       00:09:58
  Distance: (default is 110)
R1#
```

The command verifies the OSPFv2 process ID, the router ID, the interfaces explicitly configured to advertise OSPF routes, the neighbors the router is receiving updates from, and the default administrative distance, which is 110 for OSPF.

Verify OSPF Process Information (2.6.3)

The **show ip ospf** command can also be used to examine the OSPFv2 process ID and router ID, as shown in the Example 2-40.

Example 2-40   Verifying OSPF Process Information

```
R1# show ip ospf
Routing Process "ospf 10" with ID 1.1.1.1
 Start time: 00:01:47.390, Time elapsed: 00:12:32.320
 Supports only single TOS(TOS0) routes
 Supports opaque LSA
 Supports Link-local Signaling (LLS)
 Supports area transit capability
 Supports NSSA (compatible with RFC 3101)
 Supports Database Exchange Summary List Optimization (RFC 5243)
 Event-log enabled, Maximum number of events: 1000, Mode: cyclic
 Router is not originating router-LSAs with maximum metric
 Initial SPF schedule delay 5000 msecs
 Minimum hold time between two consecutive SPFs 10000 msecs
 Maximum wait time between two consecutive SPFs 10000 msecs
 Incremental-SPF disabled
 Minimum LSA interval 5 secs
 Minimum LSA arrival 1000 msecs
 LSA group pacing timer 240 secs
 Interface flood pacing timer 33 msecs
 Retransmission pacing timer 66 msecs
 EXCHANGE/LOADING adjacency limit: initial 300, process maximum 300
 Number of external LSA 1. Checksum Sum 0x00A1FF
 Number of opaque AS LSA 0. Checksum Sum 0x000000
 Number of DCbitless external and opaque AS LSA 0
 Number of DoNotAge external and opaque AS LSA 0
 Number of areas in this router is 1. 1 normal 0 stub 0 nssa
 Number of areas transit capable is 0
 External flood list length 0
 IETF NSF helper support enabled
 Cisco NSF helper support enabled
 Reference bandwidth unit is 10000 mbps
    Area BACKBONE(0)
        Number of interfaces in this area is 3
```

```
        Area has no authentication
        SPF algorithm last executed 00:11:31.231 ago
        SPF algorithm executed 4 times
        Area ranges are
        Number of LSA 3. Checksum Sum 0x00E77E
        Number of opaque link LSA 0. Checksum Sum 0x000000
        Number of DCbitless LSA 0
        Number of indication LSA 0
        Number of DoNotAge LSA 0
        Flood list length 0
R1#
```

The output verifies the OSPFv2 area information and the last time the SPF algorithm was executed.

Verify OSPF Interface Settings (2.6.4)

The **show ip ospf interface** command provides a detailed list for every OSPFv2-enabled interface. Specify an interface to display the settings of just that interface. The output in Example 2-41 is for Gigabit Ethernet 0/0/0.

Example 2-41   Verifying OSPF Interface Settings

```
R1# show ip ospf interface GigabitEthernet 0/0/0
GigabitEthernet0/0/0 is up, line protocol is up
  Internet Address 10.1.1.5/30, Area 0, Attached via Interface Enable
  Process ID 10, Router ID 1.1.1.1, Network Type POINT_TO_POINT, Cost: 10
  Topology-MTID    Cost     Disabled     Shutdown      Topology Name
        0           10        no           no             Base
  Enabled by interface config, including secondary ip addresses
  Transmit Delay is 1 sec, State POINT_TO_POINT
  Timer intervals configured, Hello 5, Dead 20, Wait 20, Retransmit 5
    oob-resync timeout 40
    Hello due in 00:00:01
  Supports Link-local Signaling (LLS)
  Cisco NSF helper support enabled
  IETF NSF helper support enabled
  Index 1/2/2, flood queue length 0
  Next 0x0(0)/0x0(0)/0x0(0)
  Last flood scan length is 1, maximum is 1
  Last flood scan time is 0 msec, maximum is 0 msec
  Neighbor Count is 1, Adjacent neighbor count is 1
    Adjacent with neighbor 2.2.2.2
  Suppress hello for 0 neighbor(s)
R1#
```

The output in this example verifies the process ID, the local router ID, the type of network, OSPF cost, DR and BDR information on multiaccess links (not shown), and adjacent neighbors.

To get a quick summary of OSPFv2-enabled interfaces, use the **show ip ospf interface brief** command, as shown in Example 2-42.

Example 2-42   Summary of OSPF Interfaces

```
R1# show ip ospf interface brief
Interface      PID   Area            IP Address/Mask     Cost   StateNbrs F/C
Lo0            10    0               10.10.1.1/24        10     P2P    0/0
Gi0/0/1        10    0               10.1.1.14/30        30     P2P    1/1
Gi0/0/0        10    0               10.1.1.5/30         10     P2P    1/1
R1#
```

This command is useful for finding important information including the following:

- Interfaces that are participating in OSPF
- Networks that are being advertised (IP address/mask)
- Cost of each link
- Network state
- Number of neighbors on each link

Syntax Checker—Verify Single-Area OSPFv2 (2.6.5)

Refer to the online course to complete this activity.

Packet Tracer—Verify Single-Area OSPFv2 (2.6.6)

In this Packet Tracer activity, you will use a variety of commands to verify the single-area OSPFv2 configuration.

Summary (2.7)

The following is a summary of the sections in this chapter.

OSPF Router ID

OSPFv2 is enabled using the **router ospf** *process-id* global configuration mode command. The *process-id* value represents a number between 1 and 65,535 and is selected by the network administrator. An OSPF router ID is a 32-bit value, represented as an IPv4 address. The router ID is used by an OSPF-enabled router to synchronize OSPF databases and participate in the election of the DR and BDR. Cisco routers derive the router ID based on one of three criteria.

The router ID is explicitly configured using the OSPF **router-id** *rid* router configuration mode command. The *rid* value is any 32-bit value expressed as an IPv4 address.

If the router ID is not explicitly configured, the router chooses the highest IPv4 address of any of the configured loopback interfaces.

If no loopback interfaces are configured, then the router chooses the highest active IPv4 address of any of its physical interfaces.

The router ID can be assigned to a loopback interface. The IPv4 address for this type of loopback interface should be configured using a 32-bit subnet mask (255.255.255.255), creating a host route. A 32-bit host route would not get advertised as a route to other OSPF routers. After a router selects a router ID, an active OSPF router does not allow the router ID to be changed until the router is reloaded or the OSPF process is reset. Use the **clear ip ospf process** privileged EXEC command to reset the adjacencies. You can then verify that R1 is using the new router ID with the **show ip protocols** command piped to display only the router ID section.

Point-to-Point OSPF Networks

The **network** command is used to determine which interfaces participate in the routing process for an OSPFv2 area. The basic syntax is **network** *network-address wildcard-mask* **area** *area-id*. Any interfaces on a router that match the network address in the **network** command can send and receive OSPF packets. When configuring single-area OSPFv2, the **network** command must be configured with the same *area-id* value on all routers. The wildcard mask is typically the inverse of the subnet mask configured on that interface. In a wildcard mask:

- **Wildcard mask bit 0:** Matches the corresponding bit value in the address
- **Wildcard mask bit 1:** Ignores the corresponding bit value in the address

Within routing configuration mode, there are two ways to identify the interfaces that will participate in the OSPFv2 routing process. One way is when the wildcard mask identifies the interface based on the network addresses. Any active interface that is configured with an IPv4 address belonging to that network will participate in the OSPFv2 routing process. The other way is that OSPFv2 can be enabled by specifying the exact interface IPv4 address using a quad-zero wildcard mask. To configure OSPF directly on the interface, use the **ip ospf** interface configuration mode command. The syntax is **ip ospf** *process-id* **area** *area-id*. Sending out unneeded messages on a LAN affects the network through inefficient use of bandwidth and resources, and it creates an increased security risk. Use the **passive-interface** router configuration mode command to stop transmitting routing messages through a router interface but still allow the network to be advertised to other routers. The **show ip protocols** command is then used to verify that the Loopback 0 interface is listed as passive. The DR/BDR election process is unnecessary as there can only be two routers on the point-to-point network between R1 and R2. Use the **ip ospf network point-to-point** interface configuration command on all interfaces where you want to disable the DR/BDR election process. Use loopbacks to simulate more networks than the equipment can support. By default, loopback interfaces are advertised as /32 host routes. To simulate a real LAN, the Loopback 0 interface is configured as a point-to-point network.

OSPF Network Types

Routers can be connected to the same switch to form a multiaccess network. Ethernet LANs are the most common example of broadcast multiaccess networks. In broadcast networks, all devices on the network see all broadcast and multicast frames. The DR is responsible for collecting and distributing LSAs. The DR uses the multicast IPv4 address 224.0.0.5, which is meant for all OSPF routers. If the DR stops producing Hello packets, the BDR promotes itself and assumes the role of DR. Every other router becomes a DROTHER. DROTHERs use the multiaccess address 224.0.0.6 (all designated routers) to send OSPF packets to the DR and BDR. Only the DR and BDR listen for 224.0.0.6. To verify the roles of the OSPFv2 router, use the **show ip ospf interface** command. To verify the OSPFv2 adjacencies, use the **show ip ospf neighbor** command. The state of neighbors in multiaccess networks can be:

- **FULL/DROTHER:** This is a DR or BDR router that is fully adjacent with a non-DR or BDR router.

- **FULL/DR:** The router is fully adjacent with the indicated DR neighbor.

- **FULL/BDR:** The router is fully adjacent with the indicated BDR neighbor.

- **2-WAY/DROTHER:** The non-DR or BDR router has a neighbor relationship with another non-DR or BDR router.

The OSPF DR and BDR election decision is based on the particular criteria. The routers in the network elect the router with the highest interface priority as the DR. The router with the second-highest interface priority is elected as the BDR. The priority can be configured to be any number between 0 and 255. If the interface priority value is set to 0, that interface cannot be elected as DR or as BDR. The default priority of multiaccess broadcast interfaces is 1. Therefore, unless otherwise configured, all routers have an equal priority value and must rely on another tie-breaking method during the DR/BDR election.

If the interface priorities are equal, then the router with the highest router ID is elected the DR. The router with the second-highest router ID is the BDR.

OSPF DR and BDR elections are not preemptive. If the DR fails, the BDR is automatically promoted to DR. This is the case even if another DROTHER with a higher priority or router ID is added to the network after the initial DR/BDR election. However, after a BDR is promoted to DR, a new BDR election occurs, and the DROTHER with the highest priority or router ID is elected as the new BDR. To set the priority of an interface, use the **ip ospf priority** *value* interface configuration command, where *value* is 0 to 255. If *value* is 0, the router will not become a DR or BDR. If *value* is 1 to 255, then the router with the higher priority value will more likely become the DR or BDR on the interface.

Modify Single-Area OSPFv2

OSPF uses cost as a metric. A lower cost indicates a better path than a higher cost. The Cisco cost of an interface is inversely proportional to the bandwidth of the interface. Therefore, a higher bandwidth indicates a lower cost. The formula used to calculate the OSPF cost is Cost = reference bandwidth / interface bandwidth. Because the OSPF cost value must be an integer, FastEthernet, Gigabit Ethernet, and 10 Gigabit Ethernet interfaces share the same cost. To correct this situation, you can adjust the reference bandwidth with the **auto-cost reference-bandwidth** router configuration command on each OSPF router or manually set the OSPF cost value with the **ip ospf cost** interface configuration command. To adjust the reference bandwidth, use the **auto-cost reference-bandwidth** *Mbps* router configuration command. The cost of an OSPF route is the accumulated value from one router to the destination network. OSPF cost values can be manipulated to influence the route chosen by OSPF. To change the cost value report by the local OSPF router to other OSPF routers, use the **ip ospf cost** *value* interface configuration command. If the Dead interval expires before the routers receive a Hello packet, OSPF removes that neighbor from its link-state database (LSDB). The router floods the LSDB with information about the down neighbor out all OSPF-enabled interfaces. Cisco uses a default of four times the Hello interval, or 40 seconds on multiaccess and point-to-point networks. To verify the OSPFv2 interface intervals, use the **show ip ospf interface** command. OSPFv2

Hello and Dead intervals can be modified manually using the following interface configuration mode commands: **ip ospf hello-interval** *seconds* and **ip ospf dead-interval** *seconds*.

Default Route Propagation

In OSPF terminology, the router located between an OSPF routing domain and a non-OSPF network is called the ASBR. To propagate a default route, the ASBR must be configured with a default static route using the **ip route 0.0.0.0 0.0.0.0** *[next-hop-address | exit-intf]* global configuration command and the **default-information originate** router configuration command. This instructs the ASBR to be the source of the default route information and propagate the default static route in OSPF updates. Verify the default route settings on the ASBR by using the **show ip route** command.

Verify Single-Area OSPFv2

The following two commands are used to verify routing:

- **show ip interface brief:** Used to verify that the desired interfaces are active with correct IP addressing.

- **show ip route:** Used to verify that the routing table contains all the expected routes.

Additional commands for determining that OSPF is operating as expected include **show ip ospf neighbor**, **show ip protocols**, **show ip ospf**, and **show ip ospf interface**.

Use the **show ip ospf neighbor** command to verify that the router has formed an adjacency with its neighboring routers. For each neighbor, this command displays:

- **Neighbor ID:** The router ID of the neighboring router.

- **Pri:** The OSPFv2 priority of the interface. This value is used in the DR and BDR election.

- **State:** The OSPFv2 state of the interface. FULL state means that the router and its neighbor have identical OSPFv2 LSDBs. On multiaccess networks, such as Ethernet, two routers that are adjacent may have their states displayed as 2WAY. The dash indicates that no DR or BDR is required because of the network type.

- **Dead Time:** The amount of time remaining that the router waits to receive an OSPFv2 Hello packet from the neighbor before declaring the neighbor down. This value is reset when the interface receives a Hello packet.

- **Address:** The IPv4 address of the neighbor's interface to which this router is directly connected.

- **Interface:** The interface on which this router has formed adjacency with the neighbor.

Using the **show ip protocols** command is a quick way to verify vital OSPF configuration information such as the OSPFv2 process ID, the router ID, the interfaces explicitly configured to advertise OSPF routes, the neighbors the router is receiving updates from, and the default administrative distance, which is 110 for OSPF. Use the **show ip ospf** command to examine the OSPFv2 process ID and router ID. This command displays the OSPFv2 area information and the last time the SPF algorithm was executed. The **show ip ospf interface** command provides a detailed list for every OSPFv2-enabled interface. Specify an interface for just one interface to display the process ID, the local router ID, the type of network, OSPF cost, DR and BDR information on multiaccess links, and adjacent neighbors.

Packet Tracer
☐ **Activity**

Packet Tracer—Single-Area OSPFv2 Configuration (2.7.1)

You are helping a network engineer test an OSPF setup by building the network in the lab where you work. You have interconnected the devices and configured the interfaces and have connectivity within the local LANs. Your job is to complete the OSPF configuration according to the requirements left by the engineer.

In this Packet Tracer activity, use the information provided and the list of requirements to configure the test network. When the task has been successfully completed, all hosts should be able to ping the internet server.

Lab—Single-Area OSPFv2 Configuration (2.7.2)

In this lab, you will complete the following objectives:

- Part 1: Build the network and configure basic device settings
- Part 2: Configure and verify single-area OSPFv2 for basic operation
- Part 3: Optimize and verify the single-area OSPFv2 configuration

Practice

The following activities provide practice with the topics introduced in this chapter. The labs are available in the companion *Enterprise Networking, Security, and Automation Labs & Study Guide (CCNAv7)*(ISBN 9780136634690). The Packet Tracer activity instructions are also in the *Labs & Study Guide*. The PKA files are found in the online course.

Lab
Lab 2.7.2: Single-Area OSPFv2 Configuration

Packet Tracer
☐ Activity

Packet Tracer Activities

Packet Tracer 2.2.13: Point-to-Point Single-Area OSPFv2 Configuration

Packet Tracer 2.3.11: Determine the DR and BDR

Packet Tracer 2.4.11: Modify Single-Area OSPFv2

Packet Tracer 2.5.3: Propagate a Default Route in OSPFv2

Packet Tracer 2.6.6: Verify Single-Area OSPFv2

Packet Tracer 2.7.1: Single-Area OSPFv2 Configuration

Check Your Understanding

Complete all the review questions listed here to test your understanding of the topics and concepts in this chapter. The appendix "Answers to the 'Check Your Understanding' Questions" lists the answers.

1. A router is participating in an OSPFv2 domain. What will always happen if the Dead interval expires before the router receives a Hello packet from an adjacent OSPF router?

   A. A new Dead interval timer of four times the Hello interval will start.

   B. OSPF will remove that neighbor from the router's link-state database.

   C. OSPF will run a new DR/BDR election.

   D. SPF will run and determine which neighbor router is down.

2. What is the first criterion used by OSPF routers to elect a DR?

   A. Highest priority

   B. Highest IP address

   C. Highest router ID

   D. Highest MAC address

3. Which wildcard mask would be used to advertise the 192.168.5.96/27 network as part of an OSPF configuration?

   A. 0.0.0.31

   B. 0.0.0.32

   C. 255.255.255.223

   D. 255.255.255.224

4. Which command would be used to determine if an OSPF routing protocol-initiated relationship had been made with an adjacent router?

   A. ping

   B. show ip interface brief

   C. show ip ospf neighbor

   D. show ip protocols

5. Which command is used to verify the OSPFv2 router ID, the interfaces explicitly configured to advertise OSPF routes, the passive interfaces, the neighbors the router is receiving updates from, and the default administrative distance, which is 110 for OSPF?

   A. show ip interface brief

   B. show ip ospf interface

   C. show ip protocols

   D. show ip route ospf

6. Two OSPFv2 routers are interconnected using a point-to-point WAN link. Which command could be used to verify the configured Hello and Dead timer intervals?

   A. show ip ospf neighbor

   B. show ip ospf interface fastethernet 0/1

   C. show ip ospf interface serial 0/0/0

   D. show ipv6 ospf interface serial 0/0/0

7. You are troubleshooting convergence and adjacency issues in an OSPFv2 network and have noticed that network route entries are missing from the routing table. Which commands provide additional information about the state of router adjacencies, timer intervals, and the area ID? (Choose two.)

   A. show ip ospf interface

   B. show ip ospf neighbor

   C. show ip protocols

   D. show ip route ospf

   E. show running-configuration

8. A network engineer has manually configured the Hello interval to 15 seconds on an interface of a router that is running OSPFv2. By default, how will the Dead interval on the interface be affected?

   A. The Dead interval will not change from the default value.

   B. The Dead interval will now be 15 seconds.

   C. The Dead interval will now be 30 seconds.

   D. The Dead interval will now be 60 seconds.

9. To establish a neighbor adjacency, two OSPF routers exchange Hello packets. Which values in the Hello packets must match on the two routers? (Choose two.)

   A. Dead interval

   B. Hello interval

   C. List of neighbors

   D. Router ID

   E. Router priority

10. What is the default router priority value for all Cisco OSPF routers?

   A. 0

   B. 1

   C. 10

   D. 255

11. What indicates to a link-state router that a neighbor is unreachable?

   A. The router no longer receives Hello packets.

   B. The router no longer receives routing updates.

   C. The router receives an LSP with previously learned information.

   D. The router receives an update with a hop count of 16.

12. Which of the following will OSPF use when it chooses its router ID?

   A. A loopback interface that is configured with the highest IP address on the router

   B. The highest active interface IP address that is configured on the router

   C. The lowest active interface IP address that is configured on the router

   D. The highest active interface that participates in the routing process because of a specifically configured **network** statement

13. An OSPF router has three directly connected networks; 10.1.0.0/16, 10.1.1.0/16, and 10.1.2.0/16. Which OSPF network command would advertise only the 10.1.1.0 network to neighbors?

   A. router(config-router)# **network 10.1.0.0 0.0.15.255 area 0**

   B. router(config-router)# **network 10.1.1.0 0.0.0.0 area 0**

   C. router(config-router)# **network 10.1.1.0 0.0.0.255 area 0**

   D. router(config-router)# **network 10.1.1.0 0.0.255.255 area 0**

14. By default, what is the OSPF cost for a link with Gigabit Ethernet interfaces?

   A. 1

   B. 100

   C. 10000

   D. 100000000

15. An administrator is configuring single-area OSPF on a router. One of the networks that must be advertised is 64.100.1.64 255.255.255.192. Which OSPF **network** statement should be configured?

   A. **network 64.100.1.64 0.0.0.15 area 0**

   B. **network 64.100.1.64 0.0.0.31 area 0**

   C. **network 64.100.1.64 0.0.0.63 area 0**

   D. **network 64.100.1.64 0.0.0.127 area 0**

16. Which of these factors will prevent two routers from forming an OSPFv2 adjacency? (Choose two.)

   A. Mismatched Cisco IOS versions

   B. Mismatched Ethernet interfaces (for example, Fa0/0 to G0/0)

   C. Mismatched OSPF Hello or Dead timers

   D. Mismatched subnet masks on the link interfaces

   E. Use of private IP addresses on the link interfaces

CHAPTER 3

Network Security Concepts

Objectives

Upon completion of this chapter, you will be able to answer the following questions:

- What is the current state of cybersecurity and vectors of data loss?
- What tools do threat actors use to exploit networks?
- What are the types of malware?
- What are common network attacks?
- How are IP vulnerabilities exploited by threat actors?
- How are TCP and UDP vulnerabilities exploited by threat actors?
- How are IP services exploited by threat actors?
- What are the best practices for protecting a network?
- What are the common cryptographic processes used to protect data in transit?

Key Terms

This chapter uses the following key terms. You can find the definitions in the Glossary.

Introduction

Perhaps you've heard one of the hundreds of news stories about data *security breaches* within a large corporation or even a government. Was your credit card number exposed by a breach? Or perhaps your private health information? Would you like to know how to prevent these data breaches? The field of network security is growing every day. This chapter provides details about the types of cybercrime and the many ways we have to fight back against *cybercriminals*. Let's get started!

Ethical Hacking Statement (3.0.3)

This chapter introduces tools and techniques used by cybercriminals to demonstrate various types of attacks. Unauthorized access to data, computer, and network systems is a crime in many jurisdictions and often is accompanied by severe consequences, regardless of the perpetrator's motivations. It is your responsibility, as the user of this material, to be cognizant of and compliant with computer use laws.

Current State of Cybersecurity (3.1)

Network breaches are now routinely reported in the media. Many of them involve high-profile organizations, celebrities, and governments. How were these attacks conducted, and what were the threat actors looking for? This section describes the current state of cybersecurity and vectors of data loss.

Current State of Affairs (3.1.1)

Cybercriminals now have the expertise and tools necessary to disrupt critical infrastructure and systems. Their tools and techniques continue to evolve.

Cybercriminals are taking *malware* to unprecedented levels of sophistication and impact. They are becoming more adept at using stealth and evasion techniques to hide their activity. In addition, cybercriminals are exploiting undefended gaps in security.

Network security breaches can disrupt e-commerce, cause the loss of business data, threaten people's privacy, and compromise the integrity of information. Corporate breaches can result in lost revenue, theft of intellectual property, and lawsuits, and they can even threaten public safety.

Maintaining a secure network ensures the safety of network users and protects commercial interests. Organizations need individuals who can recognize the speed and scale at which adversaries are amassing and refining their *cyber weaponry*. All users should be aware of the security terms in Table 3-1.

Table 3-1   Common Security Terms

Security Terms	Description
Assets	An asset is anything of value to an organization, including people, equipment, resources, and data.
Vulnerability	A vulnerability is a weakness in a system, or its design, that could be exploited by a threat.
Threat	A threat is a potential danger to a company's assets, data, or network functionality.
Exploit	An exploit is a mechanism that takes advantage of a vulnerability.
Mitigation	Mitigation refers to the countermeasures that reduce the likelihood or severity of a potential threat or risk. Network security involves multiple mitigation techniques.
Risk	Risk is the likelihood of a threat to exploit the vulnerability of an asset, with the aim of negatively affecting an organization. Risk is measured using the probability of the occurrence of an event and its consequences.

Assets must be identified and protected. Vulnerabilities must be addressed before they become threats and are exploited. Mitigation techniques are required before, during, and after an attack.

Vectors of Network Attacks (3.1.2)

An attack vector is a path by which a threat actor can gain access to a server, host, or network. Attack vectors originate from inside or outside a corporate network, as shown in Figure 3-1. For example, threat actors may target a network through the internet to disrupt network operations and create a *denial-of-service (DoS) attack*.

An internal user, such as an employee, can accidentally or intentionally:

- Steal and copy confidential data to removable media, email, messaging software, and other media.
- Compromise internal servers or network infrastructure devices.
- Disconnect a critical network connection and cause a network outage.
- Connect an infected USB drive to a corporate computer system.

Internal threats have the potential to cause greater damage than external threats because internal users have direct access to the building and its infrastructure devices. Employees may also have knowledge of the corporate network, its resources, and its confidential data.

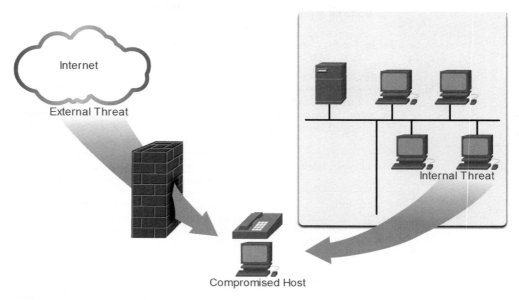

Figure 3-1   External and Internal Attack Vectors

Note

A DoS attack occurs when a network device or application is incapacitated and no longer capable of supporting requests from legitimate users.

Network security professionals must implement tools and apply techniques for mitigating both external and internal threats.

Data Loss (3.1.3)

Data is likely to be an organization's most valuable asset. Organizational data can include research and development data, sales data, financial data, human resource and legal data, employee data, contractor data, and customer data.

Data loss or *data exfiltration* occurs when data is intentionally or unintentionally lost, stolen, or leaked to the outside world. The data loss can result in:

- Brand damage and loss of reputation
- Loss of competitive advantage
- Loss of customers

- Loss of revenue
- Litigation/legal action resulting in fines and civil penalties
- Significant cost and effort to notify affected parties and recover from the breach

Table 3-2 lists common data loss vectors.

Table 3-2   Data Loss Vectors

Data Loss Vector	Description
Email/social networking	Intercepted email or IM messages could be captured and reveal confidential information.
Unencrypted devices	If the data is not stored using an encryption algorithm, then the thief can retrieve valuable confidential data.
Cloud storage devices	Sensitive data can be lost if access to the cloud is compromised due to weak security settings.
Removable media	One risk is that an employee could perform an unauthorized transfer of data to a USB drive. Another risk is that a USB drive containing valuable corporate data could be lost.
Hard copy	Confidential data should be shredded when no longer required.
Improper access control	Passwords or weak passwords which have been compromised can provide a threat actor with easy access to corporate data.

Network security professionals must protect the organization's data. Various data loss prevention (DLP) controls must be implemented to combine strategic, operational, and tactical measures.

Interactive Graphic

Check Your Understanding—Current State of Cybersecurity (3.1.4)

Refer to the online course to complete this activity.

Threat Actors (3.2)

This section describes the threat actors.

The Hacker (3.2.1)

In the previous section, you took a high-level look at the current landscape of cybersecurity, including the types of threats and vulnerabilities that plague all network administrators and architects. In this section, you will learn more details about particular types of *threat actors*.

Hacker is a common term used to describe a threat actor. Originally the term referred to someone who was a skilled computer expert such as a programmer and a hack was a clever solution. The term later evolved into what we know of it today.

As shown in Table 3-3, the terms *white hat hacker*, *black hat hacker*, and *gray hat hacker* are often used to describe types of hackers.

Table 3-3   Hacker Types

Hacker Type	Description
White hat hackers	▪ These are *ethical hackers* who use their programming skills for good, ethical, and legal purposes.
	▪ White hat hackers may perform network penetration tests in an attempt to compromise networks and systems by using their knowledge of computer security systems to discover network vulnerabilities.
	▪ Security vulnerabilities are reported to developers so they can fix them before the vulnerabilities can be exploited.
Gray hat hackers	▪ These are individuals who commit crimes and do arguably unethical things but not for personal gain or to cause damage.
	▪ Gray hat hackers may disclose a vulnerability to the affected organization after having compromised the network.
Black hat hackers	▪ These are unethical criminals who compromise computer and network security for personal gain or for malicious reasons, such as to attack networks.

Note

In this book, we do not use the term *hacker* outside of this chapter. Instead, we use the term *threat actor*. The term *threat actor* includes hackers, and it also refers to any other device, person, group, or nation-state that is, intentionally or unintentionally, the source of an attack.

Evolution of Hackers (3.2.2)

Hacking started in the 1960s with phone freaking, or phreaking, which refers to using audio frequencies to manipulate phone systems. At that time, telephone switches used various tones to indicate different functions. Early hackers realized that by mimicking a tone using a whistle, they could exploit the phone switches to make free long-distance calls.

In the mid-1980s, computer dialup modems were used to connect computers to networks. Hackers wrote "war dialing" programs that dialed each telephone number in a given area, in search of computers. When a computer was found, password-cracking programs were used to gain access.

Table 3-4 lists some modern hacking terms and a brief description of each.

Table 3-4   Common Hacking Terms

Hacking Term	Description
Script kiddies	■ These are teenagers or inexperienced hackers running existing scripts, tools, and exploits to cause harm, but typically not for profit.
Vulnerability brokers	■ These are usually gray hat hackers who attempt to discover exploits and report them to vendors, sometimes for prizes or rewards.
Hacktivists	■ These are gray hat hackers who publicly protest organizations or governments by posting articles and videos, leaking sensitive information, and performing network attacks.
Cybercriminals	■ These are black hat hackers who are either self-employed or working for large cybercrime organizations.
State-sponsored hackers	■ These are either white hat or black hat hackers who steal government secrets, gather intelligence, and sabotage networks.
	■ Their targets are foreign governments, terrorist groups, and corporations.
	■ Most countries in the world participate to some degree in state-sponsored hacking.

Cyber Criminals (3.2.3)

It is estimated that cybercriminals steal billions of dollars from consumers and businesses. Cybercriminals operate in an underground economy where they buy, sell, and trade attack toolkits, *zero-day exploit* code, *botnet* services, banking *Trojans*, *keyloggers*, and much more. They also buy and sell the private information and intellectual property they steal. Cybercriminals target small businesses and consumers, as well as large enterprises and entire industries.

Hacktivists (3.2.4)

Two examples of hacktivist groups are Anonymous and the Syrian Electronic Army. Although most hacktivist groups are not well organized, they can cause significant problems for governments and businesses. Hacktivists tend to rely on fairly basic, freely available tools.

State-Sponsored Hackers (3.2.5)

State-sponsored hackers create advanced, customized attack code, often using previously undiscovered software vulnerabilities called zero-day vulnerabilities. An example of a state-sponsored attack is the use of the Stuxnet malware to damage Iran's nuclear enrichment capabilities.

Interactive Graphic

Check Your Understanding—Threat Actors (3.2.6)

Refer to the online course to complete this activity.

Threat Actor Tools (3.3)

What do threat actors use to carry out their nefarious deeds?

This section introduces some of the tools that threat actors use to attack networks.

Video

Video—Threat Actor Tools (3.3.1)

Refer to the online course to view this video.

Introduction to Attack Tools (3.3.2)

To exploit a vulnerability, a threat actor must have a technique or tool. Over the years, attack tools have become more sophisticated and highly automated. These new tools require less technical knowledge to implement than did some of the older tools.

Figures 3-2 and 3-3 demonstrate the relationship between the sophistication of attack tools and the technical knowledge required to use them in 1985 and now.

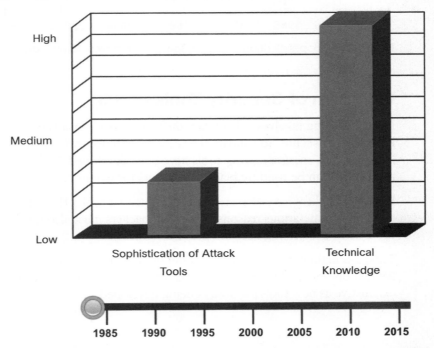

Figure 3-2   Sophistication of Attack Tools vs. Technical Knowledge (1985)

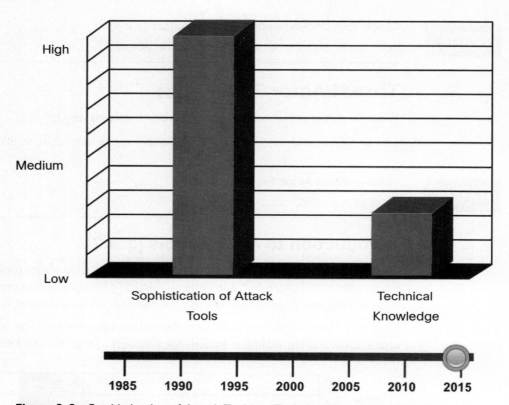

Figure 3-3   Sophistication of Attack Tools vs. Technical Knowledge (Now)

Evolution of Security Tools (3.3.3)

Ethical hacking involves using many different types of tools to test a network and keep its data secure. To validate the security of a network and its systems, many *network penetration testing* tools have been developed. Unfortunately, many of these tools can be used by black hat hackers for exploitation.

Black hat hackers have also created many hacking tools. These tools are created explicitly for nefarious reasons. White hat hackers must also know how to use these tools when performing network penetration tests.

Table 3-5 highlights categories of common penetration testing tools. Notice how some tools are used by white hats and black hats. Keep in mind that the list is not exhaustive as new tools are always being developed.

Table 3-5   Penetration Testing Tools

Penetration Testing Tool Category	Description
Password crackers	■ Password cracking tools are often referred to as password recovery tools and can be used to crack or recover a password. This is accomplished either by removing the original password, after bypassing the data encryption, or by outright discovery of the password. ■ Password crackers repeatedly make guesses in order to crack the password. ■ Examples of password cracking tools include John the Ripper, Ophcrack, L0phtCrack, THC Hydra, RainbowCrack, and Medusa.
Wireless hacking tools	■ Wireless hacking tools are used to intentionally hack into a wireless network to detect security vulnerabilities. ■ Examples of wireless hacking tools include Aircrack-ng, Kismet, InSSIDer, KisMAC, Firesheep, and NetStumbler.
Network scanning and hacking tools	■ Network scanning tools are used to probe network devices, servers, and hosts for open TCP or UDP ports. ■ Examples of scanning tools include Nmap, SuperScan, Angry IP Scanner, and NetScanTools.
Packet crafting tools	■ These tools are used to probe and test a firewall's robustness, using specially crafted forged packets. ■ Examples include Hping, Scapy, Socat, Yersinia, Netcat, Nping, and Nemesis.
Packet sniffers	■ These tools are used to capture and analyze packets in traditional Ethernet LANs or WLANs. ■ Tools include Wireshark, Tcpdump, Ettercap, Dsniff, EtherApe, Paros, Fiddler, Ratproxy, and SSLstrip.
Rootkit detectors	■ These are directory and file integrity checkers used by white hats to detect installed rootkits. ■ Examples of these tools include AIDE, Netfilter, and PF: OpenBSD Packet Filter.
Fuzzers to search vulnerabilities	■ Fuzzers are tools used by threat actors to discover a computer's security vulnerabilities. ■ Examples of fuzzers include Skipfish, Wapiti, and W3af.
Forensic tools	■ These tools are used by white hat hackers to sniff out any trace of evidence existing in a computer. ■ Examples of these tools include Sleuth Kit, Helix, Maltego, and Encase.

Penetration Testing Tool Category	Description
Debuggers	■ These tools are used by black hats to reverse engineer binary files when writing exploits. ■ They are also used by white hats when analyzing malware. ■ Debugging tools include GDB, WinDbg, IDA Pro, and Immunity Debugger.
Hacking operating systems	■ These are specially designed operating systems preloaded with tools optimized for hacking. ■ Examples of hacking operating systems include Kali Linux, Knoppix, and BackBox Linux.
Encryption tools	■ Encryption tools use algorithm schemes to encode data to prevent unauthorized access to the encrypted data. ■ Examples of these tools include VeraCrypt, CipherShed, OpenSSH, OpenSSL, Tor, OpenVPN, and Stunnel.
Vulnerability exploitation tools	■ These tools identify whether a remote host is vulnerable to a security attack. ■ Examples of vulnerability exploitation tools include Metasploit, Core Impact, Sqlmap, Social Engineer Toolkit, and Netsparker.
Vulnerability scanners	■ These tools scan a network or system to identify open ports. ■ They can also be used to scan for known vulnerabilities and scan VMs, BYOD devices, and client databases. ■ Examples of these tools include Nipper, Secunia PSI, Core Impact, Nessus v6, SAINT, and Open VAS.

Note

Many of these tools are UNIX or Linux based; therefore, a security professional should have a strong UNIX and Linux background.

Attack Types (3.3.4)

Threat actors can use the previously mentioned attack tools or a combination of tools to create attacks. Table 3-6 lists some common types of attacks. However, this list of attacks is not exhaustive as new attack vulnerabilities are constantly being discovered.

Table 3-6 Attack Types

Attack Type	Description
Eavesdropping attack	▪ A threat actor captures and "listens" to network traffic. ▪ This attack is also referred to as sniffing or snooping.
Data modification attack	▪ If threat actors have captured enterprise traffic, they can alter the data in the packet without the knowledge of the sender or receiver.
IP address spoofing attack	▪ A threat actor constructs an IP packet that appears to originate from a valid address inside the corporate intranet.
Password-based attacks	▪ If threat actors discover a valid user account, they have the same rights as the real user. ▪ Threat actors could use valid accounts to obtain lists of other users, network information, change server and network configurations, and modify, reroute, or delete data.
Denial-of-service (DoS) attack	▪ A DoS attack prevents normal use of a computer or network by valid users. ▪ A DoS attack can flood a computer or an entire network with traffic until a shutdown occurs because of the overload. ▪ A DoS attack can also block traffic, which results in a loss of access to network resources by authorized users.
Man-in-the-middle (MITM) attack	▪ This attack occurs when threat actors have positioned themselves between a source and destination. ▪ The attacker can actively monitor, capture, and transparently control communication between the source and destination.
Compromised-key attack	▪ If a threat actor obtains a secret key, that key is referred to as a compromised key. ▪ A compromised key can be used to gain access to a secured communication without the sender or receiver being aware of the attack.
Sniffer attack	▪ A sniffer is an application or a device that can read, monitor, and capture network data exchanges and read network packets. ▪ If the packets are not encrypted, a sniffer provides a full view of the data inside the packet.

Interactive Graphic

Check Your Understanding—Threat Actor Tools (3.3.5)

Refer to the online course to complete this activity.

Malware (3.4)

How do threat actors get victims to enable their attacks? They trick them into installing malicious code (malware). Malware is software that is designed to exploit a target host. There are many different types of malware, including viruses, worms, Trojan horses, ransomware, spyware, adware, and scareware.

This section describes the various types of malware used by threat actors.

Overview of Malware (3.4.1)

Now that you know about the tools that hackers use, this section introduces you to different types of malware that hackers use to gain access to end devices.

End devices are particularly prone to malware attacks. It is important to know about malware because threat actors rely on users to install malware to help exploit security gaps.

The primary vulnerabilities for end-user workstations are *virus*, *worm*, and *Trojan Horse* attacks:

- A worm executes arbitrary code and installs copies of itself in the memory of the infected computer. The main purpose of a worm is to automatically replicate itself and spread across the network from system to system.

- A virus is malicious software that executes a specific, unwanted, and often harmful function on a computer.

- A Trojan horse is a non-self-replicating type of malware. It often contains malicious code that is designed to look like something else, such as a legitimate application or file. When an infected application or file is downloaded and opened, the Trojan horse can attack the end device from within.

Viruses and Trojan Horses (3.4.2)

The most common type of computer malware is a virus. Viruses require human action to propagate and infect other computers. For example, a virus can infect a computer when a victim opens an email attachment, opens a file on a USB drive, or downloads a file.

The virus hides by attaching itself to computer code, software, or documents on the computer. When opened, the virus executes and infects the computer.

Viruses can

- Alter, corrupt, delete files, or erase entire drives

- Cause computer booting issues and corrupt applications

- Capture and send sensitive information to threat actors

- Access and use email accounts to spread themselves

- Lay dormant until summoned by the threat actor

Modern viruses are developed for specific intents, such as those listed in Table 3-7.

Table 3-7   Types of Viruses

Types of Viruses	Description
Boot sector virus	Attacks the boot sector, file partition table, or file system.
Firmware virus	Attacks the device firmware.
Macro virus	Uses the macro feature in Microsoft Office or other applications maliciously.
Program virus	Inserts itself in another executable program.
Script virus	Attacks the OS interpreter, which is used to execute scripts.

Threat actors use Trojan horses to compromise hosts. A Trojan horse is a program that looks useful but that carries malicious code. Trojan horses are often provided with free online programs such as computer games. Unsuspecting users download and install the game and get the Trojan horse, too.

As described in Table 3-8, there are several types of Trojan horses.

Table 3-8   Types of Trojan Horses

Type of Trojan Horse	Description
Remote access	Enables unauthorized remote access.
Data sending	Provides the threat actor with sensitive data, such as passwords.
Destructive	Corrupts or deletes files.
Proxy	Uses the victim's computer as the source device to launch attacks and perform other illegal activities.
FTP	Enables unauthorized file transfer services on end devices.
Security software disabler	Stops antivirus programs or firewalls from functioning.
Denial of service (DoS)	Slows or halts network activity.
Keylogger	Actively attempts to steal confidential information, such as credit card numbers, by recording keystrokes entered into a web form.

Other Types of Malware (3.4.3)

Viruses and Trojan horses are only two types of malware that threat actors use. There are many other types of malware that have been designed for specific purposes. Table 3-9 describes some of the many different types of malware.

Table 3-9   Other Types of Malware

Type of Malware	Description
Adware	■ Adware is usually distributed through online software downloads. ■ Adware can display unsolicited advertising using pop-up web browser windows or new toolbars, or it can unexpectedly redirect a webpage to a different website. ■ Pop-up windows may be difficult to control as new windows can pop up faster than the user can close them.
Ransomware	■ Ransomware typically denies a user access to his or her files by encrypting the files and then displaying a message demanding a ransom for the decryption key. ■ Users without up-to-date backups must pay the ransom to decrypt their files. ■ Payment is usually made using wire transfer or cryptocurrencies such as bitcoin.
Rootkit	■ Rootkits are used by threat actors to gain administrator account-level access to a computer. ■ They are very difficult to detect because they can alter firewall, antivirus protection, system files, and even OS commands to conceal their presence. ■ A rootkit can provide a backdoor to give a threat actor access to the PC, allowing the threat actor to upload files and install new software to be used in a DDoS attack. ■ Special rootkit removal tools must be used to remove rootkits, or a complete OS re-install may be required.
Spyware	■ Spyware is similar to adware but is used to gather information about the user and send it to threat actors without the user's consent. ■ Spyware can be a low threat, gathering browsing data, or it can be a high threat, capturing personal and financial information.
Worm	■ A worm is a self-replicating program that propagates automatically without user actions by exploiting vulnerabilities in legitimate software. ■ It uses the network to search for other victims with the same vulnerability. ■ The intent of a worm is usually to slow or disrupt network operations.

Check Your Understanding—Malware (3.4.4)

Refer to the online course to complete this activity.

Common Network Attacks (3.5)

Networks are targets. A threat actor who gains administrative access to a corporate network infrastructure can steal data, delete data, and disrupt network availability. Threat actors commonly use three types of network attacks to achieve their objectives, as discussed in this section.

Overview of Network Attacks (3.5.1)

As you have learned, there are many types of malware that hackers can use. But these are not the only ways that they can attack a network or even an organization.

When malware is delivered and installed, the payload can be used to cause a variety of network-related attacks.

To mitigate attacks, it is useful to understand the types of attacks. By categorizing network attacks, it is possible to address types of attacks rather than individual attacks.

Networks are susceptible to the following types of attacks:

- *Reconnaissance attacks*
- *Access attacks*
- DoS attacks

Video—Reconnaissance Attacks (3.5.2)

Refer to the online course to view this video.

Reconnaissance Attacks (3.5.3)

Reconnaissance is information gathering. It is analogous to a thief surveying a neighborhood by going door-to-door, pretending to sell something but actually looking for vulnerable homes to break into, such as unoccupied residences, residences with easy-to-open doors or windows, and residences without security systems or security cameras.

Threat actors use reconnaissance (or recon) attacks to do unauthorized discovery and mapping of systems, services, or vulnerabilities. Recon attacks precede access attacks or DoS attacks.

Some of the techniques used by malicious threat actors to conduct reconnaissance attacks are described in Table 3-10.

Table 3-10 Reconnaissance Attack Techniques

Technique	Description
Perform an information query of a target	■ The threat actor is looking for initial information about a target. ■ Various tools can be used, including Google search, organization websites, whois, and more.
Initiate a ping sweep of the target network	■ The information query usually reveals the target's network address. ■ The threat actor can initiate a ping sweep to determine which IP addresses are active.
Initiate a port scan of active IP addresses	■ This is used to determine which ports or services are available. ■ Examples of port scanners include Nmap, SuperScan, Angry IP Scanner, and NetScanTools.
Run vulnerability scanners	■ The threat actor queries the identified ports to determine the type and version of the application and operating system that is running on the host. ■ Examples of tools include Nipper, Secuna PSI, Core Impact, Nessus v6, SAINT, and Open VAS.
Run exploitation tools	■ The threat actor attempts to discover vulnerable services that can be exploited. ■ A variety of vulnerability exploitation tools exist, including Metasploit, Core Impact, Sqlmap, Social Engineer Toolkit, and Netsparker.

Video

Video—Access and Social Engineering Attacks (3.5.4)

Refer to the online course to view this video.

Access Attacks (3.5.5)

Access attacks exploit known vulnerabilities in authentication services, FTP services, and web services. The purpose of these types of attacks is to gain entry to web accounts, confidential databases, and other sensitive information.

Threat actors use access attacks on network devices and computers to retrieve data, gain access, or escalate access privileges to administrator status. These are the two main types of access attacks:

- **Password attack:** In a password attack, the threat actor attempts to discover critical system passwords using various methods. Password attacks are very common and can be launched using a variety of password cracking tools.

- **Spoofing attack:** In a spoofing attack, the threat actor device attempts to pose as another device by falsifying data. Common spoofing attacks include *IP spoofing*, *MAC spoofing*, and *DHCP spoofing*. These spoofing attacks are discussed in more detail later in this chapter.

Other access attacks include

- Trust exploitations

- Port redirections

- Man-in-the-middle attacks

- Buffer overflow attacks

Trust Exploitation Example

In a trust exploitation attack, a threat actor uses unauthorized privileges to gain access to a system, possibly compromising the target. Figure 3-4 shows an example of a trust exploitation.

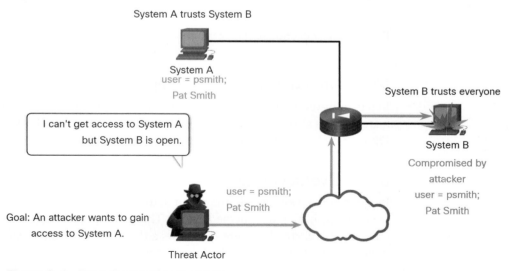

Figure 3-4   Trust Exploitation Example

Port Redirection Example

In a port redirection attack, a threat actor uses a compromised system as a base for attacks against other targets. The example in Figure 3-5 shows a threat actor using SSH (port 22) to connect to a compromised Host A. Host A is trusted by Host B and, therefore, the threat actor can use Telnet (port 23) to access it.

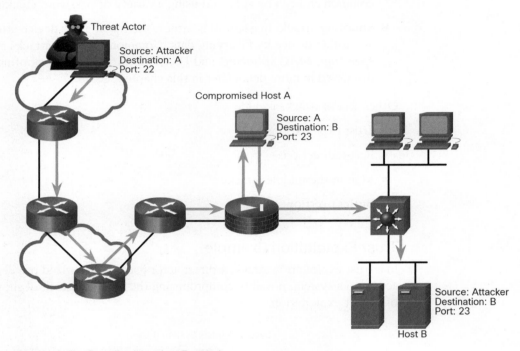

Figure 3-5   Port Redirection Example

Man-in-the-Middle Attack Example

In a man-in-the-middle attack, the threat actor is positioned in between two legitimate entities in order to read or modify the data that passes between the two parties. Figure 3-6 shows an example of a man-in-the-middle attack.

Buffer Overflow Attack

In a buffer overflow attack, the threat actor exploits the buffer memory and overwhelms it with unexpected values. This usually renders the system inoperable, creating a DoS attack. Figure 3-7 shows a threat actor sending many packets to the victim in an attempt to overflow the victim's buffer.

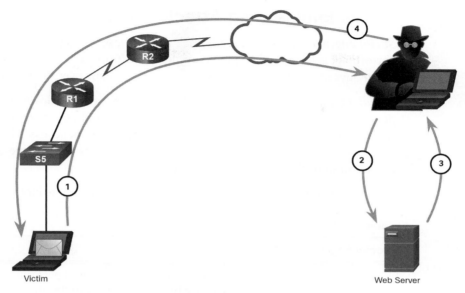

Figure 3-6   Man-in-the-Middle Attack Example

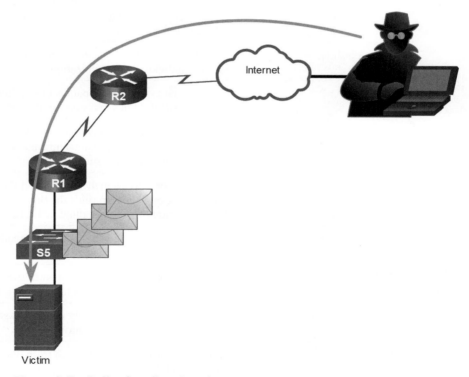

Figure 3-7   Buffer Overflow Attack

Social Engineering Attacks (3.5.6)

Social engineering is an access attack that attempts to manipulate individuals into performing actions or divulging confidential information. Some social engineering techniques are performed in person, and others occur over the telephone or internet.

Social engineers often rely on people's willingness to be helpful. They also prey on people's weaknesses. For example, a threat actor could call an authorized employee with an urgent problem that requires immediate network access. The threat actor could appeal to the employee's vanity, invoke authority using name-dropping techniques, or appeal to the employee's greed.

Information about social engineering techniques is shown in Table 3-11.

Table 3-11   Social Engineering Attacks

Social Engineering Attack	Description
Pretexting	A threat actor pretends to need personal or financial data to confirm the identity of the recipient.
Phishing	A threat actor sends fraudulent email disguised as being from a legitimate, trusted source to trick the recipient into installing malware on a device or into sharing personal or financial information.
Spear phishing	A threat actor creates a targeted phishing attack tailored for a specific individual or organization.
Spam	Also known as junk mail, spam is unsolicited email that often contains harmful links, malware, or deceptive content.
Something for something	Sometimes called *Quid pro quo*, this is an attack in which a threat actor requests personal information from a party in exchange for something such as a gift.
Baiting	A threat actor leaves a malware-infected flash drive in a public location. A victim finds the drive and inserts it into a laptop, unintentionally installing malware.
Impersonation	In this type of attack, a threat actor pretends to be someone else in order to gain the trust of a victim.
Tailgating	A threat actor quickly follows an authorized person into a secure location to gain access to a secure area.
Shoulder surfing	A threat actor inconspicuously looks over someone's shoulder to steal passwords or other information.
Dumpster diving	A threat actor rummages through trash bins to discover confidential documents.

The Social Engineering Toolkit (SET) was designed to help white hat hackers and other network security professionals create social engineering attacks to test their own networks.

Enterprises must educate their users about the risks of social engineering and develop strategies to validate identities over the phone, via email, and in person.

The following are recommended practices that should be followed by all users:

- Never give your username and password credentials to anyone.

- Never leave your username and password credentials where they can easily be found.

- Never open emails from untrusted sources.

- Never release work-related information on social media sites.

- Never reuse work-related passwords.

- Always lock or sign out of your computer when leaving it unattended.

- Always report suspicious individuals.

- Always destroy confidential information according to organization policy.

Lab—Social Engineering (3.5.7)

In this lab, you will research examples of social engineering and identify ways to recognize and prevent it.

Video

Video—Denial of Service Attacks (3.5.8)

Refer to the online course to view this video.

DoS and DDoS Attacks (3.5.9)

A denial-of-service (DoS) attack creates some sort of interruption of network services to users, devices, or applications. There are two major types of DoS attacks:

- **Overwhelming quantity of traffic:** The threat actor sends an enormous quantity of data at a rate that the network, host, or application cannot handle. This causes transmission and response times to slow down. It can also crash a device or service.

■ **Maliciously formatted packets:** The threat actor sends a maliciously formatted packet to a host or an application, and the receiver is unable to handle it. This causes the receiving device to run very slowly or crash.

DoS Attack

DoS attacks are a major risk because they interrupt communication and cause significant loss of time and money. These attacks are relatively simple to conduct, even by an unskilled threat actor.

Figure 3-8 shows an example of a DoS attack.

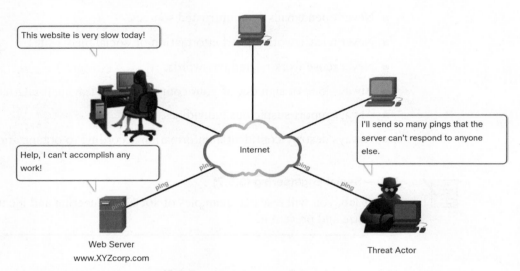

Figure 3-8   DoS Attack Example

DDoS Attack

A *distributed denial-of-service (DDoS)* attack is similar to a DoS attack, but it originates from multiple, coordinated sources. For example, a threat actor builds a network of infected hosts, known as *zombies*. The threat actor uses a *command and control (CnC)* system to send control messages to the zombies. The zombies constantly scan and infect more hosts with bot malware. The bot malware is designed to infect a host, making it a zombie that can communicate with the CnC system. The collection of zombies is called a *botnet*. Eventually, the threat actor instructs the CnC system to make the botnet of zombies carry out a DDoS attack.

Figure 3-9 shows an example of a DDoS attack.

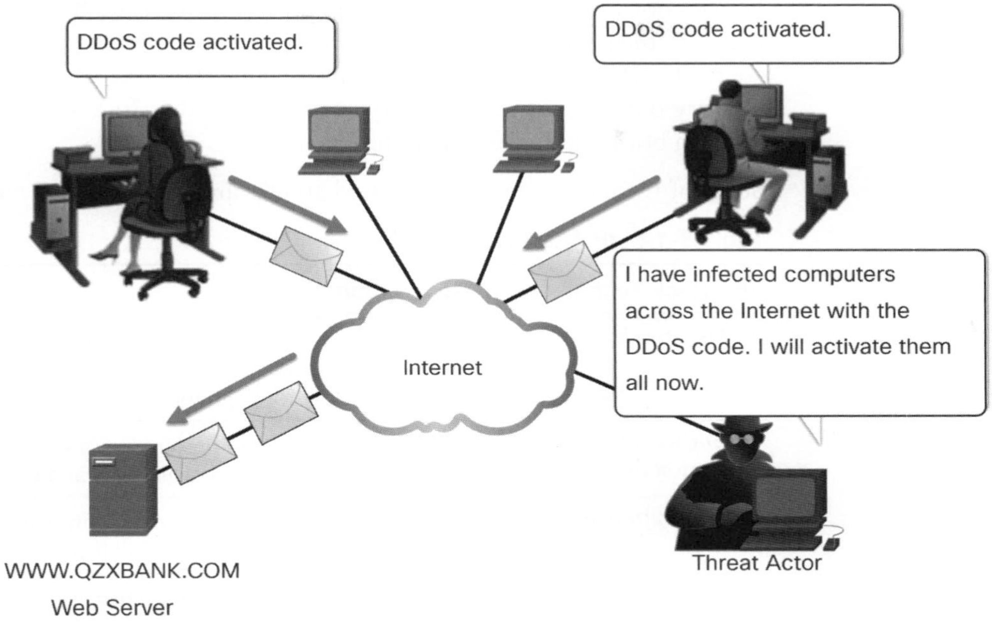

Figure 3-9 DDoS Attack Example

Interactive Graphic

Check Your Understanding—Common Network Attacks (3.5.10)

Refer to the online course to complete this activity.

IP Vulnerabilities and Threats (3.6)

Internet Protocol (IP) and Internet Control Message Protocol (ICMP) are required for network communication. Computers and networks use IP to provide the addressing for local and remote network reachability, and they use ICMP to provide messaging services for IP. However, threat actors have discovered IP and ICMP vulnerabilities that they exploit to leverage their attacks.

This section explains how IP vulnerabilities are exploited by threat actors.

Video

Video—Common IP and ICMP Attacks (3.6.1)

Refer to the online course to view this video.

IPv4 and IPv6 (3.6.2)

IP does not validate whether a packet actually came from the source IP address contained in the packet. For this reason, threat actors can send packets using a spoofed source IP address. Threat actors can also tamper with the other fields in the IP header to carry out their attacks. Security analysts must therefore understand the different fields in both the IPv4 and IPv6 headers.

Some of the most common IP-related attacks are described in Table 3-12.

Table 3-12   IP Attacks

IP Attack Techniques	Description
ICMP attacks	Threat actors use ICMP echo packets (pings) to discover subnets and hosts on a protected network, to generate DoS flood attacks, and to alter host routing tables.
Amplification and reflection attacks	Threat actors attempt to prevent legitimate users from accessing information or services by using DoS and DDoS attacks.
Address spoofing attacks	Threat actors spoof the source IP address in an IP packet to perform blind spoofing or non-blind spoofing.
Man-in-the-middle (MITM) attacks	Threat actors position themselves between a source and destination to transparently monitor, capture, and control the communication. They could eavesdrop by inspecting captured packets or alter packets and forward them to their original destination.
Session hijacking	Threat actors gain access to the physical network and then use an MITM attack to hijack a session.

ICMP Attacks (3.6.3)

Threat actors use ICMP for reconnaissance and scanning attacks. They can launch information-gathering attacks to map out a network topology, discover which hosts are active (reachable), identify the host operating system (OS fingerprinting), and determine the state of a firewall. Threat actors also use ICMP for DoS attacks.

> **Note**
>
> ICMP for IPv4 (ICMPv4) and ICMP for IPv6 (ICMPv6) are susceptible to similar types of attacks.
>
> Networks should have strict ICMP *access control list (ACL)* filtering at the network edge to avoid ICMP probing from the internet. Security analysts should be able to detect ICMP-related attacks by looking at captured traffic and log files. In the case of large networks, security devices such as firewalls and intrusion detection systems (IDSs) detect such attacks and send alerts to the security analysts.

Common ICMP messages of interest to threat actors are listed in Table 3-13.

Table 3-13   ICMP Messages as Attack Vectors

ICMP Messages Used by Hackers	Description
ICMP echo request and echo reply	Used to perform host verification and DoS attacks.
ICMP unreachable	Used to perform network reconnaissance and scanning attacks.
ICMP mask reply	Used to map an internal IP network.
ICMP redirects	Used to lure a target host into sending all traffic through a compromised device and create an MITM attack.
ICMP router discovery	Used to inject bogus route entries into the routing table of a target host.

Video

Video—Amplification, Reflection, and Spoofing Attacks (3.6.4)

Refer to the online course to view this video.

Amplification and Reflection Attacks (3.6.5)

Threat actors often use amplification and reflection techniques to create DoS attacks. The example in Figure 3-10 illustrates how an amplification and reflection technique called a Smurf attack is used to overwhelm a target host.

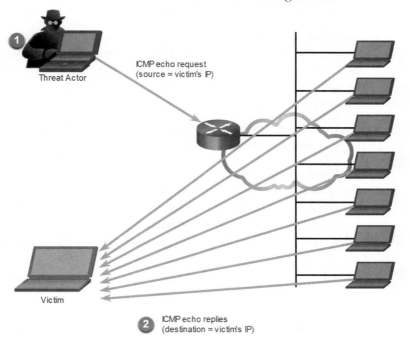

Figure 3-10   Amplification and Reflection Example

In the figure:

1. **Amplification:** The threat actor forwards ICMP echo request messages to many hosts. These messages contain the source IP address of the victim.

2. **Reflection:** These hosts all reply to the spoofed IP address of the victim to overwhelm it.

> **Note**
>
> Newer forms of amplification and reflection attacks such as DNS-based reflection and amplification attacks and Network Time Protocol (NTP) amplification attacks are now being used.

Threat actors also use resource exhaustion attacks. These attacks consume the resources of a target host to either crash it or consume the resources of a network.

Address Spoofing Attacks (3.6.6)

IP address spoofing attacks occur when a threat actor creates packets with false source IP address information to either hide the identity of the sender or to pose as another legitimate user. The threat actor can then gain access to otherwise inaccessible data or circumvent security configurations. Spoofing is usually incorporated into another attack, such as a Smurf attack.

Spoofing attacks can be non-blind or blind:

- **Non-blind spoofing:** The threat actor can see the traffic that is being sent between the host and the target. The threat actor uses non-blind spoofing to inspect the reply packet from the target victim. Non-blind spoofing determines the state of a firewall and sequence-number prediction. It can also hijack an authorized session.

- **Blind spoofing:** The threat actor cannot see the traffic that is being sent between the host and the target. Blind spoofing is used in DoS attacks.

MAC address spoofing attacks are used when threat actors have access to the internal network. Threat actors alter the MAC address of the host to match another known MAC address of a target host, as shown in Figure 3-11. The attacking host then sends a frame throughout the network with the newly configured MAC address. When the switch receives the frame, it examines the source MAC address.

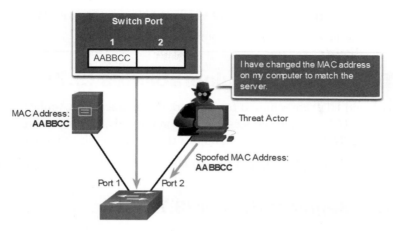

Figure 3-11   Threat Actor Spoofs a Server's MAC Address

The switch overwrites the current Content Addressable Memory (CAM) table entry and assigns the MAC address to the new port, as shown in Figure 3-12. It then forwards frames destined for the target host to the attacking host.

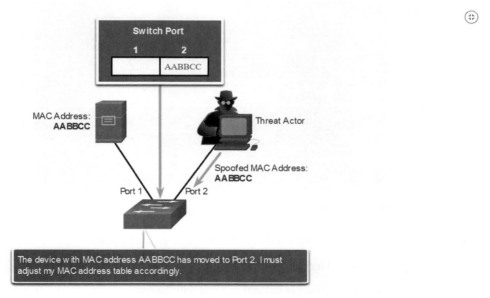

Figure 3-12   Switch Updates CAM Table with Spoofed Address

Application or service spoofing is another type of spoofing. With such an attack, a threat actor connects a rogue DHCP server to create an MITM condition.

Check Your Understanding—IP Vulnerabilities and Threats (3.6.7)

Refer to the online course to complete this activity.

TCP and UDP Vulnerabilities (3.7)

TCP and UDP are required for network communication. Application layer protocols require TCP or UDP services to function properly. However, threat actors have discovered TCP and UDP vulnerabilities that they exploit to leverage their attacks.

This section explains how TCP and UDP vulnerabilities are exploited by threat actors.

TCP Segment Header (3.7.1)

This section discusses attacks that target TCP and UDP. TCP segment information appears immediately after the IP header. The fields of the TCP segment are shown in Figure 3-13.

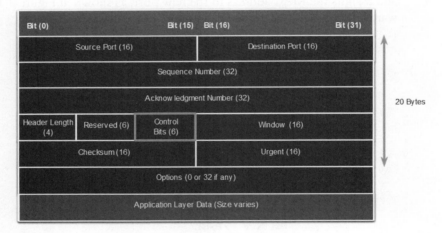

Figure 3-13   TCP Header

The flags for the six Control Bits field are as follows:

- **URG:** Urgent pointer field significant
- **ACK:** Acknowledgment field significant
- **PSH:** Push function
- **RST:** Reset the connection
- **SYN:** Synchronize sequence numbers
- **FIN:** No more data from sender

TCP Services (3.7.2)

TCP provides these services:

- **Reliable delivery:** TCP incorporates acknowledgments to guarantee delivery instead of relying on upper-layer protocols to detect and resolve errors. If a timely acknowledgment is not received, the sender retransmits the data. Requiring acknowledgments of received data can cause substantial delays. Examples of application layer protocols that make use of TCP reliability include HTTP, SSL/TLS, FTP, and DNS zone transfers.

- **Flow control:** TCP implements flow control to help minimize the delays introduced by reliable delivery. Rather than acknowledge one segment at a time, multiple segments can be acknowledged with a single acknowledgment segment.

- **Stateful communication:** TCP stateful communication between two parties occurs during the TCP three-way handshake. Before data can be transferred using TCP, a three-way handshake opens the TCP connection, as shown in Figure 3-14. If both sides agree to the TCP connection, data can be sent and received by both parties using TCP.

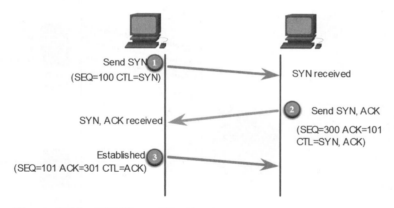

Figure 3-14   TCP Three-Way Handshake

The figure demonstrates a TCP connection established in three steps:

Step 1.   The initiating client requests a client-to-server communication session with the server.

Step 2.   The server acknowledges the client-to-server communication session and requests a server-to-client communication session.

Step 3.   The initiating client acknowledges the server-to-client communication session.

TCP Attacks (3.7.3)

Network applications use TCP or UDP ports. Threat actors conduct port scans of target devices to discover which services they offer.

TCP SYN Flood Attack

A *TCP SYN flood attack* exploits the TCP three-way handshake. Figure 3-15 shows a threat actor continually sending TCP SYN session request packets with a randomly spoofed source IP address to a target. The target device replies with a TCP SYN-ACK packet to the spoofed IP address and waits for a TCP ACK packet. Those responses never arrive. Eventually, the target host is overwhelmed with half-open TCP connections, and TCP services are denied to legitimate users.

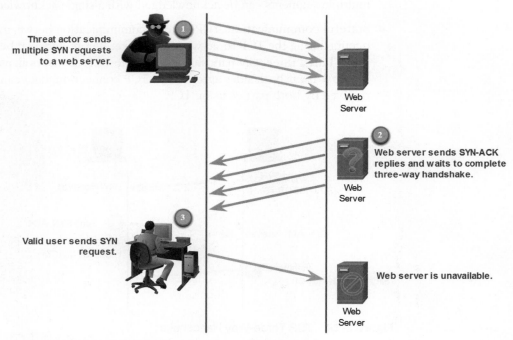

Figure 3-15   TCP SYN Flood Attack

The following steps occur in Figure 3-15:

Step 1.   The threat actor sends multiple SYN requests to a web server.

Step 2.   The web server replies with SYN-ACKs for each SYN request and waits to complete the three-way handshake. The threat actor does not respond to the SYN-ACKs.

Step 3.   A valid user cannot access the web server because the web server has too many half-opened TCP connections.

TCP Reset Attack

A *TCP reset attack* can be used to terminate TCP communications between two hosts. TCP can terminate a connection in a civilized (that is, normal) manner or in an uncivilized (that is, abrupt) manner.

Figure 3-16 shows the civilized manner, with TCP using a four-way exchange consisting of a pair of FIN and ACK segments from each TCP endpoint to close the TCP connection.

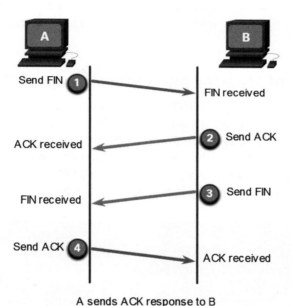

Figure 3-16   TCP Reset Attack

In the figure, terminating a TCP session uses the following four-way exchange process:

Step 1.   When the client has no more data to send in the stream, it sends a segment with the FIN flag set.

Step 2.   The server sends an ACK to acknowledge the receipt of the FIN to terminate the session from client to server.

Step 3.   The server sends a FIN to the client to terminate the server-to-client session.

Step 4.   The client responds with an ACK to acknowledge the FIN from the server.

With the uncivilized manner, a host receives a TCP segment with the RST bit set. This is an abrupt way to tear down the TCP connection and inform the receiving host to immediately stop using the TCP connection.

A threat actor could do a TCP reset attack and send a spoofed packet containing a TCP RST to one or both endpoints.

TCP Session Hijacking

TCP session hijacking takes advantage of another TCP vulnerability, although it can be difficult to conduct. A threat actor takes over an already authenticated host as it communicates with the target. The threat actor must spoof the IP address of one host, predict the next sequence number, and send an ACK to the other host. If successful, the threat actor can send (although not receive) data from the target device.

UDP Segment Header and Operation (3.7.4)

UDP is commonly used by DNS, TFTP, NFS, and SNMP. It is also used with real-time applications such as media streaming and VoIP. UDP is a connectionless transport layer protocol. It has much lower overhead than TCP because it is not connection oriented and does not offer the sophisticated retransmission, sequencing, and flow control mechanisms that provide reliability. The UDP segment structure, shown in Figure 3-17, is much smaller than TCP's segment structure.

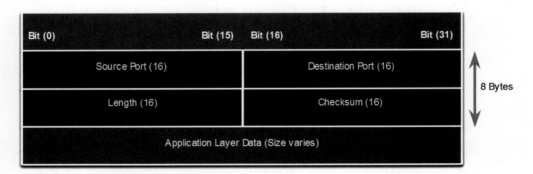

Figure 3-17   UDP Header

Although UDP is normally said to be unreliable (in contrast to TCP's reliability), this does not mean that applications that use UDP are always unreliable, nor does it mean that UDP is an inferior protocol. It means that these functions are not provided by the transport layer protocol and must be implemented elsewhere, if required.

The low overhead of UDP makes it very desirable for protocols that make simple request-and-reply transactions. For example, using TCP for DHCP would introduce unnecessary network traffic. If no response is received, the device re-sends the request.

UDP Attacks (3.7.5)

UDP is not protected by any encryption. You can add encryption to UDP, but it is not available by default. The lack of encryption means that anyone can see the traffic, change it, and send it on to its destination. Changing the data in the traffic will alter the 16-bit checksum, but the checksum is optional and is not always used. When the checksum is used, the threat actor can create a new checksum based on the new data payload and then record it in the header as a new checksum. The destination device will find that the checksum matches the data without knowing that the data has been altered. This type of attack is not widely used.

UDP Flood Attacks

You are more likely to see a *UDP flood attack*. In a UDP flood attack, all the resources on a network are consumed. The threat actor must use a tool like UDP Unicorn or Low Orbit Ion Cannon. These tools send a flood of UDP packets, often from a spoofed host, to a server on the subnet. The program sweeps through all the known ports, trying to find closed ports. This causes the server to reply with an ICMP port unreachable message. Because there are many closed ports on the server, this creates a lot of traffic on the segment, which uses up most of the bandwidth. The result is very similar to the result of a DoS attack.

Interactive Graphic

Check Your Understanding—TCP and UDP Vulnerabilities (3.7.6)

Refer to the online course to complete this activity.

IP Services

IP services include ARP, DNS, DHCP, and SLAAC. ARP resolves IPv4 addresses to MAC address, DNS resolves names to IP addresses, and DHCP and SLAAC automate the assignment of IP configurations on networks. However, threat actors have discovered IP service vulnerabilities that they exploit to leverage their attacks.

This section explains how IP services are exploited by threat actors.

ARP Vulnerabilities (3.8.1)

Earlier in this chapter, you learned about vulnerabilities with IP, TCP, and UDP. The TCP/IP protocol suite was not built for security. Therefore, the services that IP uses for addressing functions—such as ARP, DNS, and DHCP—are also not secure, as you will learn in this section.

Hosts broadcast an ARP Request to other hosts on the segment to determine the MAC address of a host with a particular IPv4 address, as shown in Figure 3-18. All hosts on the subnet receive and process the ARP Request. The host with the matching IPv4 address in the ARP Request sends an ARP Reply.

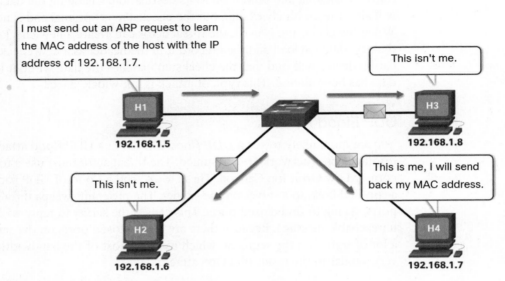

Figure 3-18　The ARP Process

Any client can send an unsolicited ARP Reply called a *gratuitous ARP*. This is often done when a device first boots up to inform all other devices on the local network of the new device's MAC address. When a host sends a gratuitous ARP, other hosts on the subnet store the MAC address and IPv4 address contained in the gratuitous ARP in their ARP tables.

This feature of ARP also means that any host can claim to be the owner of any IPv4 or MAC address. A threat actor can poison the ARP caches of devices on the local network, creating an MITM attack to redirect traffic. The goal is to target a victim host and have it change its default gateway to the threat actor's device. This positions the threat actor in between the victim and all other systems outside the local subnet.

ARP Cache Poisoning (3.8.2)

ARP cache poisoning can be used to launch various man-in-the-middle attacks.

ARP Request

Figure 3-19 shows how ARP cache poisoning works. In this example, PC-A requires the MAC address of its default gateway (R1); therefore, it sends an ARP Request for the MAC address 192.168.10.1.

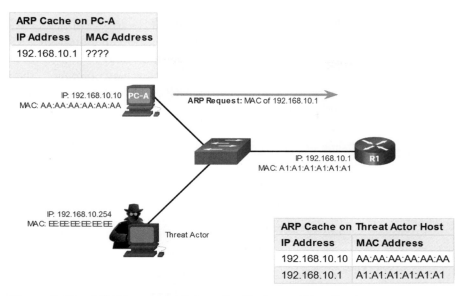

Figure 3-19   ARP Request to Poison the Cache on Other Devices

ARP Reply

In Figure 3-20, R1 updates its ARP cache with the IPv4 and MAC addresses of PC-A. R1 sends an ARP Reply to PC-A, which then updates its ARP cache with the IPv4 and MAC addresses of R1.

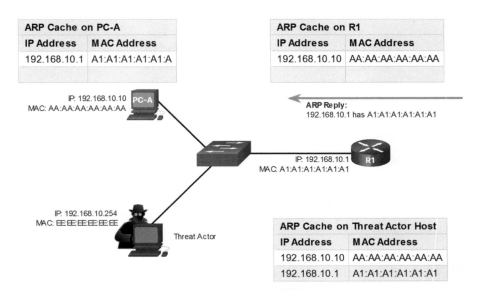

Figure 3-20   Devices Unknowingly Update the Cache with the Threat Actor's MAC Address

Spoofed Gratuitous ARP Replies

In Figure 3-21, the threat actor sends two spoofed gratuitous ARP Replies using its own MAC address for the indicated destination IPv4 addresses. PC-A updates its ARP cache with its default gateway, which is now pointing to the threat actor's host MAC address. R1 also updates its ARP cache with the IPv4 address of PC-A pointing to the threat actor's MAC address.

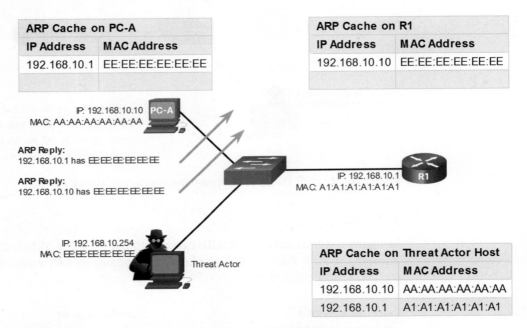

ARP Cache on PC-A	
IP Address	MAC Address
192.168.10.1	EE:EE:EE:EE:EE:EE

ARP Cache on R1	
IP Address	MAC Address
192.168.10.10	EE:EE:EE:EE:EE:EE

IP: 192.168.10.10   PC-A
MAC: AA:AA:AA:AA:AA:AA

ARP Reply:
192.168.10.1 has EE EE EE EE EE EE

ARP Reply:
192.168.10.10 has EE EE EE EE EE EE

IP: 192.168.10.1   R1
MAC: A1:A1:A1:A1:A1:A1

IP: 192.168.10.254
MAC: EE EE EE EE EE EE

Threat Actor

ARP Cache on Threat Actor Host	
IP Address	MAC Address
192.168.10.10	AA:AA:AA:AA:AA:AA
192.168.10.1	A1:A1:A1:A1:A1:A1

Figure 3-21   Threat Actor Sends Spoofed Gratuitous ARP Replies

The threat actor's host is executing an ARP poisoning attack. An ARP poisoning attack can be passive or active. With passive ARP poisoning, a threat actor steals confidential information. With active ARP poisoning, a threat actor modifies data in transit or injects malicious data.

Note

There are many tools available on the internet to create ARP MITM attacks, including dsniff, Cain & Abel, ettercap, and Yersinia.

Video

Video—ARP Spoofing (3.8.3)

Refer to the online course to view this video.

DNS Attacks (3.8.4)

The Domain Name System (DNS) protocol defines an automated service that matches resource names, such as www.cisco.com, with the required numeric network address, such as the IPv4 or IPv6 address. It includes the format for queries, responses, and data and uses resource records (RRs) to identify the type of DNS response.

Securing DNS is often overlooked. However, DNS is crucial to the operation of a network and should be secured accordingly.

DNS attacks include the following:

- *DNS open resolver attacks*
- *DNS stealth attacks*
- *DNS domain shadowing attacks*
- *DNS tunneling attacks*

DNS Open Resolver Attacks

Many organizations use the services of publicly open DNS servers such as GoogleDNS (8.8.8.8) to provide responses to queries. This type of DNS server is called an open resolver. A DNS open resolver answers queries from clients outside its administrative domain. DNS open resolvers are vulnerable to multiple malicious activities, as described in Table 3-14.

Table 3-14   DNS Resolver Attacks

DNS Resolver Attack	Description
DNS cache poisoning attack	Threat actors send spoofed, falsified resource record (RR) information to a DNS resolver to redirect users from legitimate sites to malicious sites. DNS cache poisoning attacks can be used to inform the DNS resolver to use a malicious name server that is providing RR information for malicious activities.
DNS amplification and reflection attack	Threat actors use DoS or DDoS attacks on DNS open resolvers to increase the volume of attacks and to hide the true source of an attack. Threat actors send DNS messages to the open resolvers, using the IP address of a target host. These attacks are possible because the open resolver will respond to queries from anyone asking a question.
DNS resource utilization attack	This DoS attack consumes all the available resources to negatively affect the operations of the DNS open resolver. The impact of this DoS attack may require the DNS open resolver to be rebooted or services to be stopped and restarted.

DNS Stealth Attacks

To hide their identity, threat actors may use the DNS stealth techniques described in Table 3-15 to carry out their attacks.

Table 3-15   DNS Stealth Techniques

DNS Stealth Technique	Description
Fast flux	Threat actors use this technique to hide their phishing and malware delivery sites behind a quickly changing network of compromised DNS hosts. The DNS IP addresses are continuously changed every few minutes. Botnets often employ fast flux techniques to effectively prevent malicious servers from being detected.
Double IP flux	Threat actors use this technique to rapidly change the hostname-to-IP address mappings and to also change the authoritative name server. This increases the difficulty of identifying the source of an attack.
Domain generation algorithms	Threat actors use these algorithms in malware to randomly generate domain names that can then be used as rendezvous points to their command and control (CnC) servers.

DNS Domain Shadowing Attacks

With domain shadowing, a threat actor gathers domain account credentials in order to silently create multiple subdomains to be used during attacks. These subdomains typically point to malicious servers without alerting the actual owner of the parent domain.

DNS Tunneling (3.8.5)

Threat actors who use DNS tunneling place non-DNS traffic within DNS traffic. This method is often used to circumvent security solutions when a threat actor wishes to communicate with bots inside a protected network or exfiltrate data from the organization, such as a password database. When the threat actor uses DNS tunneling, the different types of DNS records are altered. This is how DNS tunneling works for CnC commands sent to a botnet:

Step 1.   The command data is split into multiple encoded chunks.

Step 2.   Each chunk is placed into a lower-level domain name label of the DNS query.

Step 3.   Because there is no response from the local or networked DNS for the query, the request is sent to the ISP's recursive DNS servers.

Step 4. The recursive DNS service forwards the query to the threat actor's authoritative name server.

Step 5. The process is repeated until all the queries containing the chunks of data are sent.

Step 6. When the threat actor's authoritative name server receives the DNS queries from the infected devices, it sends responses for each DNS query, which contain the encapsulated, encoded CnC commands.

Step 7. The malware on the compromised host recombines the chunks and executes the commands hidden within the DNS record.

To stop DNS tunneling, the network administrator must use a filter that inspects DNS traffic. Pay close attention to DNS queries that are longer than average, as well as those that have a suspicious domain name. DNS solutions such as Cisco OpenDNS block a lot of DNS tunneling traffic by identifying suspicious domains.

DHCP (3.8.6)

DHCP servers dynamically provide IP configuration information to clients. Figure 3-22 shows the typical sequence of a DHCP message exchange between client and server.

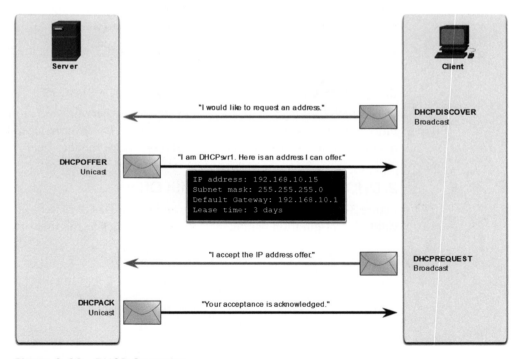

Figure 3-22 DHCP Operation

DHCP Attacks (3.8.7)

A DHCP spoofing attack occurs when a *rogue DHCP server* is connected to the network and provides false IP configuration parameters to legitimate clients. A rogue server can provide a variety of misleading information, including the following:

- **Wrong default gateway:** The threat actor provides an invalid gateway or the IPv4 address of its host to create an MITM attack. This may go entirely undetected as the intruder intercepts the data flow through the network.

- **Wrong DNS server:** The threat actor provides an incorrect DNS server address pointing the user to a malicious website.

- **Wrong IPv4 address:** The threat actor provides an invalid IP address, invalid default gateway IPv4 address, or both. The threat actor then creates a DoS attack on the DHCP client.

Note

An IPv6 device receives its default gateway address from the Router Advertisement instead of from a DHCP server.

Say that a threat actor has successfully connected a rogue DHCP server to a switch port on the same subnet as the target clients. The goal of the rogue server is to provide clients with false IPv4 configuration information.

The following sections describe the steps in a DHCP spoofing attack.

1. Client Broadcasts DHCP Discovery Messages

In Figure 3-23, a legitimate client connects to the network and requires IP configuration parameters. The client broadcasts a DHCP Discover request, looking for a response from a DHCP server. Both servers receive the message.

2. DHCP Servers Respond with Offers

Figure 3-24 shows how the legitimate and rogue DHCP servers each respond with valid IP configuration parameters. The client replies to the first offer received.

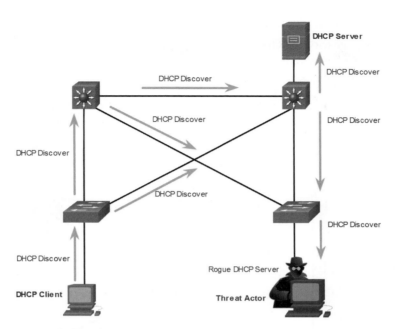

Figure 3-23   Client Broadcasts DHCP Discovery Messages

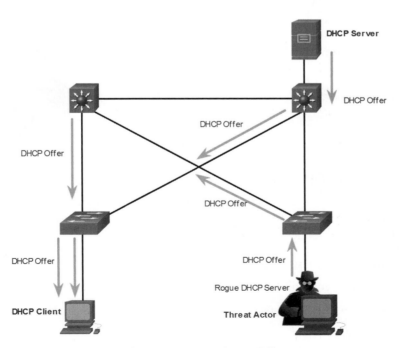

Figure 3-24   DHCP Servers Respond with Offers

3. Client Accepts Rogue DHCP Request

In this scenario, the client received the rogue offer first. It broadcasts a DHCP request accepting the parameters from the rogue server, as shown in Figure 3-25. The legitimate and rogue server each receive the request.

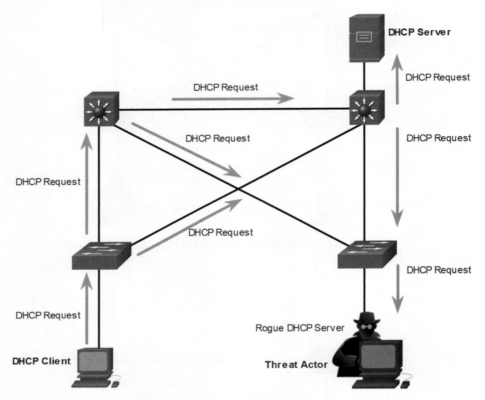

Figure 3-25   Client Accepts Rogue DHCP Request

4. Rogue DHCP Acknowledges the Request

Only the rogue server unicasts a reply to the client to acknowledge its request, as shown in Figure 3-26. The legitimate server stops communicating with the client because the request has already been acknowledged.

Lab—Explore DNS Traffic (3.8.8)

In this lab, you will complete the following objectives:

- Capture DNS traffic
- Explore DNS query traffic
- Explore DNS response traffic

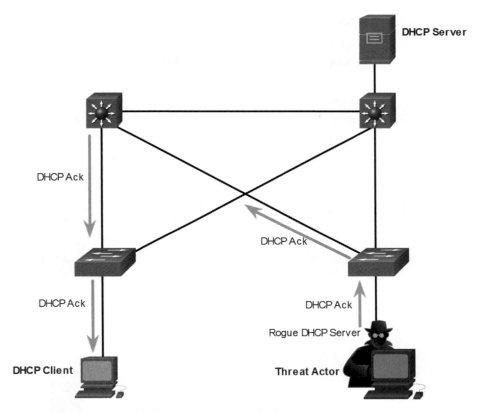

Figure 3-26   Rogue DHCP Acknowledges the Request

Network Security Best Practices (3.9)

IP services include ARP, DNS, and DHCP. ARP resolves IP addresses to MAC address, DNS resolves names to IP addresses, and DHCP automates the assignment of IP configurations on networks. Threat actors have discovered vulnerabilities in IP services that they can exploit to leverage their attacks.

This section describes the best practices for protecting a network.

Confidentiality, Integrity, and Availability (3.9.1)

It is true that the list of network attack types is long. But there are many best practices that you can use to defend your network, as you will learn in this section.

Network security consists of protecting information and information systems from unauthorized access, use, disclosure, disruption, modification, or destruction.

Most organizations follow the CIA information security triad:

- **Confidentiality:** Only authorized individuals, entities, or processes are allowed to access sensitive information. This confidentiality may require using cryptographic encryption algorithms such as AES to encrypt and decrypt data.

- **Integrity:** This refers to protecting data from unauthorized alteration. Integrity requires the use of cryptographic hashing algorithms such as SHA.

- **Availability:** Authorized users must have uninterrupted access to important resources and data. Availability requires implementing redundant services, gateways, and links.

The Defense-in-Depth Approach (3.9.2)

To ensure secure communications across both public and private networks, you must secure devices including routers, switches, servers, and hosts. Most organizations employ a *defense-in-depth approach* to security, also known as a *layered approach*. It requires a combination of networking devices and services working together. Consider the network in Figure 3-27.

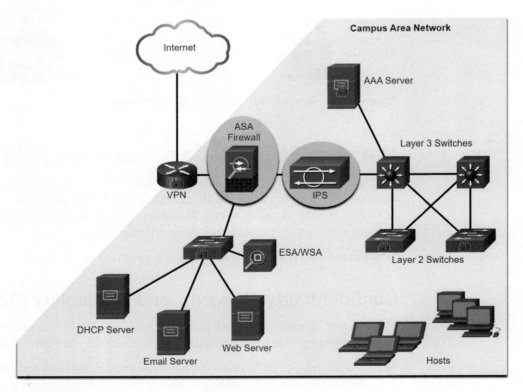

Figure 3-27   Protecting Against Network Attacks

In the network in this figure, all network devices including the router and switches are hardened, which means that they have been secured to prevent threat actors from gaining access and tampering with the devices.

It is important to secure data as it travels across various links. This may include internal traffic, but it is more important to protect the data that travels outside the organization to branch sites, telecommuter sites, and partner sites.

Firewalls (3.9.3)

A *firewall* is a system or group of systems that enforce an access control policy between networks. For example, in Figure 3-28, traffic arriving from any global sites on the internet is filtered through a firewall device. Based on configured policies, some traffic is allowed, and some traffic is denied.

Allow traffic from any external address to the web server.

Allow traffic to FTP server.

Allow traffic to SMTP server.

Allow traffic to internal IMAP server.

Deny all inbound traffic with network addresses matching internal-registered IP addresses.

Deny all inbound traffic to server from external addresses.

Deny all inbound ICMP echo request traffic.

Deny all inbound MS Active Directory queries.

Deny all inbound traffic to MS SQL server queries.

Deny all MS Domain Local Broadcasts.

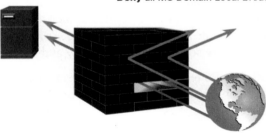

Figure 3-28   Firewall Operation

All firewalls share some common properties:

- Firewalls are resistant to network attacks.
- Firewalls are the only transit points between internal corporate networks and external networks because all traffic flows through the firewall.
- Firewalls enforce the access control policy.

There are several benefits of using firewalls in a network:

- They prevent the exposure of sensitive hosts, resources, and applications to untrusted users.

- They sanitize protocol flow, which prevents the exploitation of protocol flaws.

- They block malicious data from servers and clients.

- They reduce security management complexity by offloading most of the network access control to a few firewalls in the network.

Firewalls also present some limitations:

- A misconfigured firewall can have serious consequences for the network, such as becoming a single point of failure.

- The data from many applications cannot be passed through firewalls securely.

- Users might proactively search for ways around the firewall to receive blocked material, which can potentially expose the network to attack.

- Network performance can slow down.

- Unauthorized traffic can be tunneled or hidden so that it appears as legitimate traffic through the firewall.

IPS (3.9.4)

To defend against fast-moving and evolving attacks, you may need cost-effective detection and prevention systems, such as *intrusion detection systems (IDSs)* or the more scalable *intrusion prevention systems (IPSs)*. The network architecture integrates these solutions into the entry and exit points of the network.

IDS and IPS technologies share several characteristics. IDS and IPS technologies are both deployed as sensors. An IDS or IPS sensor can be in the form of several different devices:

- A router configured with Cisco IOS IPS software

- A device specifically designed to provide dedicated IDS or IPS services

- A network module installed in a *Cisco Adaptive Security Appliance (ASA)*, switch, or router

Figure 3-29 shows how an IPS handles denied traffic:

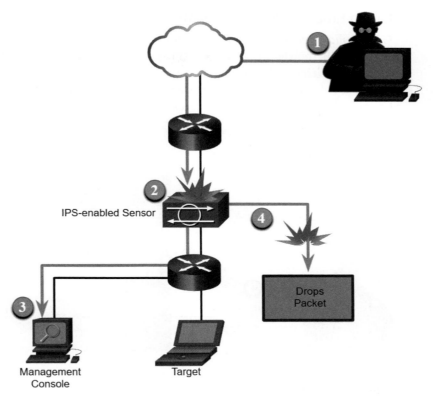

Figure 3-29   IPS Operation

Step 1.   The threat actor sends a packet destined for the target laptop.

Step 2.   The IPS intercepts the traffic and evaluates it against known threats and the configured policies.

Step 3.   The IPS sends a log message to the management console.

Step 4.   The IPS drops the packet.

IDS and IPS technologies detect patterns in network traffic by using signatures. A signature is a set of rules that an IDS or IPS uses to detect malicious activity. Signatures can be used to detect severe breaches of security, to detect common network attacks, and to gather information. IDS and IPS technologies can detect atomic signature patterns (single-packet) or composite signature patterns (multi-packet).

Content Security Appliances (3.9.5)

Content security appliances provide fine-grained control over email and web browsing for an organization's users.

Cisco Email Security Appliance (ESA)

Cisco Email Security Appliance (ESA) is a special device designed to monitor Simple Mail Transfer Protocol (SMTP). Cisco ESA is constantly updated by real-time feeds from *Cisco Talos*, which detects and correlates threats and solutions by using a worldwide database monitoring system. This threat intelligence data is pulled by the Cisco ESA every three to five minutes.

Figure 3-30 shows how ESA works:

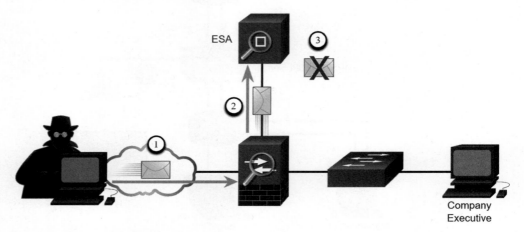

Figure 3-30   Cisco ESA in Operation

Step 1.   The threat actor sends a phishing attack to an important host on the network.

Step 2.   The firewall forwards all email to ESA.

Step 3.   ESA analyzes the email, logs it, and discards it.

Cisco Web Security Appliance (WSA)

Cisco Web Security Appliance (WSA) is a mitigation technology for web-based threats. It helps organizations address the challenges of securing and controlling web traffic. The Cisco WSA combines advanced malware protection (AMP), application visibility and control, acceptable use policy controls, and reporting.

Cisco WSA provides complete control over how users access the internet. Certain features and applications—such as chat, messaging, video, and audio—can be allowed, restricted with time and bandwidth limits, or blocked, according to the organization's requirements. WSA can perform *blacklisting* of URLs, *URL filtering*, malware scanning, URL categorization, web application filtering, and encryption and decryption of web traffic.

Figure 3-31 shows how WSA works:

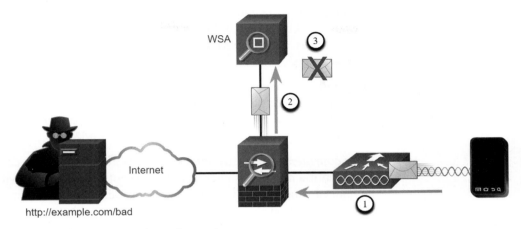

Figure 3-31   Cisco WSA in Operation

Step 1.   A corporate user attempts to connect to a website.

Step 2.   The firewall forwards the website request to WSA.

Step 3.   WSA evaluates the URL and determines that it is a known blacklisted site. WSA discards the packet and sends an access denied message to the user.

Interactive Graphic

Check Your Understanding—Network Security Best Practices (3.9.6)

Refer to the online course to complete this activity.

Cryptography (3.10)

Even if an organization has the best defense-in-depth security possible, it needs to protect its data as it leaves the network. This section describes common cryptographic processes used to protect data in transit.

Video

Video—Cryptography (3.10.1)

Refer to the online course to view this video.

Securing Communications (3.10.2)

Organizations must provide support to secure data as it travels across links. This applies to internal traffic, but it is even more important to protect the data that travels outside the organization to branch sites, telecommuter sites, and partner sites.

These are the four elements of secure communications:

- *Data integrity*: Guarantees that a message was not altered. Any changes to data in transit will be detected. Integrity is ensured by using a hash-generating algorithm such as the legacy *Message Digest version 5 (MD5)* algorithm or the more secure *Secure Hash Algorithm (SHA)* family of algorithms.

- *Origin authentication*: Guarantees that a message is not a forgery and comes from the person it purports to come from. Many modern networks ensure authentication with protocols such as *hash message authentication codes (HMACs)*.

- *Data confidentiality*: Guarantees that only authorized users can read a message, and if a message is intercepted, it cannot be deciphered within a reasonable amount of time. Data confidentiality is implemented using symmetric and asymmetric encryption algorithms.

- *Data nonrepudiation*: Guarantees that the sender cannot repudiate, or refute, the validity of a message sent. Nonrepudiation relies on the fact that only the sender has the unique characteristics or signature for how that message is treated.

Cryptography can be used almost anywhere that there is data communication. In fact, the trend is toward all communication being encrypted.

Data Integrity (3.10.3)

Hash functions are used to ensure the integrity of a message. They guarantee that message data has not changed accidentally or intentionally.

In Figure 3-32, the sender is sending a $100 money transfer to Alex.

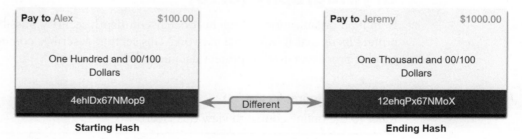

Figure 3-32   Data Integrity Example

In the figure, the sender wants to ensure that the message is not altered on its way to the receiver:

Step 1. The sending device inputs the message into a hashing algorithm and computes the fixed-length hash 4ehiDx67NMop9.

Step 2. This hash is then attached to the message and sent to the receiver. Both the message and the hash are in plaintext.

Step 3. The receiving device removes the hash from the message and inputs the message into the same hashing algorithm. If the computed hash is equal to the one that is attached to the message, the message has not been altered during transit. If the hashes are not equal, as shown in Figure 3-32, then the integrity of the message can no longer be trusted.

Note

Hashing algorithms only protect against accidental changes and do not protect data from changes deliberately made by a threat actor.

Hash Functions (3.10.4)

There are three well-known hash functions, described in this section.

MD5 with 128-Bit Digest

MD5 is a one-way function that produces a 128-bit hashed message. MD5 is a legacy algorithm that should be used only when no better alternatives are available. Use SHA-2 or SHA-3 instead.

In Figure 3-33, a plaintext message is passed through an MD5 hash function. The result is a 128-bit hashed message.

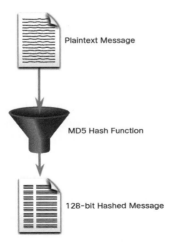

Figure 3-33   MD5 Hash Function

SHA Hashing Algorithm

SHA-1 is similar to the MD5 hash functions. Several versions exist. SHA-1 creates a 160-bit hashed message and is slightly slower than MD5. SHA-1 has known flaws and is a legacy algorithm. Use SHA-2 or SHA-3 when possible.

In Figure 3-34, a plaintext message is passed through a SHA hash function. The result is a hashed message.

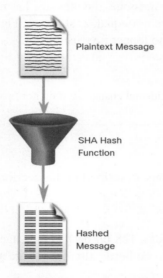

Plaintext Message

SHA Hash Function

Hashed Message

Figure 3-34 SHA Hash Function

SHA-2

SHA-2 includes SHA-224 (224 bit), SHA-256 (256 bit), SHA-384 (384 bit), and SHA-512 (512 bit). SHA-256, SHA-384, and SHA-512 are next-generation algorithms and should be used whenever possible.

SHA-3

SHA-3, which is the newest hashing algorithm, was introduced by the National Institute of Standards and Technology (NIST) as an alternative and eventual replacement for the SHA-2 family of hashing algorithms. SHA-3 includes SHA3-224 (224 bit), SHA3-256 (256 bit), SHA3-384 (384 bit), and SHA3-512 (512 bit). The SHA-3 next-generation family of algorithms should be used if possible.

While hashing can be used to detect accidental changes, it cannot be used to guard against deliberate changes. There is no unique identifying information from the sender in the hashing procedure. This means that anyone who has the correct hash function can compute a hash for any data. For example, when a message traverses a network, a potential threat actor could intercept the message, change it, recalculate the hash, and append it to the message. The receiving device would only validate against whatever hash is appended.

Therefore, hashing is vulnerable to man-in-the-middle attacks and does not provide security to transmitted data. To provide integrity and origin authentication, something more is required.

Origin Authentication (3.10.5)

To add authentication to integrity assurance, use a keyed hash message authentication code (HMAC), which uses an additional secret key as input to the hash function.

Note

Other message authentication code methods are also used. However, HMAC is used in many systems, including SSL, IPsec, and SSH.

HMAC Hashing Algorithm

As shown in Figure 3-35, an HMAC is calculated using any cryptographic algorithm that combines a cryptographic hash function with a secret key. Hash functions are the basis of the protection mechanism of HMACs.

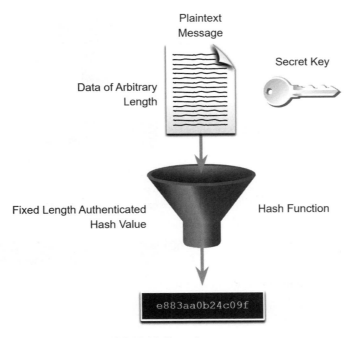

Figure 3-35 HMAC Hash Function

Only the sender and the receiver know the secret key, and the output of the hash function depends on the input data and the secret key. Only parties who have access to that secret key can compute the digest of an HMAC function. This defeats man-in-the-middle attacks and provides authentication of the data origin.

If two parties share a secret key and use HMAC functions for authentication, a properly constructed HMAC digest of a message that a party has received indicates that the other party was the originator of the message. This is because the other party possesses the secret key.

Creating the HMAC Value

As shown in Figure 3-36, the sending device inputs data (in this case, Terry Smith's $100 pay and the secret key) into the hashing algorithm and calculates the fixed-length HMAC digest. This authenticated digest is then attached to the message and sent to the receiver.

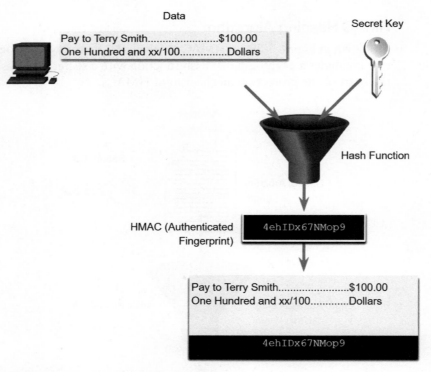

Figure 3-36   Creating the HMAC Value

Verifying the HMAC Value

As shown in Figure 3-37, the receiving device removes the digest from the message and uses the plaintext message with its secret key as input into the same hashing function. If the digest that is calculated by the receiving device is equal to the digest that was sent, the message has not been altered. In addition, the origin of the message is authenticated because only the sender possesses a copy of the shared secret key. The HMAC function has ensured the authenticity of the message.

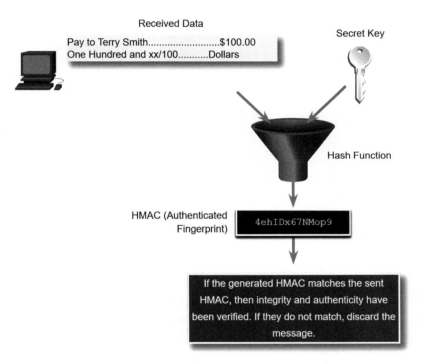

Figure 3-37   Verifying the HMAC Value

Cisco Router HMAC Example

Figure 3-38 shows how HMACs are used by Cisco routers that are configured to use Open Shortest Path First (OSPF) routing authentication.

In the figure, R1 is sending a link-state update (LSU) regarding a route to network 10.2.0.0/16:

Step 1.   R1 calculates the hash value using the LSU message and the secret key.

Step 2.   The resulting hash value is sent with the LSU to R2.

Step 3.   R2 calculates the hash value using the LSU and its secret key. R2 accepts the update if the hash values match. If they do not match, R2 discards the update.

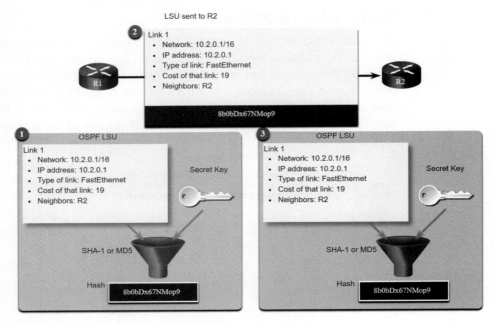

Figure 3-38   Cisco Router HMAC Example

Data Confidentiality (3.10.6)

Two classes of encryption are used to provide data confidentiality. These two classes differ in how they use keys.

Symmetric encryption algorithms such as DES, 3DES, and Advanced Encryption Standard (AES) are based on the premise that each communicating party knows the pre-shared key. Data confidentiality can also be ensured using asymmetric algorithms, including Rivest, Shamir, and Adleman (RSA) and public key infrastructure (PKI).

Figure 3-39 highlights some differences between the symmetric and asymmetric encryption algorithm methods.

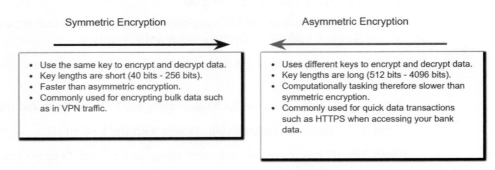

Figure 3-39   Differences Between Symmetric and Asymmetric Encryption

Symmetric Encryption (3.10.7)

Symmetric algorithms use the same *pre-shared key* to encrypt and decrypt data. A pre-shared key, also called a secret key, is known by the sender and receiver before any encrypted communications can take place.

To help illustrate how symmetric encryption works, consider an example where Alice and Bob live in different locations and want to exchange secret messages with one another through the mail system. In this example, Alice wants to send a secret message to Bob.

In Figure 3-40, Alice and Bob have identical keys to a single padlock. These keys were exchanged prior to sending any secret messages. Alice writes a secret message and puts it in a small box that she locks using the padlock and her key. She mails the box to Bob. The message is safely locked inside the box as the box makes its way through the postal system. When Bob receives the box, he uses his key to unlock the padlock and retrieve the message. Bob can use the same box and padlock to send a secret reply to Alice.

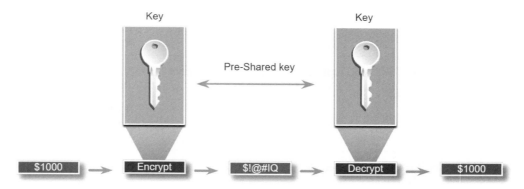

Figure 3-40 Symmetric Encryption Example

Today, symmetric encryption algorithms are commonly used with VPN traffic because symmetric algorithms use less CPU resources than asymmetric encryption algorithms. Encryption and decryption of data occur quickly on a VPN. When using symmetric encryption algorithms, like any other type of encryption, the longer the key, the longer it will take for someone to discover the key. Most encryption keys are between 112 and 256 bits. To ensure that encryption is safe, use a minimum key length of 128 bits. Use a longer key for more secure communications.

Well-known symmetric encryption algorithms are described in Table 3-16.

Table 3-16 Symmetric Encryption Algorithms

Symmetric Encryption Algorithms	Description
Data Encryption Standard (DES)	■ This is a legacy symmetric encryption algorithm. ■ It should not be used.
3DES (Triple DES)	■ This is the replacement for DES. ■ It repeats the DES algorithm process three times. ■ It should be avoided if possible as it is scheduled to be retired in 2023. ■ If implemented, use very short key lifetimes.
Advanced Encryption Standard (AES)	■ AES is a popular and recommended symmetric encryption algorithm. ■ It offers combinations of 128-, 192-, or 256-bit keys to encrypt data blocks that are 128, 192, or 256 bits long.
Software-Optimized Encryption Algorithm (SEAL)	■ SEAL is a faster symmetric encryption algorithm than AES. ■ It uses a 160-bit encryption key and has a lower impact on the CPU compared to other software-based algorithms.
Rivest Cipher (RC) series algorithms	■ RC includes several versions developed by Ron Rivest. ■ RC4 was used to secure web traffic.

Asymmetric Encryption (3.10.8)

Asymmetric encryption algorithms, also called *public key algorithms*, are designed so that the key that is used for encryption is different from the key that is used for decryption, as shown in Figure 3-41. The decryption key cannot, in any reasonable amount of time, be calculated from the encryption key and vice versa.

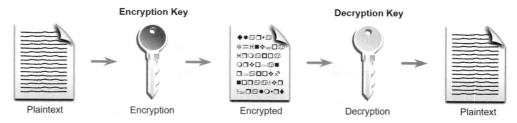

Figure 3-41   Asymmetric Encryption Example

An asymmetric algorithm uses a public key and a private key. Both keys are capable of the encryption process, but the complementary paired key is required for decryption. The process is also reversible. Data encrypted with the public key can be decrypted only with the private key. Asymmetric algorithms achieve confidentiality, authentication, and integrity by using this process.

Because the parties do not have a shared secret, very long key lengths must be used. Asymmetric encryption can use key lengths between 512 to 4096 bits. Key lengths greater than or equal to 1024 bits can be trusted, and shorter key lengths are considered unreliable.

Examples of protocols that use asymmetric key algorithms include:

- **Internet Key Exchange (IKE):** This is a fundamental component of IPsec VPNs.

- **Secure Socket Layer (SSL):** This is now implemented as the IETF standard Transport Layer Security (TLS).

- **Secure Shell (SSH):** This protocol provides a secure remote access connection to network devices.

- **Pretty Good Privacy (PGP):** This computer program provides cryptographic privacy and authentication. It is often used to increase the security of email communications.

Asymmetric algorithms are substantially slower than symmetric algorithms. Their design is based on computational problems, such as factoring extremely large numbers or computing discrete logarithms of extremely large numbers.

Because they are slow, asymmetric algorithms are typically used in low-volume cryptographic mechanisms, such as digital signatures and key exchange. However, the key management of asymmetric algorithms tends to be simpler than that for symmetric algorithms because usually one of the two encryption or decryption keys can be made public.

Common asymmetric encryption algorithms are described in Table 3-17.

Table 3-17   Asymmetric Encryption Algorithms

Asymmetric Encryption Algorithms	Key Lengths	Description
Diffie-Hellman (DH)	512, 1024, 2048, 3072, 4096	■ The algorithm enables two parties to agree on a key that they can use to encrypt messages they want to send to each other. ■ The security of this algorithm depends on the assumption that it is easy to raise a number to a certain power but difficult to compute which power was used, given the number and the outcome.
Digital Signature Standard (DSS) and Digital Signature Algorithm (DSA)	512–1024	■ DSS specifies DSA as the algorithm for digital signatures. ■ DSA is a public key algorithm based on the ElGamal signature scheme. ■ Speed of signature creation is similar to that of RSA, but the speed is 10 to 40 times slower for verification.
Rivest, Shamir, and Adleman (RSA) encryption algorithms	512–2048	■ RSA is for public key cryptography that is based on the current difficulty of factoring very large numbers. ■ It is the first algorithm known to be suitable for signing as well as encryption. ■ It is widely used in electronic commerce protocols and is believed to be secure, given sufficiently long keys and the use of up-to-date implementations.
ElGamal	512–1024	■ An asymmetric key encryption algorithm for public key cryptography that is based on the Diffie-Hellman key agreement. ■ A disadvantage of the ElGamal system is that the encrypted message becomes very big—about twice the size of the original message—and for this reason it is used only for small messages such as secret keys.
Elliptic curve techniques	160	■ Elliptic curve cryptography can be used to adapt many cryptographic algorithms, such as Diffie-Hellman or ElGamal. ■ The main advantage of elliptic curve cryptography is that the keys can be much smaller.

Diffie-Hellman (3.10.9)

Diffie-Hellman (DH) is an asymmetric mathematical algorithm in which two computers generate an identical shared secret key without having communicated before. The new shared key is never actually exchanged between the sender and receiver. However, because both parties know it, the key can be used by an encryption algorithm to encrypt traffic between the two systems.

For example, DH is commonly used when

- Data is exchanged using an IPsec VPN
- SSH data is exchanged

Figure 3-42 illustrates how DH operates. The colors in the figure will be used instead of complex long numbers to simplify the DH key agreement process. The DH key exchange begins with Alice and Bob agreeing on an arbitrary common color (in this case, yellow) that does not need to be kept secret.

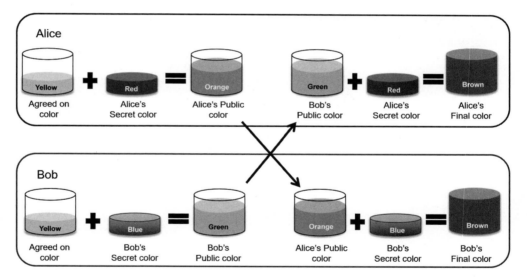

Figure 3-42   Diffie-Hellman Analogy

Next, Alice and Bob each select a secret color. Alice chooses red, and Bob chooses blue. These secret colors will never be shared with anyone. The secret color represents the chosen secret private key of each party.

Alice and Bob now mix the shared common color (yellow) with their respective secret color to produce a public color. Therefore, Alice will mix the yellow with her red color to produce a public color of orange. Bob will mix the yellow and the blue to produce a public color of green.

Alice sends her public color (orange) to Bob, and Bob sends his public color (green) to Alice.

Alice and Bob each mix the color they received with their own, original secret color (red for Alice and blue for Bob). The result is a final brown color mixture that is identical to the other's final color mixture. The brown color represents the resulting shared secret key between Bob and Alice.

DH security uses very large numbers in its calculations. For example, a DH 1024-bit number is roughly equal to a decimal number with 309 digits. Considering that a billion is 10 decimal digits (1,000,000,000), you can easily imagine the complexity of working with not one but many 309-digit decimal numbers.

Unfortunately, asymmetric key systems are extremely slow for any sort of bulk encryption. Therefore, it is common to encrypt most traffic using a symmetric algorithm, such as 3DES or AES, and use the DH algorithm to create keys that will be used by the encryption algorithm.

Interactive Graphic

Check Your Understanding—Cryptography (3.10.10)

Refer to the online course to complete this activity.

Summary (3.11)

The following is a summary of the sections in this chapter.

Current State of Cybersecurity

Network security breaches can disrupt e-commerce, cause the loss of business data, threaten people's privacy, and compromise the integrity of information. Assets must be identified and protected. Vulnerabilities must be addressed before they are exploited. Mitigation techniques are required before, during, and after an attack. An attack vector is a path by which a threat actor can gain access to a server, host, or network. Attack vectors can originate inside or outside the corporate network.

Threat Actors

The term *threat actor* includes hackers, and it also refers to any other device, person, group, or nation-state that is, intentionally or unintentionally, the source of an attack. There are white hat, gray hat, and black hat hackers. Cybercriminals operate in an underground economy where they buy, sell, and trade attack toolkits, zero-day exploit code, botnet services, banking Trojans, keyloggers, and more. Hacktivists tend to rely on fairly basic, freely available tools. State-sponsored hackers create advanced, customized attack code, often using previously undiscovered software vulnerabilities called zero-day vulnerabilities.

Threat Actor Tools

Attack tools have become more sophisticated and highly automated. These new tools require less technical knowledge to implement than did some of the older tools. Ethical hacking involves many different types of tools used to test the network and keep its data secure. To validate the security of a network and its systems, many network penetration testing tools have been developed. Common types of attacks are eavesdropping, data modification, IP address spoofing, password-based, denial-of-service, man-in-the-middle, compromised-key, and sniffer attacks.

Malware

The three most common types of malware are worms, viruses, and Trojan horses. A worm executes arbitrary code and installs copies of itself in the memory of the infected computer. A virus executes a specific unwanted, and often harmful, function on a computer. A Trojan horse is non-self-replicating. When an infected application or file is downloaded and opened, the Trojan horse can attack the end device from within. Other types of malware are adware, ransomware, rootkits, and spyware.

Common Network Attacks

Networks are susceptible to reconnaissance, access, and DoS attacks. Threat actors use reconnaissance (or recon) attacks to do unauthorized discovery and mapping of systems, services, or vulnerabilities. Access attacks exploit known vulnerabilities in authentication services, FTP services, and web services. Types of access attacks are password, spoofing, trust exploitations, port redirections, man-in-the-middle, and buffer overflow attacks. Social engineering is an access attack that attempts to manipulate individuals into performing actions or divulging confidential information. DoS and DDoS are attacks that create some sort of interruption of network services to users, devices, or applications.

IP Vulnerabilities and Threats

Threat actors can send packets by using a spoofed source IP address. Threat actors can also tamper with the other fields in the IP header to carry out their attacks. IP attack techniques include ICMP, amplification and reflection, address spoofing, MITM, and session hijacking. Threat actors use ICMP for reconnaissance and scanning attacks. They launch information-gathering attacks to map out a network topology, discover which hosts are active (reachable), identify the host operating system (OS fingerprinting), and determine the state of a firewall. Threat actors often use amplification and reflection techniques to create DoS attacks.

TCP and UDP Vulnerabilities

TCP segment information appears immediately after the IP header. TCP provides reliable delivery, flow control, and stateful communication. TCP attacks include TCP SYN flood attack, TCP reset attack, and TCP session hijacking. UDP is commonly used by DNS, TFTP, NFS, and SNMP. It is also used with real-time applications such as media streaming and VoIP. UDP is not protected by encryption. UDP flood attacks send a flood of UDP packets, often from a spoofed host, to a server on the subnet. The result is very similar to the result of a DoS attack.

IP Services

Any client can send an unsolicited ARP Reply called a gratuitous ARP. This means that any host can claim to be the owner of any IP or MAC address. A threat actor can poison the ARP caches of devices on the local network, creating an MITM attack to redirect traffic. ARP cache poisoning can be used to launch various man-in-the-middle attacks. DNS attacks include open resolver attacks, stealth attacks, domain shadowing attacks, and tunneling attacks. To stop DNS tunneling, a network administrator must use a filter that inspects DNS traffic. A DHCP spoofing attack occurs when a rogue DHCP server is connected to a network and provides false IP configuration parameters to legitimate clients.

Network Security Best Practices

Most organizations follow the CIA information security triad: confidentiality, integrity, and availability. To ensure secure communications across both public and private networks, you must secure devices including routers, switches, servers, and hosts. This is known as defense-in-depth. A firewall is a system or group of systems that enforce an access control policy between networks. To defend against fast-moving and evolving attacks, you may need an intrusion detection systems (IDS) or a more scalable intrusion prevention systems (IPS).

Cryptography

The four elements of secure communications are data integrity, origin authentication, data confidentiality, and data nonrepudiation. Hash functions guarantee that message data has not changed accidentally or intentionally. Three well-known hash functions are MD5 with 128-bit digest, SHA hashing algorithm, and SHA-2. To add authentication to integrity assurance, use a keyed hash message authentication code (HMAC), which is calculated using any cryptographic algorithm that combines a cryptographic hash function with a secret key. Symmetric encryption algorithms using DES, 3DES, AES, SEAL, and RC are based on the premise that each communicating party knows the pre-shared key. Data confidentiality can also be ensured using asymmetric algorithms, including Rivest, Shamir, and Adleman (RSA) and the public key infrastructure (PKI). Diffie-Hellman (DH) is an asymmetric mathematical algorithm for which two computers generate an identical shared secret key without having communicated before.

Practice

The following lab activities provide practice with the topics introduced in this chapter. The labs are available in the companion *Enterprise Networking, Security, and Automation Labs & Study Guide (CCNAv7)* (ISBN 9780136634690). There are no Packet Tracer activities for this chapter.

Labs

Lab 3.5.7: Social Engineering

Lab 3.8.8: Explore DNS Traffic

Check Your Understanding

Complete all the review questions listed here to test your understanding of the topics and concepts in this chapter. The appendix "Answers to the 'Check Your Understanding' Questions" lists the answers.

1. Which network security statement is true?

   A. All threats come from external networks.

   B. Internal threats are always accidental.

   C. Internal threats are always intentional.

   D. Internal threats can cause greater damage than external threats.

2. What commonly motivates cybercriminals to attack networks as compared to hacktivists or state-sponsored hackers?

   A. Fame seeking

   B. Financial gain

   C. Political reasons

   D. Status among peers

3. Which type of hacker is motivated by protesting political and social issues?

   A. Cybercriminal

   B. Hacktivist

   C. Script kiddie

   D. Vulnerability broker

4. What is Trojan horse malware?

   A. It is malware that can only be distributed over the internet.

   B. It is software that appears useful but includes malicious code.

   C. It is software that causes annoying computer problems.

   D. It is the most easily detected form of malware.

5. A user receives a call from someone in IT services, asking her to confirm her username and password for auditing purposes. Which security threat does this represent?

   A. Anonymous keylogging

   B. DDoS

   C. Social engineering

   D. Spam

6. What is a ping sweep?

   A. A DNS query and response protocol

   B. A network scanning technique that involves identifying active IP addresses

   C. A type of packet capturing software

   D. A TCP and UDP port scanner to detect open services

7. How are zombies used in security attacks?

   A. Zombies are infected machines that carry out a DDoS attack.

   B. Zombies are maliciously formed code segments used to replace legitimate applications.

   C. Zombies probe a group of machines for open ports to learn which services are running.

   D. Zombies target specific individuals to gain corporate or personal information.

8. What is used to decrypt data that has been encrypted using an asymmetric encryption algorithm public key?

   A. A different public key

   B. A digital certificate

   C. A private key

   D. DH

9. What are the SHA hash generating algorithms used for?

   A. Authentication

   B. Confidentiality

   C. Integrity

   D. Nonrepudiation

10. Which of the following is true of an IPS?

    A. It can stop malicious packets.

    B. It has no impact on latency.

    C. It is deployed in offline mode.

    D. It is primarily focused on identifying possible incidents.

11. What is the term used to describe unethical criminals who compromise computer and network security for personal gain or for malicious reasons?

   A. Black hat hackers

   B. Hacktivists

   C. Script kiddies

   D. Vulnerability broker

12. What is the term used to describe a potential danger to a company's assets, data, or network functionality?

   A. Asymmetric encryption algorithm

   B. Exploit

   C. Threat

   D. Vulnerability

13. What term is used to describe a guarantee that a message is not a forgery and does actually come from the person who is supposed to have sent it?

   A. Data nonrepudiation

   B. Exploit

   C. Mitigation

   D. Origin authentication

14. What term is used to describe a mechanism that takes advantage of a vulnerability?

   A. Asymmetric encryption algorithm

   B. Exploit

   C. Threat

   D. Vulnerability

15. Which of the following guarantees that the sender cannot repudiate, or refute, the validity of a message sent?

   A. Data nonrepudiation

   B. Exploit

   C. Mitigation

   D. Origin authentication

CHAPTER 4

ACL Concepts

Objectives

Upon completion of this chapter, you will be able to answer the following questions:

- How do ACLs filter traffic?
- How do ACLs use wildcard masks?
- How do you create ACLs?
- What are the differences between standard and extended IPv4 ACLs?

Key Terms

This chapter uses the following key terms. You can find the definitions in the Glossary.

access control entry (ACE)   page 164

inbound ACL   page 167

outbound ACL   page 167

implicit deny   page 167

wildcard mask   page 168

numbered ACL   page 175

standard ACL   page 175

extended ACL   page 175

named ACL   page 176

Introduction (4.0)

Say that you have arrived at your grandparents' residence. It is a beautiful gated community with walking paths and gardens. For the safety of the residents, no one is permitted to get into the community without stopping at the gate and presenting the guard with identification. You provide your ID, and the guard verifies that you are expected as a visitor. He documents your information and lifts the gate. Imagine if the guard had to do this for the many staff members who entered each day. The security department has simplified this process by assigning a badge to each employee that can be scanned to automatically raise the gate. You greet your grandparents, who are anxiously awaiting you at the front desk. You all get back into the car to go down the street for dinner. As you exit the parking lot, you must again stop and show your identification so that the guard will lift the gate. Rules have been put in place for all incoming and outgoing traffic.

Much like the guard in the gated community, an access control list (ACL) may be configured to permit and deny network traffic passing through an interface. The router compares the information within a packet against each access control entry (ACE), in sequential order, to determine if the packet matches one of the ACEs. This process is called *packet filtering*. Let's learn more!

Purpose of ACLs (4.1)

This section describes how ACLs filter traffic in small- to medium-sized business networks.

What Is an ACL? (4.1.1)

Routers make routing decisions based on information in each packet's header. Traffic entering a router interface is routed solely based on information in the routing table. The router compares the destination IP address with routes in the routing table to find the best match and then forwards a packet based on the best match route. A similar process can be used to filter traffic using an access control list (ACL).

An ACL is a series of IOS commands that are used to filter packets based on information found in the packet header. By default, a router does not have any ACLs configured. However, when an ACL is applied to an interface, the router performs the additional task of evaluating all network packets as they pass through the interface to determine if each packet can be forwarded.

An ACL uses a sequential list of permit or deny statements known as *access control entries (ACEs)*.

Note

ACEs are also commonly called ACL statements.

When network traffic passes through an interface configured with an ACL, the router compares the information within the packet against each ACE, in sequential order, to determine whether the packet matches one of the ACEs. This process is called packet *filtering*.

Several tasks performed by routers require the use of ACLs to identify traffic. Table 4-1 lists some of these tasks and provides examples.

Table 4-1   Tasks That Use ACLs

Task	Example
Limit network traffic to increase network performance	▪ A corporate policy prohibits video traffic on the network to reduce the network load. ▪ A policy can be enforced using ACLs to block video traffic.
Provide traffic flow control	▪ A corporate policy requires that routing protocol traffic be limited to certain links only. ▪ A policy can be implemented using ACLs to restrict the delivery of routing updates to only those that come from a known source.
Provide a basic level of security for network access	▪ Corporate policy demands that access to the human resources network be restricted to authorized users only. ▪ A policy can be enforced using ACLs to limit access to specified networks.
Filter traffic based on traffic type	▪ Corporate policy requires that email traffic be permitted into a network but that Telnet access be denied. ▪ A policy can be implemented using ACLs to filter traffic by type.
Screen hosts to permit or deny access to network services	▪ Corporate policy requires that access to some file types (such as FTP or HTTP) be limited to user groups. ▪ A policy can be implemented using ACLs to filter user access to services.
Provide priority to certain classes of network traffic	▪ Corporate traffic specifies that voice traffic be forwarded as fast as possible to avoid any interruption. ▪ A policy can be implemented using ACLs and QoS to identify voice traffic and process it immediately.

Packet Filtering (4.1.2)

Packet filtering controls access to a network by analyzing the incoming and/or outgoing packets and forwarding them or discarding them based on given criteria. Packet filtering can occur at Layer 3 or Layer 4, as shown in Figure 4-1.

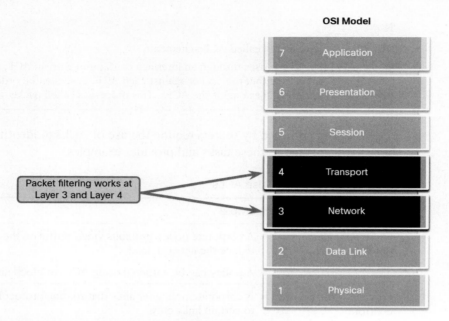

Figure 4-1   Packet Filtering in the OSI Model

Cisco routers support two types of ACLs:

- **Standard ACLs:** These ACLs only filter at Layer 3, using the source IPv4 address only.

- **Extended ACLs:** These ACLs filter at Layer 3 using the source and/or destination IPv4 address. They can also filter at Layer 4 using TCP, UDP ports, and optional protocol type information for finer control.

ACL Operation (4.1.3)

An ACL defines a set of rules that give added control for packets that enter inbound interfaces, packets relayed through the router, and packets that exit outbound interfaces of the router.

ACLs can be configured to apply to inbound traffic and outbound traffic, as shown in Figure 4-2.

Figure 4-2   ACLs on Inbound and Outbound Interfaces

Note

ACLs do not act on packets that originate from the router itself.

An *inbound ACL* filters packets before they are routed to the outbound interface. An inbound ACL is efficient because it saves the overhead of routing lookups if the packet is discarded. If a packet is permitted by the ACL, it is processed for routing. Inbound ACLs are best used to filter packets when the network attached to an inbound interface is the only source of packets that need to be examined.

An *outbound ACL* filters packets after they are routed, regardless of the inbound interface. Incoming packets are routed to the outbound interface, and they are then processed through the outbound ACL. Outbound ACLs are best used when the same filter will be applied to packets coming from multiple inbound interfaces before exiting the same outbound interface.

When an ACL is applied to an interface, it follows a specific operating procedure. For example, here are the operational steps used when traffic has entered a router interface with an inbound standard IPv4 ACL configured:

Step 1.   The router extracts the source IPv4 address from the packet header.

Step 2.   The router starts at the top of the ACL and compares the source IPv4 address to each ACE, in sequential order.

Step 3.   When a match is made, the router carries out the instruction, either permitting or denying the packet, and the remaining ACEs in the ACL, if any, are not analyzed.

Step 4.   If the source IPv4 address does not match any ACEs in the ACL, the packet is discarded because there is an *implicit deny* ACE automatically applied to all ACLs.

The last ACE statement of an ACL is always an implicit deny that blocks all traffic. By default, this statement is automatically implied at the end of an ACL even though it is hidden and not displayed in the configuration.

Note

An ACL must have at least one permit statement; otherwise, all traffic will be denied due to the implicit deny ACE statement.

Packet Tracer
☐ Activity

Packet Tracer—ACL Demonstration (4.1.4)

In this activity, you will observe how an ACL can be used to prevent a ping from reaching hosts on remote networks. After removing the ACL from the configuration, the pings will be successful.

Check Your Understanding—Purpose of ACLs (4.1.5)

Refer to the online course to complete this activity.

Wildcard Masks in ACLs (4.2)

A wildcard mask is similar to a subnet mask but the reverse. In this section, you will learn how to calculate the inverse wildcard mask.

Wildcard Mask Overview (4.2.1)

In the previous section, you learned about the purpose of ACL. This section explains how ACLs use *wildcard masks*. An IPv4 ACE uses a 32-bit wildcard mask to determine which bits of the address to examine for a match. Wildcard masks are also used by the Open Shortest Path First (OSPF) routing protocol.

A wildcard mask is similar to a subnet mask in that it uses the ANDing process to identify which bits in an IPv4 address to match. However, a wildcard mask and a subnet mask differ in the way they match binary 1s and 0s. Unlike with a subnet mask, in which binary 1 is equal to a match, and binary 0 is not a match, with a wildcard mask, the reverse is true.

Wildcard masks use the following rules to match binary 1s and 0s:

- **Wildcard mask bit 0:** Match the corresponding bit value in the address.
- **Wildcard mask bit 1:** Ignore the corresponding bit value in the address.

Table 4-2 lists some examples of wildcard masks and what they would match and ignore.

Table 4-2 Examples of Wildcard Masks

Wildcard Mask	Last Octet (in Binary)	Meaning (0—match, 1—ignore)
0.0.0.0	00000000	- Match all octets.
0.0.0.63	00111111	- Match the first three octets - Match the 2 leftmost bits of the last octet - Ignore the last 6 bits
0.0.0.15	00001111	- Match the first three octets - Match the 4 leftmost bits of the last octet - Ignore the last 4 bits of the last octet

Wildcard Mask	Last Octet (in Binary)	Meaning (0—match, 1—ignore)
0.0.0.248	11111100	■ Match the first three octets
		■ Ignore the 6 leftmost bits of the last octet
		■ Match the last 2 bits
0.0.0.255	11111111	■ Match the first three octets
		■ Ignore the last octet

Wildcard Mask Types (4.2.2)

Using wildcard masks takes some practice. The following sections provide examples to help you learn how wildcard masks are used to filter traffic for one host, one subnet, and a range IPv4 addresses.

Wildcard to Match a Host

In this example, the wildcard mask is used to match a specific host IPv4 address. Say that ACL 10 needs an ACE that only permits the host with IPv4 address 192.168.1.1. Recall that 0 equals a match, and 1 equals ignore. To match a specific host IPv4 address, a wildcard mask consisting of all zeros (that is, 0.0.0.0) is required.

Table 4-3 lists, in decimal and binary, the host IPv4 address, the wildcard mask, and the permitted IPv4 address.

Table 4-3 Wildcard to Match a Host Example

	Decimal	Binary
IPv4 address	192.168.1.1	11000000.10101000.00000001.00000001
Wildcard mask	0.0.0.0	00000000.00000000.00000000.00000000
Permitted IPv4 address	192.168.1.1	11000000.10101000.00000001.00000001

The 0.0.0.0 wildcard mask stipulates that every bit must match exactly. Therefore, when the ACE is processed, the wildcard mask will permit only the 192.168.1.1 address. The resulting ACE in ACL 10 would be **access-list 10 permit 192.168.1.1 0.0.0.0**.

Wildcard Mask to Match an IPv4 Subnet

In this example, ACL 10 needs an ACE that permits all hosts in the 192.168.1.0/24 network. The wildcard mask 0.0.0.255 stipulates that the very first three octets must match exactly, but the fourth octet does not need to match.

Table 4-4 lists, in decimal and binary, the host IPv4 address, the wildcard mask, and the permitted IPv4 addresses.

Table 4-4 Wildcard Mask to Match an IPv4 Subnet Example

	Decimal	Binary
IPv4 address	192.168.1.1	11000000.10101000.00000001.00000001
Wildcard mask	0.0.0.255	00000000.00000000.00000000.11111111
Permitted IPv4 address	192.168.1.0/24	11000000.10101000.00000001.00000000

When the ACE is processed, the wildcard mask 0.0.0.255 permits all hosts in the 192.168.1.0/24 network. The resulting ACE in ACL 10 would be **access-list 10 permit 192.168.1.0 0.0.0.255**.

Wildcard Mask to Match an IPv4 Address Range

In this example, ACL 10 needs an ACE that permits all hosts in the 192.168.16.0/24, 192.168.17.0/24, …, 192.168.31.0/24 networks. The wildcard mask 0.0.15.255 would correctly filter that range of addresses.

Table 4-5 lists, in decimal and binary the host IPv4 address, the wildcard mask, and the permitted IPv4 addresses.

Table 4-5 Wildcard Mask to Match an IPv4 Address Range Example

	Decimal	Binary
IPv4 address	192.168.16.0	11000000.10101000.00010000.00000000
Wildcard mask	0.0.15.255	00000000.00000000.00001111.11111111
Permitted IPv4 address	192.168.16.0/24 to 192.168.31.0/24	11000000.10101000.00010000.00000000 11000000.10101000.00011111.00000000

The highlighted wildcard mask bits identify which bits of the IPv4 address must match. When the ACE is processed, the wildcard mask 0.0.15.255 permits all hosts in the 192.168.16.0/24 to 192.168.31.0/24 networks. The resulting ACE in ACL 10 would be **access-list 10 permit 192.168.16.0 0.0.15.255**.

Wildcard Mask Calculation (4.2.3)

Calculating wildcard masks can be challenging. One shortcut method is to subtract the subnet mask from 255.255.255.255. The following sections provide examples to help you learn how to calculate the wildcard mask using the subnet mask.

Example 1

Say that you wanted an ACE in ACL 10 to permit access to all users in the 192.168.3.0/24 network. To calculate the wildcard mask, subtract the subnet mask (that is, 255.255.255.0) from 255.255.255.255, as shown in Table 4-6.

The solution produces the wildcard mask 0.0.0.255. Therefore, the ACE would be **access-list 10 permit 192.168.3.0 0.0.0.255.**

Table 4-6   Wildcard Mask Calculation—Example 1

Starting value	255.255.255.255
Subtract the subnet mask	−255.255.255. 0
Resulting wildcard mask	0. 0. 0.255

Example 2

In this example, say that you wanted an ACE in ACL 10 to permit network access for the 14 users in the subnet 192.168.3.32/28. Subtract the subnet (that is, 255.255.255.240) from 255.255.255.255, as shown in Table 4-7.

This solution produces the wildcard mask 0.0.0.15. Therefore, the ACE would be **access-list 10 permit 192.168.3.32 0.0.0.15.**

Table 4-7   Wildcard Mask Calculation—Example 2

Starting value	255.255.255.255
Subtract the subnet mask	−255.255.255.240
Resulting wildcard mask	0. 0. 0. 15

Example 3

In this example, say that you needed an ACE in ACL 10 to permit only networks 192.168.10.0 and 192.168.11.0. These two networks could be summarized as 192.168.10.0/23, which is a subnet mask of 255.255.254.0. Again, you subtract 255.255.254.0 subnet mask from 255.255.255.255, as shown in Table 4-8.

This solution produces the wildcard mask 0.0.1.255. Therefore, the ACE would be **access-list 10 permit 192.168.10.0 0.0.1.255.**

Table 4-8   Wildcard Mask Calculation—Example 3

Starting value	255.255.255.255
Subtract the subnet mask	−255.255.254. 0
Resulting wildcard mask	0. 0. 1.255

Example 4

Consider an example in which you need an ACL number 10 to match networks in the range 192.168.16.0/24 to 192.168.31.0/24. This network range could be summarized as 192.168.16.0/20, which is a subnet mask of 255.255.240.0. Therefore, subtract 255.255.240.0 subnet mask from 255.255.255.255, as shown in Table 4-9.

This solution produces the wildcard mask 0.0.15.255. Therefore, the ACE would be **access-list 10 permit 192.168.16.0 0.0.15.255**.

Table 4-9   Wildcard Mask Calculation—Example 4

Starting value	255.255.255.255
Subtract the subnet mask	− 255.255.240. 0
Resulting wildcard mask	0. 0. 15.255

Wildcard Mask Keywords (4.2.4)

Working with decimal representations of binary wildcard mask bits can be tedious. To simplify this task, Cisco IOS provides two keywords to identify the most common uses of wildcard masking. Keywords reduce ACL keystrokes and make it easier to read an ACE.

The two keywords are

- **host:** This keyword substitutes for the 0.0.0.0 mask and indicates that all IPv4 address bits must match to filter just one host address.
- **any:** This keyword substitutes for the 255.255.255.255 mask and indicates to ignore the entire IPv4 address or to accept any addresses.

In the command output in Example 4-1, two ACLs are configured. The ACL 10 ACE permits only the 192.168.10.10 host, and the ACL 11 ACE permits all hosts.

Example 4-1   ACLs Configured Without Keywords

```
R1(config)# access-list 10 permit 192.168.10.10 0.0.0.0
R1(config)# access-list 11 permit 0.0.0.0 255.255.255.255
R1(config)#
```

Alternatively, the keywords **host** and **any** could be used to replace the highlighted output. The commands in Example 4-2 accomplishes the same task as the commands in Example 4-1.

Example 4-2   ACLs Configured Using Keywords

```
R1(config)# access-list 10 permit host 192.168.10.10
R1(config)# access-list 11 permit any
R1(config)#
```

**Interactive
Graphic**

Check Your Understanding—Wildcard Masks in ACLs (4.2.5)

Refer to the online course to complete this activity.

Guidelines for ACL Creation (4.3)

This section provides guidelines for creating ACLs.

Limited Number of ACLs per Interface (4.3.1)

In a previous section, you learned about how wildcard masks are used in ACLs. This section discusses guidelines for ACL creation. There is a limit on the number of ACLs that can be applied on a router interface. For example, a dual-stacked (that is, IPv4 and IPv6) router interface can have up to four ACLs applied, as shown in Figure 4-3.

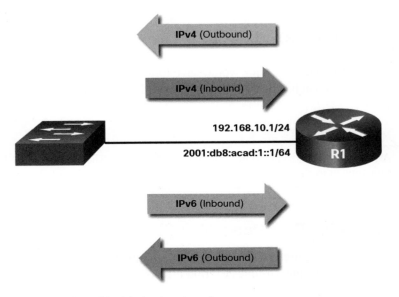

Figure 4-3   ACLs Limited on Interfaces

Specifically, a dual-stacked router interface can have

- One outbound IPv4 ACL
- One inbound IPv4 ACL
- One inbound IPv6 ACL
- One outbound IPv6 ACL

Say that R1 has two dual-stacked interfaces that need to have inbound and outbound IPv4 and IPv6 ACLs applied. As shown in Figure 4-4, R1 could have up to 8 ACLs configured and applied to interfaces.

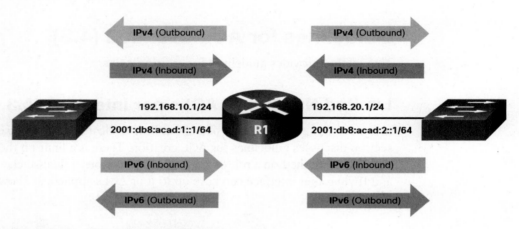

Figure 4-4   ACLs Limit Example

In this case, each interface would have four ACLs: two ACLs for IPv4 and two ACLs for IPv6. For each protocol, one ACL is for inbound traffic and one for outbound traffic.

> **Note**
>
> ACLs do not have to be configured in both directions. The number of ACLs and their direction applied to the interface will depend on the security policy of the organization.

ACL Best Practices (4.3.2)

Using ACLs requires attention to detail and great care. Mistakes can be costly in terms of downtime, troubleshooting efforts, and network service. Basic planning is required before configuring an ACL.

Table 4-10 presents some ACL best practices.

Table 4-10   Guidelines for ACLs

Guideline	Benefit
Base ACLs on the organization's security policies.	This will ensure that you implement organizational security guidelines.
Write out what you want an ACL to do.	This will help you avoid inadvertently creating potential access problems.
Use a text editor to create, edit, and save all your ACLs.	This will help you create a library of reusable ACLs.
Document ACLs by using the **remark** command.	This will help you (and others) understand the purpose of an ACE.
Test ACLs on a development network before implementing them on a production network.	This will help you avoid costly errors.

Check Your Understanding—Guidelines for ACL Creation (4.3.3)

Refer to the online course to complete this activity.

Types of IPv4 ACLs (4.4)

This section compares IPv4 standard and extended ACLs.

Standard and Extended ACLs (4.4.1)

The previous sections describe the purpose of ACLs as well as guidelines for ACL creation. This section covers standard and extended ACLs and named and *numbered ACLs*, and it provides examples of placement of these ACLs.

There are two types of IPv4 ACLs:

- *Standard ACLs*: These ACLs permit or deny packets based only on the source IPv4 address.

- *Extended ACLs*: These ACLs permit or deny packets based on the source IPv4 address and destination IPv4 address, protocol type, source and destination TCP or UDP ports, and more.

For example, Example 4-3 shows how to create a standard ACL. In this example, ACL 10 permits hosts on the source network 192.168.10.0/24. Because of the implied "deny any" at the end, all traffic except for traffic coming from the 192.168.10.0/24 network is blocked with this ACL.

Example 4-3   Standard ACL Example

```
R1(config)# access-list 10 permit 192.168.10.0 0.0.0.255
R1(config)#
```

In Example 4-4, the extended ACL 100 permits traffic originating from any host on the 192.168.10.0/24 network to any IPv4 network if the destination host port is 80 (HTTP).

Example 4-4   Extended ACL Example

```
R1(config)# access-list 100 permit tcp 192.168.10.0 0.0.0.255 any eq www
R1(config)#
```

Notice that the standard ACL 10 is only capable of filtering by source address, while the extended ACL 100 is filtering on the source and destination Layer 3 and Layer 4 protocol (for example, TCP) information.

Note

Full IPv4 ACL configuration is discussed in Chapter 5, "ACLs for IPv4 Configuration."

Numbered and Named ACLs (4.4.2)

For IPv4, there are both numbered and *named ACLs*.

Numbered ACLs

ACLs 1 to 99 and 1300 to 1999 are standard ACLs, while ACLs 100 to 199 and 2000 to 2699 are extended ACLs, as shown in Example 4-5.

Example 4-5   Available ACL Numbers

```
R1(config)# access-list ?
  <1-99>       IP standard access list
  <100-199>    IP extended access list
  <1100-1199>  Extended 48-bit MAC address access list
  <1300-1999>  IP standard access list (expanded range)
  <200-299>    Protocol type-code access list
  <2000-2699>  IP extended access list (expanded range)
  <700-799>    48-bit MAC address access list
  rate-limit   Simple rate-limit specific access list
  template     Enable IP template acls
Router(config)# access-list
```

Named ACLs

Using named ACLs is the preferred method when configuring ACLs. You can name standard and extended ACLs to provide information about the purpose of each ACL. For example, the extended ACL name FTP-FILTER is far easier to identify than the ACL number 100.

The **ip access-list** global configuration command is used to create a named ACL, as shown in Example 4-6.

Note

Numbered ACLs are created using the **access-list** global configuration command.

Example 4-6   Example of a Named ACL

```
R1(config)# ip access-list extended FTP-FILTER
R1(config-ext-nacl)# permit tcp 192.168.10.0 0.0.0.255 any eq ftp
R1(config-ext-nacl)# permit tcp 192.168.10.0 0.0.0.255 any eq ftp-data
R1(config-ext-nacl)#
```

The following are the general rules to follow for named ACLs:

- Assign a name to identify the purpose of the ACL.

- Names can contain alphanumeric characters.

- Names cannot contain spaces or punctuation.

- It is suggested that a name be written in CAPITAL LETTERS.

- Entries can be added or deleted within an ACL.

Where to Place ACLs (4.4.3)

Every ACL should be placed where it has the greatest impact on efficiency.

Figure 4-5 illustrates where standard and extended ACLs should be located in an enterprise network.

Say that the objective is to prevent traffic originating in the 192.168.10.0/24 network from reaching the 192.168.30.0/24 network. Extended ACLs should be located as close as possible to the source of the traffic to be filtered. This way, undesirable traffic is denied close to the source network, without crossing the network infrastructure.

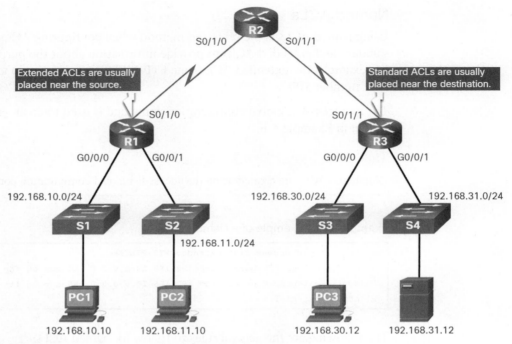

Figure 4-5   Example of Where to Place ACLs

Standard ACLs should be located as close to the destination as possible. If a standard ACL were placed at the source of the traffic, the "permit" or "deny" would occur based on the given source address, regardless of the traffic destination.

Placement of an ACL and, therefore, the type of ACL used, may also depend on a variety of factors, as listed in Table 4-11.

Table 4-11   ACL Placement Factors

Factors Influencing ACL Placement	Explanation
The extent of organizational control	▪ Placement of the ACL can depend on whether the organization has control of both the source and destination networks.
Bandwidth of the networks involved	▪ It may be desirable to filter unwanted traffic at the source to prevent transmission of bandwidth-consuming traffic.
Ease of configuration	▪ It may be easier to implement an ACL at the destination, but traffic will use bandwidth unnecessarily.
	▪ An extended ACL could be used on each router where the traffic originated. This would save bandwidth by filtering the traffic at the source, but it would require creation of extended ACLs on multiple routers.

Standard ACL Placement Example (4.4.4)

Following the guidelines for ACL placement, standard ACLs should be located as close to the destination as possible.

In Figure 4-6, the administrator wants to prevent traffic originating in the 192.168.10.0/24 network from reaching the 192.168.30.0/24 network.

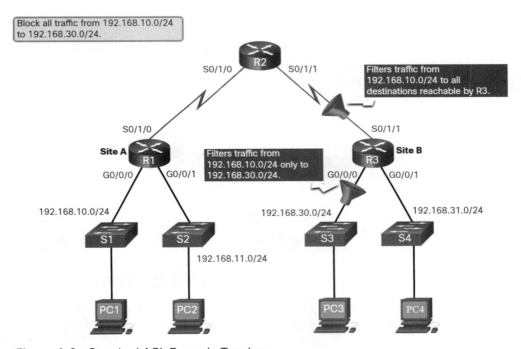

Figure 4-6   Standard ACL Example Topology

Following the basic placement guidelines, the administrator would place a standard ACL on router R3. There are two possible interfaces on R3 to which to apply the standard ACL:

- **R3 S0/1/1 interface (inbound):** The standard ACL can be applied inbound on the R3 S0/1/1 interface to deny traffic from the .10 network. However, it would also filter .10 traffic to the 192.168.31.0/24 (.31 in this example) network. Therefore, the standard ACL should not be applied to this interface.

- **R3 G0/0 interface (outbound):** The standard ACL can be applied outbound on the R3 G0/0/0 interface. This will not affect other networks that are reachable by R3. Packets from the .10 network will still be able to reach the .31 network. This is the best interface to place the standard ACL to meet the traffic requirements.

Extended ACL Placement Example (4.4.5)

Extended ACLs should be located as close to the source as possible to prevent unwanted traffic from being sent across multiple networks only to be denied when it reaches its destination.

However, an organization can only place ACLs on devices that it controls. Therefore, the extended ACL placement must be determined in the context of where organizational control extends.

In Figure 4-7, for example, Company A wants to deny Telnet and FTP traffic to Company B's 192.168.30.0/24 network from its 192.168.11.0/24 network while permitting all other traffic.

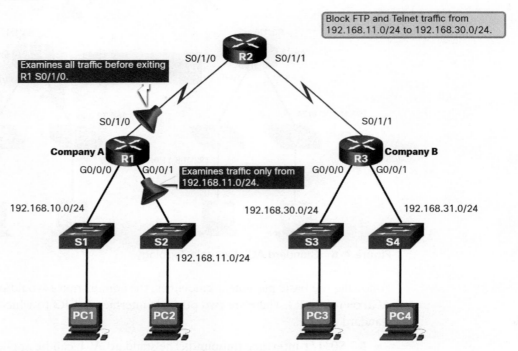

Figure 4-7 Extended ACL Example Topology

There are several ways to accomplish these goals. An extended ACL on R3 would accomplish the task, but the administrator does not control R3. In addition, this solution would allow unwanted traffic to cross the entire network, only to be blocked at the destination, which would affect overall network efficiency.

The solution is to place on R1 an extended ACL that specifies both source and destination addresses. There are two possible interfaces on R1 to apply the extended ACL:

- **R1 S0/1/0 interface (outbound):** The extended ACL can be applied outbound on the S0/1/0 interface. However, this solution would process all packets leaving R1, including packets from 192.168.10.0/24.

- **R1 G0/0/1 interface (inbound):** The extended ACL can be applied inbound on the G0/0/1, and only packets from the 192.168.11.0/24 network are subject to ACL processing on R1. Because the filter is to be limited to only those packets leaving the 192.168.11.0/24 network, applying the extended ACL to G0/1 is the best solution.

Interactive Graphic

Check Your Understanding—Guidelines for ACL Placement (4.4.6)

Refer to the online course to complete this activity.

Summary (4.5)

The following is a summary of the sections in this chapter.

Purpose of ACLs

Several tasks performed by routers require the use of ACLs to identify traffic. An ACL is a series of IOS commands that are used to filter packets based on information found in the packet header. A router does not have any ACLs configured by default. However, when an ACL is applied to an interface, the router performs the additional task of evaluating all network packets as they pass through the interface to determine whether the packets can be forwarded. An ACL uses a sequential list of permit or deny statements, known as ACEs. Cisco routers support two types of ACLs: standard ACLs and extended ACLs. An inbound ACL filters packets before they are routed to the outbound interface. If a packet is permitted by the ACL, it is then processed for routing. An outbound ACL filters packets after being routed, regardless of the inbound interface. When an ACL is applied to an interface, it follows a specific operating procedure:

Step 1.   The router extracts the source IPv4 address from the packet header.

Step 2.   The router starts at the top of the ACL and compares the source IPv4 address to each ACE, in sequential order.

Step 3.   When a match is made, the router carries out the instruction, either permitting or denying the packet, and the remaining ACEs in the ACL, if any, are not analyzed.

Step 4.   If the source IPv4 address does not match any ACEs in the ACL, the packet is discarded because there is an implicit deny ACE automatically applied to all ACLs.

Wildcard Masks

An IPv4 ACE uses a 32-bit wildcard mask to determine which bits of the address to examine for a match. Wildcard masks are also used by the Open Shortest Path First (OSPF) routing protocol. A wildcard mask is similar to a subnet mask in that it uses the ANDing process to identify which bits in an IPv4 address to match. However, a wildcard mask and a subnet mask differ in the way they match binary 1s and 0s. Wildcard mask bit 0 matches the corresponding bit value in the address. Wildcard mask bit 1 ignores the corresponding bit value in the address. A wildcard mask is used to filter traffic for one host, one subnet, and a range of IPv4 addresses. A shortcut for calculating a wildcard mask is to subtract the subnet mask from 255.255.255.255. Working with decimal representations of binary wildcard mask bits can be simplified by using the Cisco IOS keywords **host** and **any** to identify the most common uses of wildcard masking. Keywords reduce ACL keystrokes and make it easier to read ACEs.

Guidelines for ACL Creation

There is a limit on the number of ACLs that can be applied on a router interface. For example, a dual-stacked (that is, IPv4 and IPv6) router interface can have up to four ACLs applied. Specifically, a router interface can have one outbound IPv4 ACL, one inbound IPv4 ACL, one inbound IPv6 ACL, and one outbound IPv6 ACL. ACLs do not have to be configured in both directions. The number of ACLs and the direction in which they are applied to the interface depend on the security policy of the organization. Basic planning is required before configuring an ACL and includes the following best practices:

- Base ACLs on the organization's security policies.

- Write out what you want the ACL to do.

- Use a text editor to create, edit, and save all of your ACLs.

- Document ACLs by using the **remark** command.

- Test the ACLs on a development network before implementing them on a production network.

Types of IPv4 ACLs

There are two types of IPv4 ACLs: standard ACLs and extended ACLs. Standard ACLs permit or deny packets based only on the source IPv4 address. Extended ACLs permit or deny packets based on the source IPv4 address and destination IPv4 address, protocol type, source and destination TCP or UDP ports, and more. ACLs 1 to 99 and 1300 to 1999 are standard ACLs. ACLs 100 to 199 and 2000 to 2699 are extended ACLs. Using named ACLs is the preferred method when configuring ACLs. Standard and extended ACLs can be named to provide information about the purpose of each ACL.

The following are basic rules to follow for named ACLs:

- Assign a name to identify the purpose of an ACL.

- Names can contain alphanumeric characters.

- Names cannot contain spaces or punctuation.

- It is suggested that the name be written in CAPITAL LETTERS.

- Entries can be added or deleted within an ACL.

Every ACL should be placed where it has the greatest impact on efficiency. Extended ACLs should be located as close as possible to the source of the traffic to be filtered. This way, undesirable traffic is denied close to the source network without crossing the network infrastructure. Standard ACLs should be located as close to the destination as possible. If a standard ACL were placed at the source of the traffic, the "permit" or "deny" would occur based on the given source address, regardless of the traffic destination. Placement of the ACL may depend on the extent of organizational control, bandwidth of the networks, and ease of configuration.

Practice

The following Packet Tracer activity provides practice with the topics introduced in this chapter. The instructions are available in the companion *Enterprise Networking, Security, and Automation Labs & Study Guide (CCNAv7)* (ISBN 9780136634690). There are no labs for this chapter.

Packet Tracer
☐ Activity

Packet Tracer Activity

Packet Tracer 4.1.4: ACL Demonstration

Check Your Understanding Questions

Complete all the review questions listed here to test your understanding of the topics and concepts in this chapter. The appendix "Answers to the 'Check Your Understanding' Questions" lists the answers.

1. What two functions describe uses of access control lists? (Choose two.)

   A. ACLs assist a router in determining the best path to a destination.

   B. ACLs can control which areas a host can access on a network.

   C. ACLs provide a basic level of security for network access.

   D. Standard ACLs can filter traffic based on source and destination network addresses.

   E. Standard ACLs can restrict access to specific applications and ports.

2. Which three statements describe how an ACL processes packets? (Choose three.)

   A. A packet is compared with all ACEs in the ACL before a forwarding decision is made.

   B. A packet that has been denied by one ACE can be permitted by a subsequent ACE.

C. An implicit deny at the end of an ACL rejects any packet that does not match an ACE.

D. Each ACE is checked only until a match is detected or until the end of the ACL.

E. If an ACE is matched, the packet is either rejected or forwarded, as directed by the ACE.

F. If an ACE is not matched, the packet is forwarded by default.

3. Which three statements are best practices related to placement of ACLs? (Choose three.)

A. Filter unwanted traffic before it travels onto a low-bandwidth link.

B. For every inbound ACL placed on an interface, ensure that there is a matching outbound ACL.

C. Place extended ACLs close to the destination IP address of the traffic.

D. Place extended ACLs close to the source IP address of the traffic.

E. Place standard ACLs close to the destination IP address of the traffic.

F. Place standard ACLs close to the source IP address of the traffic.

4. Which two characteristics are shared by standard and extended ACLs? (Choose two.)

A. Both filter packets for a specific destination host IP address.

B. Both include an implicit deny as a final entry.

C. Both permit or deny specific services by port number.

D. They both filter based on protocol type.

E. They can be created by using either descriptive names or numbers.

5. Which two statement describes a difference between the operation of inbound and outbound ACLs? (Choose two.)

A. Inbound ACLs are processed before the packets are routed.

B. Inbound ACLs can be used in both routers and switches.

C. Multiple inbound ACLs can be applied to an interface.

D. Multiple outbound ACLs can be applied to an interface.

E. Outbound ACLs are processed after the routing is completed.

F. Outbound ACLs can be used only on routers.

G. Unlike outbound ACLs, inbound ACLs can be used to filter packets with multiple criteria.

6. In which configuration would an outbound ACL placement be preferred over an inbound ACL placement?

   A. When a router has more than one ACL

   B. When an interface is filtered by an outbound ACL and the network attached to the interface is the source network being filtered within the ACL

   C. When an outbound ACL is closer to the source of the traffic flow

   D. When the ACL is applied to an outbound interface to filter packets coming from multiple inbound interfaces before the packets exit the interface

7. What wildcard mask will match networks 10.16.0.0 through 10.19.0.0?

   A. 0.252.255.255

   B. 0.0.255.255

   C. 0.0.3.255

   D. 0.3.255.255

8. What type of ACL offers increased flexibility and control over network traffic?

   A. Extended

   B. Extensive

   C. Named standard

   D. Numbered standard

9. Which statement describes a characteristic of standard IPv4 ACLs?

   A. They can be configured to filter traffic based on both source IP addresses and source ports.

   B. They can be created with a number but not with a name.

   C. They filter traffic based on destination IP addresses only.

   D. They filter traffic based on source IP addresses only.

10. What wildcard mask will match network 10.10.100.64/26?

    A. 0.0.0.15

    B. 0.0.0.31

    C. 0.0.0.63

    D. 0.0.0.127

CHAPTER 5

ACLs for IPv4 Configuration

Objectives

Upon completion of this chapter, you will be able to answer the following questions:

- How do you configure standard IPv4 ACLs to filter traffic to meet networking requirements?

- How do you use sequence numbers to edit existing standard IPv4 ACLs?

- How do you configure a standard ACL to secure vty access?

- How do you configure extended IPv4 ACLs to filter traffic according to networking requirements?

Key Term

This chapter uses the following key term. You can find the definition in the Glossary.

stateful firewall service   *page 210*

Introduction (5.0)

In the gated community where your grandparents live, there are rules for who can enter and leave the premises. The guard will not raise the gate to let you into the community until someone confirms that you are on an approved visitor list. Much like the guard in the gated community, an access control list (ACL) may be configured to permit and deny network traffic passing through an interface. How do you configure ACLs? How do you modify them if they are not working correctly or if they require other changes? How do ACLs provide secure remote administrative access? Get started with this chapter to learn more!

Configure Standard IPv4 ACLs (5.1)

In this section, you will learn how to configure standard IPv4 ACLs.

Create an ACL (5.1.1)

In Chapter 4, "ACL Concepts," you learned what an ACL does and why it is important. In this section, you will learn about creating ACLs.

All ACLs must be planned, but planning is especially important for ACLs that require multiple access control entries (ACEs).

When configuring a complex ACL, it is suggested that you

- Use a text editor to write out the specifics of the policy to be implemented.
- Add the IOS configuration commands to accomplish those tasks.
- Include remarks to document the ACL.
- Copy and paste the commands onto the device.
- Thoroughly test each ACL to ensure that it correctly applies the desired policy.

These recommendations enable you to create an ACL thoughtfully and without impacting the traffic on the network.

Numbered Standard IPv4 ACL Syntax (5.1.2)

To create a numbered standard ACL, use the following global configuration command:

```
Router(config)# access-list access-list-number {deny | permit | remark text} source
[source-wildcard] [log]
```

Use the **no access-list** *access-list-number* global configuration command to remove a numbered standard ACL.

Table 5-1 provides a detailed explanation of the syntax used in creating a standard ACL.

Table 5-1   Syntax for Numbered Standard IPv4 ACLs

Parameter	Description
access-list-number	■ This is the decimal number of the ACL. ■ The standard ACL number range is 1 to 99 or 1300 to 1999.
deny	■ This denies access if the condition is matched.
permit	■ This permits access if the condition is matched.
remark *text*	■ (Optional) This adds a text entry for documentation purposes. ■ Each remark is limited to 100 characters.
source	■ This identifies the source network or host address to filter. ■ Use the **any** keyword to specify all networks. ■ Use the **host** *ip-address* keyword or simply enter an IP address (without the **host** keyword) to identify a specific IP address.
source-wildcard	■ (Optional) This is a 32-bit wildcard mask that is applied to the source. If this parameter is omitted, a default 0.0.0.0 mask is assumed.
log	■ (Optional) This keyword generates and sends an informational message whenever the ACE is matched. ■ The message includes the ACL number, matched condition (that is, permitted or denied), source address, and number of packets. ■ This message is generated for the first matched packet. ■ This keyword should be implemented only for troubleshooting or security reasons.

Named Standard IPv4 ACL Syntax (5.1.3)

Naming an ACL makes it easier to understand its function. To create a named standard ACL, use the following global configuration command:

```
Router(config)# ip access-list standard access-list-name
```

This command enters the named standard configuration mode where you configure the ACL ACEs.

ACL names are alphanumeric and case sensitive, and they must be unique. Capitalizing ACL names is not required but makes them stand out when viewing the running configuration output. It also makes it less likely that you will accidentally create two different ACLs with the same name but with different uses of capitalization.

> **Note**
>
> Use the **no ip access-list standard** *access-list-name* global configuration command to remove a named standard IPv4 ACL.

Example 5-1 shows the creation of a named standard IPv4 ACL called NO-ACCESS.

Example 5-1   Options for Creating a Named Standard ACL

```
R1(config)# ip access-list standard NO-ACCESS
R1(config-std-nacl)# ?
Standard Access List configuration commands:
  <1-2147483647>  Sequence Number
  default         Set a command to its defaults
  deny            Specify packets to reject
  exit            Exit from access-list configuration mode
  no              Negate a command or set its defaults
  permit          Specify packets to forward
  remark          Access list entry comment
R1(config-std-nacl)#
```

Notice that the prompt changes to named standard ACL configuration mode. ACE statements are entered in the named standard ACL subconfiguration mode. Use the help facility to view all the named standard ACL ACE options.

The three highlighted options in Example 5-1 are configured similarly to the numbered standard ACL. Unlike with the numbered ACL method, however, there is no need to repeat the initial **ip access-list** command for each ACE.

Apply a Standard IPv4 ACL (5.1.4)

After a standard IPv4 ACL is configured, it must be linked to an interface or a feature. The following interface configuration command can be used to bind a numbered or named standard IPv4 ACL to an interface:

```
Router(config-if)# ip access-group {access-list-number | access-list-name}
{in | out}
```

To remove an ACL from an interface, first enter the **no ip access-group** interface configuration command. At this point, the ACL will still be configured on the router. To remove the ACL from the router, use the **no access-list** or **no ip access-list** global configuration command.

Numbered Standard IPv4 ACL Example (5.1.5)

The topology in Figure 5-1 is used in this section to demonstrate configuring and applying numbered and named standard IPv4 ACLs to an interface. This first example shows a numbered standard IPv4 ACL implementation.

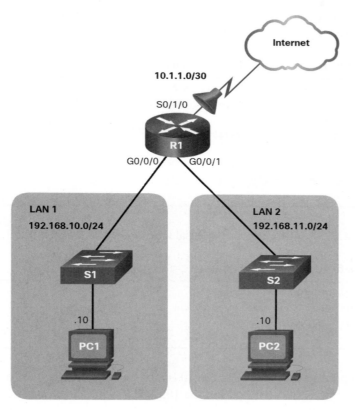

Figure 5-1   Numbered and Named Standard ACL Reference Topology

Say that only PC1 is allowed out to the internet. To enable this policy, a standard ACL ACE could be applied outbound on S0/1/0, as shown in Example 5-2.

Example 5-2   ACE to Permit PC1

```
R1(config)# access-list 10 remark ACE permits ONLY host 192.168.10.10 to the
   internet
R1(config)# access-list 10 permit host 192.168.10.10
R1(config)#
R1(config)# do show access-lists
Standard IP access list 10
    10 permit 192.168.10.10
R1(config)#
```

Notice that the output of the **show access-lists** command does not display the **remark** statements. ACL remarks are displayed in the running configuration file. Although the **remark** command is not required to enable the ACL, it is strongly suggested for documentation purposes.

Now say that a new network policy states that hosts in LAN 2 should also be permitted to the internet. To enable this policy, a second standard ACL ACE could be added to ACL 10, as shown in Example 5-3.

Example 5-3   Adding Another ACE to the ACL

```
R1(config)# access-list 10 remark ACE permits all host in LAN 2
R1(config)# access-list 10 permit 192.168.20.0 0.0.0.255
R1(config)#
R1(config)# do show access-lists
Standard IP access list 10
    10 permit 192.168.10.10
    20 permit 192.168.20.0, wildcard bits 0.0.0.255
R1(config)#
```

Apply ACL 10 outbound on the Serial 0/1/0 interface, as shown in Example 5-4.

Example 5-4   Applying the ACL

```
R1(config)# interface Serial 0/1/0
R1(config-if)# ip access-group 10 out
R1(config-if)# end
R1#
```

ACL 10 permits only host 192.168.10.10 and all hosts from LAN 2 to exit the Serial 0/1/0 interface. All other hosts in the 192.168.10.0 network are not permitted to the internet.

Use the **show running-config** command to review the ACL in the configuration, as shown in Example 5-5. Notice that the **remarks** statements are displayed in this case.

Example 5-5   Verifying the ACL in the Running Configuration

```
R1# show run | section access-list
access-list 10 remark ACE permits host 192.168.10.10
access-list 10 permit 192.168.10.10
access-list 10 remark ACE permits all host in LAN 2
access-list 10 permit 192.168.20.0 0.0.0.255
R1#
```

Finally, use the **show ip interface** command to verify whether an interface has an ACL applied to it. In Example 5-6, the output is specifically looking at the Serial 0/1/0 interface for lines that include **access list**.

Example 5-6   Verifying That the ACL Is Applied to the Interface

```
R1# show ip int Serial 0/1/0 | include access list
  Outgoing Common access list is not set
  Outgoing access list is 10
  Inbound Common access list is not set
  Inbound  access list is not set
R1#
```

Named Standard IPv4 ACL Example (5.1.6)

This section shows an example of a named standard IPv4 ACL implementation. This example uses the same topology as before, repeated in Figure 5-2 for your convenience.

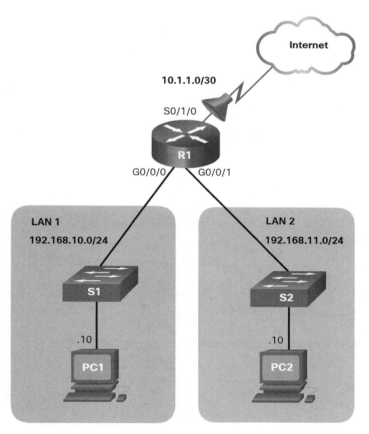

Figure 5-2   Numbered and Named Standard ACL Reference Topology

Say that only PC1 is allowed out to the internet. To enable this policy, a named standard ACL called PERMIT-ACCESS could be applied outbound on S0/1/0.

Remove the previously configured named ACL 10 and create a named standard ACL called PERMIT-ACCESS, as shown in Example 5-7.

Example 5-7   Removing an ACL and Configuring It as a Named ACL

```
R1(config)# no access-list 10
R1(config)# ip access-list standard PERMIT-ACCESS
R1(config-std-nacl)# remark ACE permits host 192.168.10.10
R1(config-std-nacl)# permit host 192.168.10.10
R1(config-std-nacl)#
```

Now add an ACE permitting only host 192.168.10.10 and another ACE permitting all LAN 2 hosts to the internet, as shown in Example 5-8.

Example 5-8   Adding an ACE to the Named ACL

```
R1(config-std-nacl)# remark ACE permits host 192.168.10.10
R1(config-std-nacl)# permit host 192.168.10.10
R1(config-std-nacl)# remark ACE permits all hosts in LAN 2
R1(config-std-nacl)# permit 192.168.20.0 0.0.0.255
R1(config-std-nacl)# exit
R1(config)#
```

Apply the new named ACL outbound to the Serial 0/1/0 interface, as shown in Example 5-9.

Example 5-9   Applying the Named ACL

```
R1(config)# interface Serial 0/1/0
R1(config-if)# ip access-group PERMIT-ACCESS out
R1(config-if)# end
R1#
```

Use the **show access-lists** and **show running-config** commands to review the ACL in the configuration, as shown in Example 5-10.

Example 5-10   Verifying the Named ACL Configuration

```
R1# show access-lists
Standard IP access list PERMIT-ACCESS
    10 permit 192.168.10.10
    20 permit 192.168.20.0, wildcard bits 0.0.0.255
R1#
```

```
R1# show run | section ip access-list
ip access-list standard PERMIT-ACCESS
 remark ACE permits host 192.168.10.10
 permit 192.168.10.10
 remark ACE permits all hosts in LAN 2
 permit 192.168.20.0 0.0.0.255
R1#
```

Finally, use the **show ip interface** command to verify whether an interface has an ACL applied to it. In Example 5-11, the output is specifically looking at the Serial 0/1/0 interface for lines that include **access list**.

Example 5-11   Verifying That the Named ACL Is Applied to the Interface

```
R1# show ip int Serial 0/1/0 | include access list
  Outgoing Common access list is not set
  Outgoing access list is PERMIT-ACCESS
  Inbound Common access list is not set
  Inbound  access list is not set
R1#
```

Syntax Check—Configure Standard IPv4 ACLs (5.1.7)

Refer to the online course to complete this activity.

Packet Tracer—Configure Numbered Standard IPv4 ACLs (5.1.8)

Standard ACLs are router configuration scripts that control whether a router permits or denies packets based on the source address. This activity focuses on defining filtering criteria, configuring standard ACLs, applying ACLs to router interfaces, and verifying and testing the ACL implementation. The routers are already configured, including IPv4 addresses and EIGRP routing.

Packet Tracer—Configure Named Standard IPv4 ACLs (5.1.9)

The senior network administrator has asked you to create a named standard ACL to prevent access to a file server. All clients from one network and one specific workstation from a different network should be denied access.

Modify IPv4 ACLs (5.2)

ACLs can be very complex and long. What happens if you notice a mistake in one ACE? Do you delete the entire ACL and re-create it? Can you change one ACE only? In this section, you will learn how to modify an existing IPv4 ACL.

Two Methods to Modify an ACL (5.2.1)

After an ACL is configured, it may need to be modified. Configuring ACLs with multiple ACEs can be complex. Sometimes the configured ACE does not yield the expected behaviors. Therefore, ACL configuration may initially require a bit of trial and error to achieve the desired filtering result.

This section discusses two methods to use when modifying an ACL:

- Using a text editor
- Using sequence numbers

Text Editor Method (5.2.2)

ACLs with multiple ACEs should be created in a text editor. Using this method allows you to plan the required ACEs, create the ACL, and then paste it into the router interface. It also simplifies the tasks involved in editing and fixing an ACL.

For example, say that ACL 1 was entered incorrectly using **19** instead of **192** for the first octet, as shown in Example 5-12.

Example 5-12   Error in the First ACE

```
R1# show run | section access-list
access-list 1 deny   19.168.10.10
access-list 1 permit 192.168.10.0 0.0.0.255
R1#
```

In this example, the first ACE should have been to deny the host at 192.168.10.10. However, the ACE was incorrectly entered.

To correct the error:

Step 1.   Copy the ACL from the running configuration and paste it into the text editor.

Step 2.   Make the necessary changes.

Step 3.   Remove the previously configured ACL on the router; otherwise, pasting the edited ACL commands will only append (that is, add) to the existing ACL ACEs on the router.

Step 4.   Copy and paste the edited ACL back to the router.

Say that ACL 1 has now been corrected. Therefore, the incorrect ACL must be deleted, and the corrected ACL 1 statements must be pasted in using global configuration mode, as shown in Example 5-13.

Example 5-13   Deleting the ACL Before Correctly Configuring the ACE

```
R1(config)# no access-list 1
R1(config)#
R1(config)# access-list 1 deny 192.168.10.10
R1(config)# access-list 1 permit 192.168.10.0 0.0.0.255
R1(config)#
```

Sequence Numbers Method (5.2.3)

An ACL ACE can be deleted or added by using the ACL sequence numbers. Sequence numbers are automatically assigned when an ACE is entered. To see these numbers listed, run the **show access-lists** command. The **show running-config** command output does not display sequence numbers.

The incorrect ACE for ACL 1 is using sequence number 10, as shown in the output of the **show access-lists** command in Example 5-14.

Example 5-14   Viewing the Sequence Number for Each ACE

```
R1# show access-lists
Standard IP access list 1
    10 deny    19.168.10.10
    20 permit 192.168.10.0, wildcard bits 0.0.0.255
R1#
```

Use the **ip access-list standard** command to edit an ACL. A statement cannot be overwritten using the same sequence number as an existing statement. Therefore, the current statement must be deleted first with the **no 10** command. Then the correct ACE can be added, using sequence number 10. Verify the changes using the **show access-lists** command, as shown in Example 5-15.

Example 5-15   Configuring and Verifying a New ACE for Sequence Number 10

```
R1# conf t
R1(config)# ip access-list standard 1
R1(config-std-nacl)# no 10
R1(config-std-nacl)# 10 deny host 192.168.10.10
R1(config-std-nacl)# end
R1#
R1# show access-lists
Standard IP access list 1
    10 deny    192.168.10.10
    20 permit 192.168.10.0, wildcard bits 0.0.0.255
R1#
```

Modify a Named ACL Example (5.2.4)

With named ACLs you can use sequence numbers to delete and add ACEs. Refer to Example 5-16 for the ACL **NO-ACCESS**.

Example 5-16   Verifying the Sequence Numbers for an ACL

```
R1# show access-lists
Standard IP access list NO-ACCESS
    10 deny   192.168.10.10
    20 permit 192.168.10.0, wildcard bits 0.0.0.255
R1#
```

Assume that host 192.168.10.5 from the 192.168.10.0/24 network should also have been denied. If you entered a new ACE, it would be appended to the end of the ACL, and the host would never be denied because ACE 20 permits all hosts from that network.

The solution is to add an ACE denying host 192.168.10.5 in between ACE 10 and ACE 20. Example 5-17 shows ACE 15 added. Notice that the new ACE was entered without using the **host** keyword; this keyword is optional when specifying a destination host.

Example 5-17   Using a Sequence Number to Insert an ACE

```
R1# configure terminal
R1(config)# ip access-list standard NO-ACCESS
R1(config-std-nacl)# 15 deny 192.168.10.5
R1(config-std-nacl)# end
R1#
R1# show access-lists
Standard IP access list NO-ACCESS
    15 deny    192.168.10.5
    10 deny    192.168.10.10
    20 permit 192.168.10.0, wildcard bits 0.0.0.255
R1#
```

The **show access-lists** command is used to verify that the ACL now has a new ACE 15 inserted appropriately before the **permit** statement.

Notice that sequence number 15 is displayed prior to sequence number 10. We might expect the order of the statements in the output to reflect the order in which they were entered. However, IOS orders host statements by using a special hashing function. The resulting order optimizes the ACL to search by host entries first, and then by network entries.

> **Note**
>
> The hashing function is only applied to host statements in an IPv4 standard access list. The details of the hashing function are beyond the scope of this book.

ACL Statistics (5.2.5)

Notice in Example 5-18 that the **show access-lists** command shows statistics for each statement that has been matched. The deny ACE in the NO-ACCESS ACL has been matched 20 times, and the permit ACE has been matched 64 times.

Example 5-18   Verifying and Clearing ACL Matches

```
R1# show access-lists
Standard IP access list NO-ACCESS
    10 deny   192.168.10.10   (20 matches)
    20 permit 192.168.10.0, wildcard bits 0.0.0.255   (64 matches)
R1#
R1# clear access-list counters NO-ACCESS
R1#
R1# show access-lists
Standard IP access list NO-ACCESS
    10 deny   192.168.10.10
    20 permit 192.168.10.0, wildcard bits 0.0.0.255
R1#
```

Note that the implied deny any in the last statement does not display any statistics. To track how many implicit denied packets have been matched, you must manually configure the **deny any** command at the end of the ACL.

Use the **clear access-list counters** command to clear the ACL statistics. This command can be used alone or with the number or name of a specific ACL.

Interactive Graphic

Syntax Checker—Modify IPv4 ACLs (5.2.6)

Refer to the online course to complete this activity.

Packet Tracer—Configure and Modify Standard IPv4 ACLs (5.2.7)

In this Packet Tracer activity, you will complete the following objectives:

- Part 1: Configure devices and verify connectivity
- Part 2: Configure and verify standard numbered and named ACLs
- Part 3: Modify a standard ACL

Secure VTY Ports with a Standard IPv4 ACL (5.3)

In this section, you will learn how to use a standard ACL to secure vty access.

The access-class Command (5.3.1)

ACLs typically filter incoming or outgoing traffic on an interface. However, an ACL can also be used to secure remote administrative access to a device using the vty lines.

Use the following two steps to secure remote administrative access to the vty lines:

Step 1.   Create an ACL to identify which administrative hosts should be allowed remote access.

Step 2.   Apply the ACL to incoming traffic on the vty lines.

Use the following line configuration mode command to apply an ACL to the vty lines:

```
R1(config-line)# access-class {access-list-number | access-list-name} {in | out}
```

The **in** keyword is the most commonly used option to filter incoming vty traffic. The **out** parameter filters outgoing vty traffic and is rarely applied.

The following should be considered when configuring access lists on vty lines:

- Both named and numbered access lists can be applied to vty lines.

- Identical restrictions should be set on all the vty lines because a user can attempt to connect to any of them.

Secure VTY Access Example (5.3.2)

The topology in Figure 5-3 is used to demonstrate how to configure an ACL to filter vty traffic. In this example, only PC1 will be allowed to Telnet in to R1.

Note
Telnet is used here for demonstration purposes only. SSH should be used in a production environment.

To increase secure access, a username and password will be created, and the **login local** authentication method will be used on the vty lines. The command in Example 5-19 creates a local database entry for user **ADMIN** and password **class**.

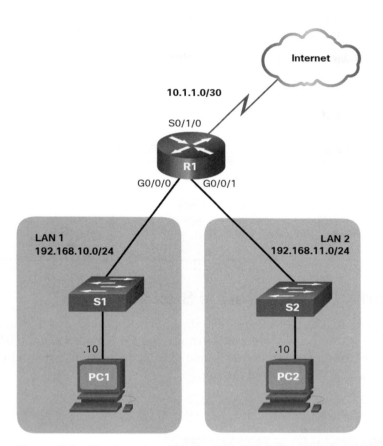

Figure 5-3   Numbered and Named Standard ACL Reference Topology

Example 5-19   Configuring and Applying an ACL to vty Lines

```
R1(config)# username ADMIN secret class
R1(config)# ip access-list standard ADMIN-HOST
R1(config-std-nacl)# remark This ACL secures incoming vty lines
R1(config-std-nacl)# permit 192.168.10.10
R1(config-std-nacl)# deny any
R1(config-std-nacl)# exit
R1(config)#
R1(config)# line vty 0 4
R1(config-line)# login local
R1(config-line)# transport input telnet
R1(config-line)# access-class ADMIN-HOST in
R1(config-line)# end
R1#
```

A named standard ACL called ADMIN-HOST is created and identifies PC1. Notice that the **deny any** has been configured to track the number of times access has been denied.

The vty lines are configured to use the local database for authentication, permit Telnet traffic, and use the ADMIN-HOST ACL to restrict traffic.

In a production environment, you would set the vty lines to only allow SSH, as shown in Example 5-20.

Example 5-20   Configuring VYT Lines for SSH Access Only

```
R1(config)# line vty 0 4
R1(config-line)# login local
R1(config-line)# transport input ssh
R1(config-line)# access-class ADMIN-HOST in
R1(config-line)# end
R1#
```

Verify the VTY Port Is Secured (5.3.3)

After an ACL to restrict access to the vty lines is configured, it is important to verify that it is working as expected. As shown in Figure 5-4, when PC1 Telnets to R1, the host is prompted for a username and password before the user on PC1 can successfully access the command prompt.

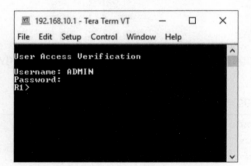

Figure 5-4   Remote Access from PC1

The R1> prompt verifies that PC1 can access R1 for administrative purposes.

Next, test the connection from PC2. As shown in Figure 5-5, when PC2 attempts to Telnet, the connection is refused.

To verify the ACL statistics, issue the **show access-lists** command. Notice the informational message displayed on the console regarding the admin user, as shown in Example 5-21. An informational console message is also generated when a user exits the vty line.

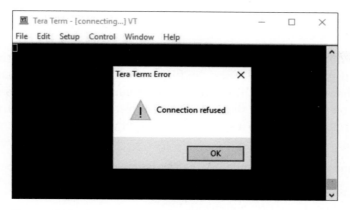

Figure 5-5   Remote Access Attempt from PC2

Example 5-21   Logging Message for Failed Login Attempt

```
R1#
Oct  9 15:11:19.544: %SEC_LOGIN-5-LOGIN_SUCCESS: Login Success [user: admin]
    [Source: 192.168.10.10] [localport: 23] at 15:11:19 UTC Wed Oct 9 2019
R1#
R1# show access-lists
Standard IP access list ADMIN-HOST
    10 permit 192.168.10.10  (2 matches)
    20 deny    any  (2 matches)
R1#
```

The matches in the **permit** line of the output result from the successful Telnet connection by PC1. The matches in the **deny** statement are due to the failed attempt to create a Telnet connection by PC2, a device on the 192.168.11.0/24 network.

Interactive Graphic

Syntax Checker—Secure the VTY Ports (5.3.4)

Refer to the online course to complete this activity.

Configure Extended IPv4 ACLs (5.4)

Extended ACLs enable more control of the filter. In this section, you configure numbered and named extended IPv4 ACLs.

Extended ACLs (5.4.1)

In the previous sections, you learned how to configure and modify standard ACLs and how to secure vty ports with a standard IPv4 ACL. Standard ACLs only filter on source address. When more precise traffic-filtering control is required, extended IPv4 ACLs can be created.

Extended ACLs are used more often than standard ACLs because they provide a greater degree of control. They can filter on source address, destination address, protocol (that is, IP, TCP, UDP, ICMP), and port number. This provides a greater range of criteria on which to base the ACL. For example, one extended ACL can allow email traffic from a network to a specific destination while denying file transfers and web browsing.

Like standard ACLs, extended ACLs can be created as either numbered or named:

- **Numbered extended ACL:** Created using the **access-list** *access-list-number* global configuration command.

- **Named extended ACL:** Created using the **ip access-list extended** *access-list-name*.

Numbered Extended IPv4 ACL Syntax (5.4.2)

The procedural steps for configuring extended ACLs are the same as for standard ACLs. The extended ACL is first configured, and then it is activated on an interface. However, the command syntax and parameters are more complex to support the additional features provided by extended ACLs.

To create a numbered extended ACL, use the following global configuration command:

```
Router(config)# access-list access-list-number {deny | permit | remark text}
protocol source source-wildcard [operator [port]] destination destination-wildcard
[operator [port]] [established] [log]
```

Use the **no ip access-list extended** *access-list-name* global configuration command to remove an extended ACL.

Although there are many keywords and parameters for extended ACLs, it is not necessary to use all of them when configuring an extended ACL. Table 5-2 provides a detailed explanation of the syntax for an extended ACL.

Table 5-2   Syntax for Numbered Extended IPv4 ACLs

Parameter	Description
access-list-number	- This is the decimal number of the ACL. - The extended ACL number range is 100 to 199 and 2000 to 2699.
deny	- This denies access if the condition is matched.

Parameter	Description
permit	▪ This permits access if the condition is matched.
remark *text*	▪ (Optional) This adds a text entry for documentation purposes. ▪ Each remark is limited to 100 characters.
protocol	▪ This is the name or number of an internet protocol. ▪ Common keywords include **ip**, **tcp**, **udp**, and **icmp**. ▪ The **ip** keyword matches all IP protocols.
source	▪ This identifies the source network or host address to filter. ▪ Use the **any** keyword to specify all networks. ▪ Use the **host** *ip-address* keyword or simply enter an IP address (without the **host** keyword) to identify a specific IP address.
source-wildcard	▪ (Optional) This is a 32-bit wildcard mask that is applied to the source.
destination	▪ This identifies the destination network or host address to filter. ▪ Use the **any** keyword to specify all networks. ▪ Use the **host** *ip-address* keyword or *ip-address*.
destination-wildcard	▪ (Optional) This is a 32-bit wildcard mask that is applied to the destination.
operator	▪ (Optional) This compares source or destination ports. ▪ Possible operands include **lt** (less than), **gt** (greater than), **eq** (equal), **neq** (not equal), and **range** (inclusive range).
port	▪ (Optional) This is the decimal number or name of a TCP or UDP port.
established	▪ (Optional) This is for TCP only. ▪ It is a first-generation firewall feature.
log	▪ (Optional) This keyword generates and sends an informational message whenever the ACE is matched. ▪ This message includes ACL number, matched condition (that is, permitted or denied), source address, and number of packets. ▪ This message is generated for the first matched packet. ▪ This keyword should be implemented only for troubleshooting or security reasons.

The command to apply an extended IPv4 ACL to an interface is the same as the command used for standard IPv4 ACLs:

```
Router(config-if)# ip access-group access-list-name {in | out}
```

To remove an ACL from an interface, first enter the **no ip access-group** interface configuration command. To remove the ACL from the router, use the **no access-list** global configuration command.

> **Note**
>
> The internal logic applied to the ordering of standard ACL statements does not apply to extended ACLs. The order in which the statements are entered during configuration is the order in which they are displayed and processed.

Protocols and Ports (5.4.3)

Extended ACLs can filter on many different types of internet protocols and ports. The following sections provide more information about the internet protocols and ports on which extended ACLs can filter.

Protocol Options

The four highlighted protocols in Example 5-22 are the most popular options.

> **Note**
>
> Use the **?** to get help when entering a complex ACE.

> **Note**
>
> If an internet protocol is not listed, then the IP protocol number could be specified. For instance, the ICMP protocol number is 1, TCP is 6, and UDP is 17.

Example 5-22   Extended ACL Protocol Options

```
R1(config)# access-list 100 permit ?
  <0-255>       An IP protocol number
  ahp           Authentication Header Protocol
  dvmrp         dvmrp
  eigrp         Cisco's EIGRP routing protocol
  esp           Encapsulation Security Payload
  gre           Cisco's GRE tunneling
  icmp          Internet Control Message Protocol
  igmp          Internet Gateway Message Protocol
```

```
ip               Any Internet Protocol
ipinip           IP in IP tunneling
nos              KA9Q NOS compatible IP over IP tunneling
object-group     Service object group
ospf             OSPF routing protocol
pcp              Payload Compression Protocol
pim              Protocol Independent Multicast
tcp              Transmission Control Protocol
udp              User Datagram Protocol
R1(config)# access-list 100 permit
```

Port Keyword Options

Selecting a protocol influences the port options. For instance, if you select

- **tcp** as the protocol, you get TCP-related ports options
- **udp** as the protocol, you get UDP-specific ports options
- **icmp** as the protocol, you get ICMP-related ports (that is, message) options

Notice how many TCP port options are available in Example 5-23. The highlighted ports are popular options.

Example 5-23   Extended ACL Port Keywords

```
R1(config)# access-list 100 permit tcp any any eq ?
  <0-65535>    Port number
  bgp          Border Gateway Protocol (179)
  chargen      Character generator (19)
  cmd          Remote commands (rcmd, 514)
  daytime      Daytime (13)
  discard      Discard (9)
  domain       Domain Name Service (53)
  echo         Echo (7)
  exec         Exec (rsh, 512)
  finger       Finger (79)
  ftp          File Transfer Protocol (21)
  ftp-data     FTP data connections (20)
  gopher       Gopher (70)
  hostname     NIC hostname server (101)
  ident        Ident Protocol (113)
  irc          Internet Relay Chat (194)
  klogin       Kerberos login (543)
  kshell       Kerberos shell (544)
```

```
    login           Login (rlogin, 513)
    lpd             Printer service (515)
    msrpc           MS Remote Procedure Call (135)
    nntp            Network News Transport Protocol (119)
    onep-plain      Onep Cleartext (15001)
    onep-tls        Onep TLS (15002)
    pim-auto-rp     PIM Auto-RP (496)
    pop2            Post Office Protocol v2 (109)
    pop3            Post Office Protocol v3 (110)
    smtp            Simple Mail Transport Protocol (25)
    sunrpc          Sun Remote Procedure Call (111)
    syslog          Syslog (514)
    tacacs          TAC Access Control System (49)
    talk            Talk (517)
    telnet          Telnet (23)
    time            Time (37)
    uucp            Unix-to-Unix Copy Program (540)
    whois           Nicname (43)
    www             World Wide Web (HTTP, 80)
R1(config)#
```

Port names or numbers can be specified. However, keep in mind that port names make it easier to understand the purpose of an ACE.

Notice that some common ports names (for example, SSH and HTTPS) are not listed. For these protocols, port numbers have to be specified.

Protocols and Port Numbers Configuration Examples (5.4.4)

Extended ACLs can filter on different port number and port name options. Example 5-24 shows the configuration of an extended ACL 100 to filter HTTP traffic. The first ACE uses the **www** port name. The second ACE uses the port number **80**. The two ACEs achieve exactly the same result.

Example 5-24   Configuring a Port with a Keyword or Port Number

```
R1(config)# access-list 100 permit tcp any any eq www
!or...
R1(config)# access-list 100 permit tcp any any eq 80
```

Configuring the port number is required when there is not a specific protocol name listed, such as SSH (port number 22) or HTTPS (port number 443), as shown in Example 5-25.

Example 5-25 Some Protocols That Must Be Configured Using a Port Number

```
R1(config)# access-list 100 permit tcp any any eq 22
R1(config)# access-list 100 permit tcp any any eq 443
R1(config)#
```

Apply a Numbered Extended IPv4 ACL (5.4.5)

The topology in Figure 5-6 is used in this section to demonstrate how to configure and apply numbered and named extended IPv4 ACLs to an interface. The first example shows a numbered extended IPv4 ACL implementation.

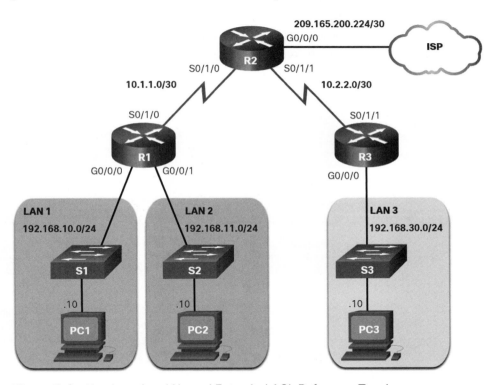

Figure 5-6 Numbered and Named Extended ACL Reference Topology

In Example 5-26, the ACL permits both HTTP and HTTPS traffic from the 192.168.10.0 network to go to any destination. Extended ACLs can be applied in various locations. However, they are commonly applied close to the source. Therefore, in Example 5-26, ACL 110 is applied inbound on the R1 G0/0/0 interface.

Example 5-26   Configuring and Applying a Numbered Extended ACL

```
R1(config)# access-list 110 permit tcp 192.168.10.0 0.0.0.255 any eq www
R1(config)# access-list 110 permit tcp 192.168.10.0 0.0.0.255 any eq 443
R1(config)#
R1(config)# interface g0/0/0
R1(config-if)# ip access-group 110 in
R1(config-if)# exit
R1(config)#
```

TCP Established Extended ACL (5.4.6)

You can have TCP perform basic *stateful firewall services* by using the TCP **established** keyword. The keyword enables inside traffic to exit the inside private network and permits the returning reply traffic to enter the inside private network, as shown in Figure 5-7.

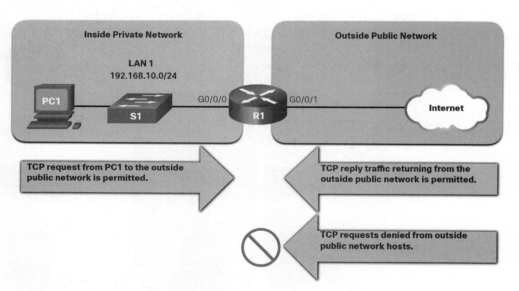

Figure 5-7   TCP Traffic Example

However, TCP traffic generated by an outside host and attempting to communicate with an inside host is denied.

The **established** keyword can be used to permit only the return HTTP traffic from requested websites and deny all other traffic.

In Figure 5-8, ACL 110, which was previously configured, filters traffic from the inside private network. ACL 120, using the **established** keyword, filters traffic coming into the inside private network from the outside public network.

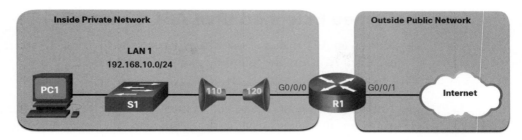

Figure 5-8   Topology Design for Inbound and Outbound Extended ACLs for Established TCP Sessions

In Example 5-27, ACL 120 is configured to only permit returning web traffic to the inside hosts. The new ACL is then applied outbound on the R1 G0/0/0 interface.

Example 5-27   Configuring an ACL to Check for a TCP-Established Session

```
R1(config)# access-list 120 permit tcp any 192.168.10.0 0.0.0.255 established
R1(config)#
R1(config)# interface g0/0/0
R1(config-if)# ip access-group 120 out
R1(config-if)# end
R1#
R1# show access-lists
Extended IP access list 110
    10 permit tcp 192.168.10.0 0.0.0.255 any eq www
    20 permit tcp 192.168.10.0 0.0.0.255 any eq 443 (657 matches)
Extended IP access list 120
    10 permit tcp any 192.168.10.0 0.0.0.255 established (1166 matches)
R1#
```

The **show access-lists** command displays both ACLs. Notice from the match statistics in Example 5-27 that inside hosts have been accessing the secure web resources from the internet. Also notice that the permit secure HTTPS counter (that is, eq 443) in ACL 110 and the return established counter in ACL 120 have increased.

The **established** parameter allows only responses to traffic that originates from the 192.168.10.0/24 network to return to that network. Specifically, a match occurs if the returning TCP segment has the ACK or reset (RST) flag bits set. This indicates that the packet belongs to an existing connection. Without the **established** parameter in the ACL statement, clients could send traffic to a web server but would not receive traffic returning from the web server.

Named Extended IPv4 ACL Syntax (5.4.7)

Naming an ACL makes it easier to understand its function. To create a named extended ACL, use the following global configuration command:

```
Router(config)# ip access-list extended access-list-name
```

This command enters the named extended configuration mode. Recall that ACL names are alphanumeric and case sensitive, and they must be unique.

In Example 5-28, a named extended ACL called NO-FTP-ACCESS is created, and the prompt changes to named extended ACL configuration mode. ACE statements are entered in the named extended ACL subconfiguration mode

Example 5-28   Applying a Named Extended ACL

```
R1(config)# ip access-list extended NO-FTP-ACCESS
R1(config-ext-nacl)#
```

Named Extended IPv4 ACL Example (5.4.8)

Named extended ACLs are created in essentially the same way that named standard ACLs are created.

The topology in Figure 5-9 is used to demonstrate configuring and applying two named extended IPv4 ACLs to an interface:

- **SURFING:** This ACL will permit inside HTTP and HTTPS traffic to exit to the internet.

- **BROWSING:** This ACL will only permit returning web traffic to the inside hosts while implicitly denying all other traffic exiting the R1 G0/0/0 interface.

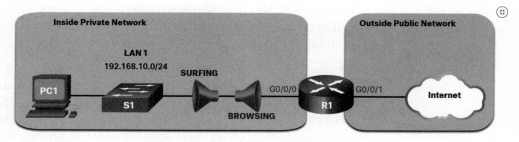

Figure 5-9   Topology Design for Named Extended ACLs

Example 5-29 shows the configuration for the inbound SURFING ACL and the outbound BROWSING ACL.

Example 5-29   Configuring Inbound and Outbound Named Extended ACLs

```
R1(config)# ip access-list extended SURFING
R1(config-ext-nacl)# Remark Permits inside HTTP and HTTPS traffic
R1(config-ext-nacl)# permit tcp 192.168.10.0 0.0.0.255 any eq 80
R1(config-ext-nacl)# permit tcp 192.168.10.0 0.0.0.255 any eq 443
R1(config-ext-nacl)# exit
R1(config)#
R1(config)# ip access-list extended BROWSING
R1(config-ext-nacl)# Remark Only permit returning HTTP and HTTPS traffic
R1(config-ext-nacl)# permit tcp any 192.168.10.0 0.0.0.255 established
R1(config-ext-nacl)# exit
R1(config)#
R1(config)# interface g0/0/0
R1(config-if)# ip access-group SURFING in
R1(config-if)# ip access-group BROWSING out
R1(config-if)# end
R1#
R1# show access-lists
Extended IP access list SURFING
    10 permit tcp 192.168.10.0 0.0.0.255 any eq www
    20 permit tcp 192.168.10.0 0.0.0.255 any eq 443 (124 matches)
Extended IP access list BROWSING
    10 permit tcp any 192.168.10.0 0.0.0.255 established (369 matches)
R1#
```

The SURFING ACL permits HTTP and HTTPS traffic from inside users to exit the G0/0/1 interface connected to the internet. Web traffic returning from the internet is permitted back into the inside private network by the BROWSING ACL.

The SURFING ACL is applied inbound, and the BROWSING ACL is applied outbound on the R1 G0/0/0 interface, as shown in the output.

Inside hosts have been accessing the secure web resources from the internet. The **show access-lists** command is used to verify the ACL statistics. Notice that the permit secure HTTPS counter (that is, eq 443) in the SURFING ACL and the return established counter in the BROWSING ACL have increased.

Edit Extended ACLs (5.4.9)

Like standard ACLs, an extended ACL can be edited using a text editor when many changes are required. Otherwise, if the edit applies to one or two ACEs, sequence numbers can be used.

In Example 5-30, say that you have just entered the SURFING and BROWSING ACLs and wish to verify their configuration by using the **show access-lists** command.

Example 5-30   Verifying the Extended ACL Configuration

```
R1# show access-lists
Extended IP access list BROWSING
    10 permit tcp any 192.168.10.0 0.0.0.255 established
Extended IP access list SURFING
    10 permit tcp 19.168.10.0 0.0.0.255 any eq www
    20 permit tcp 192.168.10.0 0.0.0.255 any eq 443
R1#
```

You notice that the ACE sequence number 10 in the SURFING ACL has an incorrect source IP network address.

To correct this error using sequence numbers, the original statement is removed with the **no** *sequence_#* command, and the corrected statement is added in place of the original statement, as shown in Example 5-31.

Example 5-31   Using a Sequence Number to Delete and Add an ACE to an Extended ACL

```
R1# configure terminal
R1(config)# ip access-list extended SURFING
R1(config-ext-nacl)# no 10
R1(config-ext-nacl)# 10 permit tcp 192.168.10.0 0.0.0.255 any eq www
R1(config-ext-nacl)# end
R1#
```

The output of the **show access-lists** command in Example 5-32 verifies the configuration change.

Example 5-32   Verifying the Edited ACL

```
R1# show access-lists
Extended IP access list BROWSING
    10 permit tcp any 192.168.10.0 0.0.0.255 established
Extended IP access list SURFING
    10 permit tcp 192.168.10.0 0.0.0.255 any eq www
    20 permit tcp 192.168.10.0 0.0.0.255 any eq 443
R1#
```

Another Named Extended IPv4 ACL Example (5.4.10)

Figure 5-10 shows another scenario for implementing a named extended IPv4 ACL. Assume that PC1 in the inside private network is permitted FTP, SSH, Telnet, DNS, HTTP, and HTTPS traffic. However, all other users in the inside private network should be denied access.

Two named extended ACLs are created in this example:

- **PERMIT-PC1:** This ACL permits only PC1 TCP access to the internet and denies all other hosts in the private network.

- **REPLY-PC1:** This ACL permits only specified returning TCP traffic to PC1 and implicitly denies all other traffic.

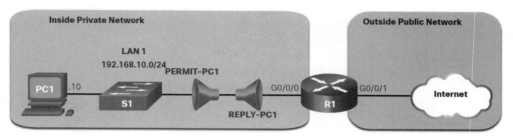

Figure 5-10   Topology Design for Another Named Extended ACL

Example 5-33 shows the configuration for the inbound PERMIT-PC1 ACL and the outbound REPLY-PC1 ACL.

The **PERMIT-PC1** ACL permits PC1 (that is, 192.168.10.10) TCP access to FTP (that is, ports 20 and 21), SSH (22), Telnet (23), DNS (53), HTTP (80), and HTTPS (443) traffic.

The **REPLY-PC1** ACL permits return traffic to PC1.

There are many factors to consider when applying an ACL, including

- The device to apply it on

- The interface to apply it on

- The direction to apply it

Careful consideration must be taken to avoid undesired filtering results. In this example, the PERMIT-PC1 ACL is applied inbound, and the REPLY-PC1 ACL is applied outbound on the R1 G0/0/0 interface.

Example 5-33   Configuring and Applying ACLs to Permit PC1 Based on the Policy

```
R1(config)# ip access-list extended PERMIT-PC1
R1(config-ext-nacl)# Remark Permit PC1 TCP access to internet
R1(config-ext-nacl)# permit tcp host 192.168.10.10 any eq 20
R1(config-ext-nacl)# permit tcp host 192.168.10.10 any eq 21
R1(config-ext-nacl)# permit tcp host 192.168.10.10 any eq 22
R1(config-ext-nacl)# permit tcp host 192.168.10.10 any eq 23
R1(config-ext-nacl)# permit tcp host 192.168.10.10 any eq 53
```

```
R1(config-ext-nacl)# permit tcp host 192.168.10.10 any eq 80
R1(config-ext-nacl)# permit tcp host 192.168.10.10 any eq 443
R1(config-ext-nacl)# deny ip 192.168.10.0 0.0.0.255 any
R1(config-ext-nacl)# exit
R1(config)#
R1(config)# ip access-list extended REPLY-PC1
R1(config-ext-nacl)# Remark Only permit returning traffic to PC1
R1(config-ext-nacl)# permit tcp any host 192.168.10.10 established
R1(config-ext-nacl)# exit
R1(config)#
R1(config)# interface g0/0/0
R1(config-if)# ip access-group PERMIT-PC1 in
R1(config-if)# ip access-group REPLY-PC1 out
R1(config-if)# end
R1#
```

Verify Extended ACLs (5.4.11)

After an ACL has been configured and applied to an interface, use Cisco IOS **show** commands to verify the configuration.

show ip interface

The **show ip interface** command is used to verify the ACL on the interface and the direction in which it was applied, as shown in Example 5-34. The command generates quite a bit of output but notice how the capitalized ACL names stand out in the output. To reduce the command output, use filtering techniques, as shown in the second command in this example.

Example 5-34   The **show ip interface** Command

```
R1# show ip interface g0/0/0
GigabitEthernet0/0/0 is up, line protocol is up (connected)
  Internet address is 192.168.10.1/24
  Broadcast address is 255.255.255.255
  Address determined by setup command
  MTU is 1500 bytes
  Helper address is not set
  Directed broadcast forwarding is disabled
  Outgoing access list is REPLY-PC1
  Inbound  access list is PERMIT-PC1
  Proxy ARP is enabled
  Security level is default
  Split horizon is enabled
  ICMP redirects are always sent
```

```
    ICMP unreachables are always sent
    ICMP mask replies are never sent
    IP fast switching is disabled
    IP fast switching on the same interface is disabled
    IP Flow switching is disabled
    IP Fast switching turbo vector
    IP multicast fast switching is disabled
    IP multicast distributed fast switching is disabled
    Router Discovery is disabled
R1#
R1# show ip interface g0/0/0 | include access list
Outgoing access list is REPLY-PC1
Inbound access list is PERMIT-PC1
R1#
```

show access-lists

The **show access-lists** command can be used to confirm that the ACLs work as expected. This command displays statistic counters that increase whenever an ACE is matched.

> **Note**
>
> Traffic must be generated to verify the operation of the ACL.

In Example 5-35, the Cisco IOS command is used to display the contents of all ACLs. Notice that IOS is displaying the keyword even though port numbers were configured. Also notice that extended ACLs do not implement the same internal logic and hashing function as standard ACLs. The output and sequence numbers displayed in the **show access-lists** command output reflect the order in which the statements were entered. Host entries are not automatically listed prior to range entries.

Example 5-35   The **show access-lists** Command

```
R1# show access-lists
Extended IP access list PERMIT-PC1
10 permit tcp host 192.168.10.10 any eq 20
20 permit tcp host 192.168.10.10 any eq ftp
30 permit tcp host 192.168.10.10 any eq 22
40 permit tcp host 192.168.10.10 any eq telnet
50 permit tcp host 192.168.10.10 any eq domain
60 permit tcp host 192.168.10.10 any eq www
70 permit tcp host 192.168.10.10 any eq 443
80 deny ip 192.168.10.0 0.0.0.255 any
Extended IP access list REPLY-PC1
10 permit tcp any host 192.168.10.10 established
R1#
```

show running-config

The **show running-config** command can be used to validate a configuration. The command also displays configured remarks. The command can be filtered to display only pertinent information, as shown in Example 5-36.

Example 5-36   The **show running-config** Command Filtered for ACL Configuration

```
R1# show running-config | begin ip access-list
ip access-list extended PERMIT-PC1
remark Permit PC1 TCP access to internet
permit tcp host 192.168.10.10 any eq 20
permit tcp host 192.168.10.10 any eq ftp
permit tcp host 192.168.10.10 any eq 22
permit tcp host 192.168.10.10 any eq telnet
permit tcp host 192.168.10.10 any eq domain
permit tcp host 192.168.10.10 any eq www
permit tcp host 192.168.10.10 any eq 443
deny ip 192.168.10.0 0.0.0.255 any
ip access-list extended REPLY-PC1
remark Only permit returning traffic to PC1
permit tcp any host 192.168.10.10 established
!
(Output omitted)
R1#
```

Packet Tracer
☐ Activity

Packet Tracer—Configure Extended IPv4 ACLs—Scenario 1 (5.4.12)

In this Packet Tracer activity, you will complete the following objectives:

- Part 1: Configure, apply, and verify an extended numbered IPv4 ACL
- Part 2: Configure, apply, and verify an extended named IPv4 ACL

Packet Tracer
☐ Activity

Packet Tracer—Configure Extended IPv4 ACLs—Scenario 2 (5.4.13)

In this Packet Tracer activity, you will complete the following objectives:

- Part 1: Configure a named extended IPv4 ACL
- Part 2: Apply and verify the extended IPv4 ACL

Summary (5.5)

The following is a summary of the sections in this chapter.

Configure Standard IPv4 ACLs

All access control lists (ACLs) must be planned, especially for ACLs requiring multiple access control entries (ACEs). When configuring a complex ACL, it is suggested that you use a text editor and write out the specifics of the policy to be implemented, add the IOS configuration commands to accomplish those tasks, include remarks to document the ACL, copy and paste the commands on a lab device, and always thoroughly test an ACL to ensure that it correctly applies the desired policy. To create a numbered standard ACL, use the **ip access-list standard** *access-list-name* global configuration command. Use the **no access-list** *access-list-number* global configuration command to remove a numbered standard ACL. Use the **show ip interface** command to verify whether an interface has an ACL applied to it. In addition to standard numbered ACLs, there are named standard ACLs. ACL names are alphanumeric and case sensitive, and they must be unique. Capitalizing ACL names is not required but makes them stand out in the running configuration output. To create a named standard ACL, use the **ip access-list standard** *access-list-name* global configuration command. Use the **no ip access-list standard** *access-list-name* global configuration command to remove a named standard IPv4 ACL. After a standard IPv4 ACL is configured, it must be linked to an interface or feature. To bind a numbered or named standard IPv4 ACL to an interface, use the **ip access-group** {*access-list-number* | *access-list-name*} { **in** | **out** } global configuration command. To remove an ACL from an interface, first enter the **no ip access-group** interface configuration command. To remove the ACL from the router, use the **no access-list** global configuration command.

Modify IPv4 ACLs

To modify an ACL, use a text editor or use sequence numbers. ACLs with multiple ACEs should be created in a text editor. Using a text editor allows you to plan the required ACEs, create the ACL, and then paste it into the router interface. An ACL ACE can also be deleted or added using the ACL sequence number. A sequence number is automatically assigned when an ACE is entered. These numbers are listed in the output of the **show access-lists** command. The **show running-config** command output does not display sequence numbers. Named ACLs can also use sequence numbers to delete and add ACEs. The **show access-lists** command shows statistics for each statement that has been matched. The **clear access-list counters** command clears the ACL statistics.

Secure VTY Ports with a Standard IPv4 ACL

ACLs typically filter incoming or outgoing traffic on an interface. However, a standard ACL can also be used to secure remote administrative access to a device using the vty lines. The two steps to secure remote administrative access to the vty lines are to create an ACL to identify which administrative hosts should be allowed remote access and to apply the ACL to incoming traffic on the vty lines. The **in** keyword is the most commonly used option to filter incoming vty traffic. The **out** parameter filters outgoing vty traffic and is rarely applied. Both named and numbered access lists can be applied to vty lines. Identical restrictions should be set on all the vty lines because a user can attempt to connect to any of them. After the ACL to restrict access to the vty lines is configured, it is important to verify that it is working as expected. Use the **show ip interface** command to verify whether an interface has an ACL applied to it. To verify ACL statistics, issue the **show access-lists** command.

Configure Extended IPv4 ACLs

Extended ACLs are used more often than standard ACLs because they provide a greater degree of control. They can filter on source address, destination address, protocol (that is, IP, TCP, UDP, ICMP), and port number. This provides a greater range of criteria on which to base the ACL. Like standard ACLs, extended ACLs can be created as numbered extended ACLs and named extended ACLs. Numbered extended ACLs are created using the same global configuration commands that are used for standard ACLs. The procedural steps for configuring extended ACLs are the same as for standard ACLs. However, the command syntax and parameters are more complex to support the additional features provided by extended ACLs. To create a numbered extended ACL, use the Router(config)# **access-list** *access-list-number* {**deny** | **permit** | **remark** *text*} *protocol source source-wildcard* [*operator* [*port*]] *destination destination-wildcard* [*operator* [*port*]] [**established**] [**log**] global configuration command. Extended ACLs can filter on many different types of internet protocols and ports. Selecting a protocol influences port options. For instance, selecting **tcp** would provide TCP-related ports options. Configuring the port number is required when there is not a specific protocol name listed, such as SSH (port number 22) or HTTPS (port number 443). TCP can also perform basic stateful firewall services with the TCP **established** keyword, which enables inside traffic to exit the inside private network and permits the returning reply traffic to enter the inside private network. After an ACL has been configured and applied to an interface, use Cisco IOS **show** commands to verify the configuration. The **show ip interface** command is used to verify the ACL on the interface and the direction in which it is applied.

Packet Tracer—IPv4 ACL Implementation Challenge (5.5.1)

In this Packet Tracer challenge, you will configure extended, standard named, and extended named IPv4 ACLs to meet specified communication requirements.

Lab—Configure and Verify Extended IPv4 ACLs (5.5.2)

In this lab, you will complete the following objectives:

- Part 1: Build the network and configure basic device settings
- Part 2: Configure and verify extended IPv4 ACLs

Practice

The following activities provide practice with the topics introduced in this chapter. The lab is available in the companion *Enterprise Networking, Security, and Automation Labs & Study Guide (CCNAv7)* (ISBN 9780136634690). The Packet Tracer activity instructions are also in the *Labs & Study Guide*. The PKA files are found in the online course.

Lab

Lab 5.5.2: Configure and Verify Extended IPv4 ACLs

Packet Tracer Activities

Packet Tracer 5.1.8: Configure Numbered Standard IPv4 ACLs

Packet Tracer 5.1.9: Configure Named Standard IPv4 ACLs

Packet Tracer 5.2.7: Configure and Modify Standard IPv4 ACLs

Packet Tracer 5.4.12: Configure Extended IPv4 ACLs—Scenario 1

Packet Tracer 5.4.13: Configure Extended IPv4 ACLs—Scenario 2

Packet Tracer 5.5.1: IPv4 ACL Implementation Challenge

Check Your Understanding Questions

Complete all the review questions listed here to test your understanding of the topics and concepts in this chapter. The appendix "Answers to the 'Check Your Understanding' Questions" lists the answers.

1. What packets match **access-list 110 permit tcp 172.16.0.0 0.0.0.255 any eq 22**?

   A. Any TCP traffic from any host to the 172.16.0.0 network

   B. Any TCP traffic from the 172.16.0.0 network to any destination network

   C. SSH traffic from any source network to the 172.16.0.0 network

   D. SSH traffic from the 172.16.0.0 network to any destination network

2. Which two keywords can be used in an access control list to replace a wildcard mask or address and wildcard mask pair? (Choose two.)

   A. **all**

   B. **any**

   C. **gt**

   D. **host**

   E. **most**

   F. **some**

3. Which two packet filters could a network administrator use on an IPv4 extended ACL? (Choose two.)

   A. Computer type

   B. Destination MAC address

   C. Destination UDP port number

   D. ICMP message type

   E. Source TCP hello address

4. In the second ACE shown in the following example, port 400 was incorrectly specified instead of port 443. What is the best way to correct this error?

   ```
   R1# show access-lists
   Extended IP access list SURFING
        10 permit tcp 192.168.10.0 0.0.0.255 any eq www
        20 permit tcp 192.168.10.0 0.0.0.255 any eq 400
   R1#
   ```

   A. Copy the ACL into a text editor, correct the ACE, and recopy the ACE to the router.

   B. Create a new named ACL and apply it to the router interface.

C. Enter **permit tcp 192.168.10.0 0.0.0.255 any eq 443**.

D. Enter the **no 20** keyword, and then enter **permit tcp 192.168.10.0 0.0.0.255 any eq 443**.

E. Remove the entire ACL and then re-create it with the correct ACE.

5. A network administrator needs to configure a standard ACL so that only the workstation of the administrator with the IP address 10.1.1.10 can access the virtual terminal of the main router. Which two configuration commands can achieve the task? (Choose two.)

A. R1(config)# **access-list 10 permit host 10.1.1.10**

B. R1(config)# **access-list 10 permit 10.1.1.10 255.255.255.0**

C. R1(config)# **access-list 10 permit 10.1.1.10 255.255.255.255**

D. R1(config)# **access-list 10 permit 10.1.1.10 0.0.0.0**

E. R1(config)# **access-list 10 permit 10.1.1.10 0.0.0.255**

6. A network administrator is writing a standard ACL to deny any traffic from the 10.10.0.0/16 network but permit all other traffic. Which two commands should be used? (Choose two.)

A. R1(config)# **access-list 55 deny any**

B. R1(config)# **access-list 55 permit any**

C. R1(config)# **access-list 55 host 10.10.0.0**

D. R1(config)# **access-list 55 deny 10.10.0.0 0.0.255.255**

E. R1(config)# **access-list 55 deny 10.10.0.0 255.255.0.0**

F. R1(config)# **access-list 55 10.10.0.0 255.255.255.255**

7. In the following example, you forgot to enter an ACE to deny the user at IP address 192.168.10.10. Which command would correctly enter the ACE to filter this address?

```
R1# show access-lists
Extended IP access list PERMIT-NET
    10 permit ip 192.168.10.0 0.0.0.255 any
    20 permit ip 192.168.11.0 0.0.0.255 any
R1#
```

A. **deny ip host 192.168.10.10**

B. **5 deny ip host 192.168.10.10**

C. **15 deny ip host 192.168.10.10**

D. **25 deny ip host 192.168.10.10**

8. You create a standard ACL called PERMIT-VTY to permit only an administrative host vty access to the router. Which line configuration command would correctly apply this ACL to the vty lines?

   A. **access-class PERMIT-VTY in**

   B. **access-class PERMIT-VTY out**

   C. **ip access-group PERMIT-VTY in**

   D. **ip access-group PERMIT-VTY out**

9. What effect does the **permit tcp 10.10.100 0.0.0.255 any eq www** extended named ACE have when implemented inbound on a G0/0 interface?

   A. All TCP traffic is permitted, and all other traffic is denied.

   B. All traffic from 10.10.100/24 is permitted anywhere on any port.

   C. The command is rejected by the router because it is incomplete.

   D. Traffic originating from 10.10.100/24 is permitted to all TCP port 80 destinations.

10. What does the CLI prompt change to after you enter the command **ip access-list extended AAA-FILTER** in global configuration mode?

   A. R1(config-ext-nacl)#

   B. R1(config-if)#

   C. R1(config-line)#

   D. R1(config-router)#

   E. R1(config-std-nacl)#

CHAPTER 6

NAT for IPv4

Objectives

Upon completion of this chapter, you will be able to answer the following questions:

- What are the purpose and function of NAT?

- How do different types of NAT operate?

- What are the advantages and disadvantages of NAT?

- How do you configure static NAT using the CLI?

- How do you configure dynamic NAT using the CLI?

- How do you configure PAT using the CLI?

- What is NAT for IPv6?

Key Terms

This chapter uses the following key terms. You can find the definitions in the Glossary.

Introduction (6.0)

IPv4 addresses are 32-bit numbers. Mathematically, this means that there can be just over 4 billion unique IPv4 addresses. In the 1980s, this seemed like more than enough IPv4 addresses. Then came the development of affordable desktop and laptop computers, smartphones and tablets, many other digital technologies, and, of course, the internet. It rather quickly became apparent that 4 billion IPv4 addresses would not be nearly enough to handle the growing demand. This is why IPv6 was developed. However, most networks today are IPv4-only or a combination of IPv4 and IPv6. The transition to IPv6-only networks is still ongoing, and *Network Address Translation (NAT)* was developed to help manage the 4 billion IPv4 addresses so that we can all use our many devices to access the internet. As you can imagine, it is important that you understand the purpose of NAT and how it works. As a bonus, this chapter contains multiple Packet Tracer activities where you get to configure different types of NAT. Let's get going!

NAT Characteristics (6.1)

Almost all networks connecting to the internet use NAT to translate IPv4 addresses. Typically, organizations assign *private IP addresses* to inside hosts. When communication exits the network, NAT translates those private addresses into *public IP addresses*. Return traffic to a public IPv4 address is re-translated to the internal private IPv4 address.

This section explains the purpose and function of NAT.

IPv4 Private Address Space (6.1.1)

As you know, there are not enough *public IPv4 addresses* to assign a unique address to each device connected to the internet. Networks are commonly implemented using *private IPv4 addresses*, as defined in RFC 1918. The RFC 1918 address classes are listed in Table 6-1. It is very likely that the computer that you use to view this course is assigned a private address.

Table 6-1   Private Internet Addresses Defined in RFC 1918

Class	RFC 1918 Internal Address Range	Prefix
A	10.0.0.0–10.255.255.255	10.0.0.0/8
B	172.16.0.0–172.31.255.255	172.16.0.0/12
C	192.168.0.0–192.168.255.255	192.168.0.0/16

These private addresses are used within an organization or site to allow devices to communicate locally. However, because these addresses do not identify any single company or organization, private IPv4 addresses cannot be routed over the internet. To allow a device with a private IPv4 address to access devices and resources outside the local network, the private address must first be translated to a public address.

NAT provides the translation of private addresses to public addresses, as shown in Figure 6-1. This allows a device with a private IPv4 address to access resources outside the private network, such as those found on the internet. Using NAT with private IPv4 addresses has been the primary method of preserving public IPv4 addresses. A single public IPv4 address can be shared by hundreds or even thousands of devices, each configured with a unique private IPv4 address.

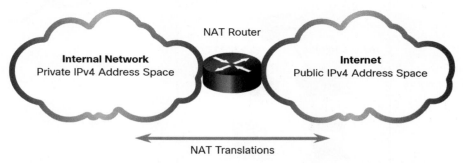

Figure 6-1   NAT Router Translating Private IPv4 Addresses to Public IPv4 Address

Without NAT, the exhaustion of the IPv4 address space would have occurred well before the year 2000. However, NAT has limitations and disadvantages, which will be explored later in this chapter. The solution to the exhaustion of IPv4 address space and the limitations of NAT is the eventual transition to IPv6.

What Is NAT? (6.1.2)

NAT has many uses, but its primary use is to conserve public IPv4 addresses. It does this by allowing networks to use private IPv4 addresses internally and providing translation to a public address only when needed. NAT has a perceived benefit of adding a degree of privacy and security to a network because it hides internal IPv4 addresses from outside networks.

NAT-enabled routers can be configured with one or more valid public IPv4 addresses. These public addresses are known as the NAT pool. When an internal device sends traffic out of the network, the NAT-enabled router translates the internal IPv4 address of the device to a public address from the NAT pool. To outside devices, all traffic entering and exiting the network appears to have a public IPv4 address from the provided pool of addresses.

A NAT router typically operates at the border of a stub network. A stub network is one or more networks with a single connection to its neighboring network, with one way in and one way out of the network. In the example in Figure 6-2, R2 is a border router. From the ISP's point of view, R2 forms a stub network.

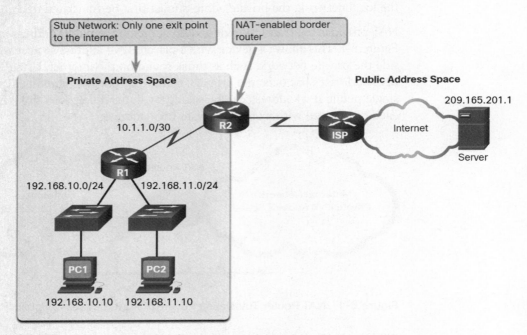

Figure 6-2   The Role NAT Plays in a Stub Network

When a device inside a stub network wants to communicate with a device outside of its network, the packet is forwarded to the border router. The border router performs the NAT process, translating the internal private address of the device to a public outside routable address.

Note

The connection to the ISP may use a private address or a public address that is shared among customers. For the purposes of this chapter, a public address is shown.

How NAT Works (6.1.3)

In Figure 6-3, PC1 with private address 192.168.10.10 wants to communicate with an outside web server with public address 209.165.201.1.

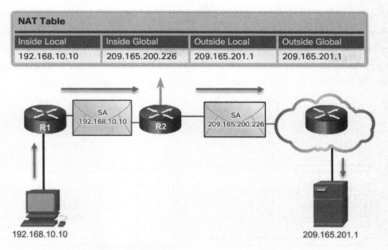

Figure 6-3   NAT in Action

NAT Terminology (6.1.4)

In NAT terminology, the *inside network* is the set of networks that is subject to translation. The *outside network* refers to all other networks.

When using NAT, IPv4 addresses have different designations based on whether they are on the private network or on the public network (internet) and whether the traffic is incoming or outgoing.

NAT includes four types of addresses:

- *Inside local address*
- *Inside global address*
- *Outside local address*
- *Outside global address*

When determining which type of address is used, it is important to remember that NAT terminology is always applied from the perspective of the device with the translated address:

- *Inside address*: The address of the device that is being translated by NAT
- *Outside address*: The address of the destination device

NAT also uses the concept of local or global with respect to addresses:

- *Local address*: Any address that appears on the inside portion of the network
- *Global address*: Any address that appears on the outside portion of the network

The terms *inside* and *outside* are combined with the terms *local* and *global* to refer to specific addresses. The NAT router R2 in Figure 6-4 is the demarcation point between the inside and outside networks. R2 is configured with a pool of public addresses to assign to inside hosts. Refer to the network and NAT table in the figure for the following discussion of each of the NAT address types.

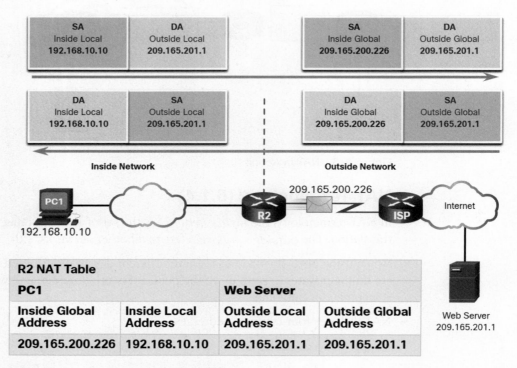

Figure 6-4 Topology for NAT Terminology

Inside Local

The inside local address is the address of the source as seen from inside the network. This is typically a private IPv4 address. In Figure 6-4, the IPv4 address 192.168.10.10 is assigned to PC1. This is the inside local address of PC1.

Inside Global

The inside global address is the address of the source as seen from the outside network. This is typically a globally routable IPv4 address. In Figure 6-4, when traffic from PC1 is sent to the web server at 209.165.201.1, R2 translates the inside local address to an inside global address. In this case, R2 changes the IPv4 source address from 192.168.10.10 to 209.165.200.226. In NAT terminology, the inside local address 192.168.10.10 is translated to the inside global address 209.165.200.226.

Outside Global

The outside global address is the address of the destination as seen from the outside network. It is a globally routable IPv4 address assigned to a host on the internet. For example, the web server is reachable at IPv4 address 209.165.201.1. Most often the outside local and outside global addresses are the same.

Outside Local

The outside local address is the address of the destination as seen from the inside network. In the example in Figure 6-4, PC1 sends traffic to the web server at the IPv4 address 209.165.201.1. While uncommon, this address could be different from the globally routable address of the destination.

PC1 has inside local address 192.168.10.10. From the perspective of PC1, the web server has outside address 209.165.201.1. When packets are sent from PC1 to the global address of the web server, the inside local address of PC1 is translated to 209.165.200.226 (inside global address). The address of the outside device is not typically translated because that address is usually a public IPv4 address.

Notice that PC1 has different local and global addresses, whereas the web server has the same public IPv4 address for both. From the perspective of the web server, traffic originating from PC1 appears to have come from 209.165.200.226, the inside global address.

Interactive Graphic

Check Your Understanding—NAT Characteristics (6.1.5)

Refer to the online course to complete this activity.

Types of NAT (6.2)

In this section, you will learn about the operation of different types of NAT.

Static NAT (6.2.1)

Now that you have learned about NAT and how it works, this section discusses the many versions of NAT that are available to you.

Static NAT uses a one-to-one mapping of local and global addresses. These mappings are configured by the network administrator and remain constant.

In Figure 6-5, R2 is configured with static mappings for the inside local addresses of Svr1, PC2, and PC3. When these devices send traffic to the internet, their inside local addresses are translated to the configured inside global addresses. To outside networks, these devices appear to have public IPv4 addresses.

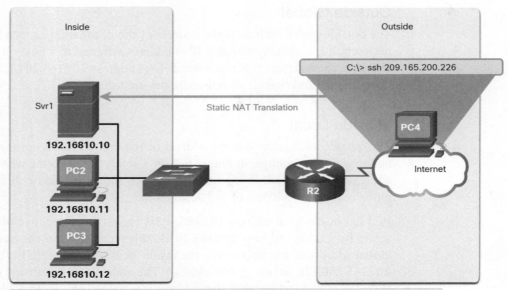

Figure 6-5   Static NAT Translation Scenario

Static NAT Table	
Inside Local Address	**Inside Global Address – Addresses reachable via R2**
192.168.10.10	209.165.200.226
192.168.10.11	209.165.200.227
192.168.10.12	209.165.200.228

Static NAT is particularly useful for web servers or devices that must have a consistent address that is accessible from the internet, such as a company web server. It is also useful for devices that must be accessible by authorized personnel when offsite but not by the general public on the internet. For example, a network administrator from PC4 can use SSH to gain access to the inside global address of Svr1 (209.165.200.226). R2 translates this inside global address to the inside local address 192.168.10.10 and connects the session to Svr1.

Static NAT requires that enough public addresses be available to satisfy the total number of simultaneous user sessions.

Dynamic NAT (6.2.2)

Dynamic NAT uses a pool of public addresses and assigns them on a first-come, first-served basis. When an inside device requests access to an outside network, dynamic NAT assigns an available public IPv4 address from the pool.

In Figure 6-6, PC3 has accessed the internet using the first available address in the dynamic NAT pool. The other addresses are still available for use. Like static NAT, dynamic NAT requires that enough public addresses be available to satisfy the total number of simultaneous user sessions.

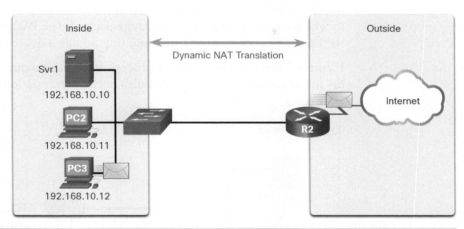

IPv4 NAT Pool

Inside Local Address	Inside Global Address Pool – Addresses reachable via R2
192.168.10.12	209.165.200.226
Available	209.165.200.227
Available	209.165.200.228
Available	209.165.200.229
Available	209.165.200.230

Figure 6-6   Dynamic NAT Translation Scenario

Port Address Translation (6.2.3)

Port Address Translation (PAT), also known as *NAT overload*, maps multiple private IPv4 addresses to a single public IPv4 address or a few addresses. This is what most home routers do. The ISP assigns one address to the router, yet several members of the household can simultaneously access the internet. This is the most common form of NAT for both the home and the enterprise.

With PAT, multiple addresses can be mapped to one address or to a few addresses because each private address is also tracked by a port number. When a device initiates a TCP/IP session, it generates a TCP or UDP source port value or a specially assigned query ID for ICMP to uniquely identify the session. When the NAT router receives a packet from the client, it uses its source port number to uniquely identify the specific NAT translation.

PAT ensures that devices use a different TCP port number for each session with a server on the internet. When a response comes back from the server, the source port number, which becomes the destination port number on the return trip, determines to which device the router forwards the packets. The PAT process also validates that the incoming packets were requested, thus adding a degree of security to the session.

Figure 6-7 demonstrates the PAT process. PAT adds unique source port numbers to the inside global address to distinguish between translations.

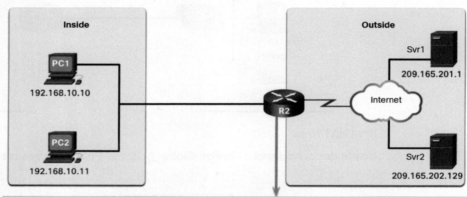

NAT Table with Overload

Inside Local IP Address	Inside Global IP Address	Outside Local IP Address	Outside Global IP Address
192.168.10.10:1555	209.165.200.226:1555	209.165.201.1:80	209.165.201.1:80
192.168.10.11:1331	209.165.200.226:1331	209.165.202.129:80	209.165.202.129:80

Figure 6-7 PAT Scenario

As R2 processes each packet, it uses a port number (such as 1331 and 1555 in this example) to identify the device from which the packet originated. The source address (SA) is the inside local address with the TCP/UDP assigned port number added. The destination address (DA) is the outside global address with the service port number added. In this example, the service port is 80, which is HTTP.

For the source address, R2 translates the inside local address to an inside global address with the port number added. The destination address is not changed but is now referred to as the outside global IPv4 address. When the web server replies, the path is reversed.

Next Available Port (6.2.4)

In the previous example, the client port numbers, 1331 and 1555, did not change at the NAT-enabled router. This is not a very likely scenario because there is a good chance that these port numbers may have already been attached to other active sessions.

PAT attempts to preserve the original source port. However, if the original source port is already used, PAT assigns the first available port number starting from the beginning of the appropriate port group 0 through 511, 512 through 1023, or 1024 through 65,535. When there are no more ports available and there is more than one external address in the address pool, PAT moves to the next address to try to allocate the original source port. This process continues until there are no more available ports or external IPv4 addresses.

In Figure 6-8, PAT has assigned the next available port (1445) to the second host address.

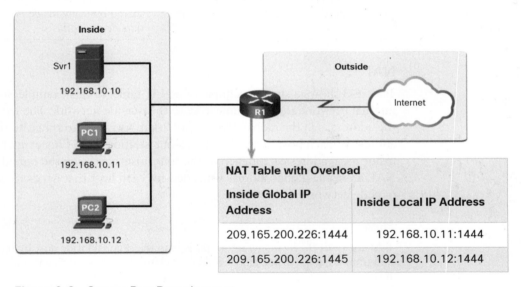

NAT Table with Overload

Inside Global IP Address	Inside Local IP Address
209.165.200.226:1444	192.168.10.11:1444
209.165.200.226:1445	192.168.10.12:1444

Figure 6-8   Source Port Reassignment

In the figure, the hosts have chosen the same port number, 1444. This is acceptable for the inside address because the hosts have unique private IPv4 addresses. However, at the NAT router, the port numbers must be changed; otherwise, packets from two different hosts would exit R2 with the same source address. This example assumes that the first 420 ports in the range 1024–65,535 are already in use, so the next available port number, 1445, is used.

When packets are returned from outside the network, if the source port number was previously modified by the NAT-enabled router, the destination port number is now changed back to the original port number by the NAT-enabled router.

NAT and PAT Comparison (6.2.5)

Table 6-2 provides a summary of the differences between NAT and PAT.

Table 6-2 NAT and PAT

NAT	PAT
One-to-one mapping between inside local and inside global addresses.	One inside global address can be mapped to many inside local addresses.
Uses only IPv4 addresses in the translation process.	Uses IPv4 addresses and TCP or UDP source port numbers in the translation process.
A unique inside global address is required for each inside host accessing the outside network.	A single unique inside global address can be shared by many inside hosts accessing the outside network.

NAT

Table 6-3 shows a simple example of a NAT table. In this example, four hosts on the internal network are communicating to the outside network. The left column lists the addresses in the global address pool that NAT uses to translate the inside local address of each host. Note the one-to-one relationship of inside global addresses to inside local addresses for each of the four hosts accessing the outside network. With NAT, an inside global address is needed for each host that needs to connect to the outside network.

Note

NAT forwards the incoming return packets to the original inside host by referring to the table and translating the inside global address back to the corresponding inside local address of the host.

Table 6-3 NAT Table

Inside Global Address	Inside Local Address
209.165.200.226	192.168.10.10
209.165.200.227	192.168.10.11
209.165.200.228	192.168.10.12
209.165.200.229	192.168.10.13

PAT

Whereas NAT only modifies the IPv4 addresses, PAT modifies both the IPv4 address and the port number. With PAT, there is generally only one or very few publicly exposed IPv4 addresses. The NAT table in Table 6-4 shows one inside global address being used to translate the inside local addresses of the four inside hosts. PAT uses the Layer 4 port number to track the conversations of the four hosts.

Table 6-4 NAT Table with PAT

Inside Global Address	Inside Local Address
209.165.200.226:2031	192.168.10.10:2031
209.165.200.226:1506	192.168.10.11:1506
209.165.200.226:1131	192.168.10.12:1131
209.165.200.226:1718	192.168.10.13:1718

Packets Without a Layer 4 Segment (6.2.6)

What about IPv4 packets carrying data other than a TCP or UDP segment? These packets do not contain a Layer 4 port number. PAT translates most common protocols carried by IPv4 that do not use TCP or UDP as transport layer protocols. The most common of these is ICMPv4. Each of these types of protocols is handled differently by PAT. For example, ICMPv4 query messages, echo requests, and echo replies include a Query ID field. ICMPv4 uses the Query ID field to identify an echo request with its corresponding echo reply. The Query ID field is incremented with each echo request sent. PAT uses the Query ID field instead of a Layer 4 port number.

> **Note**
>
> Other ICMPv4 messages do not use the Query ID field. These messages and other protocols that do not use TCP or UDP port numbers vary and are beyond the scope of this chapter.

Packet Tracer—Investigate NAT Operations (6.2.7)

You know that as a frame travels across a network, the MAC addresses change. But IPv4 addresses can also change when a packet is forwarded by a device configured with NAT. In this activity, you will see what happens to IPv4 addresses during the NAT process.

In this Packet Tracer activity, you will

- Investigate NAT operation across the intranet
- Investigate NAT operation across the internet
- Conduct further investigations

NAT Advantages and Disadvantages (6.3)

NAT solves the problem of not having enough IPv4 addresses, but it can also create other problems. This section addresses the advantages and disadvantage of NAT.

Advantages of NAT (6.3.1)

NAT provides many benefits, including the following:

- NAT conserves the legally registered addressing scheme by allowing the privatization of intranets. NAT conserves addresses through application port-level multiplexing. With NAT overload (PAT), internal hosts can share a single public IPv4 address for all external communications. In this type of configuration, very few external addresses are required to support many internal hosts.

- NAT increases the flexibility of connections to the public network. Multiple pools, backup pools, and load-balancing pools can be implemented to ensure reliable public network connections.

- NAT provides consistency for internal network addressing schemes. On a network not using private IPv4 addresses and NAT, changing the public IPv4 address scheme requires the readdressing of all hosts on the existing network. The costs of readdressing hosts can be significant. NAT allows the existing private IPv4 address scheme to remain while allowing for easy change to a new public addressing scheme. This means an organization could change ISPs and not need to change any of its inside clients.

- Using RFC 1918 IPv4 addresses, NAT hides the IPv4 addresses of users and other devices. Some people consider this a security feature; however, most experts agree that NAT does not provide security. A stateful firewall provides security on the edge of the network.

Disadvantages of NAT (6.3.2)

NAT does have drawbacks. The fact that hosts on the internet appear to communicate directly with the NAT-enabled device, rather than with the actual host inside the private network, creates a number of issues.

One disadvantage of using NAT is related to network performance, particularly for real-time protocols such as VoIP. NAT increases forwarding delays because the translation of each IPv4 address within the packet headers takes time. The first packet is always process switched, going through the slower path. The router must look at every packet to decide whether it needs translation. The router must alter the IPv4 header, and it may also alter the TCP or UDP header. The IPv4 header checksum, along with the TCP or UDP checksum, must be recalculated each time a translation is made. Remaining packets go through the fast-switched path if a cache entry exists; otherwise, they too are delayed.

The forwarding delays caused by the NAT process become more of an issue as the pools of public IPv4 addresses for ISPs become depleted. Many ISPs are having to assign customers private IPv4 addresses instead of public IPv4 addresses. Such a customer's router translates a packet from its private IPv4 address to the private IPv4 address of the ISP. Before forwarding the packet to another provider, the ISP performs NAT again, translating a private IPv4 address to one of its limited number of public IPv4 addresses. This process of two layers of NAT translation is known as carrier-grade NAT (CGN).

Another disadvantage of using NAT is that end-to-end addressing is lost. This is known as the end-to-end principle. Many internet protocols and applications depend on end-to-end addressing from the source to the destination. Some applications do not work with NAT. For example, some security applications, such as digital signatures, fail because the source IPv4 address changes before reaching the destination. Applications that use physical addresses instead of a qualified domain name do not reach destinations that are translated across the NAT router. Sometimes this problem can be avoided by implementing static NAT mappings.

Another disadvantage of using NAT is that end-to-end IPv4 traceability is also lost. It becomes much more difficult to trace packets that undergo numerous packet address changes over multiple NAT hops, making troubleshooting challenging.

Using NAT also complicates the use of tunneling protocols, such as IPsec, because NAT modifies values in the headers, causing integrity checks to fail.

Services that require the initiation of TCP connections from the outside network, or stateless protocols, such as those using UDP, can be disrupted. Unless a NAT router has been configured to support such protocols, incoming packets cannot reach their destination. Some protocols can accommodate one instance of NAT between participating hosts (passive mode FTP, for example) but fail when both systems are separated from the internet by NAT.

Interactive Graphic

Check Your Understanding—NAT Advantages and Disadvantages (6.3.3)

Refer to the online course to complete this activity.

Static NAT (6.4)

In this section, you will learn how to configure and verify static NAT. It includes a Packet Tracer activity to test your skills and knowledge. Static NAT is a one-to-one mapping between an inside address and an outside address. Static NAT allows external devices to initiate connections to internal devices using statically assigned public addresses. For instance, an internal web server may be mapped to a specific inside global address so that it is accessible from outside networks.

Static NAT Scenario (6.4.1)

Figure 6-9 shows an inside network containing a web server with a private IPv4 address. Router R2 is configured with static NAT to allow devices on the outside network (internet) to access the web server. The client on the outside network accesses the web server using a public IPv4 address. Static NAT translates the public IPv4 address to the private IPv4 address.

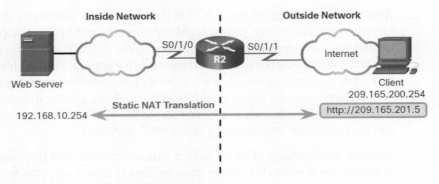

Figure 6-9 Static NAT Topology

Configure Static NAT (6.4.2)

There are two basic steps when configuring static NAT translations:

Step 1.   The first task is to create a mapping between the inside local address and the inside global addresses. In Example 6-1, the 192.168.10.254 inside local address and the 209.165.201.5 inside global address in Figure 6-9 are configured as a static NAT translation.

Example 6-1 Static NAT Configuration

```
R2(config)# ip nat inside source static 192.168.10.254 209.165.201.5
R2(config)#
```

Step 2.   After the mapping is configured, the interfaces participating in the translation are configured as inside or outside relative to NAT. In Example 6-2, the R2 Serial 0/1/0 interface is an inside interface, and Serial 0/1/1 is an outside interface.

Example 6-2   Configuring Inside and Outside NAT Interfaces

```
R2(config)# interface serial 0/1/0
R2(config-if)# ip address 192.168.1.2 255.255.255.252
R2(config-if)# ip nat inside
R2(config-if)# exit
R2(config)# interface serial 0/1/1
R2(config-if)# ip address 209.165.200.1 255.255.255.252
R2(config-if)# ip nat outside
R2(config-if)#
```

With this configuration in place, packets arriving on the inside interface of R2 (Serial 0/1/0) from the configured inside local IPv4 address (192.168.10.254) are translated and then forwarded toward the outside network. Packets arriving on the outside interface of R2 (Serial 0/1/1) that are addressed to the configured inside global IPv4 address (209.165.201.5) are translated to the inside local address (192.168.10.254) and then forwarded to the inside network.

Analyze Static NAT (6.4.3)

Using the previous configuration, Figure 6-10 illustrates the static NAT translation process between the client and the web server. Usually static translations are used when clients on the outside network (internet) need to reach servers on the inside (internal) network. The following steps are illustrated in Figure 6-10:

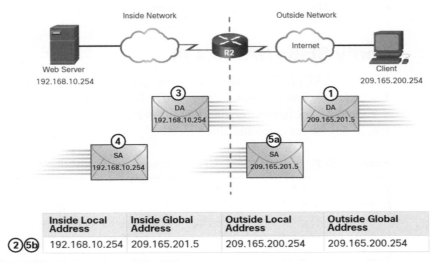

	Inside Local Address	Inside Global Address	Outside Local Address	Outside Global Address
②⑤b	192.168.10.254	209.165.201.5	209.165.200.254	209.165.200.254

Figure 6-10   Static NAT Process

Step 1. The client wants to open a connection to the web server. The client sends a packet to the web server using the public IPv4 destination address 209.165.201.5. This is the inside global address of the web server.

Step 2. The first packet that R2 receives from the client on its NAT outside interface causes R2 to check its NAT table. The destination IPv4 address 209.165.201.5 is located in the NAT table and is translated to 192.168.10.254.

Step 3. R2 replaces the inside global address 209.165.201.5 with the inside local address 192.168.10.254. R2 then forwards the packet toward the web server.

Step 4. The web server receives the packet and responds to the client using the inside local address 192.168.10.254 as the source address of the response packet.

Step 5. **a.** R2 receives the packet from the web server on its NAT inside interface with the source address of the inside local address of the web server, 192.168.10.254.

   b. R2 checks the NAT table for a translation for the inside local address. The address is found in the NAT table. R2 translates the source address 192.168.10.254 to the inside global address 209.165.201.5 and forwards the packet toward the client.

Step 6. (Not shown) The client receives the packet and continues the conversation. The NAT router performs steps 2 to 5b for each packet.

Verify Static NAT (6.4.4)

To verify NAT operation, issue the **show ip nat translations** command, as shown in Example 6-3. This command shows active NAT translations. Because the example is a static NAT configuration, the translation is always present in the NAT table, regardless of any active communications.

Example 6-3 Static NAT Translations: Always in the NAT Table

```
R2# show ip nat translations
Pro  Inside global      Inside local      Outside local      Outside global
---  209.165.201.5      192.168.10.254    ---                ---
Total number of translations: 1
R2#
```

If the command is issued during an active session, the output also indicates the address of the outside device, as shown in Example 6-4.

Example 6-4 Static NAT Translation During an Active Session

```
R2# show ip nat translations
Pro  Inside global      Inside local      Outside local      Outside
  global
tcp  209.165.201.5      192.168.10.254    209.165.200.254
  209.165.200.254
---  209.165.201.5      192.168.10.254    ---                ---
Total number of translations: 2
R2#
```

Another useful command is **show ip nat statistics**, which displays information about the total number of active translations, the NAT configuration parameters, the number of addresses in the pool, and the number of addresses that have been allocated, as shown in Example 6-5.

To verify that NAT translation is working, it is best to clear statistics from any past translations by using the **clear ip nat statistics** command before testing.

Example 6-5 NAT Statistics Before an Active Session Is Established

```
R2# show ip nat statistics
Total active translations: 1 (1 static, 0 dynamic; 0 extended)
Outside interfaces:
  Serial0/1/1
Inside interfaces:
  Serial0/1/0
Hits: 0  Misses: 0
(output omitted)
R2#
```

After the client establishes a session with the web server, the **show ip nat statistics** command displays an increase to 4 hits on the inside (Serial0/1/0) interface, as shown in Example 6-6. This verifies that the static NAT translation is taking place on R2.

Example 6-6 NAT Statistics After an Active Session Is Established

```
R2# show ip nat statistics
Total active translations: 1 (1 static, 0 dynamic; 0 extended)
Outside interfaces:
  Serial0/1/1
Inside interfaces:
  Serial0/1/0
Hits: 4  Misses: 1
(output omitted)
R2#
```

Packet Tracer—Configure Static NAT (6.4.5)

In IPv4 configured networks, clients and servers use private addressing. Before packets with private addressing can cross the internet, they need to be translated to public addressing. A server that is accessed from outside the organization is usually assigned both a public IPv4 address and a private static IPv4 address. In this activity, you will configure static NAT so that outside devices can access an inside server at its public address.

In this Packet Tracer activity, you will

- Test access without NAT
- Configure static NAT

Dynamic NAT (6.5)

In this section, you will learn how to configure and verify dynamic NAT. It includes a Packet Tracer activity to test your skills and knowledge. Whereas static NAT provides a permanent mapping between an inside local address and an inside global address, dynamic NAT automatically maps inside local addresses to inside global addresses. These inside global addresses are typically public IPv4 addresses. Dynamic NAT, like static NAT, requires the configuration of the inside and outside interfaces participating in NAT with the **ip nat inside** and **ip nat outside** interface configuration commands. However, whereas static NAT creates a permanent mapping to a single address, dynamic NAT uses a pool of addresses.

Dynamic NAT Scenario (6.5.1)

The sample topology shown in Figure 6-11 has an inside network using addresses from the RFC 1918 private address space. Attached to router R1 are two LANs, 192.168.10.0/24 and 192.168.11.0/24. Router R2, the border router, is configured for dynamic NAT, using the pool of public IPv4 addresses 209.165.200.226 through 209.165.200.240.

The pool of public IPv4 addresses (that is, the inside global address pool) is available to any device on the inside network on a first-come, first-served basis. With dynamic NAT, a single inside address is translated to a single outside address. With this type of translation, there must be enough addresses in the pool to accommodate all the inside devices needing concurrent access to the outside network. If all addresses in the pool are in use, a device must wait for an available address before it can access the outside network.

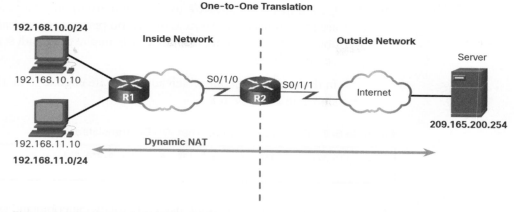

Figure 6-11 Dynamic NAT Topology

> **Note**
>
> Translating between public and private IPv4 addresses is by far the most common use of NAT. However, NAT translations can occur between pairs of IPv4 addresses.

Configure Dynamic NAT (6.5.2)

Figure 6-11 shows a sample topology where the NAT configuration allows translation for all hosts on the 192.168.0.0/16 network. This includes the 192.168.10.0 and 192.168.11.0 LANs when the hosts generate traffic that enters interface S0/1/0 and exits S0/1/1. The host inside local addresses are translated to an available pool address in the range 209.165.200.226 to 209.165.200.240.

Step 1.   Define the pool of addresses that will be used for translation using the **ip nat pool** global configuration command. This pool of addresses is typically a group of public addresses. The addresses are defined by indicating the starting IPv4 address and the ending IPv4 address of the pool. The **netmask** or **prefix-length** keyword indicates which address bits belong to the network and which bits belong to the host for that range of addresses.

In this scenario, define a pool of public IPv4 addresses under the pool name NAT-POOL1, as shown in Example 6-7.

Example 6-7   Configuring a NAT Pool

```
R2(config)# ip nat pool NAT-POOL1 209.165.200.226 209.165.200.240 netmask
  255.255.255.224
R2(config)#
```

Step 2.   Configure a standard ACL to identify (permit) only those addresses that are to be translated. An ACL that is too permissive can lead to unpredictable results. Remember that there is an implicit **deny all** statement at the end of each ACL.

In this scenario, define which addresses are eligible to be translated, as shown in Example 6-8.

Example 6-8   Defining the Traffic That Will Be Translated

```
R2(config)# access-list 1 permit 192.168.0.0 0.0.255.255
R2(config)#
```

Step 3.   Bind the ACL to the pool, using the following command syntax:

```
Router(config)# ip nat inside source list {access-list-number |
  access-list-name} pool pool-name
```

The router uses this configuration to identify which devices (**list**) receive which addresses (**pool**). In the scenario, bind NAT-POOL1 with ACL 1, as shown in Example 6-9.

Example 6-9   Binding an ACL to a Pool

```
R2(config)# ip nat inside source list 1 pool NAT-POOL1
```

Step 4.   Identify which interfaces are inside, in relation to NAT; these will be any interfaces that connect to the inside network.

In this scenario, identify interface serial 0/1/0 as an inside NAT interface, as shown in Example 6-10.

Example 6-10   Configuring the Inside NAT Interface

```
R2(config)# interface serial 0/1/0
R2(config-if)# ip nat inside
```

Step 5.   Identify which interfaces are outside, in relation to NAT; these will be any interfaces that connect to the outside network.

In this scenario, identify interface serial 0/1/1 as the outside NAT interface, as shown in Example 6-11.

Example 6-11   Configuring the Outside NAT Interface

```
R2(config)# interface serial 0/1/1
R2(config-if)# ip nat outside
```

Analyze Dynamic NAT—Inside to Outside (6.5.3)

Using the previous configuration, Figures 6-12 and 6-13 illustrate the dynamic NAT translation process between two clients and the web server.

Figure 6-12 illustrates the traffic flow from the inside network to the outside network:

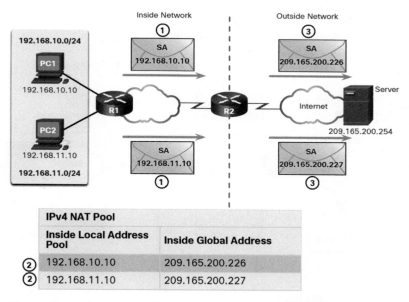

Figure 6-12   Dynamic NAT Process: Inside to Outside

Step 1.   The hosts with the source IPv4 addresses 192.168.10.10 (PC1) and 192.168.11.10 (PC2) send packets requesting a connection to the server at **the public IPv4 address 209.165.200.254.**

Step 2.   R2 receives the first packet from host 192.168.10.10. Because this packet was received on an interface configured as an inside NAT interface, R2 checks the NAT configuration to determine if this packet should be translated. The ACL permits this packet, so R2 translates the packet. R2 checks its NAT table. Because there is no current translation entry for this IPv4 address, R2 determines that the source address 192.168.10.10 must be translated. R2 selects an available global address from the dynamic address pool and creates a translation entry, 209.165.200.226. The original source IPv4 address 192.168.10.10 is the inside local address, and the translated address is the inside global address 209.165.200.226 in the NAT table. For the second host, 192.168.11.10, R2 repeats the procedure, selects the next available global address from the dynamic address pool, and creates a second translation entry, 209.165.200.227.

Step 3.   R2 replaces the inside local source address of PC1, 192.168.10.10, with the translated inside global address of 209.165.200.226 and forwards the packet. The same process occurs for the packet from PC2, using the translated address 209.165.200.227.

Analyze Dynamic NAT—Outside to Inside (6.5.4)

Figure 6-13 illustrates the remainder of the traffic flow between the clients and the server in the outside-to-inside direction:

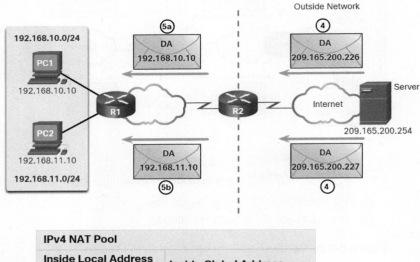

IPv4 NAT Pool	
Inside Local Address Pool	**Inside Global Address**
192.168.10.10	209.165.200.226
192.168.11.10	209.165.200.227

Figure 6-13   Dynamic NAT Process: Outside to Inside

Step 4.   The server receives the packet from PC1 and responds using the IPv4 destination address 209.165.200.226. When the server receives the second packet, it responds to PC2 using the IPv4 destination address 209.165.200.227.

Step 5.   a.   When R2 receives the packet with the destination IPv4 address 209.165.200.226, it performs a NAT table lookup. Using the mapping from the table, R2 translates the address back to the inside local address 192.168.10.10 and forwards the packet toward PC1.

   b.   When R2 receives the packet with the destination IPv4 address 209.165.200.227, it performs a NAT table lookup. Using the mapping from the table, R2 translates the address back to the inside local address 192.168.11.10 and forwards the packet toward PC2.

Step 6.   PC1 at 192.168.10.10 and PC2 at 192.168.11.10 receive the packets and continue the conversation. The router performs steps 2 to 5 for each packet. (Step 6 is not shown in the figures.)

Verify Dynamic NAT (6.5.5)

The output of the **show ip nat translations** command in Example 6-12 displays all static translations that have been configured and any dynamic translations that have been created by traffic.

Example 6-12   Verifying NAT Translations

```
R2# show ip nat translations
Pro Inside global      Inside local      Outside local      Outside global
--- 209.165.200.228    192.168.10.10     ---                ---
--- 209.165.200.229    192.168.11.10     ---                ---
R2#
```

Adding the **verbose** keyword displays additional information about each translation, including how long ago the entry was created and used, as shown in Example 6-13.

Example 6-13   Verifying Verbose NAT Translations

```
R2# show ip nat translation verbose
Pro Inside global      Inside local      Outside local      Outside global
tcp 209.165.200.228    192.168.10.10     ---                ---
    create 00:02:11, use 00:02:11 timeout:86400000, left 23:57:48, Map-Id(In): 1,
    flags:
none, use_count: 0, entry-id: 10, lc_entries: 0
tcp 209.165.200.229    192.168.11.10     ---                ---
    create 00:02:10, use 00:02:10 timeout:86400000, left 23:57:49, Map-Id(In): 1,
    flags:
none, use_count: 0, entry-id: 12, lc_entries: 0
R2#
```

By default, translation entries time out after 24 hours unless the timers have been reconfigured with the **ip nat translation timeout** *timeout-seconds* global configuration mode command.

To clear dynamic entries before the timeout has expired, use the **clear ip nat translation** privileged EXEC mode command, as shown in Example 6-14.

Example 6-14   Clearing NAT Translations

```
R2# clear ip nat translation *
R2# show ip nat translation
R2#
```

It is useful to clear the dynamic entries when testing NAT configuration. The **clear ip nat translation** command can be used with keywords and variables to control which entries are cleared, as shown in Table 6-5. Specific entries can be cleared to avoid disrupting active sessions. Use the **clear ip nat translation** * privileged EXEC command to clear all translations from the table.

Table 6-5   The **clear ip nat translation** Command

Command	Description
clear ip nat translation *	Clears all dynamic address translation entries from the NAT translation table.
clear ip nat translation inside *global-ip local-ip* [outside *local-ip global-ip*]	Clears a simple dynamic translation entry containing an inside translation or both inside and outside translation.
clear ip nat translation *protocol* inside *global-ip global-port local-ip local-port* [outside *local-ip local-port global-ip global-port*]	Clears an extended dynamic translation entry.

Note

Only the dynamic translations are cleared from the table. Static translations cannot be cleared from the translation table.

Another useful command, **show ip nat statistics**, displays information about the total number of active translations, the NAT configuration parameters, the number of addresses in the pool, and how many of the addresses have been allocated, as shown in Example 6-15.

Example 6-15   Verifying NAT Statistics

```
R2# show ip nat statistics
Total active translations: 4 (0 static, 4 dynamic; 0 extended)
Peak translations: 4, occurred 00:31:43 ago
Outside interfaces:
  Serial0/1/1
Inside interfaces:
  Serial0/1/0
Hits: 47  Misses: 0
```

```
CEF Translated packets: 47, CEF Punted packets: 0
Expired translations: 5
Dynamic mappings:
-- Inside Source
[Id: 1] access-list 1 pool NAT-POOL1 refcount 4
  pool NAT-POOL1: netmask 255.255.255.224
        start 209.165.200.226 end 209.165.200.240
        type generic, total addresses 15, allocated 2 (13%), misses 0
(output omitted)
R2#
```

Alternatively, you can use the **show running-config** command and look for NAT, ACL, interface, or pool commands with the required values. Examine these carefully and correct any errors discovered. Example 6-16 shows the NAT pool configuration.

Example 6-16   Verifying the NAT Configuration

```
R2# show running-config | include NAT
ip nat pool NAT-POOL1 209.165.200.226 209.165.200.240 netmask 255.255.255.224
ip nat inside source list 1 pool NAT-POOL1
R2#
```

> Packet Tracer
> ☐ Activity

Packet Tracer—Configure Dynamic NAT (6.5.6)

In this Packet Tracer, you will complete the following objectives:

- Configure dynamic NAT
- Verify NAT implementation

PAT (6.6)

In this section, you will learn how to configure and verify PAT. It includes a Packet Tracer activity to test your skills and knowledge.

PAT Scenario (6.6.1)

There are two ways to configure PAT, depending on how the ISP allocates public IPv4 addresses. First, the ISP can allocate a single public IPv4 address that is required for the organization to connect to the ISP; alternatively, the ISP can allocate more than one public IPv4 address to the organization. Both methods are demonstrated using the scenario shown in Figure 6-14.

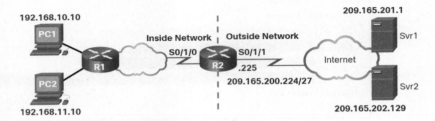

NAT Table

Inside Local Address	Inside Global Address	Outside Global Address	Outside Local Address
192.168.10.10:1444	209.165.200.225:1444	209.165.201.1:80	209.165.201.1:80
192.168.11.10:1444	209.165.200.225:1445	209.165.202.129:80	209.165.202.129:80

Figure 6-14   PAT Topology

Configure PAT to Use a Single IPv4 Address (6.6.2)

To configure PAT to use a single IPv4 address, simply add the keyword **overload** to the **ip nat inside source** global configuration command. The rest of the configuration is similar to the configuration for static and dynamic NAT except that with PAT, multiple hosts can use the same public IPv4 address to access the internet.

In Example 6-17, all hosts from network 192.168.0.0/16 (matching ACL 1) that send traffic through router R2 to the internet are translated to IPv4 address 209.165.200.225 (which is the IPv4 address of interface S0/1/1). The traffic flows are identified by port numbers in the NAT table because the **overload** keyword is configured.

Example 6-17   PAT Configuration to Overload an Interface

```
R2(config)# ip nat inside source list 1 interface serial 0/1/0 overload
R2(config)# access-list 1 permit 192.168.0.0 0.0.255.255
R2(config)#
R2(config)# interface serial0/1/0
R2(config-if)# ip nat inside
R2(config-if)# exit
R2(config)#
R2(config)# interface Serial0/1/1
R2(config-if)# ip nat outside
R2(config-if)# exit
R2(config)#
```

Configure PAT to Use an Address Pool (6.6.3)

An ISP may allocate more than one public IPv4 address to an organization. In such a case, the organization can configure PAT to use a pool of IPv4 public addresses for translation.

If a site has been issued more than one public IPv4 address, these addresses can be part of a pool that is used by PAT. The small pool of addresses is shared among a larger number of devices, with multiple hosts using the same public IPv4 address to access the internet. To configure PAT for a dynamic NAT address pool, simply add the keyword **overload** to the **ip nat inside source** global configuration command.

The same topology from the preceding example is used for this scenario and repeated in Figure 6-15 for your convenience.

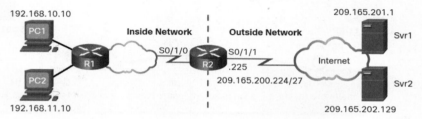

Figure 6-15   PAT with a Single Address Topology

In Example 6-18, NAT-POOL2 is bound to an ACL to permit 192.168.0.0/16 to be translated. These hosts can share an IPv4 address from the pool because PAT is enabled with the keyword **overload**.

Example 6-18   PAT Configuration to Overload a NAT Pool

```
R2(config)# ip nat pool NAT-POOL2 209.165.200.226 209.165.200.240 netmask
  255.255.255.224
R2(config)# access-list 1 permit 192.168.0.0 0.0.255.255
R2(config)# ip nat inside source list 1 pool NAT-POOL2 overload
R2(config)#
R2(config)# interface serial0/1/0
R2(config-if)# ip nat inside
R2(config-if)# exit
R2(config)#
R2(config)# interface serial0/1/0
R2(config-if)# ip nat outside
R2(config-if)# end
R2#
```

Analyze PAT—PC to Server (6.6.4)

The process of NAT overload is the same whether a single address or a pool of addresses is used. In Figure 6-16, PAT is configured to use a single public IPv4 address instead of a pool of addresses. PC1 wants to communicate with the web server Svr1. At the same time, another client, PC2, wants to establish a similar session with the web server Svr2. Both PC1 and PC2 are configured with private IPv4 addresses and with R2 enabled for PAT.

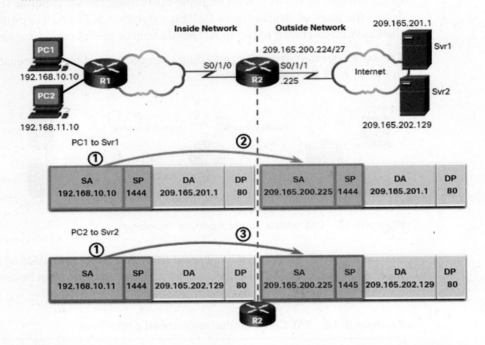

NAT Table

Inside Local Address	Inside Global Address	Outside Global Address	Outside Local Address
192.168.10.10:1444	209.165.200.225:1444	209.165.201.1:80	209.165.201.1:80
192.168.10.10:1444	209.165.200.225:1445	209.165.201.129:80	209.165.201.129:80

Figure 6-16   PAT Process: PCs to Servers

The following steps are illustrated in Figure 6-16:

Step 1.   PC1 is sending packets to Svr1, and PC2 is sending packets to Svr2. PC1 has the source IPv4 address 192.168.10.10 and is using TCP source port 1444. PC2 has the source IPv4 address 192.168.11.10 and coincidentally uses the same TCP source port, 1444.

Step 2.   The packet from PC1 reaches R2 first. Using PAT, R2 modifies the source IPv4 address to 209.165.200.225 (inside global address). There are no other devices in the NAT table using port 1444, so PAT maintains the same port number. The packet is then forwarded toward Svr1 at 209.165.201.1.

Step 3.   The packet from PC2 arrives at R2. PAT is configured to use a single inside global IPv4 address, 209.165.200.225, for all translations. Much as in the translation process for PC1, PAT changes the source IPv4 address of PC2 to the inside global address 209.165.200.225. However, PC2 has the same source port number as a current PAT entry, the translation for PC1. PAT increments the source port number until it is a unique value in its table. In this instance, the source port entry in the NAT table and the packet for PC2 receives 1445.

Analyze PAT—Server to PC (6.6.5)

Although PC1 and PC2 are using the same translated address, the inside global address 209.165.200.225, and the same source port number 1444, the modified port number for PC2 (1445) makes each entry in the NAT table unique. This becomes evident with the packets sent from the servers back to the clients, as shown in Figure 6-17.

The following steps from the servers to the PCs are illustrated in Figure 6-17:

Step 4.   The servers use the source port from the received packet as the destination port and the source address as the destination address for the return traffic. The servers seem as if they are communicating with the same host at 209.165.200.225; however, this is not the case.

Step 5.   As the packets arrive, R2 locates the unique entry in its NAT table, using the destination address and the destination port of each packet. In the case of the packet from Svr1, the destination IPv4 address 209.165.200.225 has multiple entries but only one with the destination port 1444. Using the entry in its table, R2 changes the destination IPv4 address of the packet to 192.168.10.10, with no change required for the destination port. The packet is then forwarded toward PC1.

Step 6.   When the packet from Svr2 arrives, R2 performs a similar translation. The destination IPv4 address 209.165.200.225 is located, again with multiple entries. However, using the destination port 1445, R2 is able to uniquely identify the translation entry. The destination IPv4 address is changed to 192.168.10.11. In this case, the destination port must also be modified back to its original value of 1444, which is stored in the NAT table. The packet is then forwarded toward PC2.

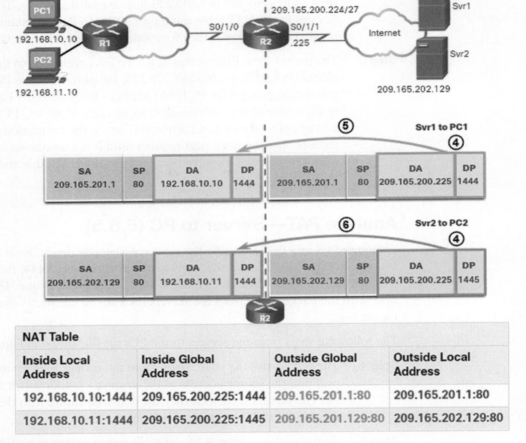

Figure 6-17   PAT Process: Servers to PCs

Verify PAT (6.6.6)

Router R2 has been configured to provide PAT to the 192.168.0.0/16 clients. When an internal host sends communication through router R2 to the internet, its address is translated to an IPv4 address from the PAT pool with a unique source port number.

The same commands used to verify static and dynamic NAT are used to verify PAT, as shown in Example 6-19. The **show ip nat translations** command displays the translations from two different hosts to different web servers. Notice that two different inside hosts are allocated the same IPv4 address, 209.165.200.226 (inside global address). The source port numbers in the NAT table differentiate the two transactions.

Example 6-19   Verifying NAT Translations

```
R2# show ip nat translations
Pro Inside global       Inside local     Outside local      Outside global
tcp 209.165.200.225:1444 192.168.10.10:1444 209.165.201.1:80   209.165.201.1:80
tcp 209.165.200.225:1445 192.168.11.10:1444 209.165.202.129:80 209.165.202.129:80
R2#
```

In Example 6-20, the **show ip nat statistics** command verifies that NAT-POOL2 has allocated a single address for both translations. The output includes information about the number and type of active translations, the NAT configuration parameters, the number of addresses in the pool, and how many have been allocated.

Example 6-20   Verifying NAT Statistics

```
R2# show ip nat statistics
Total active translations: 4 (0 static, 2 dynamic; 2 extended)
Peak translations: 2, occurred 00:31:43 ago
Outside interfaces:
  Serial0/1/1
Inside interfaces:
  Serial0/1/0
Hits: 4  Misses: 0
CEF Translated packets: 47, CEF Punted packets: 0
Expired translations: 0
Dynamic mappings:
-- Inside Source
[Id: 3] access-list 1 pool NAT-POOL2 refcount 2
 pool NAT-POOL2: netmask 255.255.255.224
        start 209.165.200.225 end 209.165.200.240
        type generic, total addresses 15, allocated 1 (6%), misses 0
(output omitted)
R2#
```

Packet Tracer—Configure PAT (6.6.7)

In this Packet Tracer activity, you will complete the following objectives:

- Part 1: Configure dynamic NAT with overload
- Part 2: Verify dynamic NAT with overload implementation
- Part 3: Configure PAT using an interface
- Part 4: Verify PAT interface implementation

NAT64 (6.7)

In this section, you will learn how NAT is used with IPv6 networks.

NAT for IPv6? (6.7.1)

Because many networks use both IPv4 and IPv6, administrators need to have a way to use IPv6 with NAT. This section discusses how IPv6 can be integrated with NAT.

IPv6, with a 128-bit address, provides 340 undecillion addresses. Therefore, address space is not an issue with IPv6 as it is with IPv4. IPv6 was developed with the intention of making NAT for IPv4—with translation between public and private IPv4 addresses—unnecessary. However, IPv6 does include its own IPv6 private address space, referred to as *unique local addresses* (*ULAs*).

IPv6 ULAs are similar to RFC 1918 private addresses in IPv4 but have a different purpose. ULAs are meant for only local communications within a site; they are not meant to provide additional IPv6 address space or to provide security.

IPv6 provides for protocol translation between IPv4 and IPv6 through *NAT64*.

NAT64 (6.7.2)

NAT for IPv6 is used in a much different context than NAT for IPv4. NAT64 is used to transparently provide access between IPv6-only and IPv4-only networks, as shown in Figure 6-18. It is not used as a form of private IPv6-to-global IPv6 translation.

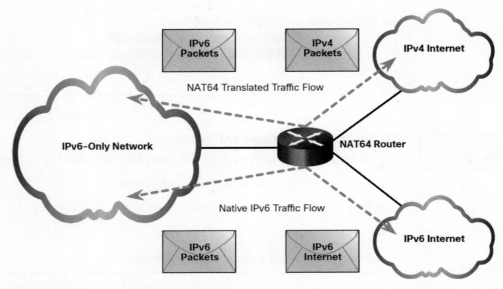

Figure 6-18   IPv6 and IPv4 Networks Translated by a NAT64 Router

Ideally, IPv6 should be run natively wherever possible; that is, IPv6 devices should communicate with each other over IPv6 networks. However, to aid in the move from IPv4 to IPv6, the IETF has developed several transition techniques to accommodate a variety of IPv4-to-IPv6 scenarios, including *dual stack*, tunneling, and translation.

With dual stack, devices run protocols associated with both IPv4 and IPv6. Tunneling for IPv6 is the process of encapsulating an IPv6 packet inside an IPv4 packet. This allows the IPv6 packet to be transmitted over an IPv4-only network.

NAT for IPv6 should not be used as a long-term strategy but as a temporary mechanism to assist in the migration from IPv4 to IPv6. Over the years, there have been several types of NAT for IPv6, including *Network Address Translation–Protocol Translation (NAT-PT)*. However, the IETF has deprecated NAT-PT and favors its replacement, NAT64. NAT64 is beyond the scope of this chapter.

Summary (6.8)

The following is a summary of the sections in this chapter.

NAT Characteristics

The limited number of public IPv4 addresses means there are not enough to assign a unique address to each device connected to the internet. Private IPv4 addresses cannot be routed over the internet. To allow a device with a private IPv4 address to access devices and resources outside the local network, the private address must be translated to a public address. NAT translates between private addresses and public addresses. The primary goal with NAT is to conserve public IPv4 addresses. It allows networks to use private IPv4 addresses internally and provides translation to a public address only when needed. When an internal device sends traffic out the network, the NAT-enabled router translates the internal IPv4 address of the device to a public address from the NAT pool. In NAT terminology, the *inside network* is the set of networks that is subject to translation, and the *outside network* is all other networks. When determining which type of address is used, it is important to remember that NAT terminology is always applied from the perspective of the device with the translated address:

- **Inside address:** The address of the device that is being translated by NAT
- **Outside address:** The address of the destination device

NAT also uses the concept of local or global with respect to addresses:

- **Local address:** Any address that appears on the inside portion of the network
- **Global address:** Any address that appears on the outside portion of the network

Types of NAT

Static NAT uses a one-to-one mapping of local and global addresses. These mappings are configured by the network administrator and remain constant. Static NAT is particularly useful for a web server or any other device that must have a consistent address that is accessible from the internet, such as a company web server. Static NAT requires that enough public addresses be available to satisfy the total number of simultaneous user sessions. Dynamic NAT uses a pool of public addresses and assigns them on a first-come, first-served basis. When an inside device requests access to an outside network, dynamic NAT assigns an available public IPv4 address from the pool. Like static NAT, dynamic NAT requires that enough public addresses be available to satisfy the total number of simultaneous user sessions. Port Address Translation (PAT), also known as NAT overload, maps multiple private IPv4 addresses to a single public IPv4 address or a few addresses. This is the most common form of NAT for both homes and enterprises. PAT ensures that devices use a different TCP port number for each session with a server on the internet. PAT attempts to preserve the original source port. However, if the original source port is already used, PAT assigns the first available port number, starting from the beginning of the appropriate port group. PAT translates most common protocols carried by IPv4 that do not use TCP or UDP as a transport layer protocol. The most common of these is ICMPv4.

Table 6-6 provides a summary of the differences between NAT and PAT.

Table 6-6   NAT and PAT

NAT	PAT
One-to-one mapping between inside local and inside global addresses.	One inside global address can be mapped to many inside local addresses.
Uses only IPv4 addresses in the translation process.	Uses IPv4 addresses and TCP or UDP source port numbers in the translation process.
A unique inside global address is required for each inside host accessing the outside network.	A single unique inside global address can be shared by many inside hosts accessing the outside network.

NAT Advantages and Disadvantages

NAT has a number of advantages: NAT conserves the legally registered addressing scheme by allowing the privatization of intranets. NAT increases the flexibility of connections to the public network. NAT provides consistency for internal network addressing schemes. NAT hides user IPv4 addresses.

NAT has a number of disadvantages: NAT increases forwarding delays because the translation of each IPv4 address within the packet headers takes time. The process of using two layers of NAT translation is known as carrier-grade NAT (CGN). End-to-end addressing is lost, but many internet protocols and applications depend on end-to-end addressing from the source to the destination. End-to-end IPv4 traceability is also lost. Using NAT also complicates the use of tunneling protocols, such as IPsec, because NAT modifies values in the headers, causing integrity checks to fail.

Static NAT

Static NAT is a one-to-one mapping between an inside address and an outside address. Static NAT allows external devices to initiate connections to internal devices using the statically assigned public address. The first task is to create a mapping between the inside local address and the inside global address, using the **ip nat inside**

source static global configuration command. After the mapping is configured, the interfaces participating in the translation are configured as inside or outside relative to NAT using the **ip nat inside** and **ip nat outside** interface configuration commands. To verify NAT operations, use the **show ip nat translations** command. To verify that NAT translation is working, it is best to clear statistics from any past translations by using the **clear ip nat statistics** privileged EXEC command before testing.

Dynamic NAT

Dynamic NAT automatically maps inside local addresses to inside global addresses. Dynamic NAT, like static NAT, requires the configuration of the inside and outside interfaces participating in NAT. Dynamic NAT uses a pool of addresses translating a single inside address to a single outside address. The pool of public IPv4 addresses (that is, the inside global address pool) is available to any devices on the inside network on a first-come, first-served basis. With this type of translation, there must be enough addresses in the pool to accommodate all the inside devices needing concurrent access to the outside network. If all addresses in the pool are in use, a device must wait for an available address before it can access the outside network.

To configure dynamic NAT, first define the pool of addresses that will be used for translation by using the **ip nat pool** global configuration command. The addresses are defined by indicating the starting IPv4 address and the ending IPv4 address of the pool. The **netmask** or **prefix-length** keyword indicates which address bits belong to the network and which bits belong to the host for the range of addresses. Configure a standard ACL to identify (permit) only those addresses that are to be translated. Bind the ACL to the pool, using the following command syntax: Router(config)# **ip nat inside source list** {*access-list-number* | *access-list-name*} **pool** *pool-name*. Identify which interfaces are inside in relation to NAT. Identify which interfaces are outside in relation to NAT.

To verify dynamic NAT configurations, use the **show ip nat translations** command to see all static translations that have been configured and any dynamic translations that have been created by traffic. Adding the **verbose** keyword brings up additional information about each translation, including how long ago the entry was created and used. By default, translation entries time out after 24 hours, unless the timers have been reconfigured with the **ip nat translation timeout** *timeout-seconds* global configuration mode command. To clear dynamic entries before the timeout has expired, use the **clear ip nat translation** privileged EXEC mode command.

PAT

There are two ways to configure PAT, depending on how the ISP allocates public IPv4 addresses. First, the ISP can allocate a single public IPv4 address that is required for the organization to connect to the ISP; alternatively, the ISP can allocate more than one public IPv4 address to the organization. To configure PAT to use a single IPv4 address, simply add the keyword **overload** to the **ip nat inside source** global configuration command. The rest of the configuration is similar to the configuration for static and dynamic NAT except that with PAT, multiple hosts can use the same public IPv4 address to access the internet. Multiple hosts can share an IPv4 address from the pool when PAT is enabled with the keyword **overload**.

To verify PAT configuration, use the **show ip nat translations** command. The source port numbers in the NAT table differentiate the transactions. The **show ip nat statistics** command verifies that the NAT-POOL has allocated a single address for multiple translations. The output includes information about the number and type of active translations, the NAT configuration parameters, the number of addresses in the pool, and how many addresses have been allocated.

NAT64

IPv6 was developed with the intention of making NAT for IPv4—with translation between public and private IPv4 addresses—unnecessary. However, IPv6 does include its own IPv6 private address space, referred to as *unique local addresses* (*ULAs*). ULAs are similar to RFC 1918 private addresses in IPv4 but have a different purpose. ULAs are meant for only local communications within a site; they are not meant to provide additional IPv6 address space or to provide security. IPv6 provides for protocol translation between IPv4 and IPv6 through NAT64. NAT for IPv6 is used in a much different context than NAT for IPv4. NAT64 is used to transparently provide access between IPv6-only and IPv4-only networks. To aid in the move from IPv4 to IPv6, the IETF has developed several transition techniques to accommodate a variety of IPv4-to-IPv6 scenarios, including dual stack, tunneling, and translation. With dual stack, devices run protocols associated with both IPv4 and IPv6. Tunneling for IPv6 is the process of encapsulating an IPv6 packet inside an IPv4 packet. This allows the IPv6 packet to be transmitted over an IPv4-only network. NAT for IPv6 should not be used as a long-term strategy but as a temporary mechanism to assist in the migration from IPv4 to IPv6.

Packet Tracer
☐ Activity

Packet Tracer—Configure NAT for IPv4 (6.8.1)

In this Packet Tracer, you will complete the following objectives:

- Configure dynamic NAT with PAT

- Configure static NAT

Lab—Configure NAT for IPv4 (6.8.2)

In this lab, you will complete the following objectives:

- Part 1: Build the network and configure basic device settings
- Part 2: Configure and verify NAT for IPv4
- Part 3: Configure and verify PAT for IPv4
- Part 4: Configure and verify static NAT for IPv4

Practice

The following activities provide practice with the topics introduced in this chapter. The labs are available in the companion *Enterprise Networking, Security, and Automation v7 Labs & Study Guide* (ISBN 9780136634690). The Packet Tracer activity instructions are also in the *Labs & Study Guide*. The PKA files are found in the online course.

Lab

Lab 6.8.2: Configure NAT for IPv4

Packet Tracer Activities

Packet Tracer 6.2.7: Investigate NAT Operation

Packet Tracer 6.4.5: Configure Static NAT

Packet Tracer 6.5.6: Configure Dynamic NAT

Packet Tracer 6.6.7: Configure PAT

Packet Tracer 6.8.1: Configure NAT for IPv4

Check Your Understanding Questions

Complete all the review questions listed here to test your understanding of the topics and concepts in this chapter. The appendix "Answers to the 'Check Your Understanding' Questions" lists the answers.

1. Typically, which network device would be used to perform NAT for a corporate environment?

   A. DHCP server

   B. Host device

   C. Router

   D. Server

   E. Switch

2. When NAT is used in a small office, which address type or types are typically used for hosts on the local LAN?

   A. Both private and public IPv4 addresses

   B. Global public IPv4 addresses

   C. Internet-routable addresses

   D. Private IPv4 addresses

3. Which version of NAT allows many hosts inside a private network to simultaneously use a single inside global address for connecting to the internet?

   A. Dynamic NAT

   B. PAT

   C. Port forwarding

   D. Static NAT

4. Which type of NAT maps a single inside local address to a single inside global address?

   A. Dynamic NAT

   B. NAT overloading

   C. Port Address Translation

   D. Static NAT

5. What is a disadvantage of NAT?

   A. The costs of readdressing hosts can be significant for a publicly addressed network.

   B. The internal hosts have to use a single public IPv4 address for external communication.

   C. The router does not need to alter the checksum of the IPv4 packets.

   D. There is no end-to-end addressing.

6. Which statement accurately describes dynamic NAT?

   A. It always maps a private IPv4 address to a public IPv4 address.

   B. It dynamically provides IPv4 addressing to internal hosts.

   C. It provides a mapping of internal hostnames to IPv4 addresses.

   D. It provides an automated mapping of inside local to inside global IPv4 addresses.

7. A network administrator configures the border router with the **ip nat inside source list 4 pool NAT-POOL** global configuration command. What is required to be configured in order for this particular command to be functional?

   A. A NAT pool named NAT-POOL that defines the starting and ending public IPv4 addresses

   B. A VLAN named NAT-POOL that is enabled and active and routed by R1

   C. An access list named NAT-POOL that defines the private addresses that are affected by NAT

   D. An access list numbered 4 that defines the starting and ending public IPv4 addresses

   E. **ip nat outside** enabled on the interface that connects to the LAN affected by NAT

8. When dynamic NAT without overloading is being used, what happens if seven users attempt to access a public server on the internet when only six addresses are available in the NAT pool?

   A. All users can access the server.

   B. No users can access the server.

   C. The first user gets disconnected when the seventh user makes the request.

   D. The request to the server for the seventh user fails.

9. Which configuration would be appropriate for a small business that has the public IPv4 address 209.165.200.225/30 assigned to the external interface on the router that connects to the internet?

   A. ```
      access-list 1 permit 10.0.0.0 0.255.255.255
      ip nat pool NAT-POOL 192.168.2.1 192.168.2.8 netmask 255.255.255.240
      ip nat inside source list 1 pool NAT-POOL
      ```
   B. ```
      access-list 1 permit 10.0.0.0 0.255.255.255
      ip nat pool NAT-POOL 192.168.2.1 192.168.2.8 netmask 255.255.255.240
      ip nat inside source list 1 pool NAT-POOL overload
      ```
   C. ```
      access-list 1 permit 10.0.0.0 0.255.255.255
      ip nat inside source list 1 interface serial 0/0/0 overload
      ```
   D. ```
      access-list 1 permit 10.0.0.0 0.255.255.255
      ip nat pool NAT-POOL 192.168.2.1 192.168.2.8 netmask 255.255.255.240
      ip nat inside source list 1 pool NAT-POOL overload
      ip nat inside source static 10.0.0.5 209.165.200.225
      ```

10. What are two of the required steps to configure PAT? (Choose two.)

    A. Create a standard access list to define applications that should be translated.

    B. Define a pool of global addresses to be used for overload translation.

    C. Define the Hello and Interval timers to match the adjacent neighbor router.

    D. Define the range of source ports to be used.

    E. Identify the inside interface.

11. What is the name for the public IPv4 addresses used on a NAT-enabled router?

    A. Inside global addresses

    B. Inside local addresses

    C. Outside global addresses

    D. Outside local addresses

CHAPTER 7

WAN Concepts

Objectives

Upon completion of this chapter, you will be able to answer the following questions:

- What is the purpose of a WAN?
- How do WANs operate?
- What are traditional WAN connectivity options?
- What are modern WAN connectivity options?
- What are internet-based connectivity options?

Key Terms

This chapter uses the following key terms. You can find the definitions in the Glossary.

Dense wavelength-division multiplexing (DWDM)   page 284

broadband   page 284

Ethernet WAN   page 285

Metro Ethernet (MetroE)   page 285

Multiprotocol Label Switching (MPLS)   page 285

Point-to-Point Protocol (PPP)   page 285

High-Level Data Link Control (HDLC)   page 285

Frame Relay   page 285

Asynchronous Transfer Mode (ATM)   page 285

data terminal equipment (DTE)   page 286

data communications equipment (DCE)   page 286

customer premises equipment (CPE)   page 286

point of presence (POP)   page 286

demarcation point   page 286

local loop (or last mile)   page 286

central office (CO)   page 286

toll network   page 286

backhaul network   page 287

backbone network   page 287

voiceband modem   page 288

DSL modem   page 288

cable modem   page 288

broadband modem   page 288

CSU/DSU   page 288

optical converter   page 288

serial communication   page 289

parallel connection   page 289

circuit-switched communication   page 290

landline   page 290

public switched telephone network (PSTN)   page 290

Integrated Services Digital Network (ISDN)   page 290

packet-switched communication   page 290

jitter   page 291

latency   page 291

light-emitting diode (LED)   page 291

multiplexing   page 292

leased line   page 294

T1   page 294

T3   page 294

E1   page 294

E3   page 294

optical carrier   page 294

voice over IP (VoIP)   page 294

modulate   page 295

demodulate   page 295

non-broadcast multiaccess (NBMA)   page 295

permanent virtual circuit (PVC)   page 295

data-link connection identifier (DLCI)   page 296

dark fiber   page 298

Ethernet over MPLS (EoMPLS)   page 299

Virtual Private LAN Service (VPLS)   page 299

teleworker   page 302

asymmetric DSL (ADSL)   page 303

Introduction (7.0)

As you know, local-area networks are called LANs. The name implies that a LAN is local to you and your small home or office business. But what if your network is for a larger business or perhaps even a global enterprise? You cannot operate a large business with multiple sites without a wide-area network, which is called a WAN. This chapter explains what WANs are and how they connect to the internet and also back to your LAN. Understanding the purpose and functions of WANs is foundational to your understanding of modern networks. Let's jump in!

Purpose of WANs (7.1)

In this section, you will learn about WAN access technologies available to small to medium-sized business networks.

LANs and WANs (7.1.1)

Whether at work or at home, we all use local-area networks (LANs). However, LANs are limited to a small geographic area. A wide-area network (WAN) is required to connect beyond the boundaries of a LAN. A WAN is a telecommunications network that spans a relatively large geographic area and operates beyond the geographic scope of a LAN.

In Figure 7-1, WAN services are required to interconnect an *enterprise campus network* to remote LANs at branch sites, telecommuter sites, and remote users.

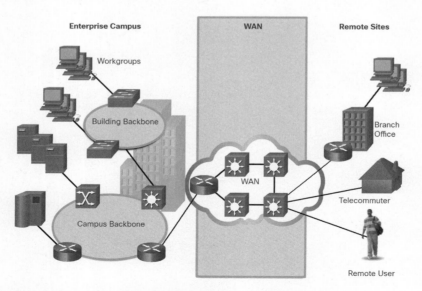

Figure 7-1   Examples of Different Types of WAN Services

Table 7-1 highlights the differences between LANs and WANs.

Table 7-1   Differences Between LANs and WANs

Local-Area Networks (LANs)	Wide-Area Networks (WANs)
LANs provide networking services within a small geographic area (such as a home network, office network, building network, or campus network).	WANs provide networking services over large geographic areas (such as in and between cities, countries, and continents).
LANs are used to interconnect local computers, peripherals, and other devices.	WANs are used to interconnect remote users, networks, and sites.
A LAN is owned and managed by an organization or a home user.	WANs are owned and managed by internet service, telephone, cable, and satellite providers.
Other than the network infrastructure costs, there is no fee to use a LAN.	WAN services are provided for a fee.
LANs provide high-bandwidth speeds using wired Ethernet and Wi-Fi services.	WANs providers offer low- to high-bandwidth speeds over long distances using complex physical networks.

Private and Public WANs (7.1.2)

WANs may be built by a variety of different types of organizations, including the following:

- An organization that wants to connect users in different locations
- An ISP that wants to connect customers to the internet
- An ISP or telecommunications provider that wants to interconnect ISPs

A *private WAN* connection is dedicated to a single customer. It provides for the following:

- Guaranteed service level
- Consistent bandwidth
- Security

A *public WAN* connection is typically provided by an ISP or a telecommunications *service provider* using the internet. With a public WAN, the service levels and bandwidth may vary, and the shared connections do not guarantee security.

WAN Topologies (7.1.3)

A physical topology describes the physical network infrastructure used by data when it is traveling from a source to a destination. The physical WAN topology used in WANs is complex and, for the most part, unknown to users. Consider a user in New York establishing a video conference call with a user in Tokyo, Japan. Other than the user's internet connection in New York, it would not be feasible to identify all the actual physical connections needed to support the video call.

A WAN topology is described using a logical topology, which includes the virtual connection between the source and destination. For example, a video conference call between a user in New York and a user in Japan would be a logical point-to-point connection.

WANs are implemented using the following logical topology designs:

- *Point-to-point topology*
- *Hub-and-spoke topology*
- *Dual-homed topology*
- *Fully meshed topology*
- *Partially meshed topology*

Note

Large networks usually deploy a combination of these topologies.

Point-to-Point Topology

A point-to-point topology, as shown in Figure 7-2, uses a point-to-point circuit between two endpoints.

Figure 7-2   Point-to-Point Topology

Point-to-point links often involve dedicated, leased-line connections from the corporate edge point to the provider networks. A point-to-point connection involves a Layer 2 transport service through the service provider network. Packets sent from one site are delivered to the other site and vice versa. A point-to-point connection is transparent to the customer network. It seems as if there is a direct physical link between two endpoints.

Point-to-point topology can become expensive if many point-to-point connections are required.

Hub-and-Spoke Topology

A hub-and-spoke topology enables a single interface on the *hub router* to be shared by all spoke circuits. *Spoke routers* can be interconnected through the hub router using *virtual circuits* and routed subinterfaces. Figure 7-3 displays a sample hub-and-spoke topology consisting of three spoke routers connecting to a hub router across a WAN cloud.

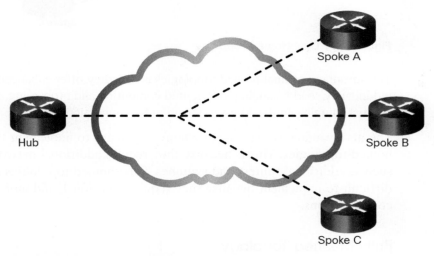

Figure 7-3   Hub-and-Spoke Topology

A hub-and-spoke topology is a *single-homed topology*. There is only one hub router, and all communication must go through it. Therefore, spoke routers can only communicate with each other through the hub router. Consequently, the hub router represents a *single point of failure*. If it fails, inter-spoke communication also fails.

Dual-homed Topology

A dual-homed topology provides redundancy. Figure 7-4 shows such a topology, with two hub routers dual-homed and redundantly attached to three spoke routers across a WAN cloud.

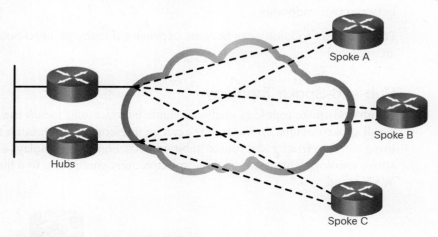

Figure 7-4   Dual-Homed Topology

The advantage of dual-homed topologies is that they offer enhanced network redundancy, load balancing, distributed computing and processing, and the ability to implement backup service provider connections.

The disadvantage is that they are more expensive to implement than single-homed topologies. This is because they require additional networking hardware, such as additional routers and switches. Dual-homed topologies are also more difficult to implement because they require additional, and more complex, configurations.

Fully Meshed Topology

A fully meshed topology uses multiple virtual circuits to connect all sites, as shown in Figure 7-5.

This is the most fault-tolerant topology of the five shown in this chapter. For instance, if site B lost connectivity to site A, it could send the data through either site C or site D.

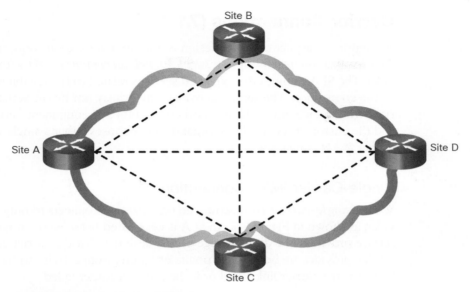

Figure 7-5   Fully Meshed Topology

Partially Meshed Topology

A partially meshed topology connects many but not all sites. For example, in Figure 7-6, sites A, B, and C are fully meshed, but site D must connect to site A to reach sites B and C.

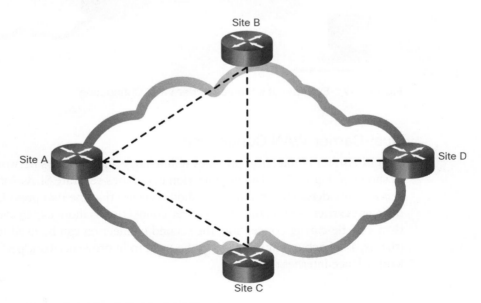

Figure 7-6   Partially Meshed Topology

Carrier Connections (7.1.4)

An important aspect of WAN design is how an organization connects to the internet. An organization usually signs a *service level agreement (SLA)* with a service provider. The SLA outlines the expected services related to the reliability and availability of the connection. The service provider may or may not be the actual carrier. A carrier owns and maintains the physical connection and equipment between the provider and the customer. Typically, an organization chooses either a single-carrier or dual-carrier WAN connection.

Single-Carrier WAN Connection

With a *single-carrier connection*, an organization connects to only one service provider, as shown in Figure 7-7. An SLA is negotiated between the organization and the service provider. The disadvantage of this design is that the carrier connection and service provider are both single points of failure. Connectivity to the internet would be lost if the carrier link failed or if the provider router failed.

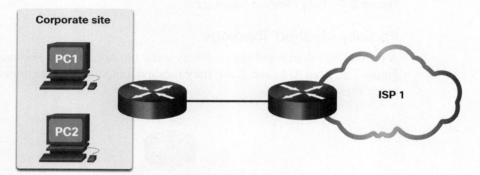

Figure 7-7   Example of a Single-Carrier WAN Connection

Dual-Carrier WAN Connection

A *dual-carrier connection* provides redundancy and increases network availability, as shown in Figure 7-8. The organization negotiates separate SLAs with two different service providers. The organization should ensure that the two providers each use a different carrier. Although a dual-carrier connection is more expensive to implement than a single-carrier connection, the second connection can be used for redundancy (that is, as a backup link). It can also be used to improve network performance and load balance internet traffic.

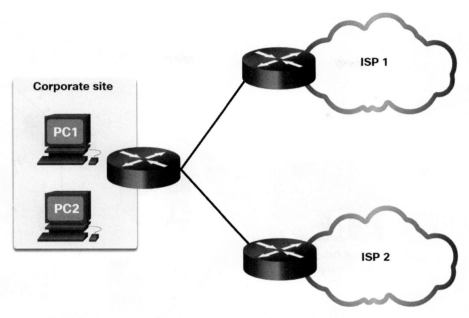

Figure 7-8   Example of a Dual-Carrier WAN Connection

Evolving Networks (7.1.5)

A company's network requirements can change dramatically as the company grows over time. Distributing employees saves costs in many ways, but it puts increased demands on the network. A network must meet the day-to-day operational needs of the business, and it also must be able to adapt and grow as the company changes. Network designers and administrators meet these challenges by carefully choosing network technologies, protocols, and service providers. They must also optimize their networks by using a variety of network design techniques and architectures.

To illustrate differences between networks of various sizes, in this chapter we use a fictitious company called SPAN Engineering and watch as it grows from a small local business into a global enterprise. SPAN Engineering, an environmental consulting firm, has developed a special process for converting household waste into electricity and is developing a small pilot project for a municipal government in its local area.

Small Network

SPAN Engineering initially consisted of 15 employees working in a small office, as shown in Figure 7-9.

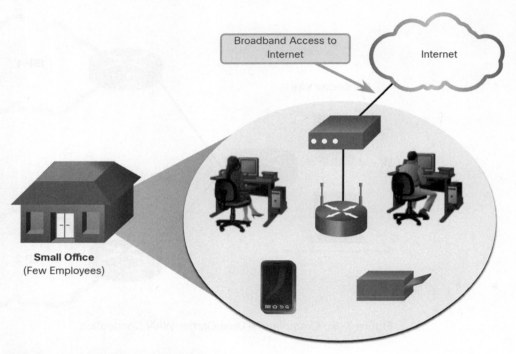

Figure 7-9 Example of a Small Network

They used a single LAN connected to a wireless router for sharing data and peripherals. The connection to the internet was through a common *broadband service* called *digital subscriber line (DSL)*, supplied by the local telephone service provider. To support the company IT requirements, SPAN contracted services from the DSL provider.

Campus Network

Within a few years, SPAN Engineering grew to require several floors of a building, as shown in Figure 7-10.

The company now required a campus-area network (CAN). A CAN interconnects several LANs within a limited geographic area. Multiple LANs are required to segment the various departments that are connecting to multiple switches in a campus network environment.

The network includes dedicated servers for email, data transfer, file storage, and web-based productivity tools and applications. A firewall secures internet access to corporate users. The business now requires in-house IT staff to support and maintain the network.

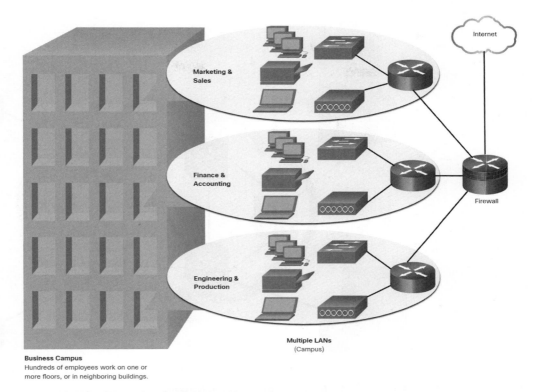

Business Campus
Hundreds of employees work on one or
more floors, or in neighboring buildings.

Figure 7-10   Example of a Campus Network

Branch Network

A few years later, SPAN Engineering expanded and added a branch site in the city
and remote and regional sites in other cities, as shown in Figure 7-11.

The company now required a metropolitan-area network (MAN) to interconnect sites
within the city. A MAN is larger than a LAN but smaller than a WAN.

To connect to the central office, branch offices in nearby cities used private
dedicated lines through their local service provider. Offices in other cities and countries require the services of a WAN or may use internet services to connect distant
locations. However, the internet introduces security and privacy issues that the IT
team must address.

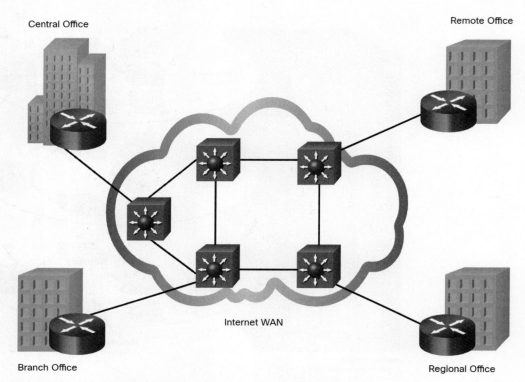

Figure 7-11   Example of a Branch Network

Distributed Network

SPAN Engineering has now been in business for 20 years and has grown to having thousands of employees distributed in offices worldwide, as shown in Figure 7-12.

To reduce network costs, SPAN encouraged *teleworking* and virtual teams using web-based applications, including web conferencing, e-learning, and online collaboration tools to increase productivity and reduce costs. Site-to-site and remote-access *virtual private networks (VPNs)* enable the company to use the internet to connect easily and securely with employees and facilities around the world.

Interactive Graphic

Check Your Understanding—Purpose of WANs (7.1.6)

Refer to the online course to complete this activity.

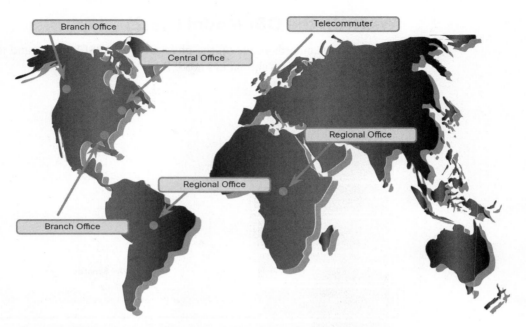

Figure 7-12   Example of a Distributed Network

WAN Operations (7.2)

Now that you understand how critical WANs are to large networks, this section discusses how they work. The concept of a WAN has been around for many years. Consider that the telegraph system was the first large-scale WAN, followed by radio, telephone system, television, and now data networks. Many of the technologies and standards developed for these WANs were used as the basis for network WANs.

WAN Standards (7.2.1)

Modern WAN standards are defined and managed by a number of recognized authorities, including the following:

- TIA/EIA, which is a combination of the *Telecommunications Industry Association (TIA)* and *Electronic Industries Alliance (EIA)*

- *International Organization for Standardization (ISO)*

- *Institute of Electrical and Electronics Engineers (IEEE)*

WANs in the OSI Model (7.2.2)

Most WAN standards focus on the physical layer (OSI Layer 1) and the data link layer (OSI Layer 2), as shown in Figure 7-13.

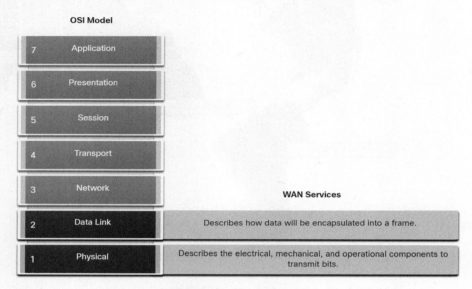

Figure 7-13   WAN Services and the OSI Model

Layer 1 Protocols

Layer 1 protocols describe the electrical, mechanical, and operational components needed to transmit bits over a WAN. For example, service providers commonly use high-bandwidth optical fiber media to span long distances (that is, long haul) using the following Layer 1 optical fiber protocol standards:

- *Synchronous Digital Hierarchy (SDH)*
- *Synchronous Optical Networking (SONET)*
- *Dense wavelength-division multiplexing (DWDM)*

SDH and SONET essentially provide the same services, and their transmission capacity can be increased by using DWDM technology.

Layer 2 Protocols

Layer 2 protocols define how data will be encapsulated into a frame. Several Layer 2 protocols have evolved over the years, including the following:

- *Broadband* (such as DSL and cable)
- Wireless

- *Ethernet WAN (Metro Ethernet [MetroE])*
- *Multiprotocol Label Switching (MPLS)*
- *Point-to-Point Protocol (PPP)* (not commonly used)
- *High-Level Data Link Control (HDLC)* (not commonly used)
- *Frame Relay* (legacy)
- *Asynchronous Transfer Mode (ATM)* (legacy)

Common WAN Terminology (7.2.3)

The WAN physical layer describes the physical connections between the company network and the service provider network.

Specific terms are used to describe WAN connections between the subscriber that is, the company/client) and the WAN service provider, as shown in Figure 7-14.

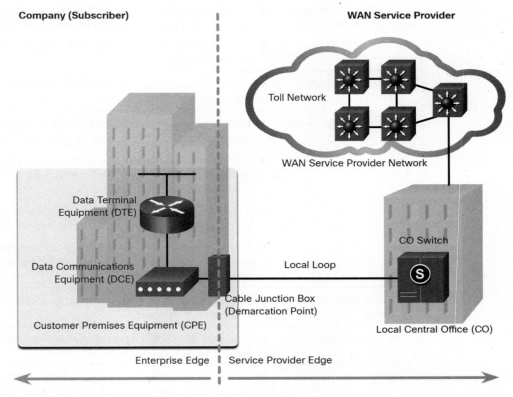

Figure 7-14   Topology Example with Common WAN Terminology

Table 7-2 explains the terms shown in Figure 7-14, as well as some additional WAN-related terms.

Table 7-2   WAN Terminology

WAN Term	Description
Data terminal equipment (DTE)	■ This is the device that connects subscriber LANs to the WAN communication device (that is, DCE).
	■ Inside hosts send their traffic to the DTE device.
	■ The DTE connects to the local loop through the DCE.
	■ The DTE device is usually a router but could be a host or server.
Data communications equipment (DCE)	■ Also called data circuit-terminating equipment, this is the device used to communicate with the provider.
	■ The DCE primarily provides an interface to connect subscribers to a communication link on the WAN cloud.
Customer premises equipment (CPE)	■ This includes the DTE and DCE devices (such as the router, modem, and optical converter) located on the enterprise edge.
	■ The subscriber either owns the CPE or leases the CPE from the service provider.
Point of presence (POP)	■ This is the point where the subscriber connects to the service provider network.
Demarcation point	■ This is a physical location in a building or complex that officially separates the CPE from service provider equipment.
	■ The demarcation point is typically a cabling junction box, located on the customer premises, that connects the CPE wiring to the local loop.
	■ It identifies the location where the network operation responsibility changes from the subscriber to the service provider.
	■ When problems arise, it is necessary to determine whether the user or the service provider is responsible for troubleshooting or repair.
Local loop (or last mile)	■ This is the copper or fiber cable that connects the CPE to the CO of the service provider.
Central office (CO)	■ This is the local service provider facility or building that connects the CPE to the provider network.
Toll network	■ This includes backhaul, long-haul, all-digital, fiber-optic communications lines, switches, routers, and other equipment inside the WAN provider network.

WAN Term	Description
Backhaul network	■ (Not shown) Backhaul networks connect multiple access nodes of the service provider network. ■ Backhaul networks can span municipalities, countries, and regions. ■ Backhaul networks are also connected to internet service providers and to the backbone network.
Backbone network	■ (Not shown) These are large, high-capacity networks used to interconnect service provider networks and to create a redundant network. ■ Other service providers can connect to the backbone directly or through another service provider. ■ Backbone network service providers are also called Tier 1 providers.

WAN Devices (7.2.4)

Many types of devices are specific to WAN environments. However, the end-to-end data path over a WAN is usually from the source DTE to the DCE, then to the WAN cloud, then to the DCE, and finally to the destination DTE, as shown in Figure 7-15.

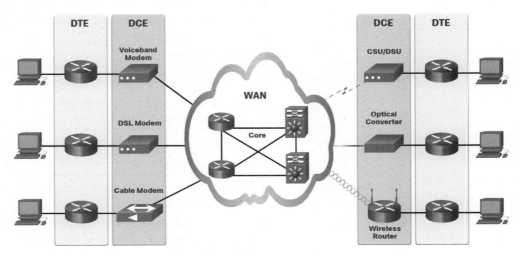

Figure 7-15   Examples of DTE and DCE in WAN Services

Table 7-3 describes the WAN devices shown in Figure 7-15.

Table 7-3   WAN Device Descriptions

WAN Device	Description
Voiceband modem	■ Also known as a dialup modem. ■ Legacy device that converted (that is, modulated) the digital signals produced by a computer into analog voice frequencies. ■ Uses telephone lines to transmit data.
DSL modem and *cable modem*	■ Collectively known as *broadband modems*, these high-speed digital modems connect to the DTE router using Ethernet. ■ DSL modems connect to the WAN using telephone lines. ■ Cable modems connect to the WAN using coaxial lines. ■ Both operate in a similar manner to the voiceband modem but use higher broadband frequencies and transmission speeds.
CSU/DSU	■ Digital-leased lines require a channel service unit (CSU) and a data service unit (DSU). ■ A CSU/DSU connects a digital device to a digital line. ■ A CSU/DSU can be a separate device like a modem, or it can be an interface on a router. ■ The CSU provides termination for the digital signal and ensures connection integrity through error correction and line monitoring. ■ The DSU converts the line frames into frames that the LAN can interpret and vice versa.
Optical converter	■ Also known as an optical fiber converter. ■ These devices connect fiber-optic media to copper media and convert optical signals to electronic pulses.
Wireless router or access point	■ These devices are used to wirelessly connect to a WAN provider. ■ Routers may also use cellular wireless connectivity.
WAN core devices	■ The WAN backbone consists of multiple high-speed routers and Layer 3 switches. ■ A router or multilayer switch must be able to support multiple telecommunications interfaces of the highest speed used in the WAN core. ■ A router or multilayer switch must also be able to forward IP packets at full speed on all those interfaces. ■ The router or multilayer switch must also support the routing protocols being used in the core.

Note

The list in Table 7-3 is not exhaustive, and other devices may be required, depending on the WAN access technology chosen.

Serial Communication (7.2.5)

Almost all network communications occur using *serial communication* delivery. Serial communication transmits bits sequentially over a single channel. In contrast, *parallel communications* simultaneously transmit several bits using multiple wires.

Figure 7-16 demonstrates the difference between serial and parallel communications.

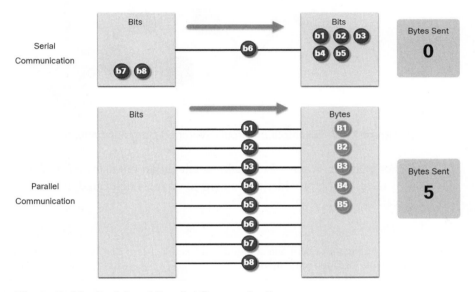

Figure 7-16   Serial and Parallel Communications

Although a parallel connection theoretically transfers data eight times faster than a serial connection, it is prone to synchronization problems. As the cable length increases, the synchronization timing between multiple channels becomes more sensitive to distance. For this reason, parallel communication is limited to very short distances only; for example, copper media is limited to less than 8 meters (that is, 26 feet).

Parallel communication is not a viable WAN communication method because of its length restriction. It is, however, a viable solution in data centers, where distances between servers and switches are relatively short. For instance, the Cisco Nexus switches in data centers support parallel optics solutions to transfer more data signals and achieve higher speeds (such as 40 Gbps and 100 Gbps).

Circuit-Switched Communication (7.2.6)

Network communication can be implemented using *circuit-switched communication*. A circuit-switched network establishes a dedicated circuit (or channel) between endpoints before the users can communicate. Specifically, circuit switching dynamically establishes a dedicated virtual connection through the service provider network before voice or data communication can start, as shown in Figure 7-17.

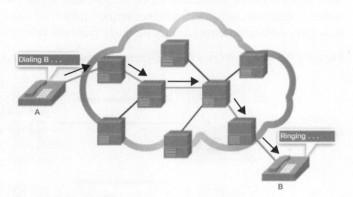

Figure 7-17   Example of Circuit-Switched Communications

For example, when a user makes a telephone call using a *landline*, the number called is used by the provider equipment to create a dedicated circuit from the caller to the called party.

> **Note**
>
> A landline is a telephone situated in a fixed location that is connected to the provider using copper or fiber-optic media.

During transmission over a circuit-switched network, all communication uses the same path. The entire fixed capacity allocated to the circuit is available for the duration of the connection, regardless of whether there is information to transmit. This can lead to inefficiencies in circuit usage. For this reason, circuit switching is generally not suited for data communication.

The two most common types of circuit-switched WAN technologies are the *public switched telephone network (PSTN)* and the legacy *Integrated Services Digital Network (ISDN)*.

Packet-Switched Communications (7.2.7)

Network communication is most commonly implemented using *packet-switched communication*. In contrast to circuit switching, packet switching segments traffic data into packets that are routed over a shared network. Packet-switched networks do not require a circuit to be established, and they allow many pairs of nodes to communicate over the same channel, as shown in Figure 7-18.

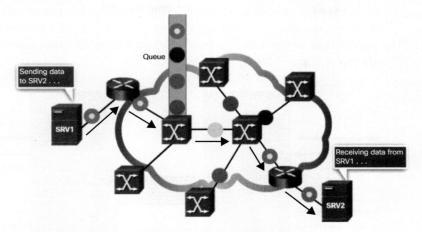

Figure 7-18   Example of Packet-Switched Communications

Packet switching is much less expensive and more flexible than circuit switching. Although susceptible to delays (*latency*) and variability of delay (*jitter*), modern packet-switching technology allows satisfactory transport of voice and video communications on these networks.

Examples of packet-switched WAN technologies are Ethernet WAN (Metro Ethernet) and Multiprotocol Label Switching (MPLS), as well as the legacy technologies Frame Relay and Asynchronous Transfer Mode (ATM).

SDH, SONET, and DWDM (7.2.8)

Service provider networks use fiber-optic infrastructures to transport user data between destinations. Fiber-optic cable is far superior to copper cable for long-distance transmissions due to its much lower attenuation and interference.

There are two optical fiber OSI Layer 1 standards available to service providers:

- **SDH:** Synchronous Digital Hierarchy (SDH) is a global standard for transporting data over fiber-optic cable.

- **SONET:** Synchronous Optical Networking (SONET) is the North American standard that provides the same services as SDH.

These two standards are essentially the same, and they are therefore often listed as SONET/SDH.

SONET and SDH define how to transfer multiple data, voice, and video communications over optical fiber using lasers or *light-emitting diodes (LEDs)* over great distances. Both standards are used on the ring network topology, which contains the redundant fiber paths that allow traffic to flow in both directions.

Dense wavelength-division multiplexing (DWDM) is a newer technology that increases the data-carrying capacity of SDH and SONET by simultaneously sending multiple streams of data (*multiplexing*) using different wavelengths of light, as shown in Figure 7-19.

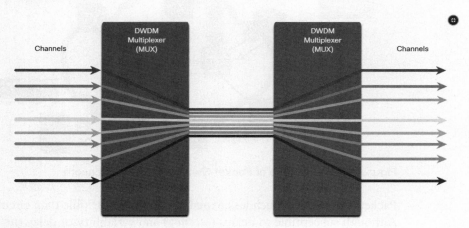

Figure 7-19   DWDM Multiplexing

DWDM has the following features:

- It supports SONET and SDH standards.
- It can multiplex more than 80 different channels of data (that is, wavelengths) onto a single fiber.
- Each channel is capable of carrying a 10 Gbps multiplexed signal.
- It assigns incoming optical signals to specific wavelengths of light (that is, frequencies).

Note

DWDM circuits are used in long-haul systems and modern submarine communications cable systems.

Check Your Understanding—WAN Operations (7.2.9)

Interactive
Graphic

Refer to the online course to complete this activity.

Traditional WAN Connectivity (7.3)

To understand the WANs of today, it helps to know where they started. This section discusses WAN connectivity options from the beginning.

Traditional WAN Connectivity Options (7.3.1)

When LANs appeared in the 1980s, organizations began to see the need to interconnect with other locations. To do so, they needed their networks to connect to the local loop of a service provider. This was accomplished by using dedicated lines or by using switched services from a service provider.

Figure 7-20 summarizes the traditional WAN connectivity options.

> **Note**
>
> There are several WAN access connection options that the enterprise edge can use to connect over the local loop to the provider. These WAN access options differ in technology, bandwidth, and cost. Each has distinct advantages and disadvantages. Familiarity with these technologies is an important part of network design.

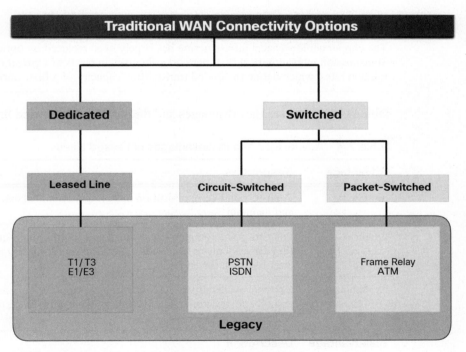

Figure 7-20   Traditional WAN Connectivity Options

Common WAN Terminology (7.3.2)

When permanent dedicated connections were required, a point-to-point link using copper media was used to provide a preestablished WAN communications path from the customer premises to the provider network. Point-to-point lines could be leased from a service provider. These lines are called *leased lines* because the organization pays a monthly lease fee to a service provider to use the lines.

Leased lines have existed since the early 1950s. They are referred to by different names, such as leased circuits, serial links, serial lines, point-to-point links, and T1/E1 or T3/E3 lines.

Leased lines are available in different fixed capacities and are generally priced based on the bandwidth required and the distance between the two connected points.

There are two systems used to define the digital capacity of a copper media serial link:

- **T-carrier:** Used in North America, T-carrier provides *T1* links supporting bandwidth up to 1.544 Mbps and *T3* links supporting bandwidth up to 43.7 Mbps.

- **E-carrier:** Used in Europe, E-carrier provides *E1* links supporting bandwidth up to 2.048 Mbps and *E3* links supporting bandwidth up to 34.368 Mbps.

Note

The copper cable physical infrastructure has largely been replaced by optical fiber networks. Transmission rates in optical fiber networks are given in terms of *Optical Carrier (OC)* transmission rates, which define the digital transmitting capacity of a fiber-optic network.

Table 7-4 summarizes the advantages and disadvantages of leased lines.

Table 7-4   Advantages and Disadvantages of Leased Lines

Advantage	Description
Simplicity	Point-to-point communication links require minimal expertise to install and maintain.
Quality	Point-to-point communication links usually offer high-quality service if they have adequate bandwidth. The dedicated capacity removes latency or jitter between the endpoints.
Availability	Constant availability is essential for some applications, such as e-commerce. Point-to-point communication links provide permanent, dedicated capacity, which is required for *voice over IP (VoIP)* or video over IP.

Disadvantage	Description
Cost	Point-to-point links are generally the most expensive type of WAN access. The cost of leased line solutions can become significant when they are used to connect many sites over increasing distances. In addition, each endpoint requires an interface on the router, which increases equipment costs.
Limited flexibility	WAN traffic is often variable, and leased lines have a fixed capacity, so that the bandwidth of the line seldom matches the need exactly. Any change to the leased line generally requires a site visit by ISP personnel to adjust capacity.

Circuit-Switched Options (7.3.3)

Circuit-switched connections are provided by public switched telephone network (PSTN) carriers. The local loop connecting the CPE to the CO is copper media. There are two traditional circuit-switched options: the PSTN and ISDN.

Public Service Telephone Network (PSTN)

Dialup WAN access uses the PSTN as its WAN connection. Traditional local loops can transport binary computer data through the voice telephone network using a voiceband modem. The modem *modulates* the digital data into an analog signal at the source and *demodulates* the analog signal to digital data at the destination. The physical characteristics of the local loop and its connection to the PSTN limit the rate of the signal to less than 56 kbps.

Dialup access is considered a legacy WAN technology. However, it may still be a viable solution when no other WAN technology is available.

Integrated Services Digital Network (ISDN)

ISDN is a circuit-switching technology that enables the PSTN local loop to carry digital signals. It provided higher-capacity switched connections than dialup access. ISDN provides for data rates from 45 Kbps to 2.048 Mbps.

ISDN has declined greatly in popularity due to high-speed DSL and other broadband services. ISDN is considered a legacy technology, and most major providers have discontinued this service.

Packet-Switched Options (7.3.4)

Packet switching segments data into packets that are routed over a shared network. Circuit-switched networks require a dedicated circuit to be established. In contrast, packet-switching networks allow many pairs of nodes to communicate over the same channel.

There are two traditional (legacy) packet-switched connectivity options: Frame Relay and ATM.

Frame Relay

Frame Relay is a simple Layer 2 *non-broadcast multiaccess (NBMA)* WAN technology that is used to interconnect enterprise LANs. A single router interface can be used to connect to multiple sites using different *permanent virtual circuits (PVCs)*. PVCs are used to carry both voice and data traffic between a source and destination, and they support data rates up to 4 Mbps, with some providers offering even higher rates.

Frame Relay creates PVCs that are uniquely identified by *data-link connection identifiers (DLCIs)*. The PVCs and DLCIs ensure bidirectional communication from one DTE device to another.

Frame Relay networks have been largely replaced by faster Metro Ethernet and internet-based solutions.

Asynchronous Transfer Mode (ATM)

Asynchronous Transfer Mode (ATM) technology is capable of transferring voice, video, and data through private and public networks. It is built on a cell-based architecture rather than on a frame-based architecture. ATM cells are always a fixed length of 53 bytes. An ATM cell contains a 5-byte ATM header followed by 48 bytes of ATM payload. Small, fixed-length cells are well suited for carrying voice and video traffic because this traffic is intolerant of delay. Video and voice traffic do not have to wait for larger data packets to be transmitted.

The 53-byte ATM cell is less efficient than the bigger frames and packets of Frame Relay. Furthermore, the ATM cell has at least 5 bytes of overhead for each 48-byte payload. When a cell is carrying segmented network layer packets, the overhead is higher because the ATM switch must be able to reassemble the packets at the destination. A typical ATM line needs almost 20% greater bandwidth than Frame Relay to carry the same volume of network layer data.

ATM networks have been largely replaced by faster Metro Ethernet and internet-based solutions.

Interactive Graphic

Check Your Understanding—Traditional WAN Connectivity (7.3.5)

Refer to the online course to complete this activity.

Modern WAN Connectivity (7.4)

This section discusses the various modern WAN services available.

Modern WANs (7.4.1)

Modern WANs have more connectivity options than traditional WANs. Enterprises now require faster and more flexible WAN connectivity options. Traditional WAN connectivity options have rapidly declined in use because they are either no longer available, too expensive, or have limited bandwidth.

Figure 7-21 displays the local loop connections most likely to be encountered today.

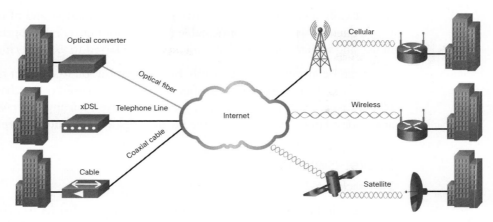

Figure 7-21   Modern WAN Connection Options

Modern WAN Connectivity Options (7.4.2)

New technologies are continually emerging. Figure 7-22 summarizes the modern WAN connectivity options.

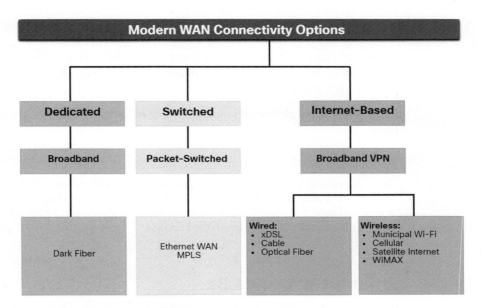

Figure 7-22   Modern WAN Connectivity Options

Dedicated Broadband

In the late 1990s, many telecommunication companies built optical fiber networks with enough fiber to satisfy projected next generation needs. However, optical technologies such as wavelength-division multiplexing (WDM) were developed and dramatically increased the transmitting ability of a single strand of optical fiber. Consequently, many fiber-optic cable runs are not in use. Fiber-optic cable that is not in use and is therefore "unlit" (that is, dark) is referred to as *dark fiber*.

Fiber can be installed independently by an organization to connect remote locations directly together. However, dark fiber could also be leased or purchased from a supplier. Leasing dark fiber is typically more expensive than any other WAN option available today. However, it provides the greatest flexibility, control, speed, and security.

Packet-Switched

Two packet-switched WAN network options are available.

Advances in Ethernet LAN technology have enabled Ethernet to expand into the MAN and WAN areas. Metro Ethernet provides fast bandwidth links and has been responsible for replacing many traditional WAN connectivity options.

Multi-protocol Label Switching (MPLS) enables the WAN provider network to carry any protocol (for example, IPv4 packets, IPv6 packets, Ethernet, DSL) as payload data. This enables different sites to connect to the provider network, regardless of its access technologies.

Internet-Based Broadband

Organizations are now commonly using the global internet infrastructure for WAN connectivity. To address security concerns, the connectivity options are often combined with VPN technologies.

Valid WAN network options include digital subscriber line (DSL), cable, wireless, and fiber.

> **Note**
>
> There are several WAN access connection options that the enterprise edge can use to connect over the local loop to the provider. These WAN access options differ in technology, bandwidth, and cost. Each has distinct advantages and disadvantages. Familiarity with these technologies is an important part of network design.

Ethernet WAN (7.4.3)

Ethernet was originally developed as a LAN access technology and was not suitable as a WAN access technology due primarily to the limited distance provided by copper media.

However, newer Ethernet standards using fiber-optic cables have made Ethernet a reasonable WAN access option. For instance, the IEEE 1000BASE-LX standard supports fiber-optic cable lengths of 5 km, and the IEEE 1000BASE-ZX standard supports cable lengths up to 70 km.

Service providers now offer Ethernet WAN service using fiber-optic cabling. The Ethernet WAN service can go by many names, including the following:

- Metropolitan Ethernet (MetroE)

- *Ethernet over MPLS (EoMPLS)*

- *Virtual Private LAN Service (VPLS)*

Figure 7-23 shows a simple Metro Ethernet topology example.

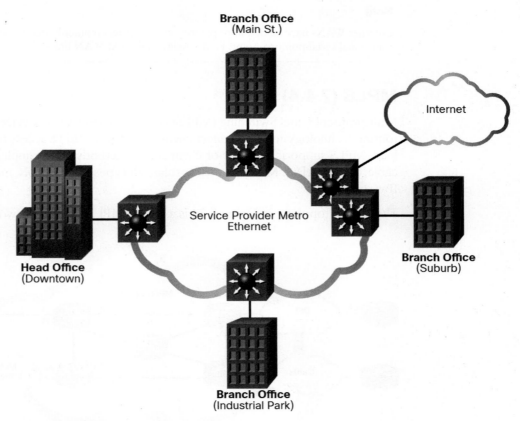

Figure 7-23   Sample Metro Ethernet Topology

The following are several benefits of an Ethernet WAN:

- **Reduced expenses and administration:** An Ethernet WAN provides a switched, high-bandwidth Layer 2 network capable of managing data, voice, and video all on the same infrastructure. This increases bandwidth and eliminates expensive conversions to other WAN technologies. The technology enables businesses to inexpensively connect numerous sites in a metropolitan area to each other and to the internet.

- **Easy integration with existing networks:** An Ethernet WAN connects easily to existing Ethernet LANs, reducing installation costs and time.

- **Enhanced business productivity:** An Ethernet WAN enables businesses to take advantage of productivity-enhancing IP applications that are difficult to implement on TDM or Frame Relay networks, such as hosted IP communications, VoIP, and streaming and broadcast video.

Note

Ethernet WANs have gained in popularity and are now commonly being used to replace the traditional serial point-to-point, Frame Relay, and ATM WAN links.

MPLS (7.4.4)

Multiprotocol Label Switching (MPLS) is a high-performance service provider WAN routing technology to interconnect clients without regard to access method or payload. MPLS supports a variety of client access methods (for example, Ethernet, DSL, cable, Frame Relay). MPLS can encapsulate all types of protocols, including IPv4 and IPv6 traffic.

The sample topology in Figure 7-24 is a simple MPLS-enabled network.

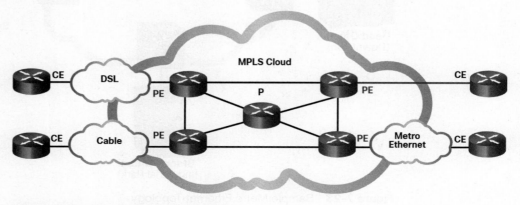

Figure 7-24 Sample MPLS Topology

An MPLS router can be a customer edge (CE) router, a provider edge (PE) router, or an internal provider (P) router. Notice that MPLS supports a variety of client access connections.

MPLS routers are label switched routers (LSRs). This means that they attach labels to packets that are then used by other MPLS routers to forward traffic. When traffic is leaving the CE, the MPLS PE router adds a short fixed-length label in between the frame header and the packet header. MPLS P routers use the label to determine the next hop of the packet. The label is removed by the egress PE router when the packet leaves the MPLS network.

MPLS also provides services for QoS support, traffic engineering, redundancy, and VPNs.

Check Your Understanding—Modern WAN Connectivity (7.4.5)

Refer to the online course to complete this activity.

Internet-Based Connectivity (7.5)

This section discusses the different internet-based connectivity services available.

Internet-Based Connectivity Options (7.5.1)

Modern WAN connectivity options do not end with Ethernet WAN and MPLS. Today, there are a host of internet-based wired and wireless options from which to choose. Internet-based broadband connectivity is an alternative to using dedicated WAN options.

Figure 7-25 lists the internet-based connectivity options.

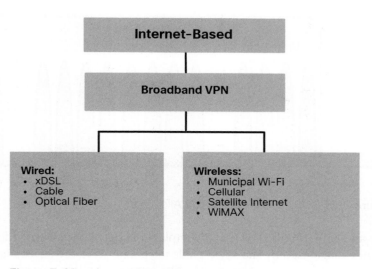

Figure 7-25   Internet-Based Connectivity Options

Internet-based connectivity can be divided into wired and wireless options.

Wired Options

Wired options use permanent cabling (such as copper or fiber) to provide consistent bandwidth and reduce error rates and latency. Examples of wired broadband connectivity are digital subscriber line (DSL), cable connections, and optical fiber networks.

Wireless Options

Wireless options are less expensive to implement compared to other WAN connectivity options because they use radio waves instead of wired media to transmit data. However, wireless signals can be negatively affected by factors such as distance from radio towers, interference from other sources, weather, and the number of users accessing the shared space. Examples of wireless broadband include cellular 3G/4G/5G and satellite internet services. Wireless carrier options vary depending on location.

DSL Technology (7.5.2)

Digital subscriber line (DSL) is a high-speed, always-on connection technology that uses existing twisted-pair telephone lines to provide IP services to users. DSL is a popular choice for home users and for enterprise IT departments to support *teleworkers*.

Figure 7-26 shows a representation of bandwidth space allocation on a copper wire for asymmetric DSL (ADSL).

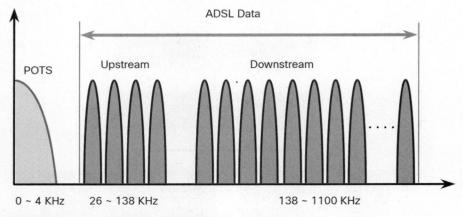

Figure 7-26   DSL Bandwidth Space Allocation

The area of the figure labeled POTS (plain old telephone system) identifies the frequency range used by the voice-grade telephone service. The area labeled ADSL represents the frequency space used by the upstream and downstream DSL signals. The area that encompasses both the POTS area and the ADSL area represents the entire frequency range supported by the copper wire pair.

There are several xDSL varieties offering different upload and download transmission rates. However, all forms of DSL are categorized as either *asymmetric DSL (ADSL)* or *symmetric DSL (SDSL)*. ADSL and ADSL2+ provide higher downstream bandwidth to the user than upload bandwidth. SDSL provides the same capacity in both directions.

The transfer rates are also dependent on the actual length of the local loop and the type and condition of the cabling. For example, an ADSL loop must be less than 5.46 km (3.39 miles) for guaranteed signal quality.

Security risks are incurred with DSL technology but can be mediated with security measures such as VPNs.

DSL Connections (7.5.3)

Service providers deploy DSL connections in the local loop. As shown in Figure 7-27, a connection is set up between the DSL modem and the *DSL access multiplexer (DSLAM)*.

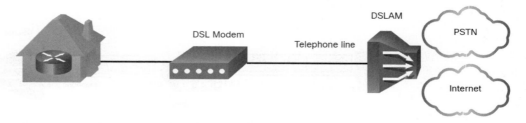

Figure 7-27   Example of a DSL Connection

A DSL modem converts the Ethernet signals from the teleworker device to a DSL signal, which is transmitted to a DSLAM at the provider location.

A DSLAM is the device located at the CO of the provider and concentrates connections from multiple DSL subscribers. A DSLAM is often built into an aggregation router.

The advantage that DSL has over cable technology is that DSL is not a shared medium. Each user has a separate direct connection to the DSLAM. Adding users does not impede performance, unless the DSLAM internet connection to the ISP or to the internet becomes saturated.

DSL and PPP (7.5.4)

Point-to-Point Protocol (PPP) is a Layer 2 protocol that was commonly used by telephone service providers to establish router-to-router and host-to-network connections over dialup and ISDN access networks.

ISPs still use PPP as the Layer 2 protocol for broadband DSL connections for several reasons:

- PPP can be used to authenticate the subscriber.

- PPP can assign a public IPv4 address and/or IPv6 prefix to the subscriber.

- PPP provides link-quality management features.

In *PPP over Ethernet (PPPoE)*, a DSL modem has a DSL interface to connect to the DSL network and an Ethernet interface to connect to the client device. However, Ethernet links do not natively support PPP.

Host with PPPoE Client

In the example in Figure 7-28, the host runs a PPPoE client to obtain a public IPv4 address and/or IPv6 prefix from a PPPoE server located at the provider site. The PPPoE client software communicates with the DSL modem using PPPoE, and the modem communicates with the ISP using PPP. In this topology, only one client can use the connection. Also, notice that there is no router to protect the inside network.

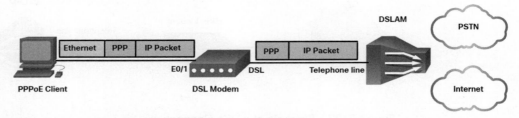

Figure 7-28   Example of a Host with PPPoE Client

Router PPPoE Client

Another solution is to configure a router to be a PPPoE client, as shown in Figure 7-29. The router is the PPPoE client and obtains its configuration from the provider. The clients communicate with the router using only Ethernet and are unaware of the DSL connection. In this topology, multiple clients can share the DSL connection.

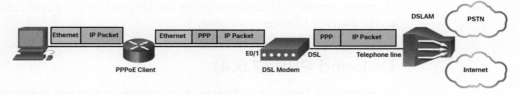

Figure 7-29   Example of a Router PPPoE Client

Cable Technology (7.5.5)

Cable technology is a high-speed always-on connection technology that uses a coaxial cable from the cable company to provide IP services to users. Like DSL, cable technology is a popular choice for home users and for enterprise IT departments to support remote workers.

Modern cable systems offer customers advanced telecommunications services, including high-speed internet access, digital cable television, and residential telephone service.

Data over Cable Service Interface Specification (DOCSIS) is the international standard for adding high-bandwidth data to an existing cable system.

Cable operators deploy *hybrid fiber-coaxial (HFC)* networks to enable high-speed transmission of data to cable modems. The cable system uses a coaxial cable to carry radio frequency (RF) signals to the end user.

HFC uses fiber-optic and coaxial cable in different portions of the network. For example, the connection between the cable modem and optical node is coaxial cable, as shown in Figure 7-30.

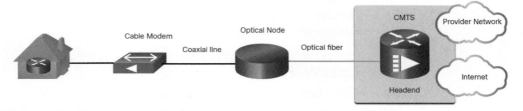

Figure 7-30   Example of Cable Technology Connections

The optical node performs optical-to-RF signal conversion. Specifically, it converts RF signals to light pulses over fiber-optic cable. The fiber media enables the signals to travel over long distances to the provider *headend*, where a *cable modem termination system (CMTS)* is located. The headend contains the databases needed to provide internet access, and the CMTS is responsible for communicating with the cable modems.

All the local subscribers share the same cable bandwidth. As more users join the service, available bandwidth may drop below the expected rate.

Optical Fiber (7.5.6)

Many municipalities, cities, and providers install fiber-optic cable to the user location. This is commonly referred to as fiber-to-the-*x* (FTTx) and includes the following:

- *Fiber-to-the-home (FTTH)*: Fiber reaches the boundary of the residence. Passive optical networks and point-to-point Ethernet are architectures that can deliver cable TV, internet, and phone services over FTTH networks directly from the service provider central office.

- *Fiber-to-the-building (FTTB)*: Fiber reaches the boundary of the building, such as the basement in a multi-dwelling unit, with the final connection to the individual living space being made via alternative means, like curb or pole technologies.

- *Fiber-to-the-node/neighborhood (FTTN)*: Optical cabling reaches an optical node that converts optical signals to a format acceptable for twisted pair or coaxial cable to the premises.

FTTx can deliver the highest bandwidth of all broadband options.

Wireless Internet-Based Broadband (7.5.7)

Wireless technology uses the unlicensed radio spectrum to send and receive data. The unlicensed spectrum is accessible to anyone who has a wireless router and wireless technology in the device he or she is using.

Until recently, one limitation of wireless access has been the need to be within the local transmission range (typically less than 100 feet) of a wireless router or a wireless modem with a wired connection to the internet.

Municipal Wi-Fi

Many cities have begun setting up municipal wireless networks. Some of these networks provide high-speed internet access for free or for substantially less than the price of other broadband services. Others are for city use only, allowing police and fire departments and other city employees to do certain aspects of their jobs remotely. To connect to *municipal Wi-Fi*, a subscriber typically needs a wireless modem, which provides a stronger radio and directional antenna than conventional wireless adapters. Most service providers provide the necessary equipment for free or for a fee, much as they do with DSL or cable modems.

Cellular

Increasingly, cellular service is another wireless WAN technology being used to connect users and remote locations where no other WAN access technology is available. Many users with smartphones and tablets can use cellular data to email, surf the web, download apps, and watch videos.

Phones, tablet computers, laptops, and even some routers can communicate through the internet using cellular technology. These devices use radio waves to communicate through a nearby mobile phone tower. The device has a small radio antenna, and the provider has a much larger antenna sitting at the top of a tower somewhere within miles of the phone.

The following are two common cellular industry terms:

- *3G/4G/5G* **wireless:** These are abbreviations for third-generation, fourth-generation, and the emerging fifth-generation mobile wireless technologies. These technologies support wireless internet access. The 4G standard supports bandwidths up to 450 Mbps download and 100 Mbps upload. The emerging 5G standard should support 100 Mbps to 10 Gbps and beyond.

- *Long-Term Evolution (LTE)*: This newer and faster technology is part of 4G technology.

Satellite Internet

Satellite internet is typically used by rural users and in remote locations where cable and DSL are not available. To access satellite internet services, subscribers need a satellite dish, two modems (uplink and downlink), and coaxial cables between the dish and the modem.

Specifically, a router connects to a satellite dish that is pointed to a service provider satellite. This satellite is in geosynchronous orbit in space. The signals must travel approximately 35,786 kilometers (22,236 miles) to the satellite and back.

The primary installation requirement is for the antenna to have a clear view toward the equator, where most orbiting satellites are stationed. Trees and heavy rains can affect signal reception.

Satellite internet provides two-way (upload and download) data communications. Upload speeds are about one-tenth of the download speed. Download speeds range from 5 Mbps to 25 Mbps.

WiMAX

Worldwide Interoperability for Microwave Access (WiMAX), described in the IEEE standard 802.16, provides high-speed broadband service with wireless access and provides broad coverage like a cellphone network rather than through small Wi-Fi hotspots.

WiMAX operates in a similar way to Wi-Fi but at higher speeds, over greater distances, and for a greater number of users. It uses a network of WiMAX towers that are like cellphone towers. To access a WiMAX network, users must subscribe to an ISP with a WiMAX tower that is within 30 miles of their location. They also need some type of WiMAX receiver and a special encryption code to get access to the base station.

WiMAX has largely been replaced by LTE for mobile access and by cable or DSL for fixed access.

VPN Technology (7.5.8)

Security risks are incurred when a teleworker or a remote office worker uses a broadband service to access the corporate WAN over the internet.

To address security concerns, broadband services provide virtual private network (VPN) connections to a network device that accepts VPN connections. The network device is typically located at the corporate site.

A VPN is an encrypted connection between private networks over a public network, such as the internet. Instead of using a dedicated Layer 2 connection, such as a leased line, a VPN uses virtual connections called VPN tunnels. VPN tunnels are routed through the internet from the private network of the company to the remote site or employee host.

The following are several benefits to using VPN:

- **Cost savings:** VPNs enable organizations to use the global internet to connect remote offices and to connect remote users to the main corporate site. This eliminates the need for expensive, dedicated WAN links and modem banks.

- **Security:** VPNs provide the highest level of security by using advanced encryption and authentication protocols that protect data from unauthorized access.

- **Scalability:** Because VPNs use the internet infrastructure within ISPs and devices, it is easy to add new users. Corporations can add large amounts of capacity without adding significant infrastructure.

- **Compatibility with broadband technology:** VPN technology is supported by broadband service providers such as DSL and cable. VPNs allow mobile workers and telecommuters to take advantage of their home high-speed internet service to access their corporate networks. Business-grade, high-speed broadband connections can also provide a cost-effective solution for connecting remote offices.

VPNs are commonly implemented as the following:

- *Site-to-site VPN*: VPN settings are configured on routers. Clients are unaware that their data is being encrypted.

- *Remote access VPN*: The user initiates remote-access connection (such as by using HTTPS in a browser to connect to the bank). Alternatively, the user can run VPN client software on his or her host to connect to and authenticate with the destination device.

Note

VPNs are discussed in more detail in Chapter 8, "VPN and IPsec Concepts."

ISP Connectivity Options (7.5.9)

This section explains the different ways an organization can connect to an ISP. The choice depends on the needs and budget of the organization.

Single-Homed

Single-homed ISP connectivity is used by the organization when internet access is not crucial to the operation. As shown in Figure 7-31, the client connects to the ISP using one link. This topology provides no redundancy, and it is the least expensive solution of the four described in this section.

Figure 7-31   Single-Homed Example

Dual-Homed

Dual-homed ISP connectivity is used by an organization when internet access is somewhat crucial to the operation. As shown in Figure 7-32, the client connects to the same ISP using two links. The topology provides both redundancy and load balancing. If one link fails, the other link can carry the traffic. If both links are operational, traffic can be load balanced over them. However, the organization loses internet connectivity if the ISP experiences an outage.

Figure 7-32   Dual-Homed Example

Multihomed

Multihomed ISP connectivity is used by an organization when internet access is crucial to the operation. The client connects to two different ISPs, as shown in Figure 7-33. This design provides increased redundancy and enables load balancing, but it can be expensive.

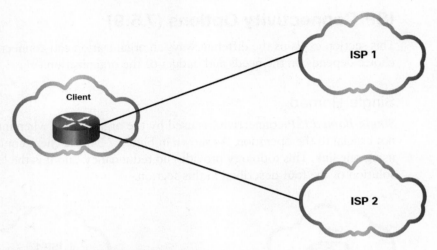

Figure 7-33   Multihomed Example

Dual-Multihomed

Dual-multihomed ISP is the most resilient topology of the four described in this section. The client connects with redundant links to multiple ISPs, as shown in Figure 7-34. This topology provides the most redundancy possible, and it is the most expensive option of the four.

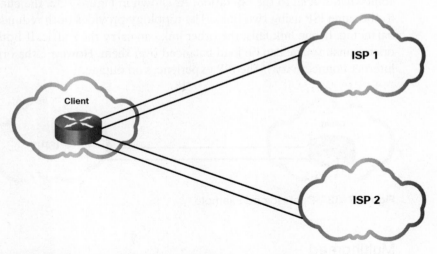

Figure 7-34   Dual-Multihomed Example

Broadband Solution Comparison (7.5.10)

Each broadband solution has advantages and disadvantages. The ideal solution is to have a fiber-optic cable directly connected to a client network. Some locations have only one option, such as cable or DSL. Some locations have only broadband wireless options for internet connectivity.

If there are multiple broadband solutions available, a cost-versus-benefit analysis should be performed to determine the best solution.

Some factors to consider include the following:

- **Cable:** Bandwidth is shared by many users. Therefore, upstream data rates are often slow during high-usage hours in areas with oversubscription.

- **DSL:** DSL has limited bandwidth and is distance sensitive (in relation to the ISP central office). The upload rate is proportionally lower than the download rate.

- **Fiber-to-the-home:** This option requires fiber installation directly to the home.

- **Cellular/mobile:** With this option, coverage is often an issue, even within a small office or home office where bandwidth is relatively limited.

- **Municipal Wi-Fi:** Most municipalities do not have a mesh Wi-Fi network deployed. If municipal Wi-Fi is available and in range, however, it is a viable option.

- **Satellite:** This option is expensive and provides limited capacity per subscriber. It is typically used when no other option is available.

Lab—Research Broadband Internet Access Options (7.5.11)

In this lab, you will complete the following objectives:

- Part 1: Investigate broadband distribution
- Part 2: Research broadband access options for specific scenarios

Summary (7.6)

The following is a summary of the sections in this chapter.

Purpose of WANs

A wide-area network (WAN) is required to connect beyond the boundaries of a LAN. A WAN is a telecommunications network that spans a relatively large geographic area. A WAN operates beyond the geographic scope of a LAN. A private WAN is a connection that is dedicated to a single customer. A public WAN connection is typically provided by an ISP or a telecommunications service provider using the internet. A WAN topology is described using a logical topology. WANs are implemented using the following logical topologies: point-to-point, hub-and-spoke, dual-homed, fully meshed, and partially meshed. With a single-carrier connection, an organization connects to only one service provider. A dual-carrier connection provides redundancy and increases network availability. The organization negotiates separate SLAs with two different service providers. Network requirements of a company can change dramatically as the company grows over time. Distributing employees saves costs in many ways, but it puts increased demands on the network. Small companies may use a single LAN connected to a wireless router to share data and peripherals. Connection to the internet is through a broadband service provider. A slightly larger company may use a campus-area network (CAN), which interconnects several LANs within a limited geographic area. An even larger company may require a metropolitan-area network (MAN) to interconnect sites within the city. A MAN is larger than a LAN but smaller than a WAN. A global company may require teleworking and virtual teams using web-based applications, including web conferencing, e-learning, and online collaboration tools. Site-to-site and remote-access virtual private networks (VPNs) enable a company to use the internet to securely connect with employees and facilities around the world.

WAN Operations

Modern WAN standards are defined and managed by a number of recognized authorities, including TIA/EIA, ISO, and IEEE. Most WAN standards focus on the physical layer (OSI Layer 1) and the data link layer (OSI Layer 2). Layer 1 protocols describe the electrical, mechanical, and operational components needed to transmit bits over a WAN. Layer 1 optical fiber protocol standards include SDH, SONET, and DWDM. Layer 2 protocols define how data is encapsulated into a frame. Layer 2 protocols include broadband, wireless, Ethernet WAN, MPLS, PPP, and HDLC. The WAN physical layer describes the physical connections between a company network and a service provider network. There are specific terms used to describe WAN connections between the subscriber (that is, the company/client) and a WAN service provider, including DTE, DCE, CPE, POP, demarcation point, local loop, CO, toll network, backhaul network, and backbone network. The end-to-end data path over a WAN is usually from source DTE to the DCE, then to the WAN cloud, then to the DCE, and finally to the destination DTE. Devices used in this path include voiceband modems, DSL and cable modems, CSUs/DSUs, optical converters, wireless routers or access points, and other WAN core devices. Serial communication transmits bits sequentially over a single channel. In contrast, parallel communications simultaneously transmit several bits using multiple wires. A circuit-switched network establishes a dedicated circuit (or channel) between endpoints before the users can communicate. During transmission over a circuit-switched network, all communication uses the same path. The two most common types of circuit-switched WAN technologies are PSTN and ISDN. Packet-switching segments traffic data into packets that are routed over a shared network. Common types of packet-switched WAN technologies are Ethernet WAN and MPLS. There are two optical fiber OSI Layer 1 standards. SDH/SONET define how to transfer multiple data, voice, and video communications over optical fiber using lasers or LEDs over great distances. Both standards are used on the ring network topology, which contains redundant fiber paths allowing traffic to flow in both directions. DWDM is a newer technology that increases the data-carrying capacity of SDH and SONET by simultaneously sending multiple streams of data (multiplexing) using different wavelengths of light.

Traditional WAN Connectivity

In the 1980s, organizations started to see the need to interconnect their LANs with other locations. They needed their networks to connect to the local loop of a service provider by using dedicated lines or by using switched services from a service provider. When permanent dedicated connections were required, a point-to-point link using copper media was used to provide a preestablished WAN communications path from the customer premises to the provider network. Dedicated leased lines were T1/E1 or T3/E3 lines. Circuit-switched connections were provided by PSTN carriers. The local loop connecting the CPE to the CO was copper media. ISDN is a circuit-switching technology that enables the PSTN local loop to carry digital signals. It provided higher-capacity switched connections than dialup access. Packet switching segments data into packets that are routed over a shared network. Packet-switching networks allow many pairs of nodes to communicate over the same channel. Frame Relay is a simple Layer 2 NBMA WAN technology used to interconnect enterprise LANs. ATM technology is capable of transferring voice, video, and data through private and public networks. It is built on a cell-based architecture rather than on a frame-based architecture.

Modern WAN Connectivity

Modern WAN connectivity options include dedicated broadband, Ethernet WAN, and MPLS (packet switched), along with various wired and wireless versions of internet-based broadband. Service providers now offer Ethernet WAN service using fiber-optic cabling. Ethernet WAN reduces expenses and administration, is easily integrated with existing networks, and enhances business productivity. MPLS is a high-performance service provider WAN routing technology for interconnecting clients. MPLS supports a variety of client access methods (such as Ethernet, DSL, cable, and Frame Relay). MPLS can encapsulate all types of protocols, including IPv4 or IPv6 traffic.

Internet-Based Connectivity

Internet-based broadband connectivity is an alternative to using dedicated WAN options. There are wired and wireless versions of broadband VPN. Wired options use permanent cabling (such as copper or fiber) to provide consistent bandwidth and reduce error rates and latency. Examples of wired broadband connectivity are digital subscriber line (DSL), cable connections, and optical fiber networks. Examples of wireless broadband include cellular 3G/4G/5G and satellite internet services. DSL is a high-speed, always-on connection technology that uses existing twisted-pair telephone lines to provide IP services to users. All forms of DSL are categorized as either ADSL or SDSL. A DSL modem converts Ethernet signals from a teleworker's device to a DSL signal, which is transmitted to a DSLAM at the provider location. The advantage that DSL has over cable technology is that DSL is not a shared medium. ISPs still use PPP as the Layer 2 protocol for broadband DSL connections. A DSL modem has a DSL interface to connect to the DSL network and an Ethernet interface to connect to the client device. Ethernet links do not natively support PPP. Cable technology is a high-speed always-on connection technology that uses a cable company coaxial cable to provide IP services to users. Cable operators deploy hybrid fiber-coaxial (HFC) networks to enable high-speed transmission of data to cable modems. The cable system uses a coaxial cable to carry radio frequency (RF) signals to the end user. Many municipalities, cities, and providers install fiber-optic cable to the user location. This is commonly referred to as fiber-to-the-x (FTTx), such as FTTH, FTTB, and FTTN.

Wireless technology uses the unlicensed radio spectrum to send and receive data. The unlicensed spectrum is accessible to anyone who has a wireless router and wireless technology in the device he or she is using. Until recently, one limitation of wireless access has been the need to be within the local transmission range (typically less than 100 feet) of a wireless router or a wireless modem that has a wired connection to the internet. Newer developments in wireless technology include municipal Wi-Fi, cellular, satellite internet, and WiMAX. To address security concerns, broadband services provide capabilities for using virtual private network (VPN) connections to a network device that accepts VPN connections, which is typically located at the corporate site. A VPN is an encrypted connection between private networks over a public network, such as the internet. Instead of using a dedicated Layer 2 connection, such as a leased line, a VPN uses virtual connections called VPN tunnels. VPN tunnels are routed through the internet from the private network of the company to the remote site or employee host. Common VPN implementations include site-to-site and remote-access VPNs. ISP connectivity options include single-homed, dual-homed, multihomed, and dual-multihomed. Cable, DSL, fiber-to-the-home, cellular/mobile, municipal Wi-Fi, and satellite internet all have advantages and disadvantages. Perform a cost-versus-benefit analysis before choosing an internet-based connectivity solution.

Packet Tracer—WAN Concepts (7.6.1)

Packet Tracer
☐ Activity

In this Packet Tracer activity, you will explore various WAN technologies and implementations.

Practice

The following activities provide practice with the topics introduced in this chapter. The labs are available in the companion *Enterprise Networking, Security, and Automation v7 Labs & Study Guide* (ISBN 9780136634690). The Packet Tracer activity instructions are also in the *Labs & Study Guide*. The PKA files are found in the online course.

Lab

Lab 7.5.11: Research Broadband Internet Access Options

Packet Tracer
☐ Activity

Packet Tracer Activity

Packet Tracer 7.6.1: WAN Concepts

Check Your Understanding Questions

Complete all the review questions listed here to test your understanding of the topics and concepts in this chapter. The appendix "Answers to 'Check Your Understanding' Questions" lists the answers.

1. Which type of internet connection would be suitable for a small 10-employee company with one local LAN?

   A. A broadband DSL or cable connection to a service provider

   B. A dialup connection to the local telephone service provider

   C. A private dedicated line to the local service provider

   D. A VSAT connection to a service provider

2. Which network scenario requires the use of a WAN?

   A. Employee workstations need to obtain dynamically assigned IP addresses.

   B. Employees in the branch office need to share files with the headquarters office that is located in a separate building on the same campus network.

   C. Employees need to access web pages that are hosted on the corporate web servers in the DMZ within their building.

   D. Traveling employees must connect to the corporate email server using a VPN.

3. Which statement is true of a WAN?

   A. A WAN operates within the same geographic scope as a LAN but has serial links.

   B. A WAN provides end-user network connectivity to the campus backbone.

   C. All serial links are considered WAN connections.

   D. WAN networks are owned by service providers.

4. Which device is needed when a digital leased line is used to provide a connection between a customer and a service provider?

   A. Access server

   B. CSU/DSU

   C. Dialup modem

   D. Layer 2 switch

5. What is a requirement of a connectionless packet-switched network?

   A. A virtual circuit is created for the duration of the packet delivery.

   B. Each packet has to carry only an identifier.

   C. Full addressing information must be carried in each data packet.

   D. The network predetermines the route for a packet.

6. What is an advantage of packet-switching technology over circuit-switching technology?

    A. Packet-switched networks are less susceptible to jitter than circuit-switched networks.

    B. Packet-switched networks can efficiently use multiple routes inside a service provider network.

    C. Packet-switched networks require an expensive permanent connection to each endpoint.

    D. Packet-switched networks usually experience lower latency than circuit-switched networks experience.

7. What is a long-distance fiber-optic media technology that supports both SONET and SDH and assigns incoming optical signals to specific wavelengths of light?

    A. ATM

    B. DWDM

    C. ISDN

    D. MPLS

8. What is the recommended technology to use over a public WAN infrastructure when a branch office is connected to a corporate site?

    A. ATM

    B. ISDN

    C. Municipal Wi-Fi

    D. VPN

9. What are two common high-bandwidth fiber-optic media standards? (Choose two.)

    A. ANSI

    B. ATM

    C. ITU

    D. SDH

    E. SONET

10. Which WAN technology establishes a dedicated constant point-to-point connection between two sites?

    A. ATM

    B. Frame Relay

    C. ISDN

    D. Leased lines

11. A hospital is looking for a solution to connect multiple newly established remote branch medical offices. Which of the following is most important when selecting a private WAN connection rather than a public WAN connection?

    A. Data security and confidentiality during transmission

    B. Higher data transmission rate

    C. Lower cost

    D. Website and file exchange service support

12. A new corporation needs a data network that must meet certain requirements. The network must provide a low-cost connection to salespeople dispersed over a large geographic area. Which two types of WAN infrastructure would meet the requirements? (Choose two.)

    A. Dedicated

    B. Internet

    C. Private infrastructure

    D. Public infrastructure

    E. Satellite

13. Which wireless technology provides internet access through cellular networks?

    A. Bluetooth

    B. LTE

    C. Municipal Wi-Fi

    D. Satellite

14. Which equipment is needed for an ISP to provide internet connections through cable service?

    A. Access server

    B. CMTS

    C. CSU/DSU

    D. DSLAM

15. A customer needs a WAN virtual connection that provides high-speed, dedicated bandwidth between two sites. Which type of WAN connection would best fulfill this need?

    A. Circuit-switched network

    B. Ethernet WAN

    C. MPLS

    D. Packet-switched network

CHAPTER 8

VPN and IPsec Concepts

Objectives

Upon completion of this chapter, you will be able to answer the following questions:

- What are the benefits of VPN technology?
- What are different types of VPNs?
- How is the IPsec framework used to secure network traffic?

Key Terms

This chapter uses the following key terms. You can find the definitions in the Glossary.

Introduction (8.0)

Have you or someone you know ever been hacked while using public Wi-Fi? It's surprisingly easy to do. But there is a solution to this problem: Use virtual private networks (VPNs) and the additional protection of *IP Security (IPsec)*. VPNs are commonly used by remote workers around the globe. There are also personal VPNs that you can use when you are on public Wi-Fi. In fact, there are many different kinds of VPNs that use IPsec to protect and authenticate IP packets between the source and destination. Want to know more? Read on!

VPN Technology (8.1)

This section discusses the benefits of VPN technology.

Virtual Private Networks (8.1.1)

To secure network traffic between sites and users, organizations use virtual private networks (VPNs) to create end-to-end private network connections. A VPN is *virtual* in that it carries information within a private network, but that information is actually transported over a public network. A VPN is *private* in that the traffic is encrypted to keep the data confidential while it is transported across the public network.

Figure 8-1 shows a collection of various types of VPNs managed by an enterprise's main site. The tunnel enables remote sites and users to access the main site's network resources securely.

In the figure, the following terms are used:

- A Cisco Adaptive Security Appliance (ASA) firewall helps organizations provide secure, high-performance connectivity, including through VPNs and always-on access for remote branches and mobile users.

- With a SOHO—which stands for small office and home office—a VPN-enabled router can provide VPN connectivity back to the corporate main site.

- *Cisco AnyConnect Secure Mobility Client* is software that remote workers can use to establish client-based VPN connections with the main site.

The first types of VPNs were strictly IP tunnels that did not include authentication or encryption of the data. For example, *Generic Routing Encapsulation (GRE)* is a tunneling protocol developed by Cisco that does not include encryption services. It is used to encapsulate IPv4 and IPv6 traffic inside an IP tunnel to create a virtual point-to-point link.

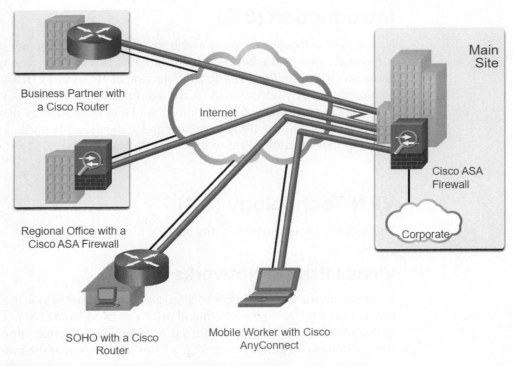

Figure 8-1   Examples of Different Types of VPNs

VPN Benefits (8.1.2)

Modern VPNs support encryption features such as Internet Protocol Security (IPsec) and *Secure Sockets Layer (SSL)* to secure network traffic between sites.

Table 8-1 lists the major benefits of VPNs.

Table 8-1   VPN Benefits

Benefit	Description
Cost savings	With the advent of cost-effective, high-bandwidth technologies, organizations can use VPNs to reduce their connectivity costs while simultaneously increasing remote connection bandwidth.
Security	VPNs provide the highest level of security available by using advanced encryption and authentication protocols that protect data from unauthorized access.

Benefit	Description
Scalability	VPNs allow organizations to use the internet, making it easy to add new users without adding significant infrastructure.
Compatibility	VPNs can be implemented across a wide variety of WAN link options, including all the popular broadband technologies. Remote workers can take advantage of these high-speed connections to gain secure access to their corporate networks.

Site-to-Site and Remote-Access VPNs (8.1.3)

VPNs are commonly deployed in one of the following configurations: site-to-site or remote-access VPNs.

Site-to-Site VPN

A site-to-site VPN is created when VPN terminating devices, called *VPN gateways*, are preconfigured with information to establish a secure tunnel. VPN traffic is only encrypted between these devices. Internal hosts have no knowledge that a VPN is being used.

Figure 8-2 shows a site-to-site VPN connection. The client laptop is connected to the network VPN gateway—in this case, a router. The VPN gateway is connected across the Internet, depicted as a cloud, to another VPN gateway (such as an ASA firewall).

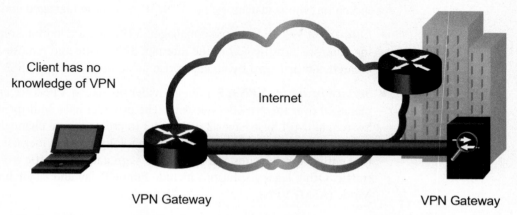

Figure 8-2   Site-to-Site VPN Topology

Remote-Access VPN

A remote-access VPN is dynamically created to establish a secure connection between a client and a VPN terminating device. For example, a remote-access SSL VPN is used when you check your banking information online.

Figure 8-3 shows a remote-access VPN connection. The client's laptop is connected through the internet, depicted as a cloud, to a VPN gateway (such as an ASA firewall).

Client initiates
VPN connection

VPN Gateway

Figure 8-3   Remote-Access VPN Topology

Enterprise and Service Provider VPNs (8.1.4)

There are many options available for securing enterprise traffic. These solutions vary depending on who is managing the VPN. VPNs can be managed and deployed as

- *Enterprise VPNs*: Enterprise-managed VPNs are a common solution for securing enterprise traffic across the internet. Site-to-site and remote-access VPNs are created and managed by an enterprise using both IPsec and SSL VPNs.

- *Service provider VPNs*: Service provider–managed VPNs are created and managed over the provider network. The provider uses Multiprotocol Label Switching (MPLS) at Layer 2 or Layer 3 to create secure channels between an enterprise's sites. MPLS is a routing technology the provider uses to create virtual paths between sites and effectively segregate the traffic from other customer traffic. Other legacy solutions include Frame Relay and Asynchronous Transfer Mode (ATM) VPNs.

Figure 8-4 lists the different types of enterprise-managed and service provider-managed VPN deployments that are discussed in more detail in this chapter.

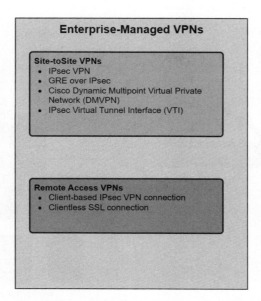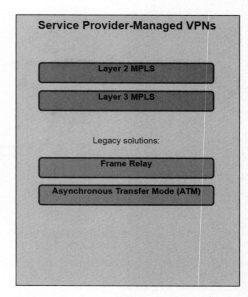

Figure 8-4   Enterprise-Managed and Server Provider–Managed VPNs

Check Your Understanding—VPN Technology (8.1.5)

Refer to the online course to complete this activity.

Types of VPNs (8.2)

In the previous section you learned about the basics of a VPN. Here you will learn about the types of VPNs.

Remote-Access VPNs (8.2.1)

VPNs have become the logical solution for remote-access connectivity for many reasons. Remote-access VPNs let remote and mobile users securely connect to the enterprise by creating an encrypted tunnel. Remote users can securely replicate their enterprise security access, including email and network applications. Remote-access VPNs also allow contractors and partners to have limited access to the specific servers, web pages, or files needed. These users can therefore contribute to business productivity without compromising network security.

A remote-access VPN is typically enabled dynamically by the user when required. Remote-access VPNs can be created using either IPsec or SSL. As shown in Figure 8-5, a remote user must initiate a remote-access VPN connection.

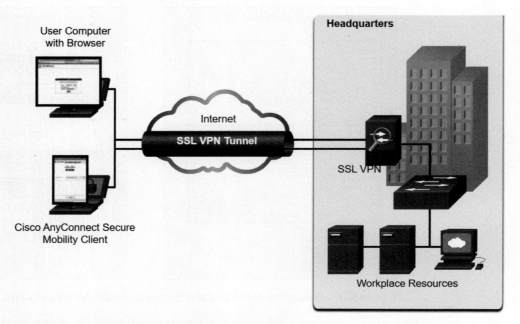

Figure 8-5   Clientless and Client-Based Connection Examples

The figure shows two ways that a remote user can initiate a remote-access VPN connection:

- *Clientless VPN* **connection:** The connection is secured using a web browser SSL connection. SSL is mostly used to protect HTTP traffic (HTTPS) and email protocols such as IMAP and POP3. HTTPS is actually HTTP using an SSL tunnel. The SSL connection is first established, and then HTTP data is exchanged over the connection.

- *Client-based VPN* **connection:** *VPN client software* such as Cisco AnyConnect Secure Mobility Client must be installed on the remote user's end device. A user must initiate a VPN connection by using the VPN client and then authenticate to the destination VPN gateway. When remote users are authenticated, they have access to corporate files and applications. The VPN client software encrypts the traffic using IPsec or SSL and forwards it over the internet to the destination VPN gateway.

SSL VPNs (8.2.2)

When a client negotiates an SSL VPN connection with the VPN gateway, it actually connects using *Transport Layer Security (TLS)*. TLS is the newer version of SSL and is sometimes expressed as SSL/TLS. However, both terms are often used interchangeably.

SSL uses the *public key infrastructure* and *digital certificates* to authenticate peers. Both IPsec and SSL VPN technologies offer access to virtually any network application or resource. However, when security is an issue, IPsec is the superior choice. If support and ease of deployment are the primary issues, consider SSL. The type of VPN method implemented depends on the access requirements of the users and the organization's IT processes. Table 8-2 compares IPsec and SSL remote-access deployments.

Table 8-2   IPsec and SSL Comparison

Feature	IPsec	SSL
Applications supported	Extensive: All IP-based applications are supported.	Limited: Only web-based applications and file sharing are supported.
Authentication strength	Strong: Uses two-way authentication with shared keys or digital certificates.	Moderate: Uses one-way or two-way authentication.
Encryption strength	Strong: Uses key lengths from 56 bits to 256 bits.	Moderate to strong: Uses key lengths from 40 bits to 256 bits.
Connection complexity	Medium: Requires a VPN client preinstalled on a host.	Low: Requires only a web browser on a host.
Connection option	Limited: Only specific devices with specific configurations can connect.	Extensive: Any device with a web browser can connect.

It is important to understand that IPsec and SSL VPNs are not mutually exclusive. Instead, they are complementary; the two technologies solve different problems, and an organization may implement IPsec, SSL, or both, depending on the needs of its telecommuters.

Site-to-Site IPsec VPNs (8.2.3)

Site-to-site VPNs are used to connect networks across another untrusted network, such as the internet. In a site-to-site VPN, end hosts send and receive normal unencrypted TCP/IP traffic through a VPN terminating device. The VPN terminating device is typically called a VPN gateway. A VPN gateway device could be a router or a firewall, as shown in Figure 8-6.

For example, the Cisco Adaptive Security Appliance (ASA) shown on the right side of the figure is a standalone firewall device that combines firewall, VPN concentrator, and intrusion prevention functionality in one software image.

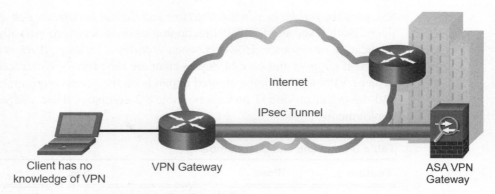

Figure 8-6 Site-to-Site IPsec VPN Topology

The VPN gateway encapsulates and encrypts all outbound traffic from a particular site. It then sends the traffic through a VPN tunnel over the internet to a VPN gateway at the target site. Upon receipt, the receiving VPN gateway strips the headers, decrypts the content, and relays the packet toward the target host inside its private network.

Site-to-site VPNs are typically created and secured using IP Security (IPsec).

GRE over IPsec (8.2.4)

Generic Routing Encapsulation (GRE) is a nonsecure site-to-site VPN tunneling protocol. It can encapsulate various network layer protocols. It also supports multicast and broadcast traffic, which may be necessary if the organization requires routing protocols to operate over a VPN. However, GRE does not by default support encryption; therefore, it does not provide a secure VPN tunnel.

A standard IPsec VPN (non-GRE) can only create secure tunnels for unicast traffic. Therefore, routing protocols do not exchange routing information over an IPsec VPN. To solve this problem, you can encapsulate routing protocol traffic using a GRE packet and then encapsulate the GRE packet into an IPsec packet to forward it securely to the destination VPN gateway. The terms used to describe the encapsulation of *GRE over IPsec tunnel* are shown in Figure 8-7:

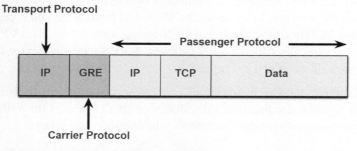

Figure 8-7 GRE over IPsec Packet

- *Passenger protocol*: This is the original packet that is to be encapsulated by GRE. It could be an IPv4 or IPv6 packet or a routing update.

- *Carrier protocol*: GRE is the carrier protocol that encapsulates the original passenger packet.

- *Transport protocol*: This is the protocol that will actually be used to forward the packet. It could be IPv4 or IPv6.

For example, in the topology shown in Figure 8-8, Branch and HQ would like to exchange OSPF routing information over an IPsec VPN.

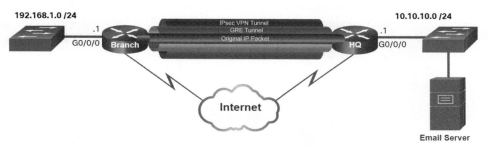

Figure 8-8   Example of Passenger, Carrier, and Transport Protocol Encapsulation

However, IPsec does not support multicast traffic. Therefore, GRE over IPsec is used to support the routing protocol traffic over the IPsec VPN. Specifically, the OSPF (the passenger protocol) packets would be encapsulated by GRE (the carrier protocol) and subsequently encapsulated in an IPsec VPN tunnel.

The Wireshark screen capture in Figure 8-9 shows an OSPF Hello packet that was sent using GRE over IPsec. In this example, the original OSPF Hello multicast packet (the passenger protocol) is encapsulated with a GRE header (the carrier protocol), which is subsequently encapsulated by another IP header (the transport protocol). This IP header can then be forwarded over an IPsec tunnel.

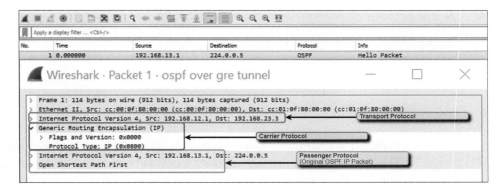

Figure 8-9   Wireshark of Encapsulated Protocols

Dynamic Multipoint VPNs (8.2.5)

Site-to-site IPsec VPNs and GRE over IPsec are adequate when there are only a few sites to securely interconnect. However, they are not sufficient when the enterprise adds many more sites. This is because each site would require static configurations to all other sites or to a central site.

Dynamic Multipoint VPN (DMVPN) is a Cisco software solution for building multiple VPNs in an easy, dynamic, and scalable manner. Like other VPN types, DMVPN relies on IPsec to provide secure transport over public networks, such as the internet.

DMVPN simplifies VPN tunnel configuration and provides a flexible option to connect a central site with branch sites. It uses a hub-and-spoke configuration to establish a full mesh topology. Spoke sites establish secure VPN tunnels with the hub site, as shown in Figure 8-10.

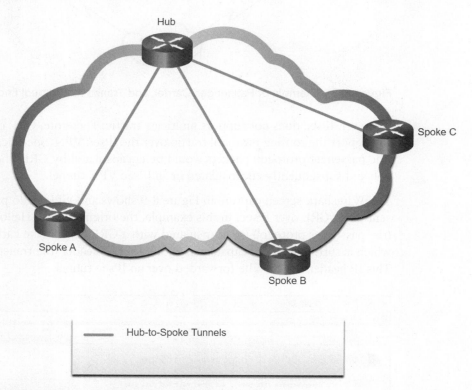

Figure 8-10   DMVPN Hub-to-Spoke Tunnels

Each site is configured using *Multipoint Generic Routing Encapsulation (mGRE)*. The mGRE tunnel interface allows a single GRE interface to dynamically support multiple IPsec tunnels. Therefore, when a new site requires a secure connection, the same configuration on the hub site would support the tunnel. No additional configuration would be required.

Spoke sites could also obtain information about other spoke sites from the central site and create virtual *spoke-to-spoke* tunnels, as shown in Figure 8-11.

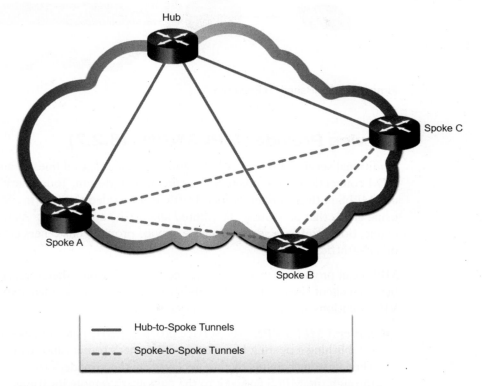

Figure 8-11   DMVPN Hub-to-Spoke and Spoke-to-Spoke Tunnels

IPsec Virtual Tunnel Interface (8.2.6)

Like DMVPN, *IPsec virtual tunnel interfaces (IPsec VTIs)* simplify the configuration process required to support multiple sites and remote access. IPsec VTI configurations are applied to a virtual interface instead of statically mapping the IPsec sessions to a physical interface.

An IPsec VTI is capable of sending and receiving both IP unicast and multicast encrypted traffic. Therefore, routing protocols are automatically supported without configuration of GRE tunnels, as shown in Figure 8-12.

An IPsec VTI can be configured between sites or in a hub-and-spoke topology.

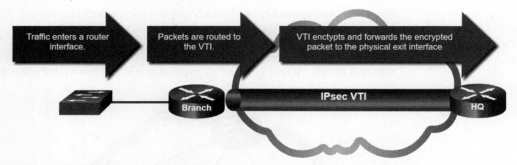

Figure 8-12   IPsec VTI Example

Service Provider MPLS VPNs (8.2.7)

Traditional service provider WAN solutions such as leased lines, Frame Relay, and ATM connections were inherently secure in their design. Today, service providers use MPLS in their core networks. Traffic is forwarded through the MPLS backbone using labels that previously distributed among the core routers. As with legacy WAN connections, traffic is secure because service provider customers cannot see each other's traffic.

MPLS can provide clients with managed VPN solutions; therefore, securing traffic between client sites is the responsibility of the service provider. Two types of MPLS VPN solutions are supported by service providers:

- *Layer 3 MPLS VPN*: The service provider participates in customer routing by establishing a peering between the customer's routers and the provider's routers. Then customer routes that are received by the provider's router are redistributed through the MPLS network to the customer's remote locations.

- *Layer 2 MPLS VPN*: The service provider is not involved in the customer routing. Instead, the provider deploys *Virtual Private LAN Service (VPLS)* to emulate an Ethernet multiaccess LAN segment over the MPLS network. No routing is involved. The customer's routers effectively belong to the same multiaccess network.

Figure 8-13 shows a service provider that offers both Layer 2 and Layer 3 MPLS VPNs.

Interactive Graphic

Check Your Understanding—Types of VPNs (8.2.8)

Refer to the online course to complete this activity.

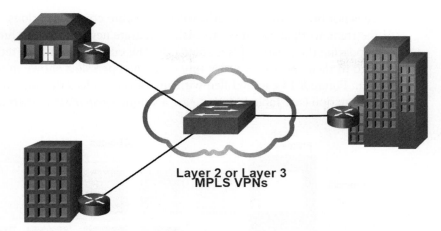

Figure 8-13   Layer 2 and Layer 3 MPLS

IPsec (8.3)

In this section, you will learn how the IPsec framework is used to secure network traffic.

Video—IPsec Concepts (8.3.1)

Refer to the online course to view this video.

IPsec Technologies (8.3.2)

IPsec is an IETF standard (RFC 2401–2412) that defines how a VPN can be secured across IP networks. IPsec protects and authenticates IP packets between source and destination. IPsec can protect traffic from Layer 4 through Layer 7.

Using the IPsec framework, IPsec provides these essential security functions:

- *Confidentiality*: IPsec uses encryption algorithms to prevent cybercriminals from reading the packet contents.

- *Integrity*: IPsec uses hashing algorithms to ensure that packets have not been altered between the source and the destination.

- **Origin authentication:** IPsec uses the *Internet Key Exchange (IKE)* protocol to authenticate the source and the destination. Methods of authentication include using *pre-shared keys (PSKs)*, digital certificates, or RSA certificates.

- **Diffie-Hellman:** Secure key exchange using the DH algorithm.

IPsec is not bound to any specific rules for secure communications. This flexibility of the framework allows IPsec to easily integrate new security technologies without updating the existing IPsec standards. The currently available technologies are aligned to their specific security function. The open slots shown in the IPsec framework in Figure 8-14 can be filled with any of the choices that are available for that IPsec function (see Table 8-3) to create a unique *security association (SA)*.

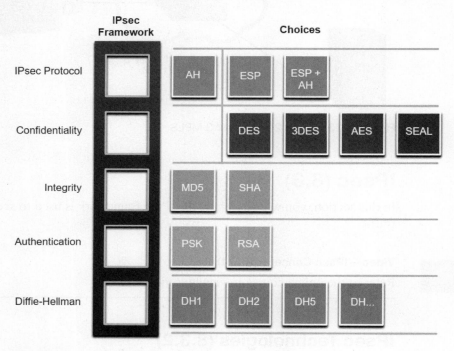

Figure 8-14   IPsec Framework

Table 8-3   The Security Functions of the IPsec Framework

IPsec Function	Description
IPsec protocol	The choices for IPsec protocol include *Authentication Header (AH)* and *Encapsulation Security Protocol (ESP)*. AH authenticates Layer 3 packets. ESP encrypts Layer 3 packets. (ESP and AH are rarely used together as this combination cannot successfully traverse a NAT device.)
Confidentiality	Encryption ensures confidentiality of Layer 3 packets. Choices include *Data Encryption Standard (DES)*, *Triple DES (3DES)*, *Advanced Encryption Standard (AES)*, and *Software-Optimized Encryption Algorithm (SEAL)*. No encryption is also an option.

IPsec Function	Description
Integrity	Integrity involves using a hashing algorithm, such as *Message Digest 5 (MD5)* or *Secure Hash Algorithm (SHA)*, to ensure that data arrives unchanged at the destination.
Authentication	IPsec uses Internet Key Exchange (IKE) to authenticate users and devices that can carry out communication independently. IKE uses several types of authentication, including username and password, one-time password, biometrics, pre-shared keys (PSKs), and digital certificates using the Rivest, Shamir, and Adleman (RSA) algorithm.
Diffie-Hellman	IPsec uses the DH algorithm to provide a public key exchange method for two peers to establish a shared secret key. There are several different groups to choose from, including DH14, 15, 16 and DH 19, 20, 21, and 24. DH1, 2, and 5 are no longer recommended.

Figure 8-15 shows examples of SAs for two different implementations.

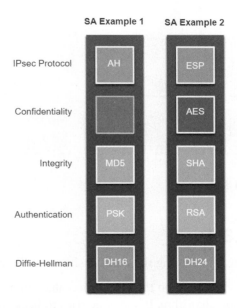

Figure 8-15   IPsec Security Association Examples

An SA is a basic building block of IPsec. When establishing a VPN link, the peers must share the same SA to negotiate key exchange parameters, establish a shared key, authenticate each other, and negotiate the encryption parameters. Notice that SA Example 1 in Figure 8-15 is using no encryption.

IPsec Protocol Encapsulation (8.3.3)

IPsec protocol encapsulation is the first building block of the framework. IPsec encapsulates packets using Authentication Header (AH) or Encapsulation Security Protocol (ESP). The choice of AH or ESP in Figure 8-16 establishes which other building blocks are available.

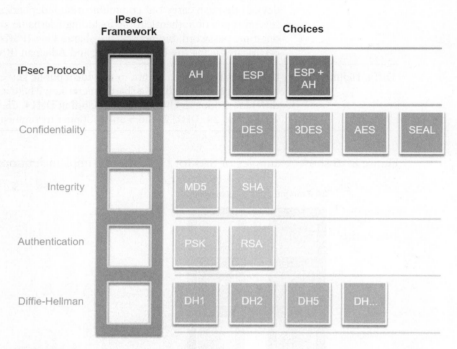

Figure 8-16   IPsec Protocol Selection

Confidentiality (8.3.4)

Confidentiality is achieved by encrypting the data, as shown in Figure 8-17.

The degree of confidentiality depends on the encryption algorithm and the length of the key used in the encryption algorithm. If someone tries to hack the key through a brute-force attack, the number of possibilities to try depends on the length of the key. The time to process all the possibilities is a function of the computer power of the attacking device. The shorter the key, the easier it is to break. A 64-bit key can take approximately a year to break with a relatively sophisticated computer. A 128-bit key with the same machine can take roughly 10^{19}, or 10 quintillion, years to decrypt.

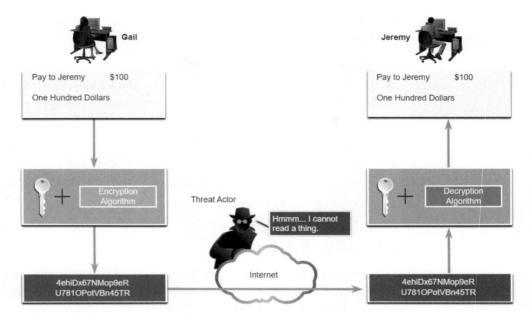

Figure 8-17   Confidentiality Example

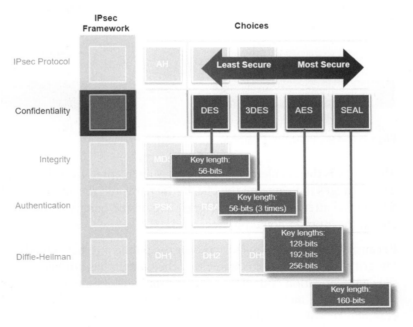

Figure 8-18   Confidentiality Encryption Algorithms

The encryption algorithms highlighted in Figure 8-18 are all symmetric key cryptosystems:

- DES uses a 56-bit key.

- 3DES is a variant of 56-bit DES that uses three independent 56-bit encryption keys per 64-bit block, which provides significantly stronger encryption strength compared to DES.

- AES provides stronger security than DES and is computationally more efficient than 3DES. AES offers three different key lengths: 128 bits, 192 bits, and 256 bits.

- SEAL is a stream cipher, which means it encrypts data continuously rather than encrypting blocks of data. SEAL uses a 160-bit key.

Integrity (8.3.5)

Data integrity means that the data that is received is exactly the same data that was sent. Data could potentially be intercepted and modified. For example, say that, as shown in Figure 8-19, a check for $100 is written to Alex.

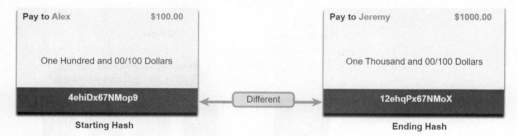

Figure 8-19   Integrity Example

The check is then mailed to Alex, but it is intercepted by a threat actor. The threat actor changes the name on the check to Jeremy and the amount on the check to $1,000 and attempts to cash it. Depending on the quality of the forgery in the altered check, the attacker could be successful.

Because VPN data is transported over the public internet, a method of proving data integrity is required to guarantee that the content has not been altered. A hash message authentication code (HMAC) is a data integrity algorithm that guarantees the integrity of the message by using a hash value. Figure 8-20 highlights the two most common HMAC algorithms:

Note

Cisco now rates SHA-1 as legacy and recommends at least SHA-256 for integrity.

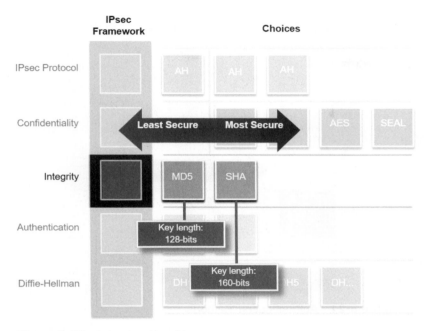

Figure 8-20   Integrity Algorithms

- Message-Digest 5 (MD5) uses a 128-bit shared-secret key. The variable-length message and 128-bit shared secret key are combined and run through the HMAC-MD5 hashing algorithm. The output is a 128-bit hash.

- Secure Hash Algorithm (SHA) uses a 160-bit secret key. The variable-length message and the 160-bit shared secret key are combined and run through the HMAC-SHA-1 algorithm. The output is a 160-bit hash.

Authentication (8.3.6)

When conducting business long distance, you must know who is at the other end of the phone, email, or fax. Similarly, with a VPN network, the device on the other end of the VPN tunnel must be authenticated before the communication path can be considered secure. Figure 8-21 highlights the two peer authentication methods:

- A pre-shared key (PSK) value can be entered into each peer manually. The PSK is combined with other information to form the authentication key. PSKs are easy to configure manually but do not scale well because each IPsec peer must be configured with the PSK of every other peer with which it communicates.

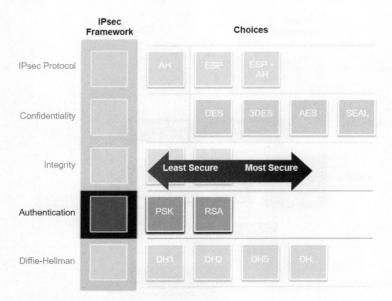

Figure 8-21 Authentication Methods

- *Rivest, Shamir, and Adleman (RSA) authentication* uses digital certificates to authenticate the peers. The local device derives a hash and encrypts it with its private key. The encrypted hash is attached to the message and is forwarded to the remote end and acts like a signature. At the remote end, the encrypted hash is decrypted using the public key of the local end. If the decrypted hash matches the recomputed hash, the signature is genuine. Each peer must authenticate its opposite peer before the tunnel is considered secure.

Figure 8-22 shows an example of PSK authentication.

At the local device, the authentication key and the identity information are sent through a hashing algorithm to form the hash for the local peer (Hash_L). One-way authentication is established by sending Hash_L to the remote device. If the remote device can independently create the same hash, the local device is authenticated. After the remote device authenticates the local device, the authentication process begins in the opposite direction, and all steps are repeated from the remote device to the local device.

Figure 8-23 shows an example of RSA authentication.

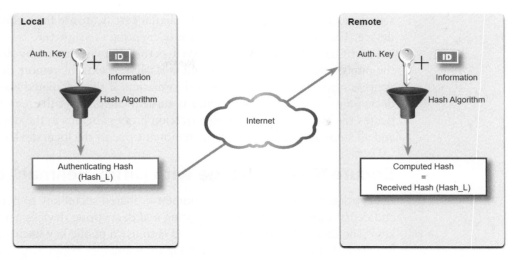

Figure 8-22   PSK Authentication

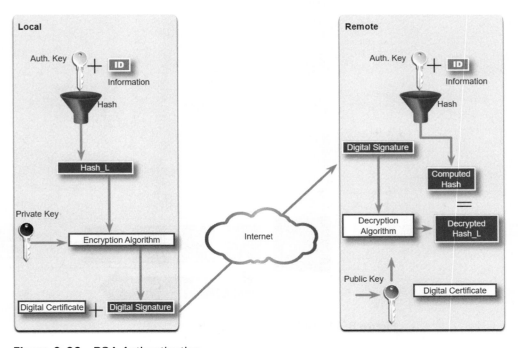

Figure 8-23   RSA Authentication

At the local device, the authentication key and identity information are sent through the hashing algorithm to form the hash for the local peer (Hash_L). Then Hash_L is encrypted using the local device's private encryption key. This creates a digital signature. The digital signature and a digital certificate are forwarded to the remote device. The public encryption key for decrypting the signature is included in the digital certificate. The remote device verifies the digital signature by decrypting it using the public encryption key. The result is Hash_L. Next, the remote device independently creates Hash_L from stored information. If the calculated Hash_L equals the decrypted Hash_L, the local device is authenticated. After the remote device authenticates the local device, the authentication process begins in the opposite direction, and all steps are repeated from the remote device to the local device.

Secure Key Exchange with Diffie-Hellman (8.3.7)

Encryption algorithms require a symmetric, shared secret key to perform encryption and decryption. How do the encrypting and decrypting devices get the shared secret key? The easiest key exchange method is to use a public key exchange method, such as Diffie-Hellman (DH), as shown in Figure 8-24.

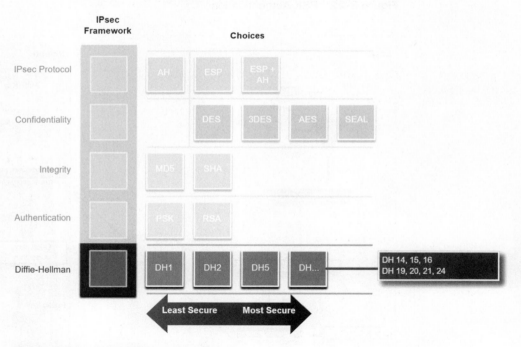

Figure 8-24   Diffie-Hellman Groups

DH provides a way for two peers to establish a shared secret key that only they know, even though they are communicating over an insecure channel. Variations of the DH key exchange are specified as DH groups:

- DH groups 1, 2, and 5 should no longer be used. These groups support key sizes of 768 bits, 1024 bits, and 1536 bits, respectively.

- DH groups 14, 15, and 16 use larger key sizes with 2048 bits, 3072 bits, and 4096 bits, respectively, and are recommended for use until 2030.

- DH groups 19, 20, 21, and 24, with respective key sizes of 256 bits, 384 bits, 521 bits, and 2048 bits, support elliptic curve cryptography (ECC), which reduces the time needed to generate keys. DH group 24 is the preferred next-generation encryption.

The DH group you choose must be strong enough, or have enough bits, to protect the IPsec keys during negotiation. For example, DH group 1 is strong enough to support DES and 3DES encryption, but not AES. For example, if the encryption or authentication algorithms use a 128-bit key, use group 14, 19, 20, or 24. However, if the encryption or authentication algorithms use a 256-bit key or higher, use group 21 or 24.

Video

Video—IPsec Transport and Tunnel Mode (8.3.8)

Refer to the online course to view this video.

Interactive Graphic

Check Your Understanding—IPsec (8.3.9)

Refer to the online course to complete this activity.

Summary (8.4)

The following is a summary of the sections in this chapter.

VPN Technology

A VPN is virtual in that it carries information within a private network, but that information is actually transported over a public network. A VPN is private in that the traffic is encrypted to keep the data confidential while it is transported across the public network. Benefits of VPNs are cost savings, security, scalability, and compatibility.

Types of VPNs

VPNs are commonly deployed in one of the following configurations: site-to-site or remote-access VPNs. VPNs can be managed and deployed as enterprise VPNs and service provider VPNs.

Remote-access VPNs let remote and mobile users securely connect to the enterprise by creating an encrypted tunnel. Remote-access VPNs can be created using either IPsec or SSL. When a client negotiates an SSL VPN connection with the VPN gateway, it actually connects using TLS. SSL uses public key infrastructure and digital certificates to authenticate peers. Site-to-site VPNs are used to connect networks across an untrusted network such as the internet. In a site-to-site VPN, end hosts send and receive normal unencrypted TCP/IP traffic through a VPN terminating device. The VPN terminating device is typically called a VPN gateway. A VPN gateway could be a router or a firewall. GRE is a nonsecure site-to-site VPN tunneling protocol. DMVPN is a Cisco software solution for easily building multiple dynamic scalable VPNs. Like DMVPN, IPsec VTIs simplify the configuration process required to support multiple sites and remote access. IPsec VTI configurations are applied to a virtual interface instead of statically mapping the IPsec sessions to a physical interface. A IPsec VTI can send and receive both IP unicast and multicast encrypted traffic. MPLS can provide clients with managed VPN solutions; therefore, securing traffic between client sites is the responsibility of the service provider. Two types of MPLS VPN solutions are supported by service providers: Layer 3 MPLS VPNs and Layer 2 MPLS VPNs.

IPsec

IPsec protects and authenticates IP packets between the source and the destination. IPsec can protect traffic from Layer 4 through Layer 7. Using the IPsec framework,

IPsec provides confidentiality, integrity, origin authentication, and Diffie-Hellman. The IPsec protocol encapsulation is the first building block of the framework. IPsec encapsulates packets using AH or ESP. The degree of confidentiality depends on the encryption algorithm and the length of the key used in the encryption algorithm. An HMAC is an algorithm that guarantees the integrity of a message by using a hash value. The device on the other end of the VPN tunnel must be authenticated before the communication path is considered secure. A PSK value is entered into each peer manually. The PSK is combined with other information to form the authentication key. RSA authentication uses digital certificates to authenticate the peers. The local device derives a hash and encrypts it with its private key. The encrypted hash is attached to the message and is forwarded to the remote end and acts like a signature. DH provides a way for two peers to establish a shared secret key that only they know, even though they are communicating over an insecure channel.

Practice

There are no labs or Packet Tracer activities for this chapter.

Check Your Understanding Questions

Complete all the review questions listed here to test your understanding of the topics and concepts in this chapter. The appendix "Answers to the 'Check Your Understanding' Questions" lists the answers.

1. A network design engineer is planning the implementation of a cost-effective method to interconnect multiple networks securely over the internet. Which type of technology is required?

    A. a dedicated ISP

    B. a GRE IP tunnel

    C. a leased line

    D. a VPN gateway

2. Which statement is true of site-to-site VPNs?

    A. Individual hosts can enable and disable the VPN connection.

    B. Internal hosts send normal, unencapsulated packets.

    C. The VPN connection is not statically defined.

    D. VPN client software is installed on each host.

3. How is the hash message authentication code (HMAC) algorithm used in an IPsec VPN?

   A. to authenticate the IPsec peers

   B. to create a secure channel for key negotiation

   C. to guarantee message integrity

   D. to protect IPsec keys during session negotiation

4. What IPsec algorithm is used to provide data confidentiality?

   A. AES

   B. Diffie-Hellman

   C. MD5

   D. RSA

   E. SHA

5. What are two hashing algorithms used with IPsec to guarantee authenticity? (Choose two.)

   A. AES

   B. DH

   C. MD5

   D. RSA

   E. SHA

6. What two IPsec algorithms provide encryption and hashing to protect interesting traffic? (Choose two.)

   A. AES

   B. DH

   C. IKE

   D. PSK

   E. SHA

7. Which protocol creates a virtual unencrypted point-to-point VPN tunnel between Cisco routers?

   A. GRE

   B. IKE

   C. IPsec

   D. OSPF

8. Which VPN solution allows the use of a web browser to establish a secure, remote-access VPN tunnel to a VPN gateway?

   A. client-based SSL

   B. clientless SSL

   C. site-to-site using a pre-shared key

   D. site-to-site using an ACL

9. Which IPsec security function utilizes encryption to protect data transfers with a key?

   A. authentication

   B. confidentiality

   C. integrity

   D. secure key exchange

10. Which of the following are service provider managed VPN solutions? (Choose two.)

    A. client-based IPsec VPN

    B. clientless SSL VPN

    C. Frame Relay

    D. Layer 3 MPLS VPN

    E. remote-access VPN

    F. site-to-site VPN

11. Which of the following are enterprise-managed remote-access VPNs? (Choose two.)

    A. client-based IPsec VPN

    B. clientless SSL VPN

    C. Frame Relay

    D. Layer 3 MPLS VPN

    E. remote-access VPN

    F. site-to-site VPN

12. Which is a requirement of a site-to-site VPN?

    A. Hosts connected using a web browser and an SSL connection

    B. Hosts connected using client-based VPN software

    C. A client/server architecture

    D. VPN gateways at each end of the tunnel

    E. VPN server at the edge of the company network

13. How is the Diffie-Hellman algorithm used in the IPsec framework?

  A. allows peers to exchange shared keys

  B. guarantees message integrity

  C. provides authentication

  D. provides strong data encryption

14. Which type of VPN involves passenger, carrier, and transport protocols?

  A. DMVPN

  B. GRE over IPsec

  C. IPsec virtual tunnel interface

  D. MPLS VPN

15. Which type of VPN supports multiple sites by applying configurations to virtual interfaces instead of physical interfaces?

  A. IPsec virtual tunnel interface

  B. DMVPN

  C. MPLS VPN

  D. GRE over IPsec

16. Which type of VPN connects using the Transport Layer Security (TLS) feature?

  A. SSL VPN

  B. GRE over IPsec

  C. DMVPN

  D. IPsec virtual tunnel interface

  E. MPLS VPN

17. Which description correctly identifies an MPLS VPN?

  A. allows multicast and broadcast traffic over a secure site-to-site VPN

  B. has both Layer 2 and Layer 3 implementations

  C. involves a nonsecure tunneling protocol being encapsulated by IPsec

  D. routes packets through virtual tunnel interfaces for encryption and forwarding.

  E. uses the public key infrastructure and digital certificates.

18. Which description correctly identifies an SSL VPN?

    A. allows multicast and broadcast traffic over a secure site-to-site VPN

    B. has both Layer 2 and Layer 3 implementations

    C. involves a nonsecure tunneling protocol being encapsulated by IPsec

    D. routes packets through virtual tunnel interfaces for encryption and forwarding

    E. uses the public key infrastructure and digital certificates

19. Which two descriptions correctly identify an IPsec VTI VPN? (Choose two.)

    A. allows multicast and broadcast traffic over a secure site-to-site VPN

    B. has both Layer 2 and Layer 3 implementations

    C. involves a nonsecure tunneling protocol being encapsulated by IPsec

    D. routes packets through virtual tunnel interfaces for encryption and forwarding

    E. uses the public key infrastructure and digital certificates

20. Which two descriptions correctly identify a GRE over IPsec VPN? (Choose two.)

    A. allows multicast and broadcast traffic over a secure site-to-site VPN

    B. has both Layer 2 and Layer 3 implementations

    C. involves a nonsecure tunneling protocol being encapsulated by IPsec

    D. routes packets through virtual tunnel interfaces for encryption and forwarding

    E. uses the public key infrastructure and digital certificates

CHAPTER 9

QoS Concepts

Objectives

Upon completion of this chapter, you will be able to answer the following questions:

- How do network transmission characteristics impact quality?

- What are the minimum network requirements for voice, video, and data traffic?

- What queuing algorithms do networking devices use?

- What are the different QoS models?

- What QoS mechanisms ensure transmission quality?

Key Terms

This chapter uses the following key terms. You can find the definitions in the Glossary.

Introduction (9.0)

Imagine driving on a heavily congested road and being in a rush to meet a friend for dinner. You hear the siren and see the lights of an ambulance behind you. You need to move off the road to let the ambulance through. The ambulance getting to the hospital takes priority over you getting to the restaurant on time.

Much like the ambulance taking priority in the traffic on the highway, some forms of network traffic need priority over others. Why? Get started with this chapter to find out!

Network Transmission Quality (9.1)

In this section, you will learn how network transmission characteristics impact quality.

Video

Video Tutorial—The Purpose of QoS (9.1.1)

Refer to the online course to view this video.

Prioritizing Traffic (9.1.2)

Quality of service (QoS) is an ever-increasing requirement of networks today. New applications, such as voice and live video transmissions, create higher expectations for quality delivery among users.

Congestion occurs when multiple communication lines aggregate onto a single device such as a router and then much of that data is placed on just a few outbound interfaces or onto a slower interface. Congestion can also occur when large data packets prevent smaller packets from being transmitted in a timely manner.

When the volume of traffic is greater than what can be transported across the network, devices queue (hold) the packets in memory until resources become available to transmit them. Queuing packets causes *delay* because new packets cannot be transmitted until previous packets have been processed. If the number of packets queued continues to increase, the memory within the device fills up, and the device drops packets. One QoS technique that can help with this problem is to classify data into multiple queues, as shown in Figure 9-1.

> **Note**
>
> A device implements QoS only when it is experiencing some type of congestion.

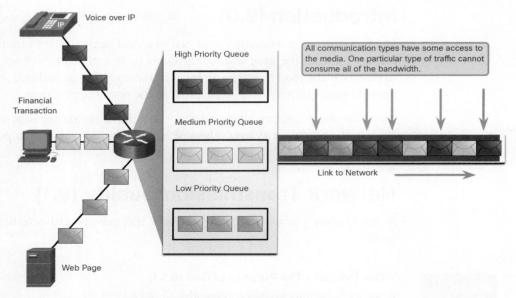

Figure 9-1   Using Queues to Prioritize Communications

Bandwidth, Congestion, Delay, and Jitter (9.1.3)

Network bandwidth is measured in the number of bits that can be transmitted in a single second, or bits per second (bps). For example, a network device may be described as having the capability to perform at 10 gigabits per second (Gbps).

Network congestion causes delay. An interface experiences congestion when it is presented with more traffic than it can handle. Network congestion points are ideal candidates for QoS mechanisms. Figure 9-2 shows three examples of typical congestion points.

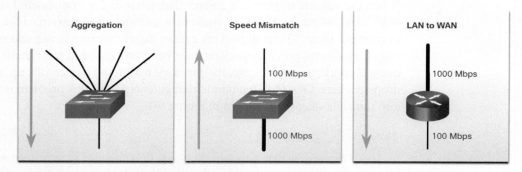

Figure 9-2   Examples of Congestion Points

Delay, or latency, refers to the time it takes for a packet to travel from the source to the destination. Two types of delays are fixed and variable. A fixed delay is a specific amount of time a specific process takes, such as how long it takes to place a bit on the transmission media. A variable delay takes an unspecified amount of time and is affected by factors such as how much traffic is being processed.

The types of delay are summarized in Table 9-1.

Table 9-1 Types of Delay

Delay Type	Description
Code delay	The fixed amount of time it takes to compress data at the source before transmitting to the first internetworking device, usually a switch.
Packetization delay	The fixed time it takes to encapsulate a packet with all the necessary header information.
Queuing delay	The variable amount of time a frame or packet waits to be transmitted on the link.
Serialization delay	The fixed amount of time it takes to transmit a frame onto the wire.
Propagation delay	The variable amount of time it takes for a frame to travel between the source and destination.
De-jitter delay	The fixed amount of time it takes to buffer a flow of packets and then send them out in evenly spaced intervals.

Jitter is the variation in the delay of received packets. At the sending side, packets are sent in a continuous stream, with the packets spaced evenly apart. Due to network congestion, improper queuing, or configuration errors, the delay between packets can vary instead of remaining constant. Both delay and jitter need to be controlled and minimized to support real-time and interactive traffic.

Packet Loss (9.1.4)

Without any QoS mechanisms in place, packets are processed in the order in which they are received. When congestion occurs, network devices such as routers and switches can drop packets. This means that time-sensitive packets, such as real-time video and voice, will be dropped with the same frequency as data that is not time sensitive, such as email and web browsing.

When a router receives a Real-Time Protocol (RTP) digital audio stream for voice over IP (VoIP), it must compensate for the jitter that is encountered. The mechanism that handles this function is the *playout delay buffer*. This buffer must buffer these packets and then play them out in a steady stream, as shown in Figure 9-3. The digital packets are later converted back to an analog audio stream.

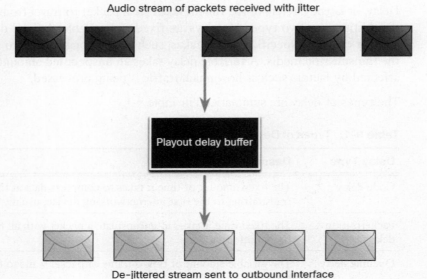

Figure 9-3   Playout Delay Buffer Compensates for Jitter

If the jitter is so severe that it causes packets to be received out of the range of this buffer, the out-of-range packets are discarded, and dropouts are heard in the audio, as shown in Figure 9-4.

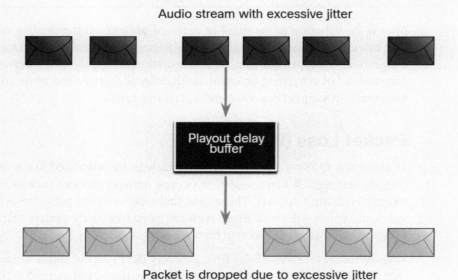

Figure 9-4   Packet Dropped Due to Excessive Jitter

For losses as small as one packet, the *digital signal processor (DSP)* interpolates what it thinks the audio should be, and no problem is audible to the user. However, when jitter exceeds what the DSP can do to make up for the missing packets, audio problems are heard.

Packet loss is a very common cause of voice quality problems on an IP network. In a properly designed network, packet loss should be near zero. The voice codecs used by the DSP can tolerate some degree of packet loss without a dramatic effect on voice quality. Network engineers use QoS mechanisms to classify voice packets for zero packet loss. Bandwidth is guaranteed for the voice calls by giving priority to voice traffic over traffic that is not sensitive to delays.

Interactive Graphic

Check Your Understanding—Network Transmission Quality (9.1.5)

Refer to the online course to complete this activity.

Traffic Characteristics (9.2)

In this section, you will learn about the minimum network requirements to support voice, video, and data traffic.

Video

Video Tutorial—Traffic Characteristics (9.2.1)

Refer to the online course to view this video.

Network Traffic Trends (9.2.2)

Earlier in this chapter, you learned about network transmission quality. In this section you will learn about traffic characteristics (voice, video, and data). In the early 2000s, the predominant types of IP traffic were voice and data. Voice traffic has a predictable bandwidth need and known packet arrival times. Data traffic is not real time and has unpredictable bandwidth need. Data traffic can temporarily burst, as when a large file is being downloaded. This bursting can consume the entire bandwidth of a link.

More recently, video traffic has become increasingly important to business communications and operations. Consider that organizations now commonly use video conferencing to meet with users and clients, high-definition video surveillance to remotely monitor facilities and equipment, and video streaming for a variety of purposes, including training. According to the *Cisco Visual Networking Index (VNI)*, by 2022 video will represent 82% of all internet traffic. In addition, mobile video traffic will reach 60.9 exabytes per month by 2022.

The type of demands that voice, video, and data traffic place on the network are very different.

Voice (9.2.3)

Voice traffic is predictable and smooth. However, voice is very sensitive to delays and dropped packets. It makes no sense to re-transmit voice if packets are lost; therefore, voice packets must receive a higher priority than other types of traffic. For example, Cisco products use the RTP port range 16,384 to 32,767 to prioritize voice traffic. Voice can tolerate a certain amount of latency, jitter, and loss without any noticeable effects. Latency should be no more than 150 milliseconds (ms). Jitter should be no more than 30 ms, and voice packet loss should be no more than 1%. Voice traffic requires at least 30 kbps of bandwidth. Table 9-2 gives a summary of voice traffic characteristics and requirements.

Table 9-2   Voice Traffic Characteristics

Characteristics	One-Way Requirements
■ Smooth	■ Latency ≤ 150 ms
■ Benign	■ Jitter ≤ 30 ms
■ Drop sensitive	■ Loss ≤ 1% bandwidth (30–128 kbps)
■ Delay sensitive	
■ UDP priority	

Video (9.2.4)

Without QoS and a significant amount of extra bandwidth capacity, video quality typically degrades. The picture appears blurry, jagged, or too slow. The audio portion of the feed may become unsynchronized with the video.

Video traffic tends to be unpredictable, inconsistent, and bursty compared to voice traffic. Compared to voice, video is less resilient to loss and has a higher volume of data per packet. Notice in Figure 9-5 that voice packets arrive every 20 ms and are a predictable 200 bytes each.

In contrast, the number and size of video packets vary every 33 ms, based on the content of the video, as shown in Figure 9-6.

For example, if the video stream consists of content that is not changing much from frame to frame, the video packets are small, and fewer of them are required to maintain acceptable user experience. However, if the video steam consists of content that is rapidly changing, such as an action sequence in a movie, the video packets are larger, and more of them are required per the 33 ms time slot to maintain an acceptable user experience.

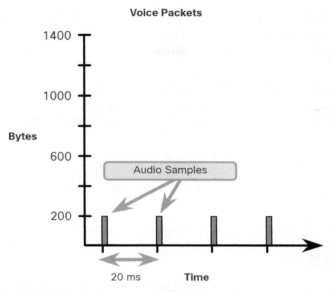

Figure 9-5   Voice Packet Size and Timing

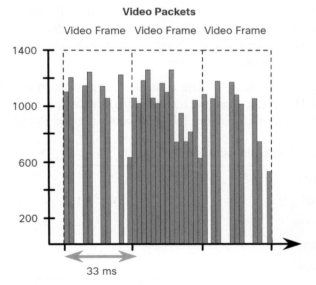

Figure 9-6   Video Packet Size and Timing

UDP ports such as 554 are used for the Real-Time Streaming Protocol (RTSP) and should be given priority over other, less delay-sensitive, network traffic. Similar to voice, video can tolerate a certain amount of latency, jitter, and loss without any noticeable effects. Latency should be no more than 400 milliseconds (ms). Jitter should be no more than 50 ms, and video packet loss should be no more than 1%. Video traffic requires at least 384 kbps of bandwidth. Table 9-3 gives a summary of video traffic characteristics and requirements.

Table 9-3   Video Traffic Characteristics

Characteristics	One-Way Requirements
■ Bursty	■ Latency ≤ 200–400 ms
■ Greedy	■ Jitter ≤ 30–50 ms
■ Drop sensitive	■ Loss ≤ 0.1–1% bandwidth (384 kbps–20 Mbps)
■ Delay sensitive	
■ UDP priority	

Data (9.2.5)

Most applications use either TCP or UDP. Unlike UDP, TCP performs error recovery. Data applications that have no tolerance for data loss, such as email and web pages, use TCP to ensure that, if packets are lost in transit, they are re-sent. Data traffic can be smooth or bursty. Network control traffic is usually smooth and predictable. When there is a topology change, the network control traffic may burst for a few seconds. But the capacity of today's networks can easily handle the increase in network control traffic as the network converges.

However, some TCP applications can consume a large portion of network capacity. For example, FTP consumes as much bandwidth as it can get when you download a large file, such as a movie or game. Table 9-4 summarizes data traffic characteristics.

Table 9-4   Data Traffic Characteristics

- Smooth/bursty
- Benign/greedy
- Drop insensitive
- Delay insensitive
- TCP retransmits

Although data traffic is relatively insensitive to drops and delays compared to voice and video, a network administrator still needs to consider the quality of the user experience, sometimes referred to as quality of experience (QoE). There are two main factors that a network administrator needs to consider about the flow of data traffic:

- Does the data come from an interactive application?
- Is the data mission critical?

Table 9-5 compares these two factors.

Table 9-5 Factors to Consider for Data Delay

Factor	Mission Critical	Not Mission Critical
Interactive	Prioritize for the lowest delay of all data traffic and strive for a 1- to 2-second response time.	Applications could benefit from lower delay.
Not interactive	Delay can vary greatly as long as the necessary minimum bandwidth is supplied.	Gets any leftover bandwidth after all voice, video, and other data application needs are met.

Interactive Graphic

Check Your Understanding—Traffic Characteristics (9.2.6)

Refer to the online course to complete this activity.

Queuing Algorithms (9.3)

The previous section covers traffic characteristics. This section explains the queuing algorithms used to implement QoS.

Video

Video Tutorial—QoS Algorithms (9.3.1)

Refer to the online course to view this video.

Queuing Overview (9.3.2)

The QoS policy implemented by a network administrator becomes active when congestion occurs on the link. Queuing is a congestion management tool that can buffer, prioritize, and, if required, reorder packets before they are transmitted to the destination.

A number of queuing algorithms are available. For the purposes of this chapter, we focus on the following:

- *First-in, first-out (FIFO)*
- *Weighted Fair Queuing (WFQ)*
- *Class-Based Weighted Fair Queuing (CBWFQ)*
- *Low Latency Queuing (LLQ)*

First-In, First Out (9.3.3)

In its simplest form, first-in, first-out (FIFO) queuing, also known as first-come, first-served queuing, buffers and forwards packets in the order of their arrival.

FIFO has no concept of priority or classes of traffic. Consequently, it makes no decision about packet priority. There is only one queue, and all packets are treated equally. Packets are sent out an interface in the order in which they arrive, as shown in Figure 9-7.

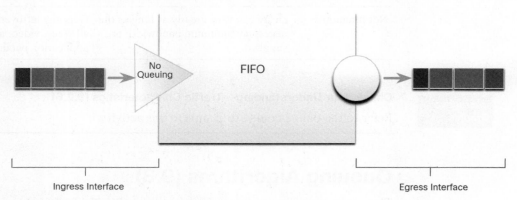

Figure 9-7   FIFO Queuing Example

Although some traffic may be more important or time-sensitive than other traffic, based on the priority *classification*, notice that the traffic is sent out in the order in which it is received.

When FIFO is used, important or time-sensitive traffic can be dropped when there is congestion on the router or switch interface. When no other queuing strategies are configured, all interfaces except serial interfaces at E1 (2.048 Mbps) and below use FIFO by default. (Serial interfaces at E1 and below use WFQ by default.)

FIFO, which is the fastest method of queuing, is effective for large links that have little delay and minimal congestion. If a link has very little congestion, FIFO queuing may be the only queuing needed.

Weighted Fair Queuing (WFQ) (9.3.4)

Weighted Fair Queuing (WFQ) is an automated scheduling method that provides fair bandwidth allocation to all network traffic. WFQ does not allow classification options to be configured. WFQ applies priority, or weights, to identified traffic and classifies it into conversations or flows, as shown in Figure 9-8.

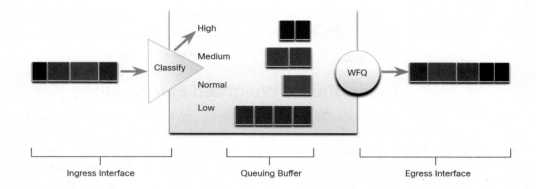

Figure 9-8   Weighted Fair Queuing Example

WFQ then determines how much bandwidth each flow is allowed, relative to other flows. The flow-based algorithm used by WFQ simultaneously schedules interactive traffic to the front of a queue to reduce response time. It then fairly shares the remaining bandwidth among high-bandwidth flows. WFQ allows you to give low-volume, interactive traffic, such as Telnet sessions and voice, priority over high-volume traffic, such as FTP sessions. When multiple file transfer flows are occurring simultaneously, the transfers are given comparable bandwidth.

WFQ classifies traffic into different flows based on packet header addressing, including characteristics such as source and destination IP addresses, MAC addresses, port numbers, protocol, and *Type of Service (ToS)* value. The ToS value in the IP header can be used to classify traffic.

Low-bandwidth traffic flows, which comprise the majority of traffic, receive preferential service that allows their entire offered loads to be sent in a timely fashion. High-volume traffic flows share the remaining capacity proportionally among themselves.

Limitations of WFQ

WFQ is not supported with tunneling and encryption because these features modify the packet content information required by WFQ for classification.

Although WFQ automatically adapts to changing network traffic conditions, it does not offer the degree of precise control over bandwidth allocation that CBWFQ offers.

Class-Based Weighted Fair Queuing (CBWFQ) (9.3.5)

Class-Based Weighted Fair Queuing (CBWFQ) extends the standard WFQ functionality to provide support for user-defined traffic classes. With CBWFQ, you define traffic classes based on match criteria including protocols, access control lists (ACLs), and input interfaces. Packets satisfying the match criteria for a class constitute the traffic for that class. A FIFO queue is reserved for each class, and traffic belonging to a class is directed to the queue for that class, as shown in Figure 9-9.

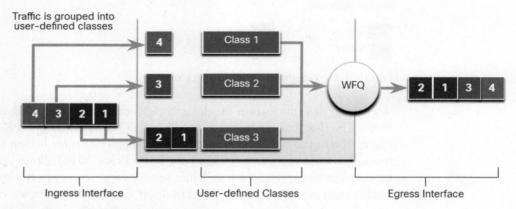

Figure 9-9   CBWFQ Example

When a class has been defined according to its match criteria, you can assign it characteristics. To characterize a class, you assign it bandwidth, weight, and a maximum packet limit. The bandwidth assigned to a class is the guaranteed bandwidth delivered to the class during congestion.

To characterize a class, you also specify the queue limit for that class, which is the maximum number of packets allowed to accumulate in the queue for the class. Packets belonging to a class are subject to the bandwidth and queue limits that characterize the class.

After a queue has reached its configured queue limit, adding more packets to the class causes tail drop or packet drop to occur, depending on how class policy is configured. Tail drop means a router simply discards any packet that arrives at the tail end of a queue that has completely used up its packet-holding resources. This is the default queuing response to congestion. Tail drop treats all traffic equally and does not differentiate between classes of service.

Low Latency Queuing (LLQ) (9.3.6)

The Low Latency Queuing (LLQ) feature brings strict priority queuing (PQ) to CBWFQ. Strict PQ allows delay-sensitive packets such as voice packets to be sent before packets in other queues. LLQ provides strict priority queuing for CBWFQ to reduce jitter in voice conversations, as shown in Figure 9-10.

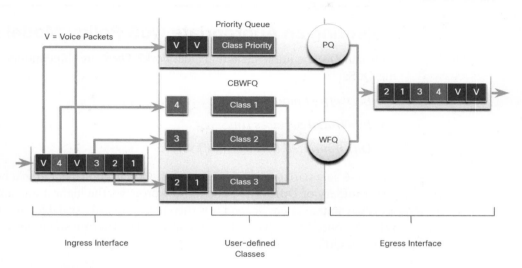

Figure 9-10 LLQ Example

Without LLQ, CBWFQ provides WFQ based on defined classes, with no strict priority queue available for real-time traffic. The weight for a packet belonging to a specific class is derived from the bandwidth you assigned to the class when you configured it. Therefore, the bandwidth assigned to the packets of a class determines the order in which packets are sent. All packets are serviced fairly, based on weight; no class of packets may be granted strict priority. This scheme poses problems for voice traffic that is largely intolerant of delay, especially variation in delay. For voice traffic, variations in delay introduce irregularities of transmission manifesting as jitter in the heard conversation.

LLQ allows delay-sensitive packets such as voice packets to be sent first (before packets in other queues), giving delay-sensitive packets preferential treatment over other traffic. Although it is possible to classify various types of real-time traffic to the strict priority PQ queue, Cisco recommends that only voice traffic be directed to the priority queue.

Check Your Understanding—Queuing Algorithms (9.3.7)

Refer to the online course to complete this activity.

Interactive
Graphic

QoS Models (9.4)

In this section, you will learn how networking devices implement QoS.

Video

Video Tutorial—QoS Models (9.4.1)

Refer to the online course to view this video.

Selecting an Appropriate QoS Policy Model (9.4.2)

How can QoS be implemented in a network? There are three models for implementing QoS:

- *Best-effort model*
- *Integrated Services (IntServ)*
- *Differentiated Services (DiffServ)*

Table 9-6 summarizes these three models. QoS is implemented in a network using either IntServ or DiffServ. While IntServ provides the highest guarantee of QoS, it is very resource intensive, and it is therefore not easily scalable. In contrast, DiffServ is less resource intensive and more scalable. The two are sometimes co-deployed in network QoS implementations.

Table 9-6 Models for Implementing QoS

Model	Description
Best-effort model	▪ This is not really an implementation as QoS is not explicitly configured. ▪ Use this when QoS is not required.
Integrated Services (IntServ)	▪ IntServ provides very high QoS to IP packets with guaranteed delivery. ▪ It defines a signaling process for applications to signal to the network that they require special QoS for a period and that bandwidth should be reserved. ▪ IntServ can severely limit the scalability of a network.
Differentiated Services (DiffServ)	▪ DiffServ provides high scalability and flexibility in implementing QoS. ▪ Network devices recognize traffic classes and provide different levels of QoS to different traffic classes.

Best Effort (9.4.3)

The basic design of the internet is best-effort packet delivery with no guarantees. This approach is still predominant on the internet today and remains appropriate for most purposes. The best-effort model treats all network packets in the same way, so an emergency voice message is treated the same way that a digital photograph attached to an email is treated. Without QoS, the network cannot tell the difference between packets and, as a result, cannot treat packets preferentially.

The best-effort model is similar in concept to sending a letter using standard postal mail. Your letter is treated exactly the same as every other letter. With the best-effort model, the letter may never arrive, and, unless you have a separate notification arrangement with the letter recipient, you may never know that the letter did not arrive.

Table 9-7 lists the benefits and drawbacks of the best-effort model.

Table 9-7   Benefits and Drawbacks of the Best-Effort Model

Benefits	Drawbacks
■ It is the most scalable model.	■ There are no guarantees of delivery.
■ Scalability is only limited by available bandwidth, in which case all traffic is equally affected.	■ Packets arrive whenever they can and in any order possible, if they arrive at all.
■ No special QoS mechanisms are required.	■ No packets have preferential treatment.
■ It is the easiest and quickest model to deploy.	■ Critical data is treated the same as casual data (such as email) is treated.

Integrated Services (9.4.4)

The Integrated Services (IntServ) architecture model (RFCs 1633, 2211, and 2212) was developed in 1994 to meet the needs of real-time applications, such as remote video, multimedia conferencing, data visualization applications, and virtual reality. IntServ is a multiple-service model that can accommodate many QoS requirements.

IntServ delivers the end-to-end QoS that real-time applications require. IntServ explicitly manages network resources to provide QoS to individual flows or streams, sometimes called *microflows*. It uses resource reservation and admission-control mechanisms as building blocks to establish and maintain QoS. This is similar to a concept known as "hard QoS." Hard QoS guarantees traffic characteristics, such as bandwidth, delay, and packet-loss rates, from end to end. Hard QoS ensures both predictable and guaranteed service levels for mission-critical applications.

Figure 9-11 shows a simple illustration of the IntServ model.

IntServ uses a connection-oriented approach inherited from telephony network design. Each individual communication must explicitly specify its traffic descriptor and requested resources to the network. The edge router performs admission control to ensure that available resources are sufficient in the network. The IntServ standard assumes that routers along a path set and maintain the state for each individual communication.

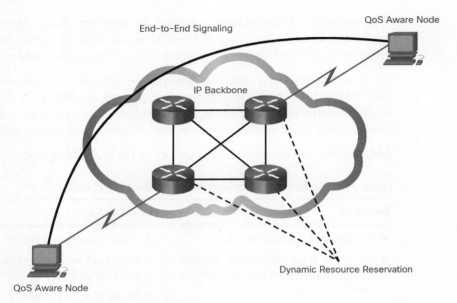

Figure 9-11   Simple IntServ Example

In the IntServ model, the application requests a specific kind of service from the network before sending data. The application informs the network of its traffic profile and requests a particular kind of service that can encompass its bandwidth and delay requirements. IntServ uses *Resource Reservation Protocol (RSVP)* to signal the QoS needs of an application's traffic along devices in the end-to-end path through the network. If network devices along the path can reserve the necessary bandwidth, the originating application can begin transmitting. If the requested reservation fails along the path, the originating application does not send any data.

The edge router performs admission control based on information from the application and available network resources. The network commits to meeting the QoS requirements of the application as long as the traffic remains within the profile specifications. The network fulfills its commitment by maintaining the per-flow state and then performing packet classification, policing, and intelligent queuing based on that state.

Table 9-8 lists the benefits and drawbacks of the IntServ model.

Table 9-8   Benefits and Drawbacks of the IntServ Model

Benefits	Drawbacks
■ Explicit end-to-end resource admission control	■ Resource intensive due to the stateful architecture requirement for continuous signaling
■ Per-request policy admission control	■ Flow-based approach not scalable to large implementations such as the internet
■ Signaling of dynamic port numbers	

Differentiated Services (9.4.5)

The Differentiated Services (DiffServ) QoS model specifies a simple and scalable mechanism for classifying and managing network traffic. For example, DiffServ can provide low-latency guaranteed service to critical network traffic such as voice or video, while providing simple best-effort traffic guarantees to non-critical services such as web traffic or file transfers.

The DiffServ design overcomes the limitations of both the best-effort and IntServ models. The DiffServ model is described in RFCs 2474, 2597, 2598, 3246, and 4594. DiffServ can provide an "almost guaranteed" QoS while still being cost-effective and scalable.

The DiffServ model is similar in concept to sending a package using a delivery service. You request (and pay for) a level of service when you send a package. Throughout the package network, the level of service you paid for is recognized, and your package is given either preferential or normal service, depending on what you requested.

DiffServ is not an end-to-end QoS strategy because it cannot enforce end-to-end guarantees. However, DiffServ QoS is a more scalable approach to implementing QoS. Unlike IntServ and hard QoS, in which the end hosts signal their QoS needs to the network, DiffServ does not use signaling. Instead, DiffServ uses a "soft QoS" approach. It works on the provisioned-QoS model, where network elements are set up to service multiple classes of traffic, each with varying QoS requirements.

Figure 9-12 shows a simple illustration of the DiffServ model.

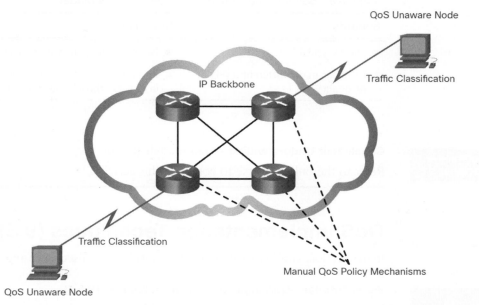

Figure 9-12 Simple DiffServ Example

As a host forwards traffic to a router, the router classifies the flows into aggregates (classes) and provides the appropriate QoS policy for the classes. DiffServ enforces and applies QoS mechanisms on a hop-by-hop basis, uniformly applying global meaning to each traffic class to provide both flexibility and scalability. For example, DiffServ could be configured to group all TCP flows as a single class and allocate bandwidth for that class rather than for the individual flows, as IntServ would do. In addition to classifying traffic, DiffServ minimizes signaling and state maintenance requirements on each network node.

Specifically, DiffServ divides network traffic into classes based on business requirements. Each of the classes can then be assigned a different level of service. As the packets traverse a network, each of the network devices identifies the packet class and services the packet according to that class. It is possible to choose many levels of service with DiffServ. For example, voice traffic from IP phones is usually given preferential treatment over all other application traffic, email is generally given best-effort service, and nonbusiness traffic can either be given very poor service or blocked entirely.

Table 9-9 lists the benefits and drawbacks of the DiffServ model.

Note

Modern networks primarily use the DiffServ model. However, due to the increasing volumes of delay- and jitter-sensitive traffic, IntServ and RSVP are sometimes co-deployed.

Table 9-9   Benefits and Drawbacks of the DiffServ Model

Benefits	Drawbacks
■ Highly scalable	■ No absolute guarantee of service quality
■ Provides many different levels of quality	■ Requires a set of complex mechanisms to work in concert throughout the network

Interactive Graphic

Check Your Understanding—QoS Models (9.4.6)

Refer to the online course to complete this activity.

QoS Implementation Techniques (9.5)

In this section, you'll learn about the QoS mechanisms used to ensure transmission quality.

Video

Video Tutorial—QoS Implementation Techniques (9.5.1)

Refer to the online course to view this video.

Avoiding Packet Loss (9.5.2)

Now that you have learned about traffic characteristics, queuing algorithms, and QoS models, it is time to learn about QoS implementation techniques.

Let's start with packet loss. Packet loss is usually the result of congestion on an interface. Most applications that use TCP experience slowdown because TCP automatically adjusts to network congestion. Dropped TCP segments cause TCP sessions to reduce their window sizes. Some applications do not use TCP and cannot handle drops (fragile flows).

The following approaches can prevent drops in sensitive applications:

- Increase link capacity to ease or prevent congestion.

- Guarantee enough bandwidth and increase buffer space to accommodate bursts of traffic from fragile flows. WFQ, CBWFQ, and LLQ can guarantee bandwidth and provide prioritized forwarding to drop-sensitive applications.

- Drop lower-priority packets before congestion occurs. Cisco IOS QoS provides queuing mechanisms, such as *weighted random early detection (WRED)*, that start dropping lower-priority packets before congestion occurs.

QoS Tools (9.5.3)

There are three categories of QoS tools, as described in Table 9-10.

Table 9-10 Tools for Implementing QoS

QoS Tools	Description
Classification and *marking* tools	■ Sessions, or flows, are analyzed to determine what traffic class they belong to.
	■ When the traffic class is determined, the packets are marked.
Congestion avoidance tools	■ Traffic classes are allotted portions of network resources, as defined by the QoS policy.
	■ The QoS policy also identifies how some traffic may be selectively dropped, delayed, or re-marked to avoid congestion.
	■ The primary congestion avoidance tool is WRED, which is used to regulate TCP data traffic in a bandwidth-efficient manner before tail drops caused by queue overflows occur.
Congestion management tools	■ When traffic exceeds available network resources, traffic is queued to await availability of resources.
	■ Common Cisco IOS-based congestion management tools include CBWFQ and LLQ algorithms.

Refer to Figure 9-13 to better understand the sequence of how these tools are used when QoS is applied to packet flows.

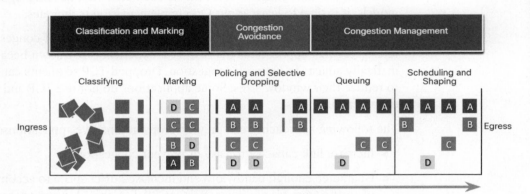

Figure 9-13   QoS Sequence

As shown in the figure, ingress packets (gray squares) are classified, and their respective IP header is marked (lettered squares). To avoid congestion, packets are then allocated resources based on defined policies. Packets are then queued and forwarded out the egress interface, based on their defined QoS shaping and policing policy.

> **Note**
>
> Classification and marking can be done on ingress or egress, whereas other QoS actions, such queuing and shaping, are usually done on egress.

Classification and Marking (9.5.4)

Before a packet can have a QoS policy applied to it, the packet has to be classified. Classification and marking allow you to identify or "mark" types of packets. Classification determines the class of traffic to which packets or frames belong. Only after traffic is marked can policies be applied to it.

How a packet is classified depends on the QoS implementation. Methods of classifying traffic flows at Layers 2 and 3 include using interfaces, ACLs, and class maps. Traffic can also be classified at Layers 4 to 7 using *Network Based Application Recognition (NBAR)*.

> **Note**
>
> NBAR is a classification and protocol discovery feature of Cisco IOS software that works with QoS features. NBAR is beyond the scope of this chapter.

Marking involves adding a value to the packet header. Devices receiving the packet look at the marked field to see if it matches a defined policy. Marking should be done as close to the source device as possible to establish the trust boundary.

How traffic is marked usually depends on the technology. Table 9-11 lists some of the marking fields used in various technologies.

Table 9-11   Traffic Marking for QoS

QoS Tool	Layer	Marking Field	Width, in Bits
Ethernet (802.1Q, 802.1p)	2	*Class of Service (CoS)*	3
802.11 (Wi-Fi)	2	Wi-Fi Traffic Identifier (TID)	3
MPLS	2	Experimental (EXP)	3
IPv4 and IPv6	3	*IP Precedence (IPP)*	3
IPv4 and IPv6	3	*Differentiated Services Code Point (DSCP)*	6

The decision of whether to mark traffic at Layer 2 or Layer 3 (or both) is not trivial and should be made after consideration of the following points:

- Layer 2 marking of frames can be performed for non-IP traffic.

- Layer 2 marking of frames is the only QoS option available for switches that are not IP aware.

- Layer 3 marking carries the QoS information from end to end.

Marking at Layer 2 (9.5.5)

802.1Q is the IEEE standard that supports VLAN tagging at Layer 2 on Ethernet networks. When 802.1Q is implemented, two fields are added to the Ethernet frame. As shown in Figure 9-14, these two fields are inserted into the Ethernet frame following the source MAC address field.

The 802.1Q standard also includes the QoS prioritization scheme known as *IEEE 802.1p*. The 802.1p standard uses the first 3 bits in the *Tag Control Information (TCI) field*. Known as the *Priority (PRI) field*, this 3-bit field identifies the Class of Service (CoS) markings. Three bits means that a Layer 2 Ethernet frame can be marked with one of eight levels of priority (values 0 through 7), as shown in Table 9-12.

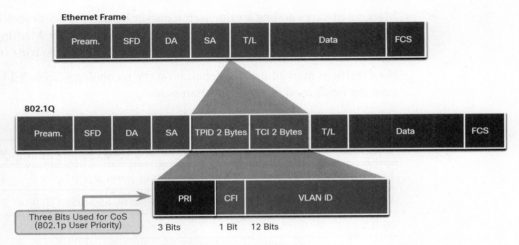

Figure 9-14 Ethernet Class of Service (CoS) Values

Table 9-12 Ethernet Class of Service (CoS) Values

CoS Value	CoS Binary Value	Description
0	000	Best-effort data
1	001	Medium-priority data
2	010	High-priority data
3	011	Call signaling
4	100	Videoconferencing
5	101	Voice bearer (voice traffic)
6	110	Reserved
7	111	Reserved

Marking at Layer 3 (9.5.6)

IPv4 and IPv6 specify an 8-bit field in their packet headers to mark packets. As shown in Figure 9-15, both IPv4 and IPv6 support an 8-bit field for marking: the *Type of Service (ToS) field* for IPv4 and the *Traffic Class field* for IPv6.

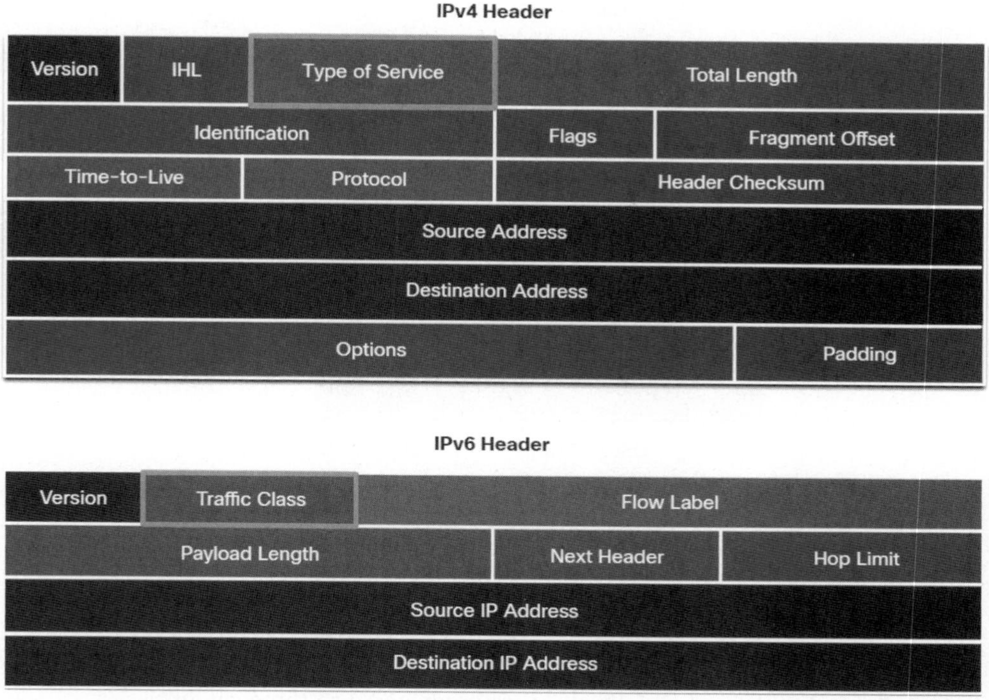

IPv4 Header

Version	IHL	Type of Service	Total Length	
Identification			Flags	Fragment Offset
Time-to-Live		Protocol	Header Checksum	
Source Address				
Destination Address				
Options				Padding

IPv6 Header

Version	Traffic Class	Flow Label		
Payload Length		Next Header		Hop Limit
Source IP Address				
Destination IP Address				

Figure 9-15   IPv4 and IPv6 Packet Headers

Type of Service and Traffic Class Field (9.5.7)

The Type of Service (IPv4) and Traffic Class (IPv6) fields carry the packet marking, as assigned by the QoS classification tools. The field is then referred to by receiving devices, which forward the packets based on the appropriate assigned QoS policy.

Figure 9-16 shows the contents of the 8-bit field. In RFC 791, the original IP standard specified the *IP Precedence (IPP) field* to be used for QoS markings. However, in practice, these 3 bits did not provide enough granularity to implement QoS.

RFC 2474 supersedes RFC 791 and redefines the ToS field by renaming and extending the IPP field. The new field, as shown in the figure, has 6 bits allocated for QoS and is called the Differentiated Services Code Point (DSCP) field. These 6 bits offer a maximum of 64 possible classes of service. The remaining 2 IP Extended Congestion Notification (ECN) bits can be used by ECN-aware routers to mark packets instead of dropping them. The ECN marking informs downstream routers that there is congestion in the packet flow.

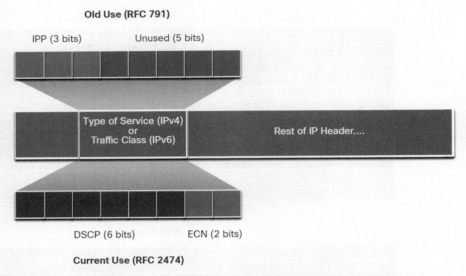

Figure 9-16 Type of Service and Traffic Class Fields in the Packet Header

DSCP Values (9.5.8)

The 64 DSCP values are organized into three categories:

- *Best Effort (BE)*: This is the default for all IP packets. The DSCP value is 0. The per-hop behavior is normal routing. When a router experiences congestion, these packets are dropped. No QoS plan is implemented.

- *Expedited Forwarding (EF)*: RFC 3246 defines EF as the DSCP decimal value 46 (binary 101110). The first 3 bits (101) map directly to the Layer 2 CoS value 5 used for voice traffic. At Layer 3, Cisco recommends that EF only be used to mark voice packets.

- *Assured Forwarding (AF)*: RFC 2597 defines AF to use the 5 most significant DSCP bits to indicate queues and drop preference. The definition of AF is illustrated in Figure 9-17.

The **AF*xy*** formula is specified as follows:

- The first 3 most significant bits are used to designate the class. Class 4 is the best queue, and Class 1 is the worst queue.

- The fourth and fifth most significant bits are used to designate the drop preference.

- The sixth most significant bit is set to 0.

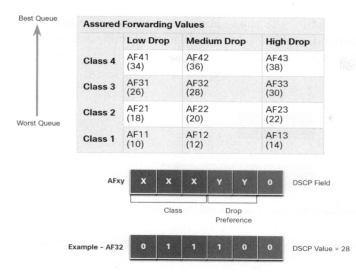

Figure 9-17   Assured Forwarding Values

For example, AF32 belongs to class 3 (binary 011) and has a medium drop preference (binary 10). The full DSCP value is 28 because you include the sixth 0 bit (binary 011100).

Class Selector Bits (9.5.9)

Because the first 3 most significant bits of the DSCP field indicate the class, these bits are also called the Class Selector (CS) bits. These 3 bits map directly to the 3 bits of the CoS field and the IPP field to maintain compatibility with 802.1p and RFC 791, as shown in Figure 9-18.

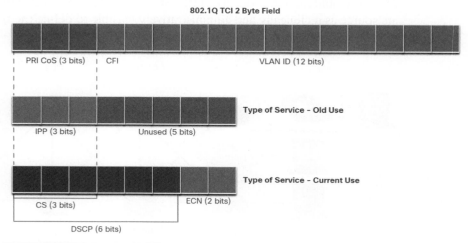

Figure 9-18   Layer 2 CoS and Layer 3 ToS

The table in Figure 9-19 shows how the CoS values map to the Class Selector bits and the corresponding DSCP 6-bit value. This same table can be used to map IPP values to the Class Selector bits.

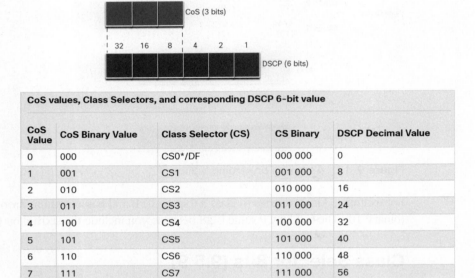

CoS values, Class Selectors, and corresponding DSCP 6-bit value

CoS Value	CoS Binary Value	Class Selector (CS)	CS Binary	DSCP Decimal Value
0	000	CS0*/DF	000 000	0
1	001	CS1	001 000	8
2	010	CS2	010 000	16
3	011	CS3	011 000	24
4	100	CS4	100 000	32
5	101	CS5	101 000	40
6	110	CS6	110 000	48
7	111	CS7	111 000	56

Figure 9-19   Mapping CoS to Class Selectors in DSCP

Trust Boundaries (9.5.10)

Where should markings occur? Traffic should be classified and marked as close to its source as technically and administratively feasible to define the trust boundary, as shown in Figure 9-20.

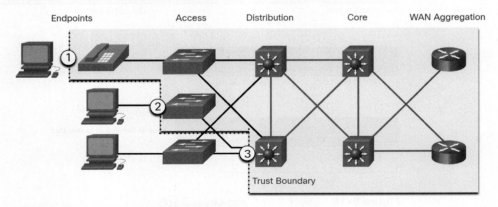

Figure 9-20   Various Trust Boundaries

The numbers in Figure 9-20 correspond to the following:

1. Trusted endpoints have the capabilities and intelligence to mark application traffic to the appropriate Layer 2 CoS and/or Layer 3 DSCP values. Examples of trusted endpoints include IP phones, wireless access points, videoconferencing gateways and systems, and IP conferencing stations.

2. Secure endpoints can have traffic marked at the Layer 2 switch.

3. Traffic can also be marked at Layer 3 switches / routers.

Re-marking traffic—for example, re-marking CoS values to IP Precedent or DSCP values—is typically necessary.

Congestion Avoidance (9.5.11)

Congestion management includes queuing and scheduling methods where excess traffic is buffered or queued (and sometimes dropped) while it waits to be sent out an egress interface. Congestion avoidance tools are simpler. They monitor network traffic loads in an effort to anticipate and avoid congestion at common network and internetwork bottlenecks before congestion becomes a problem. These tools can monitor the average depth of the queue, as represented in Figure 9-21. When the queue is below the minimum threshold, there are no drops. As the queue fills up to the maximum threshold, a small percentage of packets are dropped. When the maximum threshold is passed, all packets are dropped.

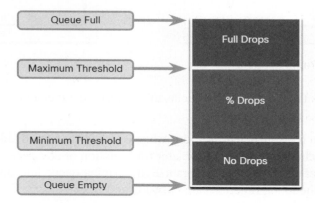

Figure 9-21 Congestion Avoidance Mechanisms

Some congestion avoidance techniques provide preferential treatment in terms of which packets will get dropped. For example, Cisco IOS QoS includes weighted random early detection (WRED) as a possible congestion avoidance solution. The

WRED algorithm allows for congestion avoidance on network interfaces by providing buffer management and allowing TCP traffic to decrease, or throttle back, before buffers are exhausted. Using WRED helps avoid tail drops and maximizes network use and TCP-based application performance. There is no congestion avoidance for User Datagram Protocol (UDP)-based traffic, such as voice traffic. In case of UDP-based traffic, methods such as queuing and compression techniques help reduce and even prevent UDP packet loss.

Shaping and Policing (9.5.12)

Traffic shaping and *traffic policing* are two mechanisms provided by Cisco IOS QoS software to prevent congestion.

Traffic shaping retains excess packets in a queue and then schedules the excess for later transmission over increments of time. The result of traffic shaping is a smoothed packet output rate, as shown in Figure 9-22.

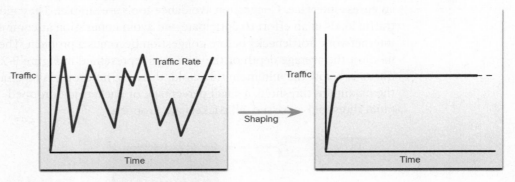

Figure 9-22   Traffic Shaping Example

Shaping implies the existence of a queue and of sufficient memory to buffer delayed packets, whereas policing does not.

Ensure that you have sufficient memory when enabling shaping. In addition, shaping requires a scheduling function for later transmission of any delayed packets. This scheduling function allows you to organize the shaping queue into different queues. Examples of scheduling functions are CBWFQ and LLQ.

Shaping is an outbound concept; packets going out an interface get queued and can be shaped. In contrast, policing is applied to inbound traffic on an interface. When the traffic rate reaches the configured maximum rate, excess traffic is dropped (or re-marked).

Policing is commonly implemented by service providers to enforce a contracted committed information rate (CIR), as shown in Figure 9-23. However, the service provider may also allow bursting over the CIR if the service provider's network is not currently experiencing congestion.

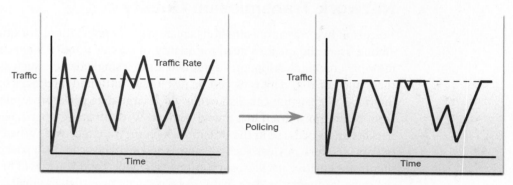

Figure 9-23   Traffic Policing Example

QoS Policy Guidelines (9.5.13)

A QoS policy must consider the full path from source to destination. If one device in the path is using a different policy than desired, then the entire QoS policy is impacted. For example, stutter in video playback could be the result of one switch in the path not having the CoS value set appropriately.

A few guidelines that help ensure the best experience for end users include the following:

- Enable queuing at every device in the path between the source and the destination.
- Classify and mark traffic as close to the source as possible.
- Shape and police traffic flows as close to their sources as possible.

Interactive Graphic

Check Your Understanding—QoS Implementation Techniques (9.5.14)

Refer to the online course to complete this activity.

Summary (9.6)

The following is a summary of the sections in this chapter.

Network Transmission Quality

Voice and live video transmissions create higher expectations for quality delivery among users and create a need for quality of service (QoS). Congestion occurs when multiple communication lines aggregate onto a single device, such as a router, and then much of that data is placed on just a few outbound interfaces or onto a slower interface. Congestion can also occur when large data packets prevent smaller packets from being transmitted in a timely manner. Without any QoS mechanisms in place, packets are processed in the order in which they are received. When congestion occurs, network devices such as routers and switches can drop packets. This means that time-sensitive packets, such as real-time video and voice, will be dropped with the same frequency as data that is not time sensitive, such as email and web browsing traffic. When the volume of traffic is greater than what can be transported across the network, devices queue (hold) the packets in memory until resources become available to transmit them. Queuing packets causes delay because new packets cannot be transmitted until previous packets have been processed. One QoS technique that can help with this problem is to classify data into multiple queues. Network congestion points are ideal candidates for QoS mechanisms to mitigate delay and latency. Two types of delays are fixed and variable. Sources of delay are code delay, packetization delay, queuing delay, serialization delay, propagation delay, and de-jitter delay. Jitter is the variation in the delay of received packets. Due to network congestion, improper queuing, or configuration errors, the delay between packets can vary instead of remaining constant. Both delay and jitter need to be controlled and minimized to support real-time and interactive traffic.

Traffic Characteristics

Voice and video traffic are two of the main reasons for QoS. Voice traffic is smooth and benign, but it is sensitive to drops and delays. Voice can tolerate a certain amount of latency, jitter, and loss without any noticeable effects. Latency should be no more than 150 milliseconds (ms). Jitter should be no more than 30 ms, and voice packet loss should be no more than 1%. Voice traffic requires at least 30 kbps of bandwidth. Video traffic is more demanding than voice traffic because of the size of the packets it sends across the network. Video traffic is bursty, greedy, drop sensitive, and delay sensitive. Without QoS and a significant amount of extra bandwidth, video quality typically degrades. UDP ports such as 554 are used for the Real-Time Streaming Protocol (RSTP) and should be given priority over other, less delay-sensitive, network traffic. Similar to voice, video can tolerate a certain amount of latency, jitter, and loss without any noticeable effects. Latency should be no more than 400 milliseconds (ms). Jitter should be no more than 50 ms, and video packet loss should be no more than 1%. Video traffic requires at least 384 kbps of bandwidth. Data traffic is not as demanding as voice and video traffic. Data packets often use TCP applications, which can retransmit data and, therefore, are not sensitive to drops and delays. Although data traffic is relatively insensitive to drops and delays compared to voice and video, a network administrator still needs to consider the quality of the user experience, sometimes referred to as quality of experience (QoE). The two main factors that a network administrator needs to consider about the flow of data traffic are whether the data comes from an interactive application and whether the data is mission critical.

Queuing Algorithms

The QoS policy implemented by a network administrator becomes active when congestion occurs on the link. Queuing is a congestion management tool that can buffer, prioritize, and, if required, reorder packets before being transmitted to the destination. This chapter focuses on the following queuing algorithms: first-in, first-out (FIFO), Weighted Fair Queuing (WFQ), Class-Based Weighted Fair Queuing (CBWFQ), and Low Latency Queuing (LLQ). FIFO queuing buffers and forwards packets in the order of their arrival. FIFO has no concept of priority or classes of traffic and, consequently, makes no decision about packet priority. When FIFO is used, important or time-sensitive traffic can be dropped when there is congestion on the router or switch interface. WFQ is an automated scheduling method that provides fair bandwidth allocation to all network traffic. WFQ applies priority, or weights, to identified traffic and classifies it into conversations or flows. WFQ classifies traffic into different flows based on packet header addressing, including such characteristics as source and destination IP addresses, MAC addresses, port numbers, protocol, and Type of Service (ToS) value. The ToS value in the IP header can be used to classify traffic. CBWFQ extends the standard WFQ functionality to provide support for user-defined traffic classes. With CBWFQ, you define traffic classes based on match criteria including protocols, access control lists (ACLs), and input interfaces. The LLQ feature brings strict priority queuing (PQ) to CBWFQ. Strict PQ allows delay-sensitive packets, such as voice, to be sent before packets in other queues, reducing jitter in voice conversations.

QoS Models

There are three models for implementing QoS: best-effort model, Integrated Services (IntServ), and Differentiated Services (DiffServ). The best-effort model is the most scalable but does not guarantee delivery and does not give any packets preferential treatment. The IntServ model was developed to meet the needs of real-time applications, such as remote video, multimedia conferencing, data visualization applications, and virtual reality. IntServ is a multiple-service model that can accommodate many QoS requirements. IntServ explicitly manages network resources to provide QoS to individual flows or streams, sometimes called microflows. It uses resource reservation and admission-control mechanisms as building blocks to establish and maintain QoS. The DiffServ QoS model specifies a simple and scalable mechanism for classifying and managing network traffic. The DiffServ design overcomes the limitations of both the best-effort and IntServ models. The DiffServ model can provide an "almost guaranteed" QoS while still being cost-effective and scalable. DiffServ divides network traffic into classes based on business requirements. Each of the classes can then be assigned a different level of service. As the packets traverse a network, each of the network devices identifies the packet class and services the packet according to that class. It is possible to choose many levels of service with DiffServ.

QoS Implementation Techniques

There are three categories of QoS tools: classification and marking tools, congestion avoidance tools, and congestion management tools. Before a packet can have a QoS policy applied to it, the packet has to be classified. Classification and marking enable you to identify, or "mark," types of packets. Classification determines the class of traffic to which packets or frames belong. Methods of classifying traffic flows at Layers 2 and 3 include using interfaces, ACLs, and class maps. Traffic can also be classified at Layers 4 to 7 using Network Based Application Recognition (NBAR). The Type of Service (IPv4) and Traffic Class (IPv6) fields carry the packet marking as assigned by the QoS classification tools. The field is then referred to by receiving devices, which forward the packets based on the appropriate assigned QoS policy. These fields have 6 bits allocated for QoS. Called the Differentiated Services Code Point (DSCP) field, these 6 bits offer a maximum of 64 possible classes of service. The field is then referred to by receiving devices, which forward the packets based on the appropriate assigned QoS policy. The 64 DSCP values are organized into three categories: Best Effort (BE), Expedited Forwarding (EF), and Assured Forwarding (AF). Because the first 3 most significant bits of the DSCP field indicate the class, these bits are also called the Class Selector (CS) bits. Traffic should be classified and marked as close to its source as technically and administratively feasible to define the trust boundary. Congestion management includes queuing and scheduling methods where excess traffic is buffered or queued (and sometimes dropped) while it waits to be sent out an egress interface. Congestion avoidance tools help to monitor network traffic loads in an effort to anticipate and avoid congestion at common network and internetwork bottlenecks before congestion becomes a problem. Cisco IOS QoS includes weighted random early detection (WRED) as a possible congestion avoidance solution. The WRED algorithm allows for congestion avoidance on network interfaces by providing buffer management and allowing TCP traffic to decrease, or throttle back, before buffers are exhausted. Traffic shaping and traffic policing are two mechanisms provided by Cisco IOS QoS software to prevent congestion.

Practice

There are no labs or Packet Tracers for this chapter.

Check Your Understanding Questions

Complete all the review questions listed here to test your understanding of the topics and concepts in this chapter. The appendix "Answers to the 'Check Your Understanding' Questions" lists the answers.

1. Under which condition does congestion occur on a converged network with voice, video, and data traffic?

   A. A user downloads a file that exceeds the file limitation that is set on the server.

   B. A request for bandwidth exceeds the amount of bandwidth available.

   C. Video traffic requests more bandwidth than voice traffic requests.

   D. Voice traffic latency begins to decrease across the network.

2. What functionality is required on routers to provide remote workers with VoIP and video-conferencing capabilities?

   A. IPsec

   B. PPPoE

   C. QoS

   D. VPN

3. What happens when a router interface ingress queue is full and new network traffic is received?

   A. The router sends the received traffic immediately.

   B. The router drops the arriving packets.

   C. The router drops all traffic in the queue.

   D. The router queues the received traffic and sends previously received traffic.

4. Which queuing method provides user-defined traffic classes where each traffic class has a FIFO queue?

   A. CBWFQ

   B. RSVP

   C. WFQ

   D. WRED

5. Which type of traffic does Cisco recommend be placed in the strict priority queue when Low Latency Queuing (LLQ) is being used?

   A. Data

   B. Management

   C. Video

   D. Voice

6. What is the default queuing method used on the LAN interfaces of Cisco devices?

   A. CBWFQ

   B. FIFO

   C. LLQ

   D. WFQ

7. What is the default queuing method used on the slower WAN interfaces of Cisco devices?

   A. CBWFQ

   B. FIFO

   C. LLQ

   D. WFQ

8. Which model is the only QoS model with no mechanism to classify packets?

   A. Best-effort

   B. DiffServ

   C. Hard QoS

   D. IntServ

9. What happens when an edge router using IntServ QoS determines that the data pathway cannot support the level of QoS requested?

    A. Data is forwarded along the pathway using a best-effort approach.

    B. Data is forwarded along the pathway using DiffServ.

    C. Data is not forwarded along the pathway.

    D. Data is forwarded along the pathway using IntServ but is not provided preferential treatment.

10. Which statement describes the QoS classification and marking tools?

    A. Classification is performed after traffic is marked.

    B. Classification should be done as close to the destination service as possible.

    C. Marking involves adding a value to a packet header.

    D. Marking involves identification of the QoS policy that should be applied to specific packets.

11. Which device would be classified as a trusted endpoint?

    A. Firewall

    B. IP conferencing station

    C. Router

    D. Switch

12. How many bits are used to identify the Class of Service (CoS) marking in a frame?

    A. 3

    B. 8

    C. 24

    D. 64

13. How many levels of priority are possible when using Class of Service (CoS) marking on frames?

    A. 3

    B. 8

    C. 24

    D. 64

CHAPTER 10

Network Management

Objectives

Upon completion of this chapter, you will be able to answer the following questions:

- How do you use CDP to map a network topology?

- How do you use LLDP to map a network topology?

- How do you implement NTP between an NTP client and an NTP server?

- How does SNMP operate?

- How does syslog operate?

- What commands are used to back up and restore an IOS configuration file?

- How do you implement protocols to manage a network?

Key Terms

This chapter uses the following key terms. You can find the definitions in the Glossary.

Introduction (10.0)

Imagine being at the helm of a spaceship. Many, many components work together to move this ship, and multiple systems manage these components. To get where you are going, you would need to have a full understanding of the components and the systems that manage them. You would probably appreciate any tools that would make managing your spaceship—*while you are also flying it*—simpler.

Like a complex spaceship, a network also needs to be managed. Happily, many tools are designed to make network management simpler. This chapter introduces you to several tools and protocols to help you manage your network—*while your users are using it*. It also includes many Packet Tracer activities and labs to test your skills. These are the tools of great network administrators, so you will definitely want to get started!

Device Discovery with CDP (10.1)

In this section, you will learn how to use CDP to map a network topology.

CDP Overview (10.1.1)

The first thing you want to know about your network is, what is in it? Where are the various components, and how are they connected? Basically, you need a map. This section explains how you can use *Cisco Discovery Protocol (CDP)* to create a map of a network.

CDP is a Cisco-proprietary Layer 2 protocol that is used to gather information about Cisco devices that share the same data link. CDP is media and protocol independent and runs on all Cisco devices, such as routers, switches, and access servers.

A device sends periodic CDP advertisements to connected devices, as shown in Figure 10-1. These advertisements share information about the type of device that is discovered, the name of the devices, and the number and type of the interfaces.

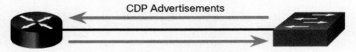

Figure 10-1 Devices Send CDP Advertisements

Most network devices are connected to other devices, and CDP can assist in network design decisions, troubleshooting, and making changes to equipment. CDP can also be used as a network discovery tool to determine information about the neighboring devices. This information gathered from CDP can help build a logical topology of a network when documentation is missing or lacking detail.

Configure and Verify CDP (10.1.2)

For Cisco devices, CDP is enabled by default. For security reasons, it may be desirable to disable CDP on a network device globally or per interface. With CDP, an attacker can gather valuable insight about the network layout, such as IP addresses, IOS versions, and types of devices.

To verify the status of CDP and display information about CDP, enter the **show cdp** command, as shown in Example 10-1.

Example 10-1   The **show cdp** Command

```
Router# show cdp
Global CDP information:
      Sending CDP packets every 60 seconds
      Sending a holdtime value of 180 seconds
      Sending CDPv2 advertisements is enabled
Router#
```

To enable CDP globally for all the supported interfaces on the device, enter **cdp run** in global configuration mode. To disable CDP for all the interfaces on a device, use the **no cdp run** command in global configuration mode, as shown in Example 10-2.

Example 10-2   Disabling and Enabling CDP Globally

```
Router(config)# no cdp run
Router(config)# exit
Router#
Router# show cdp
CDP is not enabled
Router#
Router# configure terminal
Router(config)# cdp run
Router(config)#
```

To disable CDP on a specific interface, such as the interface facing an ISP, enter **no cdp enable** in interface configuration mode. CDP is still enabled on the device; however, no more CDP advertisements are sent out that interface. To enable CDP on the specific interface again, enter **cdp enable**, as shown in Example 10-3.

Example 10-3   Enabling CDP on an Interface

```
Switch(config)# interface gigabitethernet 0/0/1
Switch(config-if)# cdp enable
Switch(config-if)#
```

To verify the status of CDP and display a list of neighbors, use the **show cdp neighbors** command in privileged EXEC mode. The **show cdp neighbors** command displays important information about the CDP neighbors. Currently, the device in Example 10-4 does not have any neighbors because it is not physically connected to any devices, as indicated by the output of the **show cdp neighbors** command.

Example 10-4   Displaying a List of CDP Neighbors

```
Router# show cdp neighbors
Capability Codes: R - Router, T - Trans Bridge, B - Source Route Bridge
                  S - Switch, H - Host, I - IGMP, r - Repeater, P - Phone,
                  D - Remote, C - CVTA, M - Two-port Mac Relay


Device ID        Local Intrfce    Holdtme    Capability  Platform  Port ID


Total cdp entries displayed : 0
Router#
```

Use the **show cdp interface** command to display the interfaces that are CDP enabled on a device. The status of each interface is also displayed. Example 10-5 shows that five interfaces are CDP enabled on the router, with only one active connection to another device.

Example 10-5   Displaying CPD Interface Information

```
Router# show cdp interface
GigabitEthernet0/0/0 is administratively down, line protocol is down
  Encapsulation ARPA
  Sending CDP packets every 60 seconds
  Holdtime is 180 seconds
GigabitEthernet0/0/1 is up, line protocol is up
  Encapsulation ARPA
  Sending CDP packets every 60 seconds
  Holdtime is 180 seconds
GigabitEthernet0/0/2 is down, line protocol is down
  Encapsulation ARPA
  Sending CDP packets every 60 seconds
  Holdtime is 180 seconds
Serial0/1/0 is administratively down, line protocol is down
  Encapsulation HDLC
  Sending CDP packets every 60 seconds
  Holdtime is 180 seconds
Serial0/1/1 is administratively down, line protocol is down
  Encapsulation HDLC
  Sending CDP packets every 60 seconds
  Holdtime is 180 seconds
```

```
GigabitEthernet0 is down, line protocol is down
  Encapsulation ARPA
  Sending CDP packets every 60 seconds
  Holdtime is 180 seconds
cdp enabled interfaces : 6
interfaces up          : 1
interfaces down        : 5
Router#
```

Discover Devices by Using CDP (10.1.3)

Consider the lack of documentation in the topology shown in Figure 10-2. The network administrator only knows that R1 is connected to another device.

Figure 10-2   R1 Topology Before Discovery

With CDP enabled on the network, the **show cdp neighbors** command can be used to determine the network layout, as shown in Example 10-6.

Example 10-6   Discovering Connected CDP Neighbors for R1

```
R1# show cdp neighbors
Capability Codes: R - Router, T - Trans Bridge, B - Source Route Bridge
                  S - Switch, H - Host, I - IGMP, r - Repeater, P - Phone,
                  D - Remote, C - CVTA, M - Two-port Mac Relay


Device ID          Local Intrfce     Holdtme     Capability  Platform   Port ID
S1                 Gig 0/0/1             179           S I    WS-C3560- Fas 0/5
R1#
```

No information is available regarding the rest of the network. The **show cdp neighbors** command provides helpful information about each CDP neighbor device, including the following:

- **Device identifiers:** This is the hostname of the neighbor device (S1).

- **Port identifier:** This is the name of the local and remote ports (G0/0/1 and F0/5, respectively).

- **Capability list:** This shows whether the device is a router or a switch (S for switch; I for IGMP [which is beyond the scope of this chapter]).

■ **Platform:** This is the hardware platform of the device (WS-C3560 for a Cisco 3560 switch).

The output shows that there is another Cisco device, S1, connected to the G0/0/1 interface on R1. Furthermore, S1 is connected through its F0/5, as shown in Figure 10-3.

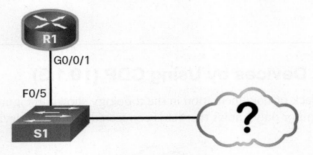

Figure 10-3   Topology from S1

The network administrator uses **show cdp neighbors detail** to discover the IP address for S1. As shown in Example 10-7, the address for S1 is 192.168.1.2.

Example 10-7   Discovering Detailed Information About S1

```
R1# show cdp neighbors detail
-------------------------
Device ID: S1
Entry address(es):
  IP address: 192.168.1.2
Platform: cisco WS-C3560-24TS,  Capabilities: Switch IGMP
Interface: GigabitEthernet0/0/1,  Port ID (outgoing port): FastEthernet0/5
Holdtime : 136 sec

Version :
Cisco IOS Software, C3560 Software (C3560-LANBASEK9-M), Version 15.0(2)SE7, R
RELEASE SOFTWARE (fc1)
Technical Support: http://www.cisco.com/techsupport
Copyright (c) 1986-2014 by Cisco Systems, Inc.
Compiled Thu 23-Oct-14 14:49 by prod_rel_team

advertisement version: 2
Protocol Hello:  OUI=0x00000C, Protocol ID=0x0112; payload len=27,
value=00000000FFFFFFFF010221FF000000000000002291210380FF0000
VTP Management Domain: ''
Native VLAN: 1
Duplex: full
```

```
Management address(es):
  IP address: 192.168.1.2

Total cdp entries displayed : 1
R1#
```

By accessing S1 either remotely through SSH or physically through the console port, the network administrator can determine what other devices are connected to S1, as shown in the output of the **show cdp neighbors** command in Example 10-8.

Example 10-8   Discovering Connected CDP Neighbors for S1

```
S1# show cdp neighbors
Capability Codes: R - Router, T - Trans Bridge, B - Source Route Bridge
                  S - Switch, H - Host, I - IGMP, r - Repeater, P - Phone,
                  D - Remote, C - CVTA, M - Two-port Mac Relay
Device ID        Local Intrfce      Holdtme    Capability  Platform  Port ID
S2               Fas 0/1            150              S I   WS-C2960- Fas 0/1
R1               Fas 0/5            179          R   S I   ISR4331/K Gig 0/0/1
S1#
```

Another switch, S2, is revealed in the output. S2 is using F0/1 to connect to the F0/1 interface on S1, as shown in Figure 10-4.

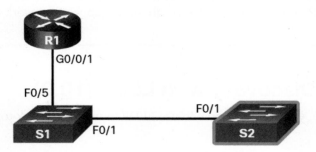

Figure 10-4   Topology from S2

Again, the network administrator can use **show cdp neighbors detail** to discover the IP address for S2 and then remotely access it. After a successful login, the network administrator uses the **show cdp neighbors** command to discover if there are more devices, as shown in Example 10-9.

Example 10-9   Discovering Connected CDP Neighbors for S2

```
S2# show cdp neighbors
Capability Codes: R - Router, T - Trans Bridge, B - Source Route Bridge
                  S - Switch, H - Host, I - IGMP, r - Repeater, P - Phone,
                  D - Remote, C - CVTA, M - Two-port Mac Relay
Device ID         Local Intrfce    Holdtme    Capability  Platform  Port ID
S1                Fas 0/1          141                S I  WS-C3560- Fas  0/1
S2#
```

The only device connected to S2 is S1. Therefore, there are no more devices to discover in the topology. The network administrator can now update the documentation to reflect the discovered devices.

Syntax Checker—Configure and Verify CDP (10.1.4)

Refer to the online course to complete this activity.

Packet Tracer—Use CDP to Map a Network (10.1.5)

A senior network administrator requires you to map the remote branch office network and discover the name of a recently installed switch that still needs to have an IPv4 address configured. Your task is to create a map of the branch office network. To map the network, you will use SSH for remote access and Cisco Discovery Protocol (CDP) to discover information about neighboring network devices, such as routers and switches.

Device Discovery with LLDP (10.2)

In this section, you will learn how to use LLDP to map a network topology.

LLDP Overview (10.2.1)

Link Layer Discovery Protocol (LLDP) does the same thing as CDP, but it is not specific to Cisco devices. Figure 10-5 shows LLDP-enabled devices sending each other LLDP advertisements.

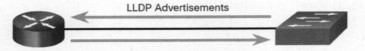

Figure 10-5   Devices Sending LLDP Advertisements

LLDP is a vendor-neutral neighbor discovery protocol similar to CDP. LLDP works with network devices, such as routers, switches, and wireless LAN access points. This protocol advertises its identity and capabilities to other devices and receives the information from a physically connected Layer 2 device.

Configure and Verify LLDP (10.2.2)

Depending on the device, LLDP may be enabled by default. To enable LLDP globally on a Cisco network device, enter the **lldp run** command in global configuration mode. To disable LLDP, enter the **no lldp run** command in global configuration mode.

Much like CDP, LLDP can be configured on specific interfaces. However, LLDP must be configured separately to transmit and receive LLDP packets.

To verify that LLDP has been enabled on a device, enter the **show lldp** command in privileged EXEC mode, as shown in Example 10-10.

Example 10-10   Configuring and Verifying LLDP

```
S1(config)# lldp run
S1(config)#
S1(config)# interface gigabitethernet 0/1
S1(config-if)# lldp transmit
S1(config-if)# lldp receive
S1(config-if)# end
S1#
S1# show lldp
Global LLDP Information:
    Status: ACTIVE
    LLDP advertisements are sent every 30 seconds
    LLDP hold time advertised is 120 seconds
    LLDP interface reinitialisation delay is 2 seconds
S1#
```

Discover Devices by Using LLDP (10.2.3)

Consider the lack of documentation in the topology shown in Figure 10-6. The network administrator only knows that S1 is connected to two devices.

Figure 10-6   S1 Topology Before Discovery

With LLDP enabled, device neighbors can be discovered by using the **show lldp neighbors** command, as shown in Example 10-11.

Example 10-11   Discovering LLDP Neighbors for S1

```
S1# show lldp neighbors
Capability codes:
    (R) Router, (B) Bridge, (T) Telephone, (C) DOCSIS Cable Device
    (W) WLAN Access Point, (P) Repeater, (S) Station, (O) Other
Device ID           Local Intf      Hold-time  Capability      Port ID
R1                  Fa0/5           117        R               Gi0/0/1
S2                  Fa0/1           112        B               Fa0/1
Total entries displayed: 2
S1#
```

The network administrator discovers that S1 has a router and a switch as neighbors. For this output, the letter B for *bridge* also indicates a switch.

From the results of **show lldp neighbors**, a topology from S1 can be constructed, as displayed in Figure 10-7.

Figure 10-7   S1 Topology After Discovery

When more details about the neighbors are needed, the **show lldp neighbors detail** command can provide information, such as the neighbor IOS version, IP address, and device capability, as shown in Example 10-12.

Example 10-12   Discovering Detailed Information about R1 and S2

```
S1# show lldp neighbors detail
------------------------------------------------
Chassis id: 848a.8d44.49b0
Port id: Gi0/0/1
Port Description: GigabitEthernet0/0/1
System Name: R1

System Description:
Cisco IOS Software [Fuji], ISR Software (X86_64_LINUX_IOSD-UNIVERSALK9-M), Version
   16.9.4, RELEASE SOFTWARE (fc2)
Technical Support: http://www.cisco.com/techsupport
Copyright (c) 1986-2019 by Cisco Systems, Inc.
Compiled Thu 22-Aug-19 18:09 by mcpre
```

```
Time remaining: 111 seconds
System Capabilities: B,R
Enabled Capabilities: R
Management Addresses - not advertised
Auto Negotiation - not supported
Physical media capabilities - not advertised
Media Attachment Unit type - not advertised
Vlan ID: - not advertised


------------------------------------------------
Chassis id: 0025.83e6.4b00
Port id: Fa0/1
Port Description: FastEthernet0/1
System Name: S2

System Description:
Cisco IOS Software, C2960 Software (C2960-LANBASEK9-M), Version 15.0(2)SE4,
  RELEASE SOFTWARE (fc1)
Technical Support: http://www.cisco.com/techsupport
Copyright (c) 1986-2013 by Cisco Systems, Inc.
Compiled Wed 26-Jun-13 02:49 by prod_rel_team

Time remaining: 107 seconds
System Capabilities: B
Enabled Capabilities: B
Management Addresses - not advertised
Auto Negotiation - supported, enabled
Physical media capabilities:
    100base-TX(FD)
    100base-TX(HD)
    10base-T(FD)
    10base-T(HD)
Media Attachment Unit type: 16
Vlan ID: 1

Total entries displayed: 2
S1#
```

Interactive Graphic

Syntax Checker—Configure and Verify LLDP (10.2.4)

Refer to the online course to complete this activity.

Interactive Graphic

Check Your Understanding—Compare CDP and LLDP (10.2.5)

Refer to the online course to complete this activity.

Packet Tracer—Use LLDP to Map a Network (10.2.6)

In this Packet Tracer activity, you will complete the following objectives:

- Build the network and configure basic device settings
- Network discovery with CDP
- Network discovery with LLDP

NTP (10.3)

In this section, you will learn how to implement *Network Time Protocol (NTP)* between an *NTP client* and an *NTP server*.

Time and Calendar Services (10.3.1)

Before you get really deep into network management, one thing that will help keep you on track is ensuring that all your components are set to the same time and date.

The *software clock* on a router or switch starts when the system boots. It is the primary source of time for the system. It is important to synchronize the time across all devices on a network because all aspects of managing, securing, troubleshooting, and planning networks require accurate timestamping. When the time is not synchronized between devices, it is impossible to determine the order of the events and the cause of an event.

Typically, the date and time settings on a router or switch can be set by using one of two methods. You can manually configure the date and time, as shown in Example 10-13, or configure Network Time Protocol (NTP).

Example 10-13   Manually Setting the Clock

```
R1# clock set 20:36:00 nov 15 2019
R1#
*Nov 15 20:36:00.000: %SYS-6-CLOCKUPDATE: System clock has been
updated from 21:32:31 UTC Fri Nov 15 2019 to 20:36:00 UTC Fri Nov 15
2019, configured from console by console.
R1#
```

As a network grows, it becomes difficult to ensure that all infrastructure devices are operating with synchronized time. Even in a smaller network environment, the manual method is not ideal. If a router reboots, how will it get an accurate date and timestamp?

A better solution is to configure NTP on the network. This protocol allows routers on the network to synchronize their time settings with an NTP server. A group of NTP clients that obtain time and date information from a single source have more consistent time settings. When NTP is implemented in the network, it can be set up to synchronize to a private master clock, or it can synchronize to a publicly available NTP server on the internet.

NTP uses UDP port 123 and is documented in RFC 1305.

NTP Operation (10.3.2)

NTP networks use a hierarchical system of time sources. Each level in this hierarchical system is called a *stratum*. The stratum level is defined as the number of hop counts from the *authoritative time source*. The synchronized time is distributed across the network by using NTP. Figure 10-8 displays a sample NTP network.

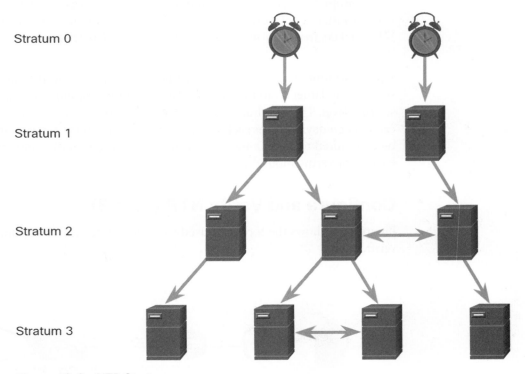

Figure 10-8   NTP Strata

In the figure, NTP servers are arranged in three levels, showing the three strata. Stratum 1 is connected to the stratum 0 clocks.

Stratum 0

An NTP network gets the time from authoritative time sources. Stratum 0 devices such as atomic and GPS clocks are the most accurate authoritative time sources. Specifically, stratum 0 devices are non-network high-precision time-keeping devices assumed to be accurate and with little or no delay associated with them. In Figure 10-8, they are represented by the clock icon.

Stratum 1

The stratum 1 devices are network devices that are directly connected to the authoritative time sources. They function as the primary network time standard to stratum 2 devices using NTP.

Stratum 2 and Lower

The stratum 2 servers are connected to stratum 1 devices through network connections. Stratum 2 devices, such as NTP clients, synchronize their time by using the NTP packets from stratum 1 servers. They could also act as servers for stratum 3 devices.

Smaller stratum numbers indicate that the server is closer to the authorized time source than larger stratum numbers. The larger the stratum number, the lower the stratum level. The max hop count is 15. Stratum 16, the lowest stratum level, indicates that a device is unsynchronized. Time servers on the same stratum level can be configured to act as a peer with other time servers on the same stratum level for backup or verification of time.

Configure and Verify NTP (10.3.3)

Figure 10-9 shows the topology used to demonstrate NTP configuration and verification.

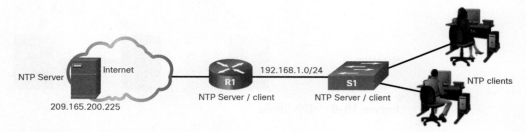

Figure 10-9 NTP Server and Client Topology

Before NTP is configured on the network, the **show clock** command displays the current time on the software clock, as shown in Example 10-14. With the **detail** option, notice that the time source is "user configuration." This means the time was manually configured using the **clock** privileged EXEC command.

Example 10-14   Displaying the Clock Source

```
R1# show clock detail
20:55:10.207 UTC Fri Nov 15 2019
Time source is user configuration
R1#
```

The **ntp server** *ip-address* global configuration command is used to configure 209.165.200.225 as the NTP server for R1. To verify that the time source is set to NTP, use the **show clock detail** command. Notice that now the time source is NTP, as shown in Example 10-15.

Example 10-15   Configuring an NTP Server for R1

```
R1(config)# ntp server 209.165.200.225
R1(config)# end
R1#
R1# show clock detail
21:01:34.563 UTC Fri Nov 15 2019
Time source is NTP
R1#
```

In Example 10-16, the **show ntp associations** and **show ntp status** commands are used to verify that R1 is synchronized with the NTP server at 209.165.200.225.

Note

The highlighted **st** in Example 10-16 stands for *stratum*.

Example 10-16   Verifying NTP on R1

```
R1# show ntp associations

  address          ref clock       st   when  poll reach  delay  offset   disp
*~209.165.200.225 .GPS.             1    61    64   377   0.481  7.480   4.261
 * sys.peer, # selected, + candidate, - outlyer, x falseticker, ~ configured


R1#
R1# show ntp status
Clock is synchronized, stratum 2, reference is 209.165.200.225
```

```
nominal freq is 250.0000 Hz, actual freq is 249.9995 Hz, precision is 2**19
ntp uptime is 589900 (1/100 of seconds), resolution is 4016
reference time is DA088DD3.C4E659D3 (13:21:23.769 PST Fri Nov 15 2019)
clock offset is 7.0883 msec, root delay is 99.77 msec
root dispersion is 13.43 msec, peer dispersion is 2.48 msec
loopfilter state is 'CTRL' (Normal Controlled Loop), drift is 0.000001803 s/s
system poll interval is 64, last update was 169 sec ago.
R1#
```

Notice that R1 is synchronized with a stratum 1 NTP server at 209.165.200.225, which is synchronized with a GPS clock. The **show ntp status** command output indicates that R1 is now a stratum 2 device that is synchronized with the NTP server at 209.165.220.225.

Next, the clock on S1 is configured to synchronize to R1 with the **ntp server** global configuration command, and then the configuration is verified with the **show ntp associations** command, as shown in Example 10-17.

Example 10-17 Configuring an NTP Server for S1

```
S1(config)# ntp server 192.168.1.1
S1(config)# end
S1#
S1# show ntp associations

  address         ref clock       st    when   poll reach  delay  offset   disp
*~192.168.1.1     209.165.200.225  2     12     64   377   1.066  13.616   3.840
 * sys.peer, # selected, + candidate, - outlyer, x falseticker, ~ configured
S1#
```

Output from the **show ntp associations** command in Example 10-18 verifies that the clock on S1 is now synchronized with R1 at 192.168.1.1 via NTP.

Example 10-18 Verifying NTP on S1

```
S1# show ntp status
Clock is synchronized, stratum 3, reference is 192.168.1.1
nominal freq is 119.2092 Hz, actual freq is 119.2088 Hz, precision is 2**17
reference time is DA08904B.3269C655 (13:31:55.196 PST Tue Nov 15 2019)
clock offset is 18.7764 msec, root delay is 102.42 msec
root dispersion is 38.03 msec, peer dispersion is 3.74 msec
loopfilter state is 'CTRL' (Normal Controlled Loop), drift is 0.000003925 s/s
system poll interval is 128, last update was 178 sec ago.
S1#
```

R1 is a stratum 2 device and NTP server to S1. Now S1 is a stratum 3 device that can provide NTP service to other devices in the network, such as end devices.

Packet Tracer—Configure and Verify NTP (10.3.4)

NTP synchronizes the time of day among a set of distributed time servers and clients. While there are a number of applications that require synchronized time, this lab focuses on the need to correlate events when listed in the system logs and other time-specific events from multiple network devices.

SNMP

Now that your network is mapped and all of your components are using the same clock, it is time to look at how you can manage your network by using *Simple Network Management Protocol (SNMP)*. This section discusses how SNMP operates.

Introduction to SNMP (10.4.1)

SNMP was developed to allow administrators to manage nodes such as servers, workstations, routers, switches, and security appliances on an IP network. It enables network administrators to monitor and manage network performance, find and solve network problems, and plan for network growth.

SNMP is an application layer protocol that provides a message format for communication between managers and agents. The SNMP system consists of three elements:

- *SNMP manager*
- *SNMP agents* (managed node)
- *Management Information Base (MIB)*

To configure SNMP on a networking device, it is first necessary to define the relationship between the manager and the agent.

The SNMP manager is part of a *network management system (NMS)*. The SNMP manager runs SNMP management software. As shown in Figure 10-10, the SNMP manager can collect information from an SNMP agent by using the "get" action and can change configurations on an agent by using the "set" action.

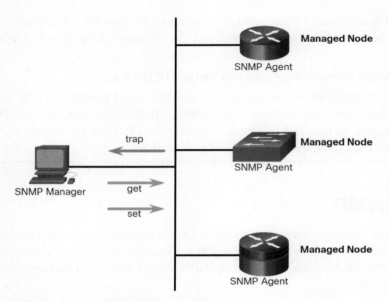

Figure 10-10   SNMP Manager and Nodes

In addition, SNMP agents can forward information directly to a network manager by using *SNMP traps*.

The SNMP agent and MIB reside on SNMP client devices. Network devices that must be managed, such as switches, routers, servers, firewalls, and workstations, are equipped with an SMNP agent software module. MIBs store data about the device and operational statistics and are meant to be available to authenticated remote users. The SNMP agent is responsible for providing access to the local MIB.

SNMP defines how management information is exchanged between network management applications and management agents. The SNMP manager polls the agents and queries the MIB for SNMP agents on UDP port 161. SNMP agents send any traps to the SNMP manager on UDP port 162.

SNMP Operation (10.4.2)

SNMP agents that reside on managed devices collect and store information about the device and its operation. The agent stores this information locally in the MIB. The SNMP manager then uses the SNMP agent to access information within the MIB.

There are two primary SNMP manager requests: get and set. An NMS uses a *get request* to query a device for data. An NMS uses a *set request* to change configuration variables in the agent device. A set request can also initiate actions within a device. For example, a set can cause a router to reboot, send a configuration file, or receive a configuration file. The SNMP manager uses the get and set actions to perform the operations described in Table 10-1.

Table 10-1   SNMP Get and Set Operations

Operation	Description
get-request	Retrieves a value from a specific variable.
get-next-request	Retrieves a value from a variable within a table; the SNMP manager does not need to know the exact variable name. A sequential search is performed to find the needed variable from within a table.
get-bulk-request	Retrieves large blocks of data, such as multiple rows in a table, that would otherwise require the transmission of many small blocks of data. (Only works with SNMPv2 or later.)
get-response	Replies to a **get-request**, **get-next-request**, and **set-request** sent by an NMS.
set-request	Stores a value in a specific variable.

The SNMP agent responds to SNMP manager requests as follows:

- **Getting an MIB variable:** The SNMP agent performs this function in response to a GetRequest-PDU from the network manager. The agent retrieves the value of the requested MIB variable and responds to the network manager with that value.

- **Setting an MIB variable:** The SNMP agent performs this function in response to a SetRequest-PDU from the network manager. The SNMP agent changes the value of the MIB variable to the value specified by the network manager. An SNMP agent reply to a set request includes the new settings in the device.

Figure 10-11 illustrates the use of an SNMP GetRequest to determine if interface G0/0/0 is up/up.

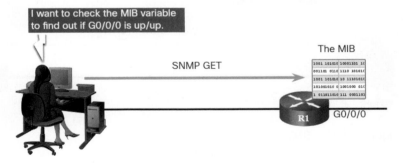

Figure 10-11   Example of an SNMP GetRequest

SNMP Agent Traps (10.4.3)

An NMS periodically polls the SNMP agents that are residing on managed devices by using the get request. The NMS queries a device for data. Using this process, a network management application can collect information to monitor traffic loads and to verify the device configurations of managed devices. The information can be displayed via a GUI on the NMS. Averages, minimums, or maximums can be calculated. The data can be graphed, or thresholds can be set to trigger a notification process when the thresholds are exceeded. For example, an NMS can monitor CPU utilization of a Cisco router. The SNMP manager samples the value periodically and presents this information in a graph for the network administrator to use in creating a *network baseline*, creating a report, or viewing real-time information.

Periodic SNMP polling does have disadvantages. First, there is a delay between the time when an event occurs and the time when it is noticed (via polling) by the NMS. Second, there is a trade-off between polling frequency and bandwidth usage. To mitigate these disadvantages, it is possible for SNMP agents to generate and send traps to immediately inform the NMS of certain events. Traps are unsolicited messages alerting the SNMP manager to a condition or an event on the network. Examples of trap conditions include, but are not limited to, improper user authentication, restarts, link status (up or down), MAC address tracking, closing of a TCP connection, loss of connection to a neighbor, and other significant events. Trap-directed notifications reduce network and agent resources by eliminating the need for some of SNMP polling requests.

Figure 10-12 illustrates the use of an SNMP trap to alert the network administrator that interface G0/0/0 has failed. The following steps occur in this figure:

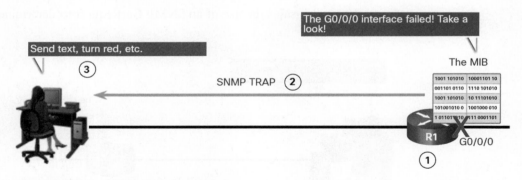

Figure 10-12 SNMP Trap Example

Step 1.   Interface G0/0/0 fails on R1.

Step 2.   R1 sends a SNMP trap message to the NMS.

Step 3.   The NMS takes necessary action.

The NMS software can send the network administrator a text message, pop up a window on the NMS software, or turn the router icon red in the NMS GUI.

The exchange of all SNMP messages is illustrated in Figure 10-13.

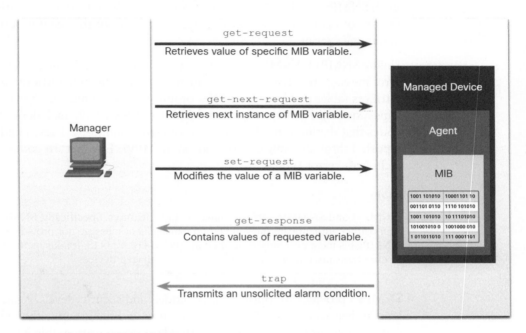

Figure 10-13   SNMP Messages

SNMP Versions (10.4.4)

There are several versions of SNMP:

- **SNMPv1:** This is the Simple Network Management Protocol, a full internet standard, that is defined in RFC 1157.

- **SNMPv2c:** This is defined in RFCs 1901 to 1908. It uses a community-string-based administrative framework.

- **SNMPv3:** This is an interoperable standards-based protocol originally defined in RFCs 2273 to 2275. It provides secure access to devices by authenticating and encrypting packets over the network. It includes a number of security features: message integrity to ensure that a packet was not tampered with in transit, authentication to determine that the message is from a valid source, and encryption to prevent the contents of a message from being read by an unauthorized source.

All versions use SNMP managers, agents, and MIBs. Cisco IOS software supports all three versions. Version 1 is a legacy solution and is not often encountered in networks today; therefore, this book focuses on versions 2c and 3.

Both SNMPv1 and SNMPv2c use a community-based form of security. The community of managers that is able to access the MIB of the agent is defined by a community string.

Unlike SNMPv1, SNMPv2c includes a bulk retrieval mechanism and more detailed error message reporting to management stations. The bulk retrieval mechanism retrieves tables and large quantities of information, minimizing the number of round trips required. The improved error handling of SNMPv2c includes expanded error codes that distinguish different kinds of error conditions. These conditions are reported through a single error code in SNMPv1. Error return codes in SNMPv2c include the error type.

Note

SNMPv1 and SNMPv2c offer minimal security features. Specifically, SNMPv1 and SNMPv2c can neither authenticate the source of a management message nor provide encryption. SNMPv3 is most currently described in RFCs 3410 to 3415. It adds methods to ensure the secure transmission of critical data between managed devices.

SNMPv3 provides for both security models and security levels. A security model is an authentication strategy set up for a user and the group within which the user resides. A security level is the permitted level of security within a security model. A combination of the security level and the security model determine which security mechanism is used when handling an SNMP packet. Available security models are SNMPv1, SNMPv2c, and SNMPv3.

Tables 10-2 through 10-6 provide information about the characteristics of the different combinations of security models and levels.

Table 10-2   SNMPv1

Characteristic	Setting
Level	noAuthNoPriv
Authentication	Community string
Encryption	No
Result	Uses a community string match for authentication

Table 10-3   SNMPv2c

Characteristic	Setting
Level	noAuthNoPriv
Authentication	Community string
Encryption	No
Result	Uses a community string match for authentication

Table 10-4   SNMPv3 noAuthNoPriv

Characteristic	Setting
Level	noAuthNoPriv
Authentication	Username
Encryption	No
Result	Uses a username match for authentication (an improvement over SNMPv2c)

Table 10-5   SNMPv3 authNoPriv

Characteristic	Setting
Level	authNoPriv
Authentication	Message Digest 5 (MD5) or Secure Hash Algorithm (SHA)
Encryption	No
Result	Provides authentication based on the HMAC-MD5 or HMAC-SHA algorithms

Table 10-6   SNMPv3 authPriv

Characteristic	Setting
Level	authPriv (requires the cryptographic software image)
Authentication	MD5 or SHA
Encryption	Data Encryption Standard (DES) or Advanced Encryption Standard (AES)

Characteristic	Setting
Result	Provides authentication based on the HMAC-MD5 or HMAC-SHA algorithms. Allows specifying the User-Based Security Model (USM) with these encryption algorithms: ■ DES 56-bit encryption in addition to authentication based on the CBC-DES (DES-56) standard ■ 3DES 168-bit encryption ■ AES 128-bit, 192-bit, or 256-bit encryption

A network administrator must configure the SNMP agent to use the SNMP version supported by the management station. Because an agent can communicate with multiple SNMP managers, it is possible to configure the software to support communications by using SNMPv1, SNMPv2c, or SNMPv3.

Interactive Graphic

Check Your Understanding—SNMP Versions (10.4.5)

Refer to the online course to complete this activity.

Community Strings (10.4.6)

For SNMP to operate, the NMS must have access to the MIB. To ensure that access requests are valid, some form of authentication must be in place.

SNMPv1 and SNMPv2c use *community strings* that control access to the MIB. Community strings are plaintext passwords. SNMP community strings authenticate access to MIB objects.

There are two types of community strings:

■ **Read-only (ro):** This type provides access to the MIB variables but does not allow these variables to be changed; they can only be read. Because security is minimal in version 2c, many organizations use SNMPv2c in read-only mode.

■ **Read-write (rw):** This type provides read and write access to all objects in the MIB.

To view or set MIB variables, the user must specify the appropriate community string for read or write access.

Figures 10-14 through 10-17 demonstrate how SNMP operates with a community string. The figures illustrate the following steps:

Step 1.   As shown in Figure 10-14, a customer calls to report that access to her web server is slow.

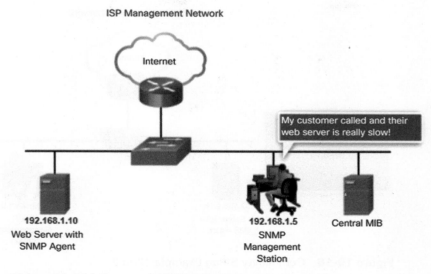

Figure 10-14   Community String Example: Step 1

Step 2.   As shown in Figure 10-15, the administrator uses the NMS to send a get request to the web server SNMP agent (get 192.168.1.10) for its connection statistics. The get request also includes the community string (2#B7!9).

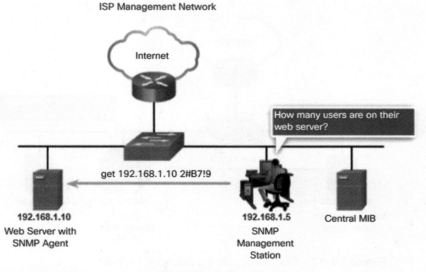

Figure 10-15   Community String Example: Step 2

Step 3. As shown in Figure 10-16, the SNMP agent verifies the received community string and IP address before replying to the get request.

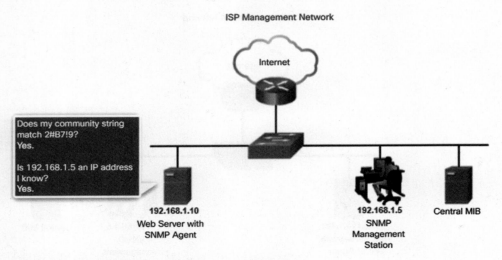

Figure 10-16   Community String Example: Step 3

Step 4. As shown in Figure 10-17, the SNMP agent sends the requested statistics to the NMS with the connection variable, reporting that 10,000 users are currently connected to the web server.

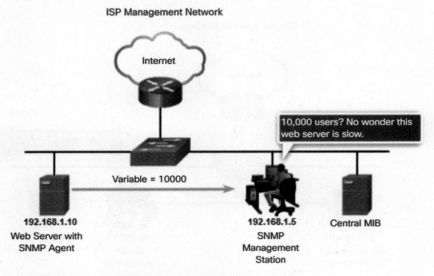

Figure 10-17   Community String Example: Step 4

Note

Plaintext passwords are not considered a security mechanism. This is because plaintext passwords are highly vulnerable to man-in-the-middle attacks, in which they are compromised through the capture of packets.

MIB Object ID (10.4.7)

The MIB organizes variables hierarchically. MIB variables enable the management software to monitor and control the network device. Formally, the MIB defines each variable as an *object ID (OID)*. OIDs uniquely identify managed objects in the MIB hierarchy. The MIB organizes the OIDs based on RFC standards into a hierarchy of OIDs, usually shown as a tree.

The MIB tree for any given device includes some branches with variables common to many networking devices and some branches with variables specific to a particular device or vendor.

RFCs define some common public variables. Most devices implement these MIB variables. In addition, networking equipment vendors, including Cisco, can define their own private branches of the tree to accommodate new variables specific to their devices.

Figure 10-18 shows portions of the MIB structure defined by Cisco.

Note that the OID can be described in words or numbers to help locate a particular variable in the tree. OIDs belonging to Cisco are numbered as follows: .iso (1), .org (3), .dod (6), .internet (1), .private (4), .enterprises (1), and .cisco (9). Therefore, the OID in this case is 1.3.6.1.4.1.9.

SNMP Polling Scenario (10.4.8)

SNMP can be used to observe CPU utilization over a period of time by polling devices. CPU statistics can then be compiled on the NMS and graphed. This creates a baseline for the network administrator. Threshold values can then be set relative to this baseline. When CPU utilization exceeds this threshold, notifications are sent. Figure 10-19 illustrates five-minute samples of router CPU utilization over the period of a few weeks.

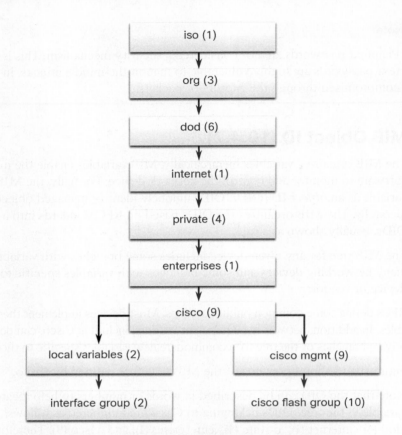

Figure 10-18   Example of an SNMP MIB Object ID Structure

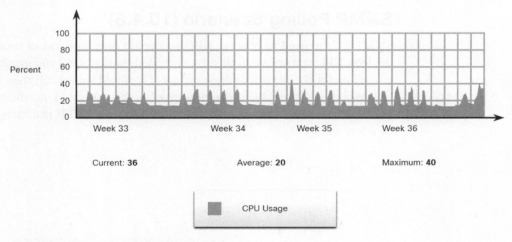

Figure 10-19   5-Minute CPU Utilization

The data is retrieved via the *snmpget* utility, issued on the NMS. By using the **snmpget** utility, you can manually retrieve real-time data or have the NMS run a report. This report would give you a period of time that you could use the data to get the average. The **snmpget** utility requires that the SNMP version, the correct community, the IP address of the network device to query, and the OID number be set. Figure 10-20 demonstrates the use of the freeware **snmpget** utility, which allows quick retrieval of information from the MIB.

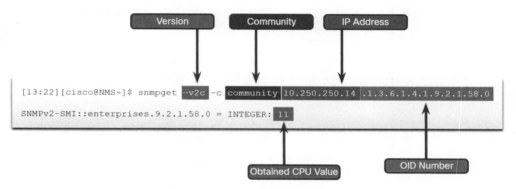

Figure 10-20   Example of the snmpget Utility

The **snmpget** command has several parameters, including:

- **-v2c:** This is the version of SNMP.

- **-c community:** This is the SNMP password, called a community string.

- **10.250.250.14:** This is the IP address of the monitored device.

- **1.3.6.1.4.1.9.2.1.58.0:** This is the OID of the MIB variable.

The last line of output shows the response. The output in Figure 10-20 shows a shortened version of the MIB variable. It then lists the actual value in the MIB location. In this case, the 5-minute moving average of the CPU busy percentage is 11%.

SNMP Object Navigator (10.4.9)

The **snmpget** utility gives some insight into the basic mechanics of how SNMP works. However, working with long MIB variable names like 1.3.6.1.4.1.9.2.1.58.0 can be problematic for the average user. More commonly, network operations staff use a network management product with an easy-to-use GUI that makes the MIB data variable naming transparent to the user.

A search for "Cisco SNMP Object Navigator tool" on the http://www.cisco.com website provides a tool that allows a network administrator to research details about a particular OID. Figure 10-21 shows an example of using Cisco SNMP Object Navigator to research the OID information for the **whyReload** object.

Figure 10-21 The SNMP Object Navigator Website

Lab—Research Network Monitoring Software (10.4.10)

In this lab, you will complete the following objectives:

- Part 1: Survey your understanding of network monitoring
- Part 2: Research network monitoring tools
- Part 3: Select a network monitoring tool

Syslog (10.5)

In this section, you will learn about the operation of syslog.

Introduction to Syslog (10.5.1)

Like a check engine light on your car dashboard, the components in your network can tell you if there is something wrong. The syslog protocol was designed to ensure that you can receive and understand such messages. When certain events occur on a network, networking devices have trusted mechanisms to notify the administrator with detailed system messages. These messages can be either non-critical or significant. Network administrators have a variety of options for storing, interpreting, and displaying these messages. They can also be alerted to the messages that could have the greatest impact on the network infrastructure.

The most common method of accessing system messages is to use a protocol called syslog.

Syslog is a term used to describe a standard. It is also used to describe the protocol developed for that standard. The syslog protocol was developed for UNIX systems in the 1980s but was first documented as RFC 3164 by the IETF in 2001. Syslog uses UDP port 514 to send event notification messages across IP networks to event message collectors, as shown in Figure 10-22.

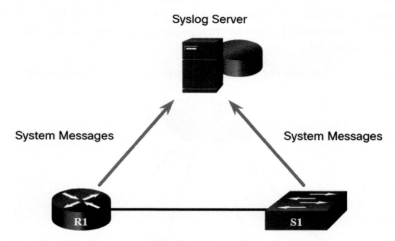

Figure 10-22   Syslog Messages Sent to the Syslog Server

Many networking devices support syslog, including routers, switches, application servers, firewalls, and other network appliances. The syslog protocol allows networking devices to send their system messages across the network to syslog servers.

There are several different syslog server software packages for Windows and UNIX. Many of them are freeware.

The syslog logging service provides three primary functions:

- The ability to gather logging information for monitoring and troubleshooting
- The ability to select the type of logging information that is captured
- The ability to specify the destinations of captured syslog messages

Syslog Operation (10.5.2)

On Cisco network devices, the syslog protocol starts by sending system messages and **debug** output to a local logging process that is internal to the device. How the logging process manages these messages and outputs depends on the device configurations. For example, syslog messages may be sent across the network to an external syslog server. These messages can be retrieved without needing to access the actual device. Log messages and outputs stored on the external server can be pulled into various reports for easier reading.

Alternatively, syslog messages may be sent to an internal buffer. Messages sent to the internal buffer are viewable only through the CLI of the device.

Finally, the network administrator may specify that only certain types of system messages be sent to various destinations. For example, a device may be configured to forward all system messages to an external syslog server. However, debug-level messages are forwarded to the internal buffer and are only accessible by the administrator from the CLI.

Figure 10-23 shows the common destinations for syslog messages

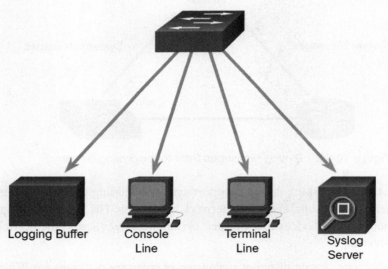

Figure 10-23   Destinations for Syslog Messages

It is possible to remotely monitor system messages by viewing the logs on a syslog server or by accessing the device through Telnet, SSH, or the console port.

Syslog Message Format (10.5.3)

Cisco devices produce syslog messages as a result of network events. Every syslog message contains a *severity level* and a *facility*.

The smaller numerical levels are the more critical syslog alarms. The severity levels of messages can be set to control where each type of message is displayed such as on the console or the other destinations). The complete list of syslog levels is shown in Table 10-7.

Table 10-7 Syslog Severity Levels

Severity Name	Severity Level	Explanation
Emergency	Level 0	System unusable
Alert	Level 1	Immediate action needed
Critical	Level 2	Critical condition
Error	Level 3	Error condition
Warning	Level 4	Warning condition
Notification	Level 5	Normal but significant condition
Informational	Level 6	Informational message
Debugging	Level 7	Debugging message

Each syslog level has its own meaning:

- **Warning Level 4—Emergency Level 0:** These messages are error messages about software or hardware malfunctions; these types of messages mean that the functionality of the device is affected. The severity of the issue determines the syslog level applied.

- **Notification Level 5:** This notification level is for normal but significant events. For example, interface up or down transitions and system restart messages are displayed at the notifications level.

- **Informational Level 6:** This is a normal information message that does not affect device functionality. For example, when a Cisco device is booting, you might see the following informational message: %LICENSE-6-EULA_ACCEPT_ALL: The Right to Use End User License Agreement is accepted.

- **Debugging Level 7:** This level indicates that the messages are output generated from issuing various **debug** commands.

Syslog Facilities (10.5.4)

In addition to specifying the severity, syslog messages also contain information on the facility. Syslog facilities are service identifiers that identify and categorize system state data for error and event message reporting. The logging facility options that are available are specific to the networking device. For example, Cisco 2960 Series switches running Cisco IOS Release 15.0(2) and Cisco 1941 routers running Cisco IOS Release 15.2(4) support 24 facility options that are categorized into 12 facility types.

Some common syslog message facilities reported on Cisco IOS routers include

- **IF:** Identifies that the syslog message was generated by an interface
- **IP:** Identifies that the syslog message was generated by IP
- **OSPF:** Identifies that the syslog message was generated by the OSPF routing protocol
- **SYS:** Identifies that the syslog message was generated by the device operating system
- **IPSEC:** Identifies that the syslog message was generated by the IPsec protocol

By default, the format of syslog messages on the Cisco IOS software is as follows:

```
%facility-severity-MNEMONIC: description
```

For example, sample output on a Cisco switch for an EtherChannel link changing state to up is:

```
%LINK-3-UPDOWN: Interface Port-channel1, changed state to up
```

Here the facility is LINK, and the severity level is 3, with a MNEMONIC of UPDOWN.

The most common messages are link up and link down messages and messages that a device produces when it exits configuration mode. If ACL logging is configured, the device generates syslog messages when packets match a parameter condition.

Configure Syslog Timestamp (10.5.5)

By default, log messages are not timestamped. In Example 10-19, the R1 GigabitEthernet 0/0/0 interface is shut down.

Example 10-19 Syslog Configuration

```
R1(config)# interface g0/0/0
R1(config-if)# shutdown
%LINK-5-CHANGED: Interface GigabitEthernet0/0/0, changed state to administratively
  down
%LINEPROTO-5-UPDOWN: Line protocol on Interface GigabitEthernet0/0/0, changed
  state to down
R1(config-if)# exit
R1(config)#
R1(config)# service timestamps log datetime
R1(config)#
R1(config)# interface g0/0/0
R1(config-if)# no shutdown
*Mar  1 11:52:42: %LINK-3-UPDOWN: Interface GigabitEthernet0/0/0, changed state to
  down
*Mar  1 11:52:45: %LINK-3-UPDOWN: Interface GigabitEthernet0/0/0, changed state to
  up
*Mar  1 11:52:46: %LINEPROTO-5-UPDOWN: Line protocol on Interface
  GigabitEthernet0/0/0,
changed state to up
R1(config-if)#
```

The message logged to the console does not identify when the interface state was changed. Log messages should be timestamped so that when they are sent to another destination, such as a syslog server, there is a record of when a message was generated.

Use the **service timestamps log datetime** global configuration command to force logged events to display the date and time. As shown in the command output in Example 10-19, when the R1 GigabitEthernet 0/0/0 interface is reactivated, the log messages contain the date and time.

Note

When using the **datetime** keyword, the clock on the networking device must be set, either manually or through NTP, as previously discussed.

Interactive Graphic

Check Your Understanding—Syslog Operation (10.5.6)

Refer to the online course to complete this activity.

Router and Switch File Maintenance (10.6)

In this section, you will use commands to back up and restore an IOS configuration file.

Router File Systems (10.6.1)

If you are thinking that you cannot possibly remember how you configured every device in your network, you are not alone. In a large network, it would not be possible to manually configure every device. Fortunately, there are many ways to copy or update your configurations and then simply paste them on other devices. To do this, you need to know how to view and manage your file systems.

Cisco IOS File System (IFS) allows an administrator to navigate to different directories and list the files in a directory. The administrator can also create subdirectories in flash memory or on a disk. The directories available depend on the device.

Example 10-20 shows the output of the **show file systems** command, which lists all the available file systems on a Cisco 4221 router.

Example 10-20   Displaying the File Systems on a Router

```
Router# show file systems
File Systems:

       Size(b)       Free(b)       Type    Flags    Prefixes
             -             -       opaque    rw      system:
             -             -       opaque    rw      tmpsys:
*   7194652672    6294822912       disk      rw      bootflash: flash:
     256589824     256573440       disk      rw      usb0:
    1804468224    1723789312       disk      ro      webui:
             -             -       opaque    rw      null:
             -             -       opaque    ro      tar:
             -             -       network   rw      tftp:
             -             -       opaque    wo      syslog:
      33554432      33539983       nvram     rw      nvram:
             -             -       network   rw      rcp:
             -             -       network   rw      ftp:
             -             -       network   rw      http:
             -             -       network   rw      scp:
             -             -       network   rw      sftp:
             -             -       network   rw      https:
             -             -       opaque    ro      cns:
Router#
```

This command provides useful information, such as the amount of total and free memory, the type of file system, and its permissions. Permissions include read only (ro), write only (wo), and read and write (rw). The permissions are shown in the Flags column of the command output.

Although there are several file systems listed, the ones that are interesting at this point are the tftp, flash, and nvram file systems.

Notice that the flash file system has an asterisk preceding it. This indicates that flash is the current default file system. The bootable IOS is located in flash; therefore, the pound symbol (#) is appended to the flash listing, indicating that it is a bootable disk.

The Flash File System

Example 10-21 shows the output of the **dir** (directory) command.

Example 10-21   Displaying the Flash File System on a Router

```
Router# dir
Directory of bootflash:/
    11   drwx          16384    Aug  2 2019 04:15:13 +00:00  lost+found
370945   drwx           4096    Oct  3 2019 15:12:10 +00:00  .installer
338689   drwx           4096    Aug  2 2019 04:15:55 +00:00  .ssh
217729   drwx           4096    Aug  2 2019 04:17:59 +00:00  core
379009   drwx           4096    Sep 26 2019 15:54:10 +00:00  .prst_sync
80641    drwx           4096    Aug  2 2019 04:16:09 +00:00  .rollback_timer
161281   drwx           4096    Aug  2 2019 04:16:11 +00:00  gs_script
112897   drwx         102400    Oct  3 2019 15:23:07 +00:00  tracelogs
362881   drwx           4096    Aug 23 2019 17:19:54 +00:00  .dbpersist
298369   drwx           4096    Aug  2 2019 04:16:41 +00:00  virtual-instance
    12   -rw-             30    Oct  3 2019 15:14:11 +00:00  throughput_monitor_params
  8065   drwx           4096    Aug  2 2019 04:17:55 +00:00  onep
    13   -rw-             34    Oct  3 2019 15:19:30 +00:00  pnp-tech-time
249985   drwx           4096    Aug 20 2019 17:40:11 +00:00  Archives
    14   -rw-          65037    Oct  3 2019 15:19:42 +00:00  pnp-tech-discovery-summary
    17   -rw-        5032908    Sep 19 2019 14:16:23 +00:00  isr4200_4300_
  rommon_1612_1r_SPA.pkg
    18   -rw-      517153193    Sep 21 2019 04:24:04 +00:00  isr4200-universalk9_ias.
  16.09.04.SPA.bin
7194652672 bytes total (6294822912 bytes free)
Router#
```

Because flash is the default file system, in this example, the **dir** command lists the contents of flash. Several files are located in flash, but of specific interest is the last listing: the name of the current Cisco IOS file image that is running in RAM.

The NVRAM File System

To view the contents of NVRAM, you must change the current default file system by using the **cd** (change directory) command, as shown in Example 10-22.

Example 10-22   Displaying the NVRAM File System on a Router

```
Router#
Router# cd nvram:
Router# pwd
nvram:/
Router#
Router# dir
Directory of nvram:/
32769   -rw-              1024                     startup-config
32770   ----                61                     private-config
32771   -rw-              1024                     underlying-config
    1   ----                 4                     private-KS1
    2   -rw-              2945                     cwmp_inventory
    5   ----               447                     persistent-data
    6   -rw-              1237                     ISR4221-2x1GE_0_0_0
    8   -rw-                17                     ecfm_ieee_mib
    9   -rw-                 0                     ifIndex-table
   10   -rw-              1431                     NIM-2T_0_1_0
   12   -rw-               820                     IOS-Self-Sig#1.cer
   13   -rw-               820                     IOS-Self-Sig#2.cer
33554432 bytes total (33539983 bytes free)
Router#
```

The present working directory command is **pwd**. This command verifies that you are viewing the NVRAM directory. Finally, the **dir** command lists the contents of NVRAM. Although there are several configuration files listed, of specific interest is the startup-configuration file.

Switch File Systems (10.6.2)

With the Cisco 2960 switch flash file system, you can copy configuration files and archive (upload and download) software images.

The command to view the file systems on a Catalyst switch is the same as on a Cisco router: **show file systems** (see Example 10-23).

Example 10-23   Displaying the File System on a Switch

```
Switch# show file systems
File Systems:

       Size(b)       Free(b)      Type    Flags   Prefixes
*   32514048     20887552      flash      rw      flash:
           -             -     opaque      rw         vb:
           -             -     opaque      ro         bs:
           -             -     opaque      rw     system:
```

```
        -              -         opaque      rw      tmpsys:
    65536          48897         nvram       rw       nvram:
        -              -         opaque      ro       xmodem:
        -              -         opaque      ro       ymodem:
        -              -         opaque      rw         null:
        -              -         opaque      ro          tar:
        -              -         network     rw         tftp:
        -              -         network     rw          rcp:
        -              -         network     rw         http:
        -              -         network     rw          ftp:
        -              -         network     rw          scp:
        -              -         network     rw        https:
        -              -         opaque      ro          cns:
Switch#
```

Use a Text File to Back Up a Configuration (10.6.3)

Configuration files can be saved to a text file by using Tera Term, as shown in Figure 10-24. To use Tera Term to back up a configuration, follow these steps:

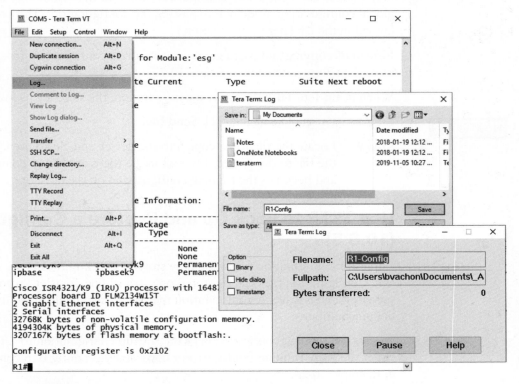

Figure 10-24   Example of Using Tera Term to Back Up a Configuration

Step 1. On the File menu, click **Log**.

Step 2. Choose the folder location and a filename for the file and click on **Save**. Tera Term opens the Tera Term: Log window and now captures all commands and output generated in the terminal window.

Step 3. To capture the current configuration, enter the **show running-config** or **show startup-config** command in privileged EXEC mode. The text displayed in the terminal window is also directed to the chosen file.

Step 4. When the capture is complete, click **Close** in the Tera Term: Log window.

Step 5. Open the file to verify that the configuration was captured properly and ensure that it is not corrupt.

Use a Text File to Restore a Configuration (10.6.4)

A configuration can be copied from a file and then directly pasted to a device. IOS executes each line of the configuration text as a command. This means that the file needs to be edited to ensure that encrypted passwords are in plaintext and that non-command text such as **--More--** and IOS messages are removed. In addition, you may want to add **enable** and **configure terminal** to the beginning of the file or enter global configuration mode before pasting the configuration. (This process is discussed in the lab later in this section.)

Instead of copying and pasting, you can restore a configuration from a text file by using Tera Term, as shown in Figure 10-25.

When using Tera Term to restore a configuration, the steps are as follows:

Step 1. On the File menu, click **Send file**.

Step 2. Locate the file to be copied to the device and click **Open**. Tera Term pastes the file to the device. The text in the file is applied as commands in the CLI and becomes the running configuration on the device.

Use TFTP to Back Up and Restore a Configuration (10.6.5)

Copies of configuration files should be stored as backup files in the event of a problem. Configuration files can be stored on a Trivial File Transfer Protocol (TFTP) server or a USB drive. A configuration file should also be included in the network documentation.

To save the running configuration or the startup configuration to a TFTP server, use either the **copy running-config tftp** or **copy startup-config tftp** command, as shown in Example 10-24.

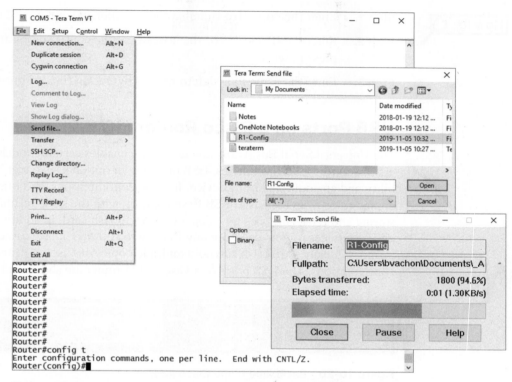

Figure 10-25 Example of Using Tera Term to Restore a Configuration

Example 10-24 Transferring the Running Configuration to a TFTP Server

```
R1# copy running-config tftp
Remote host []? 192.168.10.254
Name of the configuration file to write[R1-config]? R1-Jan-2019
Write file R1-Jan-2019 to 192.168.10.254? [confirm]
Writing R1-Jan-2019 !!!!!! [OK]
R1#
```

Follow these steps to back up the running configuration to a TFTP server:

Step 1. Enter the **copy running-config tftp** command and press Enter.

Step 2. Enter the IP address of the host where the configuration file will be stored and press Enter.

Step 3. Enter the name to assign to the configuration file and press Enter.

To restore the running configuration or the startup configuration from a TFTP server, use either the **copy tftp running-config** or **copy tftp startup-config** command. Use the following steps to restore the running configuration from a TFTP server:

Step 1. Enter the **copy tftp running-config** command and press Enter.

Step 2. Enter the IP address of the host where the configuration file is stored and press Enter.

Step 3. Enter the name to assign to the configuration file and press Enter.

USB Ports on a Cisco Router (10.6.6)

The Universal Serial Bus (USB) storage feature enables certain models of Cisco routers to support USB flash drives. USB provides an optional secondary storage capability and an additional boot device. Images, configurations, and other files can be copied to or from the Cisco USB flash memory with the same reliability as when storing and retrieving files by using a Compact Flash card. In addition, modular integrated services routers can boot any Cisco IOS software image saved on USB flash memory. Ideally, USB flash can hold multiple copies of Cisco IOS and multiple router configurations. The USB ports of a Cisco 4321 router are shown in Figure 10-26.

Figure 10-26 Backplane of the Cisco 4231

Use the **dir** command to view the contents of a USB flash drive, as shown in Example 10-25.

Example 10-25 Displaying the Contents of an Attached USB Drive

```
R1# dir usbflash0:
Directory of usbflash0:/
1 -rw- 30125020 Dec 22 2032 05:31:32 +00:00 c3825-entservicesk9-mz.123-14.T
63158272 bytes total (33033216 bytes free)
R1#
```

Use USB to Back Up and Restore a Configuration (10.6.7)

When backing up to a USB port, it is a good idea to issue the **show file systems** command to verify that the USB drive is there and confirm the name, as shown in Example 10-26.

Example 10-26   Displaying the File System to Verify That the USB Drive Is Connected

```
R1# show file systems
File Systems:

        Size(b)        Free(b)        Type   Flags   Prefixes
              -              -       opaque    rw     archive:
              -              -       opaque    rw     system:
              -              -       opaque    rw     tmpsys:
              -              -       opaque    rw     null:
              -              -      network    rw     tftp:
*    256487424      184819712         disk    rw     flash0: flash:#
              -              -         disk    rw     flash1:
       262136         249270        nvram    rw     nvram:
              -              -       opaque    wo     syslog:
              -              -       opaque    rw     xmodem:
              -              -       opaque    rw     ymodem:
              -              -      network    rw     rcp:
              -              -      network    rw     http:
              -              -      network    rw     ftp:
              -              -      network    rw     scp:
              -              -       opaque    ro     tar:
              -              -      network    rw     https:
              -              -       opaque    ro     cns:
   4050042880     3774152704     usbflash    rw     usbflash0:
R1#
```

Notice that the last line of output in Example 10-26 shows the USB port and name: usbflash0:.

Next, as shown in Example 10-27, use the **copy run usbflash0:/** command to copy the configuration file to the USB flash drive. Be sure to use the name of the flash drive, as indicated in the file system. The slash is optional but indicates the root directory of the USB flash drive.

Example 10-27   Copying the Running Configuration to a USB Drive

```
R1# copy running-config usbflash0:/
Destination filename [running-config]? R1-Config
5024 bytes copied in 0.736 secs (6826 bytes/sec)
```

IOS prompts for the filename. If the file already exists on the USB flash drive, the router prompts to overwrite, as shown in the examples.

When copying to a USB flash drive with no preexisting file, you get output similar to that shown in Example 10-27.

When copying to a USB flash drive, with the same configuration file already on the drive, you see output similar to that shown in Example 10-28.

Example 10-28   Warning When the Same Filename Already Exists on the USB Drive

```
R1# copy running-config usbflash0:
Destination filename [running-config]? R1-Config
%Warning:There is a file already existing with this name
Do you want to over write? [confirm]
5024 bytes copied in 1.796 secs (2797 bytes/sec)
R1#
```

Use the **dir** command to see the file on the USB drive and use the **more** command to see the contents, as shown in Example 10-29.

Example 10-29   Verifying That the File Is Now on the USB Drive

```
R1# dir usbflash0:/
Directory of usbflash0:/
    1  drw-       0  Oct 15 2010 16:28:30 +00:00  Cisco
   16  -rw-    5024   Jan 7 2013 20:26:50 +00:00  R1-Config
4050042880 bytes total (3774144512 bytes free)
R1#
R1# more usbflash0:/R1-Config
!
! Last configuration change at 20:19:54 UTC Mon Jan 7 2013 by
admin version 15.2
service timestamps debug datetime msec
service timestamps log datetime msec
no service password-encryption
!
hostname R1
!
boot-start-marker
boot-end-marker
!
logging buffered 51200 warnings
!
no aaa new-model
!
no ipv6 cef
R1#
```

Restore Configurations with a USB Flash Drive

To copy a file back to a device from a flash drive, you need to edit the USB R1-Config file with a text editor. For example, if the filename is **R1-Config**, use the **copy usbflash0:/R1-Config** *running-config* command to restore a running configuration.

Password Recovery Procedures (10.6.8)

Passwords are used on devices to prevent unauthorized access to those devices. For encrypted passwords, such as the enable secret passwords, the passwords must be replaced after recovery.

Note

Console access to a physical device is required to perform password recovery.

The detailed procedure for password recovery varies depending on the device. However, all the password recovery procedures follow the same basic process:

Step 1.   Enter the *ROMMON mode*.

Step 2.   Change the *configuration register*.

Step 3.   Copy the startup configuration to the running configuration.

Step 4.   Change the password.

Step 5.   Save the running configuration as the new startup configuration.

Step 6.   Reload the device.

Console access to the device through a terminal or terminal emulator software on a PC is required for password recovery. The terminal settings to access the device are:

- 9600 baud rate
- No parity
- 8 data bits
- 1 stop bit
- No flow control

Password Recovery Example (10.6.9)

The following sections describe the steps in password recovery.

Step 1. Enter the ROMMON mode.

With console access, a user can access the ROMMON mode by using a break sequence during the bootup process or by removing the external flash memory when the device is powered off. When successful, the **rommon 1 >** prompt displays, as shown in Example 10-30.

Note

The break sequence for PuTTY is Ctrl+Break. A list of standard break key sequences for other terminal emulators and operating systems can be found by searching the internet.

Example 10-30   Entering the ROMMON Mode

```
Readonly ROMMON initialized

monitor: command "boot" aborted due to user interrupt
rommon 1 >
```

Step 2. Change the configuration register.

The ROMMON software supports some basic commands, such as **confreg**. For example, the **confreg 0x2142** command sets the configuration register to 0x2142. With the configuration register at 0x2142, the device ignores the startup configuration file during startup. (The startup configuration file is where the forgotten passwords are stored.) After setting the configuration register to 0x2142, type **reset** at the prompt to restart the device. Enter the break sequence while the device is rebooting and decompressing IOS. Example 10-31 shows the terminal output of a 1941 router in the ROMMON mode after using a break sequence during the bootup process.

Example 10-31   Changing the Configuration Register

```
rommon 1 > confreg 0x2142
rommon 2 > reset

System Bootstrap, Version 15.0(1r)M9, RELEASE SOFTWARE (fc1)
Technical Support: http://www.cisco.com/techsupport
Copyright (c) 2010 by cisco Systems, Inc.
(output omitted)
```

Step 3. Copy the startup-config to the running-config.

After a device has finished reloading, copy the startup configuration to the running configuration by using the **copy startup-config running-config** command, as shown in Example 10-32.

Example 10-32   Copying the Startup Configuration to the Running Configuration

```
Router# copy startup-config running-config
Destination filename [running-config]?

1450 bytes copied in 0.156 secs (9295 bytes/sec)
R1#
```

Notice that the router prompt changes to R1# because the hostname is set to R1 in the startup configuration.

Caution

Do not enter **copy running-config startup-config**. This command erases the original startup configuration.

Step 4. Change the password.

While in privileged EXEC mode, you can configure all the necessary passwords. Example 10-33 shows how to change a password.

Note

The password **cisco** is not a strong password and is used here only as an example.

Example 10-33   Changing the Password

```
R1(config)# enable secret cisco
R1(config)#
```

Step 5. Save the running-config as the new startup-config.

After the new passwords are configured, change the configuration register back to 0x2102 by using the **config-register 0x2102** command in global configuration mode. Save the running configuration to the startup configuration, as shown in Example 10-34.

Example 10-34   Saving the Running Configuration as the New Startup Configuration

```
R1(config)# config-register 0x2102
R1(config)# end
R1#
R1# copy running-config startup-config
Destination filename [startup-config]?
Building configuration...
[OK]
R1#
```

Step 6. Reload the device.

Reload the device, as shown in Example 10-35.

Example 10-35   Reloading the Device

```
R1# reload
Proceed with reload? [confirm]

*Mar  1 13:04:53.009: %SYS-5-RELOAD: Reload requested by console. Reload Reason:
  Reload Command.
```

Notice that you are prompted to confirm the reload. To continue, press Enter. (To cancel, press Ctrl+C.) The device reboots and now uses the newly configured passwords for authentication. Be sure to use **show** commands to verify that all the configurations are still in place. For example, verify that the appropriate interfaces are not shut down after password recovery.

Note

To find detailed instructions for password recovery procedures for a specific device, search the internet.

Packet Tracer—Back Up Configuration Files (10.6.10)

In this activity, you will restore a configuration from a backup and then perform a new backup. Due to an equipment failure, a new router has been put in place. Fortunately, backup configuration files have been saved to a Trivial File Transfer Protocol (TFTP) server. You are required to restore the files from the TFTP server to get the router back online as quickly as possible.

Lab—Use Tera Term to Manage Router Configuration Files (10.6.11)

In this lab, you will complete the following objectives:

- Part 1: Configure basic device settings

- Part 2: Use terminal emulation software to create a backup configuration file

- Part 3: Use a backup configuration file to restore a router

Lab—Use TFTP, Flash, and USB to Manage Configuration Files (10.6.12)

In this lab, you will complete the following objectives:

- Part 1: Build the network and configure basic device settings

- Part 2: (Optional) Download TFTP server software

- Part 3: Use TFTP to back up and restore the switch running configuration

- Part 4: Use TFTP to back up and restore the router running configuration

- Part 5: Back up and restore running configurations using router flash memory

- Part 6: (Optional) Use a USB drive to back up and restore the running configuration

Lab—Research Password Recovery Procedures (10.6.13)

In this lab, you will complete the following objectives:

- Part 1: Research the configuration register
- Part 2: Document the password recovery procedure for a specific Cisco router

IOS Image Management

In this section, you will learn how to upgrade an IOS system image.

Video

Video—Managing Cisco IOS Images (10.7.1)

Refer to the online course to view this video.

TFTP Servers as a Backup Location (10.7.2)

Earlier in this chapter, you learned how to copy and paste a configuration. This section takes that idea one step further with IOS software images. As a network grows, Cisco IOS software images and configuration files can be stored on a central TFTP server, as shown in Figure 10-27.

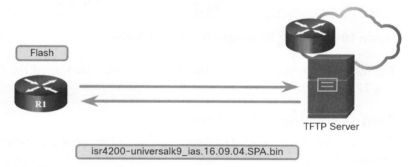

Figure 10-27   TFTP Topology

Storing the images and files centrally helps to control the number of IOS images and the revisions to those IOS images, as well as the configuration files that must be maintained.

Production internetworks usually span wide areas and contain multiple routers. For any network, it is good practice to keep a backup copy of the Cisco IOS software image in case the system image on the router becomes corrupted or accidentally erased.

Widely distributed routers need a source or backup location for Cisco IOS software images. Using a network TFTP server allows image and configuration uploads and downloads over the network. The network TFTP server can be another router, a workstation, or a host system.

Backup IOS Image to TFTP Server Example (10.7.3)

To maintain network operations with minimum downtime, it is necessary to have procedures in place for backing up Cisco IOS images. Such procedures enable a network administrator to quickly copy an image back to a router in the event of a corrupted or erased image.

In Figure 10-28, the network administrator wants to create on the TFTP server at 172.16.1.100 a backup of the current image file on the router (isr4200-universalk9_ias.16.09.04.SPA.bin).

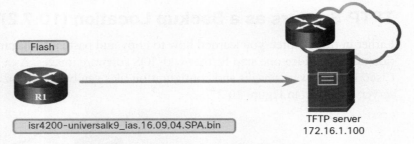

Figure 10-28   TFTP Topology—R1 to TFTP Server

The following sections describe the steps to create a backup of the Cisco IOS image to a TFTP server.

Step 1. Ping the TFTP server.

To ensure that the network TFTP server is accessible, ping the server as shown in Example 10-36.

Example 10-36   Pinging the TFTP Server

```
R1# ping 172.16.1.100
Type escape sequence to abort.
Sending 5, 100-byte ICMP Echos to 172.16.1.100, timeout is 2 seconds:
!!!!!
Success rate is 100 percent (5/5),
round-trip min/avg/max = 56/56/56 ms
R1#
```

Step 2. Verify image size in flash.

Verify that the TFTP server has sufficient disk space to accommodate the Cisco IOS software image. As shown in Example 10-37, use the **show flash0:** command on the router to determine the size of the Cisco IOS image file. The file in this example is 517153193 bytes long.

Example 10-37   Verifying Image Size in Flash

```
R1# show flash0:
-# - --length-- -----date/time------ path
8    517153193   Apr 2 2019 21:29:58  +00:00
                        isr4200-universalk9_ias.16.09.04.SPA.bin
(output omitted)
R1#
```

Step 3. Copy the image to the TFTP server.

Copy the image to the TFTP server by using the **copy** *source-url destination-url* command. After issuing the command by using the specified source and destination URLs, you are prompted for the source filename, the IP address of the remote host, and the destination filename. Typically, you press Enter to accept the source filename as the destination filename. The transfer then begins, as shown in Example 10-38.

Example 10-38   Copying the Image to the TFTP Server

```
R1# copy flash: tftp:
Source filename []? isr4200-universalk9_ias.16.09.04.SPA.bin
Address or name of remote host []? 172.16.1.100
Destination filename [isr4200-universalk9_ias.16.09.04.SPA.bin]?
Writing isr4200-universalk9_ias.16.09.04.SPA.bin...
!!!!!!!!!!!!!!!!!!!!!!!!!!!!!!!!!!!!!!!!!
(output omitted)
517153193 bytes copied in 863.468 secs (269058 bytes/sec)
R1#
```

Copy an IOS Image to a Device Example (10.7.4)

Cisco consistently releases new Cisco IOS software versions to resolve issues and provide new features. This section shows an example of using IPv6 for the transfer to show that TFTP can also be used across IPv6 networks.

Figure 10-29 illustrates the process of copying a Cisco IOS software image from a TFTP server. A new image file (isr4200-universalk9_ias.16.09.04.SPA.bin) is copied from the TFTP server at 2001:DB8:CAFE:100::99 to the router.

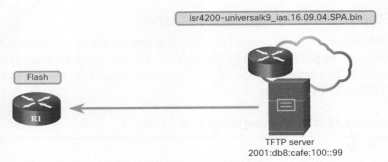

Figure 10-29 TFTP Topology—TFTP Server to R1

Select a Cisco IOS image file that meets the requirements in terms of platform, features, and software. Download the file from cisco.com and transfer it to the TFTP server. The following sections explain the process to upgrade the IOS image on the Cisco router.

Step 1. Ping the TFTP server.

To ensure that the network TFTP server is accessible, ping the server as shown in Example 10-39.

Example 10-39 Pinging the TFTP Server

```
R1# ping 2001:db8:cafe:100::99
Type escape sequence to abort.
Sending 5, 100-byte ICMP Echos to 2001:DB8:CAFE:100::99,
timeout is 2 seconds:
!!!!!
Success rate is 100 percent (5/5),
round-trip min/avg/max = 56/56/56 ms
R1#
```

Step 2. Verify the amount of free flash.

Ensure that there is sufficient flash space on the router that is being upgraded. The amount of free flash can be verified by using the **show flash:** command. Compare the free flash space with the new image file size. The **show flash:** command in Example 10-40 is used to verify free flash size. Free flash space in the example is 6294806528 bytes.

Example 10-40 Verifying the Amount of Free Flash

```
R1# show flash:
-# - --length-- -----date/time------ path
(output omitted)
6294806528 bytes available (537251840 bytes used)
R1#
```

Step 3. Copy the new IOS image to flash.

Copy the IOS image file from the TFTP server to the router by using the **copy** command, as shown in Example 10-41. After issuing this command with specified source and destination URLs, you are prompted for the IP address of the remote host, the source filename, and the destination filename. Typically, you press Enter to accept the source filename as the destination filename. The transfer of the file begins.

Example 10-41   Copying the New IOS Image to Flash

```
R1# copy tftp: flash:
Address or name of remote host []? 2001:DB8:CAFE:100::99
Source filename []?  isr4200-universalk9_ias.16.09.04.SPA.bin
Destination filename [isr4200-universalk9_ias.16.09.04.SPA.bin]?
Accessing tftp://2001:DB8:CAFE:100::99/ isr4200-
universalk9_ias.16.09.04.SPA.bin...
Loading isr4200-universalk9_ias.16.09.04.SPA.bin
from 2001:DB8:CAFE:100::99 (via
GigabitEthernet0/0/0): !!!!!!!!!!!!!!!!!!!!!

[OK - 517153193 bytes]
517153193 bytes copied in 868.128 secs (265652 bytes/sec)
R1#
```

The boot system Command (10.7.5)

To upgrade to the copied IOS image after that image is saved on the flash memory of a router, configure the router to load the new image during bootup by using the **boot system** global configuration command, as shown in Example 10-42. Save the configuration. Reload the router to boot the router with the new image.

Example 10-42   Configuring the Image to Boot

```
R1(config)# boot system flash0:isr4200-universalk9_ias.16.09.04.SPA.bin
R1(config)# exit
R1#
R1# copy running-config startup-config
R1#
R1# reload
Proceed with reload? [confirm]

*Mar  1 12:46:23.808: %SYS-5-RELOAD: Reload requested by console. Reload Reason:
  Reload Command.
```

To continue, press Enter. (To cancel, press Ctrl+C.)

During startup, the bootstrap code parses the startup configuration file in NVRAM for the **boot system** commands that specify the name and location of the Cisco IOS software image to load. Several **boot system** commands can be entered in sequence to provide a fault-tolerant boot plan.

If there are no **boot system** commands in the configuration, the router defaults to loading the first valid Cisco IOS image in flash memory and runs it.

After the router has booted, to verify that the new image has loaded, use the **show version** command, as shown in Example 10-43.

Example 10-43   Verifying That the Router Booted the Specified Image

```
R1# show version
Cisco IOS XE Software, Version 16.09.04
Cisco IOS Software [Fuji], ISR Software (X86_64_LINUX_IOSD-UNIVERSALK9_IAS-M),
  Version 16.9.4, RELEASE SOFTWARE (fc2)
Technical Support: http://www.cisco.com/techsupport
Copyright (c) 1986-2019 by Cisco Systems, Inc.
Compiled Thu 22-Aug-19 18:09 by mcpre
Cisco IOS-XE software, Copyright (c) 2005-2019 by cisco Systems, Inc.
All rights reserved.  Certain components of Cisco IOS-XE software are
licensed under the GNU General Public License ("GPL") Version 2.0.  The
software code licensed under GPL Version 2.0 is free software that comes
with ABSOLUTELY NO WARRANTY.  You can redistribute and/or modify such
GPL code under the terms of GPL Version 2.0.  For more details, see the
documentation or "License Notice" file accompanying the IOS-XE software,
or the applicable URL provided on the flyer accompanying the IOS-XE
software.

ROM: IOS-XE ROMMON
Router uptime is 2 hours, 19 minutes
Uptime for this control processor is 2 hours, 22 minutes
System returned to ROM by PowerOn
System image file is "flash:isr4200-universalk9_ias.16.09.04.SPA.bin"
(output omitted)
R1#
```

Packet Tracer
☐ Activity

Packet Tracer—Use a TFTP Server to Upgrade a Cisco IOS Image (10.7.6)

A TFTP server can help manage the storage of IOS images and revisions to IOS images. For any network, it is good practice to keep a backup copy of the Cisco IOS software image in case the system image in the router becomes corrupted or accidentally erased. A TFTP server can also be used to store new upgrades to IOS and then deployed throughout the network where needed. In this activity, you will upgrade the IOS images on Cisco devices by using a TFTP server. You will also back up an IOS image with the use of a TFTP server.

Summary (10.8)

The following is a summary of the sections in this chapter.

Device Discovery with CDP

Cisco Discovery Protocol (CDP) is a Cisco-proprietary Layer 2 protocol that is used to gather information about Cisco devices that share the same data link. The device sends periodic CDP advertisements to connected devices. CDP can be used as a network discovery tool to determine information about the neighboring devices. This information gathered from CDP can help build a logical topology of a network when documentation is missing or lacking detail. CDP can assist in network design decisions, troubleshooting, and making changes to equipment. On Cisco devices, CDP is enabled by default. To verify the status of CDP and display information about CDP, enter the **show cdp** command. To enable CDP globally for all the supported interfaces on a device, enter **cdp run** in global configuration mode. To enable CDP on a specific interface, enter the **cdp enable** global configuration command. To verify the status of CDP and display a list of neighbors, use the **show cdp neighbors** command in privileged EXEC mode. The **show cdp neighbors** command provides helpful information about each CDP neighbor device, including device identifiers, the port identifier, the capabilities list, and the platform. Use the **show cdp interface** command to display the interfaces on a device that are CDP enabled.

Device Discovery with LLDP

Cisco devices support Link Layer Discovery Protocol (LLDP), which is a vendor-neutral neighbor discovery protocol similar to CDP. This protocol advertises its identity and capabilities to other devices and receives information from a physically connected Layer 2 device. To enable LLDP globally on a Cisco network device, enter the **lldp run** command in global configuration mode. To verify that LLDP has been enabled on the device, enter the **show lldp** command in privileged EXEC mode. With LLDP enabled, you can discover device neighbors by using the **show lldp neighbors** command. When you need more details about the neighbors, use the **show lldp neighbors detail** command to find information such as the neighbor IOS version, IP address, and device capability.

NTP

The software clock on a router or switch starts when the system boots and is the primary source of time for the system. When the time is not synchronized between devices, it is impossible to determine the order of the events and the cause of an event. You can manually configure the date and time, or you can configure NTP, a protocol that allows routers on a network to synchronize their time settings with an NTP server. When NTP is implemented in a network, it can be set up to synchronize to a private master clock or it can synchronize to a publicly available NTP server on the internet. NTP networks use a hierarchical system of time sources, and each level in this system is called a stratum. The synchronized time is distributed across the network by using NTP. Authoritative time sources, also referred to as stratum 0 devices, are high-precision time-keeping devices. Stratum 1 devices are directly connected to the authoritative time sources. Stratum 2 devices, such as NTP clients, synchronize their time by using the NTP packets from stratum 1 servers. You issue the **ntp server** *ip-address* command in global configuration mode to configure a device as the NTP server. To verify the time source is set to NTP, use the **show clock detail** command. Use the **show ntp associations** and **show ntp status** commands to verify that a device is synchronized with the NTP server.

SNMP

SNMP allows administrators to manage servers, workstations, routers, switches, and security appliances on an IP network. SNMP is an application layer protocol that provides a message format for communication between managers and agents. The SNMP system consists of three elements: SNMP manager, SNMP agents, and the MIB. To configure SNMP on a networking device, you must define the relationship between the manager and the agent. The SNMP manager is part of an NMS. The SNMP manager can collect information from an SNMP agent by using the get action and can change configurations on an agent by using the set action. SNMP agents can forward information directly to a network manager by using traps. The SNMP agent responds to SNMP manager GetRequest-PDUs (to get an MIB variable) and SetRequest-PDUs (to set an MIB variable). An NMS periodically uses the get request to poll the SNMP agents by querying the device for data. A network management application can collect information to monitor traffic loads and to verify device configurations of managed devices.

SNMPv1, SNMPv2c, and SNMPv3 are all versions of SNMP. SNMPv1 is a legacy solution. Both SNMPv1 and SNMPv2c use a community-based form of security. The community of managers that is able to access the agent's MIB is defined by a community string. SNMPv2c includes a bulk retrieval mechanism and more detailed error message reporting. SNMPv3 provides for both security models and security levels. SNMP community strings are read-only (ro) and read-write (rw). They are used to authenticate access to MIB objects. The MIB organizes variables hierarchically. MIB variables enable the management software to monitor and control the network device. OIDs uniquely identify managed objects in the MIB hierarchy. The **snmpget** utility provides some insight into the basic mechanics of how SNMP works. The Cisco SNMP Navigator on the http://www.cisco.com website allows a network administrator to research details about a particular OID.

Syslog

The most common method of accessing system messages is to use a protocol called syslog. The syslog protocol uses UDP port 514 to allow networking devices to send their system messages across the network to syslog servers. The syslog logging service provides three primary functions: gather logging information for monitoring and troubleshooting, select the type of logging information that is captured, and specify the destinations of captured syslog messages. Destinations for syslog messages include the logging buffer (RAM inside a router or switch), console line, terminal line, and syslog server. Table 10-8 lists the syslog levels.

Table 10-8   Syslog Severity Levels

Severity Name	Severity Level	Explanation
Emergency	Level 0	System unusable
Alert	Level 1	Immediate action needed
Critical	Level 2	Critical condition
Error	Level 3	Error condition
Warning	Level 4	Warning condition
Notification	Level 5	Normal but significant condition
Informational	Level 6	Informational message
Debugging	Level 7	Debugging message

Syslog facilities identify and categorize system state data for error and event message reporting. Common syslog message facilities reported on Cisco IOS routers include IP, OSPF protocol, SYS operating system, IPsec, and IF. The default format of syslog messages on Cisco IOS software is %facility-severity-MNEMONIC: description. Use the **service timestamps log datetime** global configuration command to force logged events to display the date and time.

Router and Switch File Maintenance

Cisco IFS lets an administrator navigate to different directories, list the files in a directory, and create subdirectories in flash memory or on a disk. Use the **show file systems** command to display all the available file systems on a Cisco router. Use the directory command **dir** to display the directory of bootflash. Use the change directory command **cd** to view the contents of NVRAM. Use the present working directory command **pwd** to view the current directory. Use the **show file systems** command to view the file systems on a Catalyst switch or a Cisco router. Configuration files can be saved to a text file by using Tera Term. A configuration can be copied from a file and then directly pasted to a device. Configuration files can be stored on a TFTP server or a USB drive. To save the running configuration or the startup configuration to a TFTP server, use either the **copy running-config tftp** command or the **copy startup-config tftp** command. Use the **dir** command to view the contents of a USB flash drive. Use the **copy run usbflash0:/** command to copy the configuration file to the USB flash drive. Use the **dir** command to see the file on the USB drive. Use the **more** command to see the contents of the drive. For encrypted passwords, such as the enable secret passwords, the passwords must be replaced after recovery.

IOS Image Management

Cisco IOS software images and configuration files can be stored on a central TFTP server to control the number of IOS images and the revisions to those IOS images, as well as the configuration files that must be maintained. Select a Cisco IOS image file that meets the requirements in terms of platform, features, and software. Download the file from cisco.com and transfer it to the TFTP server. Ping the TFTP server. Verify the amount of free flash by using the **show flash:** command. If there is enough free flash to hold the new IOS image, copy the new IOS image to flash. To upgrade to the copied IOS image after that image is saved on the router's flash memory, configure the router to load the new image during bootup by using the **boot system** global configuration command. Save the configuration. Reload the router to boot the router with the new image. After the router has booted, to verify that the new image has loaded, use the **show version** command.

<table>
<tr><td>Packet Tracer
☐ Activity</td><td>

Packet Tracer—Configure CDP, LLDP, and NTP (10.8.1)

In this Packet Tracer activity, you will complete the following objectives:

- Build the network and configure basic device settings
- Network discovery with CDP
- Network discovery with LLDP
- Configure and verify NTP

</td></tr>
</table>

Lab—Configure CDP, LLDP, and NTP (10.8.2)

In this lab, you will complete the following objectives:

- Build the network and configure basic device settings
- Network discovery with CDP
- Network discovery with LLDP
- Configure and verify NTP

Practice

The following activities provide practice with the topics introduced in this chapter. The labs are available in the companion *Enterprise Networking, Security, and Automation Labs & Study Guide (CCNAv7)* (ISBN 9780136634690). The Packet

Tracer activity instructions are also in the *Labs & Study Guide*. The PKA files are found in the online course.

Labs

Lab 10.4.10: Research Network Monitoring Software

Lab 10.6.11: Use Tera Term to Manage Router Configuration Files

Lab 10.6.12: Use TFTP, Flash, and USB to Manage Configuration Files

Lab 10.6.13: Research Password Recovery Procedures

Lab 10.8.2: Configure CDP, LLDP, and NTP

Packet Tracer Activities

Packet Tracer 10.1.5: Use CDP to Map a Network

Packet Tracer 10.2.6: Use LLDP to Map a Network

Packet Tracer 10.3.4: Configure and Verify NTP

Packet Tracer 10.6.10: Back Up Configuration Files

Packet Tracer 10.7.6: Use a TFTP Server to Upgrade a Cisco IOS Image

Packet Tracer 10.8.1: Configure CDP, LLDP, and NTP

Check Your Understanding Questions

Complete all the review questions listed here to test your understanding of the topics and concepts in this chapter. The appendix "Answers to the 'Check Your Understanding' Questions" lists the answers.

1. Which of the following is one difference between CDP and LLDP?

    A. CDP can gather information from routers, switches, and wireless APs, whereas LLDP can only gather information from routers and switches.

    B. CDP can obtain both Layer 2 and Layer 3 information, whereas LLDP can only obtain Layer 2 information.

    C. CDP is a proprietary protocol, whereas LLDP is a vendor-neutral protocol.

    D. CDP is enabled on an interface using two commands, while LLDP requires only one command.

2. A network administrator wants to configure a router so that only a specific interface will send and receive CDP information. Which two configuration steps accomplish this? (Choose two.)

   A. R1(config)# **no cdp enable**

   B. R1(config)# **no cdp run**

   C. R1(config-if)# **cdp enable**

   D. R1(config-if)# **cdp receive**

   E. R1(config-if)# **cdp transmit**

3. What information can be gathered about a neighbor device from the **show cdp neighbors detail** command that cannot be found with the **show cdp neighbors** command?

   A. The capabilities of the neighbor

   B. The hostname of the neighbor

   C. The IP address of the neighbor

   D. The platform that is used by the neighbor

4. What is the configuration command to globally enable LLDP on a Cisco Catalyst switch?

   A. **enable lldp**

   B. **feature lldp**

   C. **lldp enable**

   D. **lldp run**

5. Which option correctly enables LLDP on an interface?

   A. R1(config-if)# **lldp enable**

   B. R1(config-if)# **lldp enable**
       R1(config-if)# **lldp receive**

   C. R1(config-if)# **lldp receive**
       R1(config-if)# **lldp transmit**

   D. R1(config-if)# **lldp enable**
       R1(config-if)# **lldp receive**
       R1(config-if)# **lldp transmit**

6. What are the most common syslog messages?

    A. Error messages about hardware or software malfunctions

    B. Link up and link down messages

    C. Output messages that are generated from debug output

    D. Messages that occur when a packet matches a parameter condition in an access control list

7. Which syslog logging severity level indicates that a device is unusable?

    A. Level 0—Emergency

    B. Level 1—Alert

    C. Level 2—Critical

    D. Level 3—Error

8. Which protocol or service allows network administrators to receive system messages that are provided by network devices?

    A. NTP

    B. NetFlow

    C. SNMP

    D. Syslog

9. Which syslog message type is accessible only to an administrator via the Cisco CLI?

    A. Alerts

    B. Debugging

    C. Emergency

    D. Errors

10. Which default destination do Cisco routers and switches use to send Syslog messages?

    A. Console

    B. Nearest syslog server

    C. NVRAM

    D. RAM

11. What is the result of configuring the **logging trap 4** global configuration command?

   A. The syslog client sends to the syslog server any event message that has a severity level of 4 or lower.

   B. The syslog client sends to the syslog server event messages with an identification trap level of only 4.

   C. The syslog client sends to the syslog server any event message that has a severity level of 4 or higher.

   D. After four events, the syslog client sends an event message to the syslog server.

12. The ntp server 10.1.1.1 global configuration command is issued on router R1. What impact does this command have?

   A. Identifies the NTP server that R1 will send system log messages to

   B. Identifies the NTP server that R1 will use to store backup configurations

   C. Identifies R1 as the NTP server using IP address 10.1.1.1

   D. Synchronizes the clock of R1 with the time server at IP address 10.1.1.1

13. Which two statements are true about NTP servers in an enterprise network? (Choose two.)

   A. All NTP servers synchronize directly to a stratum 1 time source.

   B. NTP servers at stratum 1 are directly connected to an authoritative time source.

   C. NTP servers control the mean time between failures (MTBF) for key network devices.

   D. NTP servers ensure an accurate timestamp on logging and debugging information.

   E. There can be only one NTP server on an enterprise network.

14. What can a network administrator do to access a router if the password has been lost?

   A. Access the router remotely through Telnet and use the **show running-config** command.

   B. Boot the router into ROMMON mode and reinstall IOS from a TFTP server.

   C. From ROMMON mode, configure the router to ignore the startup configuration when the router initializes.

   D. Reboot the router and use the break key sequence to bypass the password during IOS bootup.

15. What is the result of configuring the **confreg 0x2142** command at the rommon 1> prompt?

    A. Contents in NVRAM are erased.

    B. Contents in NVRAM are ignored.

    C. Contents in RAM are erased.

    D. Contents in RAM are ignored.

16. A network technician is attempting a password recovery on a router. From ROMMON mode, which command must be entered to bypass the startup configuration file?

    A. rommon> **config-register 0x2102**

    B. rommon> **confreg 0x2102**

    C. rommon> **config-register 0x2142**

    D. rommon> **confreg 0x2142**

17. What must an administrator have in order to reset a lost password on a router?

    A. A crossover cable

    B. A TFTP server

    C. Access to another router

    D. Physical access to the router

18. A network engineer is upgrading the Cisco IOS image on a 2900 Series ISR. What command could the engineer use to verify the total amount of flash memory as well as how much flash memory is currently available?

    A. **show boot memory**

    B. **show flash0:**

    C. **show interfaces**

    D. **show startup-config**

    E. **show version**

19. Which two conditions should a network administrator verify before attempting to upgrade a Cisco IOS image using a TFTP server? (Choose two.)

    A. Verify connectivity between the router and TFTP server by using the **ping** command.

    B. Verify that the checksum for the image is valid by using the **show version** command.

    C. Verify that the TFTP server is running by using the **tftpdnld** command.

    D. Verify the name of the TFTP server by using the **show hosts** command.

    E. Verify that there is enough flash memory for the new Cisco IOS image by using the **show flash** command.

20. Which statement describes SNMP operation?

    A. The SNMP agent uses a get request to query the device for data.

    B. The NMS uses a set request to change configuration variables in the agent device.

    C. An NMS periodically polls the SNMP agents that are residing on managed devices by using traps to query the devices for data.

    D. An SNMP agent that resides on a managed device collects information about the device and stores that information remotely in the MIB that is located on the NMS.

21. Which SNMP feature provides a solution to the main disadvantage of SNMP polling?

    A. SNMP community strings

    B. SNMP get messages

    C. SNMP set messages

    D. SNMP trap messages

22. When SNMPv1 or SNMPv2 is being used, which feature provides secure access to MIB objects?

    A. Community strings

    B. Message integrity

    C. Packet encryption

    D. Source validation

23. Which SNMP version uses weak community string-based access control and supports bulk retrieval?

    A. SNMPv1

    B. SNMPv2c

    C. SNMPv3

    D. SNMPv2Classic

CHAPTER 11

Network Design

Objectives

Upon completion of this chapter, you will be able to answer the following questions:

- How are data, voice, and video converged in a switched network?

- What considerations are involved in designing a scalable network?

- How do switch hardware features support network requirements?

- What types of routers are available for small to medium-sized business networks?

Key Terms

This chapter uses the following key terms. You can find the definitions in the Glossary.

Introduction (11.0)

You are a sought-after spaceship designer, and you have been asked to design a new spaceship. Your first questions are, "What will this ship be used for? How large is the crew? Will it be a war ship? Or a cargo ship? Or a science and exploration vessel?" What if you learn that the crew can be as few as 50 people, but the spaceship must be able to hold as many as 500 people, and the ship will be used in a variety of ways? How do you design a ship like this? You must design the size and configuration of the ship and the power it requires wisely.

Designing a network to meet current requirements and to adapt to future requirements is a complex task. But it can be done, thanks to hierarchical and scalable network designs that use the right components. You know you want to learn about this. Even if you have not designed your current network, knowing about network design will increase your value to the organization as a great network administrator—and who doesn't want that?

Hierarchical Networks (11.1)

Networks must be scalable, which means they must be able to accommodate increases and decreases in size. This section looks at how the hierarchical design model is used to help accomplish this task.

Video

Video—Three-Layer Network Design (11.1.1)

Refer to the online course to view this video.

The Need to Scale the Network (11.1.2)

Our digital world is changing. The ability to access the internet and the corporate network is no longer confined to physical offices, geographic locations, or time zones. In today's globalized workplace, employees can access resources from anywhere in the world, and information must be available at any time, and on any device. These requirements drive the need to build next-generation networks that are secure, reliable, and highly available. These next-generation networks must not only support current expectations and equipment but must also be able to integrate legacy platforms.

Businesses increasingly rely on their network infrastructure to provide *mission-critical services*. As businesses grow and evolve, they hire more employees, open branch offices, and expand into global markets. These changes directly affect the requirements of a network, which must be able to scale to meet the needs of business. For example, the company in Figure 11-1 has a single location with one connection to the internet.

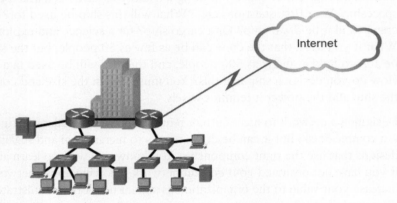

Figure 11-1   A Small, Single-Location Company

Figure 11-2 shows the company after it has grown to have multiple locations in the same city.

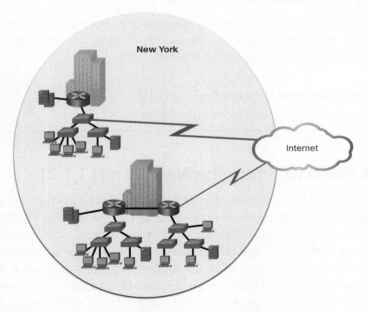

Figure 11-2   Company with Multiple Locations

Figure 11-3 shows the company continuing to grow and expanding to more cities. It also hires and connects teleworkers.

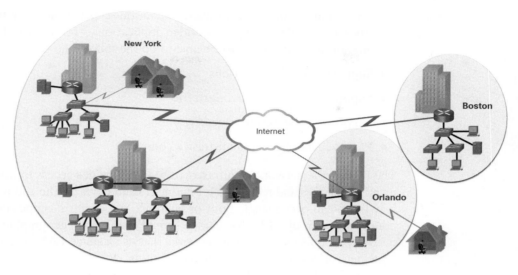

Figure 11-3   Enterprise Grows to Multiple Cities and Adds Teleworkers

Figure 11-4 shows the company expanding to other countries and centralizing management in a *network operations center (NOC)*.

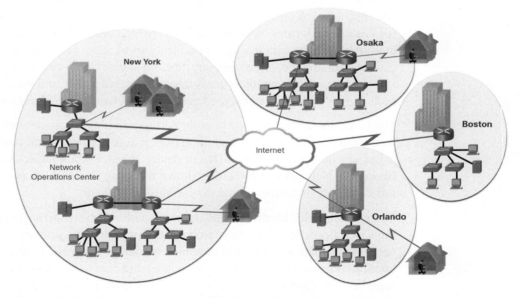

Figure 11-4   Enterprise Becomes Global and Centralizes Network Operations

A network must support the exchange of various types of network traffic—including data files, email, IP telephony, and video applications—for multiple business units. All *enterprise networks* must be able to do the following:

- Support critical applications
- Support converged network traffic
- Support diverse business needs
- Provide centralized administrative control

The LAN is the networking infrastructure that provides access to network communication services and resources for end users and devices. The end users and devices may be spread over a single floor or building. You create a campus network by interconnecting a group of LANs that are spread over a small geographic area. Campus network designs include small networks that use a single LAN switch up to very large networks with thousands of connections.

Borderless Switched Networks (11.1.3)

With the increasing demands of the *converged network*, a network must be developed with an architectural approach that embeds intelligence, simplifies operations, and is scalable to meet future demands. One recent development in network design is the *Cisco Borderless Networks architecture*, a network architecture that combines innovation and design. It allows organizations to support a borderless network that can connect anyone, anywhere, anytime, on any device—and do it securely, reliably, and seamlessly. This architecture is designed to address IT and business challenges such as supporting the converged network and changing work patterns.

The Cisco Borderless Networks architecture provides the framework to unify wired and wireless access—including policy, access control, and performance management—across many different device types. Using this architecture, the Borderless Networks architecture, shown in Figure 11-5, is built on a hierarchical infrastructure of hardware that is scalable and resilient.

By combining this hardware infrastructure with policy-based software solutions, the Cisco Borderless Networks architecture provides two primary sets of services—network services and user and endpoint services—under the umbrella of an integrated management solution. It enables different network elements to work together and allows users to access resources from any place, at any time, while providing optimization, *scalability*, and security.

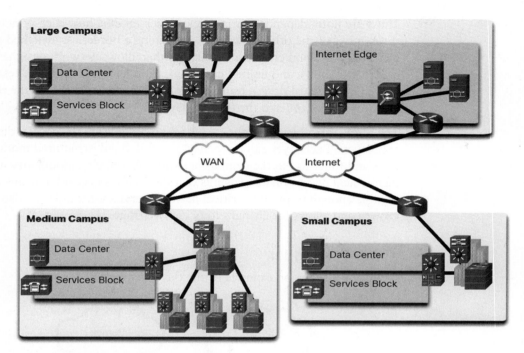

Figure 11-5 Borderless Switch Network Example

Hierarchy in the Borderless Switched Network (11.1.4)

Creating a borderless switched network requires that sound network design principles be used to ensure maximum availability, flexibility, security, and manageability. A borderless switched network must deliver on current requirements and future required services and technologies. Borderless switched network design guidelines are built on the following principles:

- **Hierarchical:** The design facilitates understanding the role of each device at every tier; simplifies deployment, operation, and management; and reduces fault domains at every tier.

- **Modularity:** The design allows seamless network expansion and integrated service enablement on an on-demand basis.

- **Resiliency:** The design satisfies user expectations for keeping the network always on.

- **Flexibility:** The design allows intelligent traffic load sharing by using all network resources.

These are not independent principles. Understanding how each principle fits in the context of the others is critical. Designing a borderless switched network in a hierarchical fashion creates a foundation that allows network designers to overlay security, mobility, and unified communication features. Two time-tested and proven hierarchical design frameworks for campus networks are the *three-layer hierarchical model* and the two-tier layer models.

The three critical layers within these tiered designs are the access, distribution, and core layers. Each layer can be seen as a well-defined, structured module with specific roles and functions in the campus network. Introducing modularity into the campus hierarchical design further ensures that the campus network remains resilient and flexible enough to provide critical network services. Modularity also helps enable growth and allows for changes to occur over time.

Three-Tier Model

Figure 11-6 shows an example of the three-tier model.

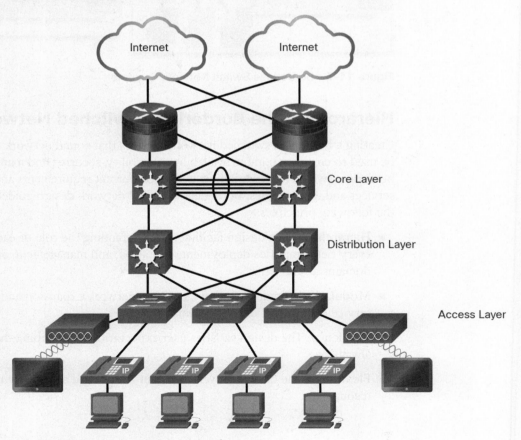

Figure 11-6   Three-Tier Model Example

At the top are two clouds depicting the internet. There are redundant links connecting to two firewall routers. The routers have redundant links to two core layer *multilayer switches*. There is an *EtherChannel* between the switches, with four links. The switches also have redundant links to two distribution layer multilayer switches. The *distribution layer switches* have redundant links to three access layer switches. Two of the switches have links to access points. Both access points have connections to tablets. The access layer switches are also connected to IP phones and PCs.

Two-Tier Model

Figure 11-7 shows an example of the two-tier model.

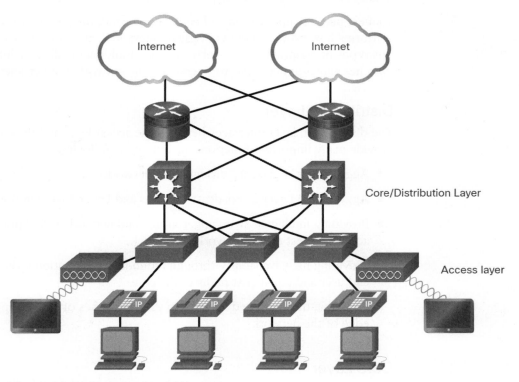

Figure 11-7   Two-Tier Model Example

At the top are two clouds depicting the internet. There are redundant links connecting to two firewall routers. The routers have redundant links to two core/distribution layer multilayer switches. The core/distribution layer switches have redundant links to three access layer switches. Two of the switches have links to access points. Both access points have connections to tablets. The access layer switches are also connected to IP phones and PCs.

Access, Distribution, and Core Layer Functions (11.1.5)

The access, distribution, and core layers perform specific functions in a *hierarchical network* design.

Access Layer

The *access layer* represents the network edge, where traffic enters or exits the campus network. Traditionally, the primary function of an access layer switch has been to provide network access to the user. Access layer switches connect to distribution layer switches, which implement network foundation technologies such as routing, quality of service, and security.

To meet network application and end-user demand, the next-generation switching platforms now provide more converged, integrated, and intelligent services to various types of endpoints at the network edge. Building intelligence into access layer switches allows applications to operate on the network more efficiently and securely.

Distribution Layer

The distribution layer interfaces between the access layer and the *core layer* to provide many important functions, including the following:

- Aggregating large-scale wiring closet networks

- Aggregating Layer 2 broadcast domains and Layer 3 routing boundaries

- Providing intelligent switching, routing, and network access policy functions to access the rest of the network

- Providing high availability through redundant distribution layer switches to the end user and equal-cost paths to the core

- Providing differentiated services to various classes of service applications at the edge of the network

Core Layer

The core layer is the network backbone. It connects several layers of the campus network. The core layer serves as the aggregator for all of the distribution layer devices and ties the campus together with the rest of the network. The primary purposes of the core layer are to provide fault isolation and high-speed backbone connectivity.

Three-Tier and Two-Tier Examples (11.1.6)

The following sections provide three-tier and two-tier design examples and explanations.

Three-Tier Example

Figure 11-8 shows a three-tier campus network design for organizations where the access, distribution, and core are each separate layers.

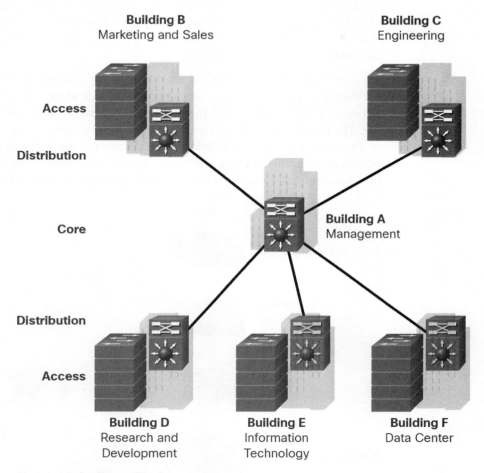

Figure 11-8   Three-Tier Example

To build a simplified, scalable, cost-effective, and efficient physical cable layout design, the recommendation is to build an extended-star physical network topology from a centralized building location to all other buildings on the same campus.

The figure shows an example of the three-tier campus network design. There are six buildings, A through F. Building A is labeled Management, Building B is Marketing and Sales, Building C is Engineering, Building D is Research and Development, Building E is Information Technology, and Building F is labeled Data Center. Buildings B through F are connected to Building A in a hub-and-spoke topology. Building A is at the core layer. Building B through F are all at the distribution and access layers.

Two-Tier Example

In some cases where extensive physical or network scalability does not exist, maintaining separate distribution and core layers is not required. In smaller campus locations where there are fewer users accessing the network, or in campus sites consisting of a single building, separate core and distribution layers may not be needed. In such a scenario, the recommendation is the two-tier campus network design, also known as the *collapsed core network design*.

Figure 11-9 shows an example of the two-tier campus network design. The figure shows the topology of a building. A router on the edge of the network has two links: one to a WAN and another to the internet. The router has a link to a multilayer switch. The router and multilayer switch make up the collapsed core/distribution layer. The multilayer switch has links to five switches at the access layer. The access layer switches are labeled Floor 6 Research and Development, Floor 5 Engineering, Floor 4 Server Farm, Floor 3 Information Technology, and Floor 2 Management.

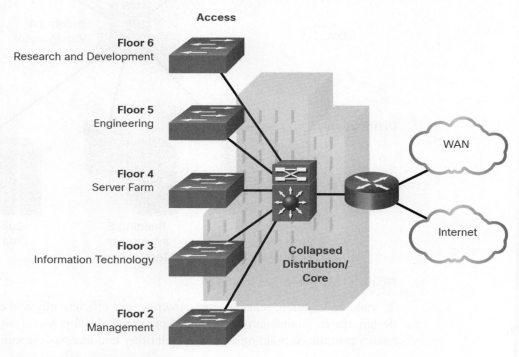

Figure 11-9   Two-Tier Example

Role of Switched Networks (11.1.7)

The role of switched networks has evolved dramatically in the past two decades. Not long ago, flat Layer 2 switched networks were the norm. These networks relied on

Ethernet and the widespread use of hub repeaters to propagate LAN traffic throughout an organization.

As shown in Figure 11-10, networks have fundamentally changed and now tend to be switched LANs in a hierarchical design.

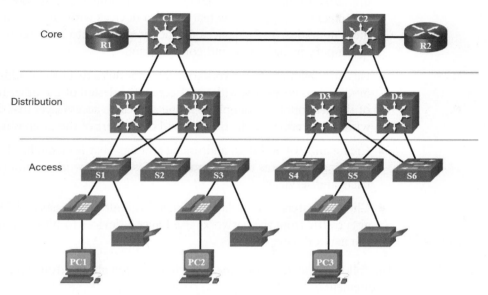

Figure 11-10   Switched Hierarchical Network Example

A switched LAN allows additional flexibility, traffic management, quality of service, and security. It also affords support for wireless networking and connectivity and support for other technologies, such as IP telephone and mobility services.

Interactive Graphic

Check Your Understanding—Hierarchical Networks (11.1.8)

Refer to the online course to complete this activity.

Scalable Networks (11.2)

In this section, you will learn about the considerations for designing a scalable network.

Design for Scalability (11.2.1)

You understand that your network is going to change. Its number of users will likely increase, those users may be located anywhere, and they will be using a wide variety of devices. Your network must be able to change along with its users. *Scalability* refers to the ability of a network to grow without losing availability and reliability.

To support a large, medium, or small network, a network designer must develop a strategy to enable the network to be available and to scale effectively and easily. Included in a basic network design strategy are the following recommendations:

- Use expandable, modular equipment or clustered devices that can be easily upgraded to increase capabilities. Device modules can be added to the existing equipment to support new features and devices without requiring major equipment upgrades. Some devices can be integrated into a cluster to act as one device to simplify management and configuration.

- Design a hierarchical network to include modules that can be added, upgraded, and modified, as necessary, without affecting the design of the other functional areas of the network (for example, creating a separate access layer that can be expanded without affecting the distribution and core layers of the campus network).

- Create an IPv4 and IPv6 addressing strategy that is hierarchical. Careful address planning eliminates the need to re-address the network to support additional users and services.

- Choose routers or multilayer switches to limit broadcasts and filter other undesirable traffic from the network. Use Layer 3 devices to filter and reduce traffic to the network core.

The following sections provide more information about advanced network design requirements.

Redundant Links

Implement redundant links in a network between critical devices and between access layer and core layer devices.

Figure 11-11 illustrates redundant links between access and core layer devices. In the wiring closet there are two switches, and in the backbone there are four switches. These six switches have redundant links. The backbone switches also have redundant links to the server farm. The server farm consists of two switches and seven servers.

Multiple Links

Implement multiple links between equipment, with either *link aggregation* (EtherChannel) or equal-cost load balancing, to increase bandwidth. Combining multiple Ethernet links into a single, load-balanced EtherChannel configuration increases available bandwidth. EtherChannel implementations can be used when budget restrictions prohibit purchasing high-speed interfaces and fiber runs.

Figure 11-12 illustrates multiple links between switches using EtherChannel. The figure has two multilayer switches with two links each to a switch. The links are aggregated together using EtherChannel.

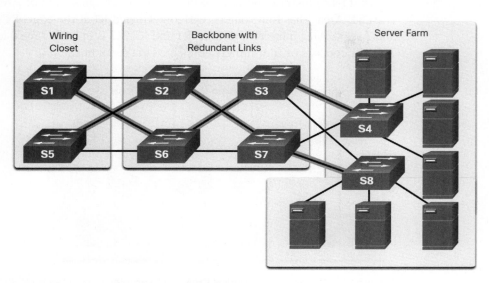

Figure 11-11   Redundant Links Example

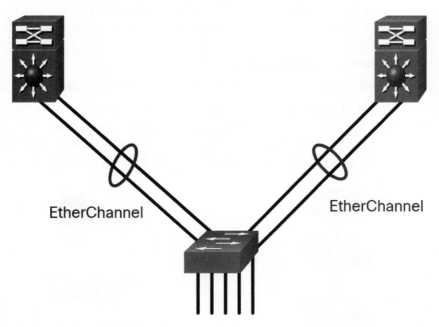

Figure 11-12   Multiple Links Example

Scalable Routing Protocol

Use a scalable routing protocol such as Open Shortest Path First (OSPF) and implement features to isolate routing updates and minimize the size of the routing table.

Figure 11-13 illustrates a three-OSPF-area network consisting of Area 1, Area 0, and Area 51. Area 1 has four routers, with one labeled R1 at the edge. R1 is in both Area 1 and Area 0. Area 0 has two routers: R1 and R2. R2 is in both Area 0 and Area 51. Area 51 consists of four routers connected via serial links.

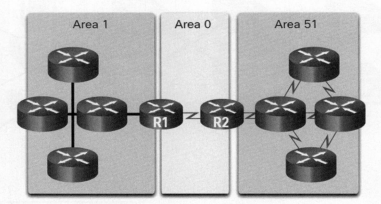

Figure 11-13   Scalable Routing Protocol Example

What if the number of routers in Area 1 and Area 51 increased to 40 routers each? OSPF provides the scalability features to support such an increase in routers.

Wireless Connectivity

Implement wireless connectivity to allow for mobility and expansion.

Figure 11-14 illustrates using wireless connectivity to allow for mobility and expansion. A router, R1, has a link to a switch, S1. S1 has redundant links to another switch, S2. S2 has links to two PCs and to a Cisco wireless access point. The Cisco wireless access point is connected wirelessly to a cellphone, a laptop, and a tablet.

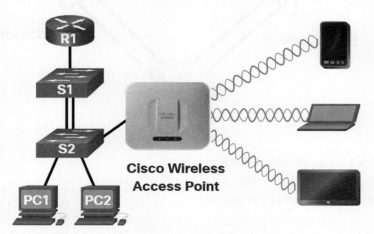

Figure 11-14   Wireless Connectivity Example

Plan for Redundancy (11.2.2)

For many organizations, the availability of the network is essential to supporting business needs. Redundancy is an important part of network design. It can prevent disruption of network services by minimizing the possibility of a single point of failure. One method of implementing redundancy is by installing duplicate equipment and providing failover services for critical devices, as in the example shown in Figure 11-15.

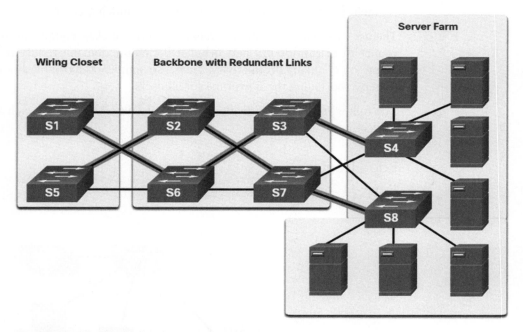

Figure 11-15   Example of a Redundant Design

Another method of implementing redundancy is by using redundant paths, as shown in the figure. Redundant paths offer alternate physical paths for data to traverse the network. Redundant paths in a switched network support high availability. However, due to the operation of switches, redundant paths in a switched Ethernet network may cause logical Layer 2 loops. For this reason, Spanning Tree Protocol (STP) is required.

STP eliminates Layer 2 loops when redundant links are used between switches. It does this by providing a mechanism for disabling redundant paths in a switched network until a path is necessary, such as when a failure occurs. STP is an open standard protocol that is used in a switched environment to create a loop-free logical topology.

Using Layer 3 in the backbone is another way to implement redundancy without the need for STP at Layer 2. Layer 3 also provides best-path selection and faster convergence during failover.

Reduce Failure Domain Size (11.2.3)

A well-designed network not only controls traffic but also limits the size of *failure domains*. A failure domain is the area of a network that is impacted when a critical device or network service experiences problems.

The function of the device that initially fails determines the impact of a failure domain. For example, a malfunctioning switch on a network segment normally affects only the hosts on that segment. However, if the router that connects the segment to other segments fails, the impact is much greater.

The use of redundant links and reliable enterprise-class equipment minimizes the chance of disruption in a network. Smaller failure domains reduce the impact of a failure on company productivity. They also simplify the troubleshooting process, thereby shortening the downtime for all users.

The following sections provide examples of failure domains of each associated device.

Edge Router

Figure 11-16 illustrates the failure domain of an edge router.

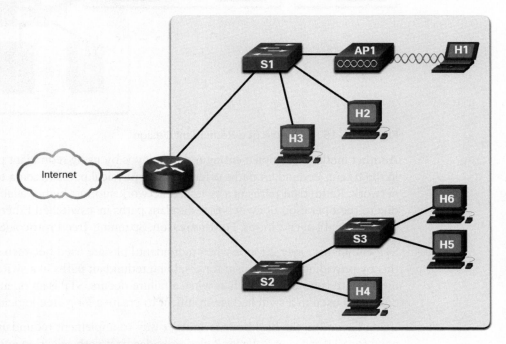

Figure 11-16 Edge Router Failure Domain

In this figure, a cloud depicting the internet is connected to an edge router. The edge router has two branched links to two switches, named S1 and S2. S1 has links to two PCs, labeled H2 and H3, and a wireless access point, labeled AP1. AP1 has a wireless connection to a laptop, labeled H1. The other switch, S2, has a link to a switch labeled S3 and a PC labeled H4. S3 has two links to two PCs, labeled H5 and H6. The failure domain for the edge router is highlighted in a square that encompasses all of the devices connected to the edge router, excluding only the link to the internet.

AP1

Figure 11-17 illustrates the failure domain of an access point, AP1.

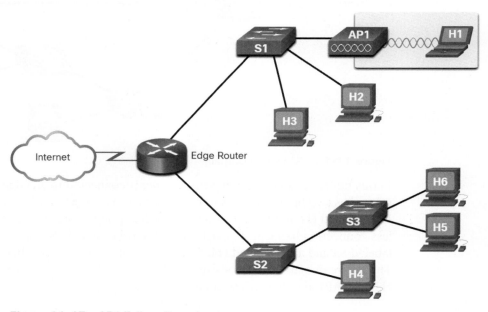

Figure 11-17   AP1 Failure Domain

In this figure, a cloud depicting the internet is connected to an edge router. The edge router has two branched links to two switches, named S1 and S2. S1 has links to two PCs, labeled H2 and H3, and a wireless access point, labeled AP1. AP1 has a wireless connection to a laptop, labeled H1. The other switch, S2, has a link to a switch labeled S3 and a PC labeled H4. S3 has two links to two PCs, labeled H5 and H6. The failure domain for AP1 consists of only the PC H1 that is wirelessly connected to AP1.

S1

Figure 11-18 illustrates the failure domain of S1.

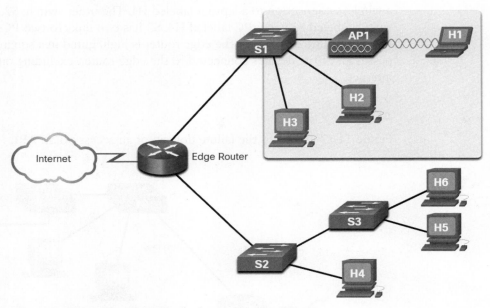

Figure 11-18 S1 Failure Domain

In this figure, a cloud depicting the internet is connected to an edge router. The edge router has two branched links to two switches, named S1 and S2. S1 has links to two PCs, labeled H2 and H3, and a wireless access point, labeled AP1. AP1 has a wireless connection to a laptop, labeled H1. The other switch, S2, has a link to a switch labeled S3 and a PC labeled H4. S3 has two links to two PCs, labeled H5 and H6. The failure domain for S1 consists of all the devices connected to S1; the PCs H2 and H3; and AP1 and its wireless connection, H1.

S2

Figure 11-19 illustrates the failure domain of S2.

In this figure, a cloud depicting the internet is connected to an edge router. The edge router has two branched links to two switches, named S1 and S2. S1 has links to two PCs, labeled H2 and H3, and a wireless access point, labeled AP1. AP1 has a wireless connection to a laptop, labeled H1. The other switch, S2, has a link to a switch labeled S3 and a PC labeled H4. S3 has two links to two PCs, labeled H5 and H6. The failure domain for S2 consists of all the devices connected to S2; the PCs H4 and H3; and S3's links to the PCs H5 and H6.

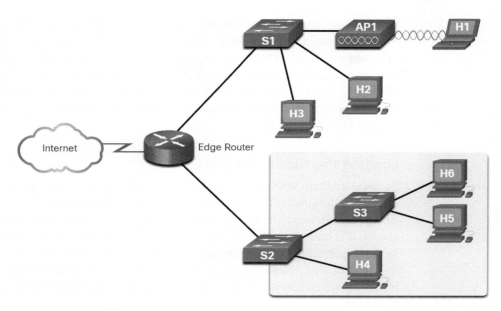

Figure 11-19   S2 Failure Domain

S3

Figure 11-20 illustrates the failure domain of S3.

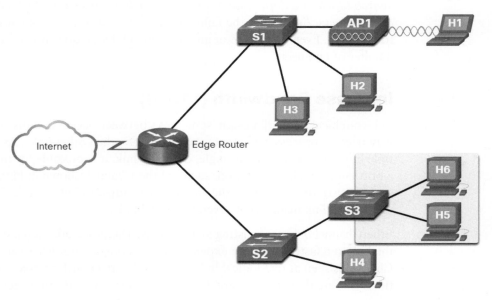

Figure 11-20   S3 Failure Domain

In this figure, a cloud depicting the internet is connected to an edge router. The edge router has two branched links to two switches, named S1 and S2. S1 has links to two PCs, labeled H2 and H3, and a wireless access point, labeled AP1. AP1 has a wireless connection to a laptop, labeled H1. The other switch, S2, has a link to a switch labeled S3 and a PC labeled H4. S3 has two links to two PCs, labeled H5 and H6. The failure domain for S3 consists of all the devices connected to S3 and the PCs H5 and H6.

Limiting the Size of Failure Domains

Because a failure at the core layer of a network can have a potentially large impact, a network designer often concentrates on efforts to prevent failures. These efforts can greatly increase the cost of implementing the network. In the hierarchical design model, it is easiest and usually least expensive to control the size of a failure domain in the distribution layer. In the distribution layer, network errors can be contained to a smaller area, thus affecting fewer users. When using Layer 3 devices at the distribution layer, every router functions as a gateway for a limited number of access layer users.

Switch Block Deployment

Routers or multilayer switches are usually deployed in pairs, with access layer switches evenly divided between them. This configuration is referred to as a *building switch block* or a *departmental switch block*. Each switch block acts independently of the others. As a result, the failure of a single device does not cause the network to go down. Even the failure of an entire switch block does not affect a significant number of end users.

Increase Bandwidth (11.2.4)

In hierarchical network design, some links between access and distribution switches may need to process a greater amount of traffic than other links. As traffic from multiple links converges onto a single, outgoing link, it is possible for that link to become a bottleneck. Link aggregation, such as EtherChannel (shown in Figure 11-21), allows an administrator to increase the amount of bandwidth between devices by creating one logical link made up of several physical links.

EtherChannel uses the existing switch ports. Therefore, additional costs to upgrade the link to a faster and more expensive connection are not necessary. The EtherChannel is seen as one logical link using an EtherChannel interface. Most configuration tasks are done on the EtherChannel interface instead of on each individual port, ensuring configuration consistency throughout the links. Finally, the EtherChannel configuration takes advantage of load balancing between links that are part of the same EtherChannel, and depending on the hardware platform, one or more load-balancing methods can be implemented.

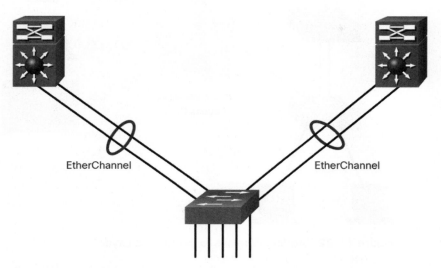

Figure 11-21   Increasing Bandwidth with EtherChannel

Expand the Access Layer (11.2.5)

The network must be designed to be able to expand network access to individuals and devices as needed. An increasingly important option for extending access layer connectivity is wireless access. Providing wireless connectivity offers many advantages, such as increased flexibility, reduced costs, and the ability to grow and adapt to changing network and business requirements.

To communicate wirelessly, an end device needs to have a wireless NIC that incorporates a radio transmitter/receiver and the required software driver to make it operational. In addition, a wireless router or a wireless access point (AP) is required for users to connect, as shown in Figure 11-22.

There are many considerations when implementing a wireless network, such as the types of wireless devices to use, wireless coverage requirements, interference considerations, and security considerations.

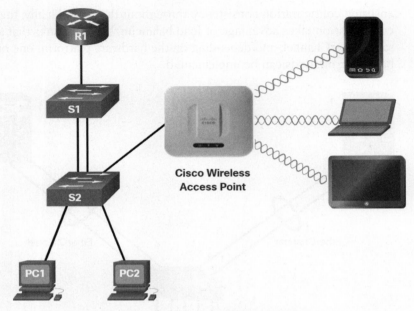

Figure 11-22   Adding Wireless to the Access Layer

Tune Routing Protocols (11.2.6)

Advanced routing protocols, such as Open Shortest Path First (OSPF), are used in large networks.

OSPF is a link-state routing protocol. As shown in Figure 11-23, OSPF works well for larger hierarchical networks where fast convergence is important.

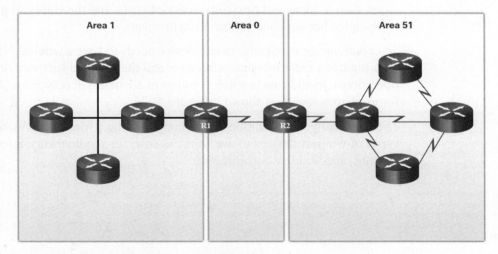

Figure 11-23   OSPF in a Large Hierarchical Network

OSPF routers establish and maintain neighbor adjacencies with other connected OSPF routers. OSPF routers synchronize their link-state database. When a network change occurs, link-state updates are sent, informing other OSPF routers of the change and establishing a new best path, if one is available.

Check Your Understanding—Scalable Networks (11.2.7)

Refer to the online course to complete this activity.

Switch Hardware (11.3)

Switches and routers are core network infrastructure devices, and selecting them may seem to be a fairly simply task. However, there are many different models of switches and routers available. Different models provide varying numbers of ports, different forwarding rates, and unique feature support.

In this section, you will learn how to select network devices based on feature compatibility and network requirement.

Switch Platforms (11.3.1)

One simple way to create hierarchical and scalable networks is to use the right equipment for the job. There are a variety of switch platforms, *form factors*, and other features that you should consider before choosing a switch.

When designing a network, it is important to select the proper hardware to meet current network requirements, as well as to allow for network growth. Within an enterprise network, both switches and routers play a critical role in network communication.

The following sections provide more information about the categories of switches for enterprise networks.

Campus LAN Switches

To scale network performance in an enterprise LAN, there are core, distribution, access, and compact switches. These switch platforms vary from fanless switches with eight fixed ports to 13-blade switches supporting hundreds of ports. *Campus LAN switch* platforms include the Cisco 2960, 3560, 3650, 3850, 4500, 6500, and 6800 Series. Figure 11-24 shows a Cisco 3650 Series switch.

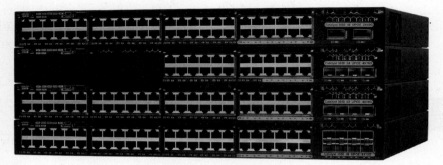

Figure 11-24   Campus LAN Switches: Cisco 3650 Series

Cloud-Managed Switches

The Cisco Meraki *cloud-managed switches*, such as the one in Figure 11-25, enable virtual stacking of switches. They monitor and configure thousands of switch ports over the web, without the intervention of onsite IT staff.

Figure 11-25   Cloud-Managed Switches: Cisco Meraki

Data Center Switches

A data center should be built using switches that promote infrastructure scalability, operational continuity, and transport flexibility. The *data center switch* platforms include the Cisco Nexus Series switches, such as the 7000 Series switch shown in Figure 11-26.

Figure 11-26   Data Center Switches: Cisco Nexus 7000 Series

Service Provider Switches

Service provider switches fall under two categories: aggregation switches and Ethernet access switches. Aggregation switches are carrier-grade Ethernet switches that aggregate traffic at the edge of a network. Service provider Ethernet access switches feature application intelligence, unified services, virtualization, integrated security, and simplified management. The Cisco ASR 9000 Series is shown in Figure 11-27.

Figure 11-27   Service Provider Switches: Cisco ASR 9000 Series

Virtual Networking

Networks are becoming increasingly virtualized. Cisco Nexus *virtual networking switch* platforms, such as the Nexus 1000v in Figure 11-28, provide secure multi-tenant services by adding virtualization intelligence technology to the data center network.

Figure 11-28   Virtual Networking: Cisco Nexus 1000v

Switch Form Factors (11.3.2)

When selecting switches, network administrators must determine the switch form factors. This includes fixed configuration, modular configuration, stackable, or non-stackable. The following sections provide more information about switch form factors.

Fixed Configuration Switches

Features and options on *fixed configuration switches* are limited to those that originally come with the switch. For example, the Cisco 3850 Series switches in Figure 11-29 are fixed configuration switches.

Figure 11-29   Fixed Configuration Switches: Cisco 3850 Series

Modular Configuration Switches

The chassis on modular switches accept field-replaceable *line cards*. The Cisco MDS 9000 Series switches in Figure 11-30 are *modular configuration switches*.

Figure 11-30   Modular Configuration Switches: Cisco MDS 9000 Series

Stackable Configuration Switches

Special cables, as shown in Figure 11-31, are used to connect *stackable configuration switches* that allow them to effectively operate as one large switch.

Figure 11-31 Stackable Configuration Switches

Thickness

The thickness of a switch, which is expressed in the number of *rack units (RUs)*, is also important for switches that are mounted in a rack. For example, each of the fixed configuration Cisco 3650 Series switches shown in Figure 11-32 is one rack units (1U), or 1.75 inches (44.45 mm) in height.

Figure 11-32 Four Switches, Each 1U Thick

Port Density (11.3.3)

The *port density* of a switch refers to the number of ports available on the switch. Figure 11-33 shows three different switches with different port densities.

Figure 11-33   Cisco Catalyst 3850 Switches with Different Port Densities

Fixed configuration switches support a variety of port density configurations. The Cisco Catalyst 3850 Series switches come in 12-, 24-, and 48-port configurations, as shown in Figure 11-33. The 48-port switch has an option for additional ports for *small form-factor pluggable (SFP)* devices.

Modular switches can support very high port densities through the addition of multiple switchport line cards. For example, the modular Catalyst 9400 switch shown in Figure 11-34 supports 384 switchport interfaces.

Large networks that support many thousands of network devices require high-density, modular switches to make the best use of space and power. Without a high-density modular switch, a network would need many fixed configuration switches to accommodate the number of devices that need network access—as well as many power outlets and a lot of closet space.

A network designer must also consider the issue of uplink bottlenecks. A series of fixed configuration switches may consume many additional ports for bandwidth aggregation between switches in order to achieve target performance. With a single modular switch, bandwidth aggregation is less of an issue because the backplane of the chassis can provide the necessary bandwidth to accommodate the devices connected to the switchport line cards.

Figure 11-34   Catalyst 9400 Switch Can Be Expanded to Provide More Ports

Forwarding Rates (11.3.4)

Forwarding rates define the processing capabilities of a switch by rating how much data a switch can process per second. Switch product lines are classified by forwarding rates. Entry-level switches have lower forwarding rates than enterprise-level switches. Forwarding rates are important to consider when selecting a switch. If the switch forwarding rate is too low, the switch cannot accommodate full wire-speed communication across all of its switch ports. *Wire speed* is the data rate that each Ethernet port on the switch is capable of attaining. Data rates can be 100 Mbps, 1 Gbps, 10 Gbps, or 100 Gbps.

For example, a typical 48-port Gigabit switch operating at full wire speed generates 48 Gbps of traffic. If the switch supports a forwarding rate of only 32 Gbps, it cannot run at full wire speed across all ports simultaneously. Fortunately, access layer switches typically do not need to operate at full wire speed because they are physically limited by their uplinks to the distribution layer. This means that less expensive, lower-performing switches can be used at the access layer, and more expensive, higher-performing switches can be used at the distribution and core layers, where the forwarding rate has a greater impact on network performance.

Power over Ethernet (11.3.5)

Power over Ethernet (PoE) allows a switch to deliver power to a device over the existing Ethernet cabling. This feature can be used by IP phones and some wireless access points, allowing them to be installed anywhere that there is an Ethernet cable. A network administrator should ensure that the PoE features are actually required for a given installation because switches that support PoE are expensive.

The following sections provide examples of PoE ports on different devices.

Switch

PoE ports look the same as any other switch ports. Check the model of a switch to determine whether its ports support PoE.

Figure 11-35 displays a Catalyst 3650 Layer 3 switch with 24 PoE-enabled ports.

Figure 11-35   PoE Ports on a Catalyst 3650 Layer 3 Switch

IP Phone

Figure 11-36 shows the external power source and PoE ports on the back of an IP phone.

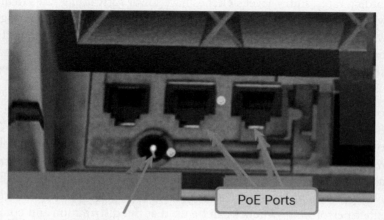

External Power Source

Figure 11-36   PoE Ports on an IP Phone

WAP

PoE ports on wireless access points look the same as any other switch ports. Check the model of the wireless access point to determine if its ports support PoE.

Figure 11-37 shows a PoE port on the back of a wireless access point.

Figure 11-37   PoE Port on a WAP

Cisco Catalyst 2960-C

The Cisco Catalyst 2960-C and 3560-C Series compact switches support PoE pass-through. PoE pass-through allows a network administrator to power PoE devices that are connected to the switch, as well as the switch itself, by drawing power from certain upstream switches.

Figure 11-38 shows PoE-enabled ports on a Cisco Catalyst 2960-C switch.

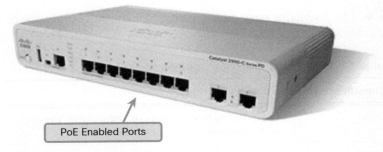

PoE Enabled Ports

Figure 11-38   PoE Ports on a Switch

Multilayer Switching (11.3.6)

Multilayer switches are typically deployed in the core and distribution layers of an organization's switched network. Multilayer switches are characterized by their ability to build a routing table, support a few routing protocols, and forward IP packets at a rate close to that of Layer 2 forwarding. Multilayer switches often support specialized hardware, such as *application-specific integrated circuits (ASICs)*. ASICs along with dedicated software data structures can streamline the forwarding of IP packets, independently of the CPU.

There is a trend in networking toward a pure Layer 3 switched environment. When switches were first used in networks, none of them supported routing. Now, almost all switches support routing. It is likely that soon every switch will incorporate a route processor because the cost of doing so is decreasing relative to other constraints.

Figure 11-39 shows a Catalyst 2960. Catalyst 2960 switches illustrate the migration to a pure Layer 3 environment. With IOS versions prior to 15.x, these switches supported only one active switch virtual interface (SVI). With IOS 15.x, these switches now support multiple active SVIs. This means that a switch can be remotely accessed via multiple IP addresses on distinct networks.

Figure 11-39 Cisco Catalyst 2960 Series Supports Multilayer Switching

Business Considerations for Switch Selection (11.3.7)

Table 11-1 highlights some of the common business considerations when selecting switch equipment.

Table 11-1 Common Business Considerations

Consideration	Description
Cost	The cost of a switch depends on the number and speed of the interfaces, supported features, and expansion capability.
Port density	Network switches must support the appropriate number of devices on the network.
Power	It is now common to power access points, IP phones, and compact switches using Power over Ethernet (PoE). In addition to PoE considerations, some chassis-based switches support redundant power supplies.
Reliability	A switch should provide continuous access to the network.

Consideration	Description
Port speed	The speed of the network connection is of primary concern to end users.
Frame buffers	The ability of a switch to store frames is important in a network where there may be congested ports to servers or other areas of the network.
Scalability	The number of users on a network typically grows over time; therefore, a switch should provide the opportunity for growth.

Interactive Graphic

Check Your Understanding—Switch Hardware (11.3.8)

Refer to the online course to complete this activity.

Router Hardware (11.4)

There are various types of router platforms available. Like switches, routers differ in physical configuration and form factor, in terms of the number and types of interfaces it supports, and be the features supported.

The focus of this section is on types of routers available to support network requirements in small to medium-sized business networks.

Router Requirements (11.4.1)

Switches are not the only component of a network that come with a variety of features. Your choice of router is another very important decision. Routers play a critical role in networking, connecting homes and businesses to the internet, interconnecting multiple sites within an enterprise network, providing redundant paths, and connecting ISPs on the internet. Routers can also act as translators between different media types and protocols. For example, a router can accept packets from an Ethernet network and re-encapsulate them for transport over a serial network.

A router uses the network portion (prefix) of the destination IP address to route packets to the proper destination. It selects an alternate path if a link goes down. All hosts on a local network specify the IP address of the local router interface in their IP configuration. This router interface is the default gateway. The ability to route efficiently and recover from network link failures is critical to delivering packets to their destination.

Routers also serve other beneficial functions, including the following:

- They provide broadcast containment by limiting broadcasts to the local network.

- They interconnect geographically separated locations.

- They group users logically by application or department within a company, based on common needs or requiring access to the same resources.

- They provide enhanced security, filtering unwanted traffic through access control lists.

Cisco Routers (11.4.2)

As a network grows, it is important to select the proper routers to meet its requirements. There are different categories of Cisco routers. The following sections provide more information about the categories of routers.

Branch Routers

Branch routers optimize branch services on a single platform while delivering an optimal application experience across branch and WAN infrastructures. Maximizing service availability at the branch requires networks designed for 24x7x365 uptime. Highly available branch networks must ensure fast recovery from typical faults while minimizing or eliminating the impact on service, and they must provide simple network configuration and management. Figure 11-40 shows Cisco Integrated Services Router (ISR) 4000 Series routers.

Figure 11-40   Cisco ISR 4000 Series

Network Edge Routers

Network edge routers enable the network edge to deliver high-performance, highly secure, and reliable services that unite campus, data center, and branch networks. Customers expect a high-quality media experience and more types of content than ever before. Customers want interactivity, personalization, mobility, and control for all content. Customers also want to access content anytime and anyplace they choose, over any device, whether at home, at work, or on the go. Network edge routers must deliver enhanced quality of service and nonstop video and mobile capabilities. Figure 11-41 shows Cisco Aggregation Services Routers (ASR) 9000 Series routers.

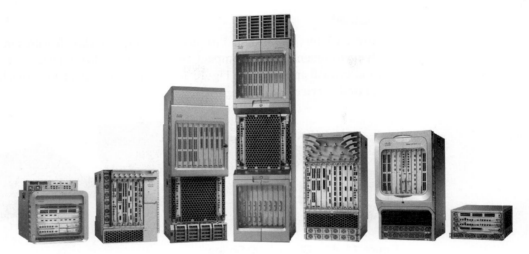

Figure 11-41   Cisco ASR 9000 Series

Service Provider Routers

Service provider routers deliver end-to-end scalable solutions and subscriber-aware services. Operators must optimize operations, reduce expenses, and improve scalability and flexibility in order to deliver next-generation internet experiences across all devices and locations. These systems are designed to simplify and enhance the operation and deployment of service-delivery networks. Figure 11-42 shows Cisco Network Convergence System (NCS) 6000 Series routers.

Door Closed   Door Open

Figure 11-42   Cisco NCS 6000 Series

Industrial

Industrial routers are designed to provide enterprise-class features in rugged and harsh environments. Their compact, modular, ruggedized design is excellent for mission-critical applications. Figure 11-43 shows Cisco 1100 Series Industrial Integrated Services routers.

Figure 11-43   Cisco 1100 Series

Router Form Factors (11.4.3)

Like switches, routers also come in many form factors. Network administrators in an enterprise environment should be able to support a variety of routers, from small desktop routers to rack-mounted or blade models. The following sections provide more information on various Cisco router platforms.

Cisco 900 Series

Figure 11-44 shows the Cisco 921-4P, which is a small branch office router. It combines WAN, switching, security, and advanced connectivity options in a compact, fanless platform for small and medium-sized businesses.

Figure 11-44   Cisco 921-4P

ASR 9000 and 1000 Series

The ASR routers in Figure 11-45 provide density and resiliency with programmability for a scalable network edge.

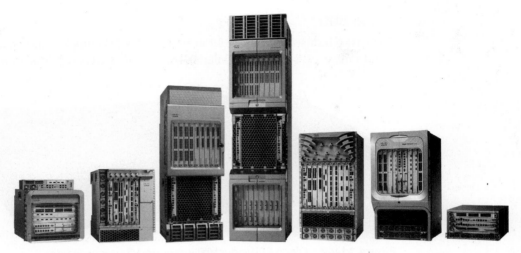

Figure 11-45   Cisco ASR 9000 and 1000 Series Aggregation Services Routers

5500 Series

The 5500 Series router in Figure 11-46 is designed to efficiently scale between large data centers and large enterprise networks, web, and service provider WAN and aggregation networks.

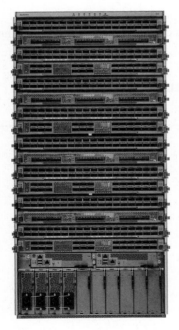

Figure 11-46   Cisco Network Convergence System 5500 Series Router

Cisco 800

The Cisco Industrial Router 829 in Figure 11-47 is compact and designed for harsh environments. It supports cellular, 2.4 GHz, and 5 GHz wireless access.

Figure 11-47   Cisco 800 Industrial Integrated Services Router

Fixed Configuration or Modular

Routers can also be categorized as fixed configuration or modular. With a fixed configuration, the desired router interfaces are built in. Modular routers come with multiple slots that allow a network administrator to change the interfaces on the router. Routers come with a variety of different interfaces, such as Fast Ethernet, Gigabit Ethernet, serial, and fiber optic.

A comprehensive list of Cisco routers can be found by searching the Cisco website, www.cisco.com.

Interactive Graphic

Check Your Understanding—Router Hardware (11.4.4)

Refer to the online course to complete this activity.

Summary (11.5)

The following is a summary of the sections in this chapter.

Hierarchical Networks

All enterprise networks must support critical applications, support converged network traffic, support diverse business needs, and provide centralized administrative control. The Cisco Borderless Networks architecture provides a framework to unify wired and wireless access—including policy, access control, and performance management—across many different device types. A borderless network is built on a hierarchical infrastructure of hardware that is scalable and resilient. Two proven hierarchical design frameworks for campus networks are the three-tier layer and the two-tier layer models. The three critical layers within these tiered designs are the access, distribution, and core layers. The access layer represents the network edge, where traffic enters or exits the campus network. Access layer switches connect to distribution layer switches, which implement network foundation technologies such as routing, quality of service, and security. The distribution layer interfaces between the access layer and the core layer. The primary purpose of the core layer is to provide fault isolation and high-speed backbone connectivity. Networks have fundamentally changed to switched LANs in a hierarchical network, providing QoS, security, support for wireless connectivity, and IP telephony and mobility services.

Scalable Networks

A basic network design strategy includes the following recommendations: Use expandable, modular equipment, or clustered devices; design a hierarchical network to include modules that can be added, upgraded, and modified; create a hierarchical IPv4 and IPv6 addressing strategy; and choose routers or multilayer switches to limit broadcasts and filter other undesirable traffic from the network. Implement redundant links in the network between critical devices and between access layer and core layer devices. Implement multiple links between equipment, with either link aggregation (EtherChannel) or equal-cost load balancing to increase bandwidth. Use a scalable routing protocol and implement features within that routing protocol to isolate routing updates and minimize the size of the routing table. Implement wireless connectivity to allow for mobility and expansion. One method of implementing redundancy is to install duplicate equipment and provide failover services for critical devices. Another method of implementing redundancy is to create redundant paths. A well-designed network not only controls traffic but limits the size of failure domains. Switch blocks act independently of the others, so the failure of a single device does not cause the network to go down. Link aggregation, such as through EtherChannel, allows an administrator to increase the amount of bandwidth between devices by creating one logical link made up of several physical links. Wireless connectivity expands the access layer. When implementing a wireless network, you must consider the types of wireless devices to use, wireless coverage requirements, interference considerations, and security. Link-state routing protocols such as OSPF work well for larger hierarchical networks where fast convergence is important. OSPF routers establish and maintain neighbor adjacencies with other connected OSPF routers; they synchronize their link-state database. When a network change occurs, link-state updates are sent, informing other OSPF routers of the change and establishing a new best path.

Switch Hardware

There are several categories of switches for enterprise networks, including campus LAN, cloud-managed, data center, service provider, and virtual networking switches. Form factors for switches include fixed configuration, modular configuration, and stackable configuration. The thickness of a switch is expressed as the number of rack units. The port density of a switch refers to the number of ports available on a single switch. The forwarding rate defines the processing capabilities of a switch by rating how much data the switch can process per second. Power over Ethernet (PoE) allows a switch to deliver power to a device over the existing Ethernet cabling. Multilayer switches are typically deployed in the core and distribution layers of an organization's switched network. Multilayer switches are characterized by their ability to build a routing table, support a few routing protocols, and forward IP packets at a rate close to that of Layer 2 forwarding. Business considerations for switch selection include cost, port density, power, reliability, port speed, frame buffers, and scalability.

Router Hardware

Routers use the network portion (prefix) of the destination IP address to route packets to the proper destination. They select an alternate path if a link or path goes down. All hosts on a local network specify the IP address of the local router interface in their IP configuration. This router interface is the default gateway. Routers also serve other beneficial functions:

- They provide broadcast containment by limiting broadcasts to the local network.

- They interconnect geographically separate locations.

- They group users logically by application or department within a company, based on common needs or requiring access to the same resources.

- They provide enhanced security by filtering unwanted traffic through access control lists.

Cisco offers several categories of routers, including branch, network edge, service provider, and industrial routers. Branch routers optimize branch services on a single platform while delivering an optimal application experience across branch and WAN infrastructures. Network edge routers deliver high-performance, highly secure, and reliable services that unite campus, data center, and branch networks. Service provider routers differentiate the service portfolio and increase revenues by delivering end-to-end scalable solutions and subscriber-aware services. Industrial routers are designed to provide enterprise-class features in rugged and harsh environments. Cisco router form factors include the Cisco 900 Series, the ASR 9000 and 1000 Series, the 5500 Series, and the Cisco 800. Routers can also be categorized as fixed configuration or modular. With fixed configuration, the desired router interfaces are built in. Modular routers come with multiple slots that allow a network administrator to change the interfaces on the router. Routers come with a variety of different interfaces, such as Fast Ethernet, Gigabit Ethernet, serial, and fiber optic.

Packet Tracer
☐ Activity

Packet Tracer—Compare Layer 2 and Layer 3 Devices (11.5.1)

In this Packet Tracer activity, you will use various commands to examine three different switching topologies and compare the similarities and differences between the 2960 and 3650 switches. You will also compare the routing table of a 4321 router with that of a 3650 switch.

Practice

The following Packet Tracer activity provides practice with the topics introduced in this chapter. The instructions are available in the companion *Enterprise Networking, Security, and Automation Labs & Study Guide (CCNAv7)* (ISBN 9780136634324). There are no labs for this chapter.

Packet Tracer
☐ Activity

Packet Tracer Activity

Packet Tracer 11.5.1: Compare Layer 2 and Layer 3 Devices

Check Your Understanding Questions

Complete all the review questions listed here to test your understanding of the topics and concepts in this chapter. The appendix "Answers to the 'Check Your Understanding' Questions" lists the answers.

1. What is a basic function of the Cisco Borderless Networks architecture distribution layer?

   A. Acting as a backbone

   B. Aggregating all the campus blocks

   C. Aggregating Layer 2 and Layer 3 routing boundaries

   D. Providing access to end-user devices

2. What is a collapsed core in a network design?

   A. A combination of the functionality of the access and core layers

   B. A combination of the functionality of the access and distribution layers

   C. A combination of the functionality of the access, distribution, and core layers

   D. A combination of the functionality of the distribution and core layers

3. Which two previously independent technologies should a network administrator attempt to combine after choosing to upgrade to a converged network infrastructure? (Choose two.)

   A. Electrical system

   B. Mobile cell phone traffic

   C. Scanners and printers

   D. User data traffic

   E. VoIP phone traffic

4. How is a two-tier LAN network design implemented?

   A. The access, distribution, and core layers are collapsed into one tier to separate the backbone layer.

   B. The access and core layers are collapsed into one tier, and the distribution layer is on a separate tier.

   C. The access and distribution layers are collapsed into one tier, and the core layer is on a separate tier.

   D. The distribution and core layers are collapsed into one tier, and the access layer is on a separate tier.

5. A local law firm is redesigning the company network so that all 20 employees can be connected to a LAN and to the internet. The law firm would prefer a low-cost and easy solution for the project. What type of switch should be selected?

   A. fixed configuration

   B. modular configuration

   C. stackable configuration

   D. data center switch

   E. service provider switch

6. What is one function of a Layer 2 switch?

   A. determining which interface is used to forward a frame, based on the destination MAC address

   B. duplicating the electrical signal of each frame to every port

   C. forwarding data based on logical addressing

   D. learning the port assigned to a host by examining the destination MAC address

7. Which network device can be used to eliminate collisions on an Ethernet network?

   A. Hub

   B. NIC

   C. Switch

   D. Wireless access point

8. Which type of address does a switch use to build the MAC address table?

   A. Destination IP address

   B. Destination MAC address

   C. Source IP address

   D. Source MAC address

9. What are two reasons a network administrator would segment a network with a Layer 2 switch? (Choose two.)

   A. To create fewer collision domains

   B. To create more broadcast domains

   C. To eliminate virtual circuits

   D. To enhance user bandwidth

   E. To isolate ARP request messages from the rest of the network

   F. To isolate traffic between segments

10. Which statement describes the microsegmentation feature of a LAN switch?

   A. All ports inside the switch form one collision domain.

   B. Each port forms a collision domain.

   C. Frame collisions are forwarded.

   D. The switch does not forward broadcast frames.

11. A _____ network is one that uses the same infrastructure to carry voice, data, and video signals.

12. In the Cisco enterprise architecture, which two functional parts of the network are combined to form a collapsed core design? (Choose two.)

   A. Access layer

   B. Core layer

   C. Distribution layer

   D. Enterprise edge

   E. Provider edge

13. Which design feature limits the impact of a distribution switch failure in an enterprise network?

   A. The installation of redundant power supplies

   B. The purchase of enterprise equipment that is designed for large traffic volume

   C. The use of a collapsed core design

   D. The use of the building switch block approach

14. What are two benefits of extending access layer connectivity to users through a wireless medium? (Choose two.)

   A. Decreased number of critical points of failure

   B. Increased bandwidth availability

   C. Increased flexibility

   D. Increased network management options

   E. Reduced costs

15. As the network administrator, you have been asked to implement EtherChannel on the corporate network. What does this configuration involve?

    A. Grouping multiple physical ports to increase bandwidth between two switches

    B. Grouping two devices to share a virtual IP address

    C. Providing redundant devices to allow traffic to flow in the event of device failure

    D. Providing redundant links that dynamically block or forward traffic

16. Which statement describes Cisco Meraki switches?

    A. They are campus LAN switches that perform the same functions as Cisco 2960 switches.

    B. They are cloud-managed access switches that enable virtual stacking of switches.

    C. They are service provider switches that aggregate traffic at the edge of the network.

    D. They promote infrastructure scalability, operational continuity, and transport flexibility.

17. What term is used to describe the thickness or height of a switch?

    A. Domain size

    B. Module size

    C. Port density

    D. Rack unit

18. What are two functions of a router? (Choose two.)

    A. It connects multiple IP networks.

    B. It controls the flow of data via the use of Layer 2 addresses.

    C. It determines the best path for sending packets.

    D. It increases the size of the broadcast domain.

    E. It manages the VLAN database.

CHAPTER 12

Network Troubleshooting

Objectives

Upon completion of this chapter, you will be able to answer the following questions:

- How is network documentation developed and used to troubleshoot network issues?

- What troubleshooting methods use a systematic, layered approach?

- What are the different networking trouble-shooting tools?

- How do you determine the symptoms and causes of network problems by using a layered model?

- How do you troubleshoot a network by using the layered model?

Key Terms

This chapter uses the following key terms. You can find the definitions in the Glossary.

Introduction (12.0)

Who is the best network administrator that you have ever seen? Why do you think this person is so good at it? Likely, it is because this person is really good at troubleshooting network problems. Good network administrators are typically experienced administrators, but that is not the whole story. Good network troubleshooters generally go about troubleshooting in a methodical fashion, and they use all of the tools available to them.

The truth is that the only way to become a good network troubleshooter is to always be troubleshooting. It takes time to get good at this. But luckily for you, there are many, many tips and tools that you can use. This chapter covers the different methods for network troubleshooting and all of the tips and tools you need to get started. This chapter also has two really good Packet Tracer activities to test your new skills and knowledge. Maybe your goal should be to become the best network administrator that someone else has ever seen!

Network Documentation (12.1)

In this section, you will learn how network documentation is developed and used to troubleshoot network issues.

Documentation Overview (12.1.1)

With network troubleshooting or any other complex activity, you need to start with good documentation. Accurate and complete network documentation is required to effectively monitor and troubleshoot networks.

Common network documentation includes the following:

- Physical and logical network topology diagrams
- Network device documentation that records all pertinent device information
- Network performance baseline documentation

All network documentation should be kept in a single location, either as hard copy or on the network on a protected server. Backup documentation should be maintained and kept in a separate location.

Network Topology Diagrams (12.1.2)

Network topology diagrams keep track of the location, function, and status of devices on a network. There are two types of network topology diagrams: physical topology and the logical topology.

Physical Topology

A physical network topology shows the physical layout of the devices connected to a network. You need to know how devices are physically connected to troubleshoot physical layer problems. Information recorded on the *physical topology diagram* typically includes the following:

- Device name
- Device location (address, room number, rack location)
- Interface and ports used
- Cable type

Figure 12-1 shows a sample physical topology diagram.

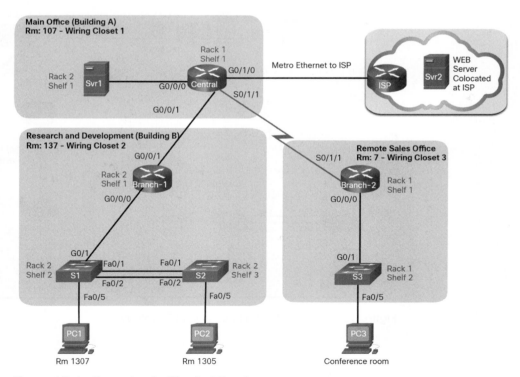

Figure 12-1   Example of a Physical Topology

Logical IPv4 Topology

A *logical topology diagram* illustrates how devices are logically connected to the network. This refers to how devices transfer data across the network when communicating with other devices. Symbols are used to represent network components, such as routers, switches, servers, and hosts. In addition, connections between multiple sites may be shown but do not represent actual physical locations.

Information recorded on a logical network topology may include the following:

- Device identifiers
- IP addresses and prefix lengths
- Interface identifiers
- Routing protocols/static routes
- Layer 2 information (for example, VLANs, trunks, EtherChannels)

Figure 12-2 displays a sample logical IPv4 network topology.

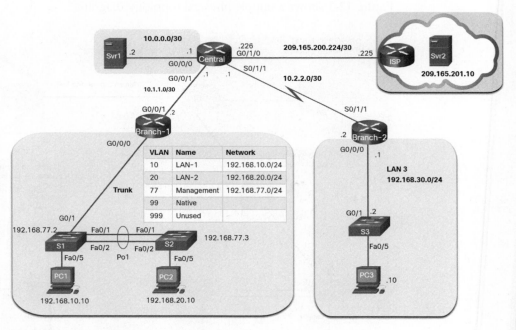

Figure 12-2 Example of a Logical IPv4 Topology

Logical IPv6 Topology

Although IPv6 addresses could also be displayed in the same IPv4 logical topology used in Figure 12-2, for the sake of clarity, we have created a separate logical IPv6 network topology in Figure 12-3.

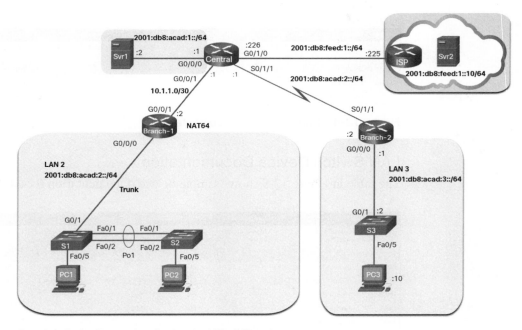

Figure 12-3 Example of a Logical IPv6 Topology

Network Device Documentation (12.1.3)

Network device documentation should contain accurate, up-to-date records of the network hardware and software. Documentation should include all pertinent information about the network devices.

Many organizations create documents with tables or spreadsheets to capture relevant device information.

The following sections look at router, switch, and end device documentation.

Router Device Documentation

The table in Figure 12-4 shows sample network device documentation for two interconnecting routers.

Device	Model	Description	Location	IOS		License
Central	ISR 4321	Central Edge Router	Building A Rm: 137	Cisco IOS XE Software, Version 16.09.04 flash:isr4300-universalk9_ias.16.09.04.SPA.bin		ipbasek9 securityk9
Interface	Description	IPv4 Address		IPv6 Address	MAC Address	Routing
G0/0/0	Connects to SVR-1	10.0.0.1/30		2001:db8:acad:1::1/64	a03d.6fe1.e180	OSPF
G0/0/1	Connects to Branch-1	10.1.1.1/30		2001:db8:acad:a001::1/64	a03d.6fe1.e181	OSPFv3
G0/1/0	Connects to ISP	209.165.200.226/30		2001:db8:feed:1::2/64	a03d.6fc3.a132	Default
S0/1/1	Connects to Branch-2	10.1.1.2/24		2001:db8:acad:2::1/64	n/a	OSPFv3
Device	Model	Description	Site	IOS		License
Branch-1	ISR 4221	Branch-2 Edge Router	Building B Rm: 107	Cisco IOS XE Software, Version 16.09.04 flash:isr4200-universalk9.16.09.04.SPA.bin		ipbasek9 securityk9
Interface	Description	IPv4 Address		IPv6 Address	MAC Address	Routing
G0/0/0	Connects to S1	Router-on-a-stick		Router-on-a-stick	a03d.6fe1.9d90	OSPF
G0/0/1	Connects to Central	10.1.1.2/30		2001:db8:acad:a001::2/64	a03d.6fe1.9d91	OSPF

Figure 12-4   Router Device Documentation

LAN Switch Device Documentation

The table in Figure 12-5 shows sample device documentation for a LAN switch.

Device	Model	Description	Mgt. IP Address	IOS		VTP	
S1	Cisco Catalyst WS-C2960-24TC-L	Branch-1 LAN1 switch	192.168.77.2/24	IOS: 15.0(2)SE7 Image: C2960-LANBASEK9-M		Domain: CCNA Mode: Server	
Port	Description	Access	VLAN	Trunk	EtherChannel	Native	Enabled
Fa0/1	Port Channel 1 trunk to S2 Fa0/1	-	-	Yes	Port-Channel 1	99	Yes
Fa0/2	Port Channel 1 trunk to S2 Fa0/2	-	-	Yes	Port-Channel 1	99	Yes
Fa0/3	*** Not in use ***	Yes	999	-	-		Shut
Fa0/4	*** Not in use ***	Yes	999	-	-		Shut
Fa0/5	Access port to user	Yes	10	-	-		Yes
...			-	-	-		-
Fa0/24	Access port to user	Yes	20	-	-		Yes
Fa0/24	*** Not in use ***	Yes	999	-	-		Shut
G0/1	Trunk link to Branch-1	-	-	Yes	-	99	Yes
G0/2	*** Not in use ***	Yes	999	-			

Figure 12-5   LAN Switch Device Documentation

End-System Documentation Files

End-system documentation focuses on the hardware and software used in servers, network management consoles, and user workstations. An incorrectly configured end system can have a negative impact on the overall performance of a network. For this reason, having access to end-system device documentation can be very useful when troubleshooting.

The table in Figure 12-6 shows an example of information that could be recorded in an end-system device document.

Device	OS	Services	MAC Address	IPv4 / IPv6 Addresses	Default Gateway	DNS
SRV1	MS Server 2016	SMTP, POP3, File services, DHCP	5475.d08e.9ad8	10.0.0.2/30 2001:db8:acad:1::2/64	10.0.0.1 2001:db8:acad:1::1	10.0.0.1 2001:db8:acad:1::1
SRV2	MS Server 2016	HTTP, HTTPS	5475.d07a.5312	209.165.201.10 2001:db8:feed:1::10/64	209.165.201.1 2001:db8:feed:1::1	209.165.201.1 2001:db8:feed:1::1
PC1	MS Windows 10	HTTP, HTTPS	5475.d017.3133	192.168.10.10/24 2001:db8:acad:1::251/64	192.168.10.1 2001:db8:acad:1::1	192.168.10.1 2001:db8:acad:1::1
...						

Figure 12-6   End-System Documentation Files

Establish a Network Baseline (12.1.4)

The purpose of network monitoring is to watch network performance in comparison to a predetermined baseline. A *baseline* is used to establish normal network or system performance to determine the "personality" of a network under normal conditions.

Establishing a network performance baseline requires collecting performance data from the ports and devices that are essential to network operation.

A network baseline should answer the following questions:

- How does the network perform during a normal or average day?
- Where are the most errors occurring?
- What part of the network is most heavily used?
- What part of the network is least used?
- Which devices should be monitored, and what alert thresholds should be set?
- Can the network meet the identified policies?

Measuring the initial performance and availability of critical network devices and links allows a network administrator to determine the difference between abnormal behavior and proper network performance as the network grows or as traffic patterns change. The baseline also provides insight into whether the current network design can meet business requirements. Without a baseline, no standard exists to measure the optimum nature of network traffic and congestion levels.

Analysis after an initial baseline also tends to reveal hidden problems. The collected data shows the true nature of congestion or potential congestion in a network. It may also reveal areas in the network that are underutilized; quite often this information can lead to network redesign efforts, based on quality and capacity observations.

The initial network performance baseline sets the stage for measuring the effects of network changes and subsequent troubleshooting efforts. Therefore, it is important to plan for it carefully.

Step 1—Determine What Types of Data to Collect (12.1.5)

When conducting the initial baseline, start by selecting a few variables that represent the defined policies. If too many data points are selected, the amount of data can be overwhelming, making analysis of the collected data difficult. Start out simply and fine-tune along the way. Some good starting variables are interface utilization and CPU utilization.

Step 2—Identify Devices and Ports of Interest (12.1.6)

Use the network topology to identify the devices and ports for which performance data should be measured. Devices and ports of interest include the following:

- Network device ports that connect to other network devices
- Servers
- Key users
- Anything else considered critical to operations

A logical network topology can be useful in identifying key devices and ports to monitor. In Figure 12-7, the network administrator has highlighted the devices and ports of interest to monitor during the baseline test.

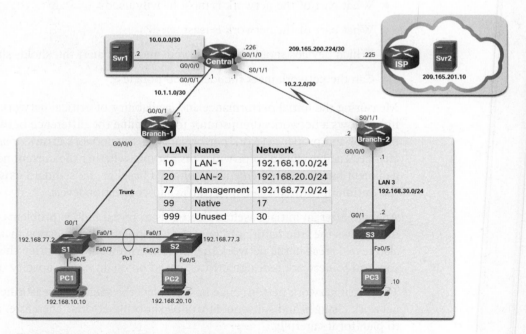

Figure 12-7   Logical Topology with Highlighted Ports of Interest

The devices of interest include PC1 (the admin terminal), and the two servers (Srv1 and Svr2). The ports of interest typically include router interfaces and key ports on switches.

Shortening the list of ports that are polled keeps the results concise and minimizes the network management load. Remember that an interface on a router or switch can be a virtual interface, such as a switch virtual interface (SVI).

Step 3—Determine the Baseline Duration (12.1.7)

The length of time for which the baseline information is gathered must be long enough to form a "normal" picture of the network. It is important to monitor for daily trends of network traffic. It is also important to monitor for trends that occur over a longer period, such as weekly or monthly. For this reason, when capturing data for analysis, the period specified should be at least seven days.

Figure 12-8 displays examples of several screenshots of CPU utilization trends captured over daily, weekly, monthly, and yearly periods.

In this example, notice that the workweek graphs are too short to reveal the recurring utilization surge every weekend on Saturday evening, when a database backup operation consumes network bandwidth. This recurring pattern is revealed in the monthly graph. A yearly graph, as shown in the figure, may include too much information to provide meaningful baseline performance details. However, it may help identify long-term patterns that should be analyzed further.

Typically, a baseline needs to last no more than six weeks, unless specific long-term trends need to be measured. Generally, a two- to four-week baseline is adequate.

Baseline measurements should not be performed during times of unique traffic patterns because the data would provide an inaccurate picture of normal network operations. Conduct an annual analysis of the entire network or baseline different sections of the network on a rotating basis. Analysis must be conducted regularly to understand how the network is affected by growth and other changes.

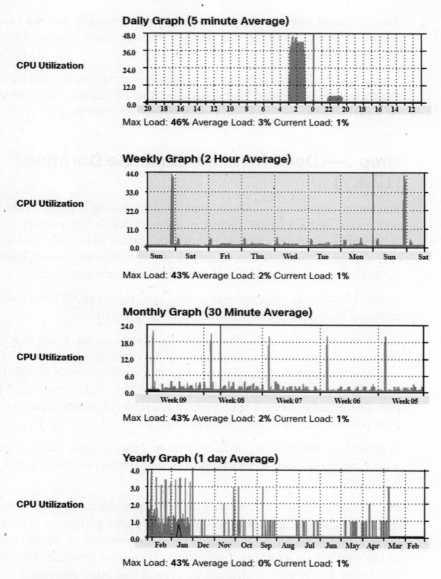

Figure 12-8 Baselines for CPU Utilization

Data Measurement (12.1.8)

When documenting a network, it is often necessary to gather information directly from routers and switches. Obvious useful network documentation commands include **ping**, **traceroute**, and **telnet**, as well as the **show** commands.

Table 12-1 lists some of the Cisco IOS commands most commonly used for data collection.

Table 12-1   IOS Commands for Data Collection

Command	Description
show version	■ Displays uptime and version information for device software and hardware.
show ip interface [brief] show ipv6 interface [brief]	■ Displays all the configuration options that are set on an interface. ■ Use the **brief** keyword to display only up/down status of IP interfaces and the IP address of each interface.
show interfaces	■ Displays detailed output for each interface. ■ To display detailed output for only a single interface, include the interface type and number in the command (for example, Gigabit Ethernet 0/0/0).
show ip route show ipv6 route	■ Displays the routing table content, including directly connected networks and learned remote networks. ■ Append **static**, **eigrp**, or **ospf** to display those routes only.
show cdp neighbors detail	■ Displays detailed information about directly connected Cisco neighbor devices.
show arp show ipv6 neighbors	■ Displays the contents of the ARP table (IPv4) and the neighbor table (IPv6).
show running-config	■ Displays the current configuration.
show vlan	■ Displays the status of VLANs on a switch.
show port	■ Displays the status of ports on a switch.
show tech-support	■ This command is useful for collecting a large amount of information about a device for troubleshooting purposes. ■ It executes multiple **show** commands, whose output can be provided to technical support representatives when reporting a problem.

Manual data collection using **show** commands on individual network devices is extremely time-consuming and is not a scalable solution. Manual collection of data should be reserved for smaller networks or limited to mission-critical network devices. For simpler network designs, baseline tasks typically use a combination of manual data collection and simple network protocol inspectors.

Sophisticated network management software is typically used to baseline large and complex networks. These software packages enable administrators to automatically create and review reports, compare current performance levels with historical observations, automatically identify performance problems, and create alerts for applications that do not provide expected levels of service.

Establishing an initial baseline or conducting a performance-monitoring analysis may require many hours or days to accurately reflect network performance. Network management software or protocol inspectors and sniffers often run continuously over the course of the data collection process.

Interactive
Graphic

Check Your Understanding—Network Documentation (12.1.9)

Refer to the online course to complete this activity.

Troubleshooting Process (12.2)

In this section, you will learn about the general troubleshooting process.

General Troubleshooting Procedures (12.2.1)

Troubleshooting can be time-consuming because networks differ, problems differ, and troubleshooting experience varies. However, experienced administrators know that using a structured troubleshooting method will shorten overall troubleshooting time.

Therefore, the troubleshooting process should be guided by structured methods. Well-defined and well-documented troubleshooting procedures can minimize wasted time associated with erratic hit-and-miss troubleshooting. However, these methods are not static. The troubleshooting steps taken to solve a problem are not always the same or executed in the exact same order.

Several troubleshooting processes can be used to solve a problem. Figure 12-9 shows the logic flowchart of a simplified three-stage troubleshooting process. Although this is a good starting point, sometimes a more detailed process may be more helpful in solving a network problem.

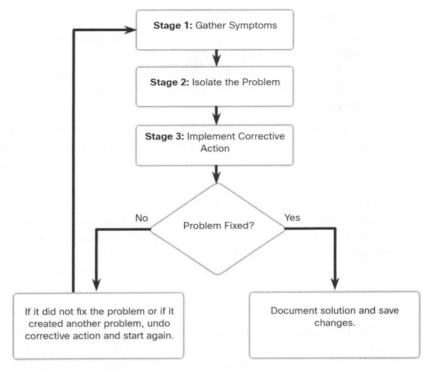

Figure 12-9   A Troubleshooting Flowchart

Seven-Step Troubleshooting Process (12.2.2)

Figure 12-10 shows a more detailed seven-step troubleshooting process. Notice how some steps interconnect. This is because some technicians may be able to jump between steps, based on their level of experience.

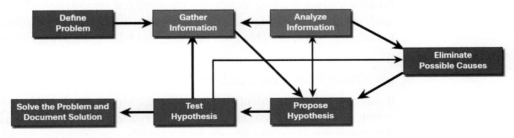

Figure 12-10   The Seven-Step Troubleshooting Flowchart

Define the Problem

The goal of the first stage is to verify that there is a problem and then properly define what the problem is. Problems are usually identified by a symptom (such as the network being slow or not working). Network symptoms may appear in many different forms, including alerts from the network management system, console messages, and user complaints.

While gathering symptoms, it is important to ask questions and investigate the issue in order to localize the problem to a smaller range of possibilities. For example, is the problem restricted to a single device, a group of devices, or an entire subnet or network of devices?

In an organization, problems are typically assigned to network technicians as trouble tickets. These tickets are created using trouble ticketing software that tracks the progress of each ticket. Trouble ticketing software may also include a self-service user portal to submit tickets, access to a searchable trouble tickets *knowledge base*, remote control capabilities to solve end-user issues, and more.

Gather Information

In the information gathering step, targets (such as hosts and devices) to be investigated must be identified, access to the target devices must be obtained, and information must be gathered. During this step, the technician may gather and document more symptoms, depending on the characteristics that are identified.

If the problem is outside the boundary of the organization's control (for example, lost internet connectivity outside the autonomous system), contact an administrator for the external system before gathering additional network symptoms.

Analyze Information

Possible causes must be identified. The gathered information can be interpreted and analyzed using network documentation, network baselines, searching organizational knowledge bases, searching the internet, and talking with other technicians.

Eliminate Possible Causes

If multiple causes are identified, then the list must be reduced by progressively eliminating possible causes to eventually identify the most probable cause. Troubleshooting experience is extremely valuable to quickly eliminate causes and identify the most probable cause.

Propose Hypothesis

When the most probable cause has been identified, a solution must be formulated. Troubleshooting experience is very valuable when proposing a plan.

Test Hypothesis

Before testing a solution, it is important to assess the impact and urgency of the problem. For instance, could the solution have an adverse effect on other systems or processes? The severity of the problem should be weighed against the impact of the solution. For example, if a critical server or router must be offline for a significant amount of time, it may be better to wait until the end of the workday to implement the fix. Sometimes, a workaround can be created until the problem is resolved.

Create a rollback plan identifying how to quickly reverse a solution. This may prove to be necessary if the solution fails.

Implement the solution and verify that it has solved the problem. Sometimes a solution introduces an unexpected problem. Therefore, it is important that a solution be thoroughly verified before proceeding to the next step.

If the solution fails, the attempted solution needs to be documented and the changes removed. The technician must now go back to the information gathering step and isolate the issue.

Solve the Problem

When the problem is solved, inform the users and anyone involved in the troubleshooting process that the problem has been resolved. Other IT team members should be informed of the solution. Appropriate documentation of the cause and the fix will assist other support technicians in preventing and solving similar problems in the future.

Question End Users (12.2.3)

Many network problems are initially reported by end users. However, the information provided is often vague or misleading. For example, users often report problems such as "the network is down," "I cannot access my email," or "my computer is slow." In most cases, additional information is required to fully understand the problem. This usually involves interacting with the affected user to discover the "who," "what," and "when" of the problem.

The following recommendations should be employed when communicating with users:

- Speak at a technical level they can understand and avoid using complex terminology.

- Always listen or read carefully what the user is saying. Taking notes can be helpful when documenting a complex problem.

- Always be considerate and empathize with users while letting them know you will help them solve their problems. Users reporting a problem may be under stress and anxious to resolve the problem as quickly as possible.

When interviewing a user, guide the conversation and use effective questioning techniques to quickly ascertain the problem. For instance, use open questions (that require detailed response) and closed questions (that is, yes-or-no questions and those that require single-word answers) to discover important facts about the network problem.

Table 12-2 provides some questioning guidelines and sample open-ended end-user questions.

When you are done interviewing a user, repeat your understanding of the problem to the user to ensure that you both agree on the problem being reported.

Table 12-2   Open-Ended User Question Guidelines

Guideline	Examples of Open-Ended End-User Questions
Ask pertinent questions.	- What does not work? - What exactly is the problem? - What are you trying to accomplish?
Determine the scope of the problem.	- Who does this issue affect? Is it just you, or are others having trouble, too? - What device is this happening on?
Determine when the problem occurred/occurs.	- When exactly does the problem occur? - When was the problem first noticed? - Were any error messages displayed?
Determine whether the problem is constant or intermittent.	- Can you reproduce the problem? - Can you send me a screenshot or video of the problem?
Determine whether anything has changed.	- What has changed since the last time it did work?
Use questions to eliminate or discover possible problems.	- What works? - What does not work?

Gather Information (12.2.4)

To gather symptoms from networking devices, use Cisco IOS commands and other tools such as packet captures and device logs.

Table 12-3 describes Cisco IOS commands commonly used to gather the symptoms of network problems.

Table 12-3   IOS Commands to Gather Information

Command	Description
ping {*host* | *ip-address*}	■ Sends an echo request packet to an address and waits for a reply. ■ The *host* or *ip-address* variable is the IP alias or IP address of the target system.
traceroute *destination*	■ Identifies the path a packet takes through the networks. ■ The *destination* variable is the hostname or IP address of the target system.
telnet {*host* | *ip-address*}	■ Connects to an IP address using the Telnet application. ■ Use SSH whenever possible instead of Telnet.
ssh -l *user-id ip-address*	■ Connects to an IP address using SSH.SSH is more secure than Telnet.
show ip interface brief show ipv6 interface brief	■ Displays a summary status of all interfaces on a device. ■ Useful for quickly identifying IP addressing on all interfaces.
show ip route show ipv6 route	■ Displays the current IPv4 and IPv6 routing tables, which contain the routes to all known network destinations.
show protocols	■ Displays the configured protocols and shows the global and interface-specific status of any configured Layer 3 protocol.
debug	■ Displays a list of options for enabling or disabling debugging events.

Note

Although the **debug** command is an important tool for gathering symptoms, it generates a large amount of console message traffic, and the performance of a network device can be noticeably affected. If the **debug** must be performed during normal working hours, warn network users that a troubleshooting effort is under way and that network performance may be affected. Remember to disable debugging when you are done.

Troubleshooting with Layered Models (12.2.5)

The OSI and TCP/IP models can be applied to isolate network problems when troubleshooting. For example, if symptoms suggest a physical connection problem, the network technician can focus on troubleshooting the circuit that operates at the physical layer.

Figure 12-11 shows some common devices and the OSI layers that must be examined during the troubleshooting process for each device.

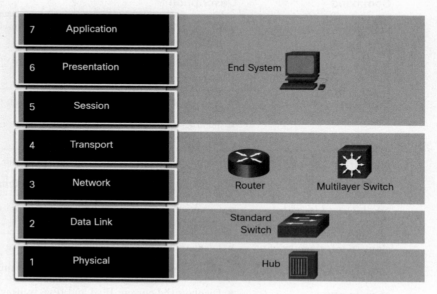

Figure 12-11   Common Devices at Each Layer of the OSI Model

Notice that routers and multilayer switches are shown at Layer 4, the transport layer. Although routers and multilayer switches usually make forwarding decisions at Layer 3, ACLs on these devices can be used to make filtering decisions using Layer 4 information.

Structured Troubleshooting Methods (12.2.6)

Several structured troubleshooting approaches can be used. Which one to use depends on the situation. Each approach has advantages and disadvantages. This section describes various methods and provides guidelines for choosing the best method for a specific situation.

Bottom-Up

In *bottom-up troubleshooting*, you start with the physical components of the network and move up through the layers of the OSI model until the cause of the problem is identified, as shown in Figure 12-12.

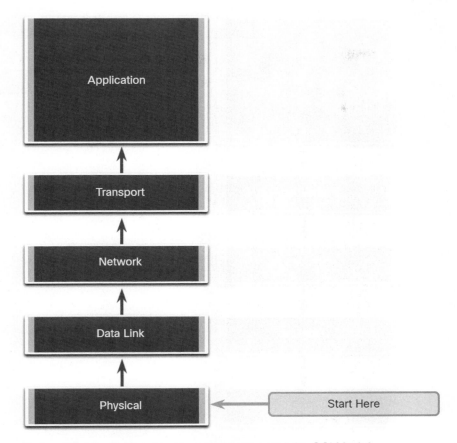

Figure 12-12   Bottom-Up Troubleshooting and the OSI Model

Bottom-up troubleshooting is a good approach to use when a physical problem is suspected. Most networking problems reside at the lower levels, so implementing the bottom-up approach is often effective.

The disadvantage with the bottom-up troubleshooting approach is that it requires you to check every device and interface on the network until the possible cause of the problem is found. Remember that each conclusion and possibility must be documented, so there can be a lot of paperwork associated with this approach. A further challenge is determining which devices to start examining first.

Top-Down

As shown in Figure 12-13, *top-down troubleshooting* starts with the end-user applications and moves down through the layers of the OSI model until the cause of the problem has been identified.

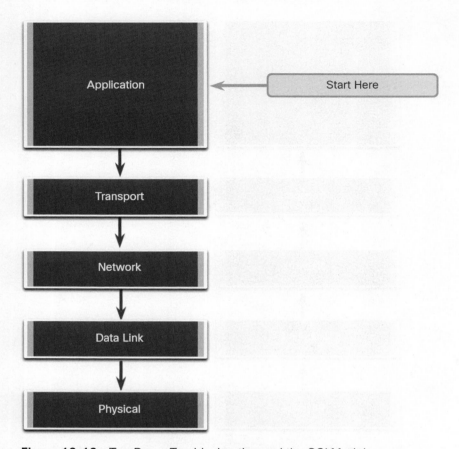

Figure 12-13   Top-Down Troubleshooting and the OSI Model

End-user applications of an end system are tested before the more specific networking pieces are tackled. Use this approach for simpler problems or when you think the problem is with a piece of software.

The disadvantage with the top-down approach is that it requires you to check every network application until the possible cause of the problem is found. Each conclusion and possibility must be documented. The challenge is to determine which application to start examining first.

Divide-and-Conquer

Figure 12-14 shows the divide-and-conquer approach to troubleshooting a networking problem.

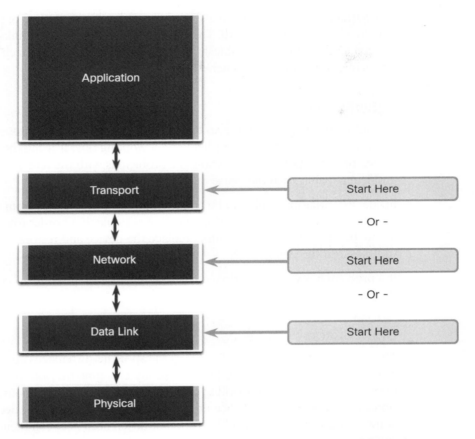

Figure 12-14   Divide-and-Conquer Troubleshooting and the OSI Model

In *divide-and-conquer troubleshooting*, the network administrator selects a layer and tests in both directions from that layer. You start by collecting user experiences of the problem, document the symptoms, and then, using that information, make an informed guess about which OSI layer should be the starting point for your investigation. When a layer is verified to be functioning properly, it can be assumed that the layers below it are functioning. The administrator can work up the OSI layers. If an OSI layer is not functioning properly, the administrator can work down the OSI layer model. For example, if users cannot access the web server, but they can ping the server, then the problem is above Layer 3. If pinging the server is unsuccessful, then the problem is likely at a lower OSI layer.

Follow-the-Path

The follow-the-path approach is one of the most basic troubleshooting techniques. With this approach, you first discover the traffic path all the way from source to destination. The scope of troubleshooting is reduced to just the links and devices that are in the forwarding path. The objective is to eliminate the links and devices that are irrelevant to the troubleshooting task at hand. This approach usually complements one of the other approaches.

Substitution

The substitution approach is also called swap-the-component because you physically swap the problematic device with a known working one. If using the replacement device fixes the problem, you know the problem is with the removed device. If the problem remains, then the cause may be elsewhere.

In specific situations, this can be an ideal method for quick problem resolution, such as with a critical single point of failure. For example, if a border router goes down, it may be more beneficial to simply replace the device and restore service than to troubleshoot the issue.

If a problem lies within multiple devices, it may not be possible to correctly isolate the problem.

Comparison

The comparison approach is also called the spot-the-differences approach because it involves attempting to resolve the problem by changing the nonoperational elements to be consistent with the working ones. You compare configurations, software versions, hardware, or other device properties, links, or processes between working and nonworking situations and spot significant differences between them.

The weakness of this method is that it might lead to a working solution without clearly revealing the root cause of the problem.

Educated Guess

The educated guess approach is also called the shoot-from-the-hip troubleshooting approach. This is a less-structured troubleshooting method that involves making an educated guess based on the symptoms of the problem. The success of this method varies based on the administrator's troubleshooting experience and ability. Seasoned technicians are more successful because they can rely on their extensive knowledge and experience to decisively isolate and solve network issues. With a less-experienced network administrator, this troubleshooting method may be more like random troubleshooting.

Guidelines for Selecting a Troubleshooting Method (12.2.7)

To quickly resolve network problems, take the time to select the most effective network troubleshooting method. Figure 12-15 illustrates which methods could be used when certain types of problem are discovered.

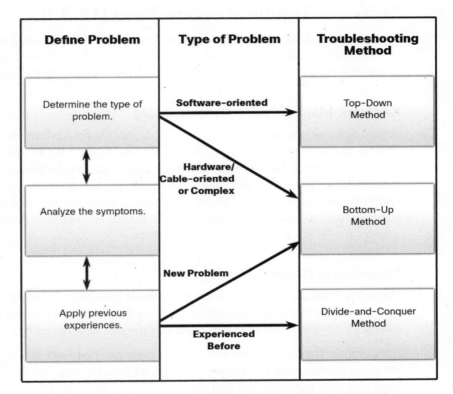

Figure 12-15   Flowchart for Selecting a Troubleshooting Method

For instance, software problems are often solved using a top-down approach, while hardware-based problems are often solved using the bottom-up approach. New problems may be solved by an experienced technician using the divide-and-conquer method. Otherwise, the bottom-up approach may be used.

Troubleshooting is a skill that is developed by doing it. Every network problem you identify and solve is added to your skill set.

Check Your Understanding—Troubleshooting Process (12.2.8)

Refer to the online course to complete this activity.

Interactive Graphic

Troubleshooting Tools (12.3)

As you know, networks are made up of software and hardware. Therefore, troubleshooting tools are available for both software and hardware. In this section, you'll learn about different networking troubleshooting tools.

Software Troubleshooting Tools (12.3.1)

A wide variety of software tools are available to make troubleshooting easier. These tools may be used to gather and analyze symptoms of network problems. They often provide monitoring and reporting functions that can be used to establish the network baseline.

Network Management System Tools

Network management system (NMS) tools include device-level monitoring, configuration, and fault-management tools. These tools can be used to investigate and correct network problems. Network monitoring software graphically displays a physical view of network devices, allowing network managers to monitor remote devices continuously and automatically. Device management software provides dynamic device status, statistics, and configuration information for key network devices. Search the internet for "NMS Tools" for more information.

Knowledge Bases

Online network device vendor knowledge bases have become indispensable sources of information. Between vendor-based knowledge bases and internet search engines, a network administrator has access to a vast pool of experience-based information.

For example, the Cisco Tools & Resources page can be found at http://www.cisco.com under the **Support** menu. This page provides tools that can be used for Cisco hardware and software.

Baselining Tools

Many tools for automating the network documentation and baselining process are available. *Baselining tools* help with common documentation tasks. For example, they can be used to draw network diagrams, help keep network software and hardware documentation up-to-date, and help to cost-effectively measure baseline network bandwidth use. Search the internet for "Network Performance Monitoring Tools" for more information.

Protocol Analyzers (12.3.2)

Protocol analyzers can be used to investigate the contents of packets while the packets are flowing through the network. A protocol analyzer decodes the various protocol layers in a recorded frame and presents this information in a relatively easy-to-use format. Figure 12-16 shows a screen capture of the Wireshark protocol analyzer.

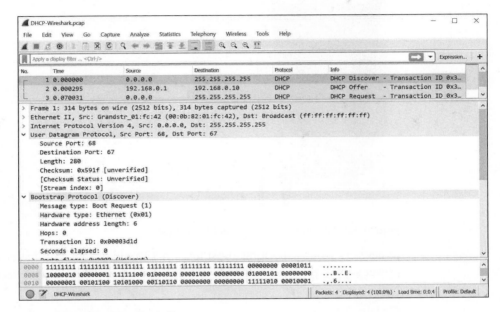

Figure 12-16   Wireshark Capture

The information displayed by a protocol analyzer includes the physical layer bit data, data link layer information, protocols, and descriptions of the frames. Most protocol analyzers can filter traffic that meets certain criteria so that all traffic to and from a device can be captured. Protocol analyzers such as Wireshark can help troubleshoot network performance problems. It is important to have both a good understanding of TCP/IP and how to use a protocol analyzer to inspect information at each TCP/IP layer.

Hardware Troubleshooting Tools (12.3.3)

There are multiple types of hardware troubleshooting tools. The following sections provide detailed descriptions of common hardware troubleshooting tools.

Digital Multimeters

Digital multimeters (DMMs), such as the Fluke 179 shown in Figure 12-17, are test instruments that are used to directly measure electrical voltage, current, and resistance values.

Figure 12-17   Fluke 179 Digital Multimeter

In network troubleshooting, most tests that would need a multimeter involve checking power supply voltage levels and verifying that network devices are receiving power.

Cable Testers

Cable testers are specialized handheld devices designed for testing the various types of data communication cabling. Figure 12-18 shows the Fluke LinkRunner AT Network Auto-Tester.

Figure 12-18   Fluke LinkRunner Cable Tester

Cable testers can be used to detect broken wires, crossed-over wiring, shorted connections, and improperly paired connections. These devices can be inexpensive continuity testers, moderately priced data cabling testers, or expensive *time-domain reflectometers (TDRs)*. TDRs are used to pinpoint the distance to a break in a cable. These devices send signals along the cable and wait for them to be reflected. The time between sending the signal and receiving it back is converted into a distance measurement. The TDR function is normally packaged with data cabling testers. TDRs used to test fiber-optic cables are known as *optical time-domain reflectometers (OTDRs)*.

Cable Analyzers

Cable analyzers, such as the Fluke DTX Cable Analyzer in Figure 12-19, are multifunctional handheld devices that are used to test and certify copper and fiber cables for different services and standards.

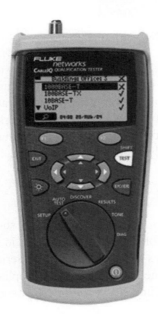

Figure 12-19   Fluke DTX Cable Analyzer

More sophisticated tools include advanced troubleshooting diagnostics that measure the distance to a performance defect such as near-end crosstalk (NEXT) or return loss (RL), identify corrective actions, and graphically display crosstalk and impedance behavior. Cable analyzers also typically include PC-based software. After field data is collected, the data from the handheld device can be uploaded so that the network administrator can create up-to-date reports.

Portable Network Analyzers

Portable network analyzers like the Fluke OptiView, shown in Figure 12-20, are used for troubleshooting switched networks and VLANs.

Figure 12-20   Fluke OptiView Portable Network Analyzer

By plugging in a network analyzer anywhere on a network, a network engineer can see the switch port to which the device is connected and the average and peak utilization. The analyzer can also be used to discover VLAN configuration, identify top network talkers (hosts generating the most traffic), analyze network traffic, and view interface details. Such a device can typically output to a PC that has network monitoring software installed for further analysis and troubleshooting.

Cisco Prime NAM

The Cisco Prime *Network Analysis Module (NAM)* portfolio, shown in Figure 12-21, includes hardware and software for performance analysis in switching and routing environments. The figure displays a Cisco Nexus 7000 Series NAM, a Cisco Catalyst 65xx Series NAM, a Cisco Prime NAM 2300 Series appliance, a Cisco Prime Virtual NAM (vNAM), a Cisco Prime NAM for Cisco Nexus 1110, and a Cisco Prime NAM for ISR G2 SRE.

The NAM includes an embedded browser-based interface that generates reports on the traffic that consumes critical network resources. In addition, the NAM can capture and decode packets and track response times to pinpoint an application problem to a network or server.

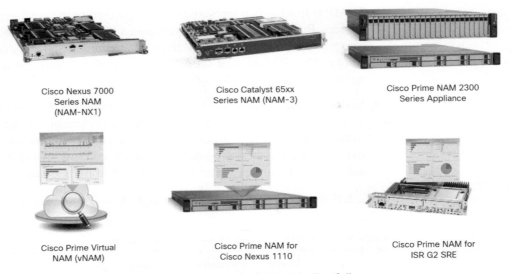

Figure 12-21   Cisco Prime Network Analysis Module Portfolio

Syslog Server as a Troubleshooting Tool (12.3.4)

Syslog is a simple protocol used by an IP device known as a syslog client to send text-based log messages to another IP device, the *syslog server*. Syslog is currently defined in RFC 5424.

Implementing a logging facility is an important part of network security and for network troubleshooting. Cisco devices can log information regarding configuration changes, ACL violations, interface status, and many other types of events. Cisco devices can send log messages to several different facilities. Event messages can be sent to one or more of the following:

- **Console:** Console logging is on by default. Messages log to the console and can be viewed when modifying or testing the router or switch using terminal emulation software while connected to the console port of the network device.

- **Terminal lines:** Enabled EXEC sessions can be configured to receive log messages on any terminal lines. Like console logging, this type of logging is not stored by the network device and, therefore, is valuable only to the user on that line.

- **Buffered logging:** Buffered logging can be useful as a troubleshooting tool because log messages are stored in memory for a time. However, log messages are cleared when the device is rebooted.

- **SNMP traps:** Certain thresholds can be preconfigured on routers and other devices. Router events such as exceeding a threshold can be processed by the router and forwarded as SNMP traps to an external SNMP network management station. SNMP traps are a viable security logging facility but require the configuration and maintenance of an SNMP system.

- **Syslog:** Cisco routers and switches can be configured to forward log messages to an external syslog service. This service can reside on any number of servers or workstations, including Microsoft Windows and Linux-based systems. Syslog is the most popular message logging facility because it provides long-term log storage capabilities and a central location for all router messages.

Cisco IOS log messages fall into one of eight levels, as shown in Table 12-4.

Table 12-4 Cisco IOS Log Message Severity Levels

	Level	Keyword	Description	Definition
Highest level	0	Emergencies	System is unusable	LOG_EMERG
	1	Alerts	Immediate action is needed	LOG_ALERT
	2	Critical	Critical conditions exist	LOG_CRIT
	3	Errors	Error conditions exist	LOG_ERR
	4	Warnings	Warning conditions exist	LOG_WARNING
Lowest level	5	Notifications	Normal (but significant) condition	LOG_NOTICE
	6	Informational	Informational messages only	LOG_NFO
	7	Debugging	Debugging messages	LOG_DEBUG

The lower the level number, the higher the severity level. By default, all messages from level 0 to 7 are logged to the console. While the ability to view logs on a central syslog server is helpful in troubleshooting, sifting through a large amount of data can be an overwhelming task. The **logging trap** *level* command (where *level* is the name or number of the severity level) limits messages logged to the syslog server based on severity. Only messages equal to or numerically lower than the specified level are logged.

In the command output in Example 12-1, system messages from level 0 (emergencies) to 5 (notifications) are sent to the syslog server at 209.165.200.225.

Example 12-1 Configuring Syslog Traps

```
R1(config)# logging host 209.165.200.225
R1(config)# logging trap notifications
R1(config)# logging on
R1(config)#
```

Check Your Understanding—Troubleshooting Tools (12.3.5)

Refer to the online course to complete this activity.

Symptoms and Causes of Network Problems (12.4)

Now that you have your documentation, some knowledge of troubleshooting methods, and the software and hardware tools to use to diagnose problems, you are ready to start troubleshooting! This section covers the most common issues that you will find when troubleshooting a network. In it, you will learn how to determine the symptoms and causes of network problems using a layered model.

Physical Layer Troubleshooting (12.4.1)

Issues on a network often present as performance problems. A performance problem means that there is a difference between the expected behavior and the observed behavior, and the system is not functioning as could be reasonably expected. Failures and suboptimal conditions at the physical layer not only inconvenience users but can impact the productivity of the entire company. Networks that experience these kinds of conditions usually shut down. Because the upper layers of the OSI model depend on the physical layer to function, a network administrator must be able to effectively isolate and correct problems at this layer.

Figure 12-22 summarizes the symptoms and causes of physical layer network problems.

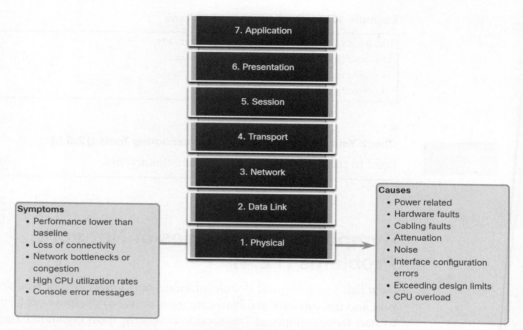

Figure 12-22   Physical Layer Symptoms and Causes

Table 12-5 lists common symptoms of physical layer network problems.

Table 12-5   Physical Layer Symptoms

Symptom	Description
Performance lower than baseline	■ Requires previous baselines for comparison. ■ The most common reasons for slow or poor performance include overloaded or underpowered servers, unsuitable switch or router configurations, traffic congestion on a low-capacity link, and chronic frame loss.
Loss of connectivity	■ Loss of connectivity could be due to a failed or disconnected cable. ■ Can be verified using a simple **ping** test. ■ Intermittent connectivity loss can indicate a loose or oxidized connection.
Network bottlenecks or congestion	■ If a router, an interface, or a cable fails, routing protocols may redirect traffic to other routes that are not designed to carry the extra capacity. ■ This can result in congestion or bottlenecks in parts of the network.

Symptom	Description
High CPU utilization rates	■ High CPU utilization rates are a symptom that a device, such as a router, switch, or server, is operating at or exceeding its design limits. ■ If not addressed quickly, CPU overloading can cause a device to shut down or fail.
Console error messages	■ Error messages reported on the device console could indicate a physical layer problem. ■ Console messages should be logged to a central syslog server.

Table 12-6 lists issues that commonly cause network problems at the physical layer.

Table 12-6   Physical Layer Causes

Problem Cause	Description
Power related	■ This is the most fundamental reason for network failure. ■ Check the operation of the fans and ensure that the chassis intake and exhaust vents are clear. ■ If other nearby units have also powered down, suspect a power failure at the main power supply.
Hardware faults	■ Faulty network interface cards (NICs) can be the cause of network transmission errors due to late collisions, short frames, and *jabber*. ■ Jabber is often defined as the condition in which a network device continually transmits random, meaningless data onto the network. ■ Other likely causes of jabber are faulty or corrupt NIC driver files, bad cabling, and grounding problems.
Cabling faults	■ Many problems can be corrected by simply reseating cables that have become partially disconnected. ■ When performing a physical inspection, look for damaged cables, improper cable types, and poorly crimped RJ-45 connectors. ■ Suspect cables should be tested or exchanged with known functioning cables.
Attenuation	■ Attenuation can be caused if a cable length exceeds the design limit for the media or when there is a poor connection resulting from a loose cable or dirty or oxidized contacts. ■ If attenuation is severe, the receiving device cannot always successfully distinguish one bit in the data stream from another bit.

Problem Cause	Description
Noise	■ Local *electromagnetic interference (EMI)* is commonly known as noise.
	■ Noise can be generated by many sources, such as FM radio stations, police radio, building security, and avionics for automated landing, crosstalk (noise induced by other cables in the same pathway or adjacent cables), nearby electric cables, devices with large electric motors, or anything that includes a transmitter more powerful than a cellphone.
Interface configuration errors	■ Many things can be misconfigured on an interface to cause it to go down, such as incorrect clock rate, incorrect clock source, and interface not being turned on.
	■ This causes a loss of connectivity with attached network segments.
Exceeding design limits	■ A component may be operating suboptimally at the physical layer because it is being utilized beyond specifications or configured capacity.
	■ When troubleshooting this type of problem, it becomes evident that resources for the device are operating at or near the maximum capacity, and there is an increase in the number of interface errors.
CPU overload	■ Symptoms include processes with high CPU utilization percentages, input queue drops, slow performance, SNMP timeouts, no remote access, or services such as DHCP, Telnet, and **ping** being slow or failing to respond.
	■ On a switch, the following could occur: spanning tree reconvergence, EtherChannel link bounce, UDLD flapping, IP SLAs failures.
	■ For routers, there could be no routing updates, route flapping, or HSRP flapping.
	■ One of the causes of CPU overload in a router or switch is high traffic.
	■ If one or more interfaces are regularly overloaded with traffic, consider redesigning the traffic flow in the network or upgrading the hardware.

Data Link Layer Troubleshooting (12.4.2)

Troubleshooting Layer 2 problems can be a challenging process. The configuration and operation of these protocols are critical to creating a functional, well-tuned network. Layer 2 problems cause specific symptoms that, when recognized, can help identify the problem quickly.

Figure 12-23 summarizes the symptoms and causes of data link layer network problems.

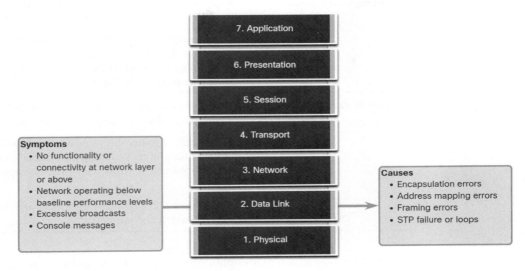

Figure 12-23 Data Link Layer Symptoms and Causes

Table 12-7 lists common symptoms of data link layer network problems.

Table 12-7 Data Link Layer Symptoms

Symptom	Description
No functionality or connectivity at the network layer or above	■ Some Layer 2 problems can stop the exchange of frames across a link, while others only cause network performance to degrade.
Network is operating below baseline performance levels	■ There are two distinct types of suboptimal Layer 2 operation that can occur in a network.
	■ First, the frames may take a suboptimal path to their destination but arrive, causing the network to experience unexpected high-bandwidth usage on links.
	■ Second, some frames may be dropped, as identified through error counter statistics and console error messages that appear on the switch or router.
	■ An extended or continuous **ping** can help reveal whether frames are being dropped.

Symptom	Description
Excessive broadcasts	■ Operating systems use broadcasts and multicasts extensively to discover network services and other hosts.
	■ Generally, excessive broadcasts result from poorly programmed or configured applications, a large Layer 2 broadcast domain, or an underlying network problem (such as STP loops or route flapping).
Console messages	■ A router recognizes that a Layer 2 problem has occurred and sends alert messages to the console.
	■ Typically, a router does this when it detects a problem with interpreting incoming frames (encapsulation or framing problems) or when keepalives are expected but do not arrive.
	■ The most common console message that indicates a Layer 2 problem is a line protocol down message.

Table 12-8 lists issues that commonly cause network problems at the data link layer.

Table 12-8   Data Link Layer Causes

Problem Cause	Description
Encapsulation errors	■ An encapsulation error occurs because the bits placed in a field by the sender are not what the receiver expects to see.
	■ This condition occurs when the encapsulation at one end of a WAN link is configured differently from the encapsulation used at the other end.
Address mapping errors	■ In topologies such as point-to-multipoint or broadcast Ethernet, it is essential that an appropriate Layer 2 destination address be given to the frame. This ensures its arrival at the correct destination.
	■ To achieve this, the network device must match a destination Layer 3 address with the correct Layer 2 address, using either static or dynamic maps.
	■ In a dynamic environment, the mapping of Layer 2 and Layer 3 information can fail because devices may have been specifically configured not to respond to ARP requests, the Layer 2 or Layer 3 information that is cached may have physically changed, or invalid ARP replies are received because of a misconfiguration or a security attack.

Problem Cause	Description
Framing errors	■ Frames usually work in groups of 8-bit bytes.
	■ A framing error occurs when a frame does not end on an 8-bit byte boundary. When this happens, the receiver may have problems determining where one frame ends and another frame starts.
	■ Too many invalid frames may prevent valid keepalives from being exchanged.
	■ Framing errors can be caused by a noisy serial line, an improperly designed cable (too long or not properly shielded), a faulty NIC, a duplex mismatch, or an incorrectly configured channel service unit (CSU) line clock.
STP failures or loops	■ The purpose of Spanning Tree Protocol (STP) is to resolve a redundant physical topology into a tree-like topology by blocking redundant ports.
	■ Most STP problems are related to forwarding loops that occur when no ports in a redundant topology are blocked and traffic is forwarded in circles indefinitely. This causes excessive flooding because of a high rate of STP topology changes.
	■ A topology change should be a rare event in a well-configured network.
	■ When a link between two switches goes up or down, there is eventually a topology change when the STP state of the port is changing to or from forwarding. However, when a port is flapping (oscillating between up and down states), this causes repetitive topology changes and flooding or slow STP convergence or reconvergence.
	■ This can be caused by a mismatch between the real topology and the documented topology, a configuration error, such as an inconsistent configuration of STP timers, an overloaded switch CPU during convergence, or a software defect.

Network Layer Troubleshooting (12.4.3)

Network layer problems include any problem that involves a Layer 3 protocol, such as IPv4, IPv6, EIGRP, OSPF, and so on. Figure 12-24 summarizes the symptoms and causes of network layer network problems.

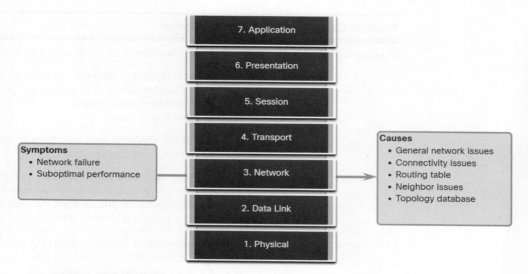

Figure 12-24   Network Layer Symptoms and Causes

Table 12-9 lists common symptoms of network layer network problems.

Table 12-9   Network Layer Symptoms

Symptom	Description
Network failure	▪ Network failure occurs when the network is nearly or completely nonfunctional, affecting all users and applications on the network. ▪ These failures are usually noticed quickly by users and network administrators and are obviously critical to the productivity of a company.
Suboptimal performance	▪ Network optimization problems usually involve a subset of users, applications, or destinations or a type of traffic. ▪ Optimization issues can be difficult to detect and even harder to isolate and diagnose. This is because they usually involve multiple layers, or even a single host computer. ▪ Determining that a problem is a network layer problem can take time.

In most networks, static routes are used in combination with dynamic routing protocols. Improper configuration of static routes can lead to less-than-optimal routing. In some cases, improperly configured static routes can create routing loops that make parts of the network unreachable.

Troubleshooting dynamic routing protocols requires a thorough understanding of how the specific routing protocols function. Some problems are common to all routing protocols, while other problems are particular to an individual routing protocol.

There is no single template for solving Layer 3 problems. Routing problems are solved with a methodical process, using a series of commands to isolate and diagnose the problems.

Table 12-10 lists areas to explore when diagnosing Layer 3 routing protocol problems.

Table 12-10 Layer 3 Routing Protocol Causes

Problem Cause	Description
General network issues	▪ Often a change in the topology, such as a down link, may have effects on other areas of the network that might not be obvious. Such changes may include the installation of new routes, static or dynamic, or removal of other routes. ▪ Determine whether anything in the network has recently changed and whether there is anyone currently working on the network infrastructure.
Connectivity issues	▪ Check for any equipment and connectivity problems, including power problems such as outages and environmental problems (for example, overheating). ▪ Also check for Layer 1 problems, such as cabling problems, bad ports, and ISP problems.
Routing table	▪ Check the routing table for anything unexpected, such as missing routes or unexpected routes. ▪ Use **debug** commands to view routing updates and routing table maintenance.
Neighbor issues	▪ If the routing protocol establishes an adjacency with a neighbor, check to see if there are any problems with the routers forming neighbor adjacencies.
Topology database	▪ If the routing protocol uses a topology table or database, check the table for anything unexpected, such as missing entries or unexpected entries.

Transport Layer Troubleshooting—ACLs (12.4.4)

Network problems can arise from transport layer problems on a router, particularly at the edge of the network, where traffic is examined and modified. For instance, both access control lists (ACLs) and Network Address Translation (NAT) operate at the network layer and may involve operations at the transport layer, as shown in Figure 12-25.

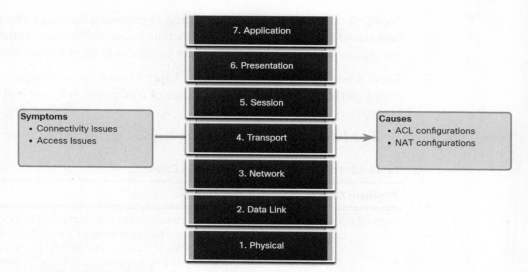

Figure 12-25 Transport Layer—ACL Symptoms and Causes

The most common issues with ACLs are caused by improper configuration, as shown in Figure 12-26.

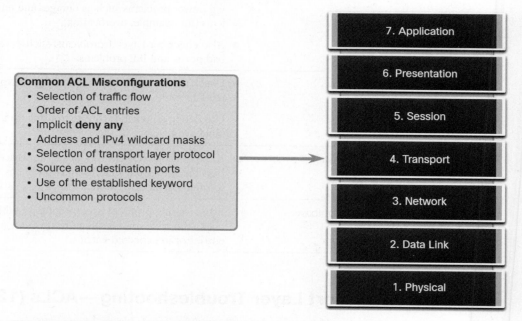

Figure 12-26 Transport Layer—Common ACL Misconfigurations

Problems with ACLs may cause otherwise working systems to fail. Table 12-11 lists areas where misconfigurations commonly occur.

Table 12-11   Transport Layer—ACL Misconfigurations

Misconfiguration	Description
Selection of traffic flow	■ Traffic is defined by both the router interface through which the traffic is traveling and the direction in which this traffic is traveling. ■ An ACL must be applied to the correct interface, and the correct traffic direction must be selected to function properly.
Order of access control entries	■ The entries in an ACL should be from specific to general. ■ Although an ACL may have an entry to specifically permit a type of traffic flow, packets never match that entry if they are being denied by another entry earlier in the list. ■ If a router is running both ACLs and NAT, the order in which each of these technologies is applied to a traffic flow is important. ■ Inbound traffic is processed by the inbound ACL before being processed by outside-to-inside NAT. ■ Outbound traffic is processed by the outbound ACL after being processed by inside-to-outside NAT.
Implicit deny any	■ When high security is not required on the ACL, this implicit access control element can be the cause of an ACL misconfiguration.
Addresses and IPv4 wildcard masks	■ Complex IPv4 wildcard masks provide significant improvements in efficiency but are more subject to configuration errors. ■ An example of a complex wildcard mask is using the IPv4 address 10.0.32.0 and wildcard mask 0.0.32.15 to select the first 15 host addresses in either the 10.0.0.0 network or the 10.0.32.0 network.
Selection of transport layer protocol	■ When configuring ACLs, it is important that only the correct transport layer protocols be specified. ■ Many network administrators, when unsure whether a type of traffic flow uses a TCP port or a UDP port, configure both. ■ Specifying both opens a hole through the firewall, possibly giving intruders an avenue into the network. ■ It also introduces an extra element into the ACL, so the ACL takes longer to process, introducing more latency into network communications.
Source and destination ports	■ Properly controlling the traffic between two hosts requires symmetric access control elements for inbound and outbound ACLs. ■ Address and port information for traffic generated by a replying host is the mirror image of address and port information for traffic generated by the initiating host.

Misconfiguration	Description
Use of the **established** keyword	■ The **established** keyword increases the security provided by an ACL. ■ However, if the keyword is applied incorrectly, unexpected results may occur.
Uncommon protocols	■ Misconfigured ACLs often cause problems for protocols other than TCP and UDP. ■ Uncommon protocols that are gaining popularity are VPN and encryption protocols.

The **log** keyword is a useful command for viewing ACL operation on ACL entries. This keyword instructs the router to place an entry in the system log whenever that entry condition is matched. The logged event includes details of the packet that matched the ACL element. The **log** keyword is especially useful for troubleshooting and provides information on intrusion attempts being blocked by the ACL.

Transport Layer Troubleshooting—NAT for IPv4 (12.4.5)

There are several problems with NAT, such as not interacting with services like DHCP and tunneling. These issues can include misconfigured NAT inside, NAT outside, or ACLs. Other issues include interoperability with other network technologies, especially those that contain or derive information from host network addressing in the packet.

Figure 12-27 summarizes common interoperability areas with NAT.

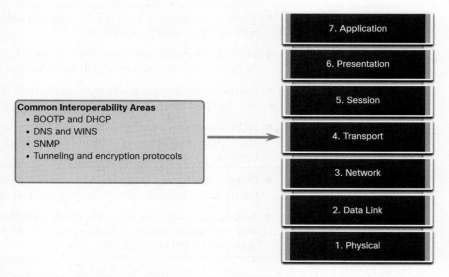

Figure 12-27 Transport Layer—Common Interoperability Areas with NAT

Table 12-12 lists common interoperability areas with NAT.

Table 12-12 Transport Layer Common Interoperability Areas

Protocol	Description
BOOTP and DHCP	▪ Both protocols manage the automatic assignment of IPv4 addresses to clients.
	▪ Recall that the first packet that a new client sends is a DHCP-Request broadcast IPv4 packet.
	▪ The DHCP-Request packet has source IPv4 address 0.0.0.0.
	▪ Because NAT requires both a valid destination IPv4 address and source IPv4 address, BOOTP and DHCP can have difficulty operating over a router running either static or dynamic NAT.
	▪ Configuring the IPv4 helper feature can help solve this problem.
DNS	▪ Because a router running dynamic NAT is changing the relationship between inside and outside addresses regularly as table entries expire and are re-created, a DNS server outside the NAT router does not have an accurate representation of the network inside the router.
	▪ Configuring the IPv4 helper feature can help solve this problem.
SNMP	▪ Like DNS packets, NAT is unable to alter the addressing information stored in the data payload of the packet.
	▪ Because of this, an SNMP management station on one side of a NAT router may not be able to contact SNMP agents on the other side of the NAT router.
	▪ Configuring the IPv4 helper feature can help solve this problem.
Tunneling and encryption protocols	▪ Encryption and tunneling protocols often require that traffic be sourced from a specific UDP or TCP port or use a protocol at the transport layer that cannot be processed by NAT.
	▪ For example, IPsec tunneling protocols and the Generic Routing Encapsulation protocol used by VPN implementations cannot be processed by NAT.

Application Layer Troubleshooting (12.4.6)

Most of the application layer protocols provide user services. Application layer protocols are typically used for network management, file transfer, distributed file services, terminal emulation, and email. New user services are often added, such as VPNs and VoIP.

Figure 12-28 shows the most widely known and implemented TCP/IP application layer protocols.

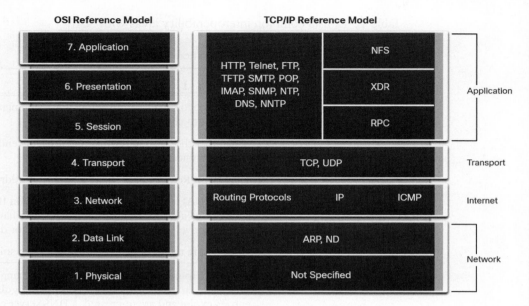

Figure 12-28 Common TCP/IP Application Layer Protocols

Table 12-13 provides a short description of each of these application layer protocols.

Table 12-13 Application Layer Protocols

Protocol	Description
SSH/Telnet	Enables users to establish terminal session connections with remote hosts.
HTTP	Supports the exchange of text, graphic images, sound, video, and other multimedia files on the web.
FTP	Performs interactive file transfers between hosts.
TFTP	Performs basic interactive file transfers, typically between hosts and networking devices.
SMTP	Supports basic message delivery services.
POP	Connects to mail servers and downloads email.
SNMP	Collects management information from network devices.
DNS	Maps IP addresses to the names assigned to network devices.
Network File System (NFS)	Enables computers to mount drives on remote hosts and operate them as if they were local drives. Originally developed by Sun Microsystems, it combines with two other application layer protocols, External Data Representation (XDR) and Remote Procedure Call (RPC), to allow transparent access to remote network resources.

The types of symptoms and causes depend on the application.

Application layer problems prevent services from being provided to application programs. A problem at the application layer can result in unreachable or unusable resources when the physical, data link, network, and transport layers are functional. It is possible to have full network connectivity but still see an application be unable to provide data.

Another type of problem at the application layer occurs when the physical, data link, network, and transport layers are functional, but the data transfer and requests for network services from a single network service or application do not meet the normal expectations of a user.

A problem at the application layer may cause users to complain that the network or an application that they are working with is sluggish or slower than usual when transferring data or requesting network services.

<table>
<tr>
<td>Interactive
Graphic</td>
<td>

Check Your Understanding—Symptoms and Causes of Network Problems (12.4.7)

Refer to the online course to complete this activity.
</td>
</tr>
</table>

Troubleshooting IP Connectivity (12.5)

In this section, you will troubleshoot a network using the layered model.

Components of Troubleshooting End-to-End Connectivity (12.5.1)

This section presents a single topology and the tools to diagnose (and in some cases solve) end-to-end connectivity problems. Diagnosing and solving problems is an essential skill for network administrators. There is no single recipe for troubleshooting, and a problem can be diagnosed in many ways. However, by employing a structured approach to the troubleshooting process, an administrator can reduce the time it takes to diagnose and solve a problem.

Throughout this section, the following scenario is used: The client host PC1 is unable to access applications on server SRV1 or server SRV2. Figure 12-29 shows the topology of this network. PC1 uses SLAAC with EUI-64 to create its IPv6 global unicast address. EUI-64 creates the interface ID using the Ethernet MAC address, inserting FFFE in the middle, and flipping the seventh bit.

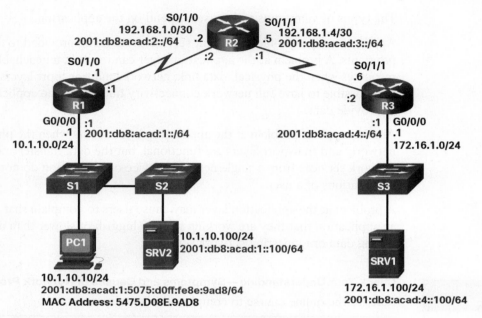

Figure 12-29   Troubleshooting Reference Topology

When there is no end-to-end connectivity, the administrator may choose to trouble-shoot with a bottom-up approach and take the following common steps:

Step 1.   Check physical connectivity at the point where network communication stops. This includes cables and hardware. The problem might be with a faulty cable or interface, or it might involve misconfigured or faulty hardware.

Step 2.   Check for duplex mismatches.

Step 3.   Check data link and network layer addressing on the local network. This includes IPv4 ARP tables, IPv6 neighbor tables, MAC address tables, and VLAN assignments.

Step 4.   Verify that the default gateway is correct.

Step 5.   Ensure that devices are determining the correct path from the source to the destination. Manipulate the routing information, if necessary.

Step 6.   Verify that the transport layer is functioning properly. Telnet can also be used to test transport layer connections from the command line.

Step 7.   Verify that there are no ACLs blocking traffic.

Step 8.   Ensure that DNS settings are correct. There should be a DNS server that is accessible.

The outcome of this process is operational, end-to-end connectivity. If all the steps have been performed without any resolution, the network administrator may either want to repeat these steps or escalate the problem to a senior administrator.

End-to-End Connectivity Problem Initiates Troubleshooting (12.5.2)

Usually what prompts a troubleshooting effort is the discovery that there is a problem with end-to-end connectivity. Two of the most common utilities used to verify a problem with end-to-end connectivity are **ping** and **traceroute**, as shown in Figure 12-30.

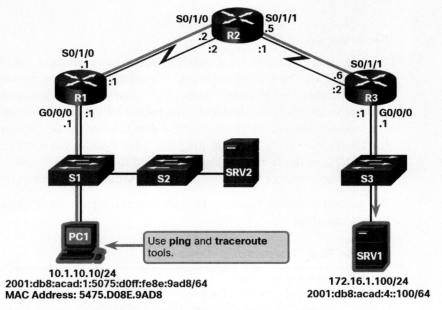

Figure 12-30   ping and **traceroute** from PC1 to SRV1

IPv4 ping

ping is probably the most widely known connectivity-testing utility in networking and has always been part of Cisco IOS software. It sends out requests for responses from a specified host address. The **ping** command uses a Layer 3 protocol called ICMP that is a part of the TCP/IP suite. **ping** uses the ICMP echo request and ICMP echo reply packets. If the host at the specified address receives the ICMP echo request, it responds with an ICMP echo reply packet. **ping** can be used to verify end-to-end connectivity for both IPv4 and IPv6. The command output in Example 12-2 shows a successful **ping** from PC1 to SRV1, at address 172.16.1.100.

Example 12-2 Successful IPv4 **ping**

```
C:\> ping 172.16.1.100
Pinging 172.16.1.100 with 32 bytes of data:
Reply from 172.16.1.100: bytes=32 time=199ms TTL=128
Reply from 172.16.1.100: bytes=32 time=193ms TTL=128
Reply from 172.16.1.100: bytes=32 time=194ms TTL=128
Reply from 172.16.1.100: bytes=32 time=196ms TTL=128
Ping statistics for 172.16.1.100:
    Packets: Sent = 4, Received = 4, Lost = 0 (0% loss),
Approximate round trip times in milli-seconds:
    Minimum = 193ms, Maximum = 199ms, Average = 195ms
C:\>
```

IPv4 traceroute

Like the **ping** command, the Cisco IOS **traceroute** command can be used for both IPv4 and IPv6. The **tracert** command is used with Windows operating systems. The trace generates a list of hops, router IP addresses, and the destination IP addresses that are successfully reached along the path. This list provides important verification and troubleshooting information. If the data reaches the destination, the trace lists the interface on every router in the path. If the data fails at some hop along the way, the address of the last router that responded to the trace is known. This address provides an indication of where the problem or security restrictions reside.

The **tracert** output in Example 12-3 illustrates the path the IPv4 packets take to reach their destination.

Example 12-3 Successful IPv4 **traceroute**

```
C:\> tracert 172.16.1.100
Tracing route to 172.16.1.100 over a maximum of 30 hops:
  1     1 ms    <1 ms    <1 ms   10.1.10.1
  2     2 ms     2 ms     1 ms   192.168.1.2
  3     2 ms     2 ms     1 ms   192.168.1.6
  4     2 ms     2 ms     1 ms   172.16.1.100
Trace complete.
C:\>
```

IPv6 ping and traceroute

When using the **ping** and **traceroute** utilities, Cisco IOS recognizes whether an address is an IPv4 or IPv6 address and uses the appropriate protocol to test connectivity. The command output in Example 12-4 shows the **ping** and **traceroute** commands on router R1 used to test IPv6 connectivity.

Example 12-4   Successful IPv6 **ping** and **traceroute**

```
R1# ping 2001:db8:acad:4::100
Type escape sequence to abort.
Sending 5, 100-byte ICMP Echos to 2001:DB8:ACAD:4::100, timeout is 2 seconds:
!!!!!
Success rate is 100 percent (5/5), round-trip min/avg/max = 56/56/56 ms
R1#
R1# traceroute 2001:db8:acad:4::100
Type escape sequence to abort.
Tracing the route to 2001:DB8:ACAD:4::100
1.    2001:DB8:ACAD:2::2 20 msec 20 msec 20 msec
2.    2001:DB8:ACAD:3::2 44 msec 40 msec 40 msec
R1#
```

Note

The **traceroute** command is commonly performed when the **ping** command fails. If **ping** succeeds, the **traceroute** command is commonly not needed because the technician knows that connectivity exists.

Step 1—Verify the Physical Layer (12.5.3)

All network devices are specialized computer systems. At a minimum, these devices consist of a CPU, RAM, and storage space, allowing the device to boot and run the operating system and interfaces. This allows for the reception and transmission of network traffic. When a network administrator determines that a problem exists on a given device, and that problem might be hardware related, it is worthwhile to verify the operation of these generic components. The Cisco IOS commands most commonly used for this purpose are **show processes cpu, show memory,** and **show interfaces.** This section discusses the **show interfaces** command.

When troubleshooting performance-related issues and hardware are suspected to be at fault, the **show interfaces** command can be used to verify the interfaces through which the traffic passes.

Example 12-5 provides command output of the **show interfaces** command.

Example 12-5   The **show interfaces** Command

```
R1# show interfaces GigabitEthernet 0/0/0
GigabitEthernet0/0/0 is up, line protocol is up
Hardware is CN Gigabit Ethernet, address is d48c.b5ce.a0c0(bia d48c.b5ce.a0c0)
Internet address is 10.1.10.1/24
(Output omitted)
Input queue: 0/75/0/0 (size/max/drops/flushes); Total output drops: 0
Queueing strategy: fifo
Output queue: 0/40 (size/max)
5 minute input rate 0 bits/sec, 0 packets/sec
5 minute output rate 0 bits/sec, 0 packets/sec
85 packets input, 7711 bytes, 0 no buffer
Received 25 broadcasts (0 IP multicasts)
0 runts, 0 giants, 0 throttles
0 input errors, 0 CRC, 0 frame, 0 overrun, 0 ignored
0 watchdog, 5 multicast, 0 pause input
10112 packets output, 922864 bytes, 0 underruns
0 output errors, 0 collisions, 1 interface resets
11 unknown protocol drops
0 babbles, 0 late collision, 0 deferred
0 lost carrier, 0 no carrier, 0 pause output
0 output buffer failures, 0 output buffers swapped out
R1#
```

Input Queue Drops

Input queue drops (and the related ignored and throttle counters) signify that, at some point, more traffic was delivered to the router than it could process. This does not necessarily indicate a problem. It could be normal traffic during peak periods. However, it could also be an indication that the CPU cannot process packets in time, so if this number is consistently high, it is worth trying to spot at which moments these counters are increasing and how this information relates to CPU usage.

Output Queue Drops

Output queue drops indicate that packets were dropped due to congestion on the interface. Seeing output drops is normal for any point where the aggregate input traffic is higher than the output traffic. During peak traffic periods, packets are dropped if traffic is delivered to the interface faster than it can be sent out. However, even if this is considered normal behavior, it leads to packet drops and queuing delays, so applications that are sensitive to those issues, such as VoIP, might suffer from performance issues. Consistent output queue drops can be an indicator that an advanced queuing mechanism is required or the current QoS setting should be modified.

Input Errors

Input errors are errors that are experienced during the reception of a frame, such as CRC errors. High numbers of CRC errors could indicate cabling problems, interface hardware problems, or, in an Ethernet-based network, *duplex mismatches*.

Output Errors

Output errors indicate errors, such as collisions, that occur during the transmission of a frame. In most Ethernet-based networks today, *full-duplex* transmission is the norm, and *half-duplex* transmission is the exception. In full-duplex transmission, operation collisions cannot occur; therefore, collisions (especially late collisions) often indicate duplex mismatches.

Step 2—Check for Duplex Mismatches (12.5.4)

A common cause of interface errors is mismatched duplex mode between two ends of an Ethernet link. In many Ethernet-based networks, point-to-point connections are now the norm, and the use of hubs and the associated half-duplex operation is becoming less common. This means that most Ethernet links today operate in full-duplex mode, and while collisions were normal for Ethernet links, collisions today often indicate that duplex negotiation has failed or that the link is not operating in the correct duplex mode.

The IEEE 802.3ab Gigabit Ethernet standard mandates the use of autonegotiation for speed and duplex. In addition, although it is not strictly mandatory, practically all Fast Ethernet NICs also use autonegotiation by default. The use of autonegotiation for speed and duplex is the current recommended practice.

However, if duplex negotiation fails for some reason, it might be necessary to set the speed and duplex manually on both ends. Typically, this would mean setting the duplex mode to full-duplex on both ends of the connection. If this does not work, running half-duplex on both ends is preferred over a duplex mismatch.

Duplex configuration guidelines include the following:

- Autonegotiation of speed and duplex is recommended.
- If autonegotiation fails, manually set the speed and duplex on interconnecting ends.
- Point-to-point Ethernet links should always run in full-duplex mode.
- Half-duplex is uncommon and typically encountered only when legacy hubs are used.

Troubleshooting Example

In the previous scenario, the network administrator needed to add additional users to the network. To incorporate these new users, the network administrator installed a second switch and connected it to the first one. Soon after S2 was added to the network, users on both switches began experiencing significant performance problems connecting with devices on the other switch, as shown in Figure 12-31.

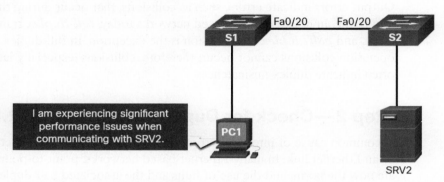

Figure 12-31 Topology for Duplex Scenario

The network administrator notices a console message on switch S2:

```
*Mar 1 00:45:08.756: %CDP-4-DUPLEX_MISMATCH: duplex mismatch discovered on FastEth-
    ernet0/20 (not half duplex), with Switch FastEthernet0/20 (half duplex).
```

Using the **show interfaces fa 0/20** command, the network administrator examines the interface on S1 that is used to connect to S2 and notices that it is set to full-duplex, as shown in the command output in Example 12-6.

Example 12-6 Checking Duplex Mode on S1 Fa0/20

```
S1# show interface fa 0/20
FastEthernet0/20 is up, line protocol is up (connected)
Hardware is Fast Ethernet, address is 0cd9.96e8.8a01 (bia 0cd9.96e8.8a01)
MTU 1500 bytes, BW 10000 Kbit/sec, DLY 1000 usec, reliability 255/255, txload
    1/255, rxload 1/255
Encapsulation ARPA, loopback not set Keepalive set (10 sec)
Full-duplex, Auto-speed, media type is 10/100BaseTX

(Output omitted)

S1#
```

The network administrator now examines the other side of the connection, the port on S2. The command output in Example 12-7 shows that this side of the connection has been configured for half-duplex.

Example 12-7   Checking Duplex Mode on S2 Fa0/20

```
S2# show interface fa 0/20
FastEthernet0/20 is up, line protocol is up (connected)
Hardware is Fast Ethernet, address is 0cd9.96d2.4001 (bia 0cd9.96d2.4001)
MTU 1500 bytes, BW 100000 Kbit/sec, DLY 100 usec, reliability 255/255, txload
  1/255, rxload 1/255
Encapsulation ARPA, loopback not set Keepalive set (10 sec)
Half-duplex, Auto-speed, media type is 10/100BaseTX

(Output omitted)

S2(config)# interface fa 0/20
S2(config-if)# duplex auto
S2(config-if)#
```

The network administrator corrects the setting to **duplex auto** to automatically negotiate the duplex. Because the port on S1 is set to full-duplex, S2 also uses full-duplex.

The users report that there are no longer any performance problems.

Step 3—Verify Addressing on the Local Network (12.5.5)

When troubleshooting end-to-end connectivity, it is useful to verify mappings between destination IP addresses and Layer 2 Ethernet addresses on individual segments. In IPv4, this functionality is provided by ARP. In IPv6, the ARP functionality is replaced by the neighbor discovery process and ICMPv6. The neighbor table caches IPv6 addresses and their resolved Ethernet physical (MAC) addresses.

This section provides an example and explanation of the commands used to verify Layer 2 and Layer 3 addressing.

Windows IPv4 ARP Table

The **arp** Windows command displays and modifies entries in the ARP cache that are used to store IPv4 addresses and their resolved Ethernet physical (MAC) addresses. As shown in the command output in Example 12-8, the **arp** Windows command lists all devices that are currently in the ARP cache.

Example 12-8 Windows IPv4 ARP Table

```
C:\> arp -a
Interface: 10.1.10.100 --- 0xd
  Internet Address      Physical Address      Type
  10.1.10.1             d4-8c-b5-ce-a0-c0     dynamic
  224.0.0.22            01-00-5e-00-00-16     static
  224.0.0.251           01-00-5e-00-00-fb     static
  239.255.255.250       01-00-5e-7f-ff-fa     static
  255.255.255.255       ff-ff-ff-ff-ff-ff     static
C:\>
```

The information that is displayed for each device includes the IPv4 address, the physical (MAC) address, and the type of addressing (static or dynamic).

To repopulate the cache with updated information, the cache can be cleared by using the **arp -d** Windows command.

Note

The **arp** commands in Linux and Mac OS X have similar syntax.

Windows IPv6 Neighbor Table

The **netsh interface ipv6 show neighbor** Windows command output in Example 12-9 lists all devices that are currently in the neighbor table.

Example 12-9 Windows IPv5 Neighbor Table

```
C:\> netsh interface ipv6 show neighbor
Internet Address                            Physical Address    Type
----------------------------------------    ----------------    -----------
fe80::9657:a5ff:fe0c:5b02                   94-57-a5-0c-5b-02   Stale
fe80::1                                     d4-8c-b5-ce-a0-c0   Reachable (Router)
ff02::1                                     33-33-00-00-00-01   Permanent
ff02::2                                     33-33-00-00-00-02   Permanent
ff02::16                                    33-33-00-00-00-16   Permanent
ff02::1:2                                   33-33-00-01-00-02   Permanent
ff02::1:3                                   33-33-00-01-00-03   Permanent
ff02::1:ff0c:5b02                           33-33-ff-0c-5b-02   Permanent
ff02::1:ff2d:a75e                           33-33-ff-2d-a7-5e   Permanent
```

The information that is displayed for each device includes the IPv6 address, the physical (MAC) address, and the type of addressing. By examining the neighbor table, the network administrator can verify that destination IPv6 addresses map to correct Ethernet addresses. The IPv6 link-local addresses on all interfaces of R1 have been manually configured to fe80::1. Similarly, R2 has been configured with the link-local address fe80::2 on its interfaces, and R3 has been configured with the link-local address fe80::3 on its interfaces. Remember, link-local addresses must be unique on the link or network.

Note

The neighbor table for Linux and Mac OS X can be displayed by using **ip neigh show** command.

IOS IPv6 Neighbor Table

The **show ipv6 neighbors** command output in Example 12-10 shows an example of the neighbor table on a Cisco IOS router.

Note

The neighbor states for IPv6 are more complex than the ARP table states in IPv4. For more information, see RFC 4861.

Example 12-10   IOS IPv6 Neighbor Table

```
R1# show ipv6 neighbors
IPv6 Address                       Age   Link-layer Addr   State    Interface
FE80::21E:7AFF:FE79:7A81           8     001e.7a79.7a81    STALE    Gi0/0
2001:DB8:ACAD:1:5075:D0FF:FE8E:9AD8 0    5475.d08e.9ad8    REACH    Gi0/0
R1#
```

Switch MAC Address Table

When a destination MAC address is found in the switch MAC address table, the switch forwards the frame only to the port of the device that has that MAC address. To do this, the switch consults its MAC address table. The MAC address table lists the MAC address connected to each port. Use the **show mac address-table** command to display the MAC address table on the switch (see Example 12-11).

Example 12-11   Switch MAC Address Table

```
S1# show mac address-table
            Mac Address Table
-------------------------------------------------
Vlan     Mac Address        Type      Ports
All      0100.0ccc.cccc     STATIC    CPU
All      0100.0ccc.cccd     STATIC    CPU
10       d48c.b5ce.a0c0     DYNAMIC   Fa0/4
10       000f.34f9.9201     DYNAMIC   Fa0/5
10       5475.d08e.9ad8     DYNAMIC   Fa0/13
Total Mac Addresses for this criterion: 5
S1#
```

Notice that the MAC address for PC1, a device in VLAN 10, has been discovered along with the S1 switch port to which PC1 attaches. Remember that the MAC address table of a switch only contains Layer 2 information, including the Ethernet MAC address and the port number. IP address information is not included.

Troubleshoot VLAN Assignment Example (12.5.6)

Another issue to consider when troubleshooting end-to-end connectivity is VLAN assignment. In a switched network, each port in a switch belongs to a VLAN. Each VLAN is considered a separate logical network, and packets destined for stations that do not belong to the VLAN must be forwarded through a device that supports routing. If a host in one VLAN sends a broadcast Ethernet frame, such as an ARP request, all hosts in the same VLAN receive the frame; hosts in other VLANs do not. Even if two hosts are in the same IP network, they will not be able to communicate if they are connected to ports assigned to two separate VLANs. In addition, if the VLAN to which a port belongs is deleted, the port becomes inactive. All hosts attached to ports belonging to the VLAN that was deleted are unable to communicate with the rest of the network. Commands such as **show vlan** can be used to validate VLAN assignments on a switch.

Say, for example, that in an effort to improve the wire management in the wiring closet, your company has reorganized the cables connected to switch S1. Almost immediately afterward, users start calling the support desk, stating that they can no longer reach devices outside their own network.

This section provides an explanation of the process used to troubleshoot this issue.

Check the ARP Table

An examination of the PC1 ARP table using the **arp** Windows command shows that the ARP table no longer contains an entry for the default gateway 10.1.10.1, as shown in the command output in Example 12-12.

Example 12-12   Checking the ARP Table

```
C:\> arp -a
Interface: 10.1.10.100 --- 0xd
  Internet Address        Physical Address        Type
  224.0.0.22              01-00-5e-00-00-16        static
  224.0.0.251             01-00-5e-00-00-fb        static
  239.255.255.250         01-00-5e-7f-ff-fa        static
  255.255.255.255         ff-ff-ff-ff-ff-ff        static
C:\>
```

Check the Switch MAC Table

There were no configuration changes on the router, so S1 is the focus of the troubleshooting. The MAC address table for S1, as shown in Example 12-13, indicates that the MAC address for R1 is on a different VLAN than the rest of the 10.1.10.0/24 devices, including PC1.

Example 12-13   Checking the Switch's MAC Table

```
S1# show mac address-table
               Mac Address Table
-------------------------------------------------
Vlan        Mac Address         Type      Ports
All         0100.0ccc.cccc      STATIC    CPU
All         0100.0ccc.cccd      STATIC    CPU
  1         d48c.b5ce.a0c0      DYNAMIC   Fa0/1
 10         000f.34f9.9201      DYNAMIC   Fa0/5
 10         5475.d08e.9ad8      DYNAMIC   Fa0/13
Total Mac Addresses for this criterion: 5
S1#
```

Correct the VLAN Assignment

During the recabling, the patch cable for R1 was moved from Fa 0/4 on VLAN 10 to Fa 0/1 on VLAN 1. When the network administrator configures the Fa 0/1 port of S1 to be on VLAN 10, as shown in Example 12-14, the problem is resolved. The MAC address table now shows VLAN 10 for the MAC address of R1 on port Fa 0/1.

Example 12-14 Correcting the VLAN Assignment

```
S1(config)# interface fa0/1
S1(config-if)# switchport mode access
S1(config-if)# switchport access vlan 10
S1(config-if)# exit
S1#
S1# show mac address-table
              Mac Address Table
-------------------------------------------------
Vlan      Mac Address      Type      Ports
All       0100.0ccc.cccc   STATIC    CPU
All       0100.0ccc.cccd   STATIC    CPU
10        d48c.b5ce.a0c0   DYNAMIC   Fa0/1
10        000f.34f9.9201   DYNAMIC   Fa0/5
10        5475.d08e.9ad8   DYNAMIC   Fa0/13
Total Mac Addresses for this criterion: 5
S1#
```

Step 4—Verify Default Gateway (12.5.7)

If there is no detailed route on a router, or if a host is configured with the wrong default gateway, then communication between two endpoints in different networks does not work. Figure 12-32 illustrates how PC1 uses R1 as its default gateway.

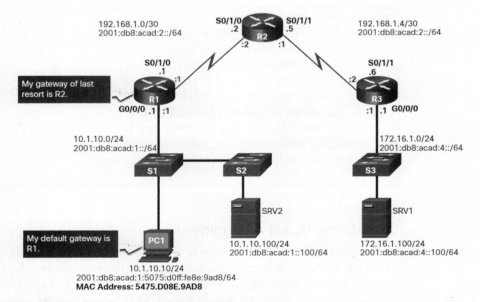

Figure 12-32 PC1 and R1 Default Gateways

Similarly, R1 uses R2 as its default gateway or gateway of last resort. If a host needs access to resources beyond the local network, the default gateway must be configured. The default gateway is the first router on the path to destinations beyond the local network.

Troubleshooting IPv4 Default Gateway Example

In this example, R1 has the correct default gateway, which is the IPv4 address of R2. However, PC1 has the wrong default gateway. PC1 should have the default gateway of R1, 10.1.10.1. This must be configured manually if the IPv4 addressing information was manually configured on PC1. If the IPv4 addressing information was obtained automatically from a DHCPv4 server, then the configuration on the DHCP server must be examined. A configuration problem on a DHCP server usually affects multiple clients.

R1 Routing Table

The command output of the **show ip route** Cisco IOS command is used to verify the default gateway of R1, as shown in Example 12-15.

Example 12-15   R1's Routing Table

```
R1# show ip route | include Gateway|0.0.0.0

Gateway of last resort is 192.168.1.2 to network 0.0.0.0
S* 0.0.0.0/0 [1/0] via 192.168.1.2

R1#
```

PC1 Routing Table

On a Windows host, the **route print** Windows command is used to verify the presence of the IPv4 default gateway, as shown in Example 12-16.

Example 12-16   PC1's Routing Table

```
C:\> route print
(Output omitted)

IPv4 Route Table
===========================================================================
Active Routes:
Network Destination        Netmask          Gateway       Interface  Metric
          0.0.0.0          0.0.0.0        10.1.10.1      10.1.10.10      11
(Output omitted)
```

Troubleshoot IPv6 Default Gateway Example (12.5.8)

In IPv6, the default gateway can be configured manually by using stateless address autoconfiguration (SLAAC) or by using DHCPv6. With SLAAC, the default gateway is advertised by the router to hosts using ICMPv6 Router Advertisement (RA) messages. The default gateway in the RA message is the link-local IPv6 address of a router interface. If the default gateway is configured manually on the host, which is very unlikely, the default gateway can be set to either the global IPv6 address or to the link-local IPv6 address.

This section provides an example and explanation of troubleshooting an IPv6 default gateway issue.

R1 Routing Table

As shown in Example 12-17, the **show ipv6 route** Cisco IOS command is used to check for the IPv6 default route on R1. R1 has a default route via R2.

Example 12-17   R1's Routing Table

```
R1# show ipv6 route

(Output omitted)

S  ::/0 [1/0]
via 2001:DB8:ACAD:2::2
R1#
```

PC1 Addressing

The **ipconfig** Windows command is used to verify that a PC1 has an IPv6 default gateway. The output in Example 12-18 shows that PC1 is missing an IPv6 global unicast address and an IPv6 default gateway. PC1 is enabled for IPv6 because it has an IPv6 link-local address. The link-local address is automatically created by the device. Checking the network documentation, the network administrator confirms that hosts on this LAN should be receiving their IPv6 address information from the router using SLAAC.

> **Note**
>
> In this example, other devices on the same LAN using SLAAC would also experience the same problem receiving IPv6 address information.

Example 12-18   PC1's Addressing

```
C:\> ipconfig
Windows IP Configuration
    Connection-specific DNS Suffix . :
    Link-local IPv6 Address . . . . : fe80::5075:d0ff:fe8e:9ad8%13
    IPv4 Address . . . . . . . . . . : 10.1.10.10
    Subnet Mask  . . . . . . . . . . : 255.255.255.0
    Default Gateway. . . . . . . . . : 10.1.10.1
C:\>
```

Check R1 Interface Settings

In Example 12-19, the command output of the **show ipv6 interface GigabitEthernet 0/0/0** command on R1 reveals that although the interface has an IPv6 address, it is not a member of the All-IPv6-Routers multicast group ff02::2. This means the router is not enabled as an IPv6 router. Therefore, it is not sending out ICMPv6 RAs on this interface.

Example 12-19   Checking R1's Interface Settings

```
R1# show ipv6 interface GigabitEthernet 0/0/0
GigabitEthernet0/0/0 is up, line protocol is up
  IPv6 is enabled, link-local address is FE80::1
  No Virtual link-local address(es):
  Global unicast address(es):
    2001:DB8:ACAD:1::1, subnet is 2001:DB8:ACAD:1::/64
  Joined group address(es):
      FF02:: 1
      FF02::1:FF00:1

(Output omitted)
R1#
```

Correct R1 IPv6 Routing

R1 is enabled as an IPv6 router using the **ipv6 unicast-routing** command. As shown in Example 12-20, the **show ipv6 interface GigabitEthernet 0/0/0** command verifies that R1 is a member of ff02::2, the All-IPv6-Routers multicast group.

Example 12-20   Correcting R1's IPv6 Routing

```
R1(config)# ipv6 unicast-routing
R1(config)# exit
R1#
R1# show ipv6 interface GigabitEthernet 0/0/0
GigabitEthernet0/0/0 is up, line protocol is up
  IPv6 is enabled, link-local address is FE80::1
  No Virtual link-local address(es):
  Global unicast address(es):
    2001:DB8:ACAD:1::1, subnet is 2001:DB8:ACAD:1::/64
  Joined group address(es):
    FF02:: 1
    FF02:: 2
    FF02::1:FF00:1
(Output omitted)
R1#
```

Verify PC1 Has an IPv6 Default Gateway

To verify that PC1 has the default gateway set, use the **ipconfig** command on the Microsoft Windows PC or the **ifconfig** command on Linux and Mac OS X. In Example 12-21, PC1 has an IPv6 global unicast address and an IPv6 default gateway. The default gateway is set to the link-local address of router R1, fe80::1.

Example 12-21   Verifying That PC1 Has an IPv6 Default Gateway

```
C:\> ipconfig
Windows IP Configuration
   Connection-specific DNS Suffix . :
   IPv6 Address. . . . . . . . . . . : 2001:db8:acad:1:5075:d0ff:fe8e:9ad8
   Link-local IPv6 Address . . . . . : fe80::5075:d0ff:fe8e:9ad8%13
   IPv4 Address . . . . . . . . . . : 10.1.10.10
   Subnet Mask  . . . . . . . . . . : 255.255.255.0
   Default Gateway. . . . . . . . . : fe80::1
                                       10.1.10.1
C:\>
```

Step 5—Verify Correct Path (12.5.9)

When troubleshooting, it is often necessary to verify the path to the destination network. Figure 12-33 shows the reference topology indicating the intended path for packets from PC1 to SRV1.

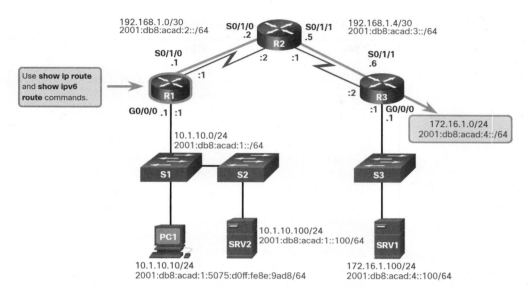

Figure 12-33 Reference Topology with the Intended Path from PC1 and SRV1

The routers in the path make the routing decision based on information in the routing tables. Examples 12-22 and 12-23 show the IPv4 and IPv6 routing tables for R1.

Example 12-22   R1's IPv4 Routing Table

```
R1# show ip route | begin Gateway
Gateway of last resort is 192.168.1.2 to network 0.0.0.0
O*E2  0.0.0.0/0 [110/1] via 192.168.1.2, 00:00:13, Serial0/1/0
      10.0.0.0/8 is variably subnetted, 2 subnets, 2 masks
C        10.1.10.0/24 is directly connected, GigabitEthernet0/0/0
L        10.1.10.1/32 is directly connected, GigabitEthernet0/0/0
      172.16.0.0/24 is subnetted, 1 subnets
O        172.16.1.0 [110/100] via 192.168.1.2, 00:01:59, Serial0/1/0
      192.168.1.0/24 is variably subnetted, 3 subnets, 2 masks
C        192.168.1.0/30 is directly connected, Serial0/1/0
L        192.168.1.1/32 is directly connected, Serial0/1/0
O        192.168.1.4/30 [110/99] via 192.168.1.2, 00:06:25, Serial0/1/0
R1#
```

Example 12-23   R1's IPv6 Routing Table

```
R1# show ipv6 route
IPv6 Routing Table - default - 8 entries
Codes: C - Connected, L - Local, S - Static, U - Per-user Static route
       B - BGP, R - RIP, H - NHRP, I1 - ISIS L1
       I2 - ISIS L2, IA - ISIS interarea, IS - ISIS summary, D - EIGRP
       EX - EIGRP external, ND - ND Default, NDp - ND Prefix, DCE - Destination
       NDr - Redirect, O - OSPF Intra, OI - OSPF Inter, OE1 - OSPF ext 1
       OE2 - OSPF ext 2, ON1 - OSPF NSSA ext 1, ON2 - OSPF NSSA ext 2
       a - Application
OE2 ::/0 [110/1], tag 1
     via FE80::2, Serial0/1/0
C    2001:DB8:ACAD:1::/64 [0/0]
     via GigabitEthernet0/0/0, directly connected
L    2001:DB8:ACAD:1::1/128 [0/0]
     via GigabitEthernet0/0/0, receive
C    2001:DB8:ACAD:2::/64 [0/0]
     via Serial0/1/0, directly connected
L    2001:DB8:ACAD:2::1/128 [0/0]
     via Serial0/1/0, receive
O    2001:DB8:ACAD:3::/64 [110/99]
     via FE80::2, Serial0/1/0
O    2001:DB8:ACAD:4::/64 [110/100]
     via FE80::2, Serial0/1/0
L    FF00::/8 [0/0]
     via Null0, receive
R1#
```

The IPv4 and IPv6 routing tables can be populated by the following methods:

- Directly connected networks
- Local host or local routes
- Static routes
- Dynamic routes
- Default routes

The process of forwarding IPv4 and IPv6 packets is based on the longest bit match or longest prefix match. The routing table process attempts to forward a packet using an entry in the routing table with the greatest number of leftmost matching bits. The number of matching bits is indicated by the prefix length of the route.

Figure 12-34 illustrates the process for both the IPv4 and IPv6 routing tables.

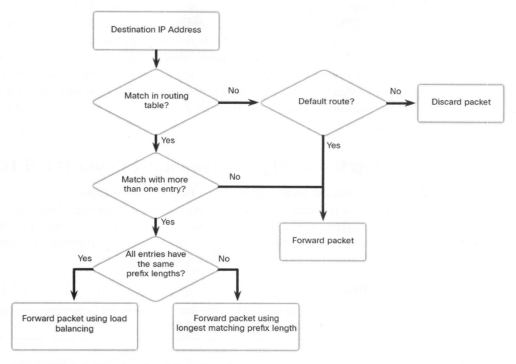

Figure 12-34   Routing Decision Flowchart

Consider the following scenarios, based on the flowchart in the figure. If the destination address in a packet:

- Does not match an entry in the routing table, then the default route is used. If there is not a default route that is configured, the packet is discarded.

- Matches a single entry in the routing table, then the packet is forwarded through the interface that is defined in this route.

- Matches more than one entry in the routing table and the routing entries have the same prefix length, then the packets for this destination can be distributed among the routes that are defined in the routing table.

- Matches more than one entry in the routing table and the routing entries have different prefix lengths, then the packets for this destination are forwarded out the interface that is associated with the route that has the longer prefix match.

Troubleshooting Example

Say that devices are unable to connect to the server SRV1 at 172.16.1.100. Using the **show ip route** command, the administrator should check to see if a routing entry exists to network 172.16.1.0/24. If the routing table does not have a specific route to the SRV1 network, the network administrator must check for the existence of a default or summary route entry in the direction of the 172.16.1.0/24 network. If none exists, then the problem may be with routing, and the administrator must verify that the network is included within the dynamic routing protocol configuration or add a static route.

Step 6—Verify the Transport Layer (12.5.10)

If the network layer appears to be functioning as expected, but users are still unable to access resources, then the network administrator must begin troubleshooting the upper layers. Two of the most common issues that affect transport layer connectivity are ACL configurations and NAT configurations. A common tool for testing transport layer functionality is the Telnet utility.

Caution

While Telnet can be used to test the transport layer, for security reasons, SSH should be used to remotely manage and configure devices.

Troubleshooting Example

A network administrator is troubleshooting a problem that involves inability to connect to a router using HTTP. The administrator pings R2, as shown in Example 12-24.

Example 12-24   Verifying Connectivity to R2

```
R1# ping 2001:db8:acad:2::2
Type escape sequence to abort.
Sending 5, 100-byte ICMP Echos to 2001:DB8:ACAD:2::2, timeout is 2 seconds:
!!!!!
Success rate is 100 percent (5/5), round-trip min/avg/max = 2/2/3 ms
R1#
```

R2 responds and confirms that the network layer and all layers below the network layer are operational. The administrator knows the issue is with Layer 4 or up and must start troubleshooting those layers.

Next, the administrator tries to use Telnet to reach R2, as shown in Example 12-25.

Example 12-25 Verifying Remote Access to R2

```
R1# telnet 2001:db8:acad:2::2
Trying 2001:DB8:ACAD:2::2 ... Open
User Access Verification
Password:
R2> exit
[Connection to 2001:db8:acad:2::2 closed by foreign host]
R1#
```

The administrator has confirmed that Telnet is running on R2. Although the Telnet server application runs on its own well-known port number 23, and Telnet clients connect to this port by default, a different port number can be specified on the client to connect to any TCP port that must be tested. Using a different port other than TCP port 23 indicates whether the connection is accepted (as indicated by the word "Open" in the output), refused, or timed out. From any of those responses, further conclusions can be made concerning the connectivity. Certain applications, if they use an ASCII-based session protocol, might even display an application banner, and it might be possible to trigger some responses from the server by typing in certain keywords, such as with SMTP, FTP, and HTTP.

For example, the administrator attempts to Telnet to R2 using port 80, as shown in Example 12-26. The output verifies a successful transport layer connection, but R2 is refusing the connection using port 80.

Example 12-26 Verifying Transport Layer Connectivity to R2

```
R1# telnet 2001:db8:acad:2::2 80
Trying 2001:DB8:ACAD:2::2, 80 ... Open
^C
HTTP/1.1 400 Bad Request
Date: Mon, 04 Nov 2019 12:34:23 GMT
Server: cisco-IOS
Accept-Ranges: none
400 Bad Request
[Connection to 2001:db8:acad:2::2 closed by foreign host]
R1#
```

Step 7—Verify ACLs (12.5.11)

On routers, there may be ACLs that prohibit protocols from passing through the interface in the inbound direction or the outbound direction.

Use the **show ip access-lists** command to display the contents of all IPv4 ACLs and the **show ipv6 access-list** command to display the contents of all IPv6 ACLs configured on a router. The specific ACL can be displayed by entering the ACL name or number as an option for this command. The **show ip interfaces** and **show ipv6 interfaces** commands display IPv4 and IPv6 interface information that indicates whether any IP ACLs are set on the interface.

Troubleshooting Example

To prevent spoofing attacks, the network administrator decided to implement an ACL that is preventing devices with source network address 172.16.1.0/24 from entering the inbound S0/0/1 interface on R3, as shown in Figure 12-35. All other IP traffic should be allowed.

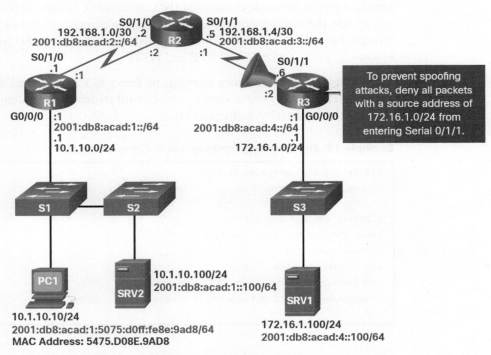

Figure 12-35   Reference Topology with ACL Placement Indicated

However, shortly after implementing the ACL, users on the 10.1.10.0/24 network are unable to connect to devices on the 172.16.1.0/24 network, including SRV1.

This section provides an example of how to troubleshoot this issue.

show ip access-lists

The **show ip access-lists** command output indicates that the ACL is configured correctly, as shown in Example 12-27.

Example 12-27   The **show ip access-lists** Command

```
R3# show ip access-lists
Extended IP access list 100
    10 deny ip 172.16.1.0 0.0.0.255 any (108 matches)
    20 permit ip any any (28 matches)
R3#
```

show ip interfaces

Next, the administrator verifies which interface has the ACL applied by using the **show ip interfaces serial 0/1/1** command and the **show ip interfaces serial 0/0/0** command. The output in Example 12-28 reveals that the ACL was never applied to the inbound interface on Serial 0/0/1, but it was accidentally applied to the G0/0/0 interface, and it is blocking all outbound traffic from the 172.16.1.0/24 network.

Example 12-28   The **show ip interfaces** Command

```
R3# show ip interface serial 0/1/1 | include access list
  Outgoing Common access list is not set
  Outgoing access list is not set
  Inbound Common access list is not set
  Inbound  access list is not set
R3#
R3# show ip interface gig 0/0/0 | include access list
  Outgoing Common access list is not set
  Outgoing access list is not set
  Inbound Common access list is not set
  Inbound  access list is 100
R3#
```

Correct the Issue

After correctly placing the IPv4 ACL on the Serial 0/0/1 inbound interface, as shown in Example 12-29 output, devices can successfully connect to the server.

Example 12-29   Correcting the Issue

```
R3(config)# interface GigabitEthernet 0/0/0
R3(config-if)# no ip access-group 100 in
R3(config-if)# exit
R3(config)#
R3(config)# interface serial 0/1/1
R3(config-if)# ip access-group 100 in
R3(config-if)# end
R3#
```

Step 8—Verify DNS (12.5.12)

The DNS protocol controls DNS, a distributed database with which you can map hostnames to IP addresses. When you configure DNS on a device, you can substitute the hostname for the IP address with all IP commands, such as **ping** or **telnet**.

To display the DNS configuration information on a switch or router, use the **show running-config** command. When there is no DNS server installed, it is possible to enter name-to-IP address mappings directly into the switch or router configuration. Use the **ip host** command to enter a name to be used instead of the IPv4 address of the switch or router, as shown in Example 12-30.

Example 12-30   Configuring a Name-to-IP Address Mapping

```
R1(config)# ip host ipv4-server 172.16.1.100
R1(config)# exit
R1#
```

Now the assigned name can be used instead of using the IP address, as shown in Example 12-31.

Example 12-31   Verifying **ping**s to the Hostname

```
R1# ping ipv4-server
Type escape sequence to abort.
Sending 5, 100-byte ICMP Echos to 172.16.1.100, timeout is 2 seconds:
!!!!!
Success rate is 100 percent (5/5), round-trip min/avg/max = 4/5/7 ms
R1#
```

To display the name-to-IP-address mapping information on a Windows-based PC, use the **nslookup** command.

Packet Tracer—Troubleshoot Enterprise Networks (12.5.13)

This activity uses a variety of technologies you have encountered during your CCNA studies, including routing, port security, EtherChannel, DHCP, and NAT. Your task is to review the requirements, isolate and resolve any issues, and then document the steps you took to verify the requirements.

Summary (12.6)

The following is a summary of the sections in this chapter.

Network Documentation

Common network documentation includes physical and logical network topologies, network device documentation recording all pertinent device information, and network performance baseline documentation. Information included on a physical topology typically includes the device name, device location (address, room number, rack location, and so on), interface and ports used, and cable type. Network device documentation for a router may include the interface, IPv4 address, IPv6 address, MAC address, and routing protocol. Network device documentation for a switch may include the port, access, VLAN, trunk, EtherChannel, native, and enabled. Network device documentation for end systems may include device name, OS, services, MAC address, IPv4 and IPv6 addresses, default gateway, and DNS. A network baseline should answer the following questions:

- How does the network perform during a normal or average day?

- Where are the most errors occurring?

- What part of the network is most heavily used?

- What part of the network is least used?

- Which devices should be monitored, and what alert thresholds should be set?

- Can the network meet the identified policies?

When conducting the initial baseline, start by selecting a few variables that represent the defined policies, such as interface utilization and CPU utilization. A logical network topology diagram can be useful in identifying key devices and ports to monitor. The length of time and the baseline information being gathered must be long enough to determine a "normal" picture of the network. When documenting the network, gather information directly from routers and switches by using the **show**, **ping**, **traceroute**, and **telnet** commands.

Troubleshooting Process

The troubleshooting process should be guided by structured methods. One method is the seven-step troubleshooting process: (1) Define the problem, (2) gather information, (3) analyze information, (4) eliminate possible causes, (5) propose a hypothesis, (6) test the hypothesis, and (7) solve the problem. When talking to end users about their network problems, ask both open and closed-ended questions. Use the **show**, **ping**, **traceroute**, and **telnet** commands to gather information from devices. Use the layered models to perform bottom-up, top-down, or divide-and-conquer troubleshooting. Other models include follow-the-path, substitution, comparison, and educated guess. Software problems are often solved using a top-down approach, while hardware-based problems are often solved using the bottom-up approach. An experienced technician may solve new problems by using the divide-and-conquer method.

Troubleshooting Tools

Common software troubleshooting tools include NMS tools, knowledge bases, and baselining tools. A protocol analyzer, such as Wireshark, decodes the various protocol layers in a recorded frame and presents this information in an easy-to-use format. Hardware troubleshooting tools include digital multimeters, cable testers, cable analyzers, portable network analyzers, and Cisco Prime NAM. A syslog server can also be used as a troubleshooting tool. With a logging facility for network troubleshooting, Cisco devices can log information regarding configuration changes, ACL violations, interface status, and many other types of events. Event messages can be sent to one or more of the following: console, terminal lines, buffered logging, SNMP traps, and syslog. The lower the level number, the higher the severity level. The **logging trap** *level* command (where *level* is the name or number of the severity level) limits messages logged to the syslog server based on severity. Only messages equal to or numerically lower than the specified level are logged.

Symptoms and Causes of Network Problems

Failures and suboptimal conditions at the physical layer usually cause networks to shut down. Network administrators must be able to effectively isolate and correct problems at this layer. Symptoms include performance lower than baseline, loss of connectivity, congestion, high CPU utilization, and console error messages. The causes are usually power related, hardware faults, cabling faults, attenuation, noise, interface configuration errors, exceeding component design limits, and CPU overload.

Data link layer problems cause specific symptoms that, when recognized, can help identify the problem quickly. Symptoms include no functionality/connectivity at Layer 2 or above, network operating below baseline levels, excessive broadcasts, and console messages. The causes are usually encapsulation errors, address mapping errors, framing errors, and STP failures or loops.

Network layer problems include any problem that involves a Layer 3 protocol, both routed protocols (such as IPv4 or IPv6) and routing protocols (such as EIGRP or OSPF). Symptoms include network failure and suboptimal performance. The causes are usually general network issues, connectivity issues, routing table problems, neighbor issues, and the topology database.

Transport layer problems can arise from transport layer problems on the router, particularly at the edge of the network, where traffic is examined and modified. Symptoms include connectivity and access issues. Causes are likely to be misconfigured NAT or ACLs. ACL misconfigurations commonly occur at the selection of traffic flow, order of access control entries, implicit deny any, addresses and IPv4 wildcard masks, selection of transport layer protocol, source and destination ports, use of the **established** keyword, and uncommon protocols. There are several problems with NAT, including misconfigured NAT inside, NAT outside, or ACL. Common interoperability areas with NAT include BOOTP and DHCP, DNS, SNMP, and tunneling and encryption protocols.

Application layer problems can result in unreachable or unusable resources when the physical, data link, network, and transport layers are functional. It is possible to have full network connectivity but still see an application be unable to provide data. Another type of problem at the application layer occurs when the physical, data link, network, and transport layers are functional, but the data transfer and requests for network services from a single network service or application do not meet the normal expectations of a user.

Troubleshooting IP Connectivity

Diagnosing and solving problems is an essential skill for network administrators. There is no single recipe for troubleshooting, and a problem can be diagnosed in many ways. However, by employing a structured approach to the troubleshooting process, an administrator can reduce the time it takes to diagnose and solve a problem.

End-to-end connectivity problems typically prompt troubleshooting efforts. Two of the utilities most commonly used to verify problems with end-to-end connectivity are **ping** and **traceroute**. The **ping** command uses a Layer 3 protocol called ICMP that is a part of the TCP/IP suite. The **traceroute** command is commonly used when the **ping** command fails.

Follow these steps when troubleshooting IP connectivity problems:

Step 1.   Verify the physical layer. The Cisco IOS commands most commonly used for this purpose are **show processes cpu**, **show memory**, and **show interfaces**.

Step 2.   Check for duplex mismatches. A common cause of interface errors is mismatched duplex mode between two ends of an Ethernet link. In many Ethernet-based networks, point-to-point connections are now the norm, and the use of hubs and the associated half-duplex operation is becoming less common. Use the **show interfaces** *interface* command to diagnose this problem.

Step 3.   Verify addressing on the local network. When troubleshooting end-to-end connectivity, it is useful to verify mappings between destination IP addresses and Layer 2 Ethernet addresses on individual segments. The **arp** Windows command displays and modifies entries in the ARP cache that are used to store IPv4 addresses and their resolved Ethernet physical (MAC) addresses. The output of the **netsh interface ipv6 show neighbor** Windows command lists all devices that are currently in the neighbor table. The **show ipv6 neighbors** command output displays an example of the neighbor table on a Cisco IOS router. Use the **show mac address-table** command to display the MAC address table on a switch.

VLAN assignment is another issue to consider when troubleshooting end-to-end connectivity. On a host, use the **arp** Windows command to see the entry for a default gateway. On a switch, use the **show mac address-table** command to check the switch MAC table and confirm that the port VLAN assignment is correct.

Step 4.   Verify the default gateway. The **show ip route** Cisco IOS command is used to verify the default gateway of a router. On a Windows host, the **route print** Windows command is used to verify the presence of the IPv4 default gateway.

In IPv6, the default gateway can be configured manually, by using stateless address autoconfiguration (SLAAC) or by using DHCPv6. The **show ipv6 route** Cisco IOS command is used to check for the IPv6 default route on a router. The **ipconfig** Windows command is used to verify whether a PC has an IPv6 default gateway. The command output of the **show ipv6 interface** *interface* command indicates whether a router is enabled as an IPv6 router. Enable a router as an IPv6 router by using the **ipv6 unicast-routing** command. To verify that a host has the default gateway set, use the **ipconfig** command on a Microsoft Windows PC or the **ifconfig** command on Linux or Mac OS X.

Step 5.   Verify the correct path. The routers in the path make routing decisions based on information in the routing tables. Use the **show ip route | begin Gateway** command for an IPv4 routing table. Use the **show ipv6 route** command for an IPv6 routing table.

Step 6.   Verify the transport layer. Two of the issues that most commonly affect transport layer connectivity are ACL configurations and NAT configurations. A common tool for testing transport layer functionality is the Telnet utility.

Step 7.   Verify ACLs. Use the **show ip access-lists** command to display the contents of all IPv4 ACLs and the **show ipv6 access-list** command to show the contents of all IPv6 ACLs configured on a router. Verify which interface has an ACL applied by using the **show ip interfaces** command.

Step 8.   Verify DNS. To display the DNS configuration information on a switch or router, use the **show running-config** command. Use the **ip host** command to enter a name-to-IPv4 address mapping in the switch or router.

Packet Tracer—Troubleshooting Challenge—Document the Network (12.6.1)

In this Packet Tracer activity, you document a network that is unknown to you:

- Test network connectivity.
- Compile host addressing information.
- Remotely access default gateway devices.
- Document default gateway device configurations.
- Discover devices on the network.
- Draw the network topology.

Packet Tracer—Troubleshooting Challenge—Use Documentation to Solve Issues (12.6.2)

In this Packet Tracer activity, you use network documentation to identify and fix network communications problems:

- Use various techniques and tools to identify connectivity issues.
- Use documentation to guide troubleshooting efforts.
- Identify specific network problems.
- Implement solutions to network communication problems.
- Verify network operation.

Practice

The following Packet Tracer activities provide practice with the topics introduced in this chapter. The instructions are available in the companion *Enterprise Networking, Security, and Automation Labs & Study Guide (CCNAv7)* (ISBN 9780136634324). There are no labs for this chapter.

Packet Tracer Activities

Packet Tracer 12.5.13: Troubleshoot Enterprise Networks

Packet Tracer 12.6.1: Troubleshooting Challenge—Document the Network

Packet Tracer 12.6.2: Troubleshooting Challenge—Use Documentation to Solve Issues

Check Your Understanding Questions

Complete all the review questions listed here to test your understanding of the topics and concepts in this chapter. The appendix "Answers to the 'Check Your Understanding' Questions" lists the answers.

1. Which statement describes the physical topology for a LAN?

   A. It defines how hosts and network devices connect to the LAN.

   B. It depicts the addressing scheme that is used in the LAN.

   C. It describes whether the LAN is a broadcast or token-passing network.

   D. It shows the order in which hosts access the network.

2. When should a network performance baseline be measured?

   A. After normal work hours to reduce possible interruptions

   B. During normal work hours of an organization

   C. Immediately after the main network devices are restarted

   D. When a denial-of-service attack on the network is detected and blocked

3. In which step of gathering symptoms does a network engineer determine whether the problem is at the core, distribution, or access layer of the network?

   A. Determine ownership.

   B. Determine the symptoms.

   C. Document the symptoms.

   D. Gather information.

   E. Narrow the scope.

4. A network technician is troubleshooting an email connection problem. Which question to the end user will help the technician get clear information to better define the problem?

   A. How big are the emails you tried to send?

   B. Is your email working now?

   C. What kind of equipment are you using to send emails?

   D. When did you first notice your email problem?

5. A team of engineers has identified a solution to a significant network problem. The proposed solution is likely to affect critical network infrastructure components. What should the team follow while implementing the solution to avoid interfering with other processes and infrastructure?

   A. Change-control procedures

   B. Knowledge base guidelines

   C. One of the layered troubleshooting approaches

   D. Syslog messages and reports

6. A network engineer is troubleshooting a network problem and can successfully **ping** between two devices. However, Telnet between the same two devices does not work. Which OSI layers should the administrator investigate next?

   A. All the layers

   B. From the network layer to the application layer

   C. From the network layer to the physical layer

   D. Only the network layer

7. Which troubleshooting method begins by examining cable connections and wiring issues?

   A. Bottom-up troubleshooting

   B. Divide-and-conquer troubleshooting

   C. Substitution troubleshooting

   D. Top-down troubleshooting

8. An administrator is troubleshooting an Internet connectivity problem on a router. The output of the **show interfaces gigabitethernet 0/0** command reveals higher-than-normal framing errors on the interface that connects to the Internet. At what layer of the OSI model is the problem likely occurring?

   A. Layer 1

   B. Layer 2

   C. Layer 3

   D. Layer 4

   E. Layer 7

9. Users report that the new website http://www.company1.biz cannot be accessed. The help desk technician checks and verifies that the website can be accessed with http://www.company1.biz:90. Which layer in the TCP/IP model is involved in troubleshooting this issue?

   A. Application

   B. Internet

   C. Network access

   D. Transport

10. A user reports that after an OS patch of the networking subsystem has been applied to a workstation, the workstation performs very slowly when connecting to network resources. A network technician tests the link with a cable analyzer and notices that the workstation sends an excessive number of frames smaller than 64 bytes and also other meaningless frames. What is the possible cause of the problem?

    A. Cabling faults

    B. Corrupted application installation

    C. Corrupted NIC driver

    D. Ethernet signal attenuation

11. A networked PC is having trouble accessing the Internet, but it can print to a local printer and **ping** other computers in the area. Other computers on the same network are not having any issues. What is the problem?

    A. The default gateway router does not have a default route.

    B. The link between the switch to which the PC connects and the default gateway router is down.

    C. The PC has a missing or incorrect default gateway.

    D. The switch port to which the PC connects has an incorrect VLAN configured.

12. Which three pieces of information are typically recorded in a logical topology diagram? (Choose three.)

A. Cable specifications

B. Device locations

C. Device models and manufacturers

D. IP addresses and prefix lengths

E. Routing protocols

F. Static routes

13. A company is setting up a website with SSL technology to protect the authentication credentials required to access the website. A network engineer needs to verify that the setup is correct and that the authentication is indeed encrypted. Which tool should be used?

A. Baselining tool

B. Cable analyzer

C. Fault-management tool

D. Protocol analyzer

14. Which number represents the most severe level of syslog logging?

A. 0

B. 1

C. 6

D. 7

CHAPTER 13

Network Virtualization

Objectives

Upon completion of this chapter, you will be able to answer the following questions:

- What is the importance of cloud computing?
- What is the importance of virtualization?
- What is virtualization of network devices and services?
- What is software-defined networking?
- What controllers are used in network programming?

Key Terms

This chapter uses the following key terms. You can find the definitions in the Glossary.

Introduction (13.0)

Imagine that you live in a two-bedroom house. You use the second bedroom for storage. The second bedroom is packed full of boxes, but you still have more to place in storage! You could consider building an addition on your house. It would be a costly endeavor, and you might not need that extra space forever. You decide to rent a storage unit for the overflow.

Similar to a storage unit, *network virtualization* and cloud services can provide a business with options other than adding servers into their own *data center*. In addition to storage, virtualization offers other advantages. Get started with this chapter to learn more about what *virtualization* and cloud services can do!

Cloud Computing (13.1)

In this section, you will learn the importance of cloud computing.

Video—Cloud and Virtualization (13.1.1)

Video

Refer to the online course to view this video.

Cloud Overview (13.1.2)

Cloud computing involves large numbers of computers connected through a network that can be physically located anywhere. Providers rely heavily on virtualization to deliver their cloud computing services. Cloud computing can reduce operational costs by using resources more efficiently. Cloud computing addresses a variety of data management issues by doing the following:

- Enabling access to organizational data anywhere and at any time
- Streamlining the organization's IT operations by allowing the organization to subscribe only to needed services
- Eliminating or reducing the need for onsite IT equipment, maintenance, and management
- Reducing costs for equipment, energy, physical plant requirements, and personnel training needs
- Enabling rapid responses to increasing data volume requirements

Cloud computing, with its "pay-as-you-go" model, allows organizations to treat computing and storage expenses as a utility rather than investing in infrastructure. It enables an organization to transform capital expenditures into operating expenditures.

Cloud Services (13.1.3)

Cloud services are available in a variety of options, tailored to meet customer requirements. The three main cloud computing services defined by the *National Institute of Standards and Technology (NIST)* in Special Publication 800-145 are as follows:

- *Software as a service (SaaS)*: The cloud provider is responsible for access to applications and services (such as email, communication, and Office 365) that are delivered over the internet. The user does not manage any aspect of the cloud services except for limited user-specific application settings. The user only needs to provide the data.

- *Platform as a service (PaaS)*: The cloud provider is responsible for providing users access to the development tools and services used to deliver the applications. These users are typically programmers and may have control over the configuration settings of the cloud provider's application-hosting environment.

- *Infrastructure as a service (IaaS)*: The cloud provider is responsible for giving IT managers access to network equipment, virtualized network services, and supporting network infrastructure. Using this cloud service allows IT managers to deploy and run software code, which can include operating systems and applications.

Cloud service providers have extended this model to also provide IT support for each of the cloud computing services. For businesses, *IT as a service (ITaaS)* can extend the capability of the network without requiring investment in new infrastructure, training of new personnel, or licensing of new software. These services are available on demand and delivered economically to any device anywhere in the world, without compromising security or function.

Cloud Models (13.1.4)

There are four primary cloud models.

- *Public cloud*: Cloud-based applications and services offered in a public cloud are made available to the general population. Services may be free or are offered on a pay-per-use model, such as paying for online storage. A public cloud uses the internet to provide services.

- *Private cloud*: Cloud-based applications and services offered in a private cloud are intended for a specific organization or entity, such as the government. A private cloud can be set up using the organization's private network, although this can be expensive to build and maintain. A private cloud can also be managed by an outside organization with strict access security.

- *Hybrid cloud*: A hybrid cloud is made up of two or more clouds (for example, part private and part public), where each part remains a separate object but the two are connected using a single architecture. Individuals on a hybrid cloud would be able to have degrees of access to various services, based on user access rights.

- *Community cloud*: A community cloud is created for exclusive use by a specific community. The differences between public clouds and community clouds are the functional needs that have been customized for the community. For example, healthcare organizations must remain compliant with policies and laws (such as HIPAA) that require special authentication and confidentiality.

Cloud Computing Versus Data Center (13.1.5)

The terms *data center* and *cloud computing* are often used incorrectly. These are the correct definitions of the two terms:

- **Data center:** Typically, a data storage and processing facility run by an in-house IT department or leased offsite.

- **Cloud computing:** Typically, an off-premises service that offers on-demand access to a shared pool of configurable computing resources. These resources can be rapidly provisioned and released with minimal management effort.

Data centers are physical facilities that provide the compute, network, and storage needs of cloud computing services. Cloud service providers use data centers to host their cloud services and cloud-based resources.

A data center can occupy one room of a building, one or more floors, or an entire building. Data centers are typically very expensive to build and maintain. For this reason, only large organizations use privately built data centers to house their data and provide services to users. Smaller organizations that cannot afford to maintain their own private data centers can reduce the overall cost of ownership by leasing cloud-based server and storage services from a larger data center organization.

Interactive Graphic

Check Your Understanding—Cloud Computing (13.1.6)

Refer to the online course to complete this activity.

Virtualization (13.2)

In this section, you will learn the importance of virtualization.

Cloud Computing and Virtualization (13.2.1)

In the previous section, you learned about cloud services and cloud models. This section explains virtualization. The terms *cloud computing* and *virtualization* are often used interchangeably; however, they mean different things. Virtualization is the foundation of cloud computing. Without it, cloud computing, as it is most widely implemented, would not be possible.

Virtualization separates the operating system (OS) from the hardware. Various providers offer virtual cloud services that can dynamically provision servers as required. For example, *Amazon Web Services (AWS)* provides a simple way for customers to dynamically provision the compute resources needed. These virtualized instances of servers are created on demand. As shown in Figure 13-1, a network administrator can deploy a variety of services from the AWS Management Console, including *virtual machines (VMs)*, web applications, virtual servers, and connections to *Internet of Things (IoT)* devices.

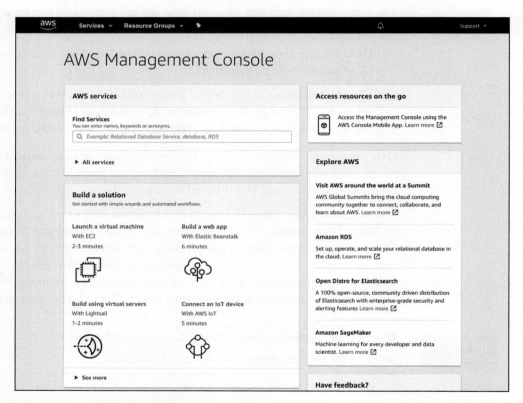

Figure 13-1   AWS Management Console

Dedicated Servers (13.2.2)

To fully appreciate virtualization, it is necessary to understand some of the history of server technology. Historically, enterprise servers consisted of a server OS, such as Windows Server or Linux Server, installed on specific hardware, as shown in Figure 13-2.

Figure 13-2   Examples of Dedicated Servers

All of a server's RAM, processing power, and hard drive space were dedicated to the service provided (for example, web services, email services). The major problem with such a configuration is that when a component fails, the service that is provided by this server becomes unavailable. This is known as a single point of failure. Another problem is that dedicated servers can be underused. Dedicated servers often sit idle for long periods of time, waiting until there is a need to deliver the specific service they provide. These servers waste energy and take up more space than is warranted by the service provided. This is known as *server sprawl*.

Server Virtualization (13.2.3)

Server virtualization takes advantage of idle resources and consolidates the number of required servers. This also allows for multiple operating systems to exist on a single hardware platform.

For example, in Figure 13-3, the eight dedicated servers shown in Figure 13-2 have been consolidated into two servers by using *hypervisors* to support multiple virtual instances of the operating systems.

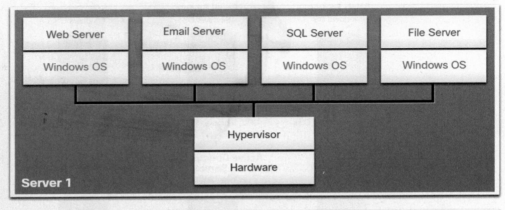

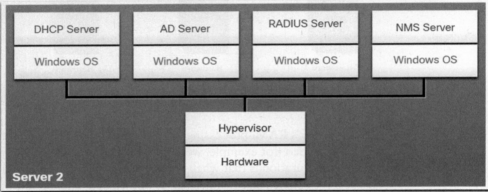

Figure 13-3   Examples of Server Virtualization

The use of virtualization normally includes redundancy to prevent single points of failure. Redundancy can be implemented in different ways. If the hypervisor fails, the VM can be restarted on another hypervisor. Also, the same VM can run on two hypervisors concurrently, copying the RAM and CPU instructions between them. If one hypervisor fails, the VM continues running on the other hypervisor. The services running on the VMs are also virtual and can be dynamically installed or uninstalled, as needed.

The hypervisor is a program, firmware, or hardware that adds an *abstraction layer* on top of the physical hardware. The abstraction layer is used to create virtual machines that have access to all the hardware of the physical machine, such as CPUs, memory, disk controllers, and NICs. Each of these virtual machines runs a complete and separate operating system. With virtualization, enterprises can now consolidate the number of servers required. For example, it is not uncommon for 100 physical servers to be consolidated as virtual machines on top of 10 physical servers that are using hypervisors.

Advantages of Virtualization (13.2.4)

One major advantage of virtualization is overall reduced cost, thanks to several factors:

- **Less equipment is required:** Virtualization enables server consolidation, requiring fewer physical servers, fewer networking devices, and less supporting infrastructure. It also means lower maintenance costs.

- **Less energy is consumed:** Consolidating servers lowers the monthly power and cooling costs. Reduced consumption helps enterprises achieve a smaller carbon footprint.

- **Less space is required:** Server consolidation with virtualization reduces the overall footprint of a data center. Fewer servers, network devices, and racks reduce the amount of floor space required.

These are additional benefits of virtualization:

- **Easier prototyping:** Self-contained labs, operating on isolated networks, can be rapidly created for testing and prototyping network deployments. If a mistake is made, an administrator can simply revert to a previous version. The testing environments can be online but isolated from end users. When testing is complete, the servers and systems can be deployed to end users.

- **Faster server provisioning:** Creating a virtual server is far faster than provisioning a physical server.

- **Increased server uptime:** Most server virtualization platforms now offer advanced redundant fault-tolerance features, such as live migration, storage migration, high availability, and distributed resource scheduling.

- **Improved disaster recovery:** Virtualization offers advanced business continuity solutions. It provides hardware abstraction capability so that the recovery site no longer needs to have hardware that is identical to the hardware in the production environment. Most enterprise server virtualization platforms also have software that can help test and automate the failover before a disaster does happen.

- **Legacy support:** Virtualization can extend the life of OSs and applications, providing more time for organizations to migrate to newer solutions.

Abstraction Layers (13.2.5)

It is useful to use layers of abstraction in computer architectures to help explain how virtualization works. A computer system consists of the abstraction layers illustrated in Figure 13-4.

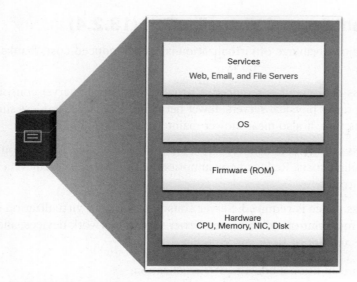

Figure 13-4 Computer Abstraction Layers

At each of these layers of abstraction, some type of programming code is used as an interface between the layer below and the layer above. For example, the C programming language is often used to program the firmware that accesses the hardware.

An example of virtualization is shown in Figure 13-5. A hypervisor is installed between the firmware and the OS. The hypervisor can support multiple instances of OSs.

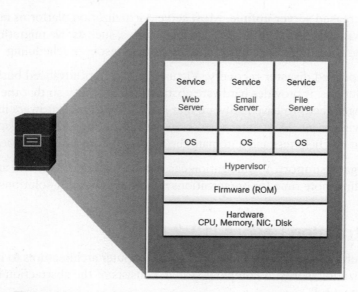

Figure 13-5 Computer with Multiple Virtualized OSs Installed

Type 2 Hypervisors (13.2.6)

A *Type 2 hypervisor* is software that creates and runs VM instances. The computer on which a hypervisor is supporting one or more VMs is a host machine. A Type 2 hypervisor is also called a hosted hypervisor because the hypervisor is installed on top of the existing host OS, such as macOS, Windows, or Linux. One or more additional guest OS instances are installed on top of the hypervisor, as shown in Figure 13-6.

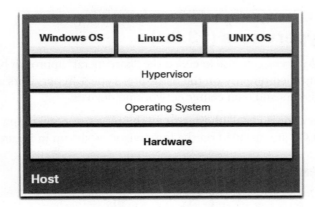

Figure 13-6   Example of a Type 2 Hypervisor

A big advantage of Type 2 hypervisors is that management console software is not required.

Type 2 hypervisors are very popular with consumers and with organizations experimenting with virtualization. Common Type 2 hypervisors include:

- Virtual PC
- VMware Workstation
- Oracle VM VirtualBox
- VMware Fusion
- Mac OS X Parallels

Many of these Type 2 hypervisors are free. However, some hypervisors offer more advanced features for a fee.

Note

It is important to make sure that a host machine is robust enough to install and run the VMs and not run out of resources.

Check Your Understanding—Virtualization (13.2.7)

Refer to the online course to complete this activity.

Virtual Network Infrastructure (13.3)

In the previous section, you learned about virtualization. This section covers the virtual network infrastructure.

Type 1 Hypervisors (13.3.1)

Using *Type 1 hypervisors* is also called the "bare metal" approach because the hypervisor is installed directly on the hardware. Type 1 hypervisors are usually used on enterprise servers and data center networking devices.

A Type 1 hypervisor is installed directly on the server or networking hardware. Instances of an OS are installed on the hypervisor, as shown in Figure 13-7.

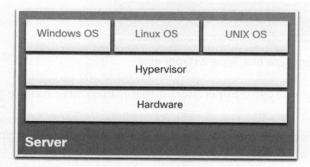

Figure 13-7   Example of a Type 1 Hypervisor

Type 1 hypervisors have direct access to the hardware resources. Therefore, they are more efficient than hosted architectures. Type 1 hypervisors improve scalability, performance, and robustness.

Installing a VM on a Hypervisor (13.3.2)

When a Type 1 hypervisor is installed and the server is rebooted, only basic information is displayed, such as the OS version, the amount of RAM, and the IP address. An OS instance cannot be created from this screen. Type 1 hypervisors require a "management console" to manage the hypervisor. Management software is used to manage multiple servers using the same hypervisor. The management console can automatically consolidate servers and power on or off servers as required.

For example, say that Server 1 in Figure 13-8 becomes low on resources.

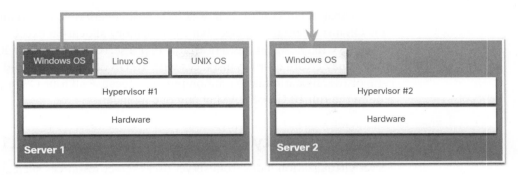

Figure 13-8   Moving a VM to Another Hardware Server

To make more resources available, the network administrator can use the management console to move the Windows instance to the hypervisor on Server 2. The management console can also be programmed with thresholds that can trigger the move automatically.

The management console enables recovery from hardware failure. If a server component fails, the management console automatically moves the VM to another server. The management console for the *Cisco Unified Computing System (UCS)* is shown in Figure 13-9. *Cisco UCS Manager* controls multiple servers and manages resources for thousands of VMs.

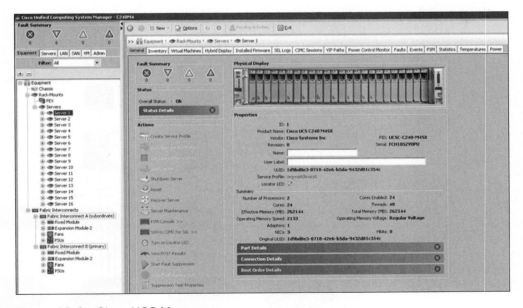

Figure 13-9   Cisco UCS Manager

Some management consoles allow server overallocation. With overallocation, multiple OS instances are installed, but their memory allocation exceeds the total amount of memory that a server has. For example, if a server has 16 GB of RAM, the administrator may create four OS instances with 10 GB of RAM allocated to each. This type of overallocation is a common practice because all four OS instances rarely require the full 10 GB of RAM at any one moment.

The Complexity of Network Virtualization (13.3.3)

Server virtualization hides from server users server resources such as the number and identity of physical servers, processors, and OSs. This practice can create problems if the data center is using traditional network architectures.

For example, virtual LANs (VLANs) used by VMs must be assigned to the same switchport as the physical server running the hypervisor. However, VMs are movable, and the network administrator must be able to add, drop, and change network resources and profiles. This process would be manual and time-consuming with traditional network switches.

Another problem is that traffic flows differ substantially from those in the traditional client/server model. Typically, a data center has a considerable amount of traffic being exchanged between virtual servers, such as the UCS servers shown in Figure 13-10.

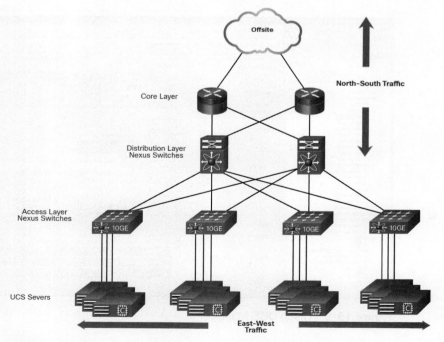

Figure 13-10   Example of North–South and East–West Traffic

These flows are called *east–west traffic* and can change in location and intensity over time. *North–south traffic* occurs between the distribution and core layers and is typically traffic destined for offsite locations such as another data center, other cloud providers, or the internet.

Dynamic ever-changing traffic requires a flexible approach to network resource management. Existing network infrastructures can respond to changing requirements related to the management of traffic flows by using quality of service (QoS) and security level configurations for individual flows. However, in large enterprises using multivendor equipment, each time a new VM is enabled, the necessary reconfiguration can be very time-consuming.

The network infrastructure can also benefit from virtualization. Network functions can be virtualized. Each network device can be segmented into multiple virtual devices that operate as independent devices. Examples include subinterfaces, virtual interfaces, VLANs, and routing tables. Virtualized routing is called *virtual routing and forwarding (VRF)*.

How is the network virtualized? The answer is found in how a networking device operates using a *data plane* and a *control plane*, as discussed in the next section.

Interactive Graphic

Check Your Understanding—Virtual Network Infrastructure (13.3.4)

Refer to the online course to complete this activity.

Software-Defined Networking (13.4)

The previous section explains virtual network infrastructure. This section covers *software-defined networking (SDN)*.

Video

Video—Software-Defined Networking (13.4.1)

Refer to the online course to view this video.

Control Plane and Data Plane (13.4.2)

A network device contains the following planes:

- **Control plane:** This is typically regarded as the brains of a device. It is used to make forwarding decisions. The control plane contains Layer 2 and Layer 3 route forwarding mechanisms, such as routing protocol neighbor tables and topology tables, IPv4 and IPv6 routing tables, STP, and the ARP table. Information sent to the control plane is processed by the CPU.

- **Data plane:** Also called the forwarding plane, this plane is typically the switch fabric connecting the various network ports on a device. The data plane of each device is used to forward traffic flows. Routers and switches use information from the control plane to forward incoming traffic out the appropriate egress interface. Information in the data plane is typically processed by a special data plane processor, without the CPU getting involved.

The following explains the differences between the operation of localized control on a Layer 3 switch and a centralized controller in SDN.

Layer 3 Switch and CEF

Figure 13-11 illustrates how *Cisco Express Forwarding (CEF)* uses the control plane and data plane to process packets.

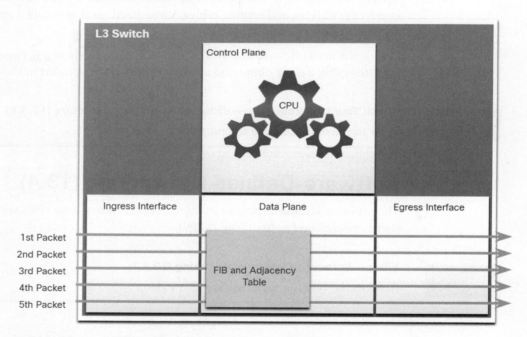

Figure 13-11   Illustration of Layer 3 Switch with CEF

CEF is an advanced Layer 3 IP switching technology that enables forwarding of packets to occur at the data plane without consulting the control plane. In CEF, the control plane's routing table prepopulates the CEF *Forwarding Information Base (FIB)* table in the data plane. The control plane's ARP table prepopulates the *adjacency table*. The data plane then forwards packets directly, based on the information contained in the FIB and adjacency table, without needing to consult the information in the control plane.

SDN and Central Controller

SDN basically involves the separation of the control plane and data plane. The control plane function is removed from each device and is performed by a centralized controller. The centralized controller communicates control plane functions to each device. Each device can then focus on forwarding data while the centralized controller manages data flow, increases security, and provides other services.

Figure 13-12 illustrates a centralized control plane communicating control plane functions to each device.

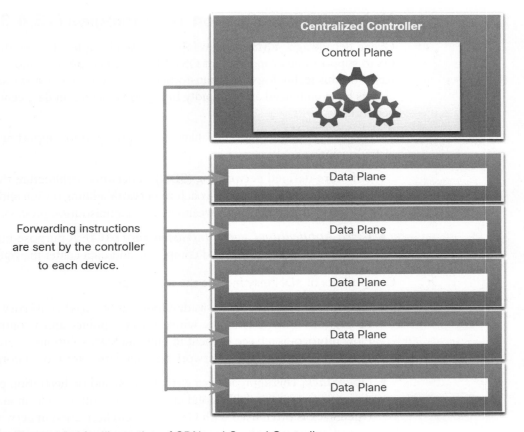

Figure 13-12 Illustration of SDN and Central Controller

At the top of the figure is the centralized control plane controller. There are arrows pointing from the control plane to five data planes. Forwarding instructions are sent by the controller to each device.

Management Plane

The *management plane* (which is not shown in the figures) is responsible for managing a device through its connection to the network. Network administrators use applications such as Secure Shell (SSH), Trivial File Transfer Protocol (TFTP), Secure FTP, and Secure Hypertext Transfer Protocol (HTTPS) to access the management plane and configure a device. In your networking studies, you have used the management plane to access and configure devices. In addition, protocols such as Simple Network Management Protocol (SNMP) use the management plane.

Network Virtualization Technologies (13.4.3)

Over a decade ago, *VMware* developed a virtualizing technology that enables a host OS to support one or more client OSs. Most virtualization technologies are now based on this technology. The transformation of dedicated servers to virtualized servers has been embraced and is rapidly being implemented in data center and enterprise networks.

Two major network architectures have been developed to support network virtualization:

- **Software-defined networking (SDN):** A network architecture that virtualizes the network, offering a new approach to network administration and management that seeks to simplify and streamline the administration process.

- *Cisco Application Centric Infrastructure (ACI)*: A purpose-built hardware solution for integrating cloud computing and data center management.

Components of SDN may include the following:

- *OpenFlow*: This approach was developed at Stanford University to manage traffic between routers, switches, wireless access points, and a controller. The OpenFlow protocol is a basic element in building SDN solutions. Search online for OpenFlow and the Open Networking Foundation for more information.

- *OpenStack*: This approach is a virtualization and orchestration platform designed to build scalable cloud environments and provide an IaaS solution. OpenStack is often used with Cisco ACI. Orchestration in networking is the process of automating the provisioning of network components such as servers, storage, switches, routers, and applications. Search online for OpenStack for more information.

- **Other components:** Other components include Interface to the Routing System (I2RS), Transparent Interconnection of Lots of Links (TRILL), Cisco FabricPath (FP), and IEEE 802.1aq Shortest Path Bridging (SPB).

Traditional and SDN Architectures (13.4.4)

In a traditional router or switch architecture, the control plane and data plane functions occur in the same device. Routing decisions and packet forwarding are the responsibility of the device operating system. In SDN, management of the control plane is moved to a centralized *SDN controller*. Figure 13-13 compares traditional and SDN architectures.

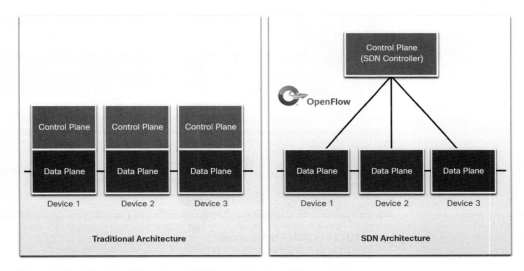

Figure 13-13   Traditional and SDN Architecture Comparison

An SDN controller is a logical entity that enables network administrators to manage and dictate how the data plane of switches and routers should handle network traffic. It orchestrates, mediates, and facilitates communication between applications and network elements.

The complete SDN framework is shown in Figure 13-14.

Note the use of *application programming interfaces (APIs)* in the SDN framework. An API is a set of standardized requests that define the proper way for an application to request services from another application.

An SDN controller uses *northbound APIs* to communicate with the upstream applications. These APIs help network administrators shape traffic and deploy services. An SDN controller also uses *southbound APIs* to define the behavior of the data planes on downstream switches and routers. OpenFlow is the original and widely implemented southbound API.

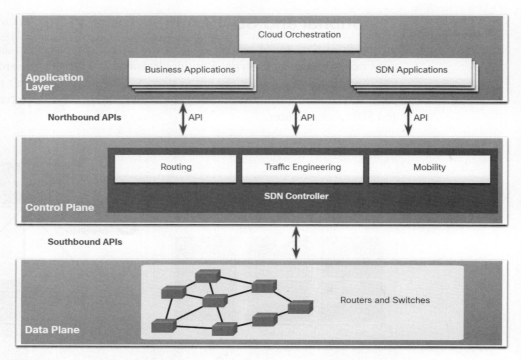

Figure 13-14   SDN Framework

Interactive Graphic

Check Your Understanding—Software-Defined Networking (13.4.5)

Refer to the online course to complete this activity.

Controllers (13.5)

The previous section covers SDN. This section explains SDN controllers.

SDN Controller and Operations (13.5.1)

An SDN controller defines the data flows between the centralized control plane and the data planes on individual routers and switches.

Each flow traveling through a network must first get permission from the SDN controller, which verifies that the communication is permissible according to the network policy. If the controller allows a flow, it computes a route for the flow to take and adds an entry for that flow in each of the switches along the path.

All complex functions are performed by the controller. The controller populates flow tables. Switches manage the flow tables. In Figure 13-15, an SDN controller communicates with OpenFlow-compatible switches using the OpenFlow protocol.

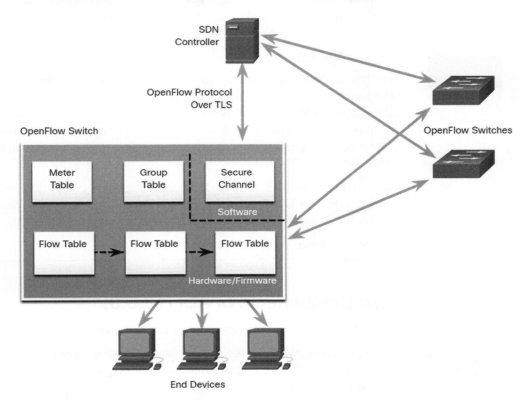

Figure 13-15   Example of SDN Controller Operations

OpenFlow uses Transport Layer Security (TLS) to securely send control plane communications over the network. Each OpenFlow switch connects to other OpenFlow switches. These switches can also connect to end-user devices that are part of a packet flow.

Within each switch, a series of tables implemented in hardware or firmware are used to manage the flows of packets through the switch. To the switch, a flow is a sequence of packets that matches a specific entry in a flow table.

Three tables types are shown in Figure 13-15:

- *Flow table*: This table matches incoming packets to a particular flow and specifies the functions that are to be performed on the packets. There may be multiple flow tables operating in a pipeline fashion.

- *Group table*: A flow table may direct a flow to a group table, which may trigger a variety of actions that affect one or more flows.

- *Meter table*: This table triggers a variety of performance-related actions on a flow, including the ability to rate limit the traffic.

Video

Video—Cisco ACI (13.5.2)

Very few organizations actually have the desire or skill to program a network using SDN tools. However, the majority of organizations want to automate their networks, accelerate application deployments, and align their IT infrastructures to better meet business requirements. Cisco developed the Application Centric Infrastructure (ACI) to meet these objectives in more advanced and innovative ways than earlier SDN approaches.

Cisco ACI is a hardware solution for integrating cloud computing and data center management. At a high level, the policy element of the network is removed from the data plane. This simplifies the way data center networks are created.

Refer to the online course to view this video.

Core Components of ACI (13.5.3)

These are the three core components of the ACI architecture:

- *Application Network Profile (ANP)*: An ANP is a collection of *endpoint groups (EPG)*, their connections, and the policies that define those connections. The EPGs, such as VLANs, web services, and applications, are just examples. An ANP is often much more complex.

- *Application Policy Infrastructure Controller (APIC)*: The APIC is considered the brains of the ACI architecture. An APIC is a centralized software controller that manages and operates a scalable ACI clustered fabric. It is designed for programmability and centralized management. It translates application policies into network programming.

- *Cisco Nexus 9000 Series switches*: These switches provide an application-aware switching fabric and work with an APIC to manage the virtual and physical network infrastructure.

An APIC is positioned between the APN and the ACI-enabled network infrastructure. The APIC translates the application requirements into a network configuration to meet those needs, as shown in Figure 13-16.

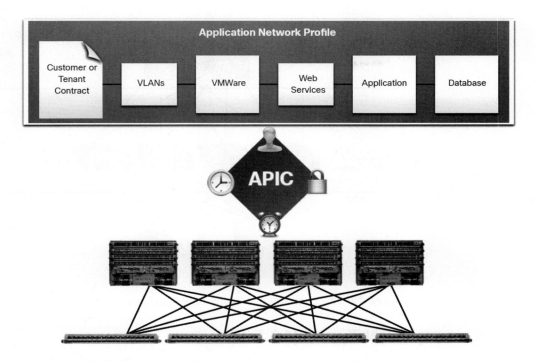

Figure 13-16   Example of APIC Operation

Spine-Leaf Topology (13.5.4)

The Cisco ACI fabric is composed of the APIC and the Cisco Nexus 9000 Series switches using two-tier *spine-leaf topology*, as shown in Figure 13-17.

The leaf switches always attach to the spines, but they never attach to each other. Similarly, the spine switches only attach to the leaf and core switches (not shown). In this two-tier topology, everything is one hop from everything else.

The Cisco APICs and all other devices in the network physically attach to leaf switches.

Unlike with SDN, the APIC controller does not manipulate the data path directly. Instead, the APIC centralizes the policy definition and programs the leaf switches to forward traffic based on the defined policies.

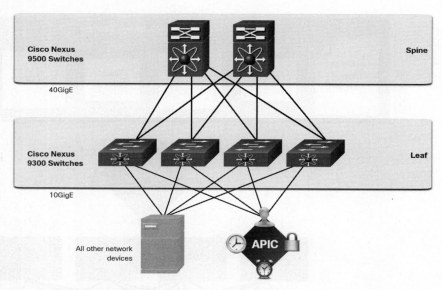

Figure 13-17   Example of a Spine-Leaf Topology

SDN Types (13.5.5)

The *Cisco Application Policy Infrastructure Controller—Enterprise Module (APIC-EM)* extends ACI aimed at enterprise and campus deployments. To better understand APIC-EM, it is helpful to take a broader look at the three types of SDN.

Device-Based SDN

In device-based SDN, the devices are programmable by applications running on the device itself or on a server in the network, as shown in Figure 13-18.

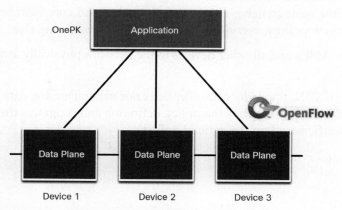

Figure 13-18   Device-Based SDN

Cisco OnePK is an example of a device-based SDN. It enables programmers to build applications using C and Java with Python to integrate and interact with Cisco devices.

Controller-Based SDN

A controller-based SDN uses a centralized controller that has knowledge of all devices in the network, as shown in Figure 13-19.

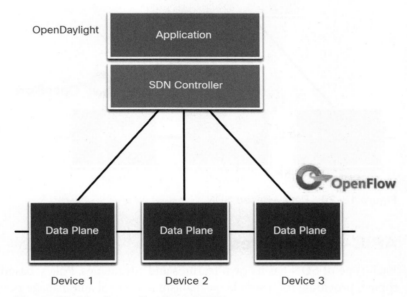

Figure 13-19   Controller-Based SDN

The applications can interface with the controller responsible for managing devices and manipulating traffic flows throughout the network. The Cisco Open SDN Controller is a commercial distribution of OpenDaylight.

Policy-Based SDN

Policy-based SDN is similar to controller-based SDN, where a centralized controller has a view of all devices in the network, as shown in Figure 13-20.

Policy-based SDN includes an additional policy layer that operates at a higher level of abstraction. It uses built-in applications that automate advanced configuration tasks via a guided workflow and user-friendly GUI. No programming skills are required. Cisco APIC-EM is an example of this type of SDN.

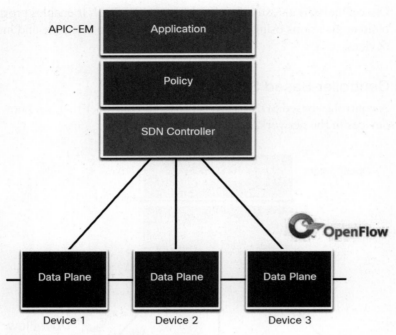

Figure 13-20   Policy-Based SDN

APIC-EM Features (13.5.6)

Each type of SDN has its own features and advantages. Policy-based SDN is the most robust, providing for a simple mechanism to control and manage policies across the entire network.

Cisco APIC-EM is an example of policy-based SDN. Cisco APIC-EM provides a single interface for network management that includes

- Discovering and accessing device and host inventories
- Viewing the topology (as shown in Figure 13-21)
- Tracing a path between end points
- Setting policies

APIC-EM Path Trace (13.5.7)

The APIC-EM Path Trace tool allows an administrator to easily visualize traffic flows and discover any conflicting, duplicate, or shadowed ACL entries. This tool examines specific ACLs on the path between two end nodes and displays any potential issues. You can see where any ACLs along the path either permitted or denied your traffic, as shown in Figure 13-22.

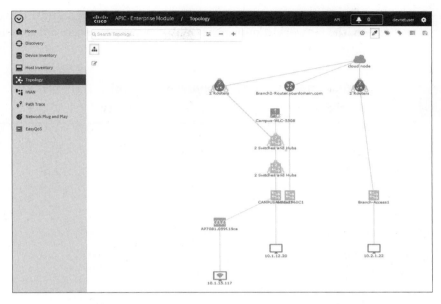

Figure 13-21   Topology Feature in the APIC-EM

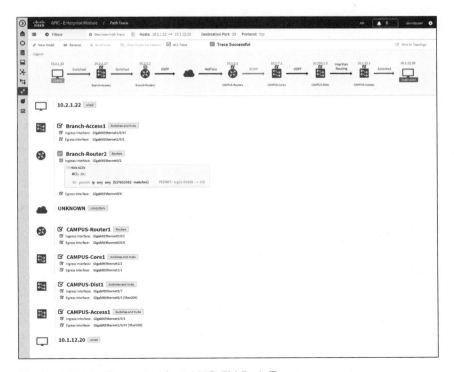

Figure 13-22   Example of an APIC-EM Path Trace

In this figure, notice how Branch-Router2 is permitting all traffic. Based on this information, the network administrator can, if necessary, make adjustments to filter traffic more effectively.

Interactive Graphic

Check Your Understanding—Controllers (13.5.8)

Refer to the online course to complete this activity.

Summary (13.6)

The following is a summary of the sections in this chapter.

Cloud Computing

Cloud computing involves large numbers of computers connected through a network that can be physically located anywhere. Cloud computing can reduce operational costs by using resources more efficiently. Cloud computing addresses a variety of data management issues:

- It enables access to organizational data anywhere and at any time.

- It streamlines the organization's IT operations by subscribing only to needed services.

- It eliminates or reduces the need for onsite IT equipment, maintenance, and management.

- It reduces costs for equipment, energy, physical plant requirements, and personnel training needs.

- It enables rapid responses to increasing data volume requirements.

The three main cloud computing services defined by the National Institute of Standards and Technology (NIST) are software as a service (SaaS), platform as a service (PaaS), and infrastructure as a service (IaaS). With SaaS, the cloud provider is responsible for access to applications and services (such as email, communication, and Office 365) that are delivered over the internet. With PaaS, the cloud provider is responsible for providing users access to the development tools and services used to deliver the applications. With IaaS, the cloud provider is responsible for giving IT managers access to the network equipment, virtualized network services, and supporting network infrastructure. The four types of clouds are public, private, hybrid, and community. Cloud-based applications and services offered in a public cloud are made available to the general population. Cloud-based applications and services offered in a private cloud are intended for a specific organization or entity, such as the government. A hybrid cloud is made up of two or more clouds (for example, part private and part public), where each part remains a separate object but the two are connected using a single architecture. A community cloud is created for exclusive use by a specific community.

Virtualization

The terms *cloud computing* and *virtualization* are often used interchangeably; however, they mean different things. Virtualization is the foundation of cloud computing.

Virtualization separates the operating system (OS) from the hardware. Historically, enterprise servers consisted of a server OS, such as Windows Server or Linux Server, installed on specific hardware. All of a server's RAM, processing power, and hard drive space were dedicated to the service. When a component fails, the service that is provided by this server becomes unavailable. This is known as a single point of failure. Another problem with dedicated servers is that they often sit idle for long periods of time, waiting until there is a need to deliver the specific service they provide. This wastes energy and resources (server sprawl). Virtualization reduces costs because less equipment is required, less energy is consumed, and less space is required. It provides for easier prototyping, faster server provisioning, increased server uptime, improved disaster recovery, and legacy support. A computer system consists of the following abstraction layers: services, OS, firmware, and hardware. A Type 1 hypervisor is installed directly on a server or networking hardware. A Type 2 hypervisor is software that creates and runs VM instances. It can be installed on top of the OS or can be installed between the firmware and the OS.

Virtual Network Infrastructure

Using Type 1 hypervisors is also called the "bare metal" approach because a hypervisor is installed directly on the hardware. Type 1 hypervisors have direct access to hardware resources and are more efficient than hosted architectures. They improve scalability, performance, and robustness. Type 1 hypervisors require a management console to manage the hypervisor. Management software is used to manage multiple servers using the same hypervisor. The management console can automatically consolidate servers and power on or off servers, as required. The management console provides recovery from hardware failure. Some management consoles also allow server overallocation. Server virtualization hides server resources, such as the number and identity of physical servers, processors, and OSs, from server users. This practice can create problems if the data center is using traditional network architectures. Another problem is that traffic flows differ substantially from those in the traditional client/server model. Typically, a data center has a considerable amount of traffic being exchanged between virtual servers. These flows are called east–west traffic and can change in location and intensity over time. North–south traffic occurs between the distribution and core layers and is typically traffic destined for offsite locations such as another data center, other cloud providers, or the internet.

Software-Defined Networking

Two major network architectures have been developed to support network virtualization: software-defined networking (SDN) and Cisco Application Centric Infrastructure (ACI). SDN is an approach to networking in which the network is remotely programmable. SDN may include OpenFlow, OpenStack, and other components.

An SDN controller is a logical entity that enables network administrators to manage and dictate how the data plane of switches and routers should handle network traffic. A network device contains a control plane and a data plane. The control plane is regarded as the brains of a device. It is used to make forwarding decisions. The control plane contains Layer 2 and Layer 3 route forwarding mechanisms, such as routing protocol neighbor tables and topology tables, IPv4 and IPv6 routing tables, STP, and the ARP table. Information sent to the control plane is processed by the CPU. The data plane, also called the forwarding plane, is typically the switch fabric connecting the various network ports on a device. The data plane of each device is used to forward traffic flows. Routers and switches use information from the control plane to forward incoming traffic out the appropriate egress interface. Information in the data plane is typically processed by a special data plane processor without the CPU getting involved. Cisco Express Forwarding (CEF) uses the control plane and data plane to process packets. CEF is an advanced Layer 3 IP switching technology that enables forwarding of packets to occur at the data plane without consultation of the control plane. SDN basically involves the separation of the control plane and data plane. The control plane function is removed from each device and is performed by a centralized controller. The centralized controller communicates control plane functions to each device. The management plane is responsible for managing a device through its connection to the network. Network administrators use applications such as Secure Shell (SSH), Trivial File Transfer Protocol (TFTP), Secure FTP, and Secure Hypertext Transfer Protocol (HTTPS) to access the management plane and configure a device. Protocols such as Simple Network Management Protocol (SNMP) use the management plane.

Controllers

An SDN controller is a logical entity that enables network administrators to manage and dictate how the data plane of switches and routers should handle network traffic. The SDN controller defines the data flows between the centralized control plane and the data planes on individual routers and switches. Each flow traveling through the network must first get permission from the SDN controller, which verifies that the communication is permissible according to the network policy. If the controller allows a flow, it computes a route for the flow to take and adds an entry for that flow in each of the switches along the path. The controller populates flow tables. Switches manage the flow tables. A flow table matches incoming packets to a particular flow and specifies the functions that are to be performed on the packets. There may be multiple flow tables that operate in a pipeline fashion. A flow table may direct a flow to a group table, which may trigger a variety of actions that affect one or more flows. A meter table triggers a variety of performance-related actions on a flow including the ability to rate limit the traffic. Cisco developed the Application Centric Infrastructure (ACI) as an advanced and innovative improvement over earlier SDN approaches. Cisco ACI is a hardware solution for integrating cloud computing and data center management. At a high level, the policy element of the network is removed from the data plane. This simplifies the way data center networks are created. The three core components of the ACI architecture are the Application Network Profile (ANP), the Application Policy Infrastructure Controller (APIC), and Cisco Nexus 9000 Series switches. The Cisco ACI fabric is composed of the APIC and the Cisco Nexus 9000 Series switches using two-tier spine-leaf topology. Unlike in SDN, the APIC controller does not manipulate the data path directly. Instead, the APIC centralizes the policy definition and programs the leaf switches to forward traffic based on the defined policies. There are three types of SDN. With device-based SDN, the devices are programmable by applications running on the device itself or on a server in the network. Controller-based SDN uses a centralized controller that has knowledge of all devices in the network. Policy-based SDN is similar to controller-based SDN, where a centralized controller has a view of all devices in the network. Policy-based SDN includes an additional policy layer that operates at a higher level of abstraction. Policy-based SDN is the most robust, providing a simple mechanism to control and manage policies across the entire network. Cisco APIC-EM is an example of policy-based SDN. Cisco APIC-EM provides a single interface for network management, including discovering and accessing device and host inventories, viewing the topology, tracing a path between endpoints, and setting policies. The APIC-EM Path Trace tool allows an administrator to easily visualize traffic flows and discover any conflicting, duplicate, or shadowed ACL entries. This tool examines specific ACLs on the path between two end nodes and displays any potential issues.

Lab—Install Linux in a Virtual Machine and Explore the GUI (13.6.1)

In this lab, you will install a Linux OS in a virtual machine, using a desktop virtualization application, such as VirtualBox. After completing the installation, you will explore the GUI interface.

Practice

The following lab provides practice with the topics introduced in this chapter. The lab is available in the companion *Enterprise Networking, Security, and Automation Labs & Study Guide (CCNAv7)* (ISBN 9780136634324). There are no Packet Tracer activities for this chapter.

Lab

Lab 13.6.1 Install Linux in a Virtual Machine and Explore the GUI

Check Your Understanding Questions

Complete all the review questions listed here to test your understanding of the topics and concepts in this chapter. The appendix "Answers to the 'Check Your Understanding' Questions" lists the answers.

1. Which of the following is the term for the extension of the internet structure to billions of connected devices?

   A. BYOD

   B. Digitization

   C. IoT

   D. M2M

2. Which cloud computing service would provide the use of network hardware such as routers and switches for a particular company?

   A. Browser as a service (BaaS)

   B. Infrastructure as a service (IaaS)

   C. Software as a service (SaaS)

   D. Wireless as a service (WaaS)

3. What technology allows users to access data anywhere and at any time?

   A. cloud computing

   B. data analytics

   C. micromarketing

   D. virtualization

4. Which cloud computing service would be best for a new organization that cannot afford physical servers and networking equipment and must purchase network services on demand?

   A. IaaS

   B. ITaaS

   C. PaaS

   D. SaaS

5. Which cloud model provides services for a specific organization or entity?

   A. community cloud

   B. hybrid cloud

   C. private cloud

   D. public cloud

6. What is a benefit of virtualization?

   A. guarantee of power

   B. improvement of business practices

   C. supply of consistent air flow

   D. support of live migration

7. What is a difference between the functions of cloud computing and virtualization?

   A. Cloud computing provides services on web-based access, whereas virtualization provides services on data access through virtualized internet connections.

   B. Cloud computing requires hypervisor technology, whereas virtualization is a fault-tolerance technology.

   C. Cloud computing separates the application from the hardware, whereas virtualization separates the OS from the underlying hardware.

   D. Cloud computing utilizes data center technology, whereas virtualization is not used in data centers.

8. Which of the following applies to a Type 2 hypervisor?

   A. best suited for enterprise environments

   B. does not require management console software

   C. has direct access to server hardware resources

   D. installs directly on hardware

9. Which is a characteristic of a Type 1 hypervisor?

   A. best suited for consumers and not for an enterprise environment

   B. does not require management console software

   C. installed directly on a server

   D. installed on an existing operating system

10. Which technology virtualizes the control plane and moves it to a centralized controller?

    A. cloud computing

    B. fog computing

    C. IaaS

    D. SDN

11. Which two layers of the OSI model are associated with SDN network control plane functions that make forwarding decisions? (Choose two.)

    A. Layer 1

    B. Layer 2

    C. Layer 3

    D. Layer 4

    E. Layer 5

12. Which type of hypervisor would most likely be used in a data center?

    A. Nexus 9000 switch

    B. Oracle VM VirtualBox

    C. Type 1

    D. Type 2

13. Which type of hypervisor would most likely be used by a consumer?

    A. Nexus 9000 switch

    B. Oracle VM VirtualBox

    C. Type 1

    D. Type 2

14. What component is considered the brains of the ACI architecture and translates application policies?

    A. Application Network Profile endpoints

    B. Application Policy Infrastructure Controller

    C. hypervisor

    D. Nexus 9000 switch

CHAPTER 14

Network Automation

Objectives

Upon completion of this chapter, you will be able to answer the following questions:

- What is automation?

- What are the JSON, YAML, and XML data formats?

- How do APIs enable computer-to-computer communications?

- How does REST enable computer-to-computer communications?

- What are the configuration management tools Puppet, Chef, Ansible, and SaltStack?

- How does Cisco DNA Center enable intent-based networking?

Key Terms

This chapter uses the following key terms. You can find the definitions in the Glossary.

Introduction (14.0)

Have you set up a home network? A small office network? Imagine doing those tasks for tens of thousands of end devices and thousands of routers, switches, and access points! Did you know that there is software that automates those tasks for an enterprise network? In fact, there is software that can automate the *design* of an enterprise network. It can automate all of the monitoring, operations, and maintenance for your network. Interested? Let's get started!

Automation Overview (14.1)

In this section, you will learn how automation impacts network management.

Video—Automation Everywhere (14.1.1)

Video

We now see automation everywhere, from self-serve checkouts at stores and automatic building environmental controls, to autonomous cars and planes. How many automated systems do you encounter in a single day?

Refer to the online course to view this video.

The Increase in Automation (14.1.2)

Automation is any process that is self-driven, that reduces and potentially eliminates the need for human intervention.

Automation was once confined to the manufacturing industry. Highly repetitive tasks, such as automobile assembly, were turned over to machines, and the modern assembly line was born. Machines excel at repeating the same task without fatigue and without the errors that humans are prone to make in such jobs.

These are some of the benefits of automation:

- Machines can work 24 hours a day without breaks, which results in greater output.

- Machines provide more uniform products than humans can.

- Automation allows the collection of vast amounts of data that can be quickly analyzed to provide information that can help guide an event or a process.

- Robots are used in dangerous conditions such as mining, firefighting, and cleaning up industrial accidents. This reduces the risk to humans.

- Under certain circumstances, smart devices can alter their own behavior to reduce energy usage, make medical diagnoses, and improve automobile driving safety.

Thinking Devices (14.1.3)

Can devices think? Can they learn from their environment? In this context, there are many definitions of the word *think*. One possible definition is the ability to connect a series of related pieces of information together and then use them to alter a course of action.

Many devices now incorporate smart technology to help govern their behavior. This can be as simple as a smart appliance lowering its power consumption during periods of peak demand or as complex as a self-driving car.

Whenever a device takes a course of action based on an outside piece of information, that device is referred to as a *smart device*. Many devices that we interact with now have the word *smart* in their names, to indicate that the devices have the ability to alter their own behavior depending on the environment.

In order for devices to "think," they need to be programmed using network automation tools.

Interactive Graphic

Check Your Understanding—Benefits of Automation (14.1.4)

Refer to the online course to complete this activity.

Data Formats (14.2)

This section compares the different types of *data formats*, including the JSON, YAML, and XML data formats.

Video

Video—Data Formats (14.2.1)

Smart devices are, in fact, tiny computers. For a smart device, such as an actuator, to react to changing conditions, it must be able to receive and interpret information sent to it by another smart device, such as a sensor. These two smart devices must share a common "language," called a *data format*. Shared data formats are also used by other devices in the network.

Refer to the online course to view this video.

The Data Formats Concept (14.2.2)

When sharing data with people, the possibilities for how to display the information are almost endless. For example, think of how a restaurant might format its menu.

It could be text-only, a bulleted list, or photos with captions, or just photos. These are just some of the ways the restaurant could format the data that makes up the menu. A well-designed form is dictated by what makes the information the easiest for the intended audience to understand. This same principle applies to shared data between computers. A computer must put the data into a format that another computer can understand.

Data formats provide a way to store and exchange data in a structured format. One such format is called *Hypertext Markup Language (HTML)*. HTML is a standard *markup language* for describing the structure of web pages, as shown Figure 14-1.

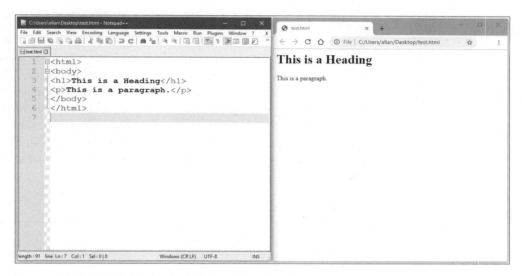

Figure 14-1   HTML Example and Resulting Web Page

These are common data formats that are used in network automation and programmability applications:

- *JavaScript Object Notation (JSON)*
- *Extensible Markup Language (XML)*
- *YAML Ain't Markup Language (YAML)*

Which data format is used depends on the format that is used by the application, tool, or script in question. Many systems can support more than one data format, and in such cases, a user can choose any of them.

Data Format Rules (14.2.3)

Data formats have rules and structure similar to those in programming and written languages. Each data format has specific characteristics, such as the following:

- Syntax, which includes the types of brackets used, such as [ ], ( ), and { }; the use of whitespace; indentation; and punctuation, such as quotes and commas.

- How objects are represented, such as by using characters, strings, lists, and *arrays*.

- How *key/value pairs* are represented. The key is usually on the left side and identifies or describes the data. The value on the right is the data itself and can be a character, a string, a number, a list, or another type of data.

Search the internet for "open notify ISS location now" to find an Open Notify website that tracks the current location of the International Space Station. At this website you can see how data formats are used and some of the similarities between them. This website includes a link for a simple application programming interface (API) call to a server, which returns the current latitude and longitude of the International Space Station, along with a UNIX timestamp. Example 14-1 shows the information returned by the server using JavaScript Object Notation (JSON). The information is displayed in a raw format, which can make it difficult to understand the structure of the data.

Example 14-1   JSON Raw Data

```
{"message": "success", "timestamp": 1560789216, "iss_position": {"latitude":
  "25.9990", "longitude": "-132.6992"}}
```

Now search the internet for the "JSONView" browser extension or any extension that allows you to view JSON in a more readable format. Example 14-2 shows this same output from Example 14-1 but now using JSONView. *Data objects* are displayed in key/value pairs. The key/value pairs are much easier to interpret than the raw data. For example, you can see the key **latitude** and its value **25.9990**.

Example 14-2   Formatted JSON Data

```
{
        "message": "success",
        "timestamp": 1560789260,
        "iss_position": {
                "latitude": "25.9990",
                "longitude": "-132.6992"
        }
}
```

> **Note**
>
> JSONView may remove the quotation marks from the key, but quotation marks are required when coding JSON key/value pairs.

Compare Data Formats (14.2.4)

To see this same data from Example 14-2 formatted as XML or YAML, search the internet for a JSON conversion tool. There are online conversion tools that can be used to convert the JASON data shown in Example 14-3 into YAML format, shown in Example 14-4, and into XML format, shown in Example 14-5. At this point, it is not important to understand the details of each data format, but you should be able to see how each data format makes use of syntax and how the key/value pairs are represented.

Example 14-3 JSON Format

```
{
    "message": "success",
    "timestamp": 1560789260,
    "iss_position": {
        "latitude": "25.9990",
        "longitude": "-132.6992"
    }
}
```

Example 14-4 YAML Format

```
message: success
timestamp: 1560789260
iss_position:
    latitude: '25.9990'
    longitude: '-132.6992'
```

Example 14-5 XML Format

```
<?xml version="1.0" encoding="UTF-8" ?>
<root>
  <message>success</message>
  <timestamp>1560789260</timestamp>
  <iss_position>
    <latitude>25.9990</latitude>
    <longitude>-132.6992</longitude>
  </iss_position>
</root>
```

JSON Data Format (14.2.5)

JSON is a human-readable data format used by applications for storing, transferring, and reading data. JSON is a very popular format used by web services and APIs to provide public data. It is popular because it is easy to parse and can be used with most modern programming languages, including Python.

Example 14-6 shows partial IOS output of the **show interface GigabitEthernet0/0/0** command on a router.

Example 14-6   IOS Router Output

```
GigabitEthernet0/0/0 is up, line protocol is up (connected)
  Description: Wide Area Network
  Internet address is 172.16.0.2/24
```

Example 14-7 shows this same information represented in JSON format.

Example 14-7   JSON Output

```
{
    "ietf-interfaces:interface": {
        "name": "GigabitEthernet0/0/0",
        "description": "Wide Area Network",
        "enabled": true,
        "ietf-ip:ipv4": {
            "address": [
                {
                    "ip": "172.16.0.2",
                    "netmask": "255.255.255.0"
                }
            ]
        }
    }
}
```

Notice that each object (that is, each key/value pair) is a different piece of data about the interface, including its name, a description, and whether the interface is enabled.

JSON Syntax Rules (14.2.6)

These are some of the characteristics of JSON:

- It uses a hierarchical structure and contains nested values.

- It uses braces, { }, to hold objects and square brackets, [ ], to hold arrays.

- Its data is written as key/value pairs.

In JSON, the data known as an object is one or more key/value pairs enclosed in braces, { }. The syntax for a JSON object includes:

- A key must be a string within double quotation marks, " ".

- A value must be a valid JSON data type (string, number, array, Boolean, null, or another object).

- A key and a value are separated by a colon.

- Multiple key/value pairs within an object are separated by commas.

- Whitespace is not significant.

At times, a key may contain more than one value. This is known as an *array*. An array in JSON is an ordered list of values. Characteristics of arrays in JSON include:

- The key is followed by a colon and a list of values and is enclosed in square brackets, [ ].

- The array is an ordered list of values.

- The array can contain multiple value types, including a string, a number, a Boolean, an object, or another array inside the array.

- Each value in the array is separated from the one before with a comma.

A JSON-formatted list of IPv4 addresses might look like the list shown in Example 14-8.

Example 14-8   JSON List of IPv4 Addresses

```
{
    "addresses": [
        {
            "ip": "172.16.0.2",
            "netmask": "255.255.255.0"
        },
        {
            "ip": "172.16.0.3",
            "netmask": "255.255.255.0"
        },
        {
            "ip": "172.16.0.4",
            "netmask": "255.255.255.0"
        }
    ]
}
```

In this example, the key is "addresses." Each item in the list is a separate object, and the objects are separated by braces, { }. The objects are two key/value pairs: an IPv4 address ("ip") and a subnet mask ("netmask"), separated by a comma. The array of objects in the list is also separated by a comma following the closing brace for each object.

YAML Data Format (14.2.7)

YAML is another type of human-readable data format that applications use for storing, transferring, and reading data. Some of the characteristic of YAML include:

■ It is like JSON and is considered a superset of JSON.

■ It has a minimalist format, which makes it easy to both read and write.

■ It uses indentation to define its structure, without the use of brackets or commas.

Consider the JSON output for a Gigabit Ethernet 2 interface in Example 14-9.

Example 14-9   JSON for GigabitEthernet2

```
{
    "ietf-interfaces:interface": {
        "name": "GigabitEthernet2",
        "description": "Wide Area Network",
        "enabled": true,
        "ietf-ip:ipv4": {
            "address": [
                {
                    "ip": "172.16.0.2",
                    "netmask": "255.255.255.0"
                },
                {
                    "ip": "172.16.0.3",
                    "netmask": "255.255.255.0"
                },
                {
                    "ip": "172.16.0.4",
                    "netmask": "255.255.255.0"
                }
            ]
        }
    }
}
```

The same data from Example 14-9 is easier to read in YAML format, as shown in Example 14-10. Much as in JSON, a YAML object is one or more key/value pairs. However, in YAML, a key and a value are separated by a colon, without the use of quotation marks. In YAML, a hyphen is used to separate each element in a list. You can see this with the three IPv4 addresses in Example 14-10.

Example 14-10   YAML for GigabitEthernet2

```
ietf-interfaces:interface:
  name: GigabitEthernet2
  description: Wide Area Network
  enabled: true
  ietf-ip:ipv4:
    address:
    - ip: 172.16.0.2
      netmask: 255.255.255.0
    - ip: 172.16.0.3
      netmask: 255.255.255.0
    - ip: 172.16.0.4
      netmask: 255.255.255.0
```

XML Data Format (14.2.8)

XML is another type of human-readable data format that applications use to store, transfer, and read data. Some of the characteristics of XML include:

- It is like HTML, which is the standardized markup language for creating web pages and web applications.

- It is self-descriptive. It encloses data within a related set of tags, such as *<tag>data</tag>*.

- Unlike HTML, XML uses no predefined tags or document structure.

An XML object is one or more key/value pairs, with the beginning tag used as the name of the key: *<key>value</key>*.

The output in Example 14-11 shows the same GigabitEthernet2 data from Examples 14-9 and 14-10 now formatted as XML.

Example 14-11   XML for GigabitEthernet2

```
<?xml version="1.0" encoding="UTF-8" ?>
<ietf-interfaces:interface>
  <name>GigabitEthernet2</name>
  <description>Wide Area Network</description>
  <enabled>true</enabled>
```

```
<ietf-ip:ipv4>
  <address>
    <ip>172.16.0.2</ip>
    <netmask>255.255.255.0</netmask>
  </address>
  <address>
    <ip>172.16.0.3</ip>
    <netmask>255.255.255.0</netmask>
  </address>
  <address>
    <ip>172.16.0.4</ip>
    <netmask>255.255.255.0</netmask>
  </address>
</ietf-ip:ipv4>
</ietf-interfaces:interface>
```

Notice that the values are enclosed within the object tags. In this example, each key/value pair is on a separate line, and some lines are indented. The indentation is not required but helps with readability. The list uses repeated instances of *<tag></tag>* for each element in the list. The elements within these repeated tags represent one or more key/value pairs.

Interactive Graphic

Check Your Understanding—Data Formats (14.2.9)

Refer to the online course to complete this activity.

APIs (14.3)

In this section, you will learn how APIs enable computer-to-computer communication.

Video

Video—APIs (14.3.1)

Data formats shared between smart devices often use an application programming interface (API). As you will learn in this section, an API is software that allows other applications to access data or services.

Refer to the online course to view this video.

The API Concept (14.3.2)

APIs are found almost everywhere. Amazon Web Services, Facebook, and home automation devices such as thermostats, refrigerators, and wireless lighting systems all use APIs. APIs are also used for building programmable network automation.

An API is software that allows other applications to access its data or services. It is a set of rules describing how one application can interact with another and the instructions to allow the interaction to occur. The user sends an API request to a server, asking for specific information, and receives an API response in return from the server, along with the requested information.

An API is similar to a waiter in a restaurant, as shown in Figure 14-2. A customer in a restaurant would like to have some food delivered to the table. The food is in the kitchen, where it is cooked and prepared. The waiter is the messenger, similar to an API. The waiter (the API) is the person who takes the customer's order (the request) and tells the kitchen what to do. When the food is ready, the waiter delivers the food (the response) to the customer.

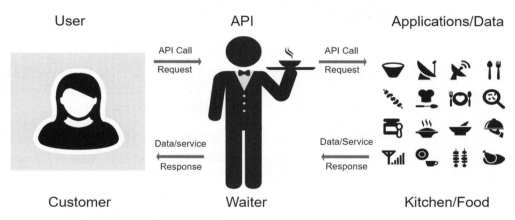

Figure 14-2   Waiter and API Analogy

Earlier in this chapter, you saw an API request to a server that returned the current latitude and longitude of the International Space Station. This was an API that Open Notify provides to access data from a web browser at the National Aeronautics and Space Administration (NASA).

An API Example (14.3.3)

To really understand how APIs can be used to provide data and services, we will look at two options for booking airline reservations. The first option uses the website of a specific airline, as shown in Figure 14-3.

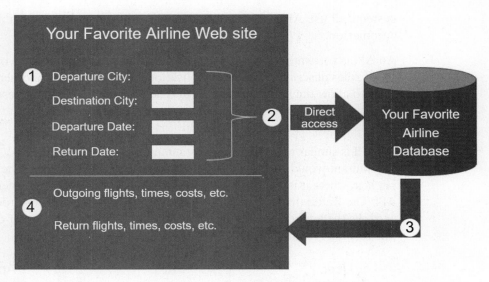

Figure 14-3   Reservation Through a Specific Airline's Website

Using the airline's website, the user enters the information needed to make a reservation request. The website interacts directly with the airline's own database and provides the user with information matching the user's request.

> **Note**
>
> This is an example of an airline website not using APIs; however, it is possible for an airline's website to achieve the same result by using APIs.

Instead of using an individual airline website that has direct access to its own information, users can use a travel site to access the same information for a variety of airlines. In this case, the user enters similar reservation information. The travel service website interacts with the various airline databases by using APIs provided by the airlines. The travel service uses each airline API to request information from that specific airline, and then it displays the information from all the airlines on the its web page, as shown in Figure 14-4.

The API acts as a kind of messenger between the requesting application and the application on the server that provides the data or service. The message from the requesting application to the server where the data resides is known as an *API call*.

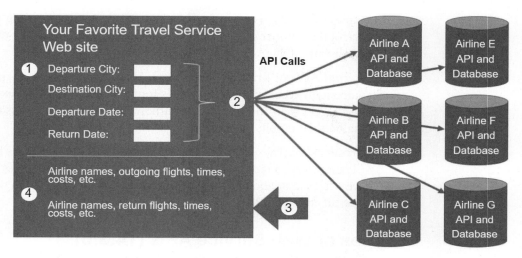

Figure 14-4 Reservation Through a Travel Site That Uses APIs to Access Various Airline Databases

Open, Internal, and Partner APIs (14.3.4)

An important consideration when developing an API is the distinction between open, internal, and partner APIs, as shown in Figure 14-5:

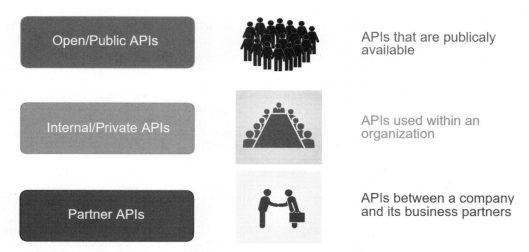

Figure 14-5 Open, Internal, and Partner APIs

- *Open APIs* or *public APIs*: These APIs are publicly available and can be used with no restrictions. The International Space Station API is an example of a public API. Because these APIs are public, many API providers, such as Google

Maps, require the user to get a free key, or token, prior to using the API to help control the number of API requests they receive and process. Search the internet for a list of public APIs.

- *Internal APIs* or *private APIs*: These APIs are used by an organization or a company to access data and services for internal use only. An example of an internal API is an API that allows authorized salespeople access to internal sales data on their mobile devices.

- *Partner APIs*: These APIs are used between a company and its business partners or contractors to facilitate business between them. The business partner must have a license or another form of permission to use the API. A travel service using an airline's API is an example of a partner API.

Types of Web Service APIs (14.3.5)

A web service is a service that is available over the internet, using the World Wide Web. There are four types of web service APIs:

- *Simple Object Access Protocol (SOAP)*
- *Representational State Transfer (REST)*
- *Extensible Markup Language–Remote Procedure Call (XML-RPC)*
- *JavaScript Object Notation–Remote Procedure Call (JSON-RPC)*

Table 14-1 lists some of the characteristics of these web service APIs.

Table 14-1 Web Service API Characteristics

Characteristic	SOAP	REST	XML-RPC	JSON-RPC
Data format	XML	JSON, XML, YAML, and others	XML	JSON
First released	1998	2000	1998	2005
Strengths	Well established	Flexible formatting and most widely used	Well established, simplicity	Simplicity

SOAP is a messaging protocol for exchanging XML-structured information, most often over HTTP or Simple Mail Transfer Protocol (SMTP). SOAP was designed by Microsoft in 1998, and SOAP APIs are considered slow to parse, complex, and rigid. The drawbacks of SOAP APIs led to the development of a simpler REST API framework that does not require XML. REST uses HTTP, is less verbose, and is easier to use than SOAP. REST refers to a style of software architecture and has become popular due to its performance, scalability, simplicity, and reliability.

REST is the most widely used web service API, accounting for over 80% of all the API types used. REST is further discussed later in this chapter.

With RPC, one system requests that another system execute some code and return the information. This occurs without having to understand the details of the network. It works much like a REST API, but there are differences in terms of formatting and flexibility. XML-RPC is a protocol developed prior to SOAP that later evolved into what became SOAP. JSON-RPC is a very simple protocol and similar to XML-RPC.

Interactive Graphic

Check Your Understanding—APIs (14.3.6)

Refer to the online course to complete this activity.

REST (14.4)

In this section, you will learn how REST enables computer-to-computer communication.

Video

Video—REST (14.4.1)

As you have just learned, REST is currently the most widely used API. This section covers REST in more detail.

Refer to the online course to view this video.

REST and RESTful API (14.4.2)

Web browsers use HTTP or HTTPS to request (GET) a web page. If successfully requested (HTTP status code 200), web servers respond to GET requests with an HTML coded web page, as shown in Figure 14-6.

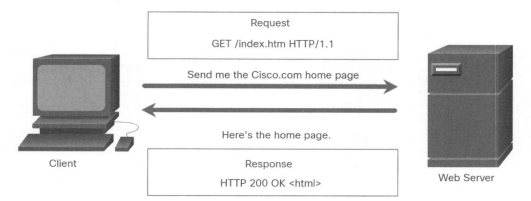

Figure 14-6   HTTP GET Request Example

REST is an architectural style for designing web service applications. It refers to a style of web architecture that has many underlying characteristics and governs the behavior of clients and servers. Simply stated, a REST API is an API that works on top of the HTTP protocol. It defines a set of functions developers can use to perform requests and receive responses via HTTP, such as GET and POST.

Conforming to the constraints of the REST architecture is generally referred to as being *RESTful*. An API can be considered RESTful if it has the following features:

- **Client/server:** The client handles the front end, and the server handles the back end. Either can be replaced independently of the other.

- **Stateless:** No client data is stored on the server between requests. The session state is stored on the client.

- **Cacheable:** Clients can cache responses to improve performance.

RESTful Implementation (14.4.3)

A RESTful web service is implemented using HTTP. It is a collection of resources with four defined aspects:

- The base *uniform resource identifier (URI)* for the web service, such as http://example.com/resources

- The data format supported by the web service, which is often JSON, YAML, or XML but could be any other data format that is a valid hypertext standard

- The set of operations supported by the web service using HTTP methods

- A hypertext-driven API

RESTful APIs use common HTTP methods including POST, GET, PUT, PATCH, and DELETE. As shown in Table 14-2, these correspond to the RESTful operations create, read, update, and delete (or CRUD).

Table 14-2   HTTP Methods and RESTful Operations

HTTP Method	RESTful Operation
POST	Create
GET	Read
PUT/PATCH	Update
DELETE	Delete

In Figure 14-7, the HTTP request asks for JSON-formatted data. If the request is successfully constructed according to the API documentation, the server responds with JSON data.

This JSON data can be used by a client's web application to display the data (for example, a smartphone mapping app shows the location of San Jose, California).

```
{
  - info: {
        statuscode: 0,
      - copyright: {
            text: "© 2019 MapQuest, Inc.",
            imageUrl: "http://api.mqcdn.com/res/mqlogo.gif",
            imageAltText: "© 2019 MapQuest, Inc."
        },
        messages: [ ]
    },
  - options: {
        maxResults: -1,
        thumbMaps: true,
        ignoreLatLngInput: false
    },
  - results: [
      - {
          - providedLocation: {
                location: "San Jose,Ca"
            },
          - locations: [
              - {
                    street: "",
                    adminArea6: "",
                    adminArea6Type: "Neighborhood",
                    adminArea5: "San Jose",
                    adminArea5Type: "City",
                    adminArea4: "Santa Clara County",
                    adminArea4Type: "County",
                    adminArea3: "CA",
                    adminArea3Type: "State",
                    adminArea1: "US",
                    adminArea1Type: "Country",
```

Figure 14-7 HTTP Request Asking for a JSON Response

URI, URN, and URL (14.4.4)

Web resources and web services such as RESTful APIs are identified using a uniform resource identifier (URI), which is a string of characters that identifies a specific network resource. As shown in Figure 14-8, a URI has two specializations:

- *Uniform resource name (URN)*: Identifies only the namespace of the resource (web page, document, image, and so on), without reference to the protocol.

- *Uniform resource locator (URL)*: Defines the network location of a specific resource on the network. HTTP or HTTPS URLs are typically used with web browsers. Other protocols, such as FTP, SFTP, and SSH, can use a URL. A URL using SFTP might look like sftp://sftp.example.com.

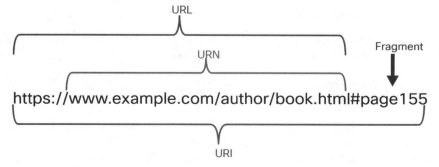

Figure 14-8 Structure of a Uniform Resource Identifier

These are the parts of a URI, as shown in the figure:

- **Protocol/scheme:** HTTPS or other protocols, such as FTP, SFTP, mailto, and NNTP

- **Hostname:** www.example.com

- **Path and filename:** /author/book.html

- **Fragment:** #page155

Anatomy of a RESTful Request (14.4.5)

In a RESTful web service, a request made to a resource's URI elicits a response. The response is a payload, typically formatted in JSON, but could be HTML, XML, or some other format. Figure 14-9 shows the URI for the MapQuest directions API. The API request is for directions from San Jose, California, to Monterey, California.

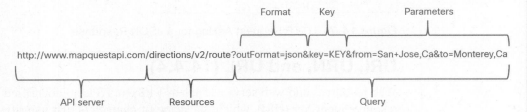

Figure 14-9 Parts of an API Request

Figure 14-10 shows part of the API response. In this example, it is the MapQuest directions from San Jose to Monterey in JSON format.

These are the different parts of the API request:

- **API server:** This is the URL for the server that answers REST requests. In this example, it is the MapQuest API server.

- **Resource:** Specifies the API that is being requested. In this example, it is the MapQuest directions API.

- **Query:** Specifies the data format and information the client is requesting from the API service. Queries can include:

  ○ **Format:** This is usually JSON but can be YAML or XML. In this example, JSON is requested.

  ○ **Key:** The key is for authorization, if required. MapQuest requires a key for its directions API. In the URI shown in Figure 14-9, you would need to replace KEY with a valid key to submit a valid request.

- ○ **Parameters:** Parameters are used to send information pertaining to the request. In this example, the query parameters include information about the directions that the API needs so it knows what directions to return: from=San+Jose,Ca and to=Monterey,Ca.

```
{
  - route: {
        hasTollRoad: false,
        hasBridge: true,
      - boundingBox: {
          - lr: {
                lng: -121.667061,
                lat: 36.596809
            },
          - ul: {
                lng: -121.897125,
                lat: 37.335358
            }
        },
        distance: 71.712,
        hasTimedRestriction: false,
        hasTunnel: false,
        hasHighway: true,
        computedWaypoints: [ ],
      - routeError: {
            errorCode: -400,
            message: ""
        },
        formattedTime: "01:12:59",
        sessionId: "5celebf7-017f-5f21-02b4-1a7b-06b08100f026",
        hasAccessRestriction: false,
        realTime: 4378,
        hasSeasonalClosure: false,
        hasCountryCross: false,
        fuelUsed: 3.29,
      - legs: [
          - {
                hasTollRoad: false,
                hasBridge: true,
                destNarrative: "Proceed to MONTEREY, CA.",
                distance: 71.712,
```

Figure 14-10   Partial JSON Payload Received from an API Request

A RESTful API, including a public API, may require a key. The key is used to identify the source of the request. Here are some reasons an API provider may require a key:

- To authenticate the source to make sure the source is authorized to use the API

- To limit the number of people using the API

- To limit the number of requests per user

- To better capture and track the data being requested by users

- To gather information on the people using the API

Note

The MapQuest API requires a key. Search the internet for the URL to obtain a MapQuest key, using the search parameter "developer.mapquest." You can also search the internet for the current MapQuest privacy policy.

RESTful API Applications (14.4.6)

Many websites and applications use APIs to access information and provide service for their customers. For example, a travel service website uses the APIs of various airlines to provide the user with airline, hotel, and other information.

Some RESTful API requests can be made by typing in the URI from within a web browser. The MapQuest directions API is an example of this. A RESTful API request can also be made in other ways, as described in the following sections.

Developer Website

Developers often maintain websites that include information about the API, parameter information, and usage examples. These sites may also allow the user to perform the API request within the developer web page by entering the parameters and other information.

Postman

Postman is an application for testing and using REST APIs. It is available as a browser app or a standalone installation. It contains everything required for constructing and sending REST API requests, including entering query parameters and keys. Postman allows you to collect and save frequently used API calls in history or as collections. Postman is an excellent tool for learning how to construct API requests and for analyzing the data that is returned from an API.

Python

APIs can be called from within a *Python* program. This allows for possible automation, customization, and app integration of the API.

Network Operating Systems

Using protocols such as NETCONF (which handles net configuration) and REST-CONF, network operating systems are beginning to provide an alternative method for configuration, monitoring, and management. The output in Example 14-12 is a typical opening response from a router after the user has established a NETCONF session at the command line.

Example 14-12   NETCONF Hello Message

```
$ ssh admin@192.168.0.1 -p 830 -s netconf
admin@192.168.0.1's password:
<hello xmlns="urn:ietf:params:xml:ns:netconf:base:1.0">
```

```
<capabilities>
  <capability>urn:ietf:params:netconf:base:1.1</capability>
  <capability>urn:ietf:params:netconf:capability:candidate:1.0</capability>
  <capability>urn:ietf:params:xml:ns:yang:ietf-netconf-monitoring</capability>
  <capability>urn:ietf:params:xml:ns:yang:ietf-interfaces</capability>
  [output omitted and edited for clarity]
</capabilities>
<session-id>19150</session-id></hello>
```

However, working at the command line is not automating the network. A network administrator can use Python scripts or other automation tools, such as *Cisco DNA Center*, to programmatically interact with a router.

Interactive Graphic

Check Your Understanding—REST (14.4.7)

Refer to the online course to complete this activity.

Configuration Management Tools (14.5)

This section compares the configuration management tools *Puppet*, *Chef*, *Ansible*, and *SaltStack*.

Video

Video—Configuration Management Tools (14.5.1)

As mentioned in the introduction to this chapter, setting up a network can be very time-consuming. Configuration management tools can help you to automate the configuration of routers, switches, firewalls, and many other aspects of your network.

Refer to the online course to view this video.

Traditional Network Configuration (14.5.2)

Network devices such as routers, switches, and firewalls have traditionally been configured by a network administrator using the CLI, as shown in Figure 14-11.

Whenever there is a change or new feature, the necessary configuration commands must be manually entered on all of the appropriate devices. In many cases, this is not only time-consuming but can also be prone to errors. This becomes a major issue on larger networks or with more complex configurations.

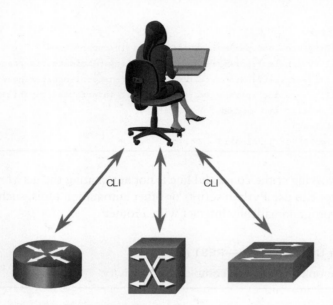

Figure 14-11   Manual Configuration Using CLI

Simple Network Management Protocol (SNMP) was developed to allow administrators to manage nodes such as servers, workstations, routers, switches, and security appliances on an IP network. Using a network management station (NMS) and SNMP, as shown in the Figure 14-12, network administrators can monitor and manage network performance, find and solve network problems, and perform queries for statistics.

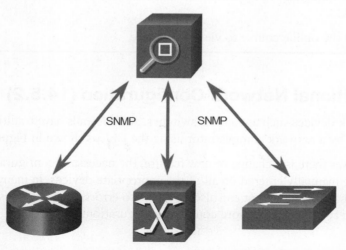

Figure 14-12   Device Configuration Through an SNMP NMS

SNMP works reasonably well for device monitoring. However, it is not typically used for configuration due to security concerns and implementation difficulty. Although SNMP is widely available, it cannot serve as an automation tool for today's networks.

You can also use APIs to automate the deployment and management of network resources. Instead of manually configuring ports, access lists, quality of service (QoS), and load-balancing policies, the network administrator can use tools to automate these configurations. These tools hook into network APIs to automate routine network provisioning tasks, enabling the administrator to select and deploy the particular network services needed. This automation can significantly reduce many repetitive and mundane tasks and free up time for network administrators to work on more important things.

Network Automation (14.5.3)

We are rapidly moving away from a world where a network administrator manages a few dozen network devices to one where an administrator is deploying and managing hundreds, thousands, and even tens of thousands of complex network devices (both physical and virtual) with the help of software. This transformation is quickly spreading from its beginnings in the data center to all places in the network. There are new and different methods for network operators to automatically monitor, manage, and configure networks. As shown in Figure 14-13, these include protocols and technologies such as REST, Ansible, Puppet, Chef, Python, JSON, and XML.

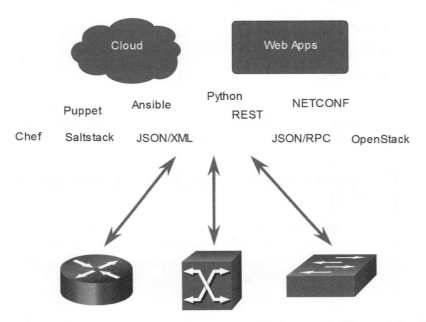

Figure 14-13 Protocols and Technologies for Automating Network Configuration

Configuration Management Tools (14.5.4)

Configuration management tools make use of RESTful API requests to automate tasks and can scale across thousands of devices. Configuration management tools maintain the characteristics of a system, or network, for consistency. These are some characteristics of the network that administrators benefit from automating:

- Software and version control
- Device attributes such as names, addressing, and security
- Protocol configurations
- ACL configurations

Configuration management tools typically include automation and orchestration. With automation, a tool automatically performs a task on a system, such as configuring an interface or deploying a VLAN. Orchestration is the process in which all these automated activities need to happen, such as the order in which they must be done, what must be completed before another task is begun, and so on. Orchestration involves arranging the automated tasks into a coordinated process or workflow.

Several tools are available to make configuration management easier, including the following:

- Ansible
- Chef
- Puppet
- SaltStack

All of these tools aim to reduce the complexity and time involved in configuring and maintaining a large-scale network infrastructure with hundreds or even thousands of devices. These same tools can benefit smaller networks as well.

Compare Ansible, Chef, Puppet, and SaltStack (14.5.5)

Ansible, Chef, Puppet, and SaltStack all come with API documentation for configuring RESTful API requests. All of them support JSON and YAML as well as other data formats. Table 14-3 compares the major characteristics of the Ansible, Puppet, Chef, and SaltStack configuration management tools.

Table 14-3 Configuration Management Tool Characteristics

Characteristic	Ansible	Chef	Puppet	SaltStack
What programming language?	Python and YAML	Ruby	Ruby	Python
Agent-based or agentless?	Agentless	Agent-based	Supports both	Supports both
How are devices managed?	Any device can be "controller"	Chef Master	Puppet Master	Salt Master
What is created by the tool?	Playbook	Cookbook	Manifest	Pillar

The following list provides more information on the characteristics compared in Table 14-3:

- **What programming language?** Ansible and SaltStack are both built on Python, whereas Puppet and Chef are built on *Ruby*. Much like Python, Ruby is an open-source, cross-platform programming language. However, Ruby is typically considered a more difficult language to learn than Python.

- **Agent-based or agentless?** Configuration management is either agent based or agentless. Agent-based configuration management is pull based, meaning that the agent on the managed device periodically connects with the master for its configuration information. Changes are made on the master and pulled down and executed by the device. Agentless configuration management is push based: A configuration script is run on the master, and the master connects to the device and executes the tasks in the script. Of the four configuration tools examined here, only Ansible is agentless.

- **How are devices managed?** Management occurs with a device called the Master in Puppet, Chef, and SaltStack. Because Ansible is agentless, any computer can be the controller.

- **What is created by the tool?** Network administrators use configuration management tools to create a set of instructions to be executed. Each tool has its own name for these instructions (for example, playbook in Ansible, cookbook in Chef). Common tool specifies a policy or a configuration that is to be applied to devices. Each device type might have its own policy. For example, all Linux servers might get the same basic configuration and security policy.

Interactive Graphic

Check Your Understanding—Configuration Management (14.5.6)

Refer to the online course to complete this activity.

IBN and Cisco DNA Center (14.6)

Explain how Cisco DNA Center enables intent-based networking.

Video—Intent-Based Networking (14.6.1)

You have learned about some of the many tools and software options that can help you automate a network. Intent-based networking (IBN) and Cisco Digital Network Architecture (DNA) Center can help you bring it all together to create an automated network.

The online course includes a video by Cisco's John Apostolopoulos and Anand Oswal, explaining how artificial intelligence and IBN can improve networks.

Refer to the online course to view this video.

Intent-Based Networking Overview (14.6.2)

Intent-based networking (IBN) is the emerging industry model for the next generation of networking. IBN builds on software-defined networking (SDN), transforming a hardware-centric and manual approach to designing and operating networks to an approach that is software centric and fully automated.

Business objectives for the network are expressed as intent. IBN captures business intent and uses analytics, machine learning, and automation to align the network continuously and dynamically as business needs change.

IBN captures and translates business intent into network policies that can be automated and applied consistently across the network.

Cisco views IBN as having three essential functions: translation, activation, and assurance. These functions interact with the underlying physical and virtual infrastructure as shown in Figure 14-14.

Network Infrastructure as Fabric (14.6.3)

From the perspective of IBN, the physical and virtual network infrastructure is a fabric. *Fabric* is a term used to describe an overlay that represents the logical topology used to virtually connect to devices, as shown in Figure 14-15.

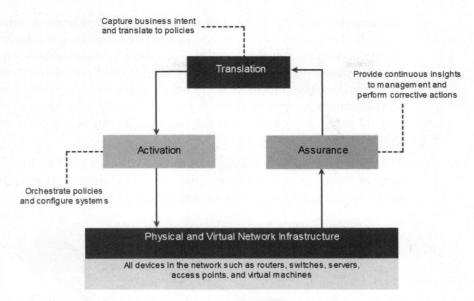

Figure 14-14   Intent-Based Networking Flowchart

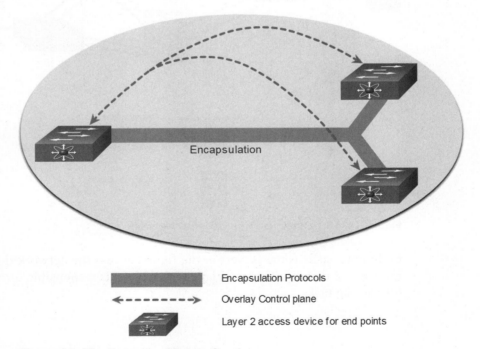

Figure 14-15   Example of Fabric Overlay

The overlay limits the number of devices the network administrator must program. It also provides services and alternative forwarding methods not controlled by the underlying physical devices. For example, the overlay is where encapsulation protocols such as IP Security (IPsec) and Control and Provisioning of Wireless Access Points (CAPWAP) occur. Using an IBN solution, the network administrator can specify through policies exactly what happens in the overlay control plane. Notice that how the switches are physically connected is not a concern of the overlay.

The underlay network is the physical topology that includes all hardware required to meet business objectives. The underlay reveals additional devices and specifies how these devices are connected, as shown in Figure 14-16.

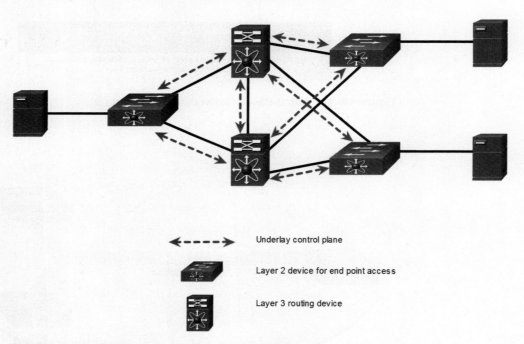

◄— — —►	Underlay control plane
	Layer 2 device for end point access
	Layer 3 routing device

Figure 14-16   Example of the Underlay Network

Endpoints, such as the servers in the figure, access the network through the Layer 2 devices. The underlay control plane is responsible for simple forwarding tasks.

Cisco Digital Network Architecture (DNA) (14.6.4)

Cisco implements the IBN fabric by using *Cisco DNA*. As displayed in Figure 14-17, the business intent is securely deployed into the network infrastructure (the fabric).

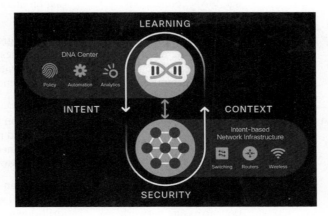

Figure 14-17   Business Intent Implemented in Cisco DNA Center

Cisco DNA then continuously gathers data from a multitude of sources (devices and applications) to provide a rich context of information. This information can be analyzed to make sure the network is performing securely at its optimal level and in accordance with business intent and network policies.

Cisco DNA is a system that is constantly learning and adapting to support the business needs. Table 14-4 lists some Cisco DNA products and solutions.

Table 14-4   Cisco DNA Solution Descriptions and Benefits

Cisco DNA Solution	Description	Benefits
SD-Access	■ First intent-based enterprise networking solution built using Cisco DNA. ■ Uses a single network fabric across the LAN and WLAN to create a consistent, highly secure user experience. ■ Segments user, device, and application traffic and automates user-access policies to establish the right policy for any user or device, with any application, across a network.	■ Enables network access in minutes for any user or device to any application without compromising security.

Cisco DNA Solution	Description	Benefits
SD-WAN	■ Uses a secure cloud-delivered architecture to centrally manage WAN connections. ■ Simplifies and accelerates delivery of secure, flexible, and rich WAN services to connect data centers, branches, campuses, and colocation facilities.	■ Delivers better user experiences for applications residing on premises or in the cloud. ■ Achieves greater agility and cost savings through easier deployments and transport independence.
Cisco DNA Assurance	■ Used to troubleshoot and increase IT productivity. ■ Applies advanced analytics and machine learning to improve performance and issue resolution and predictions to assure network performance. ■ Provides real-time notification for network conditions that require attention.	■ Allows you to identify root causes and provides suggested remediation for faster troubleshooting. ■ Provides an easy-to-use single dashboard with insights and drill-down capabilities. ■ Machine learning continually improves network intelligence to help predict problems before they occur.
Cisco DNA Security	■ Provides visibility by using the network as a sensor for real-time analysis and intelligence. ■ Provides increased granular control to enforce policy and contain threats across the network.	■ Reduces risk and protects the organization against threats—even in encrypted traffic. ■ Provides 360-degree visibility through real-time analytics for deep intelligence across the network. ■ Reduces complexity with end-to-end security.

These solutions are not mutually exclusive. For example, an organization could deploy all four solutions listed in Table 14-4. Many of these solutions are implemented using Cisco DNA Center, which provides a software dashboard for managing an enterprise network.

Cisco DNA Center (14.6.5)

Cisco DNA Center is the foundational controller and analytics platform at the heart of Cisco DNA. It supports the expression of intent for multiple use cases, including basic automation capabilities, fabric provisioning, and policy-based segmentation in the enterprise network. Cisco DNA Center is a network management and command center for provisioning and configuring network devices. It is a hardware and software platform that provides a single pane of glass (that is, single interface) that focuses on assurance, analytics, and automation.

The DNA Center interface launch page gives you an overall health summary and network snapshot, as shown in Figure 14-18. From here, a network administrator can quickly drill down into areas of interest.

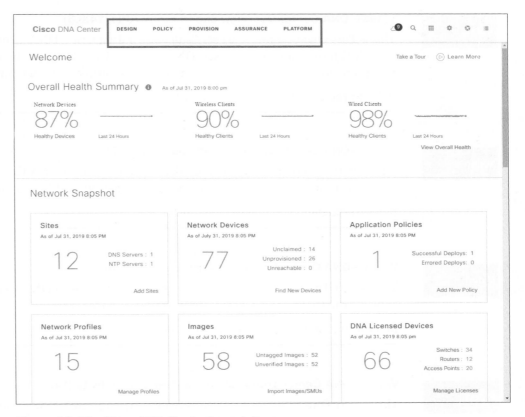

Figure 14-18   Cisco DNA Center Launch Page

Menus at the top of DNA Center provide access to five main areas:

- **Design:** Model your entire network, from sites and buildings to devices and links, both physical and virtual, across campus, branch, WAN, and cloud.

- **Policy:** Use policies to automate and simplify network management, reducing cost and risk while speeding rollout of new and enhanced services.

- **Provision:** Provide new services to users with ease, speed, and security across your enterprise network, regardless of network size and complexity.

- **Assurance:** Use proactive monitoring and insights from the network, devices, and applications to predict problems faster and ensure that policy and configuration changes achieve the business intent and the user experience you want.

- **Platform:** Use APIs to integrate with your preferred IT systems to create end-to-end solutions and add support for multivendor devices.

Video

Video—DNA Center Overview and Platform APIs (14.6.6)

This is Part One of a four-part series demonstrating Cisco DNA Center. Part One provides an overview of the Cisco DNA Center GUI. It includes the Design, Policy, Provision, and Assurance tools used to control multiple sites and multiple devices.

Refer to the online course to view this video.

Video

Video—DNA Center Design and Provision (14.6.7)

This is Part Two of a four-part series demonstrating Cisco DNA Center. Part Two provides an overview of the Cisco DNA Center Design and Provision areas.

Refer to the online course to view this video.

Video

Video—DNA Center Policy and Assurance (14.6.8)

This is Part Three of a four-part series demonstrating Cisco DNA Center. Part Three explains the Cisco DNA Center Policy and Assurance areas.

Refer to the online course to view this video.

Video

Video—DNA Center Troubleshooting User Connectivity (14.6.9)

This is Part Four of a four-part series demonstrating Cisco DNA Center. Part Four explains how to use Cisco DNA Center to troubleshoot devices.

Refer to the online course to view this video.

Interactive Graphic

Check Your Understanding—IBN and Cisco DNA Center (14.6.10)

Refer to the online course to complete this activity.

Summary (14.7)

The following is a summary of the sections in this chapter.

Automation Overview

Automation is any process that is self-driven, reducing and potentially eliminating the need for human intervention. Whenever a course of action is taken by a device based on an outside piece of information, that device is a smart device. For smart devices to "think," they need to be programmed using network automation tools.

Data Formats

Data formats make it possible to store and interchange data in a structured format. One such format is called Hypertext Markup Language (HTML). Common data formats that are used in many applications, including network automation and programmability, are JavaScript Object Notation (JSON), Extensible Markup Language (XML), and YAML Ain't Markup Language (YAML). Data formats have rules and structure similar to those of programming and written languages.

APIs

An API is a set of rules describing how one application can interact with another one and the instructions to allow the interaction to occur. Open/public APIs are, as the name suggests, publicly available. Internal/private APIs are used only within an organization. Partner APIs are used between a company and its business partners. There are four types of web service APIs: Simple Object Access Protocol (SOAP), Representational State Transfer (REST), Extensible Markup Language–Remote Procedure Call (XML-RPC), and JavaScript Object Notation–Remote Procedure Call (JSON-RPC).

REST

A REST API defines a set of functions developers can use to perform requests and receive responses via HTTP, such as GET and POST. Conforming to the constraints of the REST architecture is generally referred to as being RESTful. RESTful APIs use common HTTP methods including POST, GET, PUT, PATCH, and DELETE. These methods correspond to the RESTful operations create, read, update, and delete (or CRUD). Web resources and web services such as RESTful APIs are identified using a URI. A URI has two specializations, uniform resource name (URN) and uniform resource locator (URL). In a RESTful web service, a request made to a resource's URI elicits a response. The response is a payload typically formatted in JSON. The different parts of the API request are API servers, resources, and queries. Queries can include formats, keys, and parameters.

Configuration and Management

There are now new and different methods for network operators to automatically monitor, manage, and configure the network. These include protocols and technologies such as REST, Ansible, Puppet, Chef, Python, JSON, and XML. Configuration management tools use RESTful API requests to automate tasks and scale across thousands of devices. Characteristics of the network that benefit from automation include software and version control; device attributes such as names, addressing, and security; protocol configurations; and ACL configurations. Configuration management tools typically include automation and orchestration. Orchestration involves arranging the automated tasks into a coordinated process or workflow. Ansible, Chef, Puppet, and SaltStack all come with API documentation for configuring RESTful API requests.

IBN and Cisco DNA Center

IBN builds on SDN, taking a software-centric, fully automated approach to designing and operating networks. Cisco views IBN as having three essential functions: translation, activation, and assurance. The physical and virtual network infrastructure is a fabric—an overlay that represents the logical topology used to virtually connect to devices. The underlay network is the physical topology that includes all hardware required to meet business objectives. Cisco implements the IBN fabric using Cisco DNA. The business intent is securely deployed into the network infrastructure (the fabric). Cisco DNA continuously gathers data from a multitude of sources (devices and applications) to provide a rich context of information. Cisco DNA Center is the foundational controller and analytics platform at the heart of Cisco DNA. Cisco DNA Center is a network management and command center for provisioning and configuring network devices. It is a single-interface hardware and software platform that focuses on assurance, analytics, and automation.

Practice

There are no labs or Packet Tracer activities for this chapter.

Check Your Understanding Questions

Complete all the review questions listed here to test your understanding of the sections and concepts in this chapter. The appendix "Answers to the 'Check Your Understanding' Questions" lists the answers.

1. In the following example, which data format is used?

   ```
   message: success
   timestamp: 1560789260
   iss_position:
       latitude: '25.9990'
           longitude: '-132.6992'
   ```

   A. HTML

   B. JSON

   C. XML

   D. YAML

2. In the following example, which data format is used?

   ```
   {
       "message": "success",
       "timestamp": 1560789260,
       "iss_position": {
               "latitude": "25.9990",
               "longitude": "-132.6992"
       }
   }
   ```

   A. HTML

   B. JSON

   C. XML

   D. YAML

3. A RESTful API (for example, a public API) mat require a key. What is the function of the key?

   A. It is the top-level object of the API query.

   B. It is used in the encryption of the message by an API request.

   C. It is used to authenticate the requesting source.

   D. It represents the main query components in the API request.

4. Which two configuration management tools were developed using Python? (Choose two.)

   A. Ansible

   B. Chef

   C. Puppet

   D. RESTCONF

   E. SaltStack

5. Which configuration management tool combines a set of instructions in a manifest?

   A. Ansible

   B. Chef

   C. Puppet

   D. RESTCONF

   E. SaltStack

6. Which RESTful operation corresponds to the HTTP POST method?

   A. create

   B. delete

   C. read

   D. update

7. How does the YAML data format structure differ from JSON?

   A. YAML uses brackets and commas.

   B. YAML uses end tags.

   C. YAML uses hierarchical levels of nesting.

   D. YAML uses indentations.

8. Which configuration management tool combines a set of instructions in a playbook?

   A. Ansible

   B. Chef

   C. Puppet

   D. RESTCONF

   E. SaltStack

9. In the following example, which data format is used?

```
<root>
  <message>success</message>
  <timestamp>1560789260</timestamp>
  <iss_position>
    <latitude>25.9990</latitude>
    <longitude>-132.6992</longitude>
  </iss_position>
</root>
```

A. HTML

B. JSON

C. XML

D. YAML

10. What is a difference between the HTML and XML data formats?

A. HTML formats data in plaintext, whereas XML formats data in binary.

B. HTML uses predefined tags, and XML does not.

C. HTML requires indentation for each key/value pair, but XML does not.

D. HTML uses a pair of quotation marks to enclose data, whereas XML encloses data within a pair of tags.

11. What is REST?

A. It is a human-readable data structure that applications use for storing, transforming, and reading data.

B. It is a protocol that allows administrators to manage nodes on an IP network.

C. It is a way to store and interchange data in a structured format.

D. It is an architecture style for designing web service applications.

12. Which RESTful operation corresponds to the HTTP PUT method?

A. create

B. delete

C. read

D. update

13. What is JSON?

A. It is a compiled programming language.

B. It is a data format that is simpler than XML.

C. It is a scripting language.

D. It is a superset of YAML.

14. Which scenario describes the use of a public API?

    A. It can be used with no restrictions.

    B. It is used only within an organization.

    C. It requires a license.

    D. It is used between a company and its business partners.

Answers to the "Check Your Understanding" Questions

Chapter 1

1. B. Each OSPF router views the network differently as the root of a unique SPF tree. Each router builds adjacencies based on its own position in the topology. Each routing table in the area is developed individually through the application of the SPF algorithm. The link-state database for an area, however, must reflect the same information for all routers. Regardless of which OSPF area a router resides in, the adjacency database, routing table, and forwarding database are unique for each router. The link-state database lists information about all other routers within an area and is identical across all OSPF routers participating in that area.

2. B, C, and E. The topology table on an OSPF router is a link-state database (LSDB) that lists information about all other routers in the network and represents the network topology. All routers within an area have identical link-state databases, and the table can be viewed using the **show ip ospf database** command. The SPF algorithm uses the LSDB to produce the unique routing table for each router, which contains the lowest-cost route entries for known networks.

3. A. The adjacency database is used to create the OSPF neighbor table. The link-state database is used to create the topology table, and the forwarding database is used to create the routing table.

4. A. The OSPF Hello packet serves three primary functions: to discover OSPF neighbors and establish adjacencies, to advertise parameters that OSPF neighbors must agree on, and when necessary, to elect the DR and BDR.

5. E. Link-State Update (LSU) packets contain different types of link-state advertisements (LSAs). The LSUs are used to reply to link-state requests (LSRs) and to announce new information.

6. B and E. The OSPF router ID does not contribute to SPF algorithm calculations, nor does it facilitate the transition of the OSPF neighbor state to Full. Although the router ID is contained within OSPF messages when router adjacencies are being established, it has no bearing on the convergence process.

7. B. A multiarea OSPF network requires hierarchical network design (with two levels). The main area is called the backbone area, and all other areas must connect to the main area.

8. D and F. A multiarea OSPF network improves routing performance and efficiency in a large network. As the network is divided into smaller areas, each router maintains a smaller routing table because routes between areas can be summarized. Also, fewer updated routes means fewer LSAs are exchanged, thus reducing the need for CPU resources. Running multiple routing protocols simultaneously and implementing both IPv4 and IPv6 are not primary considerations for a multiarea OSPF network. With multiarea OSPF, only routers within an area share the same link-state database. Changes to the network topology in one area do not

impact other areas, which reduces the number of SPF algorithm calculations and the number of link-state databases.

9. A. The **show ip ospf database** command is used to verify the contents of the LSDB. The **show ip ospf interface** command is used to verify the configuration information of OSPF-enabled interfaces. The **show ip ospf neighbor** command is used to gather information regarding OSPF neighbor routers. The **show ip route ospf** command displays OSPF-related information in the routing table.

10. D. OSPF supports the concept of areas to prevent larger routing tables, excessive SPF calculations, and large LSDBs. Only routers within an area share link-state information. This allows OSPF to scale in a hierarchical fashion with all areas that connect to a backbone area.

11. D. The OSPF operation steps are establish neighbor adjacencies, exchange link-state advertisements, build the topology table, execute the SPF algorithm, and choose the best route.

12. A. The Type 2 Database Description (DBD) packet contains an abbreviated list of the LSDB of the sending router and is used by receiving routers to check against the local LSDB. The LSDB must be identical on all link-state routers within an area to construct an accurate SPF tree.

13. A, D, and F. OSPF operation progresses through seven states in establishing neighboring router adjacency, exchanging routing information, calculating the best routes, and reaching convergence. The Down, Init, and Two-Way states are involved in the phase of neighboring router adjacency establishment.

14. B. When the routers are interconnected over a common Ethernet network, a designated router (DR) and a backup DR (BDR) must be elected.

15. D. After all LSRs have been satisfied for a given router, the adjacent routers are considered synchronized and in a Full state. Updates (LSUs) are sent to neighbors only under the following conditions:

- When a network topology change is detected (incremental updates)

- Every 30 minutes

Chapter 2

1. B. On Cisco routers, the default Dead interval is four times the Hello interval, and this timer has expired in this case. SPF does not determine the state of neighbor routers; it determines which routes become routing table entries. A DR/DBR election does not always automatically run; it depends on the type of network and on whether or not the router that is no longer up was a DR or BDR.

2. A. When electing a DR, the router with the highest OSPF priority becomes the DR. If all routers have the same priority, then the router with the highest router ID is elected.

3. A. The wildcard mask can be found by subtracting the subnet mask from 255.255.255.255.

4. C. While the **show ip interface brief** and **ping** commands can be used to determine if Layer 1, 2, and 3 connectivity exists, neither command can be used to determine whether a particular OSPF or EIGRP-initiated relationship has been made. The **show ip protocols** command is useful in determining the routing parameters such as timers, router

ID, and metric information associated with a specific routing protocol. The **show ip ospf neighbor** command shows if two adjacent routers have exchanged OSPF messages in order to form a neighbor relationship.

5. C. The **show ip ospf interface** command verifies the active OSPF interfaces. The **show ip interface brief** command is used to check that the interfaces are operational. The **show ip route ospf** command displays the entries that are learned via OSPF in the routing table. The **show ip protocols** command checks that OSPF is enabled and lists the networks that are advertised.

6. C. The **show ip ospf interface serial 0/0/0** command displays the configured Hello and Dead timer intervals on a point-to-point serial WAN link between two OSPFv2 routers. The **show ipv6 ospf interface serial 0/0/0** command displays the configured Hello and Dead timer intervals on a point-to-point serial link between two OSPFv3 routers. The **show ip ospf interface fastethernet 0/1** command displays the configured Hello and Dead timer intervals on a multiaccess link between two (or more) OSPFv2 routers. The **show ip ospf neighbor** command displays the Dead interval elapsed time since the last Hello message was received, but it does not show the configured value of the timer.

7. A and B. The **show ip ospf interface** command displays routing table information that is already known. The **show ip ospf neighbors** command displays adjacency information on neighboring OSPF routers. The **show running-configuration** and **show ip protocols** commands display aspects of the OSPF configuration on the router but do not display adjacency state details or timer interval details.

8. D. Cisco IOS automatically modifies the Dead interval to four times the Hello interval.

9. A and B. The Hello and Dead interval timers contained in a Hello packet must be the same on neighboring routers in order to form an adjacency.

10. B. The router priority value is used in a DR/BDR election. The default priority for all OSPF routers is 1, but it can be manually altered to any value from 0 to 255.

11. A. OSPF routers send Hello packets to monitor the state of a neighbor. When a router stops receiving Hello packets from a neighbor, that neighbor is considered unreachable, and the adjacency is broken.

12. A. The first preference for an OSPF router ID is an explicitly configured 32-bit address. This address is not included in the routing table and is not defined by the **network** command. If a router ID that is configured through the **router-id** command is not available, OSPF routers next use the highest IPv4 address available on a loopback interface, as loopbacks used as router IDs are also not routable addresses. Lacking either of these alternatives, an OSPF router will use the highest IPv4 address from its active physical interfaces.

13. C. To advertise only the 10.1.1.0 network, the wildcard mask used in the **network** command must match the first 24 bits exactly. An alternative method of configuring this would also be to use the **network 10.1.1.0 255.255.255.0 area 0** command.

14. A. OSPF uses the formula Cost = 100,000,000 / bandwidth. Because OSPF will only use integers as cost, any bandwidth of 100 Mbps or greater will equal a cost of 1.

15. C. The correct network statement is **network 64.100.1.64 0.0.0.63 area 0**.

16. C and D. There may be several reasons two routers running OSPF will fail to form an OSPF adjacency, including subnet masks not matching, OSPF Hello or Dead timers not matching, OSPF network types not matching, and a missing or incorrect OSPF **network** command. Mismatched IOS versions, the use of private IP addresses, and different types of interface ports used are not causes for an OSPF adjacency failing to form between two routers.

Chapter 3

1. D. Internal threats can be intentional or accidental and can cause greater damage than external threats because an internal user has direct access to the internal corporate network and corporate data.

2. B. Cybercriminals are commonly motivated by money. Hackers are known to hack for status. Cyberterrorists are motivated to commit cybercrimes for religious or political reasons.

3. B. Hackers are categorized by motivating factors. Hacktivists are motivated by protesting political and social issues.

4. B. Trojan horse malware appears as useful software but hides malicious code. Trojan horse malware may cause annoying computer problems, but it can also cause fatal problems. Some Trojan horses may be distributed over the internet, but they can also be distributed by USB memory sticks and other means. Specifically targeted Trojan horse malware can be some of the most difficult malware to detect.

5. C. Social engineering involves attempting to gain the confidence of an employee and convince that person to divulge confidential and sensitive information, such as usernames and passwords. DDoS attacks, spam, and key-logging are all examples of software-based security threats, not social engineering.

6. B. A ping sweep is a technique that is used during a reconnaissance attack to locate line IP addresses. Other tools that might be used during this type of attack include a port scan or an internet information query. A reconnaissance attack is used to gather information about a particular network, usually in preparation for another type of network attack.

7. A. Zombies are infected computers that make up a botnet. They are used to deploy a distributed denial-of-service (DDoS) attack.

8. C. When an asymmetric algorithm is used, public and private keys are used for the encryption. Either key can be used for encryption, but the complementary matched key must be used for the decryption. For example, if the public key is used for encryption, the private key must be used for the decryption.

9. C. Integrity is ensured by implementing SHA hash generating algorithms. Many modern networks ensure authentication with protocols such as HMACs. Data confidentiality is ensured through symmetric encryption algorithms, including 3DES and AES. Data confidentiality can also be ensured using asymmetric algorithms.

10. A. An advantage of an intrusion prevention system (IPS) is that it can identify and stop malicious packets. However, because an IPS is deployed inline, it can add latency to the network.

11. A. Black hat hackers are unethical threat actors who use their skills to compromise computer and network security vulnerabilities. The goal is usually financial gain or personal gain, or the hacker may have malicious intent. A vulnerability broker is a gray hat hacker who attempts to discover exploits and report them to vendors, sometimes for prizes or rewards. Hacktivists are gray hat hackers who publicly protest organizations or governments by posting articles or videos, leaking sensitive information, and performing network attacks. Script kiddies are inexperienced hackers (sometimes teenagers) running existing scripts, tools, and exploits to cause harm—but typically not for profit.

12. C. A threat is a potential danger to a company's assets, data, or network functionality. An exploit is a mechanism that takes advantage of a vulnerability. A vulnerability is a weakness in a system, or its design, that could be exploited by a threat.

13. D. Origin authentication guarantees that a message is not a forgery and does actually come from the person who is supposed to have sent it. Data nonrepudiation guarantees that the sender cannot repudiate, or refute, the validity of a message sent. An exploit is a mechanism that takes advantage of a vulnerability. Mitigation describes a countermeasure to eliminate or reduce the potential of a threat or risk.

14. B. An exploit is a mechanism that takes advantage of a vulnerability. A threat is a potential danger to a company's assets, data, or network functionality. A vulnerability is a weakness in a system, or its design, that could be exploited by a threat.

15. A. Data nonrepudiation guarantees that the sender cannot repudiate, or refute, the validity of a message sent. An exploit is a mechanism that takes advantage of a vulnerability. Mitigation is a countermeasure to eliminate or reduce the potential of a threat or risk. Origin authentication guarantees that a message is not a forgery and does actually come from the person who is supposed to have sent it.

Chapter 4

1. B and C. An ACL can be configured as a simple firewall that provides security using basic traffic filtering capabilities. ACLs are used to filter host traffic by allowing or blocking matching packets to networks.

2. C, D, and E. If the information in a packet header and an ACL statement match, the rest of the statements in the list are skipped, and the packet is permitted or denied as specified by the matched statement. If a packet header does not match an ACL statement, the packet is tested against the next statement in the list. This matching process continues until the end of the list is reached. At the end of every ACL is an implicit "deny any" statement that is applied to all packets for which conditions did not test true and results in a "deny" action.

3. A, D, and E. Extended ACLs should be placed as close as possible to the source IP address so that traffic that needs to be filtered does not cross the network and use network resources. Because standard ACLs do not specify a destination address, they should be placed as close to the destination as possible. Placing a standard ACL close to the source may have the effect of filtering all traffic and limiting services to other hosts. Filtering unwanted traffic before it enters

low-bandwidth links preserves bandwidth and supports network functionality. Decisions on placing ACLs inbound or outbound are dependent on the requirements to be met.

4. B and E. Standard ACLs filter traffic based solely on a specified source IP address. Extended ACLs can filter by source or destination, protocol, or port. Both standard and extended ACLs contain an implicit deny as a final ACE. Standard and extended ACLs can be identified by either names or numbers.

5. A and E. With an inbound ACL, incoming packets are processed before they are routed. With an outbound ACL, packets are first routed to the outbound interface, and then they are processed. Thus, processing inbound is more efficient from the router's perspective. The structure, filtering methods, and limitations (that is, only one inbound and one outbound ACL can be configured on an interface) are the same for both types of ACLs.

6. D. An outbound ACL should be used when the same ACL filtering rules will be applied to packets coming from more than one inbound interface before exiting a single outbound interface. The outbound ACL will be applied on the single outbound interface.

7. D. The subnets 10.16.0.0 through 10.19.0.0 all share the same 14 high-level bits. A wildcard mask in binary that matches 14 high-order bits is 00000000.00000011.11111111.11111111. In dotted decimal, this wildcard mask is 0.3.255.255.

8. A. The two types of ACLs are standard and extended. Both types can be named or numbered, but extended ACLs offer greater flexibility. Extended ACLs provide the most

options and therefore the most filtering control.

9. D. A standard IPv4 ACL can filter traffic based on source IP addresses only. Unlike an extended ACL, it cannot filter traffic based on Layer 4 ports. However, both standard and extended ACLs can be identified with either numbers or names, and both are configured in global configuration mode.

10. C. A /26 is 255.255.255.192. Therefore, 255.255.255.255 − 255.255.255.192 = 0.0.0.63.

Chapter 5

1. D. **access-list 110 permit tcp 172.16.0.0 0.0.0.255 any eq 22** ACE matches traffic on port 22, which is for SSH, that is sourced from network 172.16.0.0/24 with any destination.

2. B and D. The **host** keyword is used when using a specific device IP address in an ACL. For example, the **deny host 192.168.5.5** command is the same as the **deny 192.168.5.5 0.0.0.0** command. The **any** keyword is used to allow any mask that meets the criteria. For example, the **permit any** command is the same as the **permit 0.0.0.0 255.255.255.255** command.

3. C and D. Extended access lists commonly filter on source and destination IPv4 addresses and TCP or UDP port numbers. Additional filtering can be provided for protocol types.

4. D. You can use the **ip access-list** command to edit an existing numbered or named ACL. The ACL ACEs can be removed using the **no** command followed by the sequence number.

5. A and D. To permit or deny one specific IPv4 address, either the wildcard mask **0.0.0.0** (used after the IP address) or the wildcard mask keyword **host** (used before the IP address) can be used.

6. B and D. To deny traffic from the 10.10.0.0/16 network, the **access-list 55 deny 10.10.0.0 0.0.255.255** command is used. To permit all other traffic, the **access-list 55 permit any** statement is added.

7. B. The host must be filtered first, so adding sequence 5 at the beginning of the ACE would insert it before the 192.168.10.0/24 network is permitted.

8. A. The **access-group** *acl-name* **in** line configuration mode command correctly applies a standard ACL to the vty interfaces.

9. D. Traffic originating from 10.10.100/24 is permitted to all destinations listening to TCP port 80 (that is, www).

10. A. After you enter the command, you go into named extended ACL configuration mode R1(config-ext-nacl).

Chapter 6

1. C. Typically, the translation from private IPv4 addresses to public IPv4 addresses is performed on routers in corporate environments. In a home environment, this device might be an access point that has routing capability or a DSL or cable router.

2. D. It is common practice to configure addresses from the 10.0.0.0/8, 172.16.0.0/12, and 192.168.0.0/16 ranges.

3. B. PAT allows many hosts on a private network to share a single public address by mapping sessions to TCP/UDP port numbers.

4. D. A one-to-one mapping of an inside local address to an inside global address is accomplished through static NAT.

5. D. Many internet protocols and applications depend on end-to-end addressing from the source to the destination. Because parts of the header of the IPv4 packets are modified, the router needs to alter the checksum of the IPv4 packets. Using a single public IPv4 address allows for the conservation of legally registered IPv4 addressing schemes. If an addressing scheme needs to be modified, it is cheaper to use private IPv4 addresses.

6. D. Dynamic NAT provides a dynamic mapping of inside local to inside global IPv4 addresses. NAT is merely the one-to-one mapping of one address to another address without consideration for whether the address is public or private. DHCP involves automatic assignment of IPv4 addresses to hosts. DNS maps hostnames to IPv4 addresses.

7. A. In order for the **ip nat inside source list 4 pool NAT-POOL** command to work, the following procedure needs to occur:

   1. Create an access list that defines the private IPv4 addresses affected by NAT.

   2. Establish a NAT pool of starting and ending public IPv4 addresses by using the **ip nat pool** command.

   3. Use the **ip nat inside source list** command to associate the access list with the NAT pool.

   4. Apply NAT to internal and external interfaces by using the **ip nat inside** and **ip nat outside** commands.

8. D. If all the addresses in the NAT pool have been used, a device must wait for an available address before it can access the outside network.

9. C. With the **ip nat inside source list 1 interface serial 0/0/0 overload** command, the router is configured to translate internal private IPv4 addresses in the range 10.0.0.0/8 to a single public IPv4 address, 209.165.200.225/30. The other options will not work because the IPv4 addresses defined in the pool, 192.168.2.0/28, are not routable on the internet.

10. B and E. The steps that are required to configure PAT are to define a pool of global addresses to be used for overload translation, to configure source translation by using the keywords **interface** and **overload**, and to identify the interfaces that are involved in the PAT.

11. A. An inside local address is the address of the source, as seen from the inside of the network. An outside global address is the address of the destination, as seen from the outside network.

Chapter 7

1. A. For this small office, an appropriate connection to the internet would be through a common broadband service such as digital subscriber line (DSL), available from the company's local telephone service provider, or a cable connection from the cable company. Because the company has so few employees, bandwidth is not a significant issue. If the company were bigger, with branch offices in remote sites, private lines would be more appropriate. VSATs are used to provide connectivity to remote locations and are typically used only when no other connectivity options are available.

2. D. When traveling employees need to connect to a corporate email server through a WAN connection, the VPN creates a secure tunnel between an employee laptop and the corporate network over the WAN connection. Obtaining dynamic IP addresses through DHCP is a function of LAN communication. Sharing files among separate buildings on a corporate campus is accomplished through the LAN infrastructure. A DMZ is a protected network inside the corporate LAN infrastructure.

3. D. WANs are used to interconnect an enterprise LAN to remote branch site LANs and telecommuter sites. A WAN is owned by a service provider. Although WAN connections are typically made through serial interfaces, not all serial links are connected to a WAN. LANs, not WANs, provide end-user network connectivity in an organization.

4. B. Digital leased lines require a channel service unit (CSU) and a data service unit (DSU). An access server concentrates dialup modem dial-in and dial-out user communications. Dialup modems are used to temporarily enable the use of analog telephone lines for digital data communications. A Layer 2 switch is used to connect a LAN.

5. C. A connection-oriented system predetermines the network path, creates a virtual circuit for the duration of the packet delivery, and requires that each packet carry an identifier. A connectionless packet-switched network, such as the internet, requires each data packet to carry addressing information.

6. B. Unlike circuit-switched networks, which typically require expensive permanent connections, packet-switched networks can

take alternate paths, if available, to reach the destination.

7. B. Dense wavelength-division multiplexing (DWDM) is a newer technology that increases the data-carrying capacity of SDH and SONET by simultaneously multiplexing data using different wavelengths of light. ISDN (Integrated Services Digital Network), ATM (Asynchronous Transfer Mode), and MPLS (Multiprotocol Label Switching) are not fiber-optic technologies.

8. D. Corporate communications over public WANs should use VPNs for security. ISDN and ATM are Layer 1 and 2 technologies that are typically used on private WANs. Municipal Wi-Fi is a wireless public WAN technology.

9. D and E. SDH and SONET are high-bandwidth fiber-optic standards that define how to transfer data, voice, and video communications using lasers or light-emitting diodes (LEDs). ATM (Asynchronous Transfer Mode) is a Layer 2 technology. ANSI (American National Standards Institute) and ITU (International Telecommunication Union) are standards organizations.

10. D. A leased line establishes a dedicated constant point-to-point connection between two sites. ATM is cell switched. ISDN is circuit switched. Frame Relay is packet switched.

11. A. A private WAN solution that involves dedicated links between sites offers the best security and confidentiality. Private and public WAN solutions offer comparable connection bandwidth, depending on the technology chosen. Connecting multiple sites with private WAN connections could be very expensive. The website and file exchange service support is not relevant.

12. B and D. VPNs over the internet provide low-cost, secure connections to remote users. VPNs are deployed over the internet public infrastructure.

13. B. LTE, or Long-Term Evolution, is a fourth-generation cellular access technology that supports internet access.

14. B. The equipment located at a cable service provider office, the cable modem termination system (CMTS), sends and receives digital cable modem signals on a cable network to provide internet services to cable subscribers. A DSLAM performs a similar function for DSL service providers. A CSU/DSU is used in leased-line connections. Access servers are needed to process multiple simultaneous dialup connections to a central office (CO).

15. B. MPLS can use a variety of technologies, such as T- and E-carriers, optical carrier, ATM, Frame Relay, and DSL, all of which support lower speeds than an Ethernet WAN. Neither a circuit-switched network, such as the public switched telephone network (PSTN) or Integrated Service Digital Network (ISDN), nor a packet-switched network is considered high speed.

Chapter 8

1. D. A GRE IP tunnel does not provide authentication or security. A leased line is not cost-effective compared to using high-speed broadband technology with VPNs. A dedicated ISP is not required when utilizing VPNs between multiple sites.

2. B. Site-to-site VPNs are statically defined VPN connections between two sites that use VPN gateways. The internal hosts do

not require VPN client software and send normal, unencapsulated packets onto the network, where they are encapsulated by the VPN gateway.

3. C. The IPsec framework uses various protocols and algorithms to provide data confidentiality, data integrity, authentication, and secure key exchange. The hash message authentication code (HMAC) is a data integrity algorithm that uses a hash value to guarantee the integrity of a message.

4. A. The IPsec framework uses various protocols and algorithms to provide data confidentiality, data integrity, authentication, and secure key exchange. Two popular algorithms that are used to ensure that data is not intercepted and modified (data integrity) are MD5 and SHA. AES is an encryption protocol and provides data confidentiality. DH (Diffie-Hellman) is an algorithm that is used for key exchange. RSA is an algorithm that is used for authentication.

5. C and E. The IPsec framework uses various protocols and algorithms to provide data confidentiality, data integrity, authentication, and secure key exchange. Two popular algorithms used to ensure that data is not intercepted and modified (data integrity and authentication) are MD5 and SHA.

6. A and E. The IPsec framework uses various protocols and algorithms to provide data confidentiality, data integrity, authentication, and secure key exchange. Two algorithms that can be used within an IPsec policy to protect interesting traffic are AES, which is an encryption protocol, and SHA, which is a hashing algorithm.

7. A. Generic Routing Encapsulation (GRE) is a tunneling protocol developed by Cisco that encapsulates multiprotocol traffic between remote Cisco routers. GRE does not encrypt data. OSPF is an open-source routing protocol. IPsec is a suite of protocols that allow for the exchange of information that can be encrypted and verified. Internet Key Exchange (IKE) is a key management standard used with IPsec.

8. B. When a web browser is used to securely access the corporate network, the browser must use a secure version of HTTP to provide SSL encryption. A VPN client is not required to be installed on the remote host, so a clientless SSL connection is used.

9. B. Confidentiality is a function of IPsec and utilizes encryption to protect data transfers with a key. Integrity is a function of IPsec and ensures that data arrives unchanged at the destination through the use of a hashing algorithm. Authentication is a function of IPsec and provides specific access to users and devices with valid authentication factors. Secure key exchange is a function of IPsec and allows two peers to maintain their private key confidentiality while sharing their public key.

10. C and D. VPNs can be managed and deployed as either enterprise VPNs (which is a common solution for securing enterprise traffic across the internet and includes site-to-site and remote-access VPNs) or service provider VPNs (that is, VPNs created and managed over the provider network, such as Layer 2 and Layer 3 MPLS VPNS, or legacy Frame Relay and ATM VPNs).

11. A and B. Enterprise managed remote-access VPNs are created dynamically when required. Remote-access VPNs include client-based IPsec VPNs and clientless SSL VPNs.

12. D. Site-to-site VPNs are static and are used to connect entire networks. Hosts have no knowledge of the VPN and send TCP/IP traffic to VPN gateways. The VPN gateway is responsible for encapsulating the traffic and forwarding it through the VPN tunnel to a peer gateway at the other end that decapsulates the traffic.

13. A. The IPsec framework uses various protocols and algorithms to provide data confidentiality, data integrity, authentication, and secure key exchange. DH (Diffie-Hellman) is an algorithm used for key exchange. DH is a public key exchange method that allows two IPsec peers to establish a shared secret key over an insecure channel.

14. B. In a GRE over IPsec tunnel, the term passenger protocol refers to the original packet that is to be encapsulated by GRE. The carrier protocol is the protocol that encapsulates the original passenger packet. The transport protocol is the protocol that will be used to forward the packet.

15. A. An IPsec VTI is a newer IPsec VPN technology that simplifies the configuration required to support multiple sites and remote access. IPsec VTI configurations use virtual interfaces to send and receive IP unicast and multicast encrypted traffic. Therefore, routing protocols are automatically supported without requiring configuration of GRE tunnels.

16. A. When a client negotiates an SSL VPN connection with the VPN gateway, it connects using Transport Layer Security (TLS). TLS is the newer version of SSL and is sometimes expressed as SSL/TLS. The two terms are often used interchangeably.

17. B. An MPLS VPN has both Layer 2 and Layer 3 implementations. A GRE over IPsec VPN involves a nonsecure tunneling protocol encapsulated by IPsec. An IPsec VTI VPN routes packets through virtual tunnel interfaces for encryption and forwarding. An IPsec VTI VPN and GRE over IPsec VPN allows multicast and broadcast traffic over a secure site-to-site VPN. An SSL VPN uses the public key infrastructure and digital certificates.

18. E. An SSL VPN uses the public key infrastructure and digital certificates. An MPLS VPN has both Layer 2 and Layer 3 implementations. A GRE over IPsec VPN involves a nonsecure tunneling protocol encapsulated by IPsec. An IPsec VTI VPN routes packets through virtual tunnel interfaces for encryption and forwarding. An IPsec VTI VPN and a GRE over IPsec VPN allow multicast and broadcast traffic over a secure site-to-site VPN.

19. A and D. An IPsec VTI VPN routes packets through virtual tunnel interfaces for encryption and forwarding. An IPsec VTI VPN and a GRE over IPsec VPN allow multicast and broadcast traffic over a secure site-to-site VPN. An MPLS VPN has both Layer 2 and Layer 3 implementations. A GRE over IPsec VPN involves a nonsecure tunneling protocol being encapsulated by IPsec. An SSL VPN uses the public key infrastructure and digital certificates.

20. A and C. A GRE over IPsec VPN involves a nonsecure tunneling protocol being encapsulated by IPsec. An IPsec VTI VPN and a GRE over IPsec VPN allow multicast and broadcast traffic over a secure site-to-site VPN. An MPLS VPN has both Layer 2 and Layer 3 implementations. An IPsec VTI VPN routes packets through virtual tunnel interfaces for encryption and forwarding. An SSL VPN uses the public key infrastructure and digital certificates.

Chapter 9

1. B. Traffic requires enough bandwidth to support services. When there is not enough bandwidth, congestion occurs and typically results in packet loss.

2. C. Quality of service (QoS) needs to be enabled on routers to provide support for VoIP and video conferencing. QoS refers to the capability of a network to provide better service to selected network traffic, such as voice and video traffic.

3. B. When the volume of traffic is greater than what can be transported across the network, devices queue, or hold, the packets in memory until resources become available to transmit them. If the number of packets to be queued continues to increase, the memory in the device fills up, and packets are dropped.

4. A. CBWFQ extends the standard WFQ functionality to provide support for user-defined traffic classes. A FIFO queue is reserved for each class, and traffic belonging to a class is directed to the queue for that class.

5. D. With LLQ, delay-sensitive data is sent first, before packets in other queues are treated. Although it is possible to enqueue various types of real-time traffic to the strict priority queue, Cisco recommends that only voice traffic be directed to the priority queue.

6. B. When no other queuing strategies are configured, all interfaces except serial interfaces at E1 (2.048 Mbps) and below use FIFO by default. Serial interfaces at E1 and below use WFQ by default.

7. D. When no other queuing strategies are configured, all interfaces except serial interfaces at E1 (2.048 Mbps) and below use FIFO by default. Serial interfaces at E1 and below use WFQ by default.

8. A. The best-effort model has no way to classify packets; therefore, all network packets are treated the same way. Without QoS, the network cannot tell the difference between packets and, as a result, cannot treat packets preferentially.

9. C. IntServ uses Resource Reservation Protocol (RSVP) to signal the QoS needs of an application's traffic along devices in the end-to-end path through the network. If network devices along the path can reserve the necessary bandwidth, the originating application can begin transmitting. If the requested reservation fails along the path, the originating application does not send any data.

10. C. Marking means adding a value to the packet header. Devices receiving the packet look at this field to see whether it matches a defined policy. Marking should be done as close to the source device as possible to establish the trust boundary.

11. B. Trusted endpoints have the capabilities and intelligence to mark application traffic to the appropriate Layer 2 CoS and/or Layer 3 DSCP values. Examples of trusted endpoints include IP phones, wireless access points, video-conferencing gateways and systems, and IP conferencing stations.

12. A. The 802.1p standard uses the first 3 bits in the Tag Control Information (TCI) field. Known as the Priority (PRI) field, this 3-bit field identifies the Class of Service (CoS) markings. Three bits means that a Layer 2 Ethernet frame can be marked with one of eight levels of priority (values 0–7).

13. D. RFC 2474 redefines the ToS field with a new 6-bit Differentiated Services Code Point (DSCP) QoS field. Six bits offers a maximum of 64 possible classes of service.

Chapter 10

1. C. LLDP requires two commands to configure an interface: **lldp transmit** and **lldp receive**.

2. B and C. The **no cdp enable** command interface configuration command cannot be executed from a global configuration prompt. Options D and E are invalid commands.

3. C. Both commands provide information for options A, B, and D. However, only **show cdp neighbors detail** provides the IP address.

4. D. Options A through C are invalid commands. The options to enable LLDP on interfaces are **lldp transmit** and **lldp receive**.

5. C. To enable LLDP on interfaces, use **lldp transmit** and **lldp receive**. The **lldp run** global configuration command enables LLDP globally. Interface LLDP configuration commands override the global command.

6. B. These are all syslog messages, but the most common ones are link up and link down messages.

7. A. The smaller the level numbers, the more critical the alarms. Emergency—Level 0 messages indicate that the system is unusable. This would be an event that has halted the system. Alert—Level 1 messages indicate that immediate action is needed, as in the case of a failed connection to the ISP. Critical—Level 2 messages indicate a critical condition, such as the failure of a backup connection to the ISP. Error—Level 3 messages indicate error conditions, such as an interface being down.

8. D. Cisco developed NetFlow for the purpose of gathering statistics on packets flowing through Cisco routers and multilayer switches. SNMP can be used to collect and store information about a device. Syslog is used to access and store system messages. NTP is used to allow network devices to synchronize time settings.

9. B. Syslog messages can be sent to the logging buffer, the console line, the terminal line, or a syslog server. However, debug-level messages are only forwarded to the internal buffer and are accessible only through the Cisco CLI.

10. A. The console receives all syslog messages by default. Syslog messages for Cisco routers and switches can be sent to memory, the console, a tty line, or a syslog server.

11. A. The logging trap level allows a network administrator to limit event messages that are being sent to a syslog server based on severity.

12. D. Option A is for syslog, B for TFTP, and the explanation for C is incorrect.

13. B and D. A is incorrect. NTP has nothing to do with MTBF, and multiple NTP servers can be identified for redundancy.

14. C. ROMMON mode must be accessed to perform password recovery on a router.

15. B. With the configuration register at 0x2142, the device ignores the startup configuration file during startup, and the startup configuration file is where the forgotten passwords are stored.

16. D. Options A and C are global configuration commands, and Option B is the default setting and looks for the startup configuration file.

17. D. An administrator must have physical access to the device along with a console connection to perform password recovery.

18. B. The **show flash0:** command displays the amount of flash available (free) and the amount of flash used. The command also displays the files stored in flash, including their size and when they were copied.

19. A and E. To upgrade Cisco IOS, you need the device IOS image file located on a reachable TFTP server. Image files are copied to flash memory. Therefore, it is important to verify the amount of flash memory available on the device.

20. B. An SNMP agent that resides on a managed device collects and stores information about the device and its operation. This information is stored by the agent locally in the MIB. An NMS periodically polls the SNMP agents that are residing on managed devices by using the get request to query the devices for data. The NMS uses a set request to change the configuration in the agent device or to initiate actions within a device.

21. D. To solve the issue of the delay that exists between when an event occurs and the time when it is noticed via polling by the NMS, you can use SNMP trap messages. SNMP trap messages are generated from SNMP agents and are sent to the NMS immediately to inform it of certain events without requiring a wait for the device to be polled by the NMS.

22. A. SNMPv1 and SNMPv2 use community strings to control access to the MIB. SNMPv3 uses encryption, message integrity, and source validation.

23. B. Both SNMPv1 and SNMPv2c use a community-based form of security consisting of community strings. However, these are plaintext passwords and are not considered a strong security mechanism. Version 1 is a legacy solution and not often encountered in networks today.

Chapter 11

1. C. One of the basic functions of the distribution layer of the Cisco Borderless Networks architecture is to perform routing between different VLANs. Acting as a backbone and aggregating campus blocks are functions of the core layer. Providing access to end-user devices is a function of the access layer.

2. D. A collapsed core design is appropriate for a small, single-building business. This type of design uses two layers (the collapsed core and distribution layers consolidated into one layer and the access layer). Larger businesses use the traditional three-tier switch design model.

3. D and E. A converged network provides a single infrastructure that combines voice, video, and data. Analog phones, user data, and point-to-point video traffic are all contained within the single network infrastructure of a converged network.

4. D. Maintaining three separate network tiers is not always required or cost-efficient. All network designs require an access layer, but a two-tier design can collapse the distribution and core layers into one layer to serve the needs of a small location with few users.

5. A. A fixed-configuration switch would meet all the requirements of the law firm in this example.

6. A. A switch builds a table of MAC addresses and associated port numbers by examining the source MAC addresses found in inbound frames. To forward a frame onward, the switch examines the destination MAC address, looks in the MAC address for a port number associated with that destination MAC address, and sends it to the specific

port. If the destination MAC address is not in the table, the switch forwards the frame out all ports except the inbound port that originated the frame.

7. C. A switch provides microsegmentation so that no other devices compete for the same Ethernet network bandwidth.

8. D. When a switch receives a frame with a source MAC address that is not in the MAC address table, the switch adds that MAC address to the table and maps that address to a specific port. Switches do not use IP addressing in the MAC address table.

9. D and F. A switch has the ability to create temporary point-to-point connections between the directly attached transmitting and receiving network devices. The two devices have full-bandwidth, full-duplex connectivity during the transmission. Segmentation adds collision domains to reduce collisions.

10. B. When a LAN switch with the microsegmentation feature is used, each port represents a segment, which in turns forms a collision domain. If each port is connected with an end-user device, there will be no collisions. However, if multiple end devices are connected to a hub and the hub is connected to a port on the switch, some collisions will occur in that particular segment—but not beyond it.

11. converged

12. B and C. The Cisco enterprise architecture consists of a hierarchical design. The network is divided into three functional layers: core, distribution, and access. In smaller networks, this three-layer division of functional layers is collapsed into two layers, with the core and distribution layers combined to form a collapsed core.

13. D. Routers or multilayer switches are usually deployed in pairs with access layer switches evenly divided between them. This configuration is referred to as a building switch block or a departmental switch block. Each switch block acts independently of the others. As a result, the failure of a single device does not cause the network to go down. Even the failure of an entire switch block does not affect a significant number of end users.

14. C and E. Providing wireless connectivity offers many advantages, such as increased flexibility, reduced costs, and the ability to grow and adapt to changing network and business requirements.

15. A. Link aggregation allows an administrator to increase the amount of bandwidth between devices by creating one logical link by grouping several physical links together. EtherChannel is a form of link aggregation used in switched networks.

16. B. Cisco Meraki cloud-managed access switches enable virtual stacking of switches. They monitor and configure thousands of switch ports over the web, without the intervention of onsite IT staff.

17. D. The thickness of a switch determines how much space on the rack it will take up and is measured in rack units.

18. A and C. Routers play a critical role in networking by determining the best path for sending packets. They connect multiple IP networks by connecting homes and businesses to the internet. They are also used to interconnect multiple sites within an enterprise network, providing redundant paths to destinations. Routers can also act as translators between different media types and protocols.

Chapter 12

1. A. A physical topology defines the way in which computers and other network devices are connected to a network.

2. B. Baseline measurements should not be performed during times of unique traffic patterns because the data would provide an inaccurate picture of normal network operations. Baseline analysis of a network should be conducted on a regular basis during normal work hours of the organization. Perform an annual analysis of the entire network or baseline different sections of the network on a rotating basis. Analysis must be conducted regularly to understand how the network is affected by growth and other changes.

3. E. In the "narrow the scope" step of gathering symptoms, a network engineer determines whether the network problem is at the core, distribution, or access layer of the network. After this step is complete and the layer is identified, the network engineer can determine which pieces of equipment are the most likely causes.

4. D. To efficiently establish exactly when the user first experienced email problems, the technician should ask an open-ended question so that the user can state the day and time that the problem was first noticed. Closed questions require only a yes or no answer, and further questions will be needed to determine the actual time of the problem.

5. A. Change-control procedures should be established and applied for each stage to ensure a consistent approach to implementing the solutions and to enable changes to be rolled back if they cause other unforeseen problems.

6. B. A successful **ping** indicates that everything is working on the physical, data link, and network layers. All of the other layers should be investigated.

7. A. In bottom-up troubleshooting, you start with the physical components of the network and move up through the layers of the OSI model until the cause of the problem is identified.

8. B. Framing errors are symptoms of problems at the data link layer (Layer 2) of the OSI model.

9. D. The issue is that the new website is configured with TCP port 90 for HTTP, which is different from the normal TCP port 80. Therefore, this is a transport layer issue.

10. C. The symptom of excessive runt packets and jabber is typically a Layer 1 issue, such as caused by a corrupted NIC driver, which could be the result of a software error during the NIC driver upgrade process. Cable faults would cause intermittent connections, but in this case, the network is not touched, and the cable analyzer has detected frame problems, not signal problems. Ethernet signal attenuation is caused by an extended or long cable, but in this case, the cable has not been changed. A NIC driver is part of the operating system; it is not an application.

11. C. Because other computers on the same network work properly, the default gateway router has a default route, and the link between the workgroup switch and the router works. An incorrectly configured switch port VLAN would not cause these symptoms.

12. D, E, and F. Information recorded on a logical network diagram may include device identifiers, IP addresses and prefix lengths,

interface identifiers, connection type, Frame Relay DLCI for virtual circuits (if applicable), site-to-site VPNs, routing protocols, static routes, data link protocols, and WAN technologies used.

13. D. Protocol analyzers are useful for investigating the contents of packets that are flowing through the network. A protocol analyzer decodes the various protocol layers in a recorded frame and presents this information in a relatively easy-to-use format.

14. A. The lower the level number, the higher the severity level. By default, all messages from levels 0 to 7 are logged to the console.

Chapter 13

1. C. The Internet of Things (IoT) is a phrase that denotes the billions of electronic devices that are now able to connect to data networks and the internet.

2. B. With IaaS, the cloud provider is responsible for access to the network equipment, virtualized network services, and supporting network infrastructure.

3. A. Cloud computing enables access to organizational data anywhere and at any time; streamlines the organization's IT operations by subscribing only the needed services; eliminates or reduces the need for onsite IT equipment, maintenance, and management; reduces costs for equipment, energy, physical plant requirements, and personnel training needs; and enables rapid responses to increasing data volume requirements.

4. A. IaaS would be the best solution because the cloud provider is responsible for access to the network equipment, virtualized

network services, and supporting network infrastructure.

5. C. A private cloud's applications and services are intended for a specific organization or entity, such as the government.

6. D. A benefit of virtualization is increased server uptime with advanced redundant fault-tolerance features such as live migration, storage migration, high availability, and distributed resource scheduling.

7. C. The terms *cloud computing* and *virtualization* are often used interchangeably; however, they mean different things. Virtualization is the foundation of cloud computing. Without it, cloud computing, as it is most widely implemented, would not be possible. Cloud computing separates the application from the hardware. Virtualization separates the OS from the hardware.

8. B. A Type 2 hypervisor, also called a hosted hypervisor, is software that creates and runs VM instances. A big advantage of Type 2 hypervisors is that management console software is not required.

9. C. A Type 1 hypervisor is installed directly on the server or networking hardware. Instances of an OS are installed on the hypervisor. Type 1 hypervisors have direct access to the hardware resources; therefore, they are more efficient than hosted architectures. Type 1 hypervisors improve scalability, performance, and robustness.

10. D. Software-defined networking (SDN) is a network architecture that has been developed to virtualize the network. For example, SDN can virtualize the control plane. It is also known as controller-based SDN. SDN moves the control plane from each network device to a central network intelligence

and policy-making entity called the SDN controller.

11. B and C. The control plane contains Layer 2 and Layer 3 route forwarding mechanisms, such as routing protocol neighbor tables and topology tables, IPv4 and IPv6 routing tables, STP, and the ARP table. Information sent to the control plane is processed by the CPU.

12. C. Using Type 1 hypervisors is also called the "bare metal" approach because the hypervisor is installed directly on the hardware. Type 1 hypervisors are usually used on enterprise servers and data center networking devices.

13. D. Type 2 hypervisors are very popular with consumers and with organizations experimenting with virtualization. Common Type 2 hypervisors include Virtual PC, VMware Workstation, Oracle VM VirtualBox, VMware Fusion, and Mac OS X Parallels.

14. B. The APIC is considered to be the brains of the ACI architecture. An APIC is a centralized software controller that manages and operates a scalable ACI clustered fabric. It is designed for programmability and centralized management. It translates application policies into network programming.

Chapter 14

1. D. YAML Ain't Markup Language (YAML) separates the key/value pairs using a colon without quotation marks. YAML also uses indentation to define the structure, without using brackets or commas. JavaScript Object Notation (JSON) encloses key/value pairs in braces, { }. Keys must be strings within double quotation marks, " ". A key is separated

from a value by a colon. Extensible Markup Language (XML) data is enclosed within a related set of tags: *<tag>data</tag>*.

2. B. JavaScript Object Notation (JSON) encloses key/value pairs in braces, { }. Keys must be strings within double quotation marks, " ". A key is separated from a value by a colon. YAML Ain't Markup Language (YAML) separates the key/value pairs using a colon without quotation marks. YAML also uses indentation to define the structure, without using brackets or commas. Extensible Markup Language (XML) data is enclosed within a related set of tags: *<tag>data</tag>*.

3. C. A RESTful API, including a public API, may require a key. The key is used to identify the source of the request through authentication.

4. A and E. Ansible and SaltStack are configuration management tools developed using Python. Chef and Puppet were developed using Ruby. Ruby is typically considered a more difficult language to learn than Python. RESTCONF is a network management protocol.

5. C. Puppet is an agent-based configuration management tool built on Ruby that allows you to create a set of instructions called a manifest. Ansible is an agentless configuration management tool built on Python that allows you to create a set of instructions called a playbook. Chef is an agent-based configuration management tool built on Ruby that allows you to create a set of instructions called a cookbook. SaltStack is an agentless configuration management tool built on Python that allows you to create a set of instructions called a pillar.

6. A. The HTTP operation POST corresponds to the RESTful operation create, GET to read, PUT/PATCH to update, and DELETE to delete.

7. D. YAML Ain't Markup Language (YAML) separates the key/value pairs using a colon without quotation marks. YAML also uses indentation to define its structure, without using brackets or commas. Extensible Markup Language (XML) data is enclosed within a related set of tags: *<tag>data</tag>*. JavaScript Object Notation (JSON) encloses key/value pairs in braces, { }. Keys must be strings within double quotation marks, " ". A key is separated from a value by a colon.

8. A. Ansible is an agentless configuration management tool built on Python that allows you to create a set of instructions called a playbook. Chef is an agent-based configuration management tool built on Ruby that allows you to create a set of instructions called a cookbook. Puppet is an agent-based configuration management tool built on Ruby that allows you to create a set of instructions called a manifest. SaltStack is an agentless configuration management tool built on Python that allows you to create a set of instructions called a pillar.

9. C. Extensible Markup Language (XML) data is enclosed within a related set of tags: *<tag>data</tag>*. JavaScript Object Notation (JSON) encloses key/value pairs in braces, { }. Keys must be strings within double quotation marks, " ". A key is from a value by a colon. YAML Ain't Markup Language (YAML) separates the key/value pairs using a colon without quotation marks. YAML also uses indentation to define its structure without using brackets or commas.

10. B. Like XML, HTML uses a related set of tags to enclose data. However, HTML uses predefined tags, whereas XML does not. XML is a human-readable data structure that applications use to store, transfer, and read data.

11. D. REST is not a protocol or service but rather a style of software architecture for designing web service applications. A REST API is an API that works on top of HTTP. It defines a set of functions developers can use to perform requests and receive responses via HTTP, such as GET and POST.

12. D. The HTTP operation PUT corresponds to the RESTful operation update, POST to create, GET to read, and DELETE to delete.

13. B. JSON is a lightweight data format for storing and transporting data. It is simpler and more readable than XML and is supported by web browsers. Like JSON, YAML Ain't Markup Language (YAML) is a data format that applications use to store and transport data. YAML is considered a superset of JSON.

14. A. Public, or open, APIs have no restrictions and are available to the public. Some API providers do require a user to obtain a free key or token prior to using the API in order to control the volume of API requests received and processed.

0–9

802.1p   *See* IEEE 802.1p.

A

abstraction layer   A virtualization layer that hides the technical implementation details of a system, allowing us to focus on the function of the layer.

access attack   A network attack that exploits known vulnerabilities in authentication services, FTP services, and web services. The purpose of this type of attack is to gain entry to web accounts, confidential databases, and other sensitive information.

access control entry (ACE)   A single line in an ACL. ACEs are also commonly called ACL statements. When network traffic passes through an interface configured with an ACL, the router compares the information within the packet against each ACE, in sequential order, to determine if the packet matches one of the ACEs.

access control list (ACL)   A series of IOS commands that controls whether a router forwards or drops packets, based on information found in the packet header.

access layer   A tier in the two- and three-layer hierarchical network design model in which devices connect to the network and that includes services such as power to network endpoints.

address spoofing attack   An attack in which a threat actor uses the IP address or MAC address of another host to impersonate that host.

adjacency table   A table in a router that contains a list of the relationships formed between selected neighboring routers and end nodes for the purpose of exchanging routing information. Adjacency is based on the use of a common media segment.

adjacency database   The database that is used to create an OSPF neighbor table.

Advanced Encryption Standard (AES)   A very secure and commonly used symmetric encryption algorithm. It provides stronger security than DES and is computationally more efficient than 3DES. *Compare with* Data Encryption Standard, Triple DES, and Software-Optimized Encryption Algorithm.

Amazon Web Services (AWS)   An Amazon company that provides on-demand cloud computing platforms to clients for a fee.

amplification and reflection attack   An attack in which a threat actor attempts to prevent legitimate users from accessing information or services by using DoS and DDoS attacks. The threat actor forwards spoofed ICMP echo request messages to many hosts, which all reply to the spoofed IP address of the victim to overwhelm it.

Ansible An agentless configuration management tool built on Python that is used to create a set of instructions called a playbook. *Compare with* Chef, Puppet, and SaltStack.

Application Network Profile (ANP) A core component of Cisco ACI architecture, which is a collection of EPGs, their connections, and the policies that define those connections.

Application Policy Infrastructure Controller (APIC) Considered to be the brains of the Cisco ACI, a centralized software controller that manages and operates a scalable and clustered ACI fabric. It is designed for programmability and centralized management and translates application policies into network programming.

application programming interface (API) A special subroutine used by an application to communicate with the operating system or some other control program. APIs use special function calls to provide the linkage to the required subroutine for execution. Open and standardized APIs are used to ensure the portability of the application code and vendor independence.

application-specific-integrated circuit (ASIC) Electronics added to a switch that allowed it to have more ports without degrading performance.

area In OSPF, part of a routing domain created to help control routing update traffic.

area border router (ABR) In OSPF, a router that connects one or more non-backbone areas to the backbone. ABRs are the routers interconnecting the areas in a multiarea OSPF network.

ARP cache poisoning A type of man-in-the-middle attack that can be used to intercept, alter, or even stop network traffic. The threat actor creates spoofed ARP messages to make legitimate hosts send frames to them.

array A data structure that contains a group of similar elements (for example, integer, string) that is used in an application to organize data to simplify sorting or searching.

asset Anything of value to an organization, including people, equipment, resources, and data (which is usually the most valuable asset).

assured forwarding (AF) A category of DSCP values consisting of four classes to provide different levels of forwarding assurances. *Compare with* best-effort (BE) and expedited forwarding (EF).

asymmetric DSL (ADSL) A type of DSL service used to connect home users and SOHO sites to ISPs. ADSL supports higher downstream speeds and slower upstream speeds. *Compare with* symmetric DSL (SDSL).

asymmetric encryption algorithm Also called a public-key algorithm, an algorithm that uses a public key and a private key. These algorithms are substantially slower than symmetric algorithms.

Asynchronous Transfer Mode (ATM) A legacy international standard for cell relay in which multiple service types (such as voice, video, or data) are conveyed in fixed-length (53-byte) cells. Fixed-length cells allow cell processing to occur in hardware, thereby reducing transit delays.

attenuation   The gradual loss in signal intensity that occurs while transmitting analog or digital signals over long distances, such as when a UTP cable exceeds the design limit of 100 meters.

Authentication Header (AH)   An IPsec packet encapsulation method that provides connection-less data integrity and data origin authentication for IP packets. It does not provide confidentiality as ESP does. *Compare with* Encapsulation Security Protocol (ESP).

authoritative time source   A high-precision timekeeping device assumed to be accurate and with little or no delay associated with it. Also referred to as a stratum 0 device.

automation   Any process that is self-driven and that reduces and potentially eliminates the need for human intervention.

autonomous system boundary router (ASBR)   In OSPF, a router that exchanges routes between OSPF and another routing domain through route redistribution. Routes are injected into OSPF from an ASBR. An ASBR communicates the OSPF routes into another routing domain. The ASBR runs OSPF and another routing protocol.

availability   A measure of the probability that a network is available for use when it is required.

B

backbone area   In OSPFv2 and OSPFv3, the special area in a multiarea design where all non-backbone areas connect. Also known as area 0. In any OSPF network design, there must be at least one area. Traditionally, this area is numbered 0. In single-area OSPF, the lone area is area 0. In multi-area OSPF, area 0 forms the core of the network,

and all other areas attach to the backbone area to facilitate interarea communication.

backbone network   A large, high-capacity network used to interconnect large Tier 1 service provider networks and to create a redundant network.

backbone router   In OSPF, a router that is con-figured to participate in area 0, or the backbone area. A backbone router can also be an ABR or ASBR.

backhaul network   A service provider network connecting multiple access nodes over municipal-ities, countries, and regions. Backhaul networks are also connected to internet service providers and to the backbone network.

backup designated router (BDR)   In OSPF, a backup to the DR in case the DR fails. The BDR is the OSPF router with the second-highest prior-ity at the time of the last DR election.

baseline   A reference used to establish normal network or system performance by collecting performance data from the ports and devices that are essential to network operation.

baselining tool   A tool that is used to help establish and measure a network's behavior.

Best Effort (BE)   A category of DSCP values with a value of 0. When a router experiences congestion, these packets are dropped. No QoS plan is implemented. *Compare with* expedited forwarding (EF) and assured forwarding (AF).

best-effort model   The default model when QoS is not explicitly configured. *Compare with* Integrated Services (IntServ) and Differentiated Services (DiffServ).

black hat hacker An unethical threat actor who compromises computer and network security vulnerabilities. The goal is usually financial gain or personal gain, though this type of hacker may simply have malicious intent.

blacklisting A process in which a firewall or security appliance (for example, IPS, ESA, WSA) is configured with access control rules to deny traffic to and from specific IP addresses.

botnet A network of infected zombies (that is, hosts) controlled by a threat actor using a CnC system.

bottom-up troubleshooting A troubleshooting method that starts with the physical components of the network and moves up through the layers of the OSI model until the cause of the problem is found. Bottom-up troubleshooting is a good approach to use when you suspect a physical problem. *Compare with* top-down troubleshooting and divide-and-conquer troubleshooting.

branch router A router platform that optimizes branch services while delivering an optimal application experience across branch and WAN infrastructures. *Compare with* network edge router and service provider router.

broadband Generic term that generally refers to DSL and cable internet technology.

broadband modem A digital modem used with DSL or cable internet service broadband communications.

broadband service Technology that provides internet access using broadband connections. Broadband service technologies include DSL, cable, and satellite access.

broadcast multiaccess A type of network configuration in which multiple routers are interconnected over an Ethernet network.

building switch block A design that deploys routers or multilayer switches in pairs, with access layer switches evenly divided between them. Each switch block operates independently of the others, so a failure of a single device does not cause the network to go down. As a result, the failure of a single device or switch block does not significantly affect end users. *See also* departmental switch block.

C

cable analyzer A multifunctional handheld device that is used to test and certify copper and fiber cables for different services and standards. More sophisticated tools include advanced troubleshooting diagnostics that measure distance to performance defect (NEXT, RL), identify corrective actions, and graphically display crosstalk and impedance behavior.

cable modem (CM) A device located at the customer premises that is used to convert an Ethernet signal from the user device to broadband cable frequencies transmitted to the headend.

cable modem termination system (CMTS) A component that exchanges digital signals with cable modems on a cable network. A headend CMTS communicates with cable modems that are located in subscribers' homes.

cable tester A specialized handheld device designed to test the various types of data communication cabling. Cabling testers can be used to detect broken wires, crossed-over wiring, shorted connections, and improperly paired connections.

campus LAN switch   Distribution, access, or compact switches that may be anywhere from a fanless switch with eight fixed ports to a 13-blade switch supporting hundreds of ports. Campus LAN switch platforms include the Cisco 2960, 3560, 3650, 3850, 4500, 6500, and 6800 Series. *Compare with* cloud-managed switch, data center switch, service provider switch, and virtual networking switch.

carrier protocol   A term used in GRE to describe the protocol (for example, GRE) that encapsulates the passenger protocol. *Compare with* passenger protocol and transport protocol.

central office (CO)   A local telephone company office to which all local loops in a given area connect and in which circuit switching of subscriber lines occurs.

Chef   An agent-based configuration management tool built on Ruby that is used to create a set of instructions called a cookbook. *Compare with* Ansible, Puppet, and SaltStack.

circuit-switched communication   A type of communication in which two network nodes establish a dedicated communications channel (circuit) through the network so that the nodes can communicate.

Cisco Adaptive Security Appliance (ASA)   A Cisco dedicated firewall appliance.

Cisco AnyConnect Secure Mobility Client   VPN software that is installed on a host to securely establish a remote-access VPN.

Cisco Application Centric Infrastructure (ACI)   A data center architecture solution originally developed by Insieme and acquired by Cisco in 2013 for integrating cloud computing and data center management. ACI is a Cisco SDN solution that includes a data center fabric built with Nexus 9000 switches running ACI Fabric OS, a cluster of APICs, and an ecosystem of integrated solutions.

Cisco Application Policy Infrastructure Controller–Enterprise Module (APIC-EM)   A policy-based SDN for enterprise and campus deployments.

Cisco Borderless Networks architecture   An architecture designed to help IT balance demanding business challenges and changing business models promoted by the influx of consumer devices into the business world. Cisco Borderless Networks can help IT evolve its infrastructure to deliver secure, reliable, and seamless user experiences in a world with many new and shifting borders.

Cisco Discovery Protocol (CDP)   A Cisco proprietary Layer 2 link discovery protocol enabled on all Cisco devices by default. It is used to discover other CDP-enabled devices for autoconfiguring connections and to troubleshoot network devices. *Compare with* Link Layer Discovery Protocol (LLDP).

Cisco DNA   An open software-driven intent-based networking platform that is constantly learning and adapting. It uses contextual insights to make sure the network continuously responds to dynamic IT and business needs.

Cisco DNA Assurance   A Cisco DNA intent-based solution to troubleshoot and increase IT productivity. It applies advanced analytics and machine learning to improve performance and issue resolution and predictions to assure network performance. It provides real-time notification for network conditions that require attention. *Compare with* SD-Access, SD-WAN, and Cisco DNA Security.

Cisco DNA Center The network management and command center for Cisco DNA.

Cisco DNA Security A Cisco DNA intent-based solution that provides visibility by using a network as a sensor for real-time analysis and intelligence. It provides increased granular control to enforce policy and contain threats across the network. *Compare with* SD-Access, SD-WAN, and Cisco DNA Assurance.

Cisco Email Security Appliance (ESA) A mitigation technology device for email-based threats. The Cisco ESA monitors SMTP traffic using real-time feeds from Cisco Talos to detect threats, block known threats, remediate when stealth malware evades initial detection, discard emails with bad links, block access to newly infected sites, and encrypt content in outgoing email to prevent data loss.

Cisco Express Forwarding (CEF) A Cisco-proprietary protocol that allows high-speed packet switching in ASICs rather than using CPUs. Cisco Express Forwarding offers "wire speed" routing of packets and load balancing.

Cisco IOS File System (IFS) The common Cisco IOS command-line interface (CLI) to all file system for all Cisco devices. The IFS provides access to file systems such as Flash memory and network file systems (for example, TFTP, rcp, and FTP).

Cisco Nexus 9000 Series switch A core component of the Cisco ACI architecture that provides an application-aware switching fabric and works with an APIC to manage the virtual and physical network infrastructure.

Cisco Talos One of the largest commercial threat intelligence teams in the world, composed of world-class researchers, analysts, and engineers. Industry-leading visibility, actionable intelligence, and vulnerability research drive rapid detection and protection for Cisco customers against known and emerging threats—and stop threats in the wild to protect the internet at large.

Cisco UCS Manager An application used to manage all software and hardware components in Cisco UCS. Cisco UCS Manager can control multiple servers and manage resources for thousands of VMs.

Cisco Unified Computing System (UCS) A product line developed specifically for a data center to manage the computing hardware, virtualization, and switching fabric. Cisco UCS is managed using Cisco UCS Manager.

Cisco Visual Networking Index (VNI) A group within Cisco that performs projections, estimates and forecasts, and direct data collection for broadband connections, video subscribers, mobile connections, and more.

Cisco Web Security Appliance (WSA) A mitigation technology device for web-based threats. Cisco WSA can perform blacklisting of URLs, URL filtering, malware scanning, URL categorization, web application filtering, and encryption and decryption of web traffic.

Class of Service (CoS) A 3-bit field inserted in a 802.1Q VLAN tagged Ethernet frame to assign a quality of service (QoS) marking. The 3-bit field identifies the CoS priority value and is used by Layer 2 switches to specify how the frame should be handled when QoS is enabled.

Class-Based Weighted Fair Queuing (CBWFQ) A QoS queuing method that permits custom policies per class of traffic, such as allowing web traffic more bandwidth than email traffic. All other unspecified traffic uses WFQ. *Compare with* first-in, first-out (FIFO), Weighted Fair Queuing (WFQ), and Low Latency Queuing (LLQ).

classification   A QoS term for the process of sorting types of packets so they can be marked and have policies applied to them.

classless   Describes a routing protocol that carries subnet mask information in its routing updates. Classless routing protocols can take advantage of VLSM and supernet routes. RIPv2, OSPF, and EIGRP are IPv4 classless routing protocols.

client-based VPN   A remote-access connection that requires IPsec or SSL VPN client software on the device. The software is used to initiate the VPN connection and authenticate to the destination VPN gateway to access corporate files and applications.

clientless VPN   A remote-access connection that is secured using a web browser SSL connection. The SSL connection is first established, and then HTTP data is exchanged over the connection.

cloud computing   The use of computing resources (hardware and software) delivered as a service over a network. An enterprise typically accesses the processing power, storage, software, or other computing services, often via a web browser, from a provider for a fee. The provider is usually an external company that hosts and manages the cloud resources.

cloud-managed switch   A switch (for example, Cisco Meraki switch) that can monitor and configure thousands of switchports over the web, without the intervention of onsite IT staff. This type of switch enables virtual stacking of

switches. *Compare with* campus LAN switch, data center switch, service provider switch, and virtual networking switch.

collapsed core layer model   A two-tier hierarchical network design model that collapses the core and distribution layers into a single layer that connects to the access layer, where wired and wireless end devices attach. Also called a two-tier campus network design.

command and control (CnC)   An attack method used by a threat actor to send control messages to a botnet of zombies and carry out a DDoS attack.

community string   A text string that is used as a password to authenticate messages sent between SNMP agents (for example, routers, switches, servers) and an NMS. The community string is sent in every packet between the NMS and agent.

confidentiality   An IPsec VPN term that describes how encryption algorithms prevent cybercriminals from reading packet contents.

configuration register   A hexadecimal value used to change the booting behavior and connection settings of a Cisco router. Common settings include 0x2102 (normal boot) and 0x2142 (bypass startup configuration for password recovery.)

congestion avoidance   A QoS method for monitoring network traffic loads in an effort to anticipate and avoid congestion. As queues fill up to the maximum threshold, a small percentage of packets are dropped. When the maximum threshold is passed, all packets are dropped.

control plane   One of the Cisco NFP functional areas that consists of managing device-generated packets required for the operation of the network itself, such as ARP message exchanges or OSPF routing advertisements. *Compare with* management plane and data plane.

converged network   (1) A network that combines voice and video with the traditional data network. (2) A network that provides a loop-free Layer 2 topology for a switched LAN through the use of spanning tree. (3) A network that provides a stable Layer 3 network where the routers have finished providing each other updates and the routing tables are complete.

convergence   The process in which a group of internetworking devices running a specific routing protocol all agree on the internetworking topology after a topology change.

core layer   A tier in the three-layer hierarchical network design model that creates the network backbone. All traffic to and from peripheral networks must pass through the core layer, which includes high-speed switching devices that can handle relatively large amounts of traffic. In a two-layer hierarchical design model, the core layer is combined with the distribution layer for small to medium-sized business networks.

CSU/DSU (channel service unit/data service unit)   A digital interface device that connects end-user equipment to the local digital telephone loop.

customer premises equipment (CPE)   Terminating equipment, such as terminals, telephones, and modems, supplied by the telephone company, installed at customer sites, and connected to the telephone company network.

cyber weaponry   The collective name for tools that threat actors may use to exploit vulnerable systems.

cybercriminal   A threat actor who commits malicious activities on networks and devices to steal sensitive information for profit. Cybercriminals can be self-employed, or they may work for large cybercrime organizations.

D

dark fiber   Unused fiber-optic cable that is unlit (that is, dark).

data center switch   A high-performance, low-latency switch that promotes infrastructure scalability, operational continuity, and transport flexibility. Data center switch platforms include the Cisco Nexus Series switches and the Cisco Catalyst 6500 Series switches. *Compare with* campus LAN switch, cloud-managed switch, service provider switch, and virtual networking switch.

data center   A facility used to house computer systems and associated components, including redundant data communications connections, high-speed virtual servers, redundant storage systems, and security devices. Only large organizations use privately built data centers. Smaller organizations lease server and storage services from data center organizations.

data communications equipment (DCE)   An EIA term for the devices and connections of a communications network that comprise the network end of the user-to-network interface. The DCE provides a physical connection to the network, forwards traffic, and provides a clocking signal used to synchronize data transmission between DCE and DTE devices. Broadband modems and interface cards are examples of DCE. The ITU refers to this device as the data circuit-terminating equipment.

data confidentiality   One of four elements of secure communication, which guarantees that only authorized users can read a message, and if a message is intercepted, it cannot be deciphered within a reasonable amount of time. Data confidentiality is implemented using symmetric and asymmetric encryption algorithms.

Data Encryption Standard (DES)   A legacy symmetric encryption algorithm that should no longer be used. DES uses a 56-bit key. *Compare with* Triple DES (3DES), Advanced Encryption Standard (AES), and Software-Optimized Encryption Algorithm (SEAL).

data exfiltration   A security term describing theft of data. It is the unauthorized copying, transfer, or retrieval of data from a compromised host by a threat actor or malware.

data format   In web programming, a way to store and exchange data in a structured format (that is, a markup language). For example, HTML describes a data format used by a web browser to display a page correctly.

data nonrepudiation   One of four elements of secure communication, which guarantees that the sender cannot repudiate, or refute, the validity of a message sent. Nonrepudiation relies on the fact that only the sender has the unique characteristics or signature for how the message is treated.

data object   In a markup language, a value or group of values displayed in a key/value pair format.

Data over Cable Service Interface Specification (DOCSIS)   An international standard developed by CableLabs, a nonprofit research and development consortium for cable-related technologies. CableLabs tests and certifies cable equipment vendor devices, such as cable modems and cable modem termination systems, and grants DOCSIS-certified or qualified status.

data plane   One of the Cisco NFP functional areas responsible for forwarding data. Data plane traffic normally consists of user-generated packets being forwarded between end devices. Most traffic travels through the router, or switch, via the data plane. Also called the forwarding plane. *Compare with* control plane and management plane.

data terminal equipment (DTE)   A device at the user end of a user-network interface that serves as a data source, destination, or both. DTE connects to a data network through a DCE device (such as a modem) and typically uses clocking signals generated by the DCE. DTE includes such devices as computers, protocol translators, and multiplexers.

database description (DBD) packet   A packet used in OSPF that contains LSA headers only and describes the contents of the entire link-state database. Routers exchange DBDs during the exchange phase of adjacency creation. A DBD is an OSPF type 2 packet.

data-link connection identifier (DLCI)   A value that specifies a PVC or SVC in a Frame Relay network. In the basic Frame Relay specification, DLCIs are locally significant. (Connected devices might use different values to specify the same connection.) In the LMI extended specification, DLCIs (which specify individual end devices) are globally significant.

dead interval   The time, in seconds, that an OSPF router waits to hear from a neighbor before declaring the neighboring router out of service.

dedicated line   A communications line that is indefinitely reserved for transmissions rather than switched as transmission is required.

defense-in-depth approach   In security, a layered approach that requires a combination of networking devices and services working together to secure a network and assets.

delay   A QoS term used to describe the time it takes for a packet to travel from the source to the destination. Fixed delay is a particular amount of time a specific process takes. A variable delay takes an unspecified amount of time and is affected by factors such as how much traffic is being processed.

demarcation point   The point where the service provider or telephone company network ends and connects with the customer's equipment at the customer's site.

demodulate   To convert an analog signal such as sound into a digital signal, such as when a modem receives data over telephone lines.

denial-of-service (DoS) attack   An attack that is used to overload specific devices and network services with illegitimate traffic, thereby preventing legitimate traffic from reaching those resources.

dense wavelength-division multiplexing (DWDM)   An optical technology used to increase bandwidth over existing fiber-optic backbones. DWDM works by combining and transmitting multiple signals simultaneously at different wavelengths on the same fiber.

departmental switch block   A design that deploys routers or multilayer switches in pairs, with access layer switches evenly divided between them. Each switch block operates independently of the others, so a failure of a single device does not cause the network to go down. As a result, the failure of a single device or switch block does not significantly affect end users. *See also* building switch block.

designated router (DR)   An OSPF router that generates LSAs for a multiaccess network and has other special responsibilities in running OSPF. Each multiaccess OSPF network that has at least two attached routers has a designated router that is elected by the OSPF Hello packet. The designated router enables a reduction in the number of adjacencies required on a multiaccess network, which in turn reduces the amount of routing protocol traffic and the size of the topology database.

DHCP spoofing   An attack in which a cybercriminal installs a fake DHCP server on the network so that legitimate clients acquire their IP confirmation from the bogus server. These types of attacks force the clients to use both a false DNS server and a computer that is under the control of the attacker as their default gateway.

dialup modem   *See* voiceband modem.

Differentiated Services (DiffServ)   A QoS model that provides high scalability and flexibility. QoS differentiates between multiple traffic flows. Network devices recognize traffic classes and provide different levels of QoS to different traffic classes. DiffServ is less resource-intensive and more scalable than IntServ. *Compare with* best-effort model and Integrated Services (IntServ).

Differentiated Services Code Point (DSCP)   A field defined in RFC 2474 to redefine the ToS field by renaming and extending the IP Precedence (IPP) field. The field has 6 bits and offers a maximum of 64 possible classes of service. The 64 DSCP values are organized into three categories: best effort (BE), expedited forwarding (EF), and assured forwarding (AF).

Diffie-Hellman (DH)   An asymmetric algorithm that enables two parties to agree on a key that they can use to encrypt messages they want to send to each other.

digital certificate A cryptographic key that has been issued by a PKI certificate authority (CA). The certificate is used to identity the communicating parties and validate the information being transferred.

digital multimeter (DMM) A test instrument that directly measures electrical values of voltage, current, and resistance. In network troubleshooting, most multimedia tests involve checking power-supply voltage levels and verifying that network devices are receiving power.

digital signal processor (DSP) A QoS algorithm used in voice networks when small packet loss is experienced. DSP analyzes and re-creates what the lost audio signal should be.

digital subscriber line (DSL) An always-on connection technology that uses existing twisted-pair telephone lines to transport high-bandwidth data and that provides IP services to subscribers. A DSL modem converts an Ethernet signal from the user device into a DSL signal, which is transmitted to the central office.

Dijkstra's algorithm An algorithm used by the OSPF routing protocol that is also called the shortest path first (SPF) algorithm.

distributed denial of service (DDoS) A coordinated attack from many devices, called zombies, that is meant to degrade or halt public access to an organization's website and resources. The threat actor uses a CnC system to send control messages to the zombies.

distribution layer A tier in the three-layer hierarchical network design model that connects the access layer to the core layer. The distribution layer aggregates connectivity from multiple access layer devices, Layer 2 broadcast domains, and Layer 3 routing boundaries. In a two-layer hierarchical design model, the distribution layer is combined with the core layer for small-to-medium-sized business networks.

divide-and-conquer troubleshooting A troubleshooting approach that starts by collecting users' experiences with a problem and documenting the symptoms. Then, using that information, you make an informed guess about the OSI layer at which to start your investigation. After you verify that a layer is functioning properly, assume that the layers below it are functioning and work up the OSI layers. If an OSI layer is not functioning properly, work your way down the OSI layer model. *Compare with* the bottom-up troubleshooting and top-down troubleshooting.

DNS domain shadowing attack A DNS attack that uses subdomains or valid domains to redirect user traffic to malicious servers.

DNS open resolver attack A DNS attack that targets publicly open available DNS resolvers such as GoogleDNS at 8.8.8.8.

DNS stealth attack A DNS attack that is used by a threat actor to hide his or her identity.

DNS tunneling attack A DNS attacks used to send non-DNS traffic (such as CnC traffic) within DNS traffic.

DROTHER A router in an OSPF multiaccess network that is neither the DR nor the BDR. DROTHERs are the other routers in the OSPF network.

DSL access multiplexer (DSLAM) A device located at the provider's CO that concentrates connections from multiple DSL subscribers.

DSL modem   A DSL device located at the customer premises that converts Ethernet signals from the internal network to DSL signals, which are transmitted to the CO.

dual-carrier connection   A setup in which an organization connects to two different service providers to provide redundancy and increase network availability. *Contrast with* single-carrier connection.

dual-homed ISP   An internet access design in which an organization has two connections to the same service provider. *Compare with* single-homed ISP, multihomed ISP, and dual-multihomed ISP.

dual-homed topology   A topology that provides redundancy such as when spoke routers are connected to two hub routers across a WAN cloud. *Contrast with* point-to-point topology, hub-and-spoke topology, and fully meshed topology.

dual-multihomed ISP   An internet access design in which an organization has multiple connections to two or more different service providers. *Compare with* single-homed ISP, dual-homed ISP, and multihomed ISP.

dual stack   An IPv4-to-IPv6 migration technique in which a device is enabled for both IPv4 and IPv6 protocols. It is a transition mechanism used when converting from IPv4 to IPv6. Basically, when using a dual stack, a router runs both IPv4 and IPv6. Other IPv6 migration techniques include translation and tunneling.

duplex mismatch   A situation in which one end of a connection is set to half duplex while the other end is set to full duplex.

Dynamic Multipoint VPN (DMVPN)   A Cisco software solution that simplifies the configuration involved in building multiple VPNs in an easy, dynamic, and scalable manner. It provides increased flexibility when connecting central office sites with branch sites in a hub-and-spoke configuration.

dynamic NAT   A type of network address translation (NAT) in which many local addresses (normally private IP addresses) are mapped to many global IP addresses (which are normally public IP addresses).

E

E1   A type of leased line available from service providers in Europe that provides bandwidth of up to 2.048 Mbps. *Contrast with* T1, T3, and E3.

E3   A type of leased line available from service providers in Europe that provides bandwidth of up to 34.368 Mbps. *Contrast with* T1, T3, and E1.

east–west traffic   A virtualization term for traffic being exchanged between virtual servers. *Compare with* north–south traffic.

edge port   A switchport that is not intended to be connected to another switch device. It immediately transitions to the forwarding state when enabled. Edge ports are conceptually similar to PortFast-enabled ports in the Cisco implementation of IEEE 802.1D.

edge router   A router that connects an inside network to an outside network (typically the internet).

electromagnetic interference (EMI)   Interference by magnetic signals caused by the flow of electricity. EMI can cause reduced data integrity and increased error rates on transmission channels. This process occurs because electrical current creates magnetic fields, which in turn cause other electrical currents in nearby wires. The induced electrical currents can interfere with proper operation of the other wire.

Electronic Industries Alliance (EIA)   An organization best known for its standards related to electrical wiring, connectors, and the 19-inch racks used to mount networking equipment. EIA standards are often combined with TIA standards and referred to as TIA/EIA standards.

Encapsulation Security Protocol (ESP)   An IPsec packet encapsulation method that provides connectionless data integrity, data origin authentication, and data confidentiality for IP packets.

endpoint group (EPG)   A Cisco ACI term for endpoints (for example, VLANs, web servers, applications).

enterprise campus network   The computing infrastructure that provides access to network communication services and resources to end users and devices spread over a single geographic location (for example, a single floor or building or even a large group of buildings spread over an extended geographic area).

enterprise network   A large and diverse network that connects most major points in a company or another organization. An enterprise network differs from a WAN in that it is privately owned and maintained.

enterprise VPN   An enterprise-managed VPN site-to-site and remote-access (that is, client based or clientless) IPsec and SSL VPN solution.

EtherChannel   A feature in which up to eight parallel Ethernet segments between the same two devices, each using the same speed, can be combined to act as a single link for forwarding and STP logic.

Ethernet over MPLS (EoMPLS)   A type of Ethernet WAN service that works by encapsulating Ethernet PDUs in MPLS packets and forwarding them across the MPLS network. Each PDU is transported as a single packet.

Ethernet WAN   A WAN in which service providers provide Ethernet-based connection options to connect subscribers to a larger service network or the internet. Also called Metro Ethernet.

ethical hacker   A white hat hacker who assesses and reports the security posture of a corporate target system.

Exchange state   An OSPF state in which OSPF routers exchange DBD packets, which contain LSA headers only and describe the contents of the entire link-state database.

expedited forwarding (EF)   A category of DSCP values with a value of 46 (binary 101110). The first 3 bits (101) map directly to the Layer 2 CoS value 5 used for voice traffic. At Layer 3, Cisco recommends that EF only be used to mark voice packets. Compare with best effort (BE) and assured forwarding (AF).

exploit   A mechanism that takes advantage of a vulnerability in a network.

ExStart state   An OSPF state in which the routers and their DR and BDR establish a master/slave relationship and choose the initial sequence number for adjacency formation. The router with the higher router ID becomes the master and starts the exchange.

extended ACL   An IOS feature that filters traffic based on multiple attributes, including protocol type, source IPv4 addresses, destination IPv4 addresses, source ports, and destination ports.

Extensible Markup Language (XML)   A markup language standard defined for the internet that defines a set of rules for encoding documents (similar to HTML) in a format that is both human readable and machine readable. In XML, the data is enclosed within a related set of tags: *<tag>data</tag>*. However, it is generally more challenging to read as it was designed to carry data and not display it. Sitemaps and configuration files often use XML files. *Compare with* JavaScript Object Notation (JSON) and YAML Ain't Markup Language (YAML).

Extensible Markup Language–Remote Procedure Call (XML-RPC)   A web service API protocol that evolved into SOAP. *Compare with* JavaScript Object Notation–Remote Procedure Call (JSON-RPC), Representational State Transfer (REST), and Simple Object Access Protocol (SOAP).

F

facility   A syslog service identifier that identifies and categorizes system state data for error and event message reporting. The logging facility options that are available are specific to the networking device.

failure domain   An area of a network that is impacted when a critical device or network service experiences problems.

fiber-to-the-building (FTTB)   An optical fiber installation term describing a situation in which fiber reaches the boundary of the building, such as the basement in a multi-dwelling unit, with the final connection to the individual living space being made via alternative means, such as curb or pole technologies.

fiber-to-the-home (FTTH)   An optical fiber installation term describing a situation in which fiber reaches the boundary of the residence. Passive optical networks and point-to-point Ethernet are architectures that can deliver cable TV, internet, and phone services over FTTH networks directly from the service provider central office.

fiber-to-the-node/neighborhood (FTTN)   An optical fiber installation term describing a situation in which fiber reaches an optical node that converts optical signals to a format acceptable for twisted-pair or coaxial cable to the premise.

firewall   A router, dedicated device, or software that denies outside traffic from entering an inside (that is, private) network. However, it permits inside network traffic to exit and return to the inside network. A firewall may use access lists and other methods to ensure the security of the private network.

first-in, first-out (FIFO)   A QoS queuing method that is often the default queuing method for a faster interface. FIFO has no concept of priority or classes of traffic and, consequently, makes no decision about packet priority. FIFO forwards packets in the order in which they arrived. *Compare with* Weighted Fair Queuing (WFQ), Class-Based Weighted Fair Queuing (CBWFQ), and Low Latency Queuing (LLQ).

fixed configuration switch   A type of switch commonly used in the access layer of the hierarchical network design model that supports only the features and options shipped with the switch. This type of switch is not upgradable. *Contrast with* modular configuration switch.

flow table An SDN table implemented in a data center switch that matches incoming packets to a particular flow and specifies the functions that are to be performed on the packets. Multiple flow tables may operate in a pipeline fashion. *Compare with* group table and meter table.

form factor The size, shape, and other physical specifications of components, particularly in consumer electronics and electronic packaging. For example, switch form factors include fixed configuration and modular configuration switch.

forwarding database The OSPF database that is used to help populate a routing table.

Forwarding Information Base (FIB) A table used with CEF to provide optimized lookups for more efficient packet forwarding.

forwarding rate A rate that defines the processing capabilities of a switch by stating how much data the switch can process per second.

frame buffer A section of memory used to store frames on congested ports.

Frame Relay A legacy industry-standard Layer 2 WAN protocol that established multiple virtual circuits between connected devices (such as routers).

Full state An OSPF state in which OSPF routers are fully adjacent with each other. All the router and network LSAs are exchanged, and the routers' databases are fully synchronized.

full-duplex An operation in which two devices can transmit and receive on the media at the same time.

fully meshed topology A network in which each network node has either a physical circuit or a virtual circuit connecting it to every other network node. A full mesh provides a great deal of redundancy, but because it can be prohibitively expensive to implement, it is usually reserved for network backbones. *Contrast with* point-to-point topology, hub-and-spoke topology, and dual-homed topology.

G

Generic Routing Encapsulation (GRE) A tunneling protocol developed by Cisco that can encapsulate a wide variety of protocol packet types inside IP tunnels. GRE creates a virtual point-to-point link to Cisco routers at remote points over an IP internetwork. GRE is designed to manage the transportation of multiprotocol and IP multicast traffic between two or more sites that may have only IP connectivity. It can encapsulate multiple protocol packet types inside an IP tunnel.

get request A type of request used by an SNMP manager to query a device for data.

gratuitous ARP An ARP reply to which no request has been made. Other hosts on the subnet store the MAC address and IP address contained in the gratuitous ARP in their ARP tables. Can be used by threat actors for nefarious reasons.

gray hat hacker A threat actor who does arguably unethical things but not for personal gain or to cause damage. For example, a gray hat hacker may disclose a vulnerability to the affected organization after having compromised the network.

GRE over IPsec tunnel Traffic encapsulated in a GRE packet that is then encapsulated into an IPsec packet so it can be forwarded securely to the destination VPN gateway. IPsec tunnels can only forward unicast traffic. GRE over IPsec enables IPsec to also send multicast and broadcast traffic, such as routing protocols.

group table   An SDN table implemented in a data center switch. A flow table may direct a flow to a group table, which may trigger a variety of actions that affect one or more flows. *Compare with* flow table and meter table.

H

hacktivist   A gray hat hacker who publicly protests organizations or governments by posting articles and videos, leaking sensitive information, and performing network attacks. Two examples of hacktivist groups are Anonymous and the Syrian Electronic Army.

half-duplex   An operation in which two devices can both transmit and receive on the media but cannot do so simultaneously.

hash message authentication code (HMAC) A code used for origin authentication to add authentication to integrity assurance by using an additional secret key as input to the hash function.

headend   A cable provider term describing where signals are first received, processed, formatted, and then distributed downstream to the cable network. The headend facility is usually unstaffed and under security fencing, and it is similar to a telephone company central office.

Hello interval   The frequency, in seconds, at which a router sends Hello packets.

hello keepalive mechanism   With OSPF and EIGRP, a small packet that is exchanged by peers to verify that a link is still operational.

Hello packet   A packet used by OSPF and EIGRP routers to discover, establish, and maintain neighbor relationships. In OSPF, Hello packets are type 1 OSPF packets and are used to establish and maintain adjacency with other OSPF routers.

hierarchical network   A design methodology for building networks in three layers: access, distribution, and core.

High-Level Data Link Control (HDLC)   An ISO bit-oriented Layer 2 WAN serial line protocol that supports router-to-router connections. It is the default encapsulation of serial interfaces on Cisco routers. *Contrast with* Point-to-Point Protocol (PPP).

hub router   Generally, a device that serves as the center of a hub-and-spoke star topology network. Connecting routers are referred to as spoke routers.

hub-and-spoke topology   A topology in which stub routers (spokes) are connected to a central hub router. A single interface to the hub can be shared by all spoke circuits. For example, spoke sites can be interconnected through the hub site using virtual circuits and routed subinterfaces at the hub. A hub-and-spoke topology is also an example of a single-homed topology. Sometimes referred to as a hub-to-spoke topology. *Contrast with* point-to-point topology, fully meshed topology, and dual-homed topology.

hybrid cloud   A cloud model that combines two or more cloud models (that is, private, community, or public). Individuals on a hybrid cloud would be able to have degrees of access to various services based on user access rights. *Compare with* public cloud, private cloud, and community cloud.

hybrid fiber-coaxial (HFC)   A telecommunications industry term for a broadband network that combines optical fiber and coaxial cable. It is commonly used by cable service providers.

Hypertext Markup Language (HTML)   The standard markup language for web browser documents. HTML describes the structure of a web page and its elements and instructs the browser on how to display the content. HTML can be enhanced using Cascading Style Sheets (CSS) and the JavaScript scripting language.

hypervisor   A program, firmware, or hardware used to create instances of VMs, which are emulated hardware including CPU, memory, storage, and networking settings in one OS. A hypervisor adds an abstraction layer on top of the real physical hardware to create VMs. Each VM runs a complete and separate operating system.

I

ICMP attack   An attack in which a threat actor uses ICMP echo packets (pings) to discover subnets and hosts on a network.

IEEE 802.1p   An IEEE standard that is used with the IEEE 802.1Q protocol to define traffic class expediting and dynamic multicast filtering. The 802.1p standard uses the first 3 bits in the 802.1Q Tag Control Information (TCI) field to create the Priority (PRI) field, which identifies the Class of Service (CoS) markings.

implicit deny   A hard-coded ACL statement in all ACLs that denies all traffic from passing through the interface. This statement is called implicit because it is not shown in output when you list ACL statements using **show** commands. It is always the last line of any ACL.

in-band management   The process of monitoring and making configuration changes to a network device over a network connection using Telnet, SSH, or HTTP access.

inbound ACL   A type of ACL that filters incoming packets. Inbound ACLs are best used to filter packets when the network attached to an inbound interface is the only source of packets that need to be examined.

infrastructure as a service (IaaS)   A cloud service in which the cloud provider is responsible for access to the network equipment, virtualized network services, and supporting network infrastructure. IaaS provides processing, storage, networking, or other fundamental computing resources to customers. *Compare with* software as a service (SaaS) and platform as a service (PaaS).

Init state   An OSPF state which specifies that the router has received a Hello packet from its neighbor, but the receiving router's ID was not included in the Hello packet.

inside address   In NAT, the address of a device that is being translated by NAT.

inside global address   In NAT for IPv4, a valid public IPv4 address that is given to the packet sourced from an inside host. Normally, the IPv4 public address is assigned as the packet exits the NAT router.

inside local address   In NAT for IPv4, an address (usually an RFC 1918 private address) that is not usually assigned by a Regional Internet Registry (RIR) or a service provider. The private IP address is assigned to a device inside a home or corporate environment.

inside network   In NAT, the internal network.

Institute of Electrical and Electronics Engineers (IEEE)   An organization dedicated to advancing technological innovation and creating standards in a wide area of industries, including power and energy, healthcare, telecommunications, and networking.

Integrated Services (IntServ)   A QoS model (sometimes called hard QoS) that provides guaranteed QoS to IP packets. However, IntServ is considered to be a legacy QoS model because it is very resource intensive and therefore limited in scalability. *Compare with* best-effort model and Differentiated Services (DiffServ).

Integrated Services Digital Network (ISDN)   A legacy communication protocol offered by telephone companies that permits telephone networks to carry data, voice, and other source traffic.

integrity   A VPN term that describes how IPsec uses hashing algorithms to ensure that packets have not been altered between source and destination.

interarea routing   In multiarea OSPF, routing that occurs between areas.

internal API   An API used by an organization or a company to access data and services for internal use only. *Compare with* open API and partner API.

International Organization for Standardization (ISO)   An international standard-setting body with members from global national standards organizations. The ISO is responsible for multiple standards, including the OSI reference model.

Internet Key Exchange (IKE)   An IPsec protocol responsible for negotiating security associations (SAs) to set up a secure, authenticated communications channel between two parties.

Internet of Things (IoT)   An architecture that connects billions of smart objects to the internet.

intent-based networking (IBN)   A type of networking that captures business intent and uses analytics, machine learning, and automation to align the network continuously to changing business needs. It can include application service levels, security policies, regulatory compliance, and operational processes.

inter-VLAN routing   The process of routing data between VLANs so that communication can occur between the different networks. It can be implemented using legacy inter-VLAN routing, a router-on-a-stick method, or a Layer 3 multilayer switch.

intrusion detection system (IDS)   A network security feature that is similar to an IPS but does not block an attack.

intrusion prevention system (IPS)   A network security feature typically deployed as a service on an ISR G2 router or by using a dedicated device (such as an IPS sensor). An IPS captures and analyzes incoming and outgoing traffic to detect traffic anomalies, detect network attacks, issue alerts, and block malicious packets.

IP Precedence   *See* IP Precedence (IPP) field.

IP Precedence (IPP) field   A field defined in the original IP standard RFC 791 to be used for QoS markings. It has now been replaced with the

Differentiated Services Code Point (DSCP) field, defined in RFC 2474.

IP Security (IPsec)   A framework of open standards that spells out the rules for secure communications. IPsec works at the network layer, protecting and authenticating IP packets between participating IPsec peers.

IP spoofing   An attack in which a threat actor alters the source IP address of a packet to impersonate another network host.

IPsec   *See* IP Security (IPsec).

IPsec Virtual Tunnel Interface (VTI)   A relatively new IPsec VPN technology that simplifies the configuration required to support multiple sites and remote access. IPsec VTI configurations use virtual interfaces to send and receive IP unicast and multicast encrypted traffic. Therefore, routing protocols are automatically supported without requiring configuration of GRE tunnels.

IT as a service (ITaaS)   A cloud service in which the cloud provider provides IT support for cloud computing. ITaaS can extend the capability of IT without requiring investment in new infrastructure, training of new personnel, or licensing of new software.

J

jabber   The condition in which a network device continually transmits random, meaningless data onto the network.

JavaScript Object Notation (JSON)   A lightweight data format for storing and transporting data. It is simpler and more readable than XML and is supported by web browsers. In JSON, the data (known as an object) is one or more key/value pairs enclosed in braces, { }. Keys must be strings within double quotation marks, " ". Keys and values are separated by a colon. *Compare with* Extensible Markup Language (XML) and YAML Ain't Markup Language (YAML).

JavaScript Object Notation-Remote Procedure Call (JSON-RPC)   A very simple web service API protocol that is similar to XML-RPC. *Compare with* Extensible Markup Language–Remote Procedure Call (XML-RPC), Representational State Transfer (REST), and Simple Object Access Protocol (SOAP).

jitter   Variation in delay (that is, latency). Ideal network conditions have little variation in the time it takes to receive packets, whereas a network experiencing congestion could have a lot of variation in latency.

K

key/value pair   A markup language term used to describe a data object. The key, on the left side, identifies or describes the data. The value on the right side is the data itself (for example, character, string, number, or list).

keylogger   A Trojan horse that actively captures confidential information (such as banking and credit card information) by recording user keystrokes on websites.

knowledge base   An information database used to assist in the use or troubleshooting of a product. Online network device vendor knowledge bases have become indispensable sources of information. When vendor-based knowledge bases are combined with internet search engines such as Google, a network administrator has access to a vast pool of experience-based information.

L

landline   A telephone line that connects to a provider network using the public switched telephone network (PSTN).

last mile   *See* local Loop.

latency   The time (in milliseconds or seconds) it takes for a packet to get from its source to its destination. Higher bandwidths typically have lower latency. Latency is sometimes displayed as RTT (round trip time) in command output.

Layer 2 MPLS VPN   An MPLS service provider VPN solution that does not involve customer routing. Instead, the MPLS provider deploys VPLS to emulate an Ethernet multiaccess LAN segment over the MPLS network. The customer's routers effectively belong to the same multiaccess network.

Layer 3 MPLS VPN   An MPLS service provider VPN solution that involves routing between the customer's routers and the provider's routers. Customer routes received by the provider's router are securely redistributed through the MPLS network to the customer's remote locations.

leased line   A type of dedicated line provided by a service provider to a client network. Leased lines are also referred to as leased circuits, serial links, serial lines, point-to-point links, and T1/E1 or T3/E3 lines. Leased lines are available in different capacities. In North America, service providers use the T-carrier system to define the digital transmission capability of a serial copper media link, while Europe uses the E-carrier system.

light-emitting diode (LED)   A semiconductor light source that is used as an indicator lamp or for general lighting.

line card   A switch card that fits into the switch chassis the way that expansion cards fit into a PC. The larger the chassis, the more modules it can support.

link aggregation   A method of aggregating (that is, combining) multiple links between equipment to increase bandwidth.

Link Layer Discovery Protocol (LLDP)   A vendor-neutral neighbor discovery protocol similar to CDP that works with network devices, such as routers, switches, and wireless LAN access points. LLDP advertises its identity and capabilities to other devices and receives the information from a physically connected Layer 2 device.

link-state acknowledgment (LSAck) packet   A packet that acknowledges receipt of LSA packets. LSAck packets are type 5 OSPF packets.

link-state advertisement (LSA)   Often referred to as a link-state packet (LSP), a broadcast packet used by link-state protocols that contains information about neighbors and path costs. LSAs are used by receiving routers to maintain their routing tables.

link-state database (LSDB)   A table used in OSPF that represents the topology of the autonomous system. It is the method by which routers "see" the state of the links in the autonomous system.

link-state information   With OSPF, information about a link, such as neighbor ID, link type, and bandwidth.

link-state packet (LSP)   *See* link-state advertisement (LSA).

link-state request (LSR) packet   A type 3 OSPF packet that is used to request the pieces of a neighbor's database that are most up to date.

link-state router   A router that uses a link-state routing protocol such as OSPF.

link-state update (LSU) packet   A type 4 OSPF packet that carries a collection of link-state advertisements (LSAs).

Loading state   An OSPF state in which peers exchange link-state information based on the neighbor DataBase Descriptor (DBD). OSPF routers send Link State Requests (LSRs) and receive Link State Updates (LSUs) containing all Link State Advertisements (LSAs).

local address   In NAT, any address that appears on the inside portion of a network.

local loop   A line from the premises of a telephone subscriber to the telephone company CO. Also referred to as the last mile.

logical topology diagram   A diagram that includes symbols to represent routers, servers, hosts, VPN concentrators, and security devices. It also includes symbols representing the type of link used to interconnect these devices, including interfaces and IP addressing. *Compare with* physical topology diagram.

Long-Term Evolution (LTE)   Usually marketed as 4G LTE, a standard for wireless communication.

Low Latency Queuing (LLQ)   A QoS queuing method that is sometimes referred to as PQ-CBWFQ (Priority Queuing CBWFQ). LLQ uses Priority Queuing (PQ) on the identified traffic to guarantee traffic bandwidth and ensure those packets are sent first. LLQ is typically used in voice networks. *Compare with* first-in, first-out (FIFO), Weighted Fair Queuing (WFQ), and Class-Based Weighted Fair Queuing (CBWFQ).

M

MAC spoofing   An attack in which a threat actor alters the source MAC address of a frame to impersonate another local network host.

malware   Software that is designed to exploit or damage end devices and networks. Malware includes computer viruses, Trojan horses, worms, ransomware, spyware, scareware, and adware.

management console   An application used with a Type 1 hypervisor to manage multiple VM servers. The management console can automatically consolidate multiple servers and power on or off servers, as required. It also provides recovery from hardware failure and can automatically and seamlessly move an unresponsive VM to another server.

Management Information Base (MIB)   A database of the objects that can be managed on a device. The managed objects, or variables, can be set or read to provide information on the network devices and interfaces.

management plane   A Cisco NFP functional area that is responsible for managing network elements. Management plane traffic is generated either by network devices or network management stations, using processes and protocols such as Telnet, SSH, TFTP, FTP, NTP, AAA, SNMP, syslog, TACACS+, RADIUS, and NetFlow. *Compare with* control plane and data plane.

man-in-the-middle attack   A type of attack in which the threat actor is positioned in between a victim and the destination.

marking   In QoS, adding a value to the packet header. Devices receiving the packet look at this field to see if it matches a defined policy.

Marking should be done as close to the source device as possible to establish the trust boundary.

markup language   A system for formatting text in a document that is syntactically distinguishable from the text. The markup language syntax is not displayed when viewing the document.

Message Digest 5 (MD5)   *See* Message Digest version 5 (MD5).

Message Digest version 5 (MD5)   A popular cryptographic hash function that produces a 128-bit (16-byte) hash value, typically expressed in text format as a 32-digit hexadecimal number. MD5 has been utilized in a wide variety of cryptographic applications and is also commonly used to verify data integrity. *Contrast with* SHA.

meter table   An SDN table implemented in data center switches that triggers a variety of performance-related actions on a flow. *Compare with* flow table and group table.

Metropolitan Ethernet (MetroE)   A WAN in which service providers provide Ethernet-based connection options to connect subscribers to a larger service network or the internet. Also called Ethernet WAN.

mission-critical service   A network service that is crucial to the operation of the enterprise.

mitigation   Countermeasures to eliminate or reduce the potential of a threat or risk. Network security involves multiple mitigation techniques.

modular configuration switch   A type of switch commonly used in the distribution and core layers of the hierarchical network design model that allows flexibility and customization by adding various line cards. *Contrast with* fixed configuration switch.

modulate   To convert digital signals to analog signals, such as when a modem sends data over telephone lines.

multiarea OSPF   A method for scaling an OSPF implementation in which as an OSPF network is expanded, other, non-backbone, areas can be created. All areas must connect to the backbone area (area 0). Routers interconnecting the areas are referred to as ABRs.

multihomed ISP   An internet access design in which an organization has connections to two or more service providers. *Compare with* single-homed ISP, dual-homed ISP, and dual-multihomed ISP.

multilayer switch   An enterprise Layer 3 switch characterized by its ability to build a routing table, support a few routing protocols, and forward IP packets at a rate close to that of Layer 2 forwarding.

multiplexing   A communication method by which multiple analog or digital signals are combined into one signal over a shared medium. DWDM transmits multiple streams of data (multiplexing) using different wavelengths of light.

Multipoint Generic Routing Encapsulation (mGRE)   A variation of GRE used with DMVPN in which an mGRE tunnel interface allows a single GRE interface to support multiple IPsec tunnels. With mGRE, dynamically allocated tunnels are created through a permanent tunnel source at the hub and dynamically allocated tunnel destinations, created as necessary, at the spokes. This reduces the size and simplifies the complexity of the configuration.

Multiprotocol Label Switching (MPLS)   A packet-forwarding technology that uses labels to make data-forwarding decisions. With MPLS, the Layer 3 header analysis is done just once (when the packet enters the MPLS domain). Label inspection drives subsequent packet forwarding.

municipal Wi-Fi   Wireless internet access provided by a city for free or for a nominal fee. Most implementations use a mesh topology, which is a series of interconnected access points located throughout a city.

N

named ACL   An ACL identified in a configuration by a descriptive name. Standard named ACLs are created using the **ip access-list standard** *acl-name* global configuration command. Extended named ACLs are created using the **ip access-list extended** *acl-name* global configuration command. *Compare with* numbered ACL.

NAT overload   See Port Address Translation (PAT).

NAT64   A NAT implementation that translates IPv6 addresses to IPv4 addresses.

National Institute of Standards and Technology (NIST)   A U.S. Department of Commerce standards agency that promotes innovation and industrial competitiveness. Its Special Publication (SP) 800-145, *The NIST Definition of Cloud Computing*, defines software as a service (SaaS), platform as a service (PaaS), and infrastructure as a service (IaaS).

neighbor table   A table in which an OSPF router records addresses and interfaces of neighbors that it discovers. In OSPF, it is created using the adjacency database.

Network Address Translation (NAT)   A mechanism for translating private addresses

into publicly usable addresses to be used within the public internet. An effective means of hiding actual device addressing within a private network.

Network Address Translation–Protocol Translation (NAT-PT)   A mechanism implemented when using both IPv4 and IPv6 addresses. This method has been deprecated by IETF in favor of NAT64.

Network Analysis Module (NAM)   An embedded browser-based interface that generates reports on the traffic that consumes critical network resources. It can be installed in Cisco Catalyst 6500 Series switches and Cisco 7600 Series routers to provide a graphical representation of traffic from local and remote switches and routers. In addition, NAM can capture and decode packets and track response times to pinpoint an application problem to the network or server.

Network Based Application Recognition (NBAR)   A classification and protocol discovery feature of Cisco IOS software that works with QoS features and classifies traffic at Layers 4 to 7.

network baseline   A reference used to efficiently diagnose and correct network problems. A network baseline documents what the network's expected performance should be under normal operating conditions. This information is captured in documentation such as configuration tables and topology diagrams.

network edge router   A router that delivers high-performance, highly secure, and reliable services to unite campus, data center, and branch networks. *Compare with* branch router, network edge router, and service provider router.

network management system (NMS)   A reasonably powerful and well-equipped computer, such as an engineering workstation, that is responsible for managing parts of a network. NMSs communicate with agents to help keep track of network statistics and resources.

network management system tools   Tools that help simplify network management; they include device-level monitoring, configuration, and fault-management tools. These tools can be used to investigate and correct network problems.

network operations center (NOC)   The central location from which a network is supervised, monitored, and maintained.

network penetration testing   Testing in which an ethical white hat hacker uses external and internal tools to test the security posture of an organization.

Network Time Protocol (NTP)   A protocol that synchronizes the time of day among a set of distributed time servers and clients so that you can correlate events when you receive system logs and other time-specific events from multiple network devices. NTP uses User Datagram Protocol (UDP) as its transport protocol.

network topology diagram   A graphical representation of a network that illustrates how devices are connected and the logical architecture of the network. A topology diagram has many of the same components as a network configuration table. Each network device should be represented on the diagram, using consistent notation or graphical symbols. Also, the logical and physical connections should be represented using simple lines or other appropriate symbols.

network virtualization   Virtualization of infrastructure hardware such as servers, routers, firewalls, switches, IPSs, WSA, and ESA. It includes IT compute, networking, and storage

that can be automatically deployed in a flexible, automated, software-controlled environment.

nonbroadcast multiaccess (NBMA)   A characterization of a type of Layer 2 network in which more than two devices connect to the network, but the network does not allow broadcast frames to be sent to all devices on the network.

northbound API   A subroutine used by an SDN controller to communicate with the upstream applications. Northbound APIs help network administrators shape traffic and deploy services.

north–south traffic   A virtualization term used to describe traffic being exchanged between external data center users and the data center server. *Compare with* east–west traffic.

NTP client   A device that obtains time and date information from a single source using NTP.

NTP server   A device that provides NTP services to clients.

numbered ACL   An ACL identified in a configuration by a number. The number also designates the type of ACL. For instance, ACLs numbered between 1 and 99 and between 1300 and 1999 are standard ACLs, whereas ACLs numbered between 100 and 199 and between 2000 and 2699 are extended ACLs. Numbered ACLs are configured using the **access-list** global configuration command. *Compare with* named ACL.

O

object ID (OID)   In SNMP, a variable (that is, object) in the MIB. OIDs uniquely identify managed objects in the MIB hierarchy, which organizes the OIDs based on RFC standards into a hierarchy of OIDs that is usually displayed as a tree.

open API A publicly available API that can be used with no restrictions. API providers typically require the user to get a free key, or token, prior to using an open API to help control the number of API requests they receive and process. *Compare with* internal API and partner API.

Open Shortest Path First (OSPF) A popular scalable, link-state routing protocol. It is based on link-state technology and introduced new concepts such as authentication of routing updates, VLSM, and route summarization.

OpenFlow A protocol developed at Stanford University that is a foundational element for building SDN solutions. The OpenFlow standard is now maintained by the Open Networking Foundation.

OpenStack A cloud operating system that is used in data centers to control large pools of compute, storage, and networking resources. OpenStack uses a web dashboard to build scalable cloud environments and provide an infrastructure as a service (IaaS) solution. OpenStack is often used with Cisco ACI.

optical carrier (OC) A term used by service providers to identify a standardized set of specifications for transmission bandwidths used with SONET fiber networks. For example, OC-1 supports bandwidths of 51.84 Mbps, OC-3 supports 155.52 Mbps, and OC-768 supports 40 Gbps.

optical converter A device that connects fiber-optic media to copper media and converts optical signals to electronic pulses.

optical time-domain reflectometer (OTDR) A TDR used to test fiber-optic cable.

origin authentication An element of secure communication which guarantees that a message

is not a forgery and actually comes from the sender who was supposed to send it. Many modern networks ensure authentication with protocols such as HMAC.

OSPF area A logical set of network segments and their attached devices. Areas are usually connected to other areas through routers to form a single autonomous system.

OSPF Hello and Dead intervals Timers in OSPF that are used to maintain neighbor adjacency. By default, if an OSPF router does not hear from its neighbor after four Hello intervals, the neighbor is considered down (dead). Configured Hello and Dead intervals must match between neighbors.

OSPFv2 Version 2 of the OSPF routing protocol, which is used to support IPv4 unicast address families.

OSPFv3 Version 3 of the OSPF routing protocol, which is used to support both IPv4 and IPv6 unicast address families.

outbound ACL An ACL that processes packets routed to the outbound interface. Outbound ACLs are best used when the same filter will be applied to packets coming from multiple inbound interfaces before exiting the same outbound interface.

outside address In NAT, the address of the destination device.

outside global address A reachable IP address used in NAT for IPv4 and assigned to a host located out on the internet.

outside local address In NAT, the address of the destination, as seen from the inside network. Although uncommon, this address could be different from the globally routable address of the destination.

outside network   In NAT, a non-internal network.

P

packet loss   A QoS term used to refer to packets that did not reach their destination because of network congestion, an invalid QoS policy that is dropping packets, physical cable problems, and more.

packet-switched communication   A type of network connection that splits traffic data into packets that are routed over a shared network. Routers determine the links that packets must be sent over based on the addressing information in each packet. Packet-switching networks do not require a circuit to be established, and they allow many pairs of nodes to communicate over the same channel.

parallel communication   A connection that uses multiple wires running parallel to each other to transfer data on all the wires simultaneously. *Contrast with* parallel connection.

partially meshed topology   A network in which each network node has either a physical circuit or a virtual circuit connecting it to many but not all other network nodes. A partial mesh provides some redundancy between key sites as it is less expensive to implement than a fully meshed topology. *Contrast with* fully meshed topology, point-to-point topology, hub-and-spoke topology, and dual-homed topology.

partner API   An API used between a company and business partners/contractors to facilitate business between them. A partner must have a license or another form of permission to use the API. *Compare with* open API and internal API.

passenger protocol   In GRE, the original IPv4, IPv6, or legacy protocol (that is, AppleTalk, DECnet, or IPX) packet that will be encapsulated by a carrier protocol. *Compare with* carrier protocol and transport protocol.

permanent virtual circuit (PVC)   A type of virtual circuit used in Frame Relay that is always ready and available for data transfer. PVCs are used to carry both voice and data traffic between a source and destination, and they support data rates of 4 Mbps or more.

phishing   A social engineering attack that aims to obtain sensitive victim information. For example, a threat actor may send fraudulent emails or messages or use social networking platforms, pretending to be trustworthy entities to trick the victims.

physical topology diagram   A diagram that documents the mapping of a network by showing the physical layout of equipment, cables, and interconnections. *Compare with* logical topology diagram.

platform as a service (PaaS)   A cloud service in which the cloud provider is responsible for access to the development tools and services used to deliver the applications. *Compare with* software as a service (SaaS) and infrastructure as a service (IaaS).

playout delay buffer   A QoS term for a mechanism that compensates for jitter by buffering packets and then playing them out in a steady stream.

point of presence (POP)   A point of interconnection between the communications facilities provided by the telephone company and a building's main distribution facility.

Point-to-Point Protocol (PPP)   A Layer 2 WAN protocol that provides router-to-router and host-to-network connections over synchronous and asynchronous circuits. It should be used on Cisco routers when connecting to other vendor routers. It also supports options such as authentication, compression, multilinking, and more. *Contrast with* High-Level Data Link Control (HDLC).

point-to-point topology   A topology in which connections connect LANs to service provider WANs and connect LAN segments within an enterprise network. *Contrast with* fully meshed topology, hub-and-spoke topology, and dual-homed topology.

Port Address Translation (PAT)   A mechanism for mapping multiple private IP addresses to a single public IP address or a few addresses. Sometimes called NAT overloading.

port density   The number of ports or interfaces supported on a switch. Network switches must support the appropriate number of devices on the network.

portable network analyzer   A portable device that is used to troubleshoot switched networks and VLANs. By plugging in a network analyzer anywhere on the network, a network engineer can see the switchport to which the device is connected and the average and peak utilization.

Postman   An application for testing and using REST APIs that is available as a browser app or a standalone installation.

Power over Ethernet (PoE)   A feature that allows a switch to deliver power to a device over the existing Ethernet cabling. This feature can be used by IP phones, security cameras, wireless access points, and other switches.

PPP over Ethernet (PPPoE)   A combination of two widely accepted standards, Ethernet and PPP, that provides an authenticated method of assigning IP addresses to client systems. PPPoE clients are typically personal computers connected to an ISP over a remote broadband connection, such as DSL or cable service. ISPs deploy PPPoE because it supports high-speed broadband access using the existing remote-access infrastructure and because it is easier for customers to use.

pre-shared key (PSK)   A secret password that two parties know in advance and use to secure communications or authenticate users.

Priority (PRI) field   A 3-bit field in the 802.1Q Tag Control field that identifies the class of service (CoS) markings of the frame.

private API   *See* internal API.

private cloud   A cloud model in which all cloud-based applications and services offered are intended for an enterprise only. A private cloud can be provisioned internally but would be expensive to build and maintain. A private cloud can also be provisioned for strict access security by a cloud provider. *Compare with* public cloud, hybrid cloud, and community cloud.

private IP address   An address assigned from a special IP address range that cannot be routed over the internet.

private IPv4 address   *See* private IP address.

private WAN   A network comprising dedicated point-to-point leased lines, circuit-switched links, such as PSTN or ISDN, and packet-switched links, such as Ethernet WAN, ATM, or Frame Relay.

propagate a default route   To advertise a default route to all other routers that use a particular dynamic routing protocol.

protocol analyzer   A tool that decodes the various protocol layers in a recorded frame and presents this information in a relatively easy-to-use format. Wireshark is a protocol analyzer.

public API   *See* open API.

public cloud   A cloud model in which all cloud-based applications and services are offered publicly to anyone. Services may be free or offered on a pay-per-use model, such as for online storage. A public cloud uses the internet to provide services. *Compare with* private cloud, hybrid cloud, and community cloud.

public IP address   An IP address that has been registered with IANA or one of its member agencies, which guarantees that the address is globally unique. Globally unique public IP addresses can be used for packets sent through the internet.

public IPv4 address   *See* public IP addresses.

public key infrastructure   A structure for authenticating and confirming the identities of users and devices using digital signatures. Trusted PKI certificate authorities (CAs) create digital signatures certifying that a particular cryptographic key belongs to a specific user or device. Devices use the key to confidently identify the user.

public WAN   A network offering broadband internet access using DSL, cable, or satellite access. Broadband connection options are typically used to connect small offices and telecommuting employees to a corporate site over the internet. Data traveling between corporate sites over the public WAN infrastructure should be protected using VPNs.

Puppet   An agent-based configuration management tool built on Ruby that is used to create a set of instructions called a manifest. *Compare with* Ansible, Chef, and SaltStack.

Python   An interpreted, high-level, general-purpose programming language that uses an object-oriented approach to help write clear, logical code for small and large-scale projects.

R

rack unit (RU)   The thickness of a device, as defined in EIA-310. One unit (U) has a standard height of 4.45 centimeters (1¾ inches) and width of 48.26 centimeters (19 inches). Therefore, a device occupying double that height would be referred to as a 2U device. Most 24-port fixed configuration switches are 1 rack unit (1U).

ransomware   A type of malware that encrypts the data on a host and locks access to it until a ransom is paid. WannaCry is an example of ransomware.

reconnaissance attack   An information-gathering attack that usually precedes an access or DoS attack. Threat actors use recon attacks to do unauthorized discovery and mapping of systems, services, or vulnerabilities.

reference bandwidth   The number, measured in Mbps, that is used by OSPF routers to calculate cost. The default reference bandwidth is 100 Mbps. Changing the reference bandwidth does not actually affect the bandwidth capacity on the link; rather, it simply affects the calculation used to determine the metric.

remote-access VPN A network that enables remote VPN clients (remote hosts) to gain secure access to the enterprise network via a VPN server device at the network edge.

Representational State Transfer (REST) The most popular architectural style for designing web service applications. A REST API works on top of the HTTP protocol and defines a set of functions developers can use to perform requests and receive responses via HTTP (for example, GET and POST). REST has become popular due to its performance, scalability, simplicity, and reliability. *Compare with* Extensible Markup Language–Remote Procedure Call (XML-RPC), JavaScript Object Notation–Remote Procedure Call (JSON-RPC), and Simple Object Access Protocol (SOAP).

Resource Reservation Protocol (RSVP) A network-control protocol used in an IntServ QoS model that enables end devices to request specific QoS from IntServ-enabled devices.

RESTful Conforming to the constraints of the REST architecture.

risk The likelihood of a threat to exploit the vulnerability of an asset, with the aim of negatively affecting an organization. Risk is measured using the probability of the occurrence of an event and its consequences.

Rivest, Shamir, and Adleman (RSA) authentication An authentication method that uses digital certificates to authenticate peers. The local device derives a hash, encrypts it with its private key, and attaches it to the message to act like a signature. The remote end decrypts the encrypted hash using the sender's public key. If the decrypted hash matches the recomputed hash, the signature is genuine. Each peer must authenticate its opposite peer before the tunnel is considered secure.

rogue DHCP server An unauthorized DHCP server connected to a corporate network to provide false IP configuration information to legitimate clients.

ROMMON mode A basic device command line that supports commands to recover a lost or forgotten password, format the flash file system, and reinstall the IOS.

route summarization The process of aggregating multiple routes into one routing advertisement to reduce the size of routing tables.

router ID A field in an OSPF Hello packet that is a 32-bit value expressed in dotted-decimal notation (an IPv4 address) used to uniquely identify the originating router.

router priority A value that is used in an OSPF DR/BDR election. The default priority for all OSPF routers is 1 but can be manually altered from 0 to 255. The higher the value, the more likely the router is to become the DR on the link.

Ruby An open-source cross-platform programming language similar to Python. Ruby is typically considered a more difficult language to learn than Python.

S

SaltStack An agentless configuration management tool built on Python that is used to create a set of instructions called a pillar. *Compare with* Ansible, Chef, and Puppet.

scalability   A network's ability to accommodate more users and data transmission requirements. For example, a scalable network can expand quickly to support new users and applications without impacting the performance of the service being delivered to existing users.

script kiddie   An inexperienced hacker (possibly a teenager) running existing scripts, tools, and exploits to cause harm but typically not for profit.

SDN controller   A controller that performs complex functions, defines the data flows that occur in the SDN data plane, and populates the data center switches' forwarding flow tables. Each flow traveling through the network must first get permission from the SDN controller, which verifies that the communication is permissible according to the network policy. If the controller allows a flow, it computes a route for the flow to take and adds an entry for that flow in each of the switches along the path.

SD-Access   A Cisco DNA intent-based solution that creates a consistent, highly secure user experience. *Compare with* SD-WAN, Cisco DNA Assurance, and Cisco DNA Security.

SD-WAN   A Cisco DNA intent-based solution that uses a secure cloud-delivered architecture to centrally manage WAN connections. *Compare with* SD-Access, Cisco DNA Assurance, and Cisco DNA Security.

Secure Hash Algorithm (SHA)   A cryptographic hash-generating algorithm that is used for data integrity and authentication.

Secure Sockets Layer (SSL)   A cryptographic protocol designed to provide communication security over the internet. It has been replaced by Transport Layer Security (TLS).

security association (SA)   A set of security attributes (that is, mutually agreed-upon keys and algorithms) shared between two devices to establish a secure VPN connection. IPsec uses the IKE protocol to create SAs between two devices.

serial connection   A connection that uses a single wire to transfer data bits one at a time. *Contrast with* parallel connection.

server sprawl   A term used to describe dedicated servers sitting idle for long periods of time, wasting energy and taking up more space than is warranted by their amount of service.

service level agreement (SLA)   A contract between a service provider and clients that identifies the services and quality of service the provider is obligated to provide.

service provider   A telecommunications company that provides access to other networks (such as the internet) to its subscribers.

service provider router   A router that is responsible for differentiating the service portfolio and increasing revenue by delivering end-to-end scalable solutions and subscriber-aware services. *Compare with* branch router and network edge router.

service provider switch   A switch that aggregates traffic at the edge of a network. Service provider Ethernet access switches provide application intelligence, unified services, virtualization, integrated security, and simplified management. *Compare with* campus LAN switch, cloud-managed switch, data center switch, and virtual networking switch.

service provider VPN   A service provider-managed VPNs solution such as a Layer 2 MPLS

VPN, a Layer 3 MPLS VPN, or a legacy solution such as a Frame Relay or Asynchronous Transfer Mode (ATM) VPN.

set request   A type of request used by an SNMP manager to change the configuration in an agent device. A set request can also initiate actions within a device.

severity level   A number in syslog messages that is used to describe the type of message. Expressed as Level 0 to Level 7, with smaller numerical levels indicating more critical syslog alarms.

shortest path first (SPF) algorithm   Often referred to as the Dijkstra's algorithm, an algorithm used by protocols such as STP and OSPF to determine a shortest path to a destination. The algorithm accumulates costs along each path, from source to destination, to determine the total cost of a route.

Simple Network Management Protocol (SNMP)   A network management protocol that is used to manage devices (that is, SNMP agents) on an IP network. The SNMP manager, which is part of the NMS, communicates with SNMP agents to monitor and manage network performance and to help find and solve network problems.

Simple Object Access Protocol (SOAP)   A web service messaging protocol for exchanging XML-structured information over HTTP or SMTP. SOAP APIs are considered slow to parse, complex, and rigid. *Compare with* Extensible Markup Language–Remote Procedure Call (XML-RPC), JavaScript Object Notation–Remote Procedure Call (JSON-RPC), and Representational State Transfer (REST).

single point of failure   A network device (for example, a router, switch, or server) that, if it

fails, will stop the entire system from working. A single point of failure is undesirable in any system with a goal of high availability or reliability.

single-area OSPF   An OSPF configuration that only uses one area, the backbone area (area 0).

single-carrier connection   An organization's connection to only one service provider. In this setup, the carrier connection and the service provider are both single points of failure. *Contrast with* dual-carrier connection.

single-homed   Term used to describe an enterprise with one connection to a service provider. *Compare with* multihomed.

single-homed ISP   An internet access design in which the organization only has one connection to a service provider. *Compare with* dual-homed ISP, multihomed ISP, and dual-multihomed ISP.

single-homed topology   A topology that provides one connection to a hub router across a WAN cloud. *Contrast with* dual-homed topology, point-to-point topology, hub-and-spoke topology, and fully meshed topology.

site-to-site VPN   A VPN that establishes a secure communication tunnel between two networks, such as a branch office network connecting to a company headquarters network.

small form-factor pluggable (SFP)   A small, compact, hot-pluggable transceiver used on switches to provide flexibility when choosing network media. SFPs are available for Ethernet, SONET/SDH, and Fibre Channel networks.

SNMP agent   An agent that resides on a managed device to collect and store information about the device and its operation.

SNMP manager   An application running on an NMS that polls SNMP agents and queries the MIB of SNMP agents using UDP port 161.

SNMP trap   An alert message sent from an SNMP agent to an SNMP manager. SNMP agents send SNMP traps to the SNMP manager using UDP port 162.

snmpget   A freeware utility used to quickly retrieve real-time information from the MIB. The **snmpget** utility requires that the SNMP version, the correct community, the IP address of the network device to query, and the OID number be set.

social engineer   A threat actor who uses social engineering techniques to exploit helpful human nature to gain access to resources.

social engineering   An access attack that attempts to manipulate individuals into performing actions or divulging confidential information. Examples include pretexting, phishing, baiting, and impersonation. Some social engineering techniques are performed in person, and others are carried out using the telephone or internet.

software as a service (SaaS)   A cloud service in which the cloud provider is responsible for providing consumers access to fully functional applications. The cloud provider manages the underlying hardware or software infrastructure and is responsible for access to services such as email, communication, and Office 365 that are delivered over the internet. Users only need to provide their data. *Compare with* platform as a service (PaaS) and infrastructure as a service (IaaS).

software clock   A clock on a router or switch that starts when the system boots and is the primary source of time for the system.

software-defined networking (SDN)   An architecture that decouples network control (control plane) from network devices (forwarding plane). SDN brings automation and programmability into data center, campus, backbone, and wide-area networks.

Software-Optimized Encryption Algorithm (SEAL)   A very secure symmetric encryption algorithm. It is a stream cipher that encrypts data continuously one byte at a time rather than encrypting blocks of data. SEAL uses a 160-bit key. *Compare with* Data Encryption Standard (DES), Triple DES (3DES), and Advanced Encryption Standard (AES).

southbound API   A routine used by an SDN controller to define the behavior of the downstream virtual switches and routers. OpenFlow is the original and widely implemented southbound API.

spam   Also known as junk mail, a social engineering attack that involves the sending of unsolicited email, which often contains harmful links, malware, or deceptive content.

spine-leaf topology   A two-tier data center topology consisting of spine switches and leaf switches. Leaf switches always attach to the spines, but they never attach to each other, and spine switches only attach to the leaf and core switches.

spoke router   Generally, a router that connects to a hub router at the center of a hub-and-spoke star topology network. Spoke routers connect to other spokes through the hub router.

stackable configuration switch   A configuration in which devices are capable of being connected to others, such as devices to provide higher port density.

standard ACL   An IOS feature used to filter traffic based on source IPv4 addresses.

stateful firewall service   A router configured with extended ACLs to support TCP state information using the TCP established keyword.

state-sponsored   A security term used to describe a white hat hacker or black hat hacker who gathers intelligence and steals secrets from foreign governments, terrorist groups, or corporations. Most countries in the world participate to some degree in state-sponsored hacking.

static NAT   A type of NAT that uses a one-to-one mapping of local and global addresses that remains constant. Static NAT is particularly useful for web servers or hosts that must have a consistent address that is accessible from the internet. These internal hosts may be enterprise servers or networking devices.

stratum   A level of the hierarchical system of time sources used by NTP. The stratum level is defined as the number of hop counts from the authoritative time source.

symmetric DSL (SDSL)   A type of DSL service used to connect corporate sites to service providers. SDSL provides the same downstream and upstream capacity in both directions. *Compare with* asymmetric DSL (ADSL).

symmetric encryption algorithm   An algorithm that uses a pre-shared key to encrypt and decrypt data. Symmetric algorithms use fewer CPU resources than asymmetric encryption algorithms.

Synchronous Digital Hierarchy (SDH)   A standard that defines how to transfer data, voice, and video traffic over optical fiber using lasers or LEDs over great distances. SDH is a European-based ETSI and ITU standard, and SONET is an American-based ANSI standard. SDH and SONET are essentially the same and, therefore, often referred to as SONET/SDH.

Synchronous Optical Networking (SONET)   A high-speed (up to 2.5 Gbps) synchronous network specification developed by Bellcore and designed to run on optical fiber. STS-1 is the basic building block of SONET. Approved as an international standard in 1988, SONET is an American-based ANSI standard, whereas SDH is a European-based ETSI and ITU standard. SDH and SONET are essentially the same and, therefore, often referred to as SONET/SDH.

syslog   A protocol that was developed for UNIX systems in the 1980s and was first documented as RFC 3164 by the IETF in 2001. Syslog uses UDP port 514 to send event notification messages across IP networks to event message collectors.

syslog server   A server that receives and stores syslog messages that can be displayed with a syslog application.

T

T1   A type of leased line available from service providers in North America that provides bandwidth of up to 1.54 Mbps. *Contrast with* T3, E1, and E3.

T3   A type of leased line available from service providers in North America that provides bandwidth of up to 44.7 Mbps. *Contrast with* T1, E1, and E3.

Tag Control Information (TCI) field   A 16-bit field in the 802.1Q header that identifies a 3-bit priority code, a 1-bit drop eligible indicator, and a 12-bit VLAN identifier.

TCP session hijacking   An attack that exploits a TCP vulnerability using IP and TCP sequence number spoofing techniques. If successful, the threat actor can send, but not receive, data from the target device.

TCP SYN flood attack   An attack that exploits the TCP three-way handshake to create a DoS attack by denying TCP services to legitimate users.

TCP SYN reset attack   An attack that exploits the TCP connection terminating flags to disrupt communicating hosts.

Telecommunications Industry Association (TIA)   An organization that develops communication standards in a variety of areas, including standards for radio equipment, cellular towers, voice over IP (VoIP) devices, satellite communications, and more. TIA standards are often combined with EIA standards and referred to as TIA/EIA standards.

teleworker   A remote user conducting work-related tasks using teleworking services. Also referred to as a telecommuter.

teleworking   Working from a nontraditional workplace such as at home. Teleworking offers many benefits to the worker and to the business. Connections are typically provided using broadband DSL or cable internet.

threat actor   An individual or a group of individuals who conduct malicious activities against individuals or organizations.

threat   A potential danger to a company's assets, data, or network functionality.

three-layer hierarchical model   A hierarchical design that maximizes performance, network availability, and the ability to scale the network design. Consists of core, distribution, and access layers.

time-domain reflectometer (TDR)   A special type of cable tester that can pinpoint the distance to a break in a cable by sending signals and measuring the time it takes the break to reflect the signal.

toll network   A network that consists of the long-haul, all-digital, fiber-optic communications lines, switches, routers, and other equipment inside the WAN provider network. There is a fee to use the services of a toll network.

top-down troubleshooting   A troubleshooting approach that starts with the end-user applications and moves down through the layers of the OSI model until the cause of the problem is found. You test end-user applications of an end system before tackling the more specific networking pieces. Use this approach for simpler problems or when you think the problem is with a piece of software. *Compare with* bottom-up troubleshooting and divide-and-conquer troubleshooting.

topology table   In OPSF, a table that contains all destinations that are advertised by neighboring routers. It is created using the OSPF LSDB.

Traffic Class field   The IPv6 equivalent of the IPv4 Type of Service (ToS) field.

traffic policing   A QoS mechanism that limits the amount of bandwidth that certain network traffic can use. Policing typically drops (discards) excess traffic. *Compare with* traffic shaping.

traffic shaping   A QoS mechanisms for preventing congestion by queueing (that is, delaying) excess traffic and sending it later. Traffic shaping retains excess packets in a queue and then schedules the excess for later transmission over increments of time. *Compare with* traffic policing.

Transport Layer Security (TLS)   A cryptographic protocol that replaces Secure Sockets Layer (SSL) but is still frequently referred to as SSL. It provides secure communications over a computer network and is commonly used to secure web access with HTTPS.

transport protocol   In GRE, a delivery protocol that encapsulates the carrier protocol. *Compare with* carrier protocol and passenger protocol.

Triple DES (3DES)   A variant of DES that provides significantly stronger encryption strength over DES. However, 3DES is now considered to be a legacy symmetric encryption algorithm that should be avoided. *Compare with* Data Encryption Standard (DES), Advanced Encryption Standard (AES), and Software-Optimized Encryption Algorithm (SEAL).

Trojan   A type of malware. *See also* Trojan horse.

Trojan horse   A type of non-self-replicating malware designed to look like a legitimate application or file to trick the user to download, install, or open the malware.

Two-Way state   An OSPF state in which communication between two routers is bidirectional and on multiaccess links, and the routers elect a DR and a BDR.

Type 1 hypervisor   A "bare metal" hypervisor installed directly on hardware. Instances of an OS are installed on the server, giving Type 1 hypervisors direct access to the hardware resources. Type 1 hypervisors improve scalability, performance, and robustness and are therefore usually used on enterprise servers and data center networking devices.

Type 2 hypervisor   Also called a "hosted hypervisor" because the hypervisor is installed on top of the existing OS (for example, Mac OS X, Windows, or Linux). Many Type 2 hypervisors are available at no cost; they are therefore popular with consumers and with organizations experimenting with virtualization.

Type of Service (ToS)   *See* Type of Service (TOS) field.

Type of Service (ToS) field   A QoS marking that exists in the Layer 3 header of an IPv4 packet and that a router can identify.

U

UDP flood attack   An attack that involves flooding UDP packets from a spoofed host to a target device, sweeping through all UDP ports and forcing the target device to reply with ICMP port unreachable messages.

uniform resource identifier (URI)   A string of characters that identifies a specific network resource. Web resources and web services such as RESTful APIs are identified using a URI. A URI contains a URL and a URN. *Compare with* uniform resource name (URN) and uniform resource locator (URL).

uniform resource locator (URL)   A string of characters that identifies the location of a specific resource on the network. HTTP and HTTPS URLs are typically used with web browsers.

Other protocols, such as FTP, SFTP, and SSH, can also use URLs. *Compare with* uniform resource identifier (URI) and uniform resource name (URN).

uniform resource name (URN)   A string of characters that identifies the namespace of a resource (web page, document, image, and so on), without reference to the protocol. *Compare with* uniform resource identifier (URI) and uniform resource locator (URL).

URL filtering   A security feature that prevents users from accessing websites based on information contained in a URL list.

V

virtual circuit   A logical circuit created to ensure reliable communication between two network devices.

virtual machine (VM)   An instance of an OS running on top of another OS. A VM runs a complete and separate operating system and has access to all the resources (that is, CPUs, memory, disk controllers, and NICs) of the host OS. VMs are a form of virtualization.

virtual networking switch   A switch such as a Cisco Nexus switch that provides secure multitenant services by adding virtualization intelligence technology to the data center network. *Compare with* campus LAN switch, cloud-managed switch, data center switch, and service provider switch.

Virtual Private LAN Services (VPLS)   A technology that supports the connection of multiple sites in a single bridged domain over a managed IP/MPLS network. VPLS presents an Ethernet interface to customers, simplifying the LAN/WAN boundary for service providers and customers, and enabling rapid and flexible service provisioning, because the service bandwidth is not tied to the physical interface. All VPLS services appear to be on the same LAN, regardless of location.

virtual private network (VPN)   A virtual point-to-point connection that uses dedicated connections, encryption, or a combination of the two between two endpoints over an unsecured network such as the internet.

virtual routing and forwarding (VRF)   An IP technology that is commonly used on service provider routers to create virtual instances of routing tables to separate network traffic between routers. VRF reduces the number of routers required, helps segment traffic, and increases network security.

virtualization   The creation of a virtual version of something, such as a hardware platform, operating system (OS), storage device, or network resources. Virtualization separates the OS from the hardware.

virus   A type of malware that executes a specific unwanted (and often harmful) function on a computer. Viruses cannot propagate and infect other computers without human action.

VMware   Commercial cloud and virtualization software and services on the x86 architecture pioneered by VMware, Inc., a subsidiary of Dell Technologies.

voice over IP (VoIP)   A voice technology that uses traditional telephones to establish telephone calling privileges over the internet. VoIP uses voice-enabled routers that convert analog voice from traditional telephone signals into IP packets. After the signals are converted into IP packets, a router sends those packets between corresponding locations.

voiceband modem   Also called a dial-up modem, an older type of modem that connects a computer to the internet via a standard telephone line.

VPN client software   Software that is installed on a host and used to establish a remote-access VPN connection.

VPN gateway   An enterprise device that is responsible for encapsulating, encrypting, and sending outbound traffic through a VPN tunnel over the internet to a peer VPN gateway that strips the headers, decrypts the content, and relays the packet toward the target host inside its private network. The VPN gateway could be a router, a firewall, or a Cisco Adaptive Security Appliance (ASA).

vulnerability broker   A gray hat hacker who attempts to discover exploits and report them to vendors, sometimes for prizes or rewards.

vulnerability   A weakness in a system or its design that could be exploited.

W

Weighted Fair Queuing (WFQ)   A QoS queuing method that attempts to balance available bandwidth between incoming flows. WFQ is often the default method applied to serial interfaces. *Compare with* first-in, first-out (FIFO), Class-Based Weighted Fair Queuing (CBWFQ), and Low Latency Queuing (LLQ).

Weighted Random Early Detection (WRED)   A QoS congestion avoidance tool that is used by TCP to regulate data traffic in a bandwidth-efficient manner before tail drops caused by queue overflows occur. WRED provides buffer management and allows TCP traffic to decrease, or throttle back, before buffers are exhausted.

white hat hacker   A threat actor who uses his or her skills for good, ethical, and legal purposes such as corporate network penetration testing to discover and report network vulnerabilities.

wildcard mask   A string of 32 binary digits used by a router to determine which bits of the address to examine for a match.

wire speed   The data rate that an Ethernet port on a switch is capable of attaining.

Worldwide Interoperability for Microwave Access (WiMAX)   IEEE standard 802.16, which offers high-speed broadband service with wireless access. It provides broad coverage like a cell phone network rather than using small Wi-Fi hotspots.

worm   A type of self-replicating malware that exploits vulnerabilities in legitimate software to consume resources and disrupt network operations.

Y

YAML Ain't Markup Language (YAML)   A newer and increasingly popular readable markup language that is commonly used for configuration files and in applications. It is similar to JSON and XML but has a minimal syntax. In YAML, the data (known as an object) is one or more key/value pairs. A key is separated from a value by a colon, without the use of quotation marks. YAML uses indentation to define the structure, without the use of brackets or commas. *Compare with* JavaScript Object Notation (JSON) and Extensible Markup Language (XML).

Z

zero-day exploit   A malware tool created by a threat actor to exploit an unknown flaw.

zombie   A compromised host device that is controlled by a threat actor for nefarious purposes such as taking part in a coordinated DDoS attack.

Numbers

A

C

CISCO

Connect, Engage, Collaborate

The Award Winning Cisco Support Community

Attend and Participate in Events

Ask the Experts
Live Webcasts

Knowledge Sharing

Documents
Blogs
Videos

Top Contributor Programs

Cisco Designated VIP
Hall of Fame
Spotlight Awards

Multi-Language Support

https://supportforums.cisco.com

REGISTER YOUR PRODUCT at CiscoPress.com/register
Access Additional Benefits and SAVE 35% on Your Next Purchase

- Download available product updates.
- Access bonus material when applicable.
- Receive exclusive offers on new editions and related products.
  (Just check the box to hear from us when setting up your account.)
- Get a coupon for 35% for your next purchase, valid for 30 days.
  Your code will be available in your Cisco Press cart. (You will also find
  it in the Manage Codes section of your account page.)

Registration benefits vary by product. Benefits will be listed on your account page
under Registered Products.

CiscoPress.com – Learning Solutions for Self-Paced Study, Enterprise, and the Classroom
Cisco Press is the Cisco Systems authorized book publisher of Cisco networking technology,
Cisco certification self-study, and Cisco Networking Academy Program materials.

At **CiscoPress.com** you can

- Shop our books, eBooks, software, and video training.
- Take advantage of our special offers and promotions (ciscopress.com/promotions).
- Sign up for special offers and content newsletters (ciscopress.com/newsletters).
- Read free articles, exam profiles, and blogs by information technology experts.
- Access thousands of free chapters and video lessons.

Connect with Cisco Press – Visit CiscoPress.com/community
Learn about Cisco Press community events and programs.

Cisco Press